KW-206-699

Table of Contents

Part III: National Studies and Trends

Part IV: State Studies and Trends

Part V: County and City Studies and Trends

Local Government Election Practices

ALSO BY ROGER L. KEMP

Managing America's Cities: A Handbook
for Local Government Productivity
(McFarland, 1998)

AS EDITOR

Economic Development in Local Government:
A Handbook for Public Officials and Citizens
(McFarland, 1995)

Strategic Planning for Local Government:
A Handbook for Officials and Citizens
(McFarland, 1993)

Privatization: The Provision of Public
Services by the Private Sector
(McFarland, 1991)

Local Government Election Practices

A Handbook for Public Officials and Citizens

Edited by
ROGER L. KEMP

McFarland & Company, Inc., Publishers
Jefferson, North Carolina, and London

Acknowledgments: Grateful acknowledgment is made to the following organizations and publishers for granting permission to reprint the material contained in this volume: American Political Science Association; Clemson University; George Mason University; International City/County Management Association; International Municipal Lawyers Association; National Civic League; National League of Cities; South Carolina Political Science Association; The Center for Voting and Democracy; The University of Georgia; University of Michigan Law School; University of Utah; University of Virginia School of Law.

British Library Cataloguing-in-Publication data are available

Library of Congress Cataloguing-in-Publication Data

Local government election practices : a handbook for public officials
   and citizens / edited by Roger L. Kemp.
        p.   cm.
   Includes index.
   ISBN 0-7864-0567-8 (library binding : 50# alkaline paper) ∞
      1. Local elections—United States.   I. Kemp, Roger L.
   JS395.L624   1999
   324.6'0973—dc21   98-20820
                                                             CIP

Manufactured in the United States of America

McFarland & Company, Inc., Publishers
   Box 611, Jefferson, North Carolina 28640

Part VI: The Future

Preface

Back when America's cities and towns were simple political jurisdictions, citizens merely voted for their favorite candidates on a city-wide basis. The representation of groups on local governing bodies was by happenstance and not by design. There was no need for complex electoral systems designed to produce legislative bodies that reflected the unique demographic characteristics of individual communities.

As local government populations grew, and the ethnic and racial composition of neighborhoods changed, the at-large election process came under increasing criticism. The simple election procedures of the past slowly changed to produce local elected leaders who reflected the racial and ethnic diversity of a community.

As cities grew in both size and population, the use of district, or ward, elections was embraced as a method to enhance voter representation. The drawing of district lines became a complex process as populations expanded and became more demographically heterogeneous. This was primarily due to the fact that since the population of these electoral districts increased over the years, the need existed occasionally to redraw their boundaries. Unrepresentative governing bodies used the various features of the district or ward system to dilute the votes generated by certain political parties and groups within a community, thereby politically disenfranchising these voters from the political process. This made it difficult, if not impossible, for some political parties and racial or ethnic groups to elect their representatives to local public office.

Advocates of the at-large election process favored this system because citizens were able to vote for all candidates running for elective office, elected officials served the needs of the entire population, the talent pool of candidates is greater on a jurisdiction-wide basis, and this can result in higher-quality office holders. From a policy perspective they claimed that policy development is focused on the broader community, and that at-large elected officials are more prone to conduct long-range planning. Some even favored this election process since the minority interests of a community are spread over the

1

entire city, as opposed to being concentrated in individual neighborhoods. Lastly, the frequent comment was made that district elections led to pork-barrel politics, which is not in the best interests of the electorate.

Those citizens who belonged to certain ethnic and racial groups that could not obtain public office under the at-large system, advocated for the district election process. They claimed campaign costs would be lower if elections were focused on single districts, increased minority representation would result from this election process, and that district advocacy provided a basis for greater equity in the delivery of public services. Also, citizens would have the opportunity to be more familiar with their elected representatives since they would be from their own neighborhoods. The idea of pork-barrel politics was downplayed since neighborhoods that had been excluded from the political process had needs that were not being considered by their at-large representatives.

To complicate matters even further, in some communities gerrymandering practices (the intentional drawing of district political boundaries to favor one party or group over another) evolved because this redistricting process was under the direct control of incumbent elected office holders. Many district election boundaries were subsequently drawn or redrawn to maintain or enhance past voting practices and thus led to the election of incumbents. Since local government populations increase in an unanticipated and unplanned manner, as district political boundaries were redrawn to reflect a constant population size, some elected officials designed district boundaries to enhance their chances of reelection. They also designed these boundaries, in some cases, purposely to exclude certain political parties or racial and ethnic groups within a local government from being elected to public office.

To solve this gerrymandering problem, good government advocates and political reformers have advanced many different proposals over the years. Nowadays, there are several distinctly different, yet highly effective, electoral systems that a community may embrace to ensure the equity of their electoral representation. All of these election practices are permitted by Congressional enactments and Supreme Court decisions, as well as a plethora of state and local laws and regulations that permit alternative local election practices within these legal guidelines. To complicate matters further, there are numerous variations to these practices. Cities and counties are also allowed to combine different election methods within their political jurisdictions. The main election systems are highlighted below, and explained in further detail in this volume.

The most common election practices include the ward system (single-member districts), at-large plurality system (voting for candidates on a jurisdiction-wide basis without single-member districts), the combined system (the use of both single-member districts and jurisdiction-wide elections), limited voting (electors vote for a fewer number of candidates than the total number to be elected), cumulative voting systems (permitting voters to cast all of their votes for a single candidate), proportional representation (where electors vote their preferences, and winners are determined by quota based on the type of representation desired), and alternative voting (a type of preferential voting where candidates are ranked according to the number of votes they receive). These election methods are further complicated by the use of partisan and non-partisan election practices (that is, political party affiliation versus no political party affiliation).

During the past few decades, many studies have been undertaken to determine the advantages and disadvantages of numerous different election methods. The purpose of this volume is to sort through and make sense out of them. To accomplish this task, and to facilitate reader references to individual topics, this book is organized into these parts: an introduction to local election practices; an overview of the laws and the systems permitting these practices; a review of national, state, county, and city studies and trends; and the future of local election practices and citizen involvement in the civic affairs of their community.

The suggested election guidelines of the National Civic League for city and county governments are set forth in the *Model City Charter* and *Model County Charter*. The elections sections of these two charters are reprinted as Appendix A and Appendix B at the end of this volume. These guidelines were developed by the Model Charter Revision Committees (for cities and counties, respectively), which included nationally respected municipal and county government experts. The National Civic League, founded over a century ago, published its first *Model City Charter* in 1899 and its first *Model County Charter* in 1956.

It is important to educate local public officials and citizens about not only the various election-system options available but also their anticipated short-term ramifications and long-range implications. The goal of all local election systems should be to afford citizens an equitable and politically acceptable electoral method for the selecting of their political leaders. Any method chosen should be determined by a plurality of the electorate. Helping public officials and citizens learn about the various election systems available, and their anticipated consequences, has been the primary focus of this volume.

Most published works on election practices focus on the federal and state levels of government. This is one of the few volumes dealing solely with election practices in local units of government—cities and counties—and it offers a codification of knowledge on this subject.

Roger L. Kemp
Fall 1998
Meriden, Connecticut

PART I
Introduction

Alternative Local Election Systems

Joseph F. Zimmerman

In an ideal polity each voter would cast a ballot for the best qualified candidates regardless of their ethnicity, race, religion, or other background characteristics. Proportional representation of groups on local governing bodies would be a happenstance and not deliberate, and there would be no need for an electoral system that self-consciously produces legislative bodies mirroring the complexion of the polity.

Unrepresentative law-making bodies unfortunately have been produced by designers of electoral systems who used their various features to "shut-out" political parties or groups, or to make it exceedingly difficult for a particular party or group to elect one of its own members to public office. Providing for direct representation of every group in a complex polity is an impossibility, and there are many citizens who contend that such representation would be undesirable. President Ronald Reagan in 1982 stated "proportional representation would, of course, be alien to the traditional political principles of our country."[1]

This chapter focuses upon the gerrymandering problems and alternative local electoral systems that can be employed to elect governing bodies and chief executives.

Gerrymandering

The widespread use of the ward or single-member district necessitates an examination of the gerrymandering problems (i.e., the intentional drawing of district lines to favor one party or group).

Reprinted with permission from National Civic Review, *Vol. 79, No. 1, January/February, 1990. Published by the National Civic League Press, Denver, Colorado.*

The representational equity problem produced by legislative districts with widely varying populations has been eliminated, except in rapidly growing communities, by the United States Supreme Court's "one person, one vote" dictum.[2] While solving one problem, the dictum intensified the traditional gerrymandering problem, as the dictum allows the violation of local government boundary lines in order to achieve equally populated districts, thereby enhancing the ability of district map makers to determine the outcome of elections.

An additional problem was created in 1977 when the United States Supreme Court upheld a deliberate racial gerrymander—labeled an "affirmative gerrymander" by David I. Wells—which encourages members of a racial group to move to districts where a majority of the voters are members of the same racial group.[3] The Court specifically ignored Justice William O. Douglas's warning that "when racial or religious lines are drawn by the State, the multiracial, multireligious communities that our Constitution seeks to weld together as one become separatist; antagonisms that relate to race or religion rather than to political issues are generated;..."[4]

Reformers were disappointed when the United States Supreme Court in 1986 failed to invalidate as unconstitutional a deliberate gerrymandering of the districts of the Indiana Legislature. While holding that such gerrymandering is subject to the equal protection clause, the Court concluded "that a threshold showing discriminatory vote dilution is required for a *prima facie* case of an equal protection violation" and the threshold was not met in this case.[5]

To solve the gerrymandering problem, reformers have advanced proposals for creation of a nonpartisan commission to draw district lines and criteria for redistricting. David I. Wells proposed criteria that would have to be adhered to by the map makers whether they are partisan or nonpartisan-contiguity, compactness, reasonable equality of population, or avoidance or excessive division of governmental jurisdictional lines.[6]

Elimination of the affirmative racial gerrymander can be achieved by congressional amendment of the Voting Rights Act of 1965 or the United States Supreme Court's reversing its 1977 decision.

Alternative Systems

Seven electoral systems have been employed to elect members of local governing bodies in the United States. There are subtypes of each system and two or more systems can be combined in a single municipality.

The ward system. The ward or single-member district system was the principal method employed to elect members of city councils until the early years of the 20th century when municipal reformers sought its replacement because the system was dominated by political bosses and machines in large cities. Some or all wards in a few cities had two council members.

In a ward system, each voter is limited to casting a ballot for one or two candidates. Hence, the system is a type of limited voting, but its results differ from the electoral system labeled limited voting examined in a subsequent section.

While the ward system provides geographical representation, citywide interests may not receive adequate consideration by the council. In addition to the gerrymandering problem, this system suffers from the plurality election problem, the citizen access problem, and the minority representation problem.[7]

The plurality election problem is most serious when the votes cast are split among a large number of candidates seeking office. The victorious candidate may be disliked by a majority of the voters and would have been defeated in a two-candidate contest. Compounding this problem is the possibility that the victorious candidate also won, with a small plurality, the primary election in which relatively few voters typically participate. Elimination of this problem by use of the run-off election or alternative vote is examined in a subsequent section.

An access problem exists in the single-member district system for the voter whose direct representative, whether a majority or plurality winner, is insensitive to the needs and desires of the voter. And the problem is most severe for the voter who publicly supported a losing candidate in the district.

The ward system may provide direct representation for a geographically concentrated group, but the system also reduces the political influence of a geographically dispersed minority group. In an at-large plurality system, a geographically dispersed minority group may be able to help determine the outcome of an election by acting as a "swing" vote, thereby allowing the group more leverage with the city council than it would have if it held a small number of council seats.

The ward system produces council members who tend to be responsive to the requests of many of their constituents. A council member, however, may be hostile to the needs of minority constituents if the group is not a majority in his district. Furthermore, experience reveals the system may distribute resources equally among districts regardless of citywide needs.[8] Districts with a large low-income minority population are disadvantaged by an equal district distribution of city resources.

The at-large plurality system. The early municipal reformers advocated the replacement of the large, ward-elected bicameral council by a small unicameral council elected at-large because they were convinced the ward system promoted "invisible" city councils controlled by corrupt machines.[9]

Each elector in the at-large system may cast a number of votes for different candidates equal to the number of council members to be elected.

Greater emphasis is placed upon the allocation of resources by the council in accordance with citywide needs. The system also offers the advantage of maximizing citizen access to decision-makers since each voter can help to elect one or more members of the council.

The system suffers the disadvantage of enabling a political party or group with the largest number of votes, perhaps only a plurality, to elect all or most council members. In this respect, the at-large and ward systems are similar in employing a "winner takes all" approach.

Pressures for geographical representation, however, led a number of cities to adopt new charters or charter amendments providing for the at-large plurality electoral system with district residency requirements. The plurality rule determines the winners of the election subject to the requirement that one member must reside in each district. If the two most popular candidates live in the same district, only the one with the most votes is elected.

By the 1960s, several political scientists and civil rights activists commenced to criticize the at-large plurality system for over-representing middle class values and neglecting the needs of blacks. In carrying out its responsibilities under the Voting Rights Act of 1965, the United States Department of Justice has promoted the ward system as a substitute for the at-large system in cities covered by the act. Interestingly, the United States Supreme Court opined in 1971 that "...it is not at all clear that the remedy is a single-member district system."[10]

The combined system. To avoid the disadvantages of the ward and at-large electoral systems, many cities adopted a combination of the two systems to ensure that both citywide and neighborhood needs would receive adequate city council consideration. Typically, a council elected by this system will have ten members elected at-large and five members elected by wards, or ten members elected by ward and five members elected at-large.

The combined system is subject to the charge that voters are deprived of their right to elect all members of a governing body. The charge is accurate, yet it must be pointed out that the single member district system is a limited voting system confining the elector's choice to a single candidate. The combined system also is criticized on the ground that it does not guarantee direct representation for minority groups because the relatively small number of districts have a winning threshold vote requirement beyond the reach of the minority groups.

Limited voting. The failure of the ward system to provide adequate two-party representation in the post–Civil War period generated interest in the adoption of a new system of voting, labeled limited voting. Under this system, each voter is allowed to vote for a number of candidates fewer than the number of candidates to be elected to the council, thereby making it impossible for the party or group with the largest number of votes to win a disproportionate share of the seats.

Typically, the voter may cast ballots for three candidates if five are to be elected or five candidates if seven are to be elected. New York City employed limited voting from 1963 to 1985 to elect one of the two "Borough" council members in each Borough to the City Council. The system currently is employed by a number of towns in Connecticut and a number of counties in Pennsylvania.

Limited voting can be utilized on an at-large or district basis, and may be employed with partisan or nonpartisan ballots. In addition, limited nomination can be employed to restrict the dominance of the largest political party.

This system is a crude method for securing minority representation. Limited voting neither guarantees that each group or party will be represented fully in proportion to its voting strength nor prevents a minority from electing a majority of the council members when several strong slates of candidates divide the votes cast. In addition, the system normally provides no representation for independent associations or minority parties other than the largest one. Further, the majority party may influence the election of a minority council member by throwing some votes to a favored minority party candidate, thereby encouraging minority party candidates to curry the favor of the majority party.

The cumulative voting system. This system was employed to elect members of the Illinois House of Representatives in the period 1870–1970.[11] The system's purpose is identical to the purpose of limited voting (i.e., to provide direct representation for the largest minority political party or group).

In Illinois, three members of the House were elected in each senatorial district and each voter had three votes which could be allocated in the following ways: three votes to one candidate, two votes to one candidate and one vote to a second candidate, one and one-half votes to each of two candidates, or one vote to each of three candidates. The majority party mathematically is unable to elect three candidates, assuming members of each party vote only for their party's candidates, unless the majority party receives over 75 percent of the votes cast.

In general, the largest party elected two candidates in a district and the second largest party elected one candidate. However, in certain districts in several elections, the minority party elected two candidates because the overconfident majority party nominated three candidates, thereby splitting the party's vote and enabling the minority party to elect two candidates.

Cumulative voting does not guarantee proportional representation because parties are unable to make their members follow instructions and, as noted, miscalculate their strength on occasion. Split-ticket voting alone, if of significant magnitude, will make proportionate representation impossible.

The system was controversial in Illinois with many citizens considering it technically complicated and confusing because the ballot can be marked in four different ways and the voter, to be informed, has to follow the activities of three legislators instead of one. Critics also maintained that inter-party competition was eliminated in some districts by so-called "sweetheart deals" and "horse trading" between the two major parties, whereby they agree to nominate a total of three candidates, thus depriving voters of any choice. The two majority party incumbents and the minority incumbent in other districts discouraged potential challengers by playing down differences and often speaking on each other's behalf.

The lack of party competition could be remedied by requiring each party to nominate at least two candidates per district, but other problems might be created. If one party has a large majority, it could have some of its members cast votes for the weaker of the minority party's candidates in order to increase the prospects of the majority party's winning three seats. The majority party can elect a candidate in such districts only if its members each cast three votes for the same candidate.

Proportional representation. The single-transferable vote (STV) system of proportional representation is a type of preferential voting designed to ensure that each political party or group will receive a number of seats on a legislative body in direct proportion to its voting strength. Voters indicate a gradation of preferences for candidates by placing numbers next to the names of the various candidates. Winners of the election are determined by a quota: the total number of valid ballots cast divided by the number of council members to be elected plus one. If 100,000 valid ballots are cast to elect a nine-member city council, the quota would be equal to

$$\frac{100,000}{9+1} + 1 = 10,001.$$

Once the quota is determined, ballots are sorted by first choices. A candidate receiving a total of "number 1" votes equal to or exceeding the quota is declared elected. Should a candidate receive more than quota, the surplus ballots are distributed to the remaining candidates.[12] Following distribution of the surplus ballots, the candidate with the smallest number of votes is declared defeated and his/her ballots are distributed by second choices to the remaining candidates. If the second choice already has been elected, the ballot is transferred to the third choice. A new count is conducted and any candidate receiving a total of "number 1" and transferred ballots exceeding the quota is declared elected. Surplus ballots of a winning candidate are transferred to the remaining candidates. The process of declaring defeated the candidate with the fewest votes and transfers of the defeated candidate's ballot is continued until the full council is elected.

The single-transferable voting system may be employed on an at-large or a district basis, and also may be employed in partisan or nonpartisan elections. The STV system must be distinguished from the "List" system of proportional representation which has not been used in the United States. Under the "List" system, voters cast ballots for political parties and the parties are allocated a number of seats in a legislative body on the basis of their respective shares of the total number of votes cast.

The principal advantage of STV is that it ensures majority rule while guaranteeing minority representation. The system recognizes that there are numerous factional divisions in cities and makes it impossible for any political party or faction with a slight electoral majority to elect all members of a city council or school board.

Following the abandonment of STV in 1947 by New York City, the Democrats won 24 of the 25 council seats in the 1949 election while polling only 52.5 percent of the votes cast. Had STV been in effect, the party division would have been thirteen Democrats, six Republicans, three Liberals, and three American Labor Party members.

The effectiveness of STV in providing minority representation is revealed by the 1989 New York City Community School Boards elections in which 30.6 percent of the seats were won by black candidates.[13] Moreover, 40.0 percent of the winning candidates were parents of school children and 54.2 percent were women.

In addition to providing a minority group—whether geographically concentrated or dispersed—with representation, STV has other advantages. Under a plurality system, a popular name at the head of a party column can carry weak or unqualified candidates into office, an outcome which is impossible under STV. The possibility of election fraud also is reduced by STV since ballots are counted centrally under close supervision.

Bullet or single-shot voting is common in at-large systems because additional choices may help defeat a group's candidate. In a STV election, second and subsequent choices are examined only if the first choice has been elected or defeated. In consequence, the presence of many preferences on the ballot has no effect on the prospect of the first choice being elected.

STV measures up well in terms of effectiveness of ballots cast as most ballots help to elect a candidate either by first choice or by transfer. In contrast, the ballots of voters in a single-member district system cast for the losing candidates—possibly amounting to a majority—may be viewed as wasted. STV, on the other hand, gives effect to voters' wishes by ensuring that each voter, with relatively few exceptions, may have an equal effect on the final outcome of the election.

STV has the additional advantage of eliminating the need for a primary or preliminary election to reduce the number of candidates, thus guaranteeing the legislators will be selected in an election with a relatively large turnout of eligible voters. Responsiveness of council members is increased as their election is dependent in large measure upon their ability to develop a program with broad citizen support instead of a one-issue platform appealing to a majority or plurality of electors in a single district. Since a vote has equal weight regardless of the polling place at which it is cast, candidates will be seeking support throughout the polity and that support will be dependent upon their responsiveness to the needs of the electorate.

STV facilitates access to decision makers. Each council member will be receptive to the views and requests of citizens regardless of their place of residence since a vote cast in any district carries an equal weight with a vote cast in any other district.

The system also measures up exceptionally well in terms of the criterion of equity: 1) majority rule with guaranteed minority representation is produced, and 2) a faction with a small majority of votes is prevented from electing all or most members of a legislative body. STV also helps to ensure equity by eliminating gerrymandering and the need for periodic reapportionment of the council.

In spite of the advantages that STV offers, it has been a controversial system and campaigns to secure its adoption have been marked by strong emotional opposition. A spurious charge is that the system is un–American because of its foreign origin. Another emotional charge is that STV permitted the election of two Communists and two American Labor Party candidates to the New York City Council in 1945. These parties accounted for 18.0 percent of the first choice votes and received 17.5 percent of the council seats.

Opponents of STV charge it promotes civic disunity and strife by fostering splinter groups and emphasizing ethnic, racial, and religious politics in contrast to a "good" electoral system which plays down divisive prejudices. A system that shuts out minority groups from direct council representation, however, does not play down divisive prejudices but does promote voter alienation. Furthermore, there is no evidence that voting along ethnic, racial, and religious lines is more common under STV than under the other electoral systems.

Objections also are raised that STV does not guarantee that each neighborhood will be represented on the city council and school board. As under at-large plurality elections, all councillors and school board members elected by STV might live in the same section of a city.

The counting of STV ballots in a large city requires several days and hence the cost of the election is higher. Development of computer programs should remove these objections in the future.

But the major argument advanced in opposition to STV is that it is a fantastically complicated system understood by relatively few citizens. STV proponents respond that the mechanics of voting are simple and few invalid ballots are cast. STV proponent George H. Hallett, Jr., pointed out that the voter "does not have to count the ballots any more than he has to make his own watch or repair his own car."[14]

The Alternative Vote

The plurality election problem results from a large number of candidates seeking an elective office and splitting the vote. The election of a local government chief executive, in common with the single-member district system, encounters this problem and some local government charters attempt to deal with it by requiring a "run-off" primary or "run-off" general election between the two highest vote getters for chief executive if no candidate receives a majority of the votes cast for the office.

The "run-off" election, however, may violate the state constitution as in Arkansas where the State Supreme Court in 1970 struck down a law providing for a "run-off" election for state offices.[15] Even if upheld as constitutional by the courts, the "run-off" election is a special election and typically suffers from a small voter turnout, resulting in the selection of a candidate representing the preference of a minority of all registered voters.

A better solution of the plurality election problem is the alternative vote, a type of preferential voting, allowing the elector to use numbers to indicate the degree of preference for each candidate. Majority preferential voting was employed successfully in New York City to elect the single member of the City Council from the Borough of Richmond (Staten Island) when STV was used to elect several members from each of the other four Boroughs of the City.

Majority preferential voting ensures that the winning candidate for a single office is the preferred candidate of the majority of the voters. Each voter places numbers after the name of each candidate to indicate the degree of preference for each candidate with "number 1" designating the most favored candidate.

The winner is determined by sorting the ballots according to "number 1" choices. Should a candidate receive a majority of the "number 1" votes, that candidate is elected. If no candidate receives a majority, the least popular candidate is declared defeated and his or her ballots are transferred to the remaining candidates by the indicated second choices. A new count of "number 1" and "number 2" choices is made, and the candidate—if any—receiving a majority of these ballots is declared elected. If no candidate is elected on this count, the remaining candidate with the smallest number of ballots is declared defeated and his or her ballots are distributed to the other candidates in accordance with the indicated second or third choices. The process of counting and transferring ballots is continued until a candidate receives a majority of the ballots.

The elected candidate admittedly may not be the individual most favored by a majority of the voters, yet the winner is the compromise person favored by a majority of the voters rather than the plurality candidate favored by one or more small group(s).

Summary and Conclusion

Eliminating malrepresentation in local governments and achieving fair representation for all groups are difficult tasks. Our review of alternative electoral systems reveals that the single-member district system is encumbered with serious problems. Nevertheless, this system will continue to be the most common electoral system within the foreseeable future because the system is supported by the two major political parties in most states and is promoted by the United States Department of Justice in political subdivisions covered by the Federal Voting Rights Act of 1965 as amended.

In view of the widespread use of the single-member district systems, state constitutions should be amended to incorporate redistricting criteria designed to eliminate or minimize deliberate gerrymandering. In local governments experiencing rapid growth, there should be a state constitutional requirement that district lines be redrawn every five years, based upon new census data, if the rate of growth exceeds a specified percentage, such as 35 or 40 percent. We also recommended that the Congress amend the Voting Rights Act to prohibit the use of the affirmative racial gerrymander.

Citizens concerned with the quality of representation in their local governments should examine carefully the alternatives to the single member district system. The semi-proportional systems—limited voting and cumulative voting—clearly have the advantage of promoting direct representation of minority groups. The ideal system, however, is STV. It permits simultaneous representation of general and particular interests, as candidates must build a citywide coalition of voters in order to win election to office.

Notes

1. "Extension of the Voting Rights Act of 1965: Statement on Action by the Senate Judiciary Committee, May 3, 1982," *Weekly Compilation of Presidential Documents*, May 7, 1982, p. 569.

2. See *Sanders v. Gray*, 372 U.S. 368 (1963); *Reynolds v. Sims*, 377 U.S. 533 (1964); and *Avery v. Midland County*, 390 U.S. 474 (1968).

3. *United Jewish Organizations v. Carey*, 430 U.S. 144 (1977). See also David I. Wells, "'Affirmative Gerrymander' Compounds Districting Problems," National Civic Review, 67:1, January 1978, pp. 16–17.

4. *Wright v. Rockefeller*, 376 U.S. 52, at 67 (1964).

5. *David v. Banemer*, 106 S. Ct. 2797, at 2816 (1986).

6. David I. Wells, "How to Inhibit Gerrymandering: The Purpose of Districting Criteria," *National Civic Review*, 71:4, April 1982, pp. 183–87.

7. Richard S. Childs, *The First 50 Years of the Council-Manager Plan of Municipal Government* (New York: National Municipal League, 1965), p. 37.

8. See the testimony of former Houston Mayor Louis Welch in *Greater Houston Civil Council et al. v. Mann*, 400 F. Supp. 696, at 700 (1977).

9. Arthur W. Bromage, *Introduction to Municipal Government and Administration*, 2nd ed. (New York: Appleton-Century-Crofts, Inc., 1957), p. 217.

10. *Whitecomb v. Chavis*, 403 U.S. 124, at 159–60 (1971).

11. George S. Blair, *Cumulative Voting: An Effective Electoral Device in Illinois Politics* (Urbana: The University of Illinois Press, 1960).

12. For a description of the two systems employed to distribute surplus ballots, see Joseph F. Zimmerman, *The Federated City: Community Control in Large Cities* (New York: St. Martin's Press, 1972), p. 75.

13. *Community School Board Elections: 1989* (Brooklyn: New York City Board of Education, 1989), Table V.

14. George H. Hallett, Jr., *Proportional Representation: The Key to Democracy* (New York: National Municipal League, 1940), pp. 72–73.

15. *Rockefeller v. Matthews*, 469 S.W. 2d 110 (1970).

At-Large vs. District Election Systems

Darrell Williams

One of the most controversial issues regarding municipal elections is the concept of switching from an at-large system to a district system. Under the at-large electoral process, council candidates are elected citywide. The latter plan divides the municipality into separate geographical districts, or wards, so that area residents can choose their representative. District advocates generally argue that this plan provides disadvantaged groups with an opportunity to select a councilperson who can voice their needs and concerns. Opponents charge that the ward plan leads to special interest politics—district elected council members tend to view local problems on a parochial basis; therefore, they support and vote for programs which benefit their area, even though such measures may not be in the best interest of the entire community.

This chapter will discuss the major concerns surrounding the debate over at-large versus district elections. First, it introduces the topic by presenting a brief background discussion. Then, it details three of the most significant issues involved in the dispute. Next, two case studies, *Bolden v. Mobile* and *McNeil v. Springfield*, are presented to illustrate what role the courts have played in trying to resolve the issue. Finally, the chapter will identify current trends relating to local election systems.

Background

The district election system has been closely identified with the nineteenth century urban political "machines." It was in cities such as Boston,

Reprinted with permission from Issue Brief, *January, 1989. Published by the National League of Cities, Washington, D.C.*

Chicago, New York and Philadelphia where political machines dominated the ward based electoral process. The machine's primary strategy included backing council candidates who were usually ward residents. More importantly, through its benevolent behavior, the machine galvanized voter support from a growing ethnic and immigrant constituency:

> The machine provided quick naturalization, jobs, social services, personal access to authority, release from surveillance of the courts, deference to ethnic pride. In return it garnered votes, herding to the polls new citizens, grateful for services rendered to and submissive to experience[d] leadership.[1]

Hence, the machine's political dominance consisted of backing its own candidates and catering to the voter's basic social and economic needs in exchange for their votes.

Besides being advantageous for the machine, the ward system appeared to be just as beneficial for the voters. In particular, the system enabled the people to elect local legislators who represented and advocated their area's concerns. Historian Samuel P. Hays explains how the ward representatives went about their mission:

> City councilmen were local leaders. They spoke for their local areas, the economic interest of their inhabitants, their residential concerns, their educational, recreational, and religious interests i.e., for those aspects of community life which mattered most to those they represented. They rolled logs in the city council to provide streets, sewers, and other public works for their local areas.[2]

It is important to note that the relationship between the ward electoral process and the political machines was more complex than described above; however, the essence of this arrangement permitted citizens to participate in a decentralized system of representation.

Around the turn of the twentieth century, commonly referred to as the Progressive Era, this form of representation came under attack from a group of structural reformers, which consisted of individuals from the business community and upper middle-class.[3] The reformers sought to reduce the power of neighborhood and ethnic leaders. Moreover, they wanted to abolish corrupt machines and establish a professional and efficient system within local government.[4] According to Hays, "These reformers were dissatisfied with existing systems of municipal government ... [t]hey objected to the structure of government which enabled local and particularistic interests to dominate."[5]

With the intent to destroy the influence of special interest politics, reformers proposed adopting new municipal voting procedures which included an at-large election system, nonpartisan elections, and the short ballot. The procedures were introduced to weaken the power base of the political machines,

remove political parties' control over the local nomination process and reduce
political organizations' influence regarding voter ballot casting.[6] Furthermore,
the new election plan was promoted as a process to elect councilmembers who
advocated efficiency in local government and preferred creating city governments that would be responsive to the needs of the over-all community. Subsequently, many jurisdictions adopted electoral reforms with the at-large system
as the center piece. In short, reformers advanced the election scheme as a
method to elect councilmembers who furthered the interests of the entire municipality and as a device to suppress the influence of special interest politics.

Present Issues

Over the past 20 years, the at-large electoral process has come under
increasing criticism and legal challenges. The center of the controversy
involves the issue of representation, election process and vote dilution. For
instance, critics charge that the system enables councilpersons to be elected
who do not represent the interest of minority groups. Also, they argue that the
system works against minority council candidates. Their most serious charge
deals with the legal issue of vote dilution—they claim that the system dilutes
the voting strength of minority groups. In accordance with these charges,
minority community leaders have filed voting rights suits to seek remedies for
violations of Section 2 of the Voting Rights Act of 1965.

The representation issue centers on the fact that most at-large-elected
councils are comprised of middle class Caucasians who reside in the same district.[7] More importantly, the council members are not always aware of, or sensitive to, minority needs; moreover, the members do not fully comprehend the
issues and problems which are unique to black and Hispanic neighborhoods.
In short, minority community leaders charge that the system fails to produce
council members who are responsive to the requests, or represent the political interest, of the minority communities.

In terms of election process, minority leaders also claim that the at-large
concept is unfavorable for their candidates. They avow that the system favors
nonminority candidates who have easier access to funds to purchase local
media time as well as operate a city-wide campaign organization. The leaders assert that the district system provides a better opportunity for election
success. Authors Albert K. Karnig and Susan Welch agree with the leaders'
assertion by pointing out, "With limited funds for buying media time, blacks
are more apt to succeed at the neighborhood [district] level than at the city-
wide level."[8] They further declared, "...district contests are advantageous to
blacks not merely because the costs are lower, but also because there is less
need for citywide name recognition or for endorsements by the media and
civic groups."[9]

The vote dilution charge involves the use of the at-large system as a mechanism to submerge minority voting strength. Specifically, because of the numerical advantage nonminority voters hold in many municipalities, minority community leaders complain that the system dilutes their influence and limits the possibility of them electing a candidate of their own choice. According to the community leaders, the election procedure enables white majority voting to nullify the effects of the votes minorities cast; as a result, minorities are prevented from gaining access to political power. In other words, white majority votes cancel the votes casted by minority voters. Thus minorities are deprived of the opportunity to influence the local decision-making process. Under such circumstances, the minority group must rely on their candidate to either attract a certain percentage of white votes along with their constituency or form an effective coalition with other racial or ethnic groups to overcome white majority voting.

Because vote dilution is a legal issue, minority leaders have used it to challenge the constitutionality of the at-large system. They have filed voting rights suits to seek remedies for violations of Section 2 of the Voting Rights Act of 1965. Although the Act does not specifically acknowledge that the at-large election system is, per se, illegal, Section 2 is one of the important sections which is concerned with dilution. The section's language states

> No voting qualification or prerequisite to voting, or standard, practice or procedure shall be imposed or applied by any State or political subdivision to deny or abridge the right of any citizen of the United States to vote on account of race or color.[10]

It is worth noting that "...Section 2 provides a private cause of action for citizens to challenge a discriminatory voting practice or procedure anywhere in the country."[11] All in all, Section 2 bans voting procedures or practices which are discriminatory and enables minority groups to challenge the at-large system under the concept of voter dilution.

Role of the Courts

The following section illustrates what role the courts have played in the dispute over the at-large election system. It highlights and discusses the importance of two widely publicized cases, *Bolden v. Mobile* and *McNeil v. Springfield*, that involve legal challenges to the at-large system. The *Bolden* case exemplifies what criteria two lower federal courts and the Supreme Court used to decide the constitutionality of at-large or multimember systems. More than anything else the case clearly defines the standard-of-proof plaintiffs had to present when challenging the election procedure. In *McNeil v. Springfield*, similar legal arguments were presented; however, the requirement of proof was different. The case demonstrates how the plaintiffs successfully use the new requirements to their benefit.

Bolden v. Mobile

In this particular case, the plaintiffs, which included Wiley L. Bolden and a class composed of all blacks in Mobile, filed a class action suit against the city of Mobile, Alabama in 1976. They claimed that the at-large system, which was used to elect the city's three-member Commission government, "abridged the voting rights of black citizens and denied blacks effective participation in the political process."[12] Furthermore, they alleged that the continued use of the system violated their rights as expressed in the 14th and 15th Amendments, and Section 2 of the Voting Rights Act of 1965.[13] Admittedly, blacks were not obstructed from voting or participating in the local political process; however, they asserted that "the at-large system diluted their vote and threatened them with continued nonrepresentation for as long as the at-large system remained in effect."[14]

The contested election system and commission form of government was established in 1911 by the Alabama State Legislature and used by the city since the law was passed.[15] Under the governing structure, commissioners are elected by a city-wide vote and each serve a four year term. The three commissioners are responsible for the city's legislative, executive, and administrative functions. For example, the administrative duties are divided among three "places"; place Number One supervises the city's finance and administration, while places Number Two and Number Three manage public safety and direct public works and related services respectively.[16] Finally, the commissioners rotate the title of mayor among themselves: each commissioner is required to serve as the mayor for 16 months out of a four year term.

The defendant contended that the system was not discriminatory by design. According to the defendant, the system was

> created by the state Legislature in 1911 at a time when blacks had already been disenfranchised. Thus, Mobil's commission form of government was created in a "race-proof" situation which preclude[d] the possibility of discriminatory intent or purpose.[17]

Additionally, the defendant argued that there was no evidence produced to suggest an invidious intent behind preserving the system.[18] Therefore, they concluded, the system was not unconstitutional.

In general, the court's findings of facts indicated the following: the slating process or candidate selection process combined with racial polarization voting limited black candidate's access, the commissioners were not adequately responding to the needs of the black community, and the pervasive effects of past discrimination discouraged blacks from participating in the political process. Although the court noted that there were no structural barriers prohibiting blacks from participating, it acknowledged that the structure combine[d] with racially polarized voting "effectively discourage[d] qualified black citizens from seeking office or being elected."[19] Citing examples of drainage and paving needs in the black community, the court expressed that "there [was] a significant difference and sluggishness in the response of the city to critical needs of the blacks compared to that in the white area."[20] Finally, the court asserted that the pervasive effects of past discrimination had "helped preclude the effective participation of blacks in the election system."[21]

After considering these and other findings, the court ruled that the city of Mobile's electoral structure was unconstitutional because it diluted the voting strength of its black citizens. Thus, it ordered the city to replace the electoral structure with a district system [in] which council members would be elected by district elections and the mayor elected city-wide.[22]

As a result of the district court's ruling, the defendants appealed the decision to the Fifth Circuit Court of Appeals. The defendants found no relief at that level—the appeals court affirmed the district court's decision and agreed with the lower court's remedy.[23] Their next step was to appeal the decision to the highest court in the land, the U.S. Supreme Court.

The Supreme Court, on a 6-to-3 vote, reversed the two lower courts rulings. Specifically, the high court's majority opinion was primarily based on the issue of "purposeful or intentional discrimination." After declaring that Mobile's black citizens' freedom to vote or to participate was not denied or abridged as provided for under the 15th Amendment, the justices focused on whether the city's electoral system violated the equal protection clause of the 14th Amendment which requires the plaintiff to present evidence of purposeful discrimination. Four of the six majority voters reasoned that the plaintiff failed to show that the city and the city commissioners "conceived or operated [a] purposeful device to further racial discrimination."[24] Writing for a four-justice plurality, Justice Potter Stewart acknowledged that the Court, in previous cases, had declined to rule that multimember or at-large systems were unconstitutional per se; instead, the Court left it up to the plaintiffs to demonstrate that the electoral system had been created or maintained for the purpose of furthering racial discrimination.[25] Hence, in order for a violation of the equal protection clause of the 14th Amendment to have occurred, plaintiffs had to prove that the commission system was adopted or preserved for the purpose of discriminating against blacks. In short, the Court reversed the lower court's decision because they failed to require the plaintiffs prove intent.

As a result of the *Bolden* case, the U.S. Congress in 1982 made it easier to challenge local election systems by broadening the concept of proof when it amended Section 2 of the 1965 Voting Rights Act. In particular, the law-makers modified the language in Section 2 so that the plaintiffs would not have to provide proof of intent. Instead, the plaintiffs must show that "an election law or procedure had been imposed or applied in a manner that 'results' in voting discrimination."[26] The provision also declared that courts would have to review the "totality of circumstances" when deciding whether a voting rights violation had been prove[n].[27] Thus, the language of Section 2 was amended so the plaintiff is not required to prove intent in a vote dilution claim.

McNeil v. Springfield

In *McNeil*, a group of black residents filed a class action suit against the City of Springfield, Illinois in 1985. The suit alleged that the city's commission form of government and election system diluted minority voting strength. The plaintiffs argued that

> based on the totality of the circumstances, the political processes leading to nomination or election in the City of Springfield, Illinois, are not equally open to participation by the plaintiffs because the plaintiffs have less opportunity than other members of the electorate to participate in the political process and to elect representatives of their choice.[28]

Consequently, the plaintiffs were seeking remedies for alleged violations of Section 2 of the Voting Rights Act of 1965, as amended June 29, 1982.

Although the plaintiffs in vote dilution cases were not required to prove intent, they had to establish the existence of three conditions:

> (1) the plaintiff's class constitute a large and geographical compact; (2) the class is politically cohesive; and (3) the white majority voting bloc usually defeats the minority's preferred candidate.[29]

In other words, the plaintiffs had to establish that they comprised a majority in a single-member district, demonstrate that they usually vote as a bloc and show that their votes are submerged as result of white majority voting.

Springfield's governmental structure consisted of the mayor and a four-member commission elected at-large. Each commissioner serves as the executive head of one of the five city executive departments. The commission form of government was adopted by referendum in 1911.

The defendants defended Springfield's structure of government by arguing that factors other than the at-large system explained why blacks were not elected to the council; and, they presented facts indicating that the city government had been responsive to the needs of the black community. They insisted that incumbency, campaign spending and the candidates' qualifications were reasons attributed to why blacks had never won a commission council position.[30] As far as responsiveness, the defendants pointed to the city's efforts to work for and promote fair housing, neighborhood renewal and hiring more black personnel.[31] Acknowledging that the blacks had suffered under discriminatory practices in the past, the defendants affirmed the city's commitment towards helping the black community overcome the disadvantages which impeded its progress.

After reviewing the findings of fact, the presiding federal district judge, Harold Baker, ruled that Springfield's commission form of government violated Section 2 of the Voting Rights Act of 1965, as amended. Judge Baker stated that the plaintiffs had established the existence of the three conditions which prove that the at-large system diluted their voting strength.[32] In terms of considering the totality of circumstances, the judge declared that other factors such as polarized voting, the persistent effects of *de facto* segregation, an election procedure which includes both nonpartisan primaries and runoff elections, the depressing socioeconomic conditions found in the black community and the fact that a black person had never been elected to the commission resulted in the conclusion that the plaintiffs' voting strength was submerged which meant they had "less opportunity than other members of the electorate to participate in the political process and to elect representatives of their choice.[33] Judge Baker further exclaimed,

> It follows that the commission form of government, with its attendant standards, practices, and procedures imposed upon the plaintiff class, results in a denial or abridgment of the plaintiffs' right to vote on account of race or color in violation of Section 2 of the Voting Rights Act of 1965, as amended.[34]

Therefore, as a violation of Section 2 of the Voting Rights Act, the plaintiffs were given a remedy. Judge Baker ordered the city to replace the at-large system with an election process chosen by the citizens. Voting in a special referendum election, the residents of Springfield chose a Mayor-Aldermanic system where the mayor will be elected citywide and ten district alderman will be elected by district.

Current Trends

The final section briefly identifies current trends relating to local election systems. In 1987, an ICMA *Base Line Data Report* presented recent information on the use of local election systems. For instance, it reported that the at-large system is more widely used by western cities.[35] Northern cities, particularly in the North Central region, most commonly use the district system. The mixed plan, in which some council members are elected at-large while others are elected by district, is used predominately in the South.

Other interesting data showed a definite correlation between form of government and election systems. In particular, the at-large system is strongly associated with both commission and council-manager forms of government.[36] The mayor-council form is utilized with the district plan.[37] Finally, mixed systems are most often used by cities with either a mayor-council or council-manager form of government.[38] Besides these indicators, the report provided informative longitudinal data.

The data indicated a decrease in both the at-large and district election systems as well as an increase in the mixed plan. For example, the statistics showed that in 1981, 66 percent of the cities surveyed used the at-large system, while only 60 percent continued to use it in 1986.[39] During the same measured period, the district system showed a slight decline—from 15 percent in 1981 to 13 percent in 1986.[40] At the time, the figures indicated an increase in the use of the mixed plan; the plan's statistic rose from 19 percent to 27 percent.[41] As the use of traditional election systems decrease, it is appropriate to discuss the significant features which contribute to increase[d] use of the mixed plan.

Providing increased minority representation and influence on local legislative bodies and creating a natural division of labor between district-based and at-large representatives are the significant features contributing to the popularity of the mixed plan's increased use. Advocates for greater minority representation have embraced the system because it is viewed as an equitable procedure to elect representatives who are responsive to minority needs and concerns. Moreover, it enables minority voters to play an important role in council contests:

> The mixed plan offers the potential for [minorities] to influence the outcome of each at-large race in addition to determining the outcome of contests in minority-majority districts. The opportunity to influence at-large positions has become more significant in recent years in light of the dispersion of the minority population, a higher incidence of black bloc voting, and higher turnout rates among blacks than whites.[42]

The other significant feature deals with the concept of division of labor. The system enables council members to simultaneously devote attention to special issue concerns and citywide problems. Authors Francine F. Rabinovitz and Edward K. Hamilton noted,

> Mixed systems could ... be a way to organize work of city councils more efficiently. At-large council members might deliberately be put in charge of issues which cut across district lines; district council members could be assigned to committees and issues which seem more narrowly defined.[43]

Conclusion

The major issues in the dispute over at-large versus district elections are representation, election process and vote dilution. Proponents of the district system claim that the at-large process produce[s] council members who fail to represent the interest of the minority communities. Moreover, they assert that the at-large system is unfavorable for minority candidates and it dilutes the voting strength of minority groups. In accordance with these charges, voting rights suits have been filed to legally challenge the at-large system.

Two of the most noticeable cases involving legal challenges are *Bolden v. Mobile* and *McNeil v. Springfield*. In *Bolden*, the U.S. Supreme Court reversed two lower courts' decision[s] because they failed to require the plaintiffs to prove that the at-large system was intentionally discriminatory. Although similar legal arguments were presented, the plaintiffs in *McNeil* were not required to prove intent. Benefiting from a 1982 amendment to the Voting Rights Act the plaintiffs successfully use[d] the new requirements to win their suit.

Finally, recent data reveal a few new developments regarding the use of local election systems. Specifically, statistics indicate that the use of both at-large and district systems is decreasing, while the use of a mixed system, in which some council members are elected at-large and others are elected by district, is increasing.

Notes

1. Richard Hofstader, *The Age of Reform* (New York: Alfred A. Knopf 1966), p. 176.

2. Samuel P. Hays, *American Political History As Social Analysis* (Knoxville: University of Tennessee Press, 1980), p. 214.

3. *Ibid.,* p. 214.

4. Chandler Davidson and George Korbel, "At-Large Elections and Minority-Group Representation," *Journal of Politics,* Vol. 43, November 1981, p. 987.

5. Hays op. cit., p. 214.

6. Tari Renner, "Municipal Election Processes: The Impact on Minority Representation," in the Municipal Yearbook 1988 (Washington, D.C.: International City Management Association, 1988), p. 13.

7. J.D. William Boyd, "Local Electoral Systems: Is there a Best Way?" *National Civic Review* (March 1976) p. 138.

8. Albert Karnig and Susan Welch, *Black Representation and Urban Policy* (Chicago: The University of Chicago Press, 1980), p.148.

9. *Ibid.,* p. 148.

10. C.E. Teasley, III, "Minority Vote Dilution: The Impact of Election System and Past Discrimination on Minority Representation," *State and Local Government Review* (Fall 1987) p.96.

11. "At-Large Elections and Vote Dilution: An Empirical Study," *Journal of Law Reform* (Summer 1986) p. 1228.

12. "*City of Mobile v. Bolden*: A setback in the fight against discrimination," *Brooklyn Law Review* p. 174.

13. *Ibid.*

14. *Ibid.*

15. Perry C. Roquemore, Jr., "Constitutionality of the At-Large Form of Government," *Alabama Municipal Journal* (December 1977) p. 16.

16. *Ibid.*

17. *Ibid.*

18. *Ibid.*

19. *Bolden v. City of Mobile, Alabama*, 423 F. Supp. 384 (1976) p. 389.

20. *Id.* at 391.

21. *Id.* at 393.

22. Wayne King, "Court Order to Revise Government Stirs Impeachment Drive in Mobile," *The New York Times* (Nov. 13, 1976) p. 1.

23. H. Russell Fox, "Achieving Fair Representation: The Rome and Mobile Decisions," *National Civic Review* (November 1980) p. 559.

24. "Court Upholds Mobile Form of Government," *City Hall Digest* (April 1980) p. 2.

25. *Brooklyn Law Review*, pp. 178–179.

26. Nadine Cohodas, "Civil Rights Victory: Voting Rights Act Extension Cleared for President Reagan," *Congressional Quarterly Weekly Report*, 40 (June 26, 1982), p. 1504.

27. *Ibid.*

28. *McNeil v. City of Springfield,* No. 86-2365, slip op. at 2 (C.D.C. January 12, 1987).

29. *Id.* at 8.

30. "Town On Trial," *Illinois Times*, Volume 12 (December 4–10) p. 5.

31. *McNeil v. City of Springfield*, op. cit., p. 43.

32. *McNeil*, op. cit., p. 46.

33. *Id.* at 46–47.

34. *Id.* at 47.

35. Tari Renner, Ph.D., "Municipal Election Processes: The Impact on Minority Representation," *Baseline Data Report,* Vol. 19, No. 6 (Washington, D. C.: International City Management Association, November/December 1987) p. 3.

36. *Ibid.* p. 4.

37. *Ibid.*

38. *Ibid.*

39. *Ibid.* p. 4.

40. *Ibid.*

41. *Ibid.*

42. A. Susan MacManus, "Mixed Electoral Systems: The Newest Reform Structure," *National Civic Review* (November 1985) pp. 487–488.

43. F. Francine Rabinovitz, and Edward K. Hamilton, "Alternative Electoral Structures and Responsiveness to Minorities," *National Civic Review* (July 1980) p. 372.

Alternative Election Systems as Voting Rights Remedies

Edward Still and Robert Richie

A municipality faced with a voting rights suit or just the desire to do the right thing before it is sued typically considers multimember districts (MMD) and single-member districts (SMD), or some combination of the two (if entire city is the district, the MMD can be called at-large voting). There are several other systems used in the United States now which may fit the needs of a community better than MMD or SMD. This chapter compares Preference Voting (PrV), Cumulative Voting (CV), and Limited Voting (LV) to the more usual alternatives by using a series of goals we believe should be fairly noncontroversial. For the rules of each system, see the accompanying sidebars. We suggest that the goal for any municipality ought to be choosing a system that works for minorities because it works for everyone.

1. **Can our election system provide racial or ethnic minorities some representation on the city council?**

    The lack of such representation is probably why the city fears being sued. If the city now uses MMD voting, this will typically cause a severe underrepresentation of racial minority groups—perhaps even a complete exclusion of the minority group.[1]

    SMDs may work if the city has a geographically concentrated minority that votes cohesively. On the other hand, the city may have a racial minority for which one district cannot be drawn. In many cities, for instance, Hispanics live in several areas of the city, but still have a distinctive and cohesive political agenda. Or the minority group may be cohesive in wishing to have its own representation, but different factions would like to have the upper hand

Reprinted with permission from Alternative Electoral Systems As Voting Rights Remedies, *1995. Published by the Center for Voting and Democracy, Washington, D.C.*

in choosing the representative. Let's assume the city council has agreed to draw one black majority district, but not all blacks can be fitted into the district. Should the district start at the northern end of the black residential area leaving out the southern end—or vice versa? What if the Booker T. Washington faction wants different district boundaries than the W.E.B. DuBois faction? How does the city council make a decision between those plans?

An alternative election system would avoid most of these problems. CV and LV give minority groups a chance to have some representation on the council, while PrV gives each group a chance at fair representation. Because a minority group will want to undertake a cautious strategy of minimizing the number of its candidates so as to maximize the votes they receive, CV and LV are likely to result in only one minority representative. On the other hand, because PrV allows votes to be transferred according to the wishes of each voter, the minority group does not need to limit the number of its candidates and may be able to win several seats on the council.

2. Will the election system discourage racial vote dilution?

Vote dilution is a process whereby election laws or practices, either singly or in concert, combine with systematic bloc voting among an identifiable group to diminish the voting strength of at least one other group. The idea is that one group, voting cohesively for its preferred candidates, is systematically outvoted by a larger group that is also cohesive.[2]

It is an unfortunate fact of life that racially polarized voting exists. Racially polarized voting simply means that two racial groups vote cohesively within the racial group and differently from the other group. The fact that the two groups vote differently and cohesively does not assign blame or even give us a reason for the difference. Racial polarization may be based on the different political interests of the two groups, or it may be based on their prejudices about the other group. It is really fruitless for election system designers to try to decide why polarization occurs; instead, they should try to alleviate its pernicious effects.

Any "winner-take-all" election will allow racially polarized voting to have an effect. Assume, for instance, that a city had two polarized groups, the Blues and Greens. If the Blues win 51 percent of the vote in an at-large election, they will win all the seats. Many cities have adopted SMD as a method of ameliorating the effect of racially polarized voting. If the Blues and Greens were residentially concentrated, it would be a simple matter to draw districts in which one group or the other had a clear majority. For instance, the Blues with 55 percent of the city's population could be the majority in three districts, and the Greens in two. This result would please many of the Greens and Blues, but the minority group in each district might be dissatisfied. (See Section 3.)

On the other hand, PrV, LV, and CV do as well as, if not better than, SMD in ameliorating the effects of racial bloc voting. Rather than drawing districts for each group, these alternative systems allow voters to group themselves into "voluntary constituencies." Such nondistricts groupings will allow the formation of bi-racial coalitions and racial crossover voting, both of which might have been frustrated by the rigid district lines imposed under SMD.

3. Will the election system allow everyone's vote to count?

If Joe Jones puts his money into a soft drink machine, he gets his money back if his selection is sold out. On the other hand, if he buys a lottery ticket and doesn't win, the money is not refunded. While we do not suggest that voters are "buying" candidates when they cast a vote, the present winner-take-all voting systems are more like a lottery than a commercial transaction. Winner-take-all inevitably leads to "wasted votes," which occur whenever a voter gets nothing back for his or her vote.

While the number of wasted votes may be diminished by districting, all the people in the minority political group in each district will still be wasting their votes—the election could have been held without their participation without changing the results. If the city creates a district with a voting majority of some minority group, it generally has to add enough voters from some other group to make the requisite number of people to meet the one-person-one-vote standard. Two law professors have called these added voters "filler people":

> These additional individuals must not be of the relevant demographic group (in order to avoid claims of packing [the district to reduce the minority group's influence in other districts]); and, in the interest of minority representation, they should not be expected to compete in any genuine sense for electoral representation in the district to which they are assigned lest they undo the preference given to the specified minority group.[3]

By avoiding both districts and winner-take-all elections, alternative election plans eliminate "filler people" and reduce wasted votes greatly. For instance, in a PrV election for five members of a city council, we know that at least ⅚ of the ballots will be counted for winning candidates. Many of the final ⅙ of the voters might have expressed a preference for one or more of the winners, so that the number of wasted votes will be even less than ⅙. Contrast that with the wasted votes in five SMDs: up to 49 percent of the voters in each district could have voted for a losing candidate.

Because of the way LV and CV work, it is much harder to predict the number of potentially wasted votes. An empirical study of the LV and CV elections in Alabama has shown that at least 73 percent of the voters in LV jurisdictions and at least 61 percent of the voters in CV jurisdictions have voted for winning candidates. The number of wasted votes will depend, of course, upon the particular conditions in the election. If there are many candidates with fairly even support in the electorate, the number of wasted votes could fall closer to or even exceed 50 percent of the electorate.

4. Can our election system encourage voter turnout?

Several political science and legal commentators have contended that SMDs depress voter turnout because of "incumbency lock." In a study of Latino politics, two political scientists said,

> Thus, in these [barrio] districts, incumbents have few electoral incentives to mobilize new voters; moreover, they are not indebted to their party for their office, and they have no reason to seek party support to win reelection. These districts are also safe districts for the incumbent's party. Thus, neither the incumbent nor the party is likely to try to mobilize voters in these districts. The design of these districts, therefore, may effectively eliminate the party's need to mobilize the grassroots.[4]

Professor Lani Guinier has taken her criticism a step earlier in time—to the creation of the district.

> [D]istricting decisions may simply reflect the arbitrary preferences of incumbent politicians who prefer packed, safe districts to ensure their reelection. Indeed, districting battles are often pitched between incumbents fighting to retain their seats, without regard to issues of voter representation. Because the choice of districts is so arbitrary, incumbents enjoy extraordinary leverage in self-perpetuation through gerrymandering.
> Thus, districting strategies often promote noncompetitive election contests, which further reduce voter participation and interest.[5]

Since alternative election systems do not use districts, they avoid the problems of incumbency lock and depressed voter turnout associated with districts. In LV, CV, and PrV elections, all candidates—incumbents and challengers alike—are running against each other. No incumbent has a "free ride," but must instead rally the faithful behind his or her candidacy.

In a recent study of municipal elections in four Massachusetts cities, George Pillsbury found that voters were like consumers of material goods— a larger set of available choices will lead to more consumption and greater satisfaction. Pillsbury found that voter turnout had declined in all four, but less in Cambridge (which uses PrV) than in the other three (which use plurality voting). Pillsbury concluded, "...the evidence certainly points to preference voting providing more incentive for voters to participate than plurality elections."[6]

5. Can we prevent a minority of the electorate from electing a majority of the council?

In some cities, a candidate can win an MMD or SMD seat by a plurality of the vote.[7] If several such candidates in an MMD election are all supported by the same group of voters, that minority of the voters can win a majority of the council. Similarly, in SMD elections, one group could win a majority of the seats with only a majority of the vote in those districts and no other votes at all—again, a plurality of the voters would have elected a majority of the council. For instance, consider the results in the 1993 Canadian election:

> In the election, Canadians clearly wanted to show the ruling Progressive Conservatives that had lost confidence in them, and the party won only 16% of the popular vote. However, the workings of the voting system turned a show of nonconfidence into a massacre. Rather than electing 46 of the 295 members that a proportional system would have provided, the Tories elected only two. By contrast, two regionally-based parties, the Bloc Quebecois and Reform, with 13% and 19% of the popular vote respectively, elected 54 and 52 Members. The voting system also turned the victorious Liberals' 41% of the vote into a very solid majority of 177 seats.[8]

LV and CV elections could also allow a minority of voters to control a majority of the council, although it is less likely than with an MMD or SMD. For instance, three of five council seats might be won by three different "single issue" groups, if each had the support of about 15 percent of the electorate, and the remainder of the electorate was fragmented in its choices for the council.

Minority control is extremely unlikely under PrV. Assume that a particular group with about 52 percent of the voters endorses five candidates for the five-member city council. If all the voters in the group cast their preferences for all five candidates of the group—in any order—the group should win three seats, since it has enough voters to fill three thresholds (each threshold would be $\frac{1}{6} + 1$, so three seats would be elected by $\frac{3}{6} + 3$ of all the votes).

6. How can we avoid gerrymandering?

Gerrymandering is defined as "political manipulation within the process of drawing district boundaries."[9] In essence, it is the effort by one group to force a disfavored group to waste its votes. Methods of gerrymandering include packing, stacking, and cracking. Cracking is splitting a political group's population concentration to prevent it from having a majority in a district. Stacking occurs when a group numerous enough to elect one representative is combined with an opposing group in a multimember district. Packing is the overconcentration of a group in one or a few districts to prevent its members from having an impact in adjoining districts.[10]

By definition, gerrymandering can only occur if there are districts. Therefore, eliminating districts eliminates gerrymanders.

Any of the non–SMD election systems may be run from the city at large or from smaller, multimember districts. A city electing fewer than a dozen members of a city council can easily run an election in the whole city. The alternative election systems have the advantage of completely eliminating the cost of redistricting.

7. Can we avoid inter-census malapportionment?

A city can spend a lot of money on a districting plan (including perhaps on a court challenge to the plan), but the plan will be malapportioned as soon as there are significant changes in the population of the city. For instance, the annexation of territory with occupied houses, the creation of new subdivisions or residential apartments in the city, the movement of people out of a decaying neighborhood—all these can cause changes in the population of the various districts. Even before the city reaches the next census, its districts can be malapportioned.

Any system without districts will avoid this creeping malapportionment problem.

8. Can the election plan provide women an equal opportunity to be elected to the council.

Studies of various types of electoral systems have shown that women do better in multimember plans than in single-member district plans.[11] Generally, the larger the number of members elected from a particular district, the more likely it is that women will be elected. Thus, any system electing several council members in the same election or district will probably elect more women than SMD.

9. Can we reduce the cost of campaigns and election administration?

There are several factors that may affect the cost of campaigns for the candidates. The first is the absolute number of people who are potential voters for a particular office. If the candidate wants to use direct mail or telephone banks to reach 5,000 voters, the cost will be less than reaching 50,000 voters by the same method. Similarly, a smaller district size may allow the candidate to make personal contact with all the voters, while she will have to use media or surrogates to contact everyone in a larger district.

The second is the number of votes the candidate expects to need to win. In a winner-take-all election, this will be one half of all the votes. This is true even if there are three or more candidates, since it is possible that some candidates could receive negligible numbers of votes. On the other hand, in the alternative election systems the usual number of votes needed is $\frac{1}{n} + 1$, where "n" is the number of seats being filled. Thus, if the candidate is able to target her direct mail, phone bank, or media campaign, she may be able to spend her money more effectively on voters who are likely to provide her margin of victory.

The third is the number of campaigns the candidate must endure to win office. For instance, a candidate will have to spend more money to run in a partisan primary, a possible runoff, and the general election than on a non-partisan election with no runoff. The alternative systems (LV, CV, and PrV) have the advantage that they can eliminate the necessity of having both partisan primaries and (general election or primary) runoffs.

Fourth, if the candidate must run a media campaign that will reach many voters who are not in her district, she might be able to share the cost with other candidates by running joint ads—for example, "Vote for the Cost-Cutting Team of Smith (District 1), Katzenbach (District 2), and Paglia (District 3)." These joint ads will be more effective if all the candidates listed are running in the same multimember district, as they would be under MMD, LV, CV, or PrV.

Fifth, candidates can win under an alternative system with the support of voters already inclined to support the candidate rather than needing the support of "swing voters" who by definition do not like either candidate. A disproportionate amount of money in SMD elections must be spent on either winning the support of these swing voters or keeping them from the polls with a negative campaign.

While there will be some tradeoffs in costs, a PrV election campaign is likely to be more cost-efficient for the candidate. She can target her campaign toward her potential supporters, wherever they live in the city, and not have to run multiple election campaigns.

Just as it costs more for the candidates to run in two or three primaries or elections, the cost to the city is greater also. By holding only one election, the city avoids the cost of the polling officials and election supplies (and in some places the rental cost of the polling places) for a second or third election.

In the past, one of the complaints about PrV has been that the counting of the ballots took too long. For instance, in Cambridge, Massachusetts, the election takes place on Tuesday and the count usually concludes on Saturday. However, the Center for Voting and Democracy has been developing a computer counting program for PrV which will allow a count within a matter of a minute or two after the computer has the choices from each ballot. The ballot information can be input manually or by using computer-readable ballots (such as computer punch cards or optical character readers). The "long count" will soon be no barrier to having the results of a PrV election by midnight on the day of the election.

10. What is a simple method for the voter to cast an effective ballot?

In terms of simplicity of marking the ballot, the "X" voting (winner-take-all) systems are likely to take the prize. But for whom should the voter cast his ballot? If he was a Perot supporter, should he stick with Perot and probably throw away his vote, or make a choice between Clinton and Bush? If he was pretty sure Perot would lose, he might switch to his least objectionable second choice.

In PrV elections the voter has only to mark first, second, third, ... (and so on) choices. Here he could have voted for Perot first and Clinton second with the assurance that his vote for Perot would "send those politicians a message" but still allow his vote to have an effect in choosing the winner.

CV voters are likely to suffer from the agonies of strategic voting, just as the winner-take-all voters do. If the voter has five votes, but thinks that her group can probably get only one or two candidates elected, should she plump all her votes behind one candidate or divide them among two candidates? If she divides her votes, which candidate gets three or four votes and which only one or two? All of these calculations have to be made trying to figure out what like-minded voters and the opposing voters are going to do. In short, the voter has to play a three-dimensional video game with a constantly moving target.

LV voters may have to make the same sort of strategic choice if there is more than one attractive candidate. Voting for a losing candidate is a wasted vote, and it is especially wasted if there was another candidate who could have been helped by the votes received by the loser.

Technical Points About Modified At-Large Voting Systems

Modified at-large voting systems describe systems in which candidates or parties win seats in close proportion to their share of the vote because as many voters as mathematically can elect candidates of choice.

Most democracies use modified at-large systems that result in nearly all votes counting toward representation. Although many of these systems allocate votes among parties rather than candidates, the following three systems are based on voting for candidates and are already used in some local elections in the United States. They require at least some seats to be elected from districts with more than one representative.

Cumulative Voting

In cumulative voting, voters cast as many votes as seats. The most common form of cumulative voting allows voters to allocate their votes however they wish, including giving all their votes to their favorite candidate.

Because voters in a minority can assign all of their votes to one candidate, that candidate can win with support from fewer voters than in a traditional at-large election. The 'threshold of exclusion' is the lowest percentage of support that ensures a candidate will win no matter what other voters do.

With cumulative voting, this threshold is equal to 1/(# of seats + 1), which is 20 percent in a four-seat race and 10 percent in a nine-seat race.

A second form of cumulative voting may promote more coalition-building and provide easier voting instructions. Voters simply vote for as many candidates as they like, and votes are allocated equally among these candidates. In a five seat race, for example, a voter choosing two candidates would give each candidate 2.5 votes, while a voter choosing four candidates would give each candidate 1.25 votes. The Illinois state legislature was elected by this form of cumulative voting from 1870 to 1980.

In recent years cumulative voting has been adopted to resolve voting rights cases in over forty localities, including Alamogordo (NM), Peoria (IL) and Chilton County (AL). A member of the covered minority won office in nearly every subsequent election.

Limited Voting

Limited voting is similar to traditional at-large elections, except voters must cast fewer votes than the number of seats or parties must nominate fewer candidates than there are seats. The greater the difference between the number of seats and the number of votes, the greater the opportunities for fair representation of those in the minority. In a race to elect five candidates in which voters had two votes, any cohesive group of voters comprising one-third of the electorate would be guaranteed to win one seat.

Notes

1. Richard L. Engstrom and Michael D. McDonald, "The Effect of At-Large versus District Elections on Racial Representation in U.S. Municipalities," in *Electoral Laws and their Political Consequences,* Bernard Grofman and Arend Lijphart, eds., 203–25 (New York: Agathon Press, 1986).
2. Chandler Davidson, "The Recent Evolution of Voting Rights Law Affecting Racial and Language Minorities," at 22, in Davidson and Grofman, eds., *Quiet Revolution in the South: The Impact of the Voting Rights Act,* 1965–1990 (Princeton: Princeton Univ. Press, 1994).
3. T. Alexander Aleinikoff and Samuel Isaacharoff, "Race and Redistricting: Drawing Constitutional Lines after *Shaw v. Reno," 92 Mich. L. Rev.* 588, 631 (1993).
4. Rodolpho O. de la Garza and Louis DeSipio, "Overview: The Link Between Individuals and Electoral Institutions in Five Latino Neighborhoods," in *Barrio Ballots: Latino Politics in the 1990 Elections,* ed. de la Garza *et al.* (Boulder, CO: Westview Press, 1994).
5. Lani Guinier, "No Two Seats: The Elusive Quest for Political Equality," *77 Va. L. Rev.* 1413, 1451–52, 1454–55 (1991) (footnotes omitted).
6. George Pillsbury, "Preference Voting and Voter Turnout," *Voting and Democracy Report* 1995, 79–80 (Washington: Center for Voting and Democracy, 1995).
7. A majority-vote requirement, along with at-large elections and nonparti-

sanship, was part of the Good Government reform movement initiated during the early part of the twentieth century. ...In 1986 Susan MacManus conducted a survey of all American cities that had a population of at least 25,000 in 1980. Most of the 946 cities contacted had a runoff provision.

Charles S. Bullock III and Loch K. Johnson, *Runoff Elections in the United States* 24–5 (Chapel Hill: University of North Carolina Press 1992). See also, National Municipal League, *Model City Charter* 51–2 (New York: National Municipal League, 6th ed. 1964).

8. Henry Milner, "Prospects for Electoral Reform in Canada," *Voting and Democracy Report 1995,* 159 (Washington: Center for Voting and Democracy, 1995).

9. Michael D. McDonald and Richard L. Engstrom, "Detecting Gerrymandering," in *Political Gerrymandering and the Courts,* Bernard Grofman, ed. (New York: Agathon Press, 1990), 178–202, at 182.

10. Gus Tyler, "Court versus Legislature: The Sociopolitics of Malapportionment," 27 *Law and Contemporary Problems* 390, 400 (1962).

11. Wilma Rule, "Electoral Systems, Contextual Factors and Women's Opportunity for Election to Parliament in Twenty Three Democracies," 40 *Western Political Quarterly* 487 (1987); Wilma Rule and Pippa Norris, "Anglo and Minority Women's Underrepresentation in Congress: Is the Electoral System the Culprit?" and Susan Welsh and Rebekah Herrick, "The Impact of At-Large Elections on the Representation of Minority Women," in *United States Electoral Systems: Their Impact on Women and Minorities,* Wilma Rule and Joseph F. Zimmerman, eds., 41–54 and 153–66 (New York: Greenwood Press, 1992).

Mixed Election Systems: The Newest Reform Structure

Susan A. MacManus

Mixed electoral systems are those in which some council members are elected at-large and others from single-member district seats, with the latter usually being the larger number. Mixed systems have gained in popularity as at-large systems have declined, being accepted by traditional good government or reform groups and by minorities and their advocates.

Mixed systems are attractive to reformers who are unwilling to go so far as to endorse exclusively single-member districts, which they regard as merely "wards in sheep's clothing." At the same time, they are increasingly reticent to defend exclusively at-large councils when they appear to have the effect of diluting minority representation. For reformers, mixed plans are an acceptable compromise which "not only furnish representation to specialized interests concentrated within particular geographic areas but also ensure the election of some representatives who will direct their priorities toward the needs of the entire city."

A lesser-known fact is that mixed systems are also being embraced by those whose primary interest is greater minority representation on city councils, school boards and county commissions. Civil rights groups, the courts and the U.S. Justice Department are more and more accepting mixed systems as mechanisms to increase and enhance levels of minority representation, whether defined in a physical sense or in a broader policy sense. In addition to electing minorities to governing bodies, they are concerned about a government's responsiveness to minority needs and priorities. Perhaps the best statement of the various types of minority representation has been made by Rufus P. Browning, Dale Rogers Marshall and David H. Tabb in *Protest Is Not*

Reprinted with permission from National Civic Review, *Vol. 74, No. 11, November, 1985. Published by the National Civic League Press, Denver, Colorado.*

Enough: The Struggle of Blacks and Hispanics for Equality in Urban Politics (Berkeley: University of California Press, 1984). In addition to representation of minority persons on councils, the authors identify two other aspects of political equality: policy responsiveness of government (responsiveness to the interest of minority groups in the distribution of benefits); and the degree of incorporation of minority groups into the political system (measured by assessing the extent to which they are represented in coalitions that dominate city policymaking on minority-related issues). Many studies have reported that mixed systems can provide these different types of representation (see bibliography).

The purpose of this chapter is to examine the growing popularity of mixed systems, focusing primarily on the features which promote minority representation. It should be noted, however, that these same features can also characterize the more traditional electoral arrangements (at-large or single-member district) depending on the political, demographic and socioeconomic setting in which they exist.

Frequency of Usage

Mixed systems are not unusual electoral arrangements, being in use in 773 (19 percent) of all U.S. cities over 2,500 population, according to the 1982 *Municipal Yearbook* (see Table 1), and in more than half of the largest cities. Using 1976 data, two studies found that 37 (35.2 percent) of the 105 central cities with more than 15 percent black population had mixed systems as did 75 (31.4 percent) of 239 central cities of all population sizes. Another study of 80 southern cities over 10,000 showed 14.5 percent had mixed systems, and, of these, 54.5 percent had at least one black city council member. A 1978 study of 264 cities over 25,000 with at least 10 percent black population reported 64 (24.2 percent) with mixed systems. Finally, a 1985 survey of all southern cities over 25,000 population found that 51 of 222 (23 percent) used mixed systems.

There is evidence that if cities change electoral setups, the choice of a mixed system is not uncommon. For example, of 41 Texas local governments that made such changes between 1970 and 1979, almost 20 percent switched to mixed systems. Likewise, 44 southern cities changed their election systems between 1970 and 1981, 43 percent to a mixed system and 57 percent to single-member districts. Between 1975 and 1985, of 50 southern cities, 38 percent changed to a mixed plan and 52 percent to a single-member district system. The overwhelming majority of those adopting a mixed system changed from a pure at-large system (see Table 2).

In 22 percent of the cases the change to a mixed system occurred because of Voting Rights Act litigation. The fact that such a plan was accepted by the plaintiffs and/or the courts confirms our contention that mixed systems may facilitate greater minority representation.

Table 1
Types of Electoral Systems

Classification	No. of cities reporting (A)	At large system No.	At large system % of (A)	Ward or district system No.	Ward or district system % of (A)	Combination system No.	Combination system % of (A)
Total, all cities	4,089	2,721	66.5	595	14.6	773	18.9
Population group							
over 1,000,000	3	0	0.0	1	33.3	2	66.7
500,000–1,000,000	12	4	33.3	2	16.7	6	50.0
250,000– 499,999	25	13	52.0	3	12.0	9	36.0
100,000– 249,999	95	48	50.5	15	15.8	32	33.7
50,000– 99,999	226	134	59.3	20	8.8	72	31.9
25,000– 49,999	463	294	63.5	61	13.2	108	23.3
10,000– 24,999	1,012	662	65.4	122	12.1	228	22.5
5,000– 9,999	1,048	706	67.4	151	14.4	191	18.2
2,500– 4,999	1,205	860	71.4	220	18.3	125	10.4
Geographic division							
New England	185	100	54.1	22	11.9	63	34.1
Mid-Atlantic	625	455	72.8	109	17.4	61	9.8
East North Central	857	463	54.0	152	17.7	242	28.2
West North Central	467	203	43.5	132	28.3	132	28.3
South Atlantic	555	425	76.6	43	7.7	87	15.7
East South Central	243	202	83.1	12	4.9	29	11.9
West South Central	451	300	66.5	62	13.7	89	19.7
Mountain	223	146	65.5	41	18.4	36	16.1
Pacific Coast	483	427	88.4	22	4.6	34	7.0
Form of government							
Mayor-council	2,111	1,199	56.8	438	20.7	474	22.5
Council-manager	1,878	1,422	75.7	157	8.4	299	15.9
Commission	100	100	100.0	0	0.0	0	0.0

Source: Heywood T. Sanders, "The Government of American Cities: Continuity and Change in Structure," *The Municipal Yearbook 1982*. Washington, D.C.: International City Management Association, 1982, Table 3/3:180.

Attractive Features

Enhancement of Minority Representation on Governing Bodies

The popularity of the mixed plan is attributable to a number of features. One of the most prominent is its success at increasing and enhancing minority representation and influence on city councils. Every scholarly investigation

Table 2
Election Systems Abandoned by Southern Cities Changing to Mixed Systems: 1975–1985

System abandoned	% Changing to mixed (N = 19)
Pure at-large	56%
At-large, from seats or positions	11
At-large, residency requirements; posts, geographically-based	22
Single member district	11
	100%

Source: Telephone survey of city clerks in cities over 25,000 population, November 1984-March 1985.

of black representation (proportional representation) has found that *average* black equity scores are considerably higher with mixed systems than with pure at-large plans, and not significantly lower than in single-member district systems. For example, in the study of black representation among southern cities changing electoral structures between 1970 and 1981, representation under mixed systems adopted was .70. (Equity is defined as a ratio: percent minority on council divided by percent minority in city population. Absolute proportional representation would yield an equity score of 1.00.) For southern cities changing to single-member district systems, the equity score was .87; for cities maintaining at-large systems, it was only .39. Another study found slightly greater minority representation in mixed systems than in wards.

Broadening of Impact and Influence Points

Another attractive feature of mixed systems is that they may increase minority impact and influence on a larger number of council races than possible under a single-member district system. The mixed plan offers the potential for blacks to influence the outcome of each at-large race in addition to determining the outcome of contests in minority-majority districts. The opportunity to influence at-large positions has become more significant in recent years in light of the dispersion of the minority population, a higher incidence of black bloc voting, and higher turnout rates among blacks than whites. These trends hold true even in the South, especially in urban areas. Migration patterns have brought in persons with more liberal racial attitudes, but several studies have found that even older native southerners have become more racially tolerant.

The Case of Sarasota, Florida

The growing tolerance on the part of white southerners may partially explain the success of a mixed plan recently adopted by Sarasota and upheld by the courts. The city adopted a ⅔ plan: two at-large and three district-based seats. The city has a black population of only 16.3 percent (12.6 percent voting age population), which is gradually spreading into white areas adjacent to predominantly black neighborhoods. The plan created one predominantly black district (50.1 percent of total population; 42.6 percent of voting age population; but only 43.3 percent of registered voters). In drawing the district, the city placed whites of lower education and income with blacks, thereby creating a more socioeconomically homogeneous district than the rest of the city. This strategy was not new. Albert Karnig and Susan Welch had earlier suggested that black candidates have better chances of winning when placed with white voters of lower socioeconomic status.

When it came time to file to run, one white candidate (a former city commissioner and mayor) and two blacks did so. Skeptics forecast a highly racially polarized election in which the white candidate would win when blacks split their votes between the two black candidates and white voters turned out in record numbers to bloc vote for the white candidate. The underlying assumption was that the whites were likely to be extremely racist. Quite the contrary occurred: 47.2 percent of the blacks turned out, compared with 18.6 percent of the whites. This demonstrates that socioeconomic indicators are much better predictors of white political participation than black. In addition, there was a much higher incidence of white crossover voting than had been projected. The white candidate received only 15 percent of the vote. The two black candidates received 85 percent, with more than 55 percent of the whites voting for a black candidate.

The higher than expected white support for the black candidates might have been the result of personal contact between the candidates and their white constituents in the course of campaigning. Or it might have been the result of whites living in fairly integrated neighborhoods which increased their racial tolerance. Whites in this area had traditionally given more support to black candidates than had whites in the rest of the city. Regardless of the reason, the result was a more equitable level of representation for the city's black population both in the short term and in the long term, as the mixed system protects the opportunity for the growing number of minorities who live outside the district to coalesce with those living in the district to influence the outcome of the at-large races.

Minority Occupancy of At-Large Seats

Another very important point to note about black influence on the at-large seats in mixed systems is that blacks often capture these seats, sometimes after serving an apprenticeship as a district-based council member. For example, in a study of Buffalo, New York, three of the six at-large representatives were black. In Houston, two of the five at-large seats are held by blacks; one previously served as a district council member. These are not isolated observations. Karnig and Welch reported that in 22 percent of 50 mixed systems they studied, the at-large seats provided greater black representation than the district seats; in 28 percent, the at-large seats provided at least some black representation. The author's 1985 survey showed that blacks held at-large seats in 35 percent of the 51 southern cities over 25,000 with mixed systems.

Protection of Geographically Dispersed Minorities

Mixed plans are also effective where minority groups are geographically dispersed. This allows minority votes "lost" in creating minority-majority districts (votes of those living outside such districts) to be "saved" through bloc voting for at-large seats or coalescing with sympathetic whites to influence at-large seat outcomes. This is an especially attractive feature if there is evidence that the minority population is spreading beyond what had been the city's traditional black enclave (as was the case in Sarasota) and where the minority population is not sufficiently concentrated to draw a majority-minority district, often more of a problem for Hispanics than blacks.

Relatedly, if the minority population is too small *and* dispersed to capture a district-based seat, the at-large posts maximize its capacity to swing vote. In *Your Voice at City Hall* (State University of New York Press, Albany, 1984) Peggy Heilig and Robert Mundt state that "a minority population must comprise about 30 percent of the total and be geographically concentrated for a [pure single-member] district plan to result in increased representation depending on the number of districts." When the minority population is small, mixed, at-large and single-member district systems produce similar levels of minority representation.

Attention to Neighborhood and Citywide Issues

A more racially neutral advantage to mixed systems is the provision of simultaneous attention to specific neighborhood-oriented and citywide issues. As noted by Francine Rabinovitz and Edward Hamilton: "A mixed system yields some natural division of labor between district-based and at-large representatives.... The smaller electorate demands and receives greater attention to more localized 'backyard' problems from the district-based than from the at-large representative.... The at-large councillor is expected to take a broader per-spective on citywide policy, and to balance off the parochial concerns of their district-based colleagues" (see the REVIEW, July 1980, page 385). Indeed, sev-eral studies have shown that district-based council members get more calls from constituents regarding day-to-day problems.

But the fact that district-based and at-large council members represent different constituencies causes a wider range of policy issues to be discussed at council meetings. This means that council members "have a better grasp of the diverse problems and concerns of residents throughout the city" (see the REVIEW, July-August 1983, page 380). It also increases citizen participation at council meetings and at the polls, although some studies have found that changing to a mixed system is no consistent guarantee that turnout will be higher. A more probable outcome of the diverse representational perspective is to increase the likelihood of policy responsiveness through council coali-tion building, especially in cities where minority voters cast the swing vote in the at-large and mayoral contests.

Summary

In summary, there is a number of reasons why mixed electoral systems are often attractive to minorities and traditional good government proponents. In a sense, mixed systems represent the American political system's tendency toward compromise; theoretically they offer something for everyone, although in certain instances so do the more traditional systems. Mixed electoral sys-tems:

- Are not unusual; they are commonly used alternatives to at-large or sin-gle-member district systems throughout the U.S.;
- Often result in higher levels of minority representation than the tradi-tional systems which they replace;
- Increase the number of council seats which can be captured and influenced by minorities, thereby expanding their representational opportunities;
- Enhance and protect the chances of electoral impact for geographically dispersed minorities;
- Promote representation of neighborhood areas and citywide concerns, operating much like a bicameral legislative body encouraging coalition building; and
- Encourage broader discussion of a wider range of policy issues.

Of course, no plan can produce the same outcome in every jurisdiction. Struc-ture almost always takes a back seat to political, demographic and socioeconomic patterns in terms of explanatory power. But, in the right setting, mixed systems can be effective mechanisms for enhancing minority representation.

Bibliography

Bullock, Charles S., III. "Feasibility of Electing a Black under Sarasota's 3-2 Plan." Report prepared for the City of Sarasota, Florida, 1984.

Browning, Rufus P., Dale Rogers Marshall, and David H. Tabb. *Protest Is Not Enough: The Struggle of Blacks and Hispanics for Equality in Urban Politics.* Berkeley: University of California Press, 1984.

Cohen, Jeffrey E., Patrick R. Cotter, and Philip B. Coulter. "The Changing Structure of Southern Political Participation: Matthews and Prothro 20 Years Later," *Social Science Quarterly* 64 (September, 1983): 536–549.

Combs, Michael W., John R. Hibbing, and Susan Welch. "Black Constituents and Congressional Roll Call Votes," *Western Political Quarterly* 37 (September, 1984): 424–434.

Davidson, Chandler, and George Korbel. "At-large Elections and Minority Group Representation: A Reexamination of Historical and Contemporary Evidence," *Journal of Politics* 43 (November, 1981): 982–1005.

Engstrom, Richard L., and Michael D. McDonald. "The Election of Blacks to City Councils: Clarifying the Impact of Electoral Arrangements on the Seats/Population Relationship," *American Political Science Review* 75 (June, 1981): 344–354.

"The Underrepresentation of Blacks on City Councils: Comparing the Structural and Socioeconomic Explanations for South/Non–South Differences," *Journal of Politics* 44 (1982): 1088–1099.

Haselwerdt, Michael V. "Voter and Candidate Reaction to District and At-Large Elections: Buffalo, New York," *Urban Affairs Quarterly* 20 (September, 1984): 31–45.

Heilig, Peggy, and Robert J. Mundt. "Changes in Representational Equity: The Effect of Adopting Districts," *Social Science Quarterly* 64 (June, 1983): 393–397.

_____. *Your Voice at City Hall: The Politics, Procedures, and Policies of District Representation.* Albany: State University of New York Press, 1984.

Karnig, Albert K. "Black Representation on City Councils: The Impact of District Elections and Socioeconomic Factors," *Urban Affairs Quarterly* 12 (December, 1976): 223–242.

Karnig, Albert K., and Susan Welch. "Electoral Structure and Black Representation of City Councils," *Social Science Quarterly* 63 (March, 1982): 99–114.

_____. *Black Representation and Urban Policy.* Chicago: The University of Chicago Press, 1980.

Latimer, Margaret K. "Black Political Representation in Southern Cities: Election Systems and Other Casual Variables," *Urban Affairs Quarterly* 15 (September 1979): 65–86.

Lyndon B. Johnson School of Public Affairs, The University of Texas. Local Government Election Systems Policy Research Project. *Local Government Election Systems.* Austin, TX: The University of Texas, Report No. 62, 1984.

MacManus, Susan A. "City Council Election Procedures and Minority Representation: Are They Related?" *Social Science Quarterly* 59 (June, 1978): 153–161.

MacManus, Susan A., and Carol A. Cassel. "Mexican Americans in City Political

Participation. Representation, and Policy Differences," *The Urban Interests* (Spring, 1982): 57–69.

Rabinovitz, Francine F., and Edward K. Hamilton. "Alternative Electoral Structures and Responsiveness to Minorities," *National Civic Review* 69 (July, 1980): 371–401.

Robinson, Theodore P., and Thomas R. Dye. "Reformism and Black Representation on City Councils," *Social Science Quarterly* 59 (June, 1978): 133–141.

Robinson, Theodore P., Robert E. England, and Kenneth J. Meier. "A Closer Look at Mixed Electoral Systems," paper presented at the annual meeting of the American Political Science Association, September 3–6, 1981.

Sanders, Heywood T. "The Government of American Cities: Continuity and Changes in Structure," *The Municipal Yearbook 1982*. Washington, D.C.: International City Management Association (1982): 178–186.

Sheffield, James F. Jr., and Charles D. Hadley. "Racial Voting in a Biracial City, A Reexamination of Some Hypotheses," *American Politics Quarterly* 17 (October, 1984): 449–464.

Stewart, Alva W., and Phung Nguyen. "Electing the City Council: Historic Change in Greensboro," *National Civic Review* 72 (July–August, 1983): 377–381.

Taebel, Delbert. "Minority Representation on City Councils: The Impact of Structure on Blacks and Hispanics," *Social Science Quarterly* 63 (June, 1978): 142–152.

Vedlitz, Arnold, and Charles A. Johnson. "Community Racial Segregation, Electoral Structure, and Minority Representation," *Social Science Quarterly* 63 (December, 1982): 729–736.

Zimmerman, Joseph F. "The Single-Member District Systems: Can It Be Reformed?" *National Civic Review* 70 (May, 1981): 255–259.

_____. "The Federal Voting Rights Act and Alternative Election Systems," *William and Mary Law Review* 19 (September, 1978): 621–660.

PART II
The Laws
and the Systems

Election Systems and Representative Democracy

Joseph F. Zimmerman

Democratic theory is premised upon representative law-making bodies, yet members of many of these bodies have been elected by systems that exclude or dilute the votes cast by members of certain racial and ethnic groups. Constructing an electoral system that will produce fair representation is a difficult task, and must commence with the removal of legal impediments to voting and replacement of electoral systems that discriminate against members of minority groups. The Voting Rights Act of 1965 as amended was designed to remedy discrimination in electoral systems and practices against blacks and members of four "foreign language minorities."

The Act is a permanent statute that also contains temporary, nationally suspensive provisions applicable to states and/or their political subdivisions if certain conditions (known informally as "triggers") are present. The "trigger provisions" originally were limited to six southern states and were designed to protect the voting rights of only blacks. Today, these provisions apply to many jurisdictions outside the South because of amendments enacted in 1975, which extend the Act's reach to jurisdictions where voter participation is low and the concentration of "protected" minorities high.

This chapter presents 1) a historical overview of the gradual liberalization of suffrage laws in the United States, 2) describes the Voting Rights Act's major provisions and their interpretation by the United States Supreme Court, and 3) examines the single-member district system, which has been promoted by implementation of the Act, vis-à-vis alternative electoral systems.

A historical review of suffrage requirements will help explain why Congress decided in 1965 to enact a statute guaranteeing the voting rights of blacks.

Reprinted with permission from National Civic Review, *Vol. 84, No. 4, Fall/Winter, 1995. Published by the National Civic League Press, Denver, Colorado.*

When the United States Constitution was ratified in 1788, voting in states was confined to male property owners or taxpayers. All other persons—women, blacks (most were slaves), indentured servants and Native Americans—lacked the right to vote.

Vermont was the first state to provide for universal male suffrage for those of "quiet and peaceable behavior."[1] A year later, the new state of Kentucky allowed suffrage for men who met a two-year residency requirement.[2] New Hampshire and Georgia abolished their constitutional taxpaying requirements in 1792 and 1798, respectively.[3] In 1809, Maryland passed a statute granting manhood suffrage without property-owning or taxpaying qualifications.

In 1821, New York enfranchised all white male residents of one year who had paid taxes and served in the State Militia, and all others who had lived in the state for three years.[4] New York, however, retained property qualifications for blacks. Thereafter, the movement for full manhood suffrage made rapid progress, and by 1860 property-owning requirements had disappeared and taxpayer prerequisites were negligible.

Before white manhood suffrage became a nationwide reality, however, a reaction set in. Alarmed at the rapid increase in the number of illiterate immigrants, particularly Irish immigrants, Connecticut in 1855 and Massachusetts in 1857 amended their constitutions to require that all voters be able to read.[5]

Black Suffrage

Few blacks were enfranchised prior to the Civil War. Maine, Massachusetts, New Hampshire, Rhode Island, and Vermont had granted suffrage to blacks, and in New York a black could vote if he possessed a freehold. The original North Carolina Constitution permitted free blacks who met other requirements to vote, but it was amended in 1835 to provide that "no free Negro, free Mulatto, or free person of mixed blood, descended from Negro ancestors to the fourth generation inclusive ... shall vote for members of the Senate or House of Commons."[6]

Immediately after the Civil War, the movement to extend the franchise to blacks gathered momentum and led to two amendments to the United States Constitution. The Fourteenth Amendment, ratified in 1868, provides that a state's representation in the U.S. House of Representatives could be reduced in the proportion that the state denied the suffrage of male citizens 21 years of age or older. The Fifteenth Amendment, ratified in 1879, prohibits the United States or any state from denying suffrage on account of race, color or previous condition of servitude.

In 1870, Congress enacted a statute, based on the Fifteenth Amendment, making private or public obstruction of the right to vote in an election a misdemeanor punishable by imprisonment of one month to one year.[7] The law was amended the following year to authorize federal oversight of the election of United States Representatives in any local government with a population exceeding 20,000 "whenever ... there shall be two citizens thereof who ... shall make known in writing, to the Judge of the Circuit Court of the United States for the Circuit wherein such city or town shall be, their desire to have said registration, or said election, or both, guarded and scrutinized."[8]

The United States Supreme Court in 1875 invalidated sections of the 1870 Act that guaranteed the voting rights of white citizens and provided for punishment of persons interfering with the voting rights of whites, holding that the Fifteenth Amendment authorized Congress to protect only the voting rights of black citizens.[9] This opinion remains in effect today. The most important remaining sections of the two statutes were repealed by Congress in 1894, thereby freeing states of direct supervision of elections by federal officials for 63 years.

With southern states in the control of whites by 1890, their state constitutions and statutes were amended to exclude most blacks from the franchise. For example, southern state legislatures revived the taxpayer qualification requiring a person to present poll tax receipts, sometimes for many years, before a person would be allowed to vote in an election; lengthened the residency requirements to debar transient blacks; and introduced the literacy test to assure the ability of voters to read or at least "understand" the constitution. To preserve the suffrage of illiterate whites, southerners invented the notorious "grandfather clause," which permitted the permanent registration of all persons who had served in the United States Army or the Confederate Army, or were descendants of veterans. The clause was declared unconstitutional by the United States Supreme Court in 1915.[10] The court in 1939 struck down state procedural obstacles to voting.

Blacks effectively were excluded from the nominating process in southern states by the "white primary," which debarred them from voting in the Democratic party's primary elections. The exclusionary device was invalidated in 1944 when the Supreme Court declared this type of primary unconstitutional, holding that a state could not cast its election laws in such a fashion as to allow a private organization, in this case a political party, to practice racial discrimination in elections.[11] Southern states, except Texas, continued to use the literacy test as a condition for voting, and several southern states had long residency requirements to disenfranchise blacks, who moved more frequently than whites. In 1949, the U.S. Supreme Court invalidated discriminatory application of voting tests.[12]

The racial gerrymander also was employed by state legislatures to reduce the voting power of black citizens. The most egregious racial gerrymander was drawn the Alabama State Legislature for Tuskegee, home of the famous black university. In 1960, the U.S. Supreme Court struck down this gerrymander, which had produced a strangely shaped, irregular district with lines drawn around houses to exclude black voters from their preexisting right to vote in municipal elections by removing them from the city's limits.[13]

Public opinion against the treatment of blacks as second-class citizens was growing, especially after the end of World War II in 1945. Reacting to this sentiment, Congress in 1957 enacted a statute authorizing the Attorney General to initiate legal action on behalf of blacks denied the opportunity to register and vote, and established the United States Commission on Civil Rights, with authority to investigate and report on devices and procedures employed by state and local governments in a discriminatory manner against blacks.[14] The Civil Rights Act of 1960 mandated that states retain federal election records for 22 months, authorized the Attorney General to inspect such records, and enabled the District Court to order registration of blacks who were victims of a pattern of voting discrimination and appoint voting referees empowered to register voters.[15] Title I of the Civil Rights Act of 1964 forbids election officials to apply registration tests or standards to applicants different from the ones administered to persons previously registered. The Act also established a rebuttable presumption of literacy for registrants with a sixth-grade, English-speaking school education, and expedited procedures for judicial resolution of voting rights cases.[16]

In 1964, the 24th Amendment, abolishing the poll tax as a condition for voting in federal elections, was ratified. Only eight blacks had been elected to the United States House of Representatives by that date, several of them during the Reconstruction Period immediately following the Civil War. Literacy tests, however, remained in use in many states, and blacks in some areas were not permitted to register and vote for candidates for state and local government offices.

The Voting Rights Act of 1965

In reaction to the growing civil rights movement in the early 1960s and actions of many southern states preventing numerous blacks from exercising the franchise, Congress in 1965 passed the Voting Rights Act to protect blacks' Fifteenth Amendment voting rights.[17] President Lyndon B. Johnson proposed that the Act contain a ten-year sunset clause, but a five-year clause was adopted as a compromise for the preclearance and other temporary provisions in order to persuade a sufficient number of senators to vote for cloture to end a filibuster.[18] Certain provisions of the Act, as amended, apply to all states and local governments, and other provisions apply only to states and political subdivisions meeting the trigger conditions. Section 4 stipulates that the Act automatically applies to any state or political subdivision of a state if the Attorney General of the United States determines that as of November 1, 1964, a test or device had been employed to abridge the right of citizens to vote, and the

Director of the United States Bureau of the Census determines that less than 50 percent of persons of voting age were registered to vote on November 1, 1964 or that less than 50 percent of persons of voting age exercised the franchise in the 1964 presidential election.[19] A "test or device" is defined as one involving literacy, morals, character, educational achievement, or knowledge of a specified subject.

Available evidence suggests that the factors incorporated as triggers deliberately were formulated to exclude Texas. Senator James B. Allen of Alabama maintained "it was first determined which states the law should be made applicable to, and then they proceeded to find the formula that would end up with those states being covered."[20] He added:

> ...by using the 50 percent voting in the election factor, that would have included the State of Texas. The President of the United States being a resident of Texas, ... it was thought inadvisable to include Texas in that formula. So they added a second circumstance, that is, that they must have a device that would hinder registration; namely the literacy test. [That] double factor ... is what took Texas out from under it, because they did not have the literacy test.[21]

The temporary provisions of the Act covered Alabama, Georgia, Louisiana, Mississippi, South Carolina, and Virginia, as well as counties in Alaska, Arizona, Hawaii, Idaho, and North Carolina. Texas was brought under the temporary provisions of the Act by the 1975 amendments.

Section 2 of the original Act is a statutory restatement of the Fifteenth Amendment's prohibition of the denial or abridgment of the right to vote based on "race, color, or previous condition of servitude."

Congress in effect imposed a federal "Dillon's Rule" on state and local governments subject to Section 5 of the Act, in that such jurisdictions may not change their electoral practices as they existed on November 1 of the year during which the prerequisite factors were met without first obtaining either the prior approval of the Attorney General, acting as an administrative surrogate of the court, or a declaratory judgment from the District Court of the District of Columbia. Actions implicating Section 5 include changing the location of a polling place, changing the existing voting system, transforming an elective office into an appointive one, annexation, and legislative redistricting, unless it is pursuant to a United States court order to correct an unconstitutional electoral system.[22] The preclearance requirement also applies to several activities of political parties, such as conduct of primary elections and selection of party officials and delegates to party conventions. Additionally, the Act directs the United States District Court to authorize appointment by the United States Civil Service Commission (now the Office of Personnel Management) of federal examiners to enforce constitutional guarantees in these state and local governments.

The Amendments

The trigger dates were expanded by the 1970 amendments to the Act to include November 1, 1968 and the 1968 presidential election; the 1975 amendments added November 1, 1972 and the 1972 presidential election.

The 1970 amendments suspended all voting tests and devices, including literacy tests, throughout the nation until August 6, 1975, and the 1975 amendments made the suspension permanent.[23] The 1970 amendments also authorize the Attorney General to seek a preliminary or permanent injunction to prevent a state or local government from enacting or administering a test or device in violation of the Act's provisions.[24]

The 1975 amendments broadened the coverage of the Act to include "language minorities," defined as "persons who are American Indian, Asian American, Alaskan Natives, or of Spanish heritage," and cited the Fourteenth and Fifteenth Amendments as the constitutional authority for the Act.[25] The language-minority trigger, providing for mandatory coverage of a governmental unit by the Act, are activated if in excess of five percent of the citizens of voting age in a state or political subdivision are members of one language minority group as of November 1, 1972 *and* less than 50 percent of all citizens of voting age participated in the presidential election of 1972. The triggers also are activated if in excess of five percent of the citizens of voting age in a state or political subdivision are members of one language minority group *and* the illiteracy rate of the group exceeds the national illiteracy rate. The definition of a test or device was expanded to include the use of only English election materials or ballots in a jurisdiction where a language minority constituted more than five percent of the voting-age population. In such jurisdictions, bilingual ballots and election materials must be provided if the group's literacy rate is lower than the national average.

The 1975 amendments also extended the preclearance and other temporary requirements for seven years. A total of 263,410 proposed changes were submitted to the Attorney General through 1994, who interposed an objection to 2,995.[26] The preclearance requirement currently applies to all or part of 16 states.

A jurisdiction's discriminatory intent may not always be apparent, since it may have maintained a racially neutral electoral system that was designed to or had the effect of diluting or eliminating the voting strength of a racial minority. In *White v. Regester*, the U.S. Supreme Court in 1973 held that the use of multimember districts in a state legislative reapportionment plan would violate the equal protection clause of the Fourteenth Amendment if "used invidiously to cancel out or minimize the voting strength of racial groups."[27]

The viability of this broad interpretation of the Act, which protected black voters without proof of deliberate or explicit desire to discriminate on the part of the jurisdiction, was weakened by subsequent Supreme Court decisions holding that proof of discrimination in violation of the Fourteenth Amendment's equal protection clause requires the establishment of "subjective intent."[28] In 1980, the Court majority in *Mobile v. Bolden* rejected the argument that voting rights discrimination should be determined by a "results" test instead of an "intent" test, as well as what the Court labeled the theory behind the former test. The Court opined that such a theory "appears to be that every political group or at least that every such group that is in the minority has a federal constitutional right to elect candidates in proportion to its numbers.... The Equal Protection Clause does not require proportional representation as an imperative of political organization."[29]

This decision generated considerable debate, and induced Congress in 1982 to amend Section 2 of the Act to incorporate a "results" test providing that "The extent to which members of a protected class have been elected to office in the state or political subdivision is one circumstance which may be considered." Congress, however, added the proviso "that nothing in this section establishes a right to have members elected in numbers equal to their proportion in the population."[30]

The 1982 amendments also modified the preclearance provisions of the Act, directed Congress to reconsider these provisions in 1997, stipulated the provisions would expire in 2007, extended the language minority provisions until August 6, 1992, stipulated that no covered jurisdiction may provide voting materials only in English prior to August 6, 2007, and guarantees a voter in need of voting assistance because "of blindness, disability, or inability to read or write may be given assistance by a person of the voter's choice, other than the voter's employer or agent of that employer or officer or agent of the voter's union."[31]

Bail-Out Provisions

Section 4(a) of the Act contains "bail-out" provisions to end the special coverage resulting from the trigger. A state or local government subject to coverage because of the racial provisions of the 1965 Act and amendments of 1970 and 1975 may file suit for a declaratory judgment in the United States District Court for the District of Columbia and offer proof that it has not discriminated against the voting right of the protected group for ten years, or establish "that any such violations were trivial, were promptly corrected, and were not repeated."[32]

In practice, it is difficult for state and local governments covered by the original Act to use the bail-out provisions successfully. Virginia attempted to obtain such exemption, but its suit for a declaratory judgment was rejected by the United States Supreme Court in 1975.[33] Of course, even if a jurisdiction is successful in bailing out, it remains subject to litigation under the results standards of Section 2 of the Act.

Court Interpretation

The constitutionality of the Act was challenged on the grounds that Congress encroached on the powers reserved to the states by the United States Constitution (Tenth Amendment), since many of its key provisions were targeted at one region of the nation. Rejecting these arguments, the United States Supreme Court in 1966 ruled that "the sections of the Act which are properly before us are an appropriate means of carrying out Congress' constitutional responsibilities and are consonant with all other provisions of the Constitution."[34]

In 1968, the Court held in *Allen v. State Board of Elections* that it was the intent of Congress that the Act be given "the broadest possible scope" to reach "any state enactment which altered the election law of a covered state in even a minor way."[35] In 1973, the Court justified its 1968 decision by maintaining:

> Had Congress disagreed with the interpretation of § 5 in *Allen*, it had ample opportunity to amend that statute. After extensive deliberations in 1970 on bills to amend the Voting Rights Act, during which the *Allen* case was repeatedly discussed, the Act was extended for five years, without substantive modifications of § 5.[36]

Neither annexation *per se* nor at-large elections *per se* have been declared unconstitutional by the courts. The Voting Rights Act of 1965, however, added a federal dimension to annexation proceedings in several states, particularly southern states, as the U.S. Supreme Court observed in its 1971 opinion in *Perkins v. Matthews*.[37] The case involved annexation of territory by the City of Canton, Mississippi, and 1965 determination by Attorney General Nicholas B. Katzenbach that Mississippi and its political subdivisions were covered by the Act.[38] In 1969, the special three-judge District Court for the Southern District of Mississippi dissolved a temporary injunction against the holding of city elections issued by a federal judge, and dismissed a complaint on the ground that "the black voters still had a majority of not less than 600 after the expansions were effected."[39] A total of 82 black voters and 331 white voters had been added to the city by annexations in 1965, 1966 and 1968; no white voters were added to the city by the 1965 annexation.

The Supreme Court overturned the decision of the three-judge District Court:

> ...changing boundary lines by annexations which enlarge the City's number of eligible voters also constitutes the change of a "standard, practice, or procedure with respect to voting." Clearly, revision of boundary lines has an effect on voting in two ways: (1) by including certain voters within the City and leaving others outside, it determines who may vote in the municipal

election and who may not; (2) it dilutes the weight of the voters to whom the franchise was limited before annexation, and "the right to suffrage can be denied by a debasement or dilution of the weight of a citizen's vote just as effectively as by wholly prohibiting the free exercise of the franchise." Moreover, § 5 was designed to cover changes having a potential for racial discrimination in voting, and such potential inheres in a change in composition of the electorate affected by an annexation.[40]

This decision resulted in a sharp decline in annexations by large southern cities, which have relatively broad state constitutional and/or statutory authority to annex territory. Subsequently, several large cities have sought the approval of the Attorney General to annex territory. Today, most southern annexations are small in terms of the size of the annexed territory and number of residents. The complexity of the issues involved with annexation are illustrated by cases involving the cities of Richmond and Petersburg, Virginia.

The first Richmond case. The 1970 annexation of territory by Richmond increased the city's population and real property tax base by 19 percent and 23 percent, respectively, but was contested as violating the Voting Rights Act of 1965. A group of black plaintiffs objected to the annexation and contended it was designed to dilute black voting strength in a city with a council elected at-large, thereby violating their rights under the Fourteenth and Fifteenth Amendments and Section 5 of the Voting Rights Act. Ninety-seven percent of the residents of the annexed area were white. Fifty percent of Richmond's pre-annexation population of 202,359 was black in 1970. This proportion was lowered to 42 percent, as the annexation added 45,705 whites and 1,557 blacks to the city's population, increasing the totals to 143,857 whites and 105,764 blacks.

The United States District Court for the Eastern District of Virginia ruled in favor of the plaintiffs: "the Fourteenth Amendment forbids a deprivation of one's vote by reason of race—this Court interprets that to mean dilution as well."[41] Declaring that de-annexation would be impractical because the city had appropriated millions of dollars for improvements in the annexed area, the court ordered that the city be divided into two districts for purposes of new councilmanic elections.[42] According to the plan, seven council members would be elected from the district comprising most of the pre-annexation territory of the city, and two members would be elected from the annexed area and a small part of the city's pre-annexation territory.

The District Court's decision was reversed by the United States Court of Appeals for the Fourth Circuit, which held that "for perfectly valid reasons Richmond's elected representatives had sought annexation since 1966."[43] The U.S. Supreme Court denied a petition for writ of certiorari, thereby upholding the decision of the Court of Appeals.[44]

The Petersburg case. In a similar case, the Supreme Court in 1973 affirmed a decision of the District Court for the District of Columbia denying

Petersburg the right to annex 14 square miles of land in Dinwiddie and Prince George's Counties, because the boundary extension would increase the proportion of white population from 45 to 54 percent in a city that elected its council members at-large, thereby discriminating against black voters by diluting their votes.[45]

The annexation ordinance, effective on December 31, 1971, was adopted unanimously in 1967 by the five-member city council. Two members, including the one who had introduced the ordinance, were black. The three-member district court found that the purpose of the annexation was to expand the city's growth and tax base, and there was no evidence that the annexation had a racial motive. The court, however, found that the city had "a long history of racial segregation and discrimination."[46]

Conceding "that an at-large system of electing city councilmen has many advantages over the ward system," the court ruled the annexation could be approved only if the city substituted ward elections for at-large elections of the council, which had been expanded from five to seven members by the 1972 Virginia Legislature.[47]

The second Richmond case. Richmond in 1972 sought court approval for its 1970 annexation, since the Attorney General twice refused to give approval for the annexation. The city council was elected at-large in 1970 with voters from the annexed area in Chesterfield County participating; only one black councilman was elected. According to the three-judge District Court for the District of Columbia, "it is conceded here that Richmond conducted these elections illegally in violation of Section 5. It did not, prior to diluting by annexation the votes of the citizens residing within the old Richmond boundaries, obtain the approval of the Attorney General or a declaratory judgment from this Court that this dilution did not have the purpose and would not have the effect of abridging the right to vote on account of race or color. Richmond has held no councilmanic elections since 1970; the illegally elected City Council continues to serve at this time."[48] During the four-year period, three members of the nine-member council resigned and their replacements were co-opted by the council.

Subsequent to the annexation, the city substituted a single-member district system for the at-large system. The District Court concluded that the change in electoral system was "discriminatory in purpose and effect and thus violative of Section 5's substantive standards as well as the section's procedural command that prior approval be obtained from the Attorney General or this Court."[49]

The Supreme Court in 1975 reversed the lower court decision and made a distinction between the Petersburg and Richmond cases:

> Petersburg was correctly decided. On the facts here presented, the annexation of an area with a white majority, combined with at-large councilmanic

elections and racial voting, created or enhanced the power of the white majority to exclude Negroes totally from participation in the governing of the city
through membership on the city council. We agreed, however, that the consequence would be satisfactorily obviated if at-large elections were replaced
by a ward system of choosing councilmen....

We can not accept the position that such a single-member ward system
would nevertheless have the effect of denying or abridging the right to vote
because Negroes would constitute a lesser proportion of the population after
the annexation than before, and given racial bloc voting, would have fewer
seats on the city council.[50]

This decision constitutes a significant departure from the *Perkins* decision because the Court indicated it was no longer concerned that the pre-
annexation black vote would be diluted, provided blacks were represented
"fairly" in a city's governing body following annexation. New elections, held
on March 1, 1977, resulted in the selection of five blacks and four whites as
members of the city council.

While annexation may be viewed as an "indirect" form of racial gerrymandering, since annexation may have as its purpose and its effect the dilution of the voting rights of blacks living within the pre-annexation boundaries
of the city, the Supreme Court in 1976 and 1977 was faced with the question
of whether a "reverse racial gerrymander"—one that deliberately created a
"safe" black district—was constitutional.

The Hasidic Jews case. Although the Voting Rights Act was designed to
end voting discrimination in the southern states, the Attorney General in 1970
made a determination that New York State had maintained a test or device on
November 1, 1968, as defined by Section 4(c) of the Act as amended. Moreover, the Director of the Bureau of the Census determined that Bronx, Kings
(Brooklyn) and New York (Manhattan) Counties were subject to Sections 4
and 5 of the Act, since fewer than 50 percent of the residents of voting age
cast a ballot in the 1968 presidential election and a literacy test had been used
in the counties prior to 1970.[51] The specific reasons for applying the Act were
the 1970 amendments changing the trigger date to 1968, and the fact that ballots were printed only in English. The District Court for the Southern District
of New York ruled that "plaintiffs can not cast an effective vote without being
able to comprehend fully the registration and election forms and the ballot
itself."[52] The decision was affirmed by the United States Supreme Court.[53]

New York filed a complaint in the District Court for the District of Columbia seeking a declaratory judgment exempting the counties from coverage by
the Act. With the approval of the United States Department of Justice, the
court granted the judgment. Denied leave to intervene in the case, the National
Association for the Advancement of Colored People (NAACP) unsuccessfully
appealed the denial to the U.S. Supreme Court. However, on remand the
NAACP's motion was granted.[54]

The NAACP, after reopening the declaratory judgment action, obtained an order from the District Court for the District of Columbia holding that the Act, as amended in 1970, applied to congressional and state legislative districts in Manhattan, Brooklyn and the Bronx, and the decision was affirmed by the Supreme Court.[55] These judgments necessitated a special session of the New York State Legislature, which on May 29, 1974 redrew congressional and state legislative district lines drawn in 1972.[56] Although the 1974 redistricting did not change the number of state senate and assembly districts with no-white voting majorities, it did increase the nonwhite majority *percentage* in two senate districts and two assembly districts, and decreased the nonwhite majority percentage in one senate district and two assembly districts.

Objections to several of the new district lines were advanced by representatives of Brooklyn's Hasidic Jews, who argued that the new assembly districts divided the Hasidic community and made it the victim of a racial gerrymander, thereby diluting the value of their votes in violation of the equal protection clause of the Fourteenth Amendment to the United States Constitution.[57] The Hasidic community, which had been able to elect one of its members to the state assembly, also challenged the assumption that only black legislators can represent the interests of blacks. In response to questioning in the District Court, Executive Director Richard S. Scolaro of the State Legislative Committee that drew the district lines stated that the United States Justice Department's insistence on a proportion of black voters of 65 percent was the "sole reason" why the Hasidic community was split between two assembly districts.[58]

On July 1, 1974, the Attorney General approved the new districts and dismissed the objections of Hasidic Jews and Irish, Italian and Polish groups on the grounds that the Voting Rights Act was designed to prohibit voting discrimination on the basis of race, not ethnic origin or religious beliefs.[59] In carrying out his duties under Section 5 of the Act, the Attorney General emphasized that it was not his function "to dictate to the State of New York specific actions, steps, or lines with respect to its own redistricting plan."[60]

The District Court dismissed the complaint of the Hasidic Jews on the grounds that the petitioners were not disenfranchised and that race could be considered in redistricting in order to correct previous racial discrimination.[61] The Court of Appeals affirmed the District Court's decision by reasoning that the redistricting did not under-represent whites, who composed 65 percent of the population, since approximately 70 percent of the state assembly and senate districts in Brooklyn would have white majorities.[62]

The Court of Appeals was convinced that it would be an impossible task for a legislature to reapportion itself if "a state must in a reapportionment draw lines so as to preserve ethnic community unity."[63]

The Supreme Court heard oral arguments in *United Jewish Organizations of Williamsburg v. Wilson* on October 6, 1976. Justice White asked Nathan

Lewin, the plaintiffs' attorney, a question relative to the establishment of leg-islative districts with a specified percentage of blacks to help them elect mem-bers of their own race. Chief Justice Warren E. Burger interjected and inquired whether this action "would have the unfortunate effect to cut against the whole effort to achieve an integrated society?"[64] After Mr. Lewin responded in the affirmative, the Chief Justice added that "it does more than that. It pushes peo-ple to move into blocks" where others of the same race live.[65]

On March 1, 1977, the Court, by a seven-to-one vote, upheld the lower court ruling that the 1974 redistricting was constitutional, and ruled that the Act "was itself broadly remedial," and the use of racial considerations in draw-ing district lines often would be necessary.[66] The Court specifically opined that "neither the Fourteenth nor the Fifteenth Amendment mandates any *per se* rule against using racial factors in districting and apportionment."[67]

Many observers were disturbed by the Court's opinion because it appeared to overturn its 1960 decision in *Gomillion v. Lightfoot*, which invalidated racial gerrymandering. Justice Frankel of the District Court of the Southern District of New York, sitting by designation on the Court of Appeals for the Second Circuit, in his dissent offered penetrating insight into the nature of the case:

> The case is one where no preexisting wrong was shown of such a character as to justify, or render congruent, presumptively odious concept of racial "critical mass" as the principle of the fashioning of electoral districts. Indeed, it is a case where no official is willing to accept, let alone to claim, respon-sibility for the requirement of 65 [percent] or over nonwhite.[68]

The Court also was faulted for its uncritical acceptance of the 65 percent "nonwhite" majority as the magic percentage needed to ensure that the vot-ing rights of "nonwhites" are not abridged. The Court presented state and local governments with a difficult choice between concentrating members of a protected minority into a single district until they constitute 65 percent of the population and spreading them out among two or more districts to permit them to exercise a "balance of power."

Evidence is lacking that white voters and black voters form respective homogeneous entities for voting purposes. Interestingly, many of the Puerto Rican voters in the Williamsburg district were described as "nonwhites," and the assumption apparently was made that blacks and Puerto Ricans have identi-cal interests. Nevertheless, this decision provided a powerful incentive for the adoption of single-member districts apportioned solely on the basis of race.

The subject of racial gerrymandering remains a contentious one. The Supreme Court in *Shaw v. Reno* in 1993 remanded a case involving a North Carolina "serpentine" congressional district, which stretched 160 miles along Interstate 85, for a determination of whether the obvious racial gerrymander violated the equal protection clause of the Fourteenth Amendment. Writing for the majority, Justice Sandra Day O'Connor opined:

Racial classifications ... reinforce the belief, held by too many for too much of our history, that individuals should be judged on the color of their skin. Racial gerrymandering, even for remedial purposes, may balkanize us into competing racial factions; it threatens to carry us further from the goal of a political system in which race no longer matters....[69]

Building upon its 1993 voting rights decision, the Supreme Court announced its 5-to-4 opinion in *Miller v. Johnson* on June 29, 1995, which invalidated the boundary lines of Georgia's 11th congressional district because race was the predominant factor in drawing them.[70] Writing for the majority, Justice Anthony Kennedy opined that race cannot be "the predominant factor motivating the legislature's decision to place a significant number of voters within a particular district." The majority announced the Court would employ "strict scrutiny" in future voting rights cases to determine whether districts were tailored narrowly to achieve a compelling state interest. The Kennedy opinion was particularly critical of the role of the United States Department of Justice and rejected the State of Georgia's argument that the plan was enacted to comply with the demands of the Department. The Department's performance, the Court concluded, "raises a serious constitutional question" and is "unsupportable."

Summary and Conclusion

The Voting Rights Act has succeeded in removing insidious barriers to voting by blacks and foreign language minorities, but has resulted in the remedial employment of the single-member district system, which constitutes a significant source of current political and legal controversy. Proportional representation, limited voting and cumulative voting can promote the election of minority candidates without encouraging segregation. The ideal system for candidate-based election in the United States is the single-transferable vote form of PR, which permits simultaneous representation of general and particular interests as candidates must build jurisdiction-wide coalitions in order to win election to office.

Merely changing electoral systems, however, will not necessarily increase dramatically the election of minorities to office. There are barriers to election other than the electoral system, many of which inhere to the advantages of incumbency. Incumbents in large jurisdictions have staff who spend part of their time promoting the re-election of their employers. In addition, elected officers attract media attention by presenting speeches and attending various public functions. They also may communicate with voters in their districts through newsletters printed and posted at government expense, and may make public service announcements which reinforce their name recognition. The most critical barrier to the effective challenge of an incumbent elected official often is lack of funds to mount a major campaign. Records filed with election officials in the various states reveal that incumbents, with few exceptions, possess a vastly superior ability to raise funds.[71]

The task for reformers today is to measure the quality of representation produced by various electoral systems and evaluate them in terms of the following criteria: effectiveness of ballots cast, maximization of voter participation, representation of competing interests, maximization of citizen access to elected decision makers, equity in interest group members' representation, and legitimacy of the legislative body.

Notes

1. *Vermont Constitution of 1791*, Chap. II, § 21.
2. *Kentucky Constitution of 1972*, Art. III, § 1.
3. *New Hampshire Constitution of 1784*, Part Second, Arts. 13 and 27 (1792) and *Georgia Constitution of 1798*, Art. IV, § 1.
4. *New York Constitution of 1821*, Art II, § 1.
5. *Massachusetts Constitution of 1780*, Art. XX of Articles of Amendments.
6. *North Carolina Constitution of 1776*, Art. I of Amendments, § 3.
7. 16 Stat. 140 (1870).
8. 16 Stat. 433 (1871).
9. *United States v. Reese*, 92 U.S. 214 (1875).
10. *Guinn v. United States*, 238 U.S. 347 (1915).
11. *Smith v. Allwright*, 321 U.S. 649 (1944).
12. *Schell v. Davis*, 336 U.S. 933 (1949).
13. *Gomillion v. Lightfoot*, 364 U.S. 339 (1960).
14. *Civil Rights Act of 1957*, 71 Stat. 634, 42 U.S.C.A. § 1975 (1958 Supp.).
15. *Civil Rights Act of 1960*, 74 Stat. 86, 42 U.S.C.A. § 1971 (1961 Supp.).
16. *Civil Rights Act of 1964*, 78 Stat. 241, 42 U.S.C.A. § 2000a (1965 Supp.).
17. *Voting Rights Act of 1965*, 79 Stat. 437, 42 U.S.C.A. § 1973 (1966 Supp.).
18. *Voting Rights Extension: Hearings Before Subcommittee No. 5 of the Committee on the Judiciary, House of Representatives* (Washington, D.C.: United States Government Printing Office, 1969), Serial No. 3, p. 265.
19. *Voting Rights Act of 1965*, 79 Stat. 437, 42 U.S.C.A. § 19 (1966 Supp.).
20. *Extension of the Voting Rights Act of 1965: Hearings Before Sub-Committee on Constitutional Rights of the Committee of the Judiciary, United States Senate* (Washington, D.C.: United States Government Printing Office, 1975), p. 24.
21. *Ibid.*
22. See, 28 CFR § 51 (1993).
23. *Voting Rights Act Amendments of 1970*, 84 Stat. 312, 42 U.S.C.A. § 1973 (1971 Supp.) and *Voting Rights Act Amendments of 1975,* 89 Stat. 401, 42 U.S.C.A. § 1973b (1994).
24. *Voting Rights Act Amendments of 1970*, 84 Stat. 312, 28 U.S.C.A. §§ 1391–393 (1971 Supp.).
25. *Voting Rights Act Amendments of 1975*, 89 Stat. 402, 42 U.S.C.A. §§ 1973a, 1973d, and 1973i (1976 Supp.)
26. Data supplied to author by attorney David H. Hunter, Voting Section, United States Department of Justice, 17 January 1995.

27. *White v. Regester*, 412 U.S. 755 (1973).

28. *Washington v. Davis*, 426 U.S. 229 at 238–39 (1976) and *Village of Arlington Heights v. Metropolitan Housing Development Corporation*, 429 U.S. 252 at 256 (1977).

29. *City of Mobile v. Bolden*, 446 U.S. 55 at 75 (1980).

30. *Voting Rights Act Amendments of 1982*, 96 Stat. 134, 42 U.S.C.A. § 1973(b) (1994).

31. *Ibid.*, 96 Stat. 133–35, 42 U.S.C.A. §§ 1973b and 1973aa–6 (1994).

32. *Ibid.*, 96 Stat. 132, 42 U.S.C.A. § 1973C (1994).

33. *Virginia v. United States*, 386 F.Supp. 1319 (1974) and *Virginia v. United States* U.S. 901 (1975).

34. *South Carolina v. Katzenbach*, 383 U.S. 301 at 308 (1966).

35. *Allen v. State Board of Elections*, 393 U.S. 544 at 566–67 (1968).

36. *Georgia v. United States*, 411 U.S. 526 at 533 (1973).

37. *Perkins v. Matthews*, 400 U.S. 379 (1971).

38. 20 *Federal Register* 9897 (August 6, 1965).

39. *Perkins v. Matthews*, 301 F.Supp. 565 (S.D. Miss. 1969).

40. *Perkins v. Matthews*, 400 U.S. 379 at 388–89 (1971).

41. *Holt v. City of Richmond*, 334 F.Supp 228 at 236 (1971).

42. *Ibid.*, pp. 238–40.

43. *Holt v. Richmond*, 459 F. 2d 1093 at 1099 (4th Cir., 1972).

44. *Holt v. Richmond*, 408 U.S. 931 (1972).

45. *City of Petersburg Virginia v. United States et al.*, 354 F.Supp. 1021 (1972); *City of Petersburg Virginia v. United States et al.*, 410 U.S. 962 (1973).

46. *City of Petersburg Virginia v. Untied States et al.*, 354 F.Supp. 1021 at 1025 (1972).

47. *Ibid.*, at 1027.

48. *City of Richmond v. United States*, 376 F.Supp. 1344 at 1351 (1974).

49. *Ibid.*, at 1352. Under the ward plan, blacks would have a majority of at least 64.0 percent in four wards and would constitute 40.9 percent of the population in a fifth ward. Whites would have a majority in four wards.

50. *City of Richmond v. United States*, 422 U.S. 358 at 370–71 (1975).

51. 35 *Federal Register*, 12354 (July 31, 1970) and 36 *Federal Register,* 5809 (March 21, 1971).

52. *Torres v. Sachs*, 381 F.Supp. 309 at 312 (1973).

53. *Torres v. Sachs*, 419 U.S. 888 (1974).

54. *NAACP v. New York*, 413 U.S. 345 (1973).

55. *New York v. United States*, 419 U.S. 888 (1974).

56. *New York Laws of 1974*, Chaps. 585–91 and 599.

57. Emanuel Perlmutter, "Hasidic Groups File Suit to Bar Redistricting as 'Gerrymander,'" *The New York Times*, 12 June, 1974, p. 28.

58. Linda Greenhouse, "Hasidic Jews are Called 'Victims of Racial Gerrymander' at Hearing on Suit," *The New York Times*, 21 June 1974, p. 19.

59. *Memorandum of Decision* (Washington, D.C.: Civil Rights Division, United States Department of Justice, 1 July 1974), unpublished.

60. *Ibid.*, p. 17.

61. *United Jewish Organizations of Williamsburg, Incorporated v. Wilson*, 377 F.Supp. 1164 at 1165–166 (1974).

62. *United Jewish Organizations of Williamsburg, Incorporated v. Wilson*, 510 F. 2d 512 at 523. (1975).

63. *Ibid.*, at 521.

64. Lesley Oelsner, "Brooklyn's Hasidim Argue Voting Rights Case Before the Supreme Court," *The New York Times*, 7 October 1976, p. 47.

65. *Ibid.*

66. *United Jewish Organizations of Williamsburg, Incorporated v. Carey*, 430 U.S. 144 at 156 and 159–60 (1977).

67. *Ibid.*, at 161.

68. *United Jewish Organizations of Williamsburg, v. Wilson*, 510 F. 2d 512 at 526 (1975).

69. *Shaw v. Reno*, 113S.ct.2816 at 2832 (1993).

70. The Miller decision has not been published, but may be identified by its case numbers: 94–631, 94–797 and 94–929.

71. For additional details, see, Joseph F. Zimmerman, "Fair Representation for Minorities and Women" in Wilma Rule and Joseph Zimmerman, eds., *United States Electoral Systems: Their Impact on Women and Minorities* (Westport, Conn.: Greenwood Press, 1992), pp. 1–11.

The Supreme Court and the Voting Rights Act

Olethia Davis

Minority vote dilution continues to be a hotly debated issue 30 years after passage of the Voting Rights Act. Responsibility has fallen largely to the judiciary to determine whether unlawful vote dilution has occurred in jurisdictions covered by Sections 2 and 5 of the Act. Yet, a review of case law reveals that the Court has been inconsistent in its interpretation of Sections 2 and 5. This ambiguity has provided ammunition for opponents of voting rights and intensified the debate over federal civil rights guarantees.

In the context of voting rights, this debate centers around such issues as the appropriate evidence required to prove minority vote dilution, the types of election systems that might be challenged on the grounds of Section 2 and/or Section 5, and whether the three-pronged test devised by the Supreme Court in *Thornburg v. Gingles* is a supplement to the 1982 revised version of Section 2 or a reiteration of the legislative intent of the U.S. Senate.[1]

Judicial Interpretation of Section 5

Most challenges to vote dilution have been brought on grounds other than Section 5 because of its limited scope. Until 1987, the required test of retrogression—whether a change in electoral laws or structures has a dilutionary effect—and proof of intentional discrimination were difficult and in many cases impossible to prove.

In 1987, however, the U.S. Department of Justice adopted the language of the Senate report on voting rights, which indicated that the legislative intent

Reprinted with permission from National Civic Review, *Vol. 84, No. 4, Fall/Winter, 1995. Published by the National Civic League Press, Denver, Colorado.*

of the amended Act was to incorporate the results standard of Section 2 into the preclearance requirement of Section 5.[2] This interpretation is based on that portion of Section 2 that mandates that a "totality of circumstances" must be met in order for jurisdictions to receive declaratory judgment as mandated by Section 2 and set forth in Section 4(f)(2).[3]

The Court in several earlier rulings expanded the scope of Section 5, thus protecting the voting rights of minorities. In *Allen v. State Board of Elections*, the Court required preclearance when a jurisdiction attempted to replace elections with appointment of officials.[4] The Court's opinion shifted the focus of Section 5 challenges from vote denial—disenfranchisement—to vote dilution, and indicated that Section 5 encompassed a broad range of voting practices and procedures. The Court's holding in *Georgia v. United States* reinforced its decision in *Allen*.[5] In *Georgia,* the Court contended that "had Congress disagreed with the interpretations of Section 5 in *Allen*, it had ample opportunity to amend the statute, [therefore,] we can only conclude ... that *Allen* [was] correctly interpreted."[6] In *Hadnott v. Amos*, the Court required federal approval of a change in the declaration deadline for independent candidates.[7] In *Perkins v. Matthews*, the Court required preclearance of a change in location of polling places as well as approval of a change from single-member district to at-large elections.[8] In *City of Petersburg, Virginia v. United States*, the Court ruled that annexations that diluted minority voting strength were illegal, even in the absence of an invidious or discriminatory intent.[9] Likewise, in *City of Rome v. United States*, the Court ruled that annexations violated the Voting Rights Act.[10] In *Rome*, the Court held that the change in electoral structure "would lead to a retrogression in the position of racial minorities with respect to their *effective* [emphasis added] exercise of the [franchise]."[11]

However, in *City of Richmond, Virginia v. United States* and *Beer v. United States*, the Court began to limit the scope of its interpretation of Section 5.[12] In both of these cases, the Court rejected Section 5 voting rights claims. In contrast to its preclearance inclusion of a broad range of election procedures in *Allen* and *Georgia*, the Court placed limitations on the types of changes it considered violative of Section 5 in *Beer* and *Richmond*. In *Beer*, the Court placed weight on the retrogression test of Section 5. In *Richmond*, the Court upheld an annexation that decreased the percentage of blacks in the population of Richmond, Virginia. According to the Court, "as long as the ward system fairly represents the voting strength of the Negro community as it exists after annexation we cannot hold ... that such an annexation is nevertheless barred by Section 5."[13] Despite the Court's ruling in *Richmond*, its focus on the dilutive effect of a reapportionment plan resulted in a deviation from a strict application of the *Beer* retrogression standard to a "dilutive effect" standard.[14]

The Court's ambiguity in Section 5 litigation reached its peak in *Presley v. Etowah County Commission*.[15] According to the Court, shifts in power on local governmental bodies were not covered by the preclearance provisions of Section 5 unless such changes resulted in disenfranchisement of a protected class. The Court concluded that the Voting Rights Act covers only four types of voting changes: 1) the manner of voting, such as switching from single-member districts to at-large elections; 2) candidate qualifications; 3) voter registration; and 4) creation or abolition of an elected office.[16] Furthermore, the Court held that election changes, in order to be declared violative of Section 5, must have a direct impact on the electoral process.

In *Presley*, Justice Stevens disagreed with the Court's interpretation of Section 5. In his dissenting opinion, Stevens emphasized that *Presley* resulted in the Court's ignoring "the broad scope of Section 5 coverage" established by its ruling in *Allen*.[17] Stevens concluded that "the reallocation of decision making authority of an elective office that is taken 1) after the victory of a black candidate, and 2) after the entry of a consent decree designed to give black voters an opportunity to have representation on an elective body [should be] covered by Section 5."[18]

The 1982 Amendment of Section 2

As a result of problems encountered by individuals and organizations pursuing voting rights complaints under Section 5, the case law of the Court on vote dilution mostly involves allegations of Section 2 violations. In 1982, Congress revised the language of Section 2 in an attempt to diminish the possible consequences of the Supreme Court's decision in *City of Mobile v. Bolden*, which placed a heavy evidentiary burden of proof on the plaintiffs in vote-dilution litigation.[19] Congress also relied on the Supreme Court's previous decision in *White v. Regester* and the decision of the Fifth Circuit Court of Appeals in *Zimmer v. McKeithen* in drafting the 1982 amendment.[20]

In *Mobile*, the Supreme Court employed a strict constructionist interpretation of the Fifteenth Amendment, holding that it ensured only the right to register and vote, and offered no protection against vote dilution. Moreover, the Court concluded that the Fourteenth Amendment did prohibit vote dilution, but only in those cases where it could be proved that an electoral procedure had been established for racially discriminatory purposes.

Not only did the Court devise the "intent" standard in *Mobile*, it also distinguished between disenfranchisement and vote dilution. According to the Court, the former prevents or discourages a group from voting, while the latter may exist even though people are permitted to vote. The Court held that proof of intentional discrimination was necessary to successfully demonstrate the employment of discriminatory voting practices. This standard placed an evidentiary burden of proof on plaintiffs in vote-dilution lawsuits.

The *Mobile* Court also rejected the *Zimmer* test, devised by the Fifth Circuit

Court of Appeals in *Zimmer v. McKeithen*, thus requiring plaintiffs to provide proof of invidious or intentional discrimination in order to prevail in vote-dilution claims.[21] In *Zimmer*, the Fifth Circuit augmented the Supreme Court's ruling in *White* by providing a list of guidelines to be met in proving a vote-dilution claim. It is specifically Section 2(b) of the amended Act that contains the language of both *White* and *Zimmer*. Proof of a "totality of circumstances" as outlined in *Zimmer* is required to prove that "a voting qualification or prerequisite to voting or standard practice, or procedure ... imposed by any State or political subdivision ... results in a denial or abridgment of the right of any citizen of the United States to vote...."[22] Section 4(f)(2) of the Act extended this coverage to language minorities.

According to the *Zimmer* test, unconstitutional dilution is proved when an aggregate of these factors occurs: 1) lack of access to the process of slating candidates, 2) unresponsiveness of legislators to the particularized interests of the minority community, 3) a tenuous state policy underlying the preference for multimember or at-large districting, and 4) existence of past discrimination that generally precluded the effective participation of minorities in the political process.[23] Additional *Zimmer* factors that may be considered by the courts are anti-single shot voting requirements, existence of unusually large districts, majority vote requirements, and omission of provisions for residency requirements in geographical sub-districts in at-large elections.[24]

Section 2 originally protected only the act of voting, but Section 2 as amended in 1982 provided for the right to participate at every level (e.g., nomination, election, holding political office) of the political process. In short, the overall purpose of revising Section 2 was to reinstate and reinforce the legislative intent of the Voting Rights Act following the *Mobile* decision. According to the Senate report, "this amendment is designed to make clear that proof of discriminatory intent is not required to establish a violation of Section 2." It thereby restores the legal standards, based on the controlling Supreme Court precedents, which applied to voting discrimination claims prior to the litigation involved in *Mobile v. Bolden*.[25]

Additionally, Congress was very much aware of the Court's past inconsistency in deciding challenges to at-large election structures, and sought in its 1982 amendments to eliminate that ambiguity.[26] Accordingly, Congress devised a "results" standard to be utilized by the courts in resolving voting rights claims. The components of this new standard were outlined in the Senate report.[27] In effect, the results standard nullified the intent standard devised by the Supreme Court in *Mobile*.

According to Congress, if "as a result of the challenged practice or structure plaintiffs do not have an equal opportunity to elect candidates of their choice, such a practice will be considered in violation of the Act, specifically Section 2."[28] Additionally, the language of Section 2 prohibited both vote dilution and disenfranchisement.

The Court's Interpretation of Section 2 as Amended

Congress's amendment of Section 2 resulted in the filing of numerous lawsuits. The first case to reach the U.S. Supreme Court involving allegations of a Section 2 violation following the 1982 amendments was *Thornburg v. Gingles.*[29] It is important to emphasize that prior to *Gingles,* the Court had adjudicated a case involving the subject of minority vote dilution, but the complaint in that instance was based on constitutional grounds, not the Voting Rights Act.[30] The Court ruled in *Rogers v. Lodge* that an at-large election system utilized by Burke County, Georgia resulted in minority vote dilution and was thus violative of the equal protection of the laws guaranteed by the Fourteenth Amendment.

Gingles originally was a 1984 case filed by black registered voters in North Carolina challenging one single-member district and six multimember districts in the state's reapportionment plan.[31] The plaintiffs alleged that the plan concentrated blacks into a majority-white multimember district resulting in vote dilution. Relying on the Senate report factors, the District Court upheld the plaintiff's Section 2 claim, concluding that the totality of circumstances were consistent with vote dilution. The court's ruling with respect to five of the multimember districts was appealed by the State of North Carolina.

On appeal to the United States Supreme Court, the state alleged that the District Court incorrectly concluded that the legislative reapportionment plan violated Section 2. The Court unanimously affirmed the District Court ruling in four of the five multimember districts, but the justices split on the evidentiary standard to be applied in vote-dilution cases. This split resulted in the filing of four separate opinions, indicating a continued lack of consensus in judicial review of key Voting Rights Act provisions.

Despite its lack of consensus, the *Thornburg* Court devised a three-pronged test—the *Gingles* test—to detect justifiable vote dilution in multi-member/at-large districts. This test requires plaintiffs alleging vote dilution to meet three criteria: The protected minority must demonstrate that 1) it is sufficiently large and geographically compact to constitute a majority in one or more single-member districts, 2) it is politically cohesive and tends to vote as a bloc, and 3) the majority vote sufficiently as a bloc to defeat the minority's preferred candidate.[32] The Court ruled that the *Gingles* factors were prerequisites that must be met to secure a determination of vote dilution.

Using similar reasoning as the Fifth Circuit in *Jones* and *McMillan* and the Eleventh Circuit in *Marengo* and *Dallas County,* the *Gingles* Court placed importance on the degree of racial bloc voting in vote-dilution cases.[33] In each of these cases, the circuit courts emphasized the importance of a finding of racial polarization in voting and pointed out that Section 2 did not require a demonstration of the existence of all of the factors included in Section 2.

According to the courts, a showing of racial bloc voting is a prerequisite for a vote-dilution claim.

Of significance in *Gingles* was the Supreme Court's distinction between *legally significant* racial bloc voting (i.e., the degree of bloc voting required to prove a dilution claim) and racial polarization per se. Legally significant racial bloc voting requires plaintiffs to provide evidence of the existence of racial polarization that results in the inability of minorities to elect candidates of their choice.

In rendering a definition of legally significant racial bloc voting, the Court rejected the contention that proof of racial bloc voting should rest on the ability of minority voters to elect *minority* candidates of choice. According to the Court, "the fact that race of voter and race of candidate is often correlated is not directly pertinent to a Section 2 inquiry. Under Section 2, it is the *status* of the candidate as the *chosen representative of a particular racial group*, not the race of the candidate, that is important."[34]

Gingles provided clarity with regard to the accepted definition of racial polarization. The Court accepted a less stringent definition than that accepted by the lower courts in *Collins* and *McCord*.[35] The *Gingles* Court accepted the definition provided by the plaintiffs' expert witness, Dr. Bernard Grofman. According to Grofman, racial polarization is "a consistent relationship between race of the voter and the way in which he votes ... [or when] black voters and white voters vote differently."[36]

The *Gingles* Court also addressed the question of whether bivariate or multivariate analysis should be utilized to prove vote dilution. The lower courts had employed both methods.[37] The Supreme Court rejected the requirement of multivariate analysis, or the consideration of multiple factors in proving differential racial voting patterns. According to the Court, the proper question to ask is *whether* voters have divergent voting patterns on the basis of race, not *why* they vote differently. The court concluded that "it is the *difference* between the choices made by black and white voters and not the reasons for the differences that leads to blacks' having less opportunity to elect their candidates of choice."[38] Despite the *Gingles* Court's attempt to specify criteria that must be met by plaintiffs alleging vote dilution, its actual decision in *Thornburg v. Gingles* resulted in numerous unresolved questions, which have catalyzed additional debate over voting rights.[39] Some of the questions posed as a result of the *Gingles* decision include:

1. Should the courts be interested only in the presence of racial bloc voting, and not explanations for such differences?
2. Did the three-pronged *Gingles* test replace or complement the "totality of circumstances" test incorporated into the amended Section 2?
3. Are plaintiffs required to provide evidence of the presence of any of the factors included in Section 2 as amended in 1982?

4. Since *Gingles* focused primarily on the second factor in Section 2, how should the courts adjudicate cases involving the other inclusive factors of Section 2?

These unanswered questions resulted in conflicting decisions rendered by lower courts.[40]

Post-Thornburg Interpretation of Section 2

The United States Supreme Court did not revisit Section 2 until the early 1990s, in cases involving challenges to judicial election structures and processes.[41] These lawsuits forced the Court to provide clarity on its interpretation of Section 2, since the Fifth and Sixth Circuits differed in their respective interpretations of the applicability of Section 2 to the election of judges. The Fifth Circuit concluded in *Chisom v. Roemer* that Section 2 coverage did not extend to judicial contests since the explicit language of the Section—"to elect *representatives* of choice"—did not include judges, who are not viewed as representatives.[42] On the other hand, the Sixth Circuit held that Section 2 did apply to the election of judges.[43] In response to these conflicting rulings, the Supreme Court held in a Justice Department appeal of the *Chisom* ruling that Section 2 does indeed apply to judicial elections, opining that Section 2 "protected the right to vote … without making any distinctions or imposing any limitations as to which elections would fall within its purview."[44]

To a certain degree, *Chisom* lessened the evidentiary burden imposed by the Court in *Gingles*. Even though the Court's decision in *Chisom* did not over-rule *Gingles*, the fact remains that although the plaintiffs in judicial challenges provided the Court with evidence to fulfill the results standard of Section 2, the majority opinion of the Court focused primarily on whether judges were representatives, rather than the issue of vote dilution. By centering on statutory interpretation of the legislative intent of Congress in revising Section 2, the Court, in effect, shifted the question in cases involving the election of judges from a results standard proving vote dilution to the ability of minorities to elect their preferred candidates—an influence standard. As a result, the Court opened a Pandora's Box which eventually led to what is considered by a number of observers to be one of its most infamous voting rights determinations.[45]

In response to the Court's decision in *Chisom*, many jurisdictions devised majority-minority single-member election districts. Opponents of such districts challenged their constitutionality by relying on the equal protection clause of the Fourteenth Amendment. As a result, the Court was faced with the formidable task of interpreting and balancing the protections set out in Section 2 of the Voting Rights Act with those provided by the Fourteenth Amendment.

The result has been an unwillingness to provide definitive and consistent rulings with regard to voting rights.

This ambiguity leads to a discussion of the most recent case law involving vote dilution.[46] In *Growe*, the Court rendered a decision with negative implications for minority voting rights. Even though the decision was cloaked in a consideration of judicial federalism, with the Court holding that states should have autonomy in reapportionment, the overall ruling resulted in an attack on the creation of majority-minority legislative districts. This case represented the initial reluctance of the Court to render a decision involving its interpretation of either Section 2 or the *Gingles* standard. Then, in *Voinovich*, a unanimous Court upheld the creation of black-majority voting districts,[47] but during the same term questioned the constitutionality of race-conscious districting in *Shaw v. Reno*.[48]

In *Shaw*, the Court was asked to determine the constitutionality of the actions of the United States Department of Justice in its efforts to secure minority voting rights. *Shaw* represented a departure from a reliance on the Voting Rights Act and the Court's own precedents, since the plaintiffs in this case were not required to provide any evidentiary proof under Section 2 or in compliance with the *Gingles* test to prove the existence of vote dilution.[49] The results standard was completely ignored by the *Shaw* Court.

In subsequent voting rights cases, the Court's fragmentation has continued, with the dissenters emphasizing the Court's tenuousness and disregard of precedents. In the *Johnson* and *Holder* cases, a splintered Court narrowed the scope of Section 2 by concluding, respectively, that minorities in Florida were not entitled to additional majority-minority districts and that a grant of ultimate power to a single white county commissioner in Georgia did not deny African-Americans a voice in local government policy.[50]

The Court's decision in *Johnson* to a certain degree mirrored its reasoning in *Voinovich*, in which the Court concluded that the creation of majority-minority districts was permissible if it did not diminish minority voting strength. The *Voinovich* Court, however, included a qualifier by opining that a case-by-case approach should be employed to determine the constitutionality of such districts because the facts and circumstances of each might differ. Nonetheless, *Johnson* dramatizes the unwillingness of the Court to declare *all* majority-minority districts unconstitutional after its controversial ruling in *Shaw*.

Holder provided a clear indication that the members of the Court differ in their interpretations of Section 2 of the Voting Rights Act. Justice Souter's reasoning in *Johnson* led to his dissension in *Holder*. In *Johnson*, Souter, writing for the Court's majority, held the creation of majority-minority districts permissible in order to increase minority representation. However, this same reasoning was not applied in *Holder*. Three Justices provided separate concurring opinions. In fact, Justice Thomas, in his dissenting opinion, advocated judicial restraint in voting rights cases, a narrow judicial interpretation of the Act, and the overturning of *Allen*.

Holder had been brought by black plaintiffs challenging a single-member county commission form of government in Bleckly, Georgia. The Court of Appeals for the Eleventh Circuit, finding that the form of government constituted an obstacle to minority voting and thus violated Section 2, ordered an expansion of the county commission. The Supreme Court reversed the appellate court's decision, holding that changes to the size of the governmental body or organization are not covered by the Voting Rights Act.

In *Miller*,[51] the Court declared a majority-minority congressional district in Georgia unconstitutional. The opinion of the Court rested on constitutional grounds—the Equal Protection Clause of the Fourteenth Amendment—rather than an interpretation of Section 2 of the Voting Rights Act or the three-pronged *Gingles* test. The *Miller* Court contended that neither *Shaw* nor *Miller* involved vote dilution claims, but equal protection claims, because states had employed race as a basis for "segregating" voters.

In essence, the *Miller* Court failed to recognize that it is impossible to comply with the mandates of Sections 2 and 5 of the Voting Rights Act without a consideration of race (in many cases race may be the paramount factor). The Court has therefore made it very difficult for jurisdictions to meet the requirements of the Voting Rights Act without violating the equal protection guarantees of the Fourteenth Amendment.

Conclusion

The United States Supreme Court has been consistently vague in its interpretation of Sections 2 and 5 of the Voting Rights Act. This ambiguity has resulted in both plaintiffs and defendants in vote-dilution cases attempting to meet evidentiary proof requirements as the Court continues to devise new modes of interpretation, ignores precedents, and fails to uniformly apply provisions of the Act.

In light of the fact that the Court has in many cases abandoned its own voting rights precedents, lower courts—as well as parties involved in vote-dilution claims—lack clear guidance to follow in such cases.

In addition, the Court's holdings in the most recent cases have had serious ramifications relative to the political gains of minorities. These decisions have carried minority voting rights back to the second era of vote-dilution litigation, during which the Court rendered its *Mobile* decision. In fact, the Court's interpretation and application of the three-pronged test in *Gingles* has resulted in a return to the "intent" standard of *Bolden*.

Additionally, an overwhelming impact of the Court's tenuousness on the issue of voting rights constitutes what this author refers to as "vote dilutigation," in which attorneys and others opposed to ensuring the full electoral participation of minorities have devised standards and statistical interpretations that serve the same purpose as earlier barriers to voting, such as large, multi-member districts and anti-single-shot provisions.

It is time to refocus the voting rights debate on the proper role of the judiciary in extending and enforcing minority political access. Such a reframing of the debate will require legislative involvement, just as it did when the Supreme Court rendered its decision in *Mobile*. However, the ultimate question is this: Will a conservatively oriented legislative branch place limitations on a conservative court?

Notes

1. *Thornburg v. Gingles*, 478 U.S. 30 (1986).
2. H.R. Rep. Ser. No. 9, 99th Cong., 2d Sess. 11 (1986). See also, 28 C.F.R. Section 51.55. The amended Section 5 reads: "(a) Section 5 of the Voting Rights Act of 1965 as amended, 42 U.S.C. 1973c [1988], prohibits the enforcement in any jurisdiction covered by Section 4(b) of the Act, 42 U.S.C. 1973b(b), of any voting qualification or prerequisite of voting or standard, practice, or procedure with respect to voting different from that in force or effect on the date used to determine coverage, until either: (1) A declaratory judgment is obtained from the U.S. District Court for the District of Columbia that such qualification, prerequisite, standard, practice, or procedure does not have the purpose and will not have the effect of denying or abridging the right to vote on account of race, color, or membership in a language minority group, or (2) It has been submitted to the Attorney General and the Attorney General has interposed no objection within a 60-day period following submission. (b) In order to make clear the responsibilities of the Attorney General under Section 5 and the interpretation of the Attorney General of the responsibility imposed on other under this Section, the procedures in this part have been established to govern the administration of Section 5."
3. Section 4(f)(2) reads: "(2) To assist the Court in determining whether to issue a declaratory judgment under this subsection, the plaintiff shall present evidence of minority participation, including evidence of the levels of minority group registration and voting, changes in such levels over time, and disparities between minority-group and non-minority-group participation." See also, C.F.R. Section 51.2.
4. *Allen v. State Board of Elections*, 393 U.S. 544 (1969).
5. *Georgia v. United States*, 411 U.S. 526 (1973).
6. *Georgia v. United States,* 411 U.S. at 534.
7. *Hadnott v. Amos*, 394 U.S. at 358 (1969).
8. *Perkins v. Matthews*, 400 U.S. at 379 (1971).
9. *Petersburg v. United States*, 410 U.S. at 962 (1973).
10. *City of Rome v. United States*, 446 U.S. at 156 (1980).
11. *City of Rome v. United States*, 446 U.S. at 156.
12. *City of Richmond v. United States*, 422 U.S. at 358 (1975); *Beer v. United States*, 425 U.S. at 130 (1976).
13. *City of Richmond v. United States*, 422 U.S. at 371.

14. This standard was developed by the Court in *Petersburg* and first applied in *Richmond.*

15. *Presley v. Etowah County Commission,* 112 S. Ct. at 820 (1992). *Presley* involved separate challenges by black commissioners of Etowah and Russell Counties, Alabama. These commissioners filed a single complaint alleging that the restructuring of the county commissions resulted in racial discrimination in violation of the U.S. Constitution, civil rights statutes, court orders, and Section 5 of the Voting Rights Act.

16. *Presley v. Etowah County Commission,* 112 S. Ct. at 828.

17. *Presley v. Etowah County Commission,* 112 S. Ct. at 836.

18. *Presley v. Etowah County Commission,* 112 S. Ct at 839.

19. *Voting Rights Act of 1982,* 96 Stat. 131, 42 U.S.C.A. Section 1973.

20. *White v. Regester,* 412 U.S. 755 (1973) and *Zimmer v. McKeithen,* 485 F.2d 1297 (5th Cir. 1973).

21. *Zimmer v. McKeithen,* 485 F.2d 1297 (5th Cir. 1973).

22. See, *Voting Rights Act of 1982,* 96 Stat. 134, 42 U.S.C. Section 1973 (1988).

23. *Zimmer v. McKeithen,* 485 F.2d 1297 (5th Cir. 1973).

24. *Zimmer v. McKeithen,* 485 F.2d 1297 (5th Cir. 1973).

25. U.S. Senate, 1982, p. 2.

26. See, Senate Judiciary Report on the Extension of the Voting Rights Act, Rep. No. 97–417, 97th Cong., 2d Sess., pp. 19–27 (1982).

27. Senate Judiciary Report on the Extension of the Voting Rights Act, Rep. No. 97–417, 97th Cong., 2d Sess. at 19–27 (1982).

28. House of Representatives 1981 at 29; Senate 1982b at 28, 36–37.

29. *Thornburg v. Gingles,* 478 U.S. at 30 (1986).

30. *Rogers v. Lodge,* 458 U.S. at 613 (1982).

31. *Gingles v. Edmisten,* 590 F.Supp. at 345 (E.D.N.C. 1984), *aff'd sub nom Thornburg v. Gingles,* 478 U.S. at 30 (1986).

32. *Gingles v. Edmisten,* 590 F.Supp. at 345 (E.D.N.C. 1984), *aff'd sub nom Thornburg v. Gingles,* 478 U.S. at 30 (1986).

33. *Jones v. City of Lubbock, Texas,* 727 F.2d at 364 (5th Cir. 1984); *U.S. v. Marengo County Commission,* 731 F.2d at 1546 (11th Cir. 1984); *McMillan v. Escambia County,* 748 F.2d at 1037 (5th Cir. 1984); *Lee County Branch of NAACP v. City of Opelika,* 748 F.2d at 147 (11th Cir. 1984).

34. *Gingles v. Edmisten,* 590 F.Supp. at 345 (E.D.N.C. 1984), *aff'd sub nom Thornburg v. Gingles,* 478 U.S. at 30 (1986).

35. *Collins v. City of Norfolk,* 605 F.Supp. at 377 (E.D.Va. 1984); *aff'd* 768 F.2d at 572 (4th Cir. 1985); *rev'd* 816 F.2d at 932 (4th Cir. 1987); 679 F.Supp. (E.D. Va. 1988); 883 F.2d at 1232 (4th Cir. 1989); *McCord v. City of Fort Lauderdale,* 787 F.2d at 1528 (11th Cir. 1986).

36. *Thornburg v. Gingles,* 478 U.S. at 53.

37. Bivariate analysis was utilized in *Jones, Marengo County* and *McMillan.* On the other hand, multivariate analysis was employed in *Opelika, Collins* and *McCord.*

38. *Thornburg v. Gingles,* 478 U.S. at 63.

39. See, Bernard Grofman, Lisa Handley and Richard Niemi, *Minority Representation and the Quest for Voting Equality* (Cambridge University Press, 1992). For a discussion of the unresolved issues flowing from the *Gingles* test, see, Robert Heath, "*Thornburg v. Gingles*: The Unresolved Issues," *National Civic Review,* January–February 1990, pp. 50–71.

40. *Buckanaga v. Sisseton Independent School District*, 804 F.2d at 469 (8th Cir. 1989).

41. See, *Georgia State Board of Elections v. Brooks*, 498 U.S. at 916 (1990); *Chisom v. Roemer*, 111 S.Ct. at 2354 (1991), and companion cases *United States v. Roemer*, 111 S.Ct. at 2354 (1991) and *Houston Lawyers' Association v. Texas Attorney General*, 501 U.S. at 419 (1991).

42. *League of United Latin American Citizens Council No. 4434 [LULAC] v. Clements*, 914 F.2d at 620 (5th Cir. 1990).

43. *Mallory v. Eyrich*, 839 F.2d at 275 (6th Cir. 1988).

44. *United States v. Roemer*, 111 S.Ct. at 2354 (1991).

45. *Shaw v. Reno*, 113 S.Ct. at 2816 (1993).

46. *Growe, Secretary of State of Minnesota v. Emison*, 113 S.Ct. at 1075 (1993). See also, *Shaw v. Reno*, 113 S.Ct. at 2816 (1993); *In re Voinovich et al.*, 114 S.Ct. at 2156 (1994); *Johnson v. DeGrandy*, 114 S.Ct. at 2647 (1994); *Miller et al. v. Johnson et al.*, No. 94–631, (1995).

47. *In re Voinovich et al.*, 114 S.Ct. at 2156 (1994).

48. *Shaw v. Reno*, 113 S.Ct. at 2816 (1993).

49. See dissenting opinions of Justices White, Blackmun, Stevens, and Souter.

50. *Johnson v. DeGrandy*, 114 S.Ct. at 2647 (1994) and *Holder v. Hall*, 114 S.Ct. at 2581 (1994).

51. The *Miller* decision has not yet been published, but may be identified by its case number 94–631.

The Supreme Court on Redistricting

Richard L. Engstrom

Contiguity, compactness, and respect for both communities of interest and formal political subdivisions are districting criteria that have been elevated in importance recently by the United States Supreme Court. Although none of these criteria is required by the federal constitution or any federal statute, the Court identified them in *Miller v. Johnson* as "traditional, race-neutral districting principles" that, absent extraordinary justification, are not to be "subordinated" to racial considerations when representational districts are constructed.[1] These traditional criteria now serve, in Justice Sandra Day O'Connor's words, as "a crucial frame of reference" in the evaluation of districts.[2] If they are accorded less weight than race in the design of a district, the district must satisfy the strict scrutiny standard for compliance with the Fourteenth Amendment, which means the district must be "narrowly tailored" to further a "compelling governmental interest." Strict scrutiny is popularly described as "strict in theory but fatal in fact."

Miller involved a challenge to the Eleventh Congressional District in Georgia. The plaintiffs alleged that this majority African-American district was a "racial gerrymander." The allegation was not based on a claim that any racial group's voting strength had been diluted by the location of the district lines, but simply that this particular district had been deliberately constructed to have an African-American majority. The Court found that race had indeed been "the predominant factor" in the design of the district, and that this had occurred at the expense of the traditional districting criteria.[3] Strict scrutiny was therefore applied, and the district was found to be fatally flawed.

Miller is the progeny of *Shaw v. Reno*, a 1993 decision involving majority

Reprinted with permission from National Civic Review, *Vol. 84, No. 4, Fall/Winter, 1995. Published by the National Civic League Press, Denver, Colorado.*

African-American congressional districts in North Carolina.[4] The Court held in *Shaw* that race-based districting could be challenged as a violation of the equal protection clause even though there is no allegation that the voting strength of any racial group is adversely affected by the districts. Although *Shaw* failed to resolve this new type of "gerrymandering" claim, it succeeded in attracting increased attention to the criteria for drawing districts by holding that strict scrutiny will be required when "traditional districting principles such as compactness, contiguity, and respect for political subdivisions" are disregarded in the design of districts.[5] *Miller* was the first application of the *Shaw* precedent by the Supreme Court. The principle of respecting "communities defined by actual shared interests" was added to the list of traditional districting criteria in *Miller*.[6]

The explicit recognition of these criteria will no doubt make them more important referents for future districting decisions. Those who design and/or adopt districting plans will not want to subject their product to strict scrutiny, and therefore will be less inclined to deviate from these criteria. This will not, however, make the districting task any easier. It is, in contrast, likely to make districting more difficult, because what exactly these criteria entail is far from certain.

The absence of clear definitions for some of these criteria, as well as clear standards for identifying when they have been "respected" and when they have been "subordinated," leaves districting cartographers, litigators, advocates, and judges in a conceptual thicket. This is already apparent in the post–*Shaw* decisions of the lower federal courts. This ambiguity is exacerbated by the fact that these traditional criteria are often in conflict rather than in harmony. Emphasizing one criterion, quite simply, can interfere with implementing another. Communities of interest, for example, may not be geographically distributed in a compact fashion and can be split by county and municipal boundaries. No agreed-upon hierarchy of these criteria exists to help resolve such conflicts.

Even assuming that these criteria can be clearly defined and readily measured, and therefore capable of providing an unambiguous "frame of reference," what exactly the standard for comparison will be also remains unclear. Will courts compare the respect accorded these criteria to some absolute standard, or to the respect actually accorded them in the past? Given that the Supreme Court has acknowledged that none of these criteria is constitutionally required,[7] it is not likely that some absolute standard will be judicially imposed. Nor, presumably, will the tolerance for deviations from these criteria be less because a gerrymandering allegation concerns race. Justice O'Connor's statement, in her concurrence in *Miller*, that "certainly the standard does not treat efforts to create majority-minority districts *less* favorably than similar efforts on behalf of other groups"[8] indicates that deviations tolerated in the past, for non-racial purposes, will continue to be acceptable in the racial context. If that is the law, then the frame of reference will have to allow substantial deviations in many states and local political jurisdictions, for the application of these criteria has not been particularly strict. Indeed, their subordination to political considerations has been substantial, even when explicitly required by state constitutions or statutes or by city charters.

The conceptual ambiguity surrounding these districting criteria, and the new subordination standard, is a cause for serious concern. Adherence to these traditional principles does not extricate those responsible for districting from the "political thicket," but rather confronts them with capricious definitions and contrasting measurements, as evident in the litigation spawned by *Shaw*. Elevating the legal importance of these criteria, without more precise guidelines for their application, will not bring us closer to the goal of "fair and effective representation."[9] While these criteria may be facially neutral, districting is, unfortunately, an activity in which "the potential for mischief in the name of neutrality is substantial."[10]

This chapter reviews the criteria identified in the *Shaw* and *Miller* decisions. Special attention will be given to their treatment by the federal district courts in the gerrymandering litigation following the *Shaw* decision, and to their new role as a "frame of reference" in the post–*Miller* districting process.

Contiguity

Contiguity and compactness are criteria widely invoked in the evaluation of districts. They are conceptually distinct criteria that concern different aspects of the geographical form of districts. Many state constitutions, statutes, and local charters require representational districts to be contiguous; far fewer require them to be compact.[11]

Contiguity is, or at least was, the most straightforward of the criteria identified by the Court. It is a simple dichotomous concept. A district is either contiguous or it is not. The test for determining this is not complicated, "A contiguous district is one in which a person can go from any point within the district to any other point [within the district] without leaving the district."[12] In short, contiguity requires that districts not be divided into discrete geographical parts.

The lack of confusion over what contiguity entails rarely has resulted in controversy. The major issue concerning contiguity involves whether the ability to travel throughout a district is a theoretical or a literal requirement. This usually arises when bodies of water serve to connect what are otherwise separate parts of a district. Some contiguity provisions require an actual transportation linkage across any water separating parts of a district, such as that in the New York City Charter, which specifies that "there shall be a connection by a bridge, a tunnel, a tramway or by regular ferry service."[13] Additional controversy has arisen over whether having parts of a district connecting only at a point satisfies the criterion of contiguity.

Until *Shaw*, it could be said that "Contiguity is a relatively trivial require-ment and usually a noncontroversial one."[14] Lower court decisions following *Shaw,* however, have created confusion about what "contiguity" now requires. Some judges have not been convinced that districts that meet the traditional definition of contiguity satisfy this criterion. In a case involving Louisiana's congressional districts, for example, a federal court held that a majority African-American district that was only 80 feet wide in places complied with this criterion, "but only hypertechnically and thus cynically," and that "Such tokenism mocks the traditional criterion of contiguity."[15] The expression "tech-nical contiguity" has been applied to other majority-minority districts in other post–*Shaw* decisions.[16] Some courts even have begun to treat contiguity as a continuous concept, as if some districts can be viewed as "more" or "less" contiguous than others.[17]

This approach to contiguity has been an unfortunate development. It com-mingles the notion of contiguity with that of compactness, treating the two as if they are synonymous. A district that is never less than 80 miles wide may well be more compact than one that is 80 feet wide at points, but it should not be considered "more contiguous" for that reason as well. These are distinct criteria that concern different aspects of the geographical form that districts can assume. A district should not be found to violate the contiguity criterion simply because its shape violates the compactness criterion.

Compactness

In contrast to contiguity, the compactness criterion has always been a matter of considerable ambiguity. It concerns the shape of districts, not whether they contain geographically discrete parts. Compactness is a continuous con-cept. Districts can be considered more or less compact, and therefore this cri-terion, unlike contiguity, has been the object of a great variety of quantitative measurements. In fact, there is "no generally accepted definition" of what exactly compactness entails, and therefore no generally accepted measure of it either.[18]

Compactness is legally required less often than contiguity,[19] and there is far less consensus about its importance in the design of districts. The linkage between the shapes districts assume and the quality of representation district residents receive has long been questioned. As candidly expressed by one set of commentators:

> It is, in truth, hard to develop a powerful case for the intrinsic value of hav-ing compact districts: If the representative lived at the center of a compact district, he or she wouldn't have to travel any more than absolutely neces-sary to campaign door-to-door or meet with constituents, but other than that, uncompactness does not seem to affect representation in any way.[20]

A compactness requirement is widely touted, however, as an impediment to gerrymandering. It will rarely preclude gerrymandering, at least the dilutive kind, because that type of gerrymandering is not limited to funny-shaped districts. Indeed, a compactness rule, in some circumstances, could even serve as an excuse for this type of gerrymander.[21] But it is at least a constraint on the way in which district lines can be drawn and therefore an impediment of the manipulation of those lines for political advantage. Odd-shaped districts do stimulate suspicions of deliberate manipulation, and therefore districting is an area, as Justice O'Connor observed in *Shaw*, "in which appearances do matter."[22]

Since *Shaw* elevated the concern for compactness, lower courts have been confronted with a wide array of quantitative indicators that supposedly reveal the relative compactness of districts.[23] These measures emphasize different aspects of shapes, however, and therefore can and do result in conflicting conclusions. Even bizarrely shaped districts can satisfy some of the tests. The measures also vary greatly in complexity. The simplest is based on the length of district boundaries. The shorter the length, the more compact a district is considered to be. Other measures examine the extent to which district shapes deviate from some specified standard, such as a circle or a square, or the extent to which a district fills the area of a polygon encasing it.

New measures have been proposed that depart from the notion of geographical appearances, focusing instead on the physical distances between the homes of the people residing within a district.[24] A federal court in California recently departed even further from the traditional concern for shape and adopted the notion of "functional compactness," holding the "Compactness does not refer to geometric shapes but the ability of citizens to relate to each other and their representatives and the ability of representatives to relate effectively to their constituency."[25]

The variation in approaches does not end here, either. Just as the federal court in Louisiana commingled contiguity with compactness, the federal court handling the *Miller* case commingled communities of interest with compactness. After reviewing several approaches to measuring geographical compactness, that court chose to rely instead on a population-based approach that would "require an assessment of population densities, shared history and common interests; essentially, whether the populations roped into a particular district are close enough geographically, economically, and culturally to justify their being held in a single district."[26] The Supreme Court affirmed both the California decision (rejecting a *Shaw*–type claim) and the *Miller* decision without commenting on what compactness actually entails.

With this type of confusion over the concept of "compactness," requiring that districts not be subordinated to a compactness standard will not simplify the districting task. Districting decisions are likely to be more, not less, difficult in this context. Without some clarity concerning this constraint, those designing and/or adopting districts cannot be expected to know the limitations under which they must work.

Communities of Interest

Many sets of equi-populous districts can usually be created, even when contiguity is required and some type of compactness constraint is applied. Ideally, however, districts should be more than arbitrary aggregations of individuals. The use of geographically based districts is premised on the notion that people who reside close to one another share interests. Geographical proximity is assumed to either cause or reflect, distinct interests and policy preferences. When such "communities of interest" exist, it is often suggested that they be maintained intact within representational districts.

The communities of interest standard is unfortunately "probably the least well defined" criterion for drawing districts.[27] Serious problems arise in identifying such communities, as well as deciding which ones deserve to be recognized in the design of districts. This criterion was not listed among the traditional districting principles in *Shaw*, and therefore has not received as much attention from the lower courts as has compactness. Respect for "communities defined by actual shared interests" was added to the list in *Miller*, however, with little indication of how this concept is to be applied.

One of the principle questions in light of *Miller* is whether this criterion concerns "shared interests" among people living in geographical proximity to each other, or whether it concerns the degree to which districts themselves are homogeneous along some dimension or dimensions. In *Miller*, Justice Anthony Kennedy said that "A State is free to recognize communities that have a particular racial makeup, provided its action is directed toward some common thread of relevant interests."[28] The fact that this comment was immediately followed by a quote from *Shaw* indicating that it would be legitimate to concentrate minority group members in a single district—when they "live together in one community"—suggests that the concept may require geographic proximity.[29] But when Justice Kennedy concluded that the district at issue in *Miller* "tells a tale of disparity, not community," he was explicitly referencing "the social, political and economic makeup" of the district as a whole. African-Americans in the Savannah area had been joined with African-Americans in metropolitan Atlanta, thereby linking, according to Kennedy, African-Americans who were "worlds apart in culture."[30]

This issue is central to the North Carolina congressional districting case, which will be reviewed by the Supreme Court during its 1995–96 term. In North Carolina the district court identified the state's two majority African-American congressional districts as distinctive in character, one being rural and the other urban. This resulted from the legislature's concern that districts

reflect "significant communities of interest."[31] The application of this criterion
to these districts was very systematic; a guideline was adopted that at least 80
percent of the population of one district reside outside cities with populations
exceeding 20,000, and at least 80 percent of the population of the other reside
within cities exceeding 20,000. This resulted in districts that are far from compact, but which, according to the district court, have "substantial, relatively
high degrees of homogeneity of shared socio-economic—hence political—
interests and needs among [their] citizens."[32]

Justice Kennedy did state that the "mere recitation of purported communities of interest" will not successfully invoke this criterion.[33] Simply referencing well known geographical place names presumably will not suffice.
Identifying an area as containing people with particular traits, such as ethnic
or religious identifications or life-style preferences, may be sufficient, provided the particular interest shared are documented. But which "shared interests" deserve recognition in districting, and whether this recognition extends
to people who share an applicable interest but do not reside in close geographical proximity to each other, remain to be determined. This is a districting criterion that has never been well specified, and is unlikely to be clearly
defined prior to the next round of redistricting following the 2000 census.

Political Subdivisions

The final traditional criterion on the Supreme Court's list is respect for
political subdivisions. Local units of government, especially counties, have
often served as building blocks for state legislative and congressional districts.
Prior to the Supreme Court's adoption of the "one person, one vote" principle, counties were even the units to which legislative seats were apportioned
in many of the states.[34] Not dividing counties among districts, unless necessary to equalize populations, has been a common districting constraint.[35] Following established political boundaries such as these is said to keep districts
more cognizable to voters.

Political subdivisions are recognized by law, and there should be no problem in identifying them and in determining whether or not they have been
divided by representational district lines. This is a simple matter of counting.
There may be arguments, however, over which political subdivisions to include
in the count. Counties, as noted, had been the major focus prior to *Shaw* and
Miller, but the treatment of other subdivisions could be examined as well. The
district court in Louisiana, for example, referenced how the state's congressional districts divided "major municipalities" as well as counties.[36] The list
could include other units as well, such as school districts, other types of special districts, or townships. Where the list ends is an issue in need of resolution.

Simply counting the number of units divided by a district or districts may not be the appropriate basis for evaluation, either. Whereas the court in Louisiana found the splitting of municipalities to be objectionable *per se*, the federal court in the Texas congressional districting case responded very differently. The fact that cities in Texas had been divided between districts was not viewed as a negative, despite the divisions being along racial lines. The court noted instead that these divisions "gave the Congressmen a toe-hold in such cities and effectively doubled the cities' representation in Congress."[37] Other issues include such things as "How many splits are too many?" and "Is a little split from a single unit as bad as a big split?"[38]

Another related issue is the respect to be accorded precinct lines. Precincts are not governmental jurisdictions, but merely administrative units for elections. It is often argued that precincts should not be divided by districts, but this is simply a matter of administrative convenience. Requiring districts to follow preexisting precinct boundaries can impede the achievement of other, more important districting goals, such as creating majority-minority districts, and courts should not allow this constraint to be a pretext for discriminatory districting. Precincts can be changed relatively easily to accommodate more important districting criteria.

Frame of Reference

Traditional race-neutral districting criteria are now supposed to provide a frame of reference for evaluating *Shaw*– and *Miller*–type gerrymandering allegations. The districting criteria discussed above are those that the Supreme Court has explicitly recognized as falling within that category. The Court made it clear in *Miller*, however, that it did not consider these to be an exhaustive list of such principles.[39] While the Court provided no indication of the other types of criteria that might be employed to evaluate these allegations, it did leave some of Georgia's expressed criteria off the list, perhaps indicating that these criteria are not to be included.

The Georgia legislature had adopted districting "guidelines" that included, in addition to contiguity and respect for political subdivisions, the protection of incumbent office holders. This was expressed through two separate guidelines. One was "avoiding contests between incumbents," the other was "preserving the core of existing districts," which functions largely as a euphemism for incumbent protection.[40] Georgia had elevated one of the venerable unwritten rules of redistricting—save the incumbents!—to the status of an explicit guideline.[41] Indeed, even the federal court in Georgia had included "protecting incumbents" among its list of "traditional districting principles."[42] The absence of this criterion in the Supreme Court's recitation of principles may reflect the fact that this criterion, while traditional, has hardly been "race-neutral" in application, given the over-representation of whites (or Anglos) in elected offices.

Another question concerning the use of the recognized criteria as a frame of reference concerns, as noted above, the standard for comparison. While protecting incumbents may not make the list of traditional criteria, it is not by itself an impermissible districting goal,[43] and has often been a reason for deviating from the other criteria. The federal court in Louisiana, for example, acknowledged that the compactness criterion, not required by any Louisiana law, had been trumped by incumbent protection considerations in previous congressional districting schemes of that state. The "Old Eighth" district, which the court described as "certainly bizarre" in shape, was admittedly "crafted for the purpose of ensuring the reelection of Congressman Gillis Long."[44] Will districts drawn to enhance the electoral opportunities of African-Americans in Louisiana therefore also be allowed to be bizarre or at least no more bizarre, or will such districts be held to a higher standard?[45]

Traditional districting principles often have been subordinated to nonracial political goals, of course, without any requirement that such subordination be justified. This is illustrated by another Supreme Court case, *Gaffney v. Cummings,* which involved districts for the lower house of the Connecticut state legislature.[46] The parallels between *Gaffney* and the *Shaw* and *Miller* cases are striking, except the issue in *Gaffney* is the deliberate manipulation of district boundaries for partisan rather than racial reasons.

In designing Connecticut's legislative districts, two of the traditional criteria cited in *Shaw* and *Miller*, compactness and respect for political subdivisions (the latter even a requirement of the Connecticut Constitution), were clearly subordinated to a purported goal of providing "proportional representation." The proportionality in this case concerned the representation of the state's Republican and Democratic voters. The Supreme Court found that "The record abounds with evidence, and it is frankly admitted by those who prepared the plan, that virtually every Senate and House district line was drawn with the conscious intent to create a districting plan that would achieve a rough approximation of the statewide political strengths of the Democratic and Republican Parties."[47]

While the Connecticut plan has been described as "a bipartisan gerrymander,"[48] it was not, in fact, the product of any bipartisan agreement. It was developed by the Republican party's representative to a three-person apportionment board, with the assistance of counsel to the state Republican party, and was vigorously opposed by the Democratic party's representative on the board. (The decisive vote was provided by the third member of the board, who had been selected by the two party appointees.) The plans were subsequently challenged by Democratic plaintiffs as "a gigantic gerrymander."[49] A large number of Republican party supporters were concentrated in one geographical area of the state, and therefore districts based on neutral districting principles would result in many Republican votes being wasted in safe Republican districts. The plaintiffs argued that the architects of the plan had deliberately gerrymandered the districts across the state in order to offset this unfavorable (for districting purposes) geographical pattern of Republican support.[50]

The federal district court in Connecticut found that districts in the plan had "highly irregular and bizarre outlines."[51] The state acknowledged the fact that districts had been made less compact than otherwise necessary in order to achieve the desired partisan balance among the districts. This was also "frankly admitted by those who prepared the plan."[52] Indeed, in defending the distorted shapes of the districts, the state rejected the notion that districts should be held to a compactness standard, of any type, stating:

> Compactness has no necessary relation to the devising of districts to provide fair and effective representation because the crucial variables are the residential patterns of the persons to be represented. Noncompactness could be the only way to provide even minimal representation of a scattered minority.[53]

Another neutral districting criterion, respect for political subdivisions, was also subordinated to the proportionality goal. In this case, the criterion was actually a state constitutional requirement. The Connecticut Constitution contained a prohibition against dividing towns when creating state assembly districts, and this criterion was also violated more than necessary so that districts would have particular partisan configurations.[54] This was also frankly acknowledged by the authors of the plan. Its chief architect testified, "We considered keeping the breaking of town lines within as reasonable limits as we could but where there were other considerations of fairness [proportional representation] that overrode that, I did not insist the town lines be maintained exact."[55] His assistant likewise testified:

> A. I cut town lines which were in my opinion necessary.
> Q. In order to achieve the political balance?
> A. In order to achieve the balance, yes.[56]

The subordination of these traditional criteria in this context produced no adverse comment by the Supreme Court. They certainly did not constitute "a crucial frame of reference" for the Courts' evaluation of these state legislative districts.

The districting criteria the Court has recognized as constituting the frame of reference have not been rigidly adhered to in the past. They have, in contrast, often been subordinated to political considerations. In light of Justice O'Connor's comment that majority-minority districts will not be held to a higher standard, presumably past practices rather than political science texts will be the point of comparison. Whether deviations from these criteria resulting from nondilutive racial considerations will be no less tolerable than past, or even present, deviations due to other acceptable political considerations, however, remains to be seen. While Justice O'Connor's words no doubt were meant to reassure minority voters that a double standard was not being adopted, no other justice in the majority joined her in that gesture.[57]

Conclusion

The *Shaw* and *Miller* decisions have made several districting criteria the frame of reference for adjudicating allegations of racial gerrymandering. These criteria, unfortunately, are neither well defined nor easily measured; moreover, they have not all been strictly applied prior to these decisions. Even contiguity, which was once the clearest of the criteria, is now clouded in ambiguity and no longer readily distinguishable from compactness.

The confusion surrounding these criteria themselves, as well as the standards for determining when they are respected and when they are subordinated, are a cause for concern. The districting task is difficult enough without adding this additional complexity to the process. The Supreme Court will review cases concerning congressional districts in North Carolina and Texas during its next term. Hopefully the Court will see the need to begin clarifying the components and application of the new frame of reference it has created. Without such clarification, redistricting in the post–*Miller* era will indeed be, as Justice Ruth Bader Ginsburg has predicted, "perilous work for state legislatures,"[58] not to mention county boards, city councils, school boards, and any other person or group who may be responsible for structuring representational districts.

Notes

1. The decision in *Miller v. Johnson* has not yet been published but the "slip opinion" may be identified by the following case numbers: 94–631, 94–797 and 94–929.

2. *Miller*, sl. op. at 1 (O'Connor, concurring).

3. *Miller*, sl. op. at 17–18.

4. *Shaw v. Reno*, 113 S.Ct. 2816 (1993).

5. *Shaw*, sl. op. at 15.

6. *Miller*, sl. op. at 15.

7. *Shaw*, sl. op. at 15.

8. *Miller*, sl. op. at 1 (O'Connor, J., concurring) (emphasis in original).

9. *Reynolds v. Sims*, 377 U.S. 533, 565–566 (1964).

10. David Butler and Bruce Cain, *Congressional Redistricting: Comparative and Theoretical Perspectives* (New York: MacMillan Publishing Co., 1992), p. 150.

11. See Bernard Grofman, "Criteria for Districting: A Social Science

Perspective," 33 *UCLA Law Review* (October 1985), pp. 177–183; Richard H. Pildes and Richard G. Niemi, "Expressive Harms 'Bizarre Districts,' and Voting Rights: Evaluating Election-District Appearances after *Shaw v. Reno*," 92 *Michigan Law Review* (December 1992), pp. 528–531; and W. E. Lyons and Malcolm E. Jewell, "Redrawing Council Districts in American Cities," 18 *State and Local Government Review,* (Spring 1986), p. 76.

12. Note, "Reapportionment," 79 *Harvard Law Review,* (April, 1966), p. 1284.

13. N.Y.C. Charter ch. 2, sec. 52 (2).

14. Bernard Grofman, "Criteria for Districting," p. 84.

15. *Hayes v. State of Louisiana,* 839 F. Supp. 1188, 1200 (E.D. La. 1993).

16. *Shaw v. Hunt,* 861 F. Supp. 408, 468 (E.D. N.C. 1994) and *Johnson v. Miller,* 864 F. Supp. 1354, 1368 (S.D. Ga. 1994).

17. *Shaw,* at 452. See also *Vera v. Richards,* 861 F. Supp. 1304, 1338, 1342 (S.D. Tex. 1994). It has also been suggested that "... 'contiguity' is not an abstract or geometric technical phase. It assumes meaning when seen in combination with concepts of 'regional integrity' and 'community of interest.'" *DeWitt v. Wilson,* 856 F. Supp. 1409, 1414 (E.D. Cal. 1994).

18. *Shaw v. Hunt,* at 452; see also *Johnson,* at 1388.

19. See Lyons and Jewell, "Redrawing Council Districts," at 76.

20. Charles Backstrom, Leonard Robbins, and Scott Eller, "Establishing a Statewide Electoral Effects Baseline," in Benard Grofman (ed.) *Political Gerrymandering and the Courts* (New York: Agathon Press, 1990), p. 152.

21. See David Butler and Bruce Cain, *Congressional Redistricting,* pp. 149–150.

22. *Shaw,* sl. op. at 15.

23. See especially *Johnson,* at 1388–1390, and *Vera,* at 1329–1330.

24. See generally Richard G. Niemi, Bernard Grofman, Carl Carlucci, and Thomas Hofeller, "Measuring Compactness and the Role of a Compactness Standard in a Test for Partisan and Racial Gerrymandering," 52 *Journal of Politics,* (November 1990), 1155–1181, and H.P. Young, "Measuring the Compactness of Legislative Districts," 13 *Legislative Studies Quarterly,* (February 1988), 105–115.

25. *DeWitt,* at 1414.

26. *Johnson,* at 1389; see also *Vera* at 1341.

27. *DeWitt v. Wilson,* (unsigned, one-paragraph order, issued by Supreme Court on June 29, 1995, upholding California's 1992 redistricting plan).

28. Richard Morrill, "A Geographer's Perspective," in Bernard Grofman, ed., *Political Gerrymandering and the Courts* (New York: Agathon Press, 1990), p. 215.

29. *Miller,* sl. op. at 18.

30. *Shaw v. Reno,* sl. op. at 14.

31. *Shaw v. Hunt,* at 471.

32. *Shaw v. Hunt,* at 470.

33. *Miller,* sl. op. at 15, 18.

34. See Malcolm E. Jewell, "Constitutional Provisions for State Legislative Apportionment," 8 *Western Political Quarterly* (June 1955), 271–279.

35. See Grofman, "Criteria for Districting," at 177–183.

36. *Hayes,* (1993), at 1201, and *Hayes v. State of Louisiana,* 862 F. Supp. 119, 121 (W.D. La. 1994).

37. *Vera,* at 1345; compare, however, the same court's comments at 1334–1335 n. 43.

38. Backstrom, Leonard, and Robbins, "Establishing a Statewide Electoral Effects Base," at 153.

39. *Miller,* sl. op. at 15.

40. *Miller,* sl. op. at 4.

41. See, for example, Royce Hanson, *The Political Thicket: Reapportionment and Constitutional Democracy* (Englewood Cliffs, N.J.: Prentice-Hall, Inc., 1966), p. 35.

42. *Johnson,* at 1369.

43. See *Burns v. Richardson,* 384 U.S. 73, 89 n. 16 (1966) and *White v. Weiser,* 412 U.S. 783, 791 (1973).

44. *Hayes* (1994), at 122.

45. One judge on the *Hayes* court stated that the old eighth district "has no application to this case," presumably because it "was never challenged on constitutionality by any court in the United States." *Hayes* (1994), at 127 (Shaw, J., concurring). The main opinion in that case also mentioned that the old eighth was "before *Shaw* and never challenged." *Id.,* at 122. The grounds for such a constitutional challenge remain unclear, however, given that the only features of the district referenced by the court were that it was (1) not compact and (2) protected an incumbent, neither of which violates the Constitution. See notes 7 and 44, *supra.*

46. *Gaffney v. Cummings,* 412 U.S. 735 (1973).

47. *Gaffney,* at 753.

48. *Davis v. Bandemer,* 478 U.S. 109, 154 (1986) (O'Connor, J., concurring).

49. Brief for a Appellees at 47, *Gaffney v. Cummings,* 412 U.S. 735 (1973).

50. See Richard L. Engstrom, "The Supreme Court and Equipopulous Gerrymandering: A Remaining Obstacle in the Quest for Fair and Effective Representation," 1976 *Arizona State Law Journal* (No. 2, 1976), 277, 301–304.

51. *Cummings v. Meskill,* 341 F. Supp. 139, 147 (D. Conn. 1972).

52. See depositions of Judge George A. Saden and James F. Collins, Appendix at 54–55, 100–101, 153–170, Record, *Gaffney v. Cummings,* 412 U.S. 735 (1973).

53. Brief for a Appellant at 51, *Gaffney v. Cummings,* 412 U.S. 735 (1973).

54. *Cummings v. Meskill,* at 148.

55. Saden deposition, *supra* note 50, at 53.

56. Collins deposition, *supra* note 50, at 99; see also deposition testimony at 92, 95, and 98.

57. Some courts have held that the "narrow tailoring" portion of the strict scrutiny test requires a majority-minority district to adhere as closely as possible to neutral districting criteria. See *Vera,* at 1343, and *Hayes* (1993), at 1208–1209. In *Shaw v. Hunt,* however, narrow tailoring is viewed as requiring only compliance with constitutionally mandated criteria. *Shaw v. Hunt,* at 449–454.

58. *Miller,* sl. op. at 17 (Ginsburg, J., dissenting).

Cumulative Voting and the Voting Rights Act

Edward Still and Pamela Karlan

Having found in April of 1994 that Worcester County, Maryland's practice of electing its commission at-large violated Section 2 of the Voting Rights Act, U.S. District Court Judge Joseph H. Young offered the commissioners the opportunity to propose a plan that "completely remedies the prior dilution of minority voting strength and fully provides equal opportunity for minority citizens to participate and elect candidates of their choice."[1] The Worcester County Commission responded only with a cosmetic change that required every commissioner to live in a defined residency area while continuing to seek election at-large.

In light of the commission's abdication of its responsibility, Judge Young was obligated to draft a plan. After considering proposals advanced by the plaintiffs, he adopted a plan that retains the at-large election system preferred by the county, but modifies the way in which individual voters cast their ballots to provide *all* voters, regardless of race or place of residence, with an absolutely equal opportunity to elect the candidates of their choice. Under the circumstances of this case, *Honnis W. Cane, Jr. v. Worcester County, Maryland*,[2] Judge Young's decision to order the use of cumulative voting within the county's existing at-large system represents a sensitive response to the needs of all the various litigants.

At-Large Voting without Exclusionary Tendencies

Cumulative voting preserves many of the distinctive and valuable features of at-large elections. For example, candidates can live anywhere in the

Reprinted with permission from National Civic Review, *Vol. 84, No. 4, Fall/Winter, 1995. Published by the National Civic League Press, Denver, Colorado.*

jurisdiction and vote for any candidate running for office, rather than being restricted to voting for a candidate from a designated district. Thus, candidates retain the incentive to compete for support throughout the county and, after election, continue to represent the entire county rather than a geographic subdivision.[3]

The sole significant difference between cumulative voting and traditional at-large voting is that in a cumulative voting system voters can "cumulate" their votes—that is, cast more than one vote for a candidate about whom they feel strongly. For example, a voter who strongly supports candidate Jones could cast all five of his votes for Jones. A voter remains free, of course, to cast one vote for each of five candidates, precisely as in a traditional at-large scheme.[4]

The suggestion that cumulative voting is confusing to voters is baseless. A study of recently adopted cumulative voting plans shows that nearly all the voters understood the proper way to cast a ballot, and only a small minority found the system more complex than other election systems.[5] Ninety-five percent of the voters knew they could cast all their votes for one candidate; a mere 13 percent found the cumulative voting plan "more difficult to understand" than systems utilized in other local elections in which they had voted.

The ability of voters to "plump" their votes behind a single candidate (or a few candidates) dampens the winner-take-all element of traditional at-large systems that enables a bloc-voting majority to capture all the available seats even when substantial numbers of voters prefer other candidates. As Judge Young explained in his opinion, all election systems have a "threshold of exclusion" equal in size to the smallest possible number of minority individuals needed to elect a candidate of their choice in a given jurisdiction.[6] In a traditional at-large system, the threshold of exclusion is 50 percent; unless a group constitutes a *majority* of the electorate, the remainder of the electorate—by voting strategically—can shut that group out completely. Similarly, within each district of a single-member district plan, the threshold of exclusion is again 50 percent—only the group that constitutes the majority of the electorate within the district can elect its preferred candidate.[7] By contrast, the threshold of exclusion in a cumulative voting system can be described by the equation $1/(s + 1)$, where s equals the number of seats to be filled in the election.[8] In the case of Worcester County, with a five-member commission, the threshold of exclusion using cumulative voting would be 16.67 percent.[9]

This substantially smaller figure means that any politically cohesive group, regardless of who its members are or where they live, can, by plumping their votes behind a single candidate, elect a representative of their choice. Thus, cumulative voting modifies the traditional at-large election plan to give minority groups a real opportunity to elect the candidates they favor.[10] Nonetheless, cumulative voting does not guarantee proportional representation in the sense of setting aside seats for particular groups. It simply gives a greater number of groups a chance to elect the candidates they prefer.

Thus, cumulative voting is not "proportional representation." Cumulative voting is sometimes called a "semi-proportional" system. A recent book advocating the adoption of proportional representation in the United States noted with regard to cumulative voting and another semi-proportional system called limited voting:

> Both systems are designed to make it more difficult for one party to elect all the representatives in an election, and both *may* produce more proportional results than single-member or at-large plurality elections. But full representation is not guaranteed.... That is why these are called *semi*-proportional and why most proponents of... [proportional representation] considered them crude systems....[11]

Contrary to suggestions contained in the Worcester County Commission's appeal brief, cumulative voting is not a novel system. Corporations, for example, often use cumulative voting to elect their boards of directors,[12] and an increasing number of jurisdictions have adopted cumulative voting to remediate Voting Rights Act violations.[13]

Cumulative Voting and Inclusion

Cumulative voting does an excellent job of fostering the notion of "civic inclusion." As Pamela Karlan has written:

> [The Supreme Court's long-standing] emphasis on equal political access for all voters ... rests on a belief that the distinctive values of inclusion in governmental decision making bring a sense of connectedness to the community and greater dignity; greater readiness to acquiesce in governmental decisions and hence broader consent and legitimacy; and more informed, equitable and intelligent governmental decision making.
> [Civic inclusion] accepts the bedrock diversity of modern America and seeks to bring diverse groups into the governing circle because, quite simply, the best way to ensure that all points of view are taken into account is to create decision-making bodies in which all points of view are represented by people who embody them. It is not enough that there are people who can only imagine what minority interests might require.[14]

Modifying an at-large system to provide for cumulative voting often can meet the goals of civic inclusion better than single-member districts. First, empirical studies of recent cumulative voting elections show that they fully cure Voting Rights Act violations by enabling members of traditionally excluded racial and ethnic minorities to elect candidates of their choice.[15] At the same time, cumulative voting avoids the necessity for deliberately drawing districts along racial lines, with the significant legal problems that practice can incur. Cumulative voting retains the at-large principle and allows *voters,* rather than governments, to form "voluntary districts" with other, like-minded voters.[16] Moreover, unlike districting schemes, which are imposed on voters by outside groups (e.g., legislatures, city councils, courts) and usually last for a decade or more, cumulative voting elections allow voters to make their affiliative decisions for themselves, on the occasion of every regular election.

Geographic districting plans are based on the implicit assumption that voters have an identity of interest with their geographical neighbors. While neighbors may have a common interest in whether the city repaves the street in front of their houses or rezones the lot on the corner for use as a fraternity house, on other issues voters may have more in common with residents of other neighborhoods than with people who live down the street. Districting relies on geographical proximity, while cumulative voting allows the voters themselves to decide whether and when geography is more important than other connections or common interests. Under a modified at-large cumulative voting plan, a like-minded group of voters enjoys a chance to elect its preferred representatives regardless of where its members live.

The rule of *Connor v. Johnson,* requiring courts to adopt single-member districts, is not applicable to the case of Worcester County, Maryland.[17] *Connor* involved a state legislative redistricting plan consisting of both single-member and multimember districts. The U.S. District Court, in rendering its decision, was forced to consider strong evidence that multimember districts were dilutive of minority voting strength.[18] By imposing single-member districts as the presumptive standard, the court was following a trend in American politics, thereby insulating itself from the charge that a single-member district—because it "allows the majority to defeat the minority on all fronts"—allows a court to pick the eventual majority of the legislative body.[19] Worcester County had employed a county-wide election system for a number of years and expressed a strong preference for continued use of an at-large plan. Thus, Judge Young, in imposing the cumulative voting plan, deferred to the local jurisdiction's policy choices. This decision followed the precedent of preserving existing practices and structures to the extent practicable, making only such changes as are necessary to eradicate any discriminatory features.[20]

Avoidance of Undesirable
Side Effects of District Remedies

In *Thornburg v. Gingles,*[21] the U.S. Supreme Court held that plaintiffs in racial vote dilution cases must *usually* show that "the minority group ... is sufficiently large and geographically compact to constitute a majority in a single-member district." The "geographically compact" requirement (which is not found in the Voting Rights Act) makes sense if the plaintiffs' sole claim is that the use of at-large elections rather than single-member district elections dilutes their voting strength. But as both the Supreme Court and Congress have recognized, a group's voting strength can be diluted by other practices as well. For example, majority-vote requirements and numbered-post provisions can dilute a group's voting power.[22] Thus, sometimes it is the voting rules *within* an at-large system, rather than the at-large nature of the constituency, that dilutes the minority's voting strength. Modifying the winner-take-all rules, by switching, for example, to cumulative voting, can offer a complete remedy. Such modifications can provide equal electoral opportunity while retaining the legitimate interests served by at-large elections (e.g., the preservation of jurisdiction-wide constituencies).

Any election plan that depends on districts is subject to gerrymandering and dilution (and sometimes inflation) of a minority group's voting power. Moreover, race-conscious districting sometimes can send an unfortunate message to voters about the salience of race in the political process.[23] Finally, when a court is called upon to make the decisions about how to draw districts (because, as in the Worcester County case, a defendant jurisdiction has defaulted on its obligation to provide a remedy), it often is plunged into a political thicket of competing, overlapping and sensitive interests.[24]

Far from accentuating racially polarized voting, cumulative voting ameliorates its effects. The use of cumulative voting in the British Empire supports this claim:

> The name "cumulative vote" appears for the first time in 1853, but three years earlier the system was recommended by a committee of the Privy Council for preventing the monopoly of colonial Legislative Councils by one party, and was applied in the Cape Colony. It continued to be used there for the election of the Legislative Council until that [body] disappeared under the new constitution of the Union of South Africa in 1909, and Lord Milner contrasted its effects most favorably with those of the majority system used to elect the House of Assembly (Lower House). In the Assembly, the division between Dutch and British stock was accentuated, for one part of the Colony returned only Boer representatives, the other part only non–Boers; in the Legislative Council, on the contrary, the minority in each region had representation.[25]

The principal purpose of Section 2 of the Voting Rights Act is to ameliorate the effects of discriminatory actions, without requiring discriminatory voters to change the way they vote:

> By contrast [to other anti-discrimination statutes], the Voting Rights Act seeks to alter the consequences of racial bloc voting patterns without governing the way individual voters cast their ballots; the primary conduct—the racial patterns in voting—is unaffected.[26]

Thus, while the employment discrimination laws tell employers not to make choices on the basis of race, religion, etc., the Voting Rights Act allows the voter to make discriminatory *decisions*, but tries to prevent all the discriminatory *consequences* those decisions might otherwise engender.

Another consideration that favors cumulative voting and similar remedies is the recent hostility of the U.S. Supreme Court to the conventional single-member district approach to minority electoral empowerment. With regard to racial gerrymandering, Justice Sandra Day O'Connor, in her majority opinion, wrote, "Put differently, we believe that reapportionment is one area in which appearances do matter."[27] With the Supreme Court taking the position that oddly shaped electoral districts may be considered presumptively unconstitutional, lower courts and legislative bodies are constrained in the boundaries they may draw. If the only remedy for an instance of racially polarized voting is single-member districts, and if the only district providing a reasonable chance for black voters to elect candidates of their choice is one with a "bizarre" appearance, blacks will be left without an effective remedy to cure a proven violation of Voting Rights Act. If the Supreme Court is not to gut the Voting Rights Act of all meaning and power, the answer is that there must be a way to introduce electoral opportunity without Balkanizing the population. Cumulative voting is such a system.

Cumulative voting permits jurisdictions to avoid race-conscious district drawing. Individual voters decide whether, and to what extent, to be race conscious. Furthermore, cumulative voting does not freeze existing race consciousness into place, because the system does not institutionalize the divisions in society by drawing a "black district," a "Latino district" or a "white district." The system also does not leave voters who are in the numerical minority in a given district feeling as if their votes do not count. In a district that is 65 percent or more black and in which there is racially polarized voting, the white minority is apt to feel as closed out of the political process as blacks felt when they were the minority in the multimember/at-large plan. Single-member districts shift the burden of the election plan from a minority group in a multimember district to the new minorities in each of the single-member districts or sub-districts. The members of the jurisdiction-wide majority who are minorities in their own districts may harbor a resentment for the "affirmative action" that has placed them in a powerless minority.[28] By contrast, cumulative voting allows *all* voters to vote for the candidates of their choice, and makes it quite probable that *most* voters will cast at least some of their votes for a candidate who actually wins, thereby increasing their sense of effective participation in electoral politics.

Finally, modifying at-large elections to permit cumulative voting allows bi-racial coalitions to form. Racially homogeneous single-member districts tend to preserve the racial divisions in society by making it unnecessary for candidates to appeal to any group other than their own and requiring all compromises (if any) to take place at the legislative/policy-making level, rather than among the voting public.[29] Professor Lani Guinier of the University of Pennsylvania School of Law offers a stinging criticism of single-member districts in a recent article:

> [T]he districting strategy excludes the possibility of representation for those whose interests are not defined by, or consistent with, those in the geographically defined district. Subdistricting simply assumes a linkage between interest and residence that is not necessarily as fixed as racial segregation patterns might otherwise suggest....
>
> [D]istricting decisions may simply reflect the arbitrary preferences of incumbent politicians who prefer packed, safe districts to ensure their reelection. Indeed, districting battles are often pitched between incumbents fighting to retain their seats, without regard to issues of voter representation. Because the choice of districts is so arbitrary, incumbents enjoy extraordinary leverage in self-perpetuation through gerrymandering.
>
> Thus, districting strategies often promote noncompetitive election contests, which further reduce voter participation and interest.[30]

By contrast, in a cumulative voting system, candidates of all races have the incentive to appeal to all voters.

Cumulative voting is not prohibited by the so-called anti-proportional representation disclaimer of Section 2 of the Voting Rights Act. That disclaimer provides:

> The extent to which members of a protected class have been elected to office in the State of political subdivision is one circumstance which may be considered: Provided, That nothing in this section establishes a right to have members of a protected class elected in numbers equal to their proportion in the population.[31]

Since cumulative voting allows the racial minority the same power to elect candidates of their choice as the racial majority, but does not guarantee the racial make-up of the governmental body, there is no violation of the proviso. It was added to the text of the 1982 Voting Rights Act amendments bill to counter any tendency to establish a quota system in elections; that is, requirements that the results of an election be invalidated if a certain percentage of protected minorities failed to win office. As the Senate Judiciary Committee noted:

> This disclaimer is entirely consistent with the above mentioned Supreme Court and Court of Appeals precedents, which contain similar statements regarding the absence of any right to proportional representation. It puts to rest any concerns that have been voiced about racial quotas.[32]

As noted above, cumulative voting does not guarantee who will win; black voters may form a coalition with another group and choose a non-black; or black voters may split into warring ideological camps. In either case, cumulative voting allows them more opportunity to elect a candidate of their choice than does a winner-take-all system such as the at-large and single-member district plans.

Conclusion

Cumulative voting is a promising alternative to both traditional at-large elections, with their tendency to exclude minority groups from the political process, and single-member district systems, with their fragmentation of the electorate and requirement that courts or politicians allocate voters among constituencies. Moreover, as in Worcester County, Maryland, cumulative voting offers courts a tool for striking an appropriate balance between the interests of the plaintiffs in remedying racial vote dilution, and those of the county in retaining the benefits of at-large elections and a city-wide constituency.

Notes

1. S. Rep. No. 97–417, p. 31 (1982).
2. *Honnis W. Cane, Jr. v. Worcester County, Maryland,* 35 F.3d at 921 (1994).
3. For general information on cumulative voting, see, Richard L. Engstrom, Delbert A. Taebel and Richard L. Cole, "Cumulative Voting as a Remedy for Minority Vote Dilution: The Case of Alamogordo, New Mexico," *Journal of Law and Politics,* Vol. 5 (1989), pp. 469–497.
4. Other combinations also are possible. A voter who was part of a coalition, for example, might cast three votes for candidate Smith and two for candidate Wilson.
5. Richard L. Cole, Delbert A. Taebel and Richard L. Engstrom, "Alternatives to Single-Member Districts," *Western Political Quarterly,* March 1990, pp. 191–199.
6. Pamela Karlan, "Maps and Misreadings: The Role of Geographic Compactness in Racial Vote Dilution Litigation," *Harvard Civil Rights-Civil Liberties Law Review,* Vol. 24 (1989), p. 222; Edward Still, "Alternatives to Single-Member Districts," in Chandler Davidson, ed., *Minority Vote Dilution* (Washington, D.C.: Howard University Press, 1984), pp. 253–258.
7. The threshold of exclusion assumes that all voters are voting strategically; that is, that every group of voters is trying to maximize its share of the seats. If the majority group does not vote strategically, a minority group may be able to win a seat even if its numerical strength lies below the threshold. For example, black candidates for the Chilton County, Alabama Commission were able to win in a cumulative voting system even though blacks had less than the threshold of exclusion because the white majority spread its votes among more than seven candidates.
8. Karlan, "Maps and Misreadings," p. 222.
9. There are five available seats. Hence, the formula for the threshold of exclusion in Worcester County is $1/(1 + 5)$, or $\frac{1}{6}$.

10. "Minority" is not a euphemism for "black." In a cumulative system, a minority group might consist of a politically cohesive black community, but it can also consist of any group that is less than a majority of the relevant voting population, such as Republicans, people who feel strongly about environmental issues, or advocates of a single-payer health care plan.

11. Douglas J. Amy, *Real Choices/New Voices: The Case for Proportional Representation Elections in the United States* (New York: Columbia University Press, 1993), p. 186.

12. See the American Bar Association's "Model Business Corporation Act," §33. See also, Lani Guinier, "The Triumph of Tokenism: The Voting Rights Act and the Theory of Black Electoral Success," *Michigan Law Review,* Vol. 89 (1991), pp. 1077, 1139 n. 298.

13. The Justice Department has also precleared under Section 5 the use of cumulative voting in 18 Texas jurisdictions during the last two years, including counties and school districts.

14. Karlan, "Maps and Misreadings," p. 180 and n. 27.

15. Richard L. Engstrom et al., "Cumulative Voting as a Remedy..."; Richard L. Engstrom and Charles Barrilleaux, "Native Americans and Cumulative Voting: the Sisseton-Wahpeton Sioux," *Social Science Quarterly,* June 1991, p. 338; and Still, "Cumulative and Limited Voting in Alabama," in Wilma Rule and Joseph F. Zimmerman, eds., *United States Electoral Systems: Their Impact on Minorities and Women* (Westport, Conn.: Greenwood Press, 1992), pp. 183–196.

16. Karlan, "Maps and Misreadings," p. 226 and n. 24.

17. "We agree that when district courts are forced to fashion apportionment plans, single-member districts are preferable to large multimember districts as a general matter." *Connor v. Johnson,* 402 U.S. at 690 (1971).

18. Frank Parker, in *Black Votes Count: Political Empowerment in Mississippi After 1965* (Chapel Hill: University of North Carolina Press, 1990) writes, "The lawyers for the [*Connor v. Johnson*] plaintiffs had made a strong case that multimember districts in Hind County [Mississippi] were racially discriminatory.... [T]he Supreme Court could order single-member districts without departing from its repeatedly expressed position that multimember districts are not *per se* unconstitutional or from the line of precedent rejecting the Fourteenth Amendment challenges to such districts." (p. 14)

19. *Kilgarlin v. Hill,* 386 U.S. 120 at 126 (1967), Douglas, J. concurring. See also, Robert G. Dixon, Jr. *Democratic Representation: Reapportionment in Law and Politics* (New York: Oxford University Press, 1968).

20. As the Supreme Court noted in another context, "[W]henever a covered jurisdiction submits a proposal reflecting the policy choices of the elected representatives of the people—no matter what constraints have limited the choices available to them—the preclearance requirement of the Voting Rights Act is applicable." *McDaniel v. Sanchez,* 452 U.S. 139 at 153 (1981).

21. *Thornburg v. Gingles,* 478 U.S. 30 at 48 (1986).

22. See, for example, *City of Rome v. United States,* 446 U.S. 156 at 183–184 (1980) and S. Rep. No. 97–417, p. 28 (1982).

23. See, for example, *Shaw v. Reno,* 113 S.Ct. 2816 at 2827 (1993).

24. See, *Connor v. Johnson,* 402 U.S. 690 (1971), which requires courts to avoid the inherently political considerations that decisions about multimember constituencies would raise.

25. Enid Lakeman and James D. Lambert, *Voting in Democracies: A Study of*

the Majority and Proportional Electoral Systems (London: Harcourt Brace, 1955), pp. 79–80.

26. T. Alexander Aleinikof and Samuel Issacharoff, "Race and Redistricting: Drawing Constitutional Lines after *Shaw v. Reno," Michigan Law Review,* Vol. 92 (1993), pp. 588, 634.

27. *Shaw v. Reno*, 113, S.Ct. 2816 at 2817 (1993).

28. See, "Affirmative Action and Electoral Reform," *Yale Law Journal,* Vol. 90 (1981), pp. 1811, 1828–1829.

29. See, *United Jewish Organizations v. Carey*, 430 U.S. 134 at 172–173 (1977). Justice Brennan, in his concurring opinion, wrote that racially safe districts may frustrate "potentially successful effort at coalition building across racial lines." See also, Guinier, *The Triumph of Tokensim,* pp. 1139 n. 30, 1148 n. 331, and accompanying text.

30. Lani Guinier, "No Two Seats: The Elusive Quest for Political Equality," *Virginia Law Review,* Vol. 77 (1991), pp. 1413, 1451–1452 and 1454–1455.

31. *Voting Rights Act Amendments of 1982,* 96 Stat. 134, 42 U.S.C. §1973 (1988).

32. S. Rep. No. 97–417, p. 31 (1982), citing *Whitcomb v. Chavis,* 403 U.S. 124 (1971); *White v. Regester,* 412 U.S. 755 (1973); *Zimmer v. McKeithen,* 485 F 2d 1297 (5th Cir. 1973) *en banc* affirmed on other grounds *sub nomine East Carroll Parish School District Board v. Marshall,* 424 U.S. 636 (1976).

At-Large Elections and Vote Dilution

Richard A. Walawender

A central premise of the American political system of representative democracy is that each person's vote be meaningful and efficacious. Indeed, in a truly "equal democracy," a "majority of the electors would always have a majority of the representatives; but a minority of the electors would always have a minority of the representatives."[1] If the vote of one individual is accorded but a fraction of another's vote, or if an entire segment of society is disenfranchised, as is arguably the case in many municipal at-large electoral schemes, the government cannot be deemed truly representative.

Although no single type of electoral system[2] can be deemed perfectly representative, the ideals of true representation and voting equality are recognized as so important to the American democratic system that the Supreme Court[3] has found it imperative for the judiciary to protect against vote dilution.[4] Vote dilution can be characterized as consisting of two types: interdistrict and intradistrict. Interdistrict vote dilution occurs when an individual voter's electoral strength is either greater or lesser than that of a voter in another district because the populations of the two districts are unequal in number.[5] The Supreme Court has controlled this type of vote dilution through application of the "one person, one vote" principle,[6] requiring the populations of all legislative districts to be numerically equal to one another.

Intradistrict vote dilution,[7] by contrast, occurs when an individual's vote is effectively diluted within his or her own district. This occurs when the votes of an identifiable racial, ethnic, political, or geographic group are assimilated into a large electorate, thereby diminishing that group's collective electoral strength. For example, when several legislative districts are consolidated into

Reprinted with permission from Journal of Law Reform, *Vol. 19, No. 4, Summer, 1986. Published by the University of Michigan School of Law, Ann Arbor, Michigan.*

one, and the several legislators representing the consolidated district are elected on an at-large basis,[8] the enlarged electoral base hampers the ability of a group of voters to elect from among itself its proportionate share of representation. Accordingly, a group of voters who previously constituted a majority in their smaller district becomes a minority in a larger district, no longer able to elect its representative.

The Supreme Court has not established a basic constitutional principle for remedying intradistrict vote dilution and has consistently refused to declare local at-large election schemes unconstitutional per se.[9] As a result, the federal courts have vacillated among various interpretations of the Fourteenth and Fifteenth Amendments as to what standard of proof is required to prove local at-large election schemes discriminatory. Concurrently with the Court's search for a way to assure all Americans a right to an equally effective vote, Congress enacted the Voting Rights Act in 1965.[10] In passing the Act, Congress, pursuant to the enforcement clause of the Fifteenth Amendment, set out to eliminate racial discrimination in voting. In 1982, Congress amended Section 2 of the Act, providing a standard to prove at-large election schemes discriminatory upon a showing that the system "results" in denying minority groups the opportunity to elect their representatives to office.[11]

The 1982 amendments to the Act, however, have remained a subject of controversy. Opponents of the Act misperceive municipal at-large electoral systems, believing they provide as much minority representation as single-member district systems. This chapter addresses that misperception with data showing that at-large schemes provide significantly less minority representation than other schemes. The various standards used by federal courts in reviewing the constitutionality of at-large election systems are outlined in Part I. Part II sets forth an analysis of Congress's response to the judicial ambivalence toward at-large elections—the 1982 amendments to Section 2 of the Voting Rights Act.[12] Part III presents empirical data illustrating that, generally, blacks are significantly more underrepresented on city councils in cities with at-large election systems than in cities with district systems. Part IV discusses the implications of the empirical findings in light of the congressional amendments to the Voting Rights Act. The chapter concludes that the congressional reimposition of the "results" standard for proving at-large election systems discriminatory was a necessary step forward because municipal at-large election systems remain systematically underrepresentative of significant population groups.

I. Judicial Response to Vote Dilution Claims of At-Large Elections

Before the 1982 amendments to the Voting Rights Act, the Supreme Court analyzed claims of vote dilution in at-large electoral systems in terms of the Fourteenth Amendment's equal protection clause. The first Supreme Court case addressing vote dilution in an at-large election system was *Fortson v. Dorsey*.[13] At issue was Georgia's state senate apportionment plan, which divided fifty-four seats among fifty-four districts, drawn predominantly along county lines. To avoid mathematical disparity among the districts, the plan provided that where more than one district existed in a single county all the county's districts would be conglomerated into a single district for voting purposes, and the senators for each of the districts would be elected at-large by a countywide vote. The plaintiffs claimed that the at-large, multimember scheme unconstitutionally diluted their right to vote because it could "[nullify] the unanimous choice of the voters of a district, thereby thrusting upon them a senator for whom no one in the district had voted."[14]

Justice Brennan, however, writing for the majority, failed to comprehend the plaintiff's intradistrict vote dilution claim. He insisted on analyzing the problem strictly in terms of the "one person, one vote" principle.[15] So long as the population of a multimember district was proportionately equal to the populations of other districts, the Court reasoned, the election scheme passed constitutional muster.[16] Thus, extending the Court's analysis to its logical conclusion, because mathematical disparity can only arise when there are at least two districts to compare, there can be no intradistrict vote dilution. The Court's reasoning failed to recognize and distinguish a central difference of at-large districting from single-member districting: while vote dilution in single-member districting schemes occurs *between* several districts, vote dilution in at-large schemes occurs *within* the single district.[17]

Only Justice Douglas, the lone dissenter, correctly analyzed the case in terms of intradistrict vote dilution. He concluded that "to allow some candidates to be chosen by the electors in their districts and others to be defeated by the voters of foreign districts" clearly constituted invidious discrimination.[18]

Subsequent Supreme Court decisions[19] established that an at-large election scheme could be subject to constitutional attack if its "invidious effect"[20] minimizes the voting strength of racial or political groups of voters.[21] Elaborating on the "invidious effect" standard in the only case where it invalidated a multimember election scheme,[22] the Court stated that racial and political groups are not constitutionally entitled to proportionate representation. Such groups are entitled only to an equal opportunity to participate effectively in the election process.[23]

Apparently unsatisfied with the Supreme Court's analysis of the intradistrict vote dilution problem, the Fifth Circuit developed a more concrete test in *Zimmer v. McKeithen*.[24] The *Zimmer* court enumerated a list of factors[25] to aid in assessing the constitutionality of a particular at-large scheme.[26]

1) the extent to which the election scheme is rooted in racial discrimination;

2) accessibility of the candidate slating process to minorities;

3) degree of legislative unresponsiveness to particularized needs of minorities;

4) tenuousness of the state policy underlying the preference of at-large districting;

5) existence of past discrimination hampering effective minority participation in election process;

6) use of unusually large districts, majority vote requirements, anti-single-shot voting provisions, or lack of provisions guaranteeing geographical representation within the district.

But the Supreme Court then rejected the "invidious effect" standard and the *Zimmer* factor analysis approach in *City of Mobile v. Bolden*.[27] Basing its opinion on recent decisions holding that the due process and equal protection clauses of the Fourteenth Amendment require a showing of discriminatory intent in order to prove a constitutional violation,[28] the plurality stated that proof of racially discriminatory *intent* was required to overturn, as violative of the Fourteenth Amendment, an at-large districting scheme. The Court also noted that because showing a violation of the Fifteenth Amendment required proof of a racially discriminatory motive as well,[29] to overturn at-large districting systems would require a showing that the system was established primarily for a discriminatory purpose.[30] Moreover, because the plurality deemed the Voting Rights Act to be coextensive with the Fifteenth Amendment,[31] it concluded that the Act supplied no additional authority from which to overturn an at-large election system absent proof of discriminatory intent.

Prior to the *Mobile* decision, and in anticipation of the Supreme Court's application of an intent test for Section 2 of the Voting Rights Act, several circuit court of appeals decisions[32] held that meeting the *Zimmer* criteria raised an inference of discriminatory purpose or intent. Although in *Mobile* the Supreme Court left unclear whether or not it rejected this approach,[33] in a subsequent case,[34] the Court held that the discriminatory intent necessary to prove unconstitutional group vote dilution could be inferred from the totality of factors and circumstances surrounding the particular at-large scheme. Moreover, because the Court also noted that appellate courts should defer to this factually based inference, the post–*Mobile* constitutional standard for analyzing at-large electoral systems became confusing, at best, or virtually impossible to overcome, at worst.

II. Section 2 of the Voting Rights Act

The legislative response to electoral systems that dilute minority voting power was the Voting Rights Act of 1965. Section 5 of the Act[35] gives the United States Attorney General authority to review certain proposed changes to voting practices in specifically "covered" jurisdictions and "preclear" the changes before they may be implemented.[36] The Attorney General will not preclear any voting or electoral practice that has the "effect of denying or abridging the right to vote on account of race or color."[37]

In contrast to Section 5's limited jurisdictional scope, Section 2 provides a private cause of action for citizens to challenge a discriminatory voting practice or procedure anywhere in the country.[38] Section 2 of the Voting Rights Act was intended to secure the right of every citizen to participate fully in the electoral process.[39] Prior to the 1982 amendments, the language of Section 2 did not clearly evince a particular standard for proving unconstitutional group vote dilution,[40] even though Congress provided for a right of action for private citizens or the government to challenge allegedly discriminatory voting practices or procedures.[41]

In direct response to the Supreme Court's imposition of an "intent" test for Section 2 in *Mobile v. Bolden*,[42] Congress amended the Act in 1982 to provide expressly for a more lenient "results" test.[43] Basically, the amendment codified the *White* and *Zimmer*[44] factor analysis approach as the standard of proof for claims of intradistrict vote dilution in at-large election schemes.[45] Not only does the amended statute's "results" standard call for a consideration of the totality of circumstances surrounding a particular election scheme, it also speaks in terms of a right for minorities to have an equal opportunity to elect representatives of their own choosing:

> (b) A violation of subsection (a) of this section is established if, based on the totality of circumstances, it is shown that the political processes leading to nomination or election ... are not equally open to participation by members of a class of citizens protected by subsection (a) of this section in that its members have less opportunity than other members of the electorate to participate in the political process and to elect representatives of their choice.[46]

The amendment thus makes it clear that underrepresentation of a minority group should be an important factor to consider in determining the validity of an at-large system.[47]

Several congressmen were concerned that the proposed amendment's express "results" standard and reference to equal opportunity to participate may be interpreted as requiring a system of proportional representation.[48] To ward off their concerns, the sponsors of the bill agreed to include a proviso to the amendment[49] disclaiming the idea that the amendment created any right to proportionate representation.[50]

In effect, Congress recognized the Court's unwillingness to use the equal protection clause as a sword with which to strike down at-large electoral systems that effectively prevent substantial minority groups from electing representatives. The 1982 amendments to Section 2 were designed to provide a method of preventing at-large schemes that do, in fact, result in vote dilution for minority groups, and to eliminate any speculation as to what standard of proof should be applied.

III. Empirical Analysis of Minority Representation in At-Large Elections

Congressional opponents of the 1982 amendments to Section 2 of the Voting Rights Act feared that the new language would mandate proportional representation,[51] and that Congress was usurping the Court's power to interpret the Constitution.[52] The opponents also believed that Congress should not intervene to protect minorities from the voting dilution caused by at-large electoral schemes.[53] After all, the opponents argued, because the use of the at-large electoral system, with origins in reform efforts to stop the abuses of political machines,[54] is so widespread,[55] any resulting minority vote dilution is insignificant and does not justify using the more lenient "results" standard.[56]

Congress debated, on an abstract, theoretical level, the seriousness of the diluting effects that at-large electoral schemes had on minority voting and representation.[57] But whether or not at-large election systems present structural barriers to minority representation is best demonstrated by empirical analysis. An empirical study on the effect that at-large election systems have on minority representation, as compared to single-member and mixed district systems,[58] will show whether the 1982 amendments to Section 2 were or were not, in fact, justifiable.

A. Data Collection and Methodology

Rather than relying on any one technique for measuring minority representation on city councils, this chapter utilizes several social science techniques to determine the structural representativeness of municipal election systems.[59] This chapter, incorporating more recent, 1980 Census figures into the statistical analysis, updates the findings of other studies.[60] Recent data on black council representation in cities were derived from the *National Roster of Black Elected Officials, 1982.*[61] Population and socioeconomic data were drawn from the *U.S. Census of Population, 1980.*[62] Information on individual city election type was derived from the 1982 edition of *The Municipal Yearbook*[63] and *The Encyclopedia of American Cities.*[64]

The sample tested comprised 268 municipalities with populations of 25,000 or more and a black population of at least ten percent.[65] The electoral systems used in all the cities were characterized as either at-large, district, or mixed.[66] An at-large system is one where each citizen votes from among all the council candidates running in the city for as many as there are council seats up for election that year.[67] A district system allows the voter to cast only one vote for a council candidate residing in the voter's district. A mixed system, as its name suggests, employs a combination of at-large and district voting.

B. Findings

Many cities throughout the country now employ at-large systems.[68] Nearly 60 percent of all U.S. cities with populations over 25,000 utilize an at-large system for electing council members, while 12.4 percent use a pure district system.[69] Western cities employ at-large schemes most often (81.3 percent), while midwestern cities utilize at-large systems least frequently (50.3 percent).[70] Cities with higher percentages of black populations use at-large election systems as frequently as cities with smaller black populations.[71]

1. Comparing proportionate measures of black representation for at-large, district, and mixed cities—Similar to some of the other empirical studies,[72] a standardized variable is used to measure the proportion of black representation on city councils to that of white representation. This variable, the Black Council Penetration (BCP), is the ratio of a city's percentage of black city council members to the percentage of the city's black population. A ratio of 1.00 for a particular city, for instance, would indicate that the black share of the city's council would be exactly equal to the black share of the city's population. Ratios exceeding 1.00 indicate overrepresentation of blacks on the council, while ratios below 1.00 indicate underrepresentation.[73] Thus, a BCP ratio of 0.50 indicates that the percentage of blacks on the city's council is half the percentage of blacks in the city's population.

The average BCP for all cities with populations over 25,000 and at least a 10 percent black population, regardless of election type, is 0.504.[74] On the average, then, blacks receive only about one-half the representation on city councils that their population percentages would have predicted as proportional.

As compared to the BCP found for district systems, the BCP for at-large systems is significantly lower.[75] Cities with at-large systems have an average BCP of only 0.399. In contrast, the BCP for district cities is 0.771. Eliminating cities in which the black population exceeds 50 percent of the population, the average BCP for at-large cities is only 0.385, compared with a much more proportional BCP of 0.764 for district cities.[76] The BCP averages for mixed cities, as expected, fall between at-large and district cities.[77]

The effect of election type on black representation in city councils is most dramatically illustrated in those cities where blacks constitute 31 to 40 percent of the population.[78] The BCP for cities in this population range is higher for district cities but lower for at-large cities than in any other category. In district cities of this type the BCP is 0.830, over two times as great as the corresponding 0.362 BCP for at-large cities.

Isolating cities by region reveals some interesting findings. Contrary to widely held beliefs,[79] the underrepresentation of blacks is not a problem confined only to the South, but exists in nearly equal proportion throughout all regions of the country.[80] At-large cities of the West prove most inequitable for black representation, holding an average BCP of only 0.237.[81] In comparison, the average BCP for southern at-large cities is 0.391, while for midwestern at-large cities it is 0.402, and for northeastern at-large cities it is 0.561. Southern district cities, however, are the most underrepresentative district cities in the country.

Most significantly, the analysis shows that district cities in every region have significantly higher BCP ratios than counterpart at-large cities.[82] The disparity between BCP ratios of at-large and district cities is most pronounced in the West.[83]

2. Illustrating the underrepresentation of blacks in at-large systems by regression analysis—Relying merely on BCP ratios, however, can be somewhat misleading. The BCP ratio average, while a useful tool to give a general perspective on minority representation, is somewhat artificially skewed lower because it automatically scores every city without a black person on its council at zero, regardless of whether that city's population is 25,000 or one million.[84] Accordingly, the overall BCP average for a group of cities can reflect a much lower value than would result from totaling the number of black council members and black populations for the entire group of cities prior to calculating the BCP ratio.

Regression-based analysis can correct this deficiency and provide a clearer indication of the effect of city electoral schemes on the ability of blacks to get elected to office.[85] Regression analysis takes into account the fact that cities without black council members have different black population percentages.[86] Moreover, a regression-based analysis makes it possible to examine the electoral system as a variable across a range of black population percentages.[87] Thus, in contrast with the BCP ratio methodology, cities of differing black populations are not accorded the same weight for determining the minority representativeness of a particular electoral system. Rather, the differences in black population percentages are taken into account in deriving the resultant index of representativeness.

In this regression analysis, each city's black population percentage is directly compared to its black council percentage. The data are then fit into a set of linear relationships, described by an equation.[88] The slope of the equation reveals how proportionately representative the particular election system is in general. Thus, true proportional representation, where the percentage of a city's black population is equal to its percentage of black council members, yields a slope of 1.00. The smaller the slope value, the less proportionally representative is the system.

The analysis of cities in the three electoral systems reveals once again that district cities provide the most proportional representation for blacks (slope = 0.900), at-large cities provide the least (slope = 0.589), and mixed cities are in between (slope = 0.844).[89] A graph of the equations more vividly illustrates the disparity of representativeness between district, at-large, and mixed electoral systems revealed by regression analysis.[90] The graph shows that district systems are much closer to the line of perfect proportional representation than either at-large or mixed systems, with at-large systems being the least representative.

IV. Implications

An analysis of the empirical data based on the 1980 Census corroborates the findings of several other political science analyses of at-large election systems[91]: namely, that at-large systems reflect more underrepresentation for minority groups than do mixed or district systems. Yet, even so, the congressional action in amending the Voting Rights Act would not be justified unless it can also be shown that at-large election schemes are the cause of the underrepresentation, i.e., at-large election systems are structurally and inherently less representative.

Undoubtedly, factors apart from the electoral structure of a city affect the ability and desire of minority groups to elect members of their group to office. For example, education level, income level, partisan activity, and occupational characteristics may play some role. Nevertheless, each of these socioeconomic factors can be controlled to permit a measurement of the impact of electoral schemes on the ability of minority groups to achieve representation on city legislatures. One recent study,[92] controlling for socioeconomic characteristics, found the relationship between electoral structure and black representation unaffected.[93] Given that, in and of themselves, at-large electoral systems impede electoral opportunities for minorities, the 1982 congressional amendment to Section 2, codifying the "results" test as the standard for showing a violation of the Voting Rights Act, was timely and justified for several reasons.

First, the "results" standard is an appropriate means of enforcing the Fourteenth and Fifteenth Amendments' guarantees of due process and equal protection. The burden of proving discriminatory intent, which the Supreme Court attempted to impose, is practically insurmountable unless evidence showing discriminatory effect can raise a presumption of discriminatory purpose.[94] Many at-large electoral systems were adopted during the municipal reform movement in the early part of the 20th century to prevent the establishment of or to destroy existing political machines. Undoubtedly, some of the appeal of the reformist proposal of at-large electoral schemes stemmed from prejudice and racism, but many cities had genuine problems of political corruption and viewed at-large elections as a possible solution.[95] Thus, proving exactly why a particular municipality adopted an at-large electoral scheme is not only difficult, such an inquiry is blind to the present diluting effects that the system imposes on minorities.

Secondly, the data suggest that there is no evidence of a substantial movement toward at-large systems. Once a city reaches a certain minority population,[96] dilution of minority voting strength is not an apparent, widespread purpose. This does not mean, however, that Congress should be prohibited from dealing effectively with the rampant problem of minority voting dilution currently existing in at-large electoral systems. Although Section 5 of the Voting Rights Act puts a check on intentional switching over to at-large systems having a discriminatory effect,[97] at-large electoral schemes are so widespread already that denying the federal government the power to provide for a reasonable means of challenging election schemes that blatantly dilute minority voting power would allow a significant amount of official discrimination to flourish in the nation's cities.

Finally, the findings of this study as to the underrepresentativeness of at-large electoral systems can be analogously applied to other "minority" groups, such as geographic or economic minority groups, although the Voting Rights Act does not protect them. For instance, an older section of a city with distinct concerns, such as infrastructure renovation, housing, or urban renewal, may be entirely ignored by a city council elected at-large because no councilperson resides in that part of the city and the citizens of that section cannot, as a group, garner enough votes to elect someone from their own community.[98] Cities contemplating implementing or changing their existing system of council election should consider the fact that at-large systems, generally, are not as representative of the different segments of the citizenry as district or mixed systems.

Conclusion

Black representation levels on city councils with at-large systems are strikingly low for cities of all sizes. The evidence illustrates that at the local level, at-large electoral systems do not result in representation of blacks to the same degree as whites. Analogously, it is probable that other groups holding some kind of minority status in an at-large city face the same sorts of structural problems in obtaining the representation of their choice. Thus, the most practical and reasonably effective way of ensuring minority groups an equal opportunity to elect local legislators of their choice, short of declaring at-large systems unconstitutional per se or mandating proportional representation, is to prohibit any system that "results" in vote dilution, as provided in Section 2 of the Voting Rights Act.[99]

Ample evidence exists showing that at-large electoral systems dilute minority votes throughout the entire nation, not just in southern cities. Actually, voting dilution is even more acute in other parts of the country. Thus, Section 2 appropriately applies to the whole nation and should not be limited to areas where a history of discrimination exists.

In amending Section 2 to provide for a "results" test, Congress helped provide minorities with a more equal opportunity to elect representation to local government by subjecting to judicial scrutiny at-large electoral schemes that, in fact, result in vote dilution. In a political culture that generally disfavors proportional representation electoral schemes, the "results" standard of Section 2 is perhaps the best alternative.

Appendix

Table 1*
Distribution by Population of U.S. Cities with Over 25,000 People Electing Councils Under At-Large, District, and Mixed Electoral Schemes

Population	Total Number of Cities Reporting	Percent of Total Number of Cities†		
		At-Large	District	Mixed
Over 25,000	(824)	59.8 (493)	12.4 (102)	27.8 (229)
25,000–49,999	(463)	63.5 (294)	13.2 (61)	23.3 (108)
50,000–99,999	(226)	59.3 (134)	8.8 (20)	31.9 (72)
100,000–249,999	(95)	50.5 (48)	15.8 (15)	33.7 (32)
Over 250,000	(40)	42.5 (17)	15.0 (6)	42.5 (17)

*Source: International City Mgmt. Ass'n, Municipal Year Book, 1982.
†Numbers in parentheses are the number of cities constituting category.

Table 2*
Distribution by Region of Country of
U.S. Cities Electing Councils Under At-Large,
District, and Mixed Electoral Schemes

Geographic Location†	Total Number of Cities Reporting§	Percent of Total Number of Cities†		
		At-Large	District	Mixed
Northeast	(810)	68.5 (555)	16.2 (131)	15.3 (124)
Midwest	(1324)	50.3 (666)	21.5 (284)	28.2 (374)
South	(1249)	74.2 (927)	9.4 (117)	16.4 (205)
West	(706)	81.3 (574)	8.9 (63)	9.9 (70)

*Source: International City Mgmt. Ass'n, Municipal Year Book, 1982. Includes all cities with over a 25,000 population.
†In accordance with U.S. Census delineation of regions.
§Numbers in parentheses are the number of cities comprising category.

Table 3
Mean BCP* of Cities† by
Type of Electoral System

	Total	At-Large	District	Mixed
Number:	268	144	43	81
Mean BCP:	.504	.399	.771	.549

$*BCP = \dfrac{\text{Black Percentage of City Council}}{\text{Black Percentage of City Population}}$
†Cities with population of at least 25,000 and at least 10 percent black population.

Table 4
Mean BCP* of Cities† by
Percent of Black Population

Percent of Black Population	Total	At-Large	District	Mixed
1–100	.504 (268)	.399 (144)	.771 (43)	.549 (81)
10–20	.490 (110)	.368 (60)	.778 (16)	.531 (34)
21–30	.485 (62)	.405 (34)	.733 (9)	.511 (19)
31–40	.462 (46)	.362 (29)	.830 (8)	.457 (9)
41–50	.579 (25)	.492 (9)	.685 (6)	.595 (10)

Table 4 (cont.)

Percent of Black Population	Total	At-Large	District	Mixed
0–50	.487 (243)	.385 (132)	.764 (39)	.525 (72)
51–100	.670 (25)	.561 (12)	.845 (4)	.737 (9)

Notes: Numbers in parentheses refer to number of cities in category.

*BCP = $\dfrac{\text{Black Percentage of City Council}}{\text{Black Percentage of City Population}}$

†Cities with population of at least 25,000.

Table 5
Mean BCP* of Cities† by
Region of Country

	Total	South	West	Midwest	Northeast
Number:	268	133	25	65	45
Mean BCP:	.504	.472	.470	.540	.569

*BCP = $\dfrac{\text{Black Percentage of City Council}}{\text{Black Percentage of City Population}}$

†Cities with population of at least 25,000 and at least 10 percent black population.

Table 6
Mean BCP* of Cities† by
Region of Country and Type of Electoral System

	Total	South	West	Midwest	Northeast
Total:	.504 (268)	.472 (133)	.470 (25)	.540 (65)	.569 (45)
At-large:	.399 (144)	.391 (82)	.237 (14)	.402 (30)	.561 (18)
District:	.771 (43)	.689 (19)	.927 (7)	.807 (10)	.787 (7)
Mixed:	.549 (81)	.549 (32)	.485 (4)	.599 (25)	.499 (20)

Note: Numbers in parentheses refer to number of cities in category.

*BCP = $\dfrac{\text{Black Percentage of City Council}}{\text{Black Percentage of City Population}}$

†Cities with population of at least 25,000 and at least 10 percent black population.

Graph 1
Relationship Between Percentage of Black Population and Percentage of Blacks on City Councils in At-large, District, and Mixed Election Cities

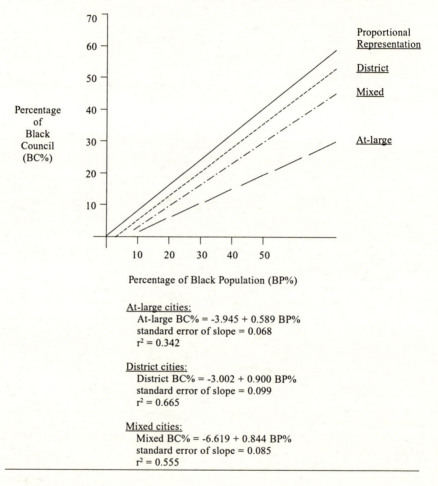

At-large cities:
  At-large BC% = -3.945 + 0.589 BP%
  standard error of slope = 0.068
  r^2 = 0.342

District cities:
  District BC% = -3.002 + 0.900 BP%
  standard error of slope = 0.099
  r^2 = 0.665

Mixed cities:
  Mixed BC% = -6.619 + 0.844 BP%
  standard error of slope = 0.085
  r^2 = 0.555

Notes

1. J.S. Mill, "Representative Government," in *On Liberty and Considerations on Representative Government* 105, 190 (R. McCallum ed. 1946) (1861).

2. Nearly all local governments in the United States utilize either at-large, district, or mixed electoral systems to elect legislators. *See infra* note 8 and text accompanying notes 66–68. Electoral systems based on proportional representation, while common in Europe, are nearly nonexistent among American localities.

3. In *Baker v. Carr,* 369 U.S. 186 (1962), the Court held a challenge to a reapportionment scheme based on the equal protection clause of the Fourteenth Amendment to be justicable. Prior to *Baker*, the Court had considered reapportionment to be a political question. *See Colegrove v. Green,* 328 U.S. 549, 556 (1946) (Frankfurter, J., concurring).

4. Vote dilution is the result of a set of "techniques for reducing or nullifying the effects of the votes that minorities do cast." S. Wasby, *Vote Dilution, Minority Voting Rights, and the Courts* 1 (1982). The minorities whose votes can be diluted include ethnic and racial groups, as well as geographically or economically distinct segments of a larger constituency. *See also* Washington, "Does the Constitution Guarantee Fair and Effective Representation to All Interest Groups Making Up the Electorate," 17 *How. L.J.* 91 (1971). Washington argues: "Fair and effective representation as a political supposition, therefore, is the ability of individual votes to be a component of an interest group which has sufficient muscle to ... win the election." *Id.* at 116 (citation omitted).

5. Consider, for example, a situation where voter *A* lives in a more populous legislative district than voter *B*. *A* has less voting strength than *B* because *A*'s vote is a smaller fraction of the total, thereby affording *A* less opportunity to cast a tie-breaking vote. *See generally* R. Dixon, *Democratic Representation: Reapportionment in Law and Politics* (1968).

6. *Reynolds v. Sims,* 377 U.S. 533, 567–68 (1964) (holding that the equal protection clause of the Fourteenth Amendment requires state legislative seats to be apportioned with districts of relatively equal populations); *Lucas v. Forty-Fourth Gen. Assembly,* 377 U.S. 713, 736 (1964) ("An individual's constitutionally protected right to cast an equally weighted vote cannot be denied....").

7. Some commentators have labeled intradistrict vote dilution as "group" vote dilution, due to the fact that the resultant dilution effectively shuts out identifiable groups from representation. *See generally* R. Dixon, *supra* note 5.

8. Several variants of the multimember or at-large scheme exist. One is where all the candidates for several legislative seats compete against each other. Another is where all the voters cast their votes for a candidate in each of several subdistricts comprising the at-large district.

9. *See* cases cited *infra* notes 13, 19 and 27.

10. Pub. L. No. 89–110, 79 Stat. 437 (codified as amended at 42 U.S.C. §§ 1971, 1973 to 1973bb–1 [1982 & Supp. II 1984]).

11. Voting Rights Act Amendments of 1982, Pub. L. No. 97–205, § 3, 96 Stat. 131, 134 (codified at 42 U.S.C. § 1973(a) [1982]).

The 1982 amendment of § 2 prohibits the application of any voting practice that "results in a denial or abridgment of the right of any citizen of the United States to vote on account of race or color." *Id.* Prior to the 1982 amendments, the Act did not expressly set forth a standard for showing when a voting practice denied the right to vote in contravention of the Act. *See infra* Part II.

12. 42 U.S.C. § 1973 (1982).

13. 379 U.S. 433 (1965).

14. *Id.* at 437.

15. *Id.* at 436. Justice Brennan quoted from dicta in *Reynolds v. Sims,* 377 U.S. 533 (1964), where the Court stated that "[o]ne body could be composed of single-member districts while the other could have *at least some* multimember districts." *Id.* at 577 (emphasis added by Brennan, J.).

16. *Fortson,* 379 U.S. at 437. The Court did leave open the possibility of finding

an at-large system in violation of the equal protection clause if it "designedly or otherwise" operated to "cancel out the voting strength of racial or political elements of the voting population." *Id.* at 439.

17. Justice Harlan, in concurrence, noted that the majority's opinion suggested the constitutionality of a state legislative reapportionment plan "must, in the last analysis, always be judged in terms of simple arithmetic." *Id.* at 439–40.

18. *Id.* at 441–42 (Douglas, J., dissenting). Although Justice Douglas did not use the term "intradistrict" vote dilution, he clearly had the concept in mind when analyzing the multimember scheme at issue: "[E]ven if a candidate for one of those districts obtained all of the votes in that district, he could still be defeated by the foreign vote, while he would of course be elected if he were running in a district in the first group." *Id.* at 441.

19. *Whitcomb v. Chavis,* 403 U.S. 124 (1971) (reversing a district court's redistricting of Indiana's legislature into all single-member districts); *Burns v. Richardson,* 384 U.S. 73 (1966) (reversing a district court's overturning of Hawaii's multimember legislative districting).

20. *See Burns,* 384 U.S. at 88. The *Burns* Court listed examples of the invidious effect of discrimination caused by at-large election systems: "if ... districts are large in relation to the total number of legislators, if districts are not appropriately sub-districted to assure distribution of legislators that are resident over the entire district, or if districts characterized both houses of a bicameral legislature rather than one." *Id.*

21. Theoretical and mathematical arguments alone are not sufficient to prove of violation of the Fourteenth Amendment; rather, "[t]he real-life impact of multimember districts on individual voting power" must be demonstrated. *Whitcomb v. Chavis,* 403 U.S. 124, 146 (1971).

22. *White v. Regester,* 412 U.S. 755 (1973) (upholding district court's findings and conclusions that the black and Mexican-American communities were "effectively excluded from participation in the Democratic primary election process" because of a Texas House of Representatives reapportionment plan establishing multimember districts).

23. Mere evidence that a particular group lacks proportional representation, the Court stated, is not enough to render the system unconstitutional. *Id.* at 765–66 (quoting *Whitcomb,* 403 U.S. at 149–50):

> [I]t is not enough that a racial group allegedly discriminated against has not had legislative seats in proportion to its voting potential. The plaintiffs' burden is to produce evidence to support findings that the political processes leading to nomination and election were not equally open to participation by the group in question—that its members had less opportunity than did other residents in the districts to participate in the political processes and to elect legislators of their choice.

24. 485 F.2d. 1297 (5th Cir. 1973), *aff'd sub nom. East Carroll Parish School Board v. Marshall,* 424 U.S. 636 (1976).

25. These factors have been subsequently referred to by other courts as the *Zimmer* factors.

26. The court in *Zimmer* noted that the presence of all the factors is not necessary to establish an unconstitutional vote dilution. Rather, courts should evaluate the factors on an aggregate basis. 485 F.2d. at 1305.

27. 446 U.S. 55 (1980). For a more detailed discussion of the case law leading to *Bolden*, see Parker, "The 'Results' Test of Section 2 of the Voting Rights Act: Abandoning the Intent Standard," 69 *Va. L. Rev.* 715 (1983).

28. *Arlington Heights v. Metropolitan Hous. Dev. Corp.*, 429 U.S. 252 (1977) (requiring proof of discriminatory intent to demonstrate that a zoning law violated equal protection of minorities); *Washington v. Davis*, 426 U.S. 229 (1976) (requiring proof of intent or purpose to sustain a due process claim that black plaintiffs were racially discriminated against by a police department's written personnel test used in employee recruitment).

29. In support of its assertion that the Fifteenth Amendment requires a showing of discriminatory intent, the Court cited *Guinn v. United States*, 238 U.S. 347 (1915) (finding Oklahoma "grandfather" clause exempting from voting literacy requirement anyone entitled to vote before 1866 unconstitutional because its purpose was to circumvent the Fifteenth Amendment); *Gomillion v. Lightfoot*, 364 U.S. 339 (1960) (holding that the drawing of municipal boundaries might be found unconstitutional because drafters were solely concerned with segregating black and white voters); *Wright v. Rockefeller*, 376 U.S. 52 (1964) (upholding state reapportionment scheme because there was no proof that the legislature drew districts on racial lines or that the legislature was motivated by racial consideration); *Smith v. Allwright*, 321 U.S. 649 (1944) (implicating Texas in conduct of a racially exclusionary Texas Democratic Party primary election scheme); and *Terry v. Adams* 345 U.S. 461 (1953) (holding that a state involved in purposeful exclusion of blacks from participating in the election process violated the Fifteenth Amendment even though the election was conducted by a private political organization neither authorized nor regulated by the state).

30. *Mobile*, 446 U.S. at 65: The Fifteenth Amendment "prohibits only purposefully discriminatory denial or abridgment by government of the freedom to vote 'on account of race, color, or previous condition of servitude.'"

31. *Id.* at 60.

32. *McIntosh County Branch of the NAACP v. City of Darien*, 605 F.2d 753 (5th Cir. 1979); *Cross v. Baxter*, 604 F.2d 875 (5th Cir. 1979); *Nevett v. Sides*, 571 F.2d 209 (5th Cir. 1978), cert. denied, 446 U.S. 951 (1980).

33. The plurality in *Mobile* stated that the presence of *Zimmer* factors may afford some evidence of a discriminatory purpose. *Mobile*, 446 U.S. at 73. Justice Stevens, concurring, rejected the plurality's "subjective intent" standard and stated that the proper test for determining whether an electoral scheme was unconstitutional "should focus on the objective effects of the political decision [that instituted the scheme]." *Id.* at 90.

For detailed discussions of the *Mobile* decision, see Parker, "The Impact of *City of Mobile v. Bolden* and Strategies and Legal Arguments for Voting Rights Cases in its Wake," in *The Right to Vote 98* (Rockefeller Found. Conf. Rep. 1981); Comment, "The Standard of Proof in At-Large Vote Dilution Discrimination Cases After *City of Mobile v. Bolden*," 10 *Fordham Urb. L.J.* 103 (1981); "The Supreme Court, 1979 Term," 94 *Harv. L. Rev.* 75, 149 (1980).

34. *Rogers v. Lodge*, 458 U.S. 613, 618–22 (1982) (holding a district court's inference of intentional discrimination from totality of factors not clearly erroneous requiring reversal; hence, multimember district was properly invalidated as violative of the equal protection clause of the fourteenth amendment). Justices Powell and Rehnquist dissented on the ground that discriminatory intent must be proven primarily by objective evidence.

Cf. Note, "The Constitutional Significance of the Discriminatory Effects of

At-Large Elections," 91 *Yale L.J.* 974 (1982) (perceptively observing that *Rogers* failed to state what discriminatory effects of an at-large election system are necessary to raise the presumption of discriminatory purpose, and proposing that either racially polarized voting patterns or lack of proportional representation should be sufficient to raise the presumption).

35. 42 U.S.C. § 1973c (1982).

36. *Id.*

37. *Id.* Section 5's "effects" standard prevents voting procedure changes that "would lead to a retrogression in the position of racial minorities with respect to their effective exercise of the electoral franchise." *Beer v. United States,* 425 U.S. 130, 141 (1976). For further discussion of the "effects" standard, see *infra* note 43.

38. 42 U.S.C. § 1973 (1982).

39. *Senate Comm. on the Judiciary, Report on S. 1992, S. Rep. No. 417,* 97th Cong., 2d Sess. 4 [hereinafter cited as *S. Rep.*], reprinted in 1982 *U.S. Code Cong. & Ad. News* 177, 181.

40. Prior to the 1982 amendments, § 2 read: "No voting qualification or prerequisite to voting, or standard, practice or procedure shall be imposed or applied by any State or political subdivision to deny or abridge the right of any citizen of the United States to vote on account of race or color...." *Voting Acts Amendments of 1975,* Pub. L. No. 94–73, tit. II, § 206, 89 Stat. 400, 402 (current version at 42 U.S.C. § 1973 (1982)).

41. *See id.*

42. 446 U.S. 55 (1980). For a discussion of the *Mobile* case, see *supra* text accompanying notes 27–31.

43. *S. Rep., supra* note 39, at 15. In opposing enactment of the 1982 amendments to § 2 of the Voting Rights Act, the Subcommittee on the Constitution of the Senate Committee on the Judiciary expressed several legal concerns about the amendment's constitutionality including: (1) improper federal infringement on state authority; (2) over-breadth of scope, because it applies to areas of the country were there is no history of official discrimination; (3) "results" standard inappropriate means of enforcing the Fourteenth and Fifteenth Amendments; and (4) violation of separation of powers between the judiciary and the legislature. *See id.* at 169–73.

For a comprehensive analysis of the legal arguments in favor of the constitutionality of the § 2 amendments, see McKenzie & Krauss, "Section 2 of the Voting Rights Act: An Analysis of the 1982 Amendment," 19 *Harv. C.R.–C.L. L. Rev.* 155 (1984). See also *United States v. Marengo County Comm'n,* 731 F.2d 1546 (11th Cir.) (upholding the constitutionality of amended § 2) *cert. denied,* 105 S.Ct. 375 (1984).

The "results" standard of § 2 is generally regarded as separate and distinct from § 5's "effects" standard. The difference between the two standards is succinctly stated by McKenzie & Krauss, *supra,* at 169: "Proof of liability under section 2 ... requires a review of the totality of the circumstances surrounding the challenged practice or procedure. Unlike section 5, section 2 does not necessarily entail a comparison of the numerical voting strength of minorities before and after a voting scheme is adopted." For further discussion of the differences between the two standards, see Jones, "Redistricting and the Voting Rights Act: A Limited but Important Impact," 73 *Nat'l. Civic Rev.* 176 (1984).

44. *See supra* notes 22 (discussing *White v. Regester,* 412 U.S. 755 (1973)) & 24–26 and accompanying text (discussing *Zimmer v. McKeithen,* 485 F.2d 1297 (5th Cir. 1973)).

45. The amended § 2 (a) now reads: "No voting qualification or prerequisite

to voting or standard, practice, or procedure shall be imposed or applied by any State or political subdivision in a manner which results in a denial or abridgment of the right of any citizen of the United States to vote on account of race or color....." 42 U.S.C. § 1973 (a) (1982).

The Senate Judiciary Committee stated its intention in amending the Act: "The 'results' standard is meant to restore the pre–*Mobile* legal standard which governed cases challenging election systems or practices as an illegal dilution of the minority vote. Specifically, subsection (b) embodies the test laid down by the Supreme Court in *White.*" *S.Rep., supra* note 39, at 27 (footnote omitted).

46. 42 U.S.C. § 1973 (b) (1982).

47. *Id.*

48. *See S. Rep., supra* note 39, at 142–43.

49. The proviso, known as the "Dole Compromise," expressly disclaims any right to proportional representation: "*Provided*, That nothing is this section establishes the right to have members of a protected class elected in numbers equal to their proportion in the population." 42 U.S.C. § 1973 (b) (1982).

50. Despite the proviso's disclaimer, Senator Hatch still expressed concern that a § 2 violation could be established under the results test merely with evidence of "the absence of proportional representation *plus* the existence of 'one or more objective factors of discrimination', such as an at-large system of government." *S.Rep., supra* note 39, at 97.

51. *See supra* notes 48–50 and accompanying text.

52. *See supra* note 43.

53. *See Subcomm. on the Constitution of the Senate Comm. on the Judiciary, Report on the Voting Rights Act* [hereinafter cited as *Voting Rights Act Report*], *reprinted in S. Rep. supra* note 39, at 139.

54. *See infra* note 95 and accompanying text.

55. *See* table 1 in the appendix.

56. *See Voting Rights Act Report, supra* note 53.

57. *See S. Rep., supra* note 39.

58. For definitions of at-large, single-member district, and mixed electoral systems, see *infra* notes 66–67 and accompanying text.

59. *See* Cole, "Electing Blacks to Municipal Office: Structural and Social Determinants," 10 *Urb. Aff. Q.* 17 (1974); Karnig, "Black Representation on City Councils: The Impact of District Elections and Socioeconomic Factors," 12 *Urb. Aff. Q.* 223 (1976); MacManus, "City Council Election Procedures and Minority Representation: Are They Related?," 59 *Soc. Sci. Q.* 153 (1978); Robinson & Dye, "Reformism and Black Representation on City Councils," 59 *Soc. Sci. Q.* 133 (1978); *see also* Jones, "The Impact of Local Election Systems on Black Political Representation," 11 *Urb. Aff. Q.* 345 (1976); Taebel, "Minority Representation on City Councils: The Impact of Structure on Blacks and Hispanics," 59 *Soc. Sci. Q* 142 (1978). *Cf.* Banzhaf, "Multimember Electoral Districts—Do They Violate the 'One Man, One Vote' Principle," 75 *Yale L.J.* 1309 (1966).

60. The studies cited *supra* note 59 used data from the 1960 or 1970 Census.

61. *Joint Center for Political Studies National Roster of Black Elected Officials,* 1982.

62. *Bureau of the Census, U.S. Dep't of Commerce, U.S. Census of Population,* 1980.

63. *International City Mgmt. Ass'n., The Municipal Yearbook,* 1982.

64. *The Encyclopedia of American Cities* (O. Nergal ed. 1980).

65. This sample of 268 cities includes all those cities for which adequate data were available from the above sources. Some cities that met the sample criteria were nevertheless excluded from the sample because data for those cities were not available.

66. This categorization follows that employed in the studies cited *supra* note 59.

67. For further discussion of the most widely utilized at-large election schemes, *see supra* note 8.

68. *See* Table 1 in the appendix.

69. *Id.*

70. *See* Table 2 in the appendix.

71. Cities whose black populations comprise between 10 percent and 25 percent of the total population were as likely to have at-large electoral systems as cities whose black populations constituted a greater percentage of the population. *See* Table 4 in the appendix.

72. *See* studies cited *supra* note 59.

73. Essentially, a BCP ratio of 1.00 would mean perfect proportional representation for blacks.

74. *See* Table 3 in the appendix.

75. *Id.*

76. *See* Table 4 in the appendix.

77. *Id.*

78. *Id.*

79. Including the contentions of the opponents of the 1982 amendments to § 2 in Congress. *See S. Rep. supra* note 39.

80. *See* Table 5 in the appendix.

81. *See* Table 6 in the appendix.

82. *Id.*

83. In the West, at-large cities average a BCP of only 0.237 while district cities average a BCP of 0.927. *Id.*

84. *See* Engstrom & McDonald, "The Election of Blacks to City Councils: Clarifying the Impact of Electoral Arrangements on the Seats/Population Relationship," 75 *Am. Pol. Sci. Rev.* 344, 346 (1981).

85. *Id.*

86. *Id.*

87. "A regression-based analysis also permits one to examine the impact of electoral arrangements in the conceptually most appropriate way, as a *specifying variable* which establishes conditions under which the seats/population relationship varies, rather than as an independent variable with a direct impact." *Id.* (emphasis in original).

88. Using a model similar to the one espoused by Engstrom & McDonald, *supra* note 84, at 347, equation is in the following form:

$$BCC\% = [\text{y-intercept}] + x BP\%$$

were BCC% is the percentage of blacks on the council and BP% is the percentage of blacks in the population. The x is the slope of the equation y-intercept describes the linear equation's intersection point with the vertical axis.

89. *See* graph 1 and accompanying explanations in the appendix.

90. *Id.*

91. *See supra* note 59.

92. Engstrom & McDonald, *supra* note 84.

93. The Engstrom and McDonald study, *id.,* controlled for population size, rate of population change from 1960 to 1970, median family income, median school years completed by those over 25 years old, and the percentage of the white-collar labor force. These factors were added to the regression equation and tested for both uniform impact across all electoral systems and conditional impact in each system. The slopes for the representativeness of blacks for each of the three electoral systems remained virtually unaffected, and the regression coefficients for the socioeconomic factors suggested very slight impact.

The Engstrom and McDonald study refuted the findings of Cole, *supra* note 59, and MacManus, *supra* note 59, which concluded that electoral structures have only minimal impact when size, growth rate, income, education, and occupation characteristics are considered. Perhaps the reason for the divergent findings, Engstrom and McDonald point out, is that the other studies used a subtractive measure of proportionality, which understates the level of underrepresentation in cities with smaller black populations. Engstrom & McDonald, *supra* note 84, at 350–51.

94. *But see Rogers v. Lodge,* 458 U.S. 613, 618 (1982).

95. *See generally* H. Alderfer, *American Local Government and Administration* 298–309 (1956); D. Lockard, *The Politics of State and Local Government* 337–40 (1st ed. 1963).

96. *See* Table 3 in the appendix.

97. 42 U.S.C. § 1973c (1982). Section 5 requires certain state and local voting procedure changes to be " precleared" by the Attorney General. The section is limited to states that use certain testing devices to qualify voters after 1964. *See supra* note 43 (discussing the differences between the "effects" and "results" standards of proving voting dilution under the Voting Rights Act).

98. *S. Rep. supra* note 39.

99. 42 U.S.C. § 1973 (1982).

Voting Rights Litigation

Lee L. Blackman and Erich R. Luschei[1]

In the United States, especially in the West, many cities, school districts, and other public entities use at-large election systems to elect public officials. Once viewed as a solution to problems associated with ward politics, the at-large system of electing representatives has become the object of numerous challenges in the federal courts.[2] The cases have challenged the at-large election process on the ground that such elections eliminate or dilute the voting strength of minority groups.

A significant number of voting rights lawsuits are expected in the wake of the 1990 Census results. The Census figures document growth of minority populations throughout the country. There is little doubt that the Census and the subsequent redistricting of jurisdictions as a result of it, will spawn dozens of voting rights lawsuits in jurisdictions with sizable minority populations.

Voting rights lawsuits attacking at-large election systems typically involve formidable plaintiffs' attorneys, complicated issues of fact and law, sensitive political considerations, and huge litigation expenses.

This chapter provides background information about cases involving at-large election systems. In addition, it discusses the applicable legal standards and the evidence typically offered on the fundamental issues, and presents an overview of the considerations facing elected officials and their counsel when deciding whether to avoid, defend, or settle voting rights lawsuits.[3]

Every citizen of voting age has the right to cast a vote that is equal in dignity to the votes cast by fellow voters.[4] Commonly known as "one person, one vote," this essential right was first recognized by the United States Supreme Court as a proper subject of judicial consideration in the 1962 decision of *Baker v. Carr.*[5]

Reprinted with permission from Municipal Attorney, *Vol. 32, Nos. 5 and 6, September/December, 1991. Published by the International Municipal Lawyers Association, Washington, D.C.*

Under the one person, one vote rule, if voters are divided into districts, each district must be substantially equal in population to each other district which elects a representative.[6] For example, if a jurisdiction's governing body has five members elected from five districts and there are 500 voters, each district must contain 100 people. A system which has unequal populations in the electoral districts causes the votes in an "over-populated" district to be worth less, or be "diluted," when compared to the votes of people in "under-populated" districts. An alternative at-large system also may cause problems. Under the at-large system, all five representatives are elected by the entire population.[7]

Racial Vote Dilution as a Justicable Claim

The one person, one vote rule only protects equality in the weight of a person's vote. It does not protect group interests, such as the interests of Democrats or Republicans, women or men, pro-choice or pro-life advocates, or the interests of any other group united by shared political, social, economic, or other concerns.

However, some groups, mainly racial and ethnic minorities, have received special federal protection against electoral systems which lead to group interest dilution. The vast majority of racial vote dilution cases have involved African Americans and, to an increasing extent, Hispanic Americans.

Racial vote dilution cases grew out of the one person, one vote rule and first became prevalent in the federal courts in the early 1970's. Racial vote dilution occurs when an election system allows a white majority to minimize or cancel out the votes of a cohesive minority group.[8] This occurs when the minority group is submerged in a larger population that votes against minority candidates. In an environment of racially polarized voting, an at-large election system allows a group that is only marginally larger to select all of the representatives. This can prevent even a relatively large and cohesive minority group from electing any of its preferred candidates. This is racial vote dilution.

Under federal law, racial vote dilution is as violative of minority voting rights as the use of a poll tax, a literacy test, or any other device that directly impairs an individual's right to vote. The remedy preferred by the federal courts for curing racial vote dilution is use of a single-member district system in which at least one political district encompasses the geographic concentrations of minorities.[9] Such a system allows minority voters to comprise a majority of the voters in at least one district, and thus control the electoral outcome for at least one of the seats on the governing board.

Modern Standards for Claims

There are three sources for the substantive right in an electoral system free of racial vote dilution. First, Section 2 of the Voting Rights Act (42 U.S.C. § 1973) prohibits the use of any election system that denies minority voters an equal opportunity to elect candidates of their choice. Under Section 2, it does not matter whether the system was developed or maintained with the intent to harm the minority group. Rather, liability may be imposed if it is determined that, without the existing electoral system, the minority group would be expected, as a result of its own size, concentration, and cohesiveness, to elect representatives of its choice.

The other two sources of law are the equal protection clause of the Fourteenth Amendment and the Fifteenth Amendment of the United States Constitution. These constitutional provisions make unlawful any election system that was adopted or maintained for the purpose of reducing minority voting strength when such system has some adverse effect.

The Statutory Claim

Under Section 2, there are three primary elements of proof which a plaintiff must satisfy to prevail in a voting rights action. Those elements are: 1) the minority group must be large in number and geographically concentrated enough to form an effective voting majority in one district; 2) the minority group must be politically cohesive; and 3) the minority group must prove that the majority group votes as a block against minority candidates.[10]

Under the first requirement for a Section 2 claim is that the minority group must be sufficiently numerous and sufficiently concentrated so that under a single-member district system at least one district could be created in which that minority group is a majority of those eligible to vote.[11]

It is a simple arithmetic fact that some groups do not have enough members to influence the outcome of any but the closest elections, no matter how cohesively they might vote or how favorable the electoral system might be to their interests. Other groups are large and cohesive, but are not residentially concentrated. That is, they may be dispersed throughout a political jurisdiction or integrated within the majority group. In either case, the lines of a single-member district simply could not be drawn in a way that would concentrate a sufficient number of the minority group's members to permit them to form a majority.

There are three principal factors that must be considered in assessing whether this first requirement for a Voting Rights Act claim has been satisfied.

First, the current number of seats on the governing body is assumed to be an appropriate number and will be used as the number of districts in the proposed single-member district plan.[12]

Second, each district must be allocated an equivalent portion of the population. If there are 10,000 people in the city with a five member governing board, then each district must contain 2,000 people. Taking these two quantitative considerations into account, the minority group in this hypothetical case must be able to comprise at least 1,001 of the people in one of the districts.[13]

Third, voting eligibility must be considered. If a minority group has a disproportionate number of noncitizens or citizens below the voting age, then a mere population majority will not be sufficient to demonstrate the group's ability to elect a candidate. In such circumstances, the group must be numerous enough and geographically concentrated enough to constitute an eligible voter majority in a district.[14]

Whether the district majority requirement can be established is usually the easiest issue in a Section 2 case. The evidence is readily accessible using the United States Census data. A demographer may be retained to evaluate census tracts as to racial, ethnic, and age composition. A demographer tries to determine whether a district may be drawn in which the minority group will have an effective voting majority, using the factors mentioned above.

If it appears that this first Section 2 requirement cannot be established, summary judgment may be obtained. If it appears that this requirement can be established, the second element of the claim must be satisfied. Thus the inquiry becomes whether or not voting in the jurisdiction is racially polarized. The components of racially polarized voting include political cohesion within the minority group and white bloc voting by the majority.[15] These components are described below.

Minority Political Cohesion

The political process is generally able to accommodate competing concerns. If a minority group does not have a distinct set of interests or is not intent on selecting certain candidates to champion those interests, its views generally are deemed to receive adequate representation within the general process of government. However, if the minority group does have distinct interests which the group attempts to advance, the group's submergence in the majority structure may deny representation or political responsiveness to the group's special interests.[16]

The standard and preferred method of proving minority political cohesion is analysis of the electoral behavior of the minority group in the jurisdiction under scrutiny. The question is whether minority voters vote as a reasonably unified group.

There are three primary means to determine how people vote: 1) voters are asked (through exit polls and other surveys), 2) prior voting behavior is assessed in precincts which are almost exclusively minority (homogeneous precinct analysis), or 3) the percentage of the voters that the minority group represents in each precinct is compared to the votes cast for each candidate in each precinct to infer overall minority voter preferences (ecological regression analysis).[17]

None of these methods provides direct evidence of the actual votes cast by minority and nonminority voters in specific elections. Indeed, it is not possible to know, as a matter of mathematical certainty, which person voted for which candidate because ballots are not designated by minority affiliation.

The method most commonly used in voting rights cases is ecological regression analysis. Under this statistical method, when the percentage of the vote received by a minority candidate increases as the percentage of minority group members in the precincts increases, an inference is drawn that the increase in the percent of support for the minority candidate has been provided by the increase in the percentage of minority voters. Statistical measures of significance are then used to identify the strength of the correlation.

The principal vice of this method is that one never knows whether the people actually voting are representative of the racial composition of the precinct. Thus, differences between racial groups in eligibility (i.e., age and citizenship), registration, and turnout undermine the strength of the model and the inference that those who actually cast ballots mirror the precinct population becomes attenuated.[18]

Homogeneous precinct analysis is similar to ecological regression analysis, except that it only examines precincts in which the minority group comprises 80% or more of the people in the precinct. The fundamental assumption of homogeneous precinct analysis is that voters in homogeneous precincts will mirror the preferences expressed by the minority group as a whole. If minority voters in homogeneous precincts are cohesive, it is inferred that the minority group is cohesive in the jurisdiction as a whole.[19]

Exit polls or telephone polls are a third inferential method for ascertaining how a minority group votes. People are asked their racial background and how they voted.[20]

Whatever method is used, a level of agreement among minority voters which would allow one to conclude that the minority group has distinctive interests expressed through voting patterns must exist. There is no quantitative threshold that serves as a bright line to determine cohesiveness, but only one case has determined that less than majority support demonstrated cohesion.[21]

Majority Bloc Voting

White bloc voting is the primary evil at which challenges to at-large election systems are aimed. If white voters are the majority of the electorate and consistently vote contrary to the manner in which minority voters vote, an at-large electoral system will allow white bloc voting to consistently prevent the minority group from electing its preferred candidates.[22]

To be legally significant, white bloc voting must rise to a level that routinely results in the defeat of candidates that the minority group prefers. The degree of white bloc voting which may be legally significant depends on a number of factors, including the relative numeric proportion of minority and white voters in the electorate, the extent of cross-over voting, and the size of the districts.[23]

Additional Factors

The original line of Supreme Court voting rights cases made a finding of intentional discrimination essential to a plaintiff's success.[24] The focus was on issues such as the motive of those who authored the plan under attack; the presence of racial appeals in elections, reflecting a societal attitude approving discrimination by those elected; the presence of voting on the basis of race, evidencing both an attitude of discrimination likely to be represented in those elected and the essential circumstance under which an at-large system could effectively be used to accomplish a racially discriminatory desire to deny electoral opportunity to minority candidates; and the responsiveness of the jurisdiction to the specialized needs of the minority group, with nonresponsiveness demonstrating that the minority group was being treated differently by the elected leaders and was effectively unrepresented by the leaders elected by the majority.[25]

When Congress adopted the results test in amending Section 2, it stated that all of the factors which had been developed by the courts along the way remained pertinent to a Section 2 case. The Supreme Court's clarification of the results standard in *Thornburg v. Gingles*, however, made it clear that the three *Thornburg* preconditions are the heart of the results analysis, with the other factors being secondary or tertiary. At this juncture, it would seem that evidence concerning the factors not encompassed within the three essential elements of Section 2 will not be crucial to the outcome of a Section 2 case. Nevertheless, they are likely to be the subject of pretrial discovery, even if no constitutional claim is presented, and evidence on these issues may be effective in encouraging the finder of fact to be receptive to the plaintiff's case.

The Constitutional Claim

The earlier discussion identified the principal prerequisite to a constitutional case—evidence that the electoral system was adopted or is being maintained for a racially discriminatory purpose.[26] It is not necessary that the discriminatory purpose be the sole, compelling, or even leading motive in adopting or maintaining an electoral system. However, proof is required that the system was adopted or is being maintained, at least in part, because of, rather than in spite of the adverse impact on the minority's opportunity to elect candidates of their choice.[27]

The evidence supporting a constitutional intent claim is likely to cover each of the issues referred to during the above discussion of the statutory cause of action.[28] But the greatest emphasis will be on the events surrounding the original adoption of the electoral system and the latest modifications or reconsiderations of it. The inquiry will encompass the full legislative process, including pre-and post-deliberative conversations among legislators (although purely internal thoughts and unarticulated considerations may be protected from judicial scrutiny).

The history of the treatment of minorities in and by the political jurisdiction will be subject to judicial examination. This includes the establishment and accomplishment of affirmative action goals relating to government hiring and contracting. The claim that government services are provided on a less than evenhanded basis is also likely to be litigated (providing an opportunity for the plaintiffs to collect documents and data for other potential uses).

No simple guide to the evidentiary prerequisites for an intentional vote dilution case is possible. Badly chosen language that sounds racially hostile by one of the authors of the system may be enough to convince a judge that the system was adopted, at least in part, to disadvantage a minority group's efforts to elect candidates. And, a finding that the authors were acting with the race-neutral political objectives to disadvantage every group (political or ethnic) which might mount an effective challenge to those presently in power is not likely to be sufficient to avoid the intentional discrimination claim.[29]

Litigate Or Settle

The merits of a Section 2 case can be assessed by using estimates of minority group demographics and political cohesion. A demographer can be consulted. The demographer will have to look at census tract population data broken down by ethnicity and age. He or she will also consider citizenship rate estimates for each ethnic group in the jurisdiction. The demographer can be asked if a contiguous district can be drawn in which 50% or more of the voting age citizens are members of the minority group.

To assess voting cohesion and polarization, experienced political observers can be consulted to assess the number of minority voters who will select a candidate whose race is the same as theirs unless there is some strong reason to the contrary. The same question can be asked with respect to majority group voters. If there is no clear answer, data regarding voting patterns in precincts known to be ethnically homogeneous can be considered. Previous exit polls in the community can be considered. If essential, results of elections can be subjected to ecological regression analysis.

If the answer to the demographic question is that a minority majority district can be drawn, and the answer to the cohesion question is not clear, the electoral system is likely to face a serious challenge unless members of the minority community have been elected frequently and consistently.

Evaluating a constitutional case is enormously more subjective, mainly because it is often only through the pretrial discovery that it is determined whether there are the psychologically crucial anchors (what plaintiffs might consider to be warm if not smoking guns) which are essential to such a case. It is also hard to predict how well the witnesses will do and how well the various trial attorneys will do. Nevertheless, given the Supreme Court's establishment of significant preconditions to Section 2 cases, it is likely that a constitutional claim will be pursued even if the Section 2 claim appears weak.

The appropriateness of pursuing a compromise settlement will also be affected by one consideration which does not bear directly on the strength of the plaintiffs' case, namely the costs of defense and the possible obligation to pay the plaintiffs' attorneys' fees should they ultimately prevail (either by judgment or settlement). Voting rights cases are expert and discovery intensive. Each side can spend several hundred thousand dollars or more simply on pretrial discovery and preparation. The trial process can consume weeks, at a cost of several thousand dollars per day. The cost, of course, is no reason to settle a case that lacks merit. However, these tend to be cases in which the outcome is in doubt as long as the matter is pending.

While chances of success and cost are critical issues, decision makers in this area must deal with a number of other considerations, the most significant of which is the fact that the choice of an electoral system alone has profound political consequences, some of which are subtle. This consideration will probably determine whether, and how, settlement may be accomplished. Frequently, the lawsuit threatens to dissolve a partisan balance of power. Sometimes, it merely threatens individual incumbents.[30]

Two other aspects of these battles merit special comment. First, these cases intrude on governmental operations. Many documents must be collected and produced. Many individuals (usually those who run the government) must take time away from their work to prepare and to testify. Legislators and their closest aides will be asked, and are likely to be instructed to respond to, a broad collection of inquiries that they would rather not address. In addition, the press is likely to publicize every aspect of the case and to editorialize in favor of the outcome it thinks best.

Settlement Approaches

If there is no consensus on whether to defend or to settle, one possible alternative is to place the issue before the voters. If the voters decide to retain the at-large system, they will have done so with an understanding of the costs that will be incurred. They also will have provided the city council or board with a mandate on how to proceed. If the voters decide to eliminate the at-large system, further costs of litigation may be avoided and the council will be released from the responsibility for having made a potentially unpopular decision. Attorneys for the plaintiffs are often willing to forestall proceedings if a commitment is made to place an acceptable proposal before the voters in an expeditious manner.[31] The ballot measure approach is usually attractive to plaintiffs and their attorneys.[32]

In assessing the settlement option, there are a number of alternatives which can be considered short of shifting to a pure district system. The at-large system can be retained, but cumulative or single-shot voting permitted. Systems in which some seats are elected from multimember districts and some from single-member districts can be adopted. At-large systems may be modified to provide for district by district primaries, but at-large run-offs. District systems may be modified by the addition of a strong mayor, elected city wide. Even where the at-large system must be removed, one option which tends to preserve the political balance of power, as well as all of the incumbents' seats, is to increase the size of the council or board.[33]

The decision to settle and the choice of alternative arrangements will not involve an easy legal, let alone an easy political, judgment. Nevertheless, there are alternatives to lengthy, expensive, and unhappy litigation.

Conclusion

There is no litigation with the same mix of challenging legal issues, complicated factual questions, colorful personalities, serious social consequences, and omnipresent risk of miscalculation as is present in a voting rights case. Conducting a trial in such a case is inherently dangerous, but then so is trying to settle it. In many instances, the potential for settlement exists only for a limited period of time, generally at the onset of the proceedings. Settlement usually requires an act of political statesmanship at a time when elected leaders are inclined to be doctrinaire.

To the extent counsel can influence the outcome of the process, it is usually a matter of helping the participants find a way to do what they are already inclined to do rather than a matter of acting as the moving force in changing personal attitudes. Jurisdictions are well served when they avoid the circumstance where the 20% of the people who feel strongly about the issue are permitted to perpetuate a fight that the 80% who are in the middle would be perfectly ready to compromise. In such a circumstance, there is usually a way to settle the matter while still preserving to the principal participants an opportunity to retain or obtain the political outcome they seek.

Notes

1. Mr. Blackman is a partner (Los Angeles), and Mr. Luschei an associate (Boston), in the national law firm of McDermott, Will & Emery. Both have represented a number of governmental entities in litigation under the Voting Rights Act and the Fourteenth and Fifteenth Amendments of the United States Constitution.

2. This is true with regard to both the number of cases filed and the geographic reach of the cases. Prior to the mid-1980's, at-large system litigation was generally confined to jurisdictions in the South. During the 1985 to 1989 time frame, however, at-large systems in California were challenged in the cities of Watsonville, Salinas, Stockton, Pomona, Chula Vista, National City and San Diego. *See Romero v. City of Pomona*, 883 F.2d 1418 (9th Cir. 1989); *Gomez v. City of Watsonville*, 863 F.2d 1407 (9th Cir. 1988); *Skorepa v. City of Chula Vista*, 723 F.Supp. 1384 (S.D. Cal. 1989). Similarly, the Midwest began to see the spread of this litigation. *See, e.g. Sanchez v. Bond*, 875 F.2d 1488 (10th Cir. 1989) (Colorado); *McNeil v. Springfield Park Dist.*, 851 F.2d 937 (7th Cr. 1988) (Illinois); *Duchanage v. Sisseton Ind. School Dist.*, 804 F.2d 469 (8th Cir. 1986) (South Dakota). Regions in the South continued to see substantial litigation in this area. *See, e.g., Overton v. City of Austin*, 871 F.2d 529 (5th Cir. 1989) (Texas); *Citizens for a Better Gretna v. City of Gretna*, 834 F.2d 496 (5th Cir. 1987) (Louisiana); *Concerned Citizens of Hardee County v. Hardee County Board of Commissioners*, 906 F.2d 524 (11th Cir. 1990) (Florida).

3. This is not an exhaustive treatment of these subjects. In almost every situation, there is more to say, at least one qualifier which could be added, or at least one more alternative than those presented here. Much of the discussion also is applicable to reapportionment cases where a minority group contends that district lines are situated in a manner that dilutes minority voting strength either through dividing the group into two or more districts or packing the group into a single district when it has the electoral power to control two districts.

4. *Baker v. Carr*, 369 U.S. 186 (1962).

5. *Id.*

6. *Reynolds v. Sims*, 377 U.S. 533, 579 (1964). "[T]he overriding objective [of reapportionment] must be substantial equality of population among the various districts, so that the vote of any citizen is approximately equal in weight to that of any other citizen."

7. See note 1 and note 5 and accompanying text. *See also, Thornburg v. Gingles*, 478 U.S. 30 (1986).

8. *Thornburg v. Gingles*, 478 U.S. 48 (1986).

9. This is not the exclusive remedy, but generally is the remedy that the plaintiffs request in their complaint. For a discussion of common issues that arise on the remedy side of these cases, *see McGhee v. Granville County*, 860 F.2d 110 (4th Cir. 1988). In *McGhee*, the district court adopted a cumulative voting proposal

where it was apparent that African American voters were too dispersed in the community to comprise a "safe" majority in more than one of seven districts, even though the African American voting age population comprised 40% of the total. Cumulative voting would have allowed African American voters to control three of seven seats on the legislative body. The court of appeals reversed, finding that the government's proposed district plan was adequate even though it did not provide African American voters with their maximum potential voting strength.

10. The three essential elements of a Section 2 case are enumerated in the Supreme Court's most recent and most profound examination of Section 2 of the Voting Rights Act, *Thornburg v. Gingles*, 478 U.S. 30 (1986). These elements, sometimes referred to as the *Thornburg* preconditions, were derived from prior case law and the Senate Report on the 1982 amendments to the Voting Rights Act, Congress' last significant action in the voting rights arena. *Thornburg* at 49–50, stated succinctly, a bloc voting majority must usually be able to defeat candidates supported by a politically cohesive, geographically insular minority group.

11. While it is possible for a group that is less than a majority of the voters to elect its preferred candidate by securing cross-over support from other groups, and even though a plurality of voters may be able to exert strong influence in a close election, the critical consideration in a Section 2 case is the presence of an ability, on the basis of the minority group's own votes, to elect a representative but for the impact of the electoral system.

12. *Romero v. City of Pomona*, 883 F.2d 1418, 1425 n.10 (9th Cir. 1989).

13. This hypothetical assumes only one minority group. Where there are multiple minority groups, the calculus changes—there may be circumstances where a group without a population majority nevertheless does have an electoral majority.

14. *Romero, supra*, 883 F.2d at 1424. This may be a significant hurdle. If, for example, a minority group is one-third noncitizen, it must comprise 60 percent of a district's population in order to be a majority of those eligible to vote.

15. *Thornburg* at 51–51, 56. "The purpose of inquiring into the existence of racially polarized voting is two fold: to ascertain whether minority group members constitute a politically cohesive unit and to determine whether whites vote sufficiently as a bloc usually to defeat the minority's preferred candidate."

16. However, it is not a defense to a Section 2 case that the political jurisdiction is responsive to the special needs of the minority group. Similarly, it is no defense that minority group members are appointed to local boards and commissions and are fairly represented in the ranks of government employees. Section 2 is not focused on policy, or even on policy making, but rather on the impact that the electoral system has on the opportunity of a minority group to elect candidates that are distinctively the preferred choice of the minority group.

17. *See, e.g., Thornburg*, 478 U.S. at 52–53 (recognizing homogeneous or "extreme case" analysis and ecological regression analysis as standard methods for ascertaining whether voting is racially polarized); *Romero v. City of Pomono*, 665 F.Supp. 853 (C.D. Cal. 1987), aff'd., 883 F.2d 1418 (9th Cir. 1989) (finding that results of exit polls were more reliable tha[n] results of homogeneous precinct and ecological regression analysis); *Gomez v. City of Watsonville*, 863 F.2d 1407 (9th Cir. 1988) (holding that evidence of expected preferences inferred from socioeconomic and cultural factors could not outweigh actual voting results presented through undisputed ecological regression and homogeneous precinct analysis).

18. Ecological regression is not highly regarded by statisticians. However, it

is well liked by lawyers and social scientists when it tends to confirm what they intuitively believe.

19. The principal vice of homogeneous precinct analysis is its assumption that members of the minority group who live in precincts which are not ethnically homogeneous vote the same way as the usually smaller number of minority group members who reside in different precincts. In addition, rates of eligibility, registration, and turnout also undermine the method.

20. Telephone polls are subject to question because the passage of time and the actual outcome of the election tend to color the recollections of those contacted. The lack of complete anonymity has also been raised as an issue. Exit polls are the best means to assess actual voting behavior. However, such polls (which must be conducted on the day of the election) are both expensive and limited in coverage.

21. Other means to predict voting cohesiveness have been used, including attitudinal surveys and lay or expert opinions on the existence of minority group agreement on current issues. These are not irrelevant to a voting rights case, but they are useful only to the extent they contribute to the determination of voting cohesiveness. The appearance of unity on issues which affect the minority community will not prevail over demonstrated disagreement in voting patterns. Nor will obviously disparate views within different components of a minority group defeat a claim where agreement in voting preference is expressed when it comes time to vote. *Citizens for a Better Gretna v. City of Gretna,* 834 F.2d 496, 501–02 (5th Cir. 1987) (holding that 49% support by black voters for a black candidate was enough to demonstrate that the black candidate was the preferred candidate of black voters).

22. Of course, minority candidates could still be elected from time to time in such an at-large system. But the election of such candidates will not necessarily defeat a Section 2 claim. There are, for example, minority candidates who appeal to the majority and may be selected as the preferred candidate of the majority, even though that candidate is not the preferred minority choice. Such an election will not demonstrate an absence of polarized voting or that the failure of other minority candidates to be elected is unrelated to the use of an at-large system.

23. *Thornburg,* 478 U.S. at 56–57.

24. For a discussion of the historical evolution of these standards, *see generally, City of Mobile v. Bolden,* 446 U.S. 56 (1980) and *Thornburg* at 43–46.

25. Other factors that were important included candidate slating requirements, the size of the districts, the use of run-offs in primary elections, restrictions against cumulative or single-shot voting, the use of other voting provisions or restrictions which could enhance the adverse effects on minorities of an at-large structure, the extent to which historically ended discrimination had continuing impacts which diminished the opportunity of minority groups to be politically effective, and the strength of the race-neutral policy which was said to support use of the at-large system.

26. *Mobile v. Bolden,* 446 U.S. 55 (1980).

27. *Personnel Administrator v. Feeney,* 442 U.S. 256, 278 (1979).

28. Evidence will likely address the events leading to adoption of the system, the history of intentional discrimination in and by the jurisdiction and the state, the presence of racial appeals in elections, the presence of voting on the basis of race (minority cohesion and majority bloc voting), the responsiveness of the jurisdiction to the specialized needs of the minority group, past electoral success or failure by minority candidates, candidate slating processes, the size of the districts, the use of run-offs in primary elections, restrictions against cumulative or single-shot voting,

the use of other voting provisions or restrictions which could enhance the adverse effects on minorities of an at-large system, the continuing impact of historical discrimination on the ability of minorities to participate effectively in the political process, the tenuousness of the policy underlying the electoral system, and the extent of the minority group's residential concentration or dispersion. "Any evidence which tends to demonstrate the presence of a discriminatory motive is probative on the intent issue." *See, e.g., Rodgers v. Lodge*, 458 U.S. 613 (1982); *Garza v. County of Los Angeles*, 756 F.Supp. 1298, aff'd, 918 F.2d 763 (9th Cir. 1990), *cert. denied*, 111 S.Ct. 681 (1991).

29. *Garza v. County of Los Angeles*, 756 F.Supp. 1298, aff'd, 918 F.2d 763 (9th Cir. 1990), *cert. denied*, 111 S.Ct. 681 (1991).

30. Incumbents have legitimate reason to favor incumbency. The people who elect the incumbents do so in order that they might serve, not in order that they might restructure the system in a way which deprives the electorate of the people they have chosen.

31. There is little certainty in most litigated cases. Plaintiffs' attorneys advance their time and significant costs. They all but invariably have a genuine concern about the effect of a negative outcome on the group they represent.

32. If such an approach is taken, the parties should stipulate to a conditional stay of proceedings and obtain a stay order from the court to avoid misunderstandings that are otherwise sure to arise. Plaintiffs' attorneys are entitled to recover fees and costs if a case is settled, whether by ballot or otherwise. Pre-filing investigations are routine and plaintiffs' attorneys probably will have spent substantial time preparing the case. For this reason, a firm commitment should be obtained from the plaintiffs' attorneys concerning fees in the event that the proposal is adopted. Unless a firm figure is agreed to, and made part of the stay order or a contemporaneous contract, the city will be faced with an unnegotiated claim for fees even after the plaintiffs obtain the relief they desired without having prevailed on the merits at trial. In addition, fees incurred by the plaintiffs' attorneys to obtain their fees are generally recoverable in themselves.

33. The range of options will depend on a number of facts, including whether the city is operated under the state's general law or a charter (in California, for example, charter cities have a broader array of options). The willingness of the elected officials to stipulate to a finding of liability may also affect the range of settlement options, because a stipulation for judgment may allow the court to order a remedy without a vote of the residents of the jurisdiction.

PART III
National Studies and Trends

Election Processes and Minority Representation

Tari Renner

Elections are at the core of any democratic system of governance. In concept, elections provide a communications process enabling people to transmit their values, attitudes, and beliefs about how and by who[m] the government should be managed. While this may be true at the conceptual level, in practice elections are not an ideal communication device. Some of the most important mitigating factors are the lack of voter knowledge about candidates, issues, government operations, and the absence of meaningful political dialogue between candidates seeking public office. Voters must possess information on the candidates and on the issues in order for the communications process to function effectively. Adequate information enables choices, but even if we assume the conditions of extensive knowledge and clear alternatives, the rules and procedures for transmitting people's votes into representation are critical in determining the outcome. In a pragmatic world of indirect representative democracy, these rules are especially important.

Electoral Procedures

Any set of election procedures will be biased in translating voter preferences. Biases of various systems are not necessarily obvious. There may be perception of a bias rather than an actual bias determined by empirical research.

Electoral Reform. The structural reform movement of the early twentieth

Reprinted with permission from Baseline Data Report, *Vol. 19, No. 6, November/December, 1987. Published by the International City/County Management Association, Washington, D.C.*

century pushed for changes in municipal election procedures because of a perception that changes would weaken the urban political machines. These reforms included introducing at-large elections to weaken the geographic base of power developed in city ward organizations, nonpartisan elections and direct primaries to cripple the political parties' control over the nomination of candidates for public office; and the short ballot to reduce the influence of the machine's choices as a voting cue to citizens. In the latter example, it was presumed that voters would be able to focus greater attention upon a few races and therefore be less likely to follow the organization's list when casting ballots.

It seems logical that these electoral reforms should have reduced the power of the urban political machines, and it appears that the dawning of these reforms occurred simultaneously with the decline of machine influence. Yet there is little systematic, empirical evidence to indicate that they actually caused the decline. There were many other important factors such as an increase in education levels, the rise of the mass media, a change in immigration patterns, and the development of federal social welfare programs.

There is scholarly research emerging that examines other effects of the election procedures developed during the reform era. This research indicates that there have been both intended and unintended consequences of these electoral reforms. One group of these empirical studies has examined the correlation between city election systems and government decisions. (Existence of a correlation does not necessarily indicate a causal relationship.) The most famous study was conducted in the late sixties by Robert Lineberry and Edmund Fowler.[1] The researchers found that cities with reformed electoral institutions (at-large and nonpartisan elections) tended to spend less and tax less than cities[2] without these procedures. They also concluded that the cities with at-large and nonpartisan elections were less responsive to ethnic and socioeconomic divisions in their populations than the cities that did not have reformed electoral procedures. Other researchers, such as William Lyons[3] obtained similar results in more recent projects.

Some of the more recent research, however, has focused on the impact of at-large and district elections upon minority representation of city councils. Using a variety of techniques but a rather limited number of cities researchers have generally found that minorities are more likely to win seats on councils with either district or mixed elections than with at-large systems.

Impact of the Voting Rights Act. The controversy over the effect of electoral reforms has increasing importance for local governments in light of the Voting Rights Act amendments and subsequent broad interpretation of these amendments by the Supreme Court in *Thornburg v. Gingles*, 106 S.Ct. 2752 (1986). Portions of the 1982 amendments to the Voting Rights Act were passed, despite strong opposition by the Reagan Administration, in reaction to the Supreme Court's decision in *City of Mobile v. Bolden*, 446 U.S. 55 (1980). The

Mobile ruling stated that in order for an election system to be overturned it must be demonstrated that there was some *intent* to discriminate. The demonstration that the results of an election procedure were discriminatory was not deemed by the Court to be sufficient to invalidate the system. In response to this case, the amendments to Section 2 of the Voting Rights Act make it clear that laws that result in diluting minority votes are just as impermissible as those that are accompanied by discriminatory intent. This section states that a system is invalid if, based upon all known circumstances, it is apparent that minorities have fewer opportunities than others to participate in the electoral process and elect candidates of their choosing. When the Supreme Court was again faced with the responsibility of deciding this question in light of changes in the law, it provided a broad activist interpretation in *Thornburg v. Gingles*. After analyzing all of the surrounding circumstances, the Court struck down several multimember state legislative districts in North Carolina based upon their discriminatory voting results. The factors that were considered included the degree of historical discrimination; the degree of racially polarized block voting; racial appeals in political campaign rhetoric; the proportion of minorities elected to public office (although the Court made it clear that minorities do not have a right to have a fixed percentage of elected positions); and the extent to which there is responsiveness to minorities on the part of public officials in a community.

Subsequent decisions in the lower federal courts indicate a willingness of the judiciary to aggressively enforce this law. In *Dillard v. Crenshaw County*, U.S. District Central Alabama, 649 F.Supp. p. 289 (1986), a U.S. District Court ordered several Alabama counties to elect all their county commissioners from single-member districts. The existing election procedures in these counties were found to substantially reduce the number of blacks on these local governing bodies. In *McNeal v. Springfield*, U.S. District Central Illinois, 658 F.Supp. p. 1015 (1987), the central Illinois U.S. District Court ruled that Springfield must change its election system to a district plan and expand the size of the council in order to create a black majority district in the city. Springfield is just over 10% black, and it would have been virtually impossible to create a black majority constituency with only five districts. A similar decision was reached in *Derrickson v. City of Danville*, U.S. District Central Illinois, 87–2007 (1987). In this case, Danville, Illinois, was also ordered to elect representatives by district and expand its legislative body. The city had previously elected three commissioners and a mayor using the at-large scheme. They currently have 14 alderman chosen from seven districts. The change to this plan resulted in the election, on 15 September 1987, of the first two blacks in history to serve on Danville's council.

However, establishing district or mixed plans with black majority constituencies does not necessarily guarantee that minority representation will increase in local legislative bodies. After a recent switch to the district plan in Cambridge, Maryland, a black majority ward elected a white candidate to the city council. There are numerous additional obstacles, other than election systems, that may prevent or inhibit minorities from winning council seats. In Annapolis, Maryland, Alderman Carl Snowden, a new black council member elected as a result of the city's conversion to a ward system, said: "You've got to demonstrate to the black voters in an area that it makes a difference who represents them on the council."[4]

Black Proportion of Voters. Another problem is that there is generally a gap between the percentage of the black population in a given area and the percentage of black eligible voters. (Blacks tend to comprise a disproportionate share of the population that is under 18.) Other reductions might occur in the black proportion of the voting electorate if the minority community is less likely to register and vote than the population as a whole. Consider a hypothetical district which has a 58% black population. Blacks probably only compose about 54% of the voting age population. In addition if whites are even slightly more likely to register, the proportion of registered voters who are black might be only 51%. Finally, suppose that on election day, whites are slightly more likely to turn out. The voting electorate could easily be only 48% or 49% black in a district where blacks compose 58% of the total population. Therefore, unless the black percentage of a the population is a very substantial majority, it is by no means certain that a majority of those actually casting ballots on election day will be black.

Effect of Constituency Perspectives. Minority representation is obviously not the only consequence of using at-large or district elections. While there is little systematic, empirical data on the question, from a conceptual standpoint it appears that council members elected from the two systems would tend to make very different decisions. Consider the hypothetical data in Table 1. Assume there is a five member council (one member from each of the four districts and the mayor who is elected at-large). Each of these elected officials uses the same decision-making rule: support programs with the highest success rate in my constituency. Two programs and the numbers of people that have been helped and harmed by each program in the four council districts are reflected in Table 1. It is clear that Program A has a higher success rate than Program B in every council district. However, Program B has a higher citywide success rate. Program B actually helps more people than it harms overall, while the reverse is true for Program A. In fact, Program B helps more people and harms fewer people (in absolute numbers) than Program A. If the council has the task of deciding which of these programs to eliminate and which to continue, what decision will they make? From the perspective of the individual council members, each may want to continue the program that produces the highest success rate in their constituency. Consequently, the logical response to the above data would be the unanimous selection of Program A by the four council members. The mayor, whose constituency is the entire city,

Table 1
Hypothetical Data for Council Decision

Council district	Program A			Program B		
	No. of people helped	*No. of people harmed*	*Success rate (%)*	*No. of people helped*	*No. of people harmed*	*Success rate (%)*
Total, all districts	225	305	42	285	265	52
1	80	40	67	100	100	50
2	75	225	25	10	40	20
3	40	20	67	65	35	65
4	30	20	60	110	90	55

would logically prefer Program B. While this is a purely hypothetical example which ignores other variables that affect council decisions, it does illustrate the potential differences in decisions resulting from different constituency perspectives.

This chapter does not attempt to resolve the controversies surrounding the types and consequences of municipal election systems. However, it attempts to shed some additional light on the subject by examining the most current and comprehensive data available from ICMA's 1986 Form of Government survey. (See Methodology in Appendix.) The first section of this chapter will analyze the current cross-sectional patterns of election methods (at-large, district, mixed, partisan, and nonpartisan) and the longitudinal changes in these patterns since ICMA's 1981 survey. The second section examines the effect of these election systems upon black representation on city councils.

Patterns of Municipal Electoral Systems

The survey data on at-large, district, and mixed election systems are presented in Table 2. Respondents were asked the number of council members that were elected using various procedures. If it was reported that all members were nominated and elected at-large, then they are included in the at-large category. If it was reported that all council members were nominated and elected by ward or district, then they are included in the district category. All other responses are considered to be a mixed system election process. This latter category includes situations in which a council is composed of four members elected from districts and the mayor, a full voting member, elected at-large.

Prevalence of Different Systems. In the total for all cities, 60.4% elect council members by the at-large system; 12.8% use the district system; and

Table 2
Method* of Election

Classification	No. of cities reporting (A)	At-large No.	At-large % of (A)	District No.	District % of (A)	Mixed No.	Mixed % of (A)
Total, all cities	3,895	2,354	60.4	497	12.8	1,044	26.8
Population group							
500,000 and over	13	2	15.4	3	23.1	8	61.5
250,000– 499,999	23	8	34.8	4	17.4	11	47.8
100,000– 249,999	93	35	37.6	24	17.2	42	45.2
50,000– 99,999	227	121	53.3	16	10.6	82	36.1
25,000– 49,999	472	264	55.9	54	11.4	154	32.6
10,000– 24,999	986	575	58.3	114	11.6	297	30.1
5,000– 9,999	955	597	62.5	118	12.4	240	25.1
2,500– 4,999	1,126	752	66.8	164	14.6	210	18.7
Geographic region							
Northeast	742	492	66.3	101	13.6	149	20.1
North Central	1,260	616	48.9	247	19.6	397	31.5
South	1,179	698	59.2	103	8.7	378	32.1
West	714	548	76.8	46	6.4	120	16.8
Geographic division							
New England	148	72	48.6	17	11.5	59	39.9
Mid-Atlantic	594	420	70.7	84	14.1	90	15.2
East North Central	781	419	53.6	122	15.6	240	30.7
West North Central	479	197	41.1	125	26.1	157	32.8
South Atlantic	517	319	61.7	36	7.0	162	20.6
East South Central	233	167	71.7	18	7.7	48	31.3
West South Central	429	212	49.4	49	11.4	168	39.2
Mountain	235	143	60.9	26	11.1	66	28.1
Pacific Coast	479	405	84.6	20	4.2	54	11.3
Metro status							
Central	372	148	39.8	58	15.6	166	44.6
Suburban	2,101	1,450	69.0	214	10.2	437	20.8
Independent	1,422	756	53.2	225	15.8	441	31.0
Form of government							
Mayor-council	1,686	827	49.1	359	21.3	500	29.7
Council-manager	2,095	1,427	68.1	132	6.3	536	25.6
Commission	114	100	87.7	6	5.3	8	7.0

*Election method refers to at-large, district, or mixed.

26.8% have some combination of the two. This pattern of responses for the aggregate is by no means uniform. When election methods are analyzed in the context of population size, the proportion of cities using at-large systems decreases as population increases. There is a consistent linear increase of the percentage of cities with this system as we examine descending population categories. Only 15.4% of those cities with over 500,000 residents report using at-large elections, compared to 34.8% for the 250,000 to 499,999 population range; 37.6% for the 100,000 to 249,999 group; 53.3% for the 50,000 to 99,999 range; 55.9% for 25,000 to 49,999 population group; 58.3% for the 10,000 to 24,999 range; 62.5% for cities with 5,000 to 9,999 residents; and 66.8% for the respondents in the smallest population group surveyed—communities of 2,500 to 4,999 people. We find the inverse for the proportion of mixed systems. These percentages increase consistently as population increases, from a low of 18.7% for the 2,500 to 4,999 category, to a high of 61.5% for the cities with populations of 500,000 and above. The district plan cities exhibit a curvilinear pattern. The percentages of respondents with this plan decrease steadily with population decreases, from a high of 23.1% for the largest cities to a low of 10.6% in the 50,000 to 99,999 population category. At this point the proportion of district systems begins to rise again up to 14.6% for the group of respondents in the 2,500 to 4,999 population range (Figure 1).

There are also some clear regional patterns to this data. The overall percentage ratios of at-large to district to mixed systems for the regions[5] are shown in Table 2. It is clear that the highest proportions of at-large systems and the lowest proportions of district and mixed systems are found in the West. The district system is most prevalent in the North Central area and the highest figures for mixed systems are in the South.

The smaller divisional breakdowns indicate an even greater dispersion. At-large systems range from a high of 84.6% in the Pacific Coast division[6] to a low of 41.1% in the West North Central division. The proportions of the elections by district methods range from a high of 26.1% in the West North Central area to a low of 4.2% on the Pacific Coast. Mixed systems range in use from 39.9% in New England to 11.3% on the Pacific Coast.

The at-large procedure is most likely to be found in suburban cities (69%) and least likely in central cities (39.8%). More central cities have mixed systems (44.6%) than at-large systems (39.8%). The proportion of cities reporting district plans does not appear to vary noticeably between the central, suburban, and independent cities. There is only a 5.6 percentage point gap between the high and low values of this metro status[7] variable.

Not surprisingly, form of government[8] also appears to be correlated with method of election system. At-large elections are almost universally used in commission cities (87.7%) and are very likely to be found in council-manager cities (68.1%). However, less than a majority of reporting mayor-council cities (49.1%) use the at-large procedure. The district plan is by far the most

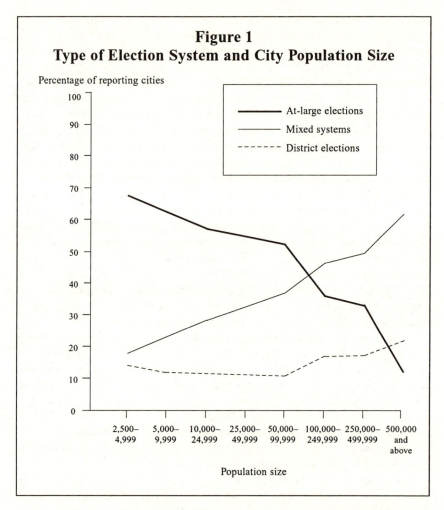

Figure 1
Type of Election System and City Population Size

Percentage of reporting cities

Legend:
——— At-large elections
——— Mixed systems
- - - - - District elections

Population size

prevalent in mayor-council cities (21.3%), whereas only 6.3% of the respondents from council-manager municipalities use the district system, and 5.3% of the respondents from local governments operating under the commission form use the district system. Mixed election systems are also most likely in mayor-council forms of government (29.7%) but are found almost as often in council-manager cities (25.6%). The proportion of commission cities with mixed procedures is only 7%.

There are some very clear longitudinal shifts between the 1981 and 1986 data. As Figure 2 demonstrates, the proportion of cities using the at-large system has decreased over time. The national figure in 1981 was 66.5% compared to 60.4% in 1986. This is somewhat predictable since the system has been embroiled in the representation controversy discussed earlier. In addition, the

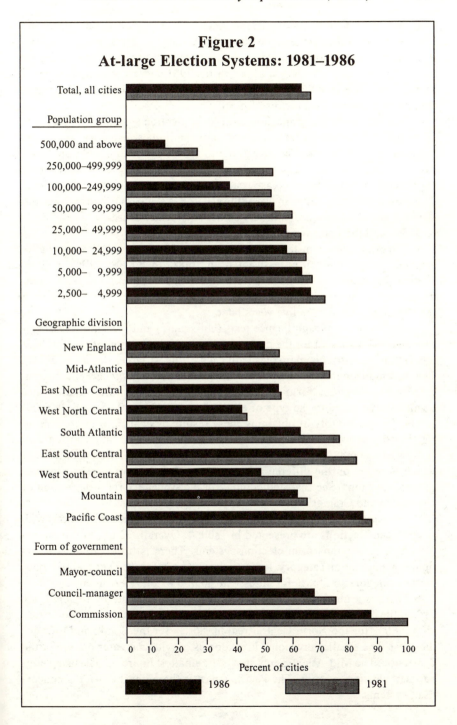

Figure 2
At-large Election Systems: 1981–1986

1982 amendments to the Voting Rights Act were passed during this period and have led to several direct legal challenges to at-large systems. It is also apparent that the proportion of ward or district systems has not shown a corresponding increase. The 14.6% figure in the 1981 survey actually decreased slightly to 12.8% in 1986. The only national increase has been in the proportion of mixed systems. This rose from 18.9% to 26.8%.

The decline in the proportion of at-large election systems is apparent at all population levels. In fact, it is not until the highest category of at-large systems in the 1986 data (the 66.8% figure for the 2,500 to 4,999 population group) is examined that a figure is found equivalent to the national average for the 1981 survey. This decrease is also evident in the geographic divisions. The most precipitous drops in use of the at-large system are found in the South Atlantic and West South Central divisions. The former decreased from 76.6% to 61.7% and the latter from 66.5% to 49.4%.

The proportion of at-large systems has also declined for all forms of government. Mayor-council cities went from 56.8% in 1981 to 49.1% in 1986. Council-manager cities decreased from 75.7% in 1981 to 68.1% in 1986. Commission cities dropped from using exclusively the at-large election system in the 1981 survey to 87.7% five years later.

Table 3 presents significance tests (chi-square) and measure of association data (Cramer's V) for the cross-tabulation of the method of election system (at-large, district, and mixed) with each of the variables discussed above. The data indicate that all five of the variables (population, geographic region, geographic division, form of government, and metropolitan status) are significantly related to the type of election system at the 0.05, 0.01, or 0.001 levels. The probability of obtaining these results by chance, if there were no relationship between the variables, is infinitesimal. These relationships are all fairly weak as measured by Cramer's V. The highest correlation is only 0.213 which is based on the difference between type of election system and geographic division. (See the Methodology in the Appendix for a discussion of chi-square and Cramer's V.)

Partisan and Nonpartisan. The 1986 data on the percentage of cities with nonpartisan elections are presented in Table 4. Overall, 72.6% of the reporting cities have nonpartisan election systems. There is little variance in this figure by population category. It ranges from 84.6% for the over 500,000 population category to 68.8% for cities with 10,000 to 24,999 residents.

There is a much more substantial variation in the data by region. Only 21% of the cities in the Northeast have nonpartisan election systems compared with 77.9% for the North Central region, 86.1% for the South, and 94% for the West. The smaller divisional breakdowns provide a clearer picture of the dispersion. The Mid-Atlantic area shows the smallest figure, 12.5%, using nonpartisan election systems. The Pacific Coast is the highest at 97.7% nonpartisan systems.

Table 3
Relationship of Variables to Method* of Election

| Variable | Chi square | | | Cramer's V |
	Value	Degrees† of freedom	Significance	Value
Population	103.442	14	0.000	0.115
Geographic region	209.423	6	0.000	0.164
Geographic division	354.250	16	0.000	0.213
Metro status	169.706	4	0.000	0.148
Form of government	263.300	4	0.000	0.184

*Election method refers to at-large, district, or mixed.
†The value of chi square is not just a function of the relationship between two variables. It is also affected by the size of each cross tabulation table. Higher levels of chi square are necessary to reject null hypotheses as table size increases. Degrees of freedom are an indication of table size. Degrees of freedom are calculated by multiplying the number of rows minus one, by the number of columns minus one. The formula is df = (r-1)(c-1).

Suburban cities are the least likely to have nonpartisan elections. But even among this group, 68% use the procedure. Central cities report slightly higher use of nonpartisan elections with 74% indicating this method which is slightly below the independent cities with 79% reporting nonpartisan elections.

Form of government is also correlated with the occurrence of nonpartisan elections. Council-manager cities are the most likely to have them (81.9%) followed by commission cities (74.6%). Mayor-council governments are the least likely to have nonpartisan systems. In fact, over 20 percent points separate these cities from the council-manager respondents (61% to 81.9%).

Table 5 presents significance tests and measure of association for the cross-tabulations of type of election procedure (partisan, nonpartisan) with the five variables used throughout this analysis which are population, geographic region, geographic division, [metro status], and form of government. Each of the variables is significantly related to type of election procedure at either the 0.05 or 0.01 levels, and all except population are significant at the 0.001 level. However, the strength of these correlations varies substantially. Population, metro status and form of government are weakly correlated with type of election procedure. The Cramer's V measures of association values are only 0.072, 0.116, and 0.230, for the respective variables. The geographic variables of region and division are rather strongly correlated 0.572 and 0.620, respectively.

The patterns in this data have not changed much since 1981. Nationally there was only about 2% in the results of the 1981 and 1986 surveys. In the earlier survey, 70.2% of the total reported using nonpartisan elections. In the 1986 survey, the figure increases slightly to 72.6%. This trend of slight increases is apparent in each of the separate population and regional categories,

Table 4
Type of Election*

Classification	No. of cities reporting (A)	Partisan No.	Partisan % of (A)	Nonpartisan No.	Nonpartisan % of (A)
Total, all cities	3,927	1,076	27.4	2,851	72.6
Population group					
500,000 and over	13	2	15.4	11	84.6
250,000– 499,999	23	7	30.4	16	69.6
100,000– 249,999	93	22	23.7	71	76.3
50,000– 99,999	229	52	22.7	177	77.3
25,000– 49,999	475	122	25.7	353	74.3
10,000– 24,999	1,004	313	31.2	691	68.8
5,000– 9,999	955	283	29.6	672	70.4
2,500– 4,999	1,135	275	24.2	860	75.8
Geographic region					
Northeast	739	584	79.0	155	21.0
North Central	1,292	286	22.1	1,006	77.9
South	1,176	163	13.9	1,013	86.1
West	720	43	6.0	677	94.0
Geographic division					
New England	145	64	44.1	81	55.9
Mid-Atlantic	594	520	87.5	74	12.5
East North Central	798	254	31.8	544	68.2
West North Central	494	32	6.5	462	93.5
South Atlantic	528	57	10.8	471	89.2
East South Central	226	48	21.2	178	78.8
West South Central	422	58	13.7	364	86.3
Mountain	239	32	13.4	207	86.6
Pacific Coast	481	11	2.3	470	97.7
Metro status					
Central	375	97	25.9	278	74.1
Suburban	2,115	677	32.0	1,438	68.0
Independent	1,437	302	21.0	1,135	79.0
Form of government					
Mayor-council	1,707	666	39.0	1,041	61.0
Council-manager	2,102	380	18.1	1,722	81.9
Commission	118	30	25.4	88	74.6

*Type refers to partisan or nonpartisan.

Table 5
Relationship of Variables to Type of Election*

| Variable | Chi square | | | Cramer's V |
	Value	Degrees† of freedom	Significance	Value
Population	20.269	7	0.005	0.072
Geographic region	1,282.679	3	0.000	0.572
Geographic division	1,510.215	8	0.000	0.620
Metro status	52.475	2	0.000	0.116
Form of government	207.840	2	0.000	0.230

*Type refers to partisan or nonpartisan.

but this is not the case for the form of government information. While the proportion of nonpartisan election systems is basically the same in both surveys, there was a very slight decrease for the reporting council-manager cities (83.1% in 1981, and 81.9% in 1986).

It is apparent from the preceding data that while changes have occurred from 1981 to 1986 in the proportion of cities with at-large, district, and mixed systems—the figures for nonpartisan elections have remained relatively stable (Figure 3).

Election Systems and Minority Representation of City Councils

The second section of this chapter examines the different levels of minority representation for the different types of election systems. Although the existing research on this question is rather extensive and uses a much more elaborate set of statistical controls than is possible here, this project is distinguished by the fact that the data set used is the most comprehensive in existence. The analysis is not meant to be definitive. To the contrary, it is designed to present a broad overview of a subject that offers opportunities for extensive scholarly research and exploration.

In order to consider levels of minority representation, the percentage of blacks in the municipal legislature is collapsed into low, medium, and high categories. Cities with fewer than 20% blacks are included in the low category; those with between 20% and 39% are in the medium category; and the high category represents cities with councils that are 40% or more black. It should be clear, however, that the proportion of blacks on the council is not only a function of the type of election system. There are additional variables

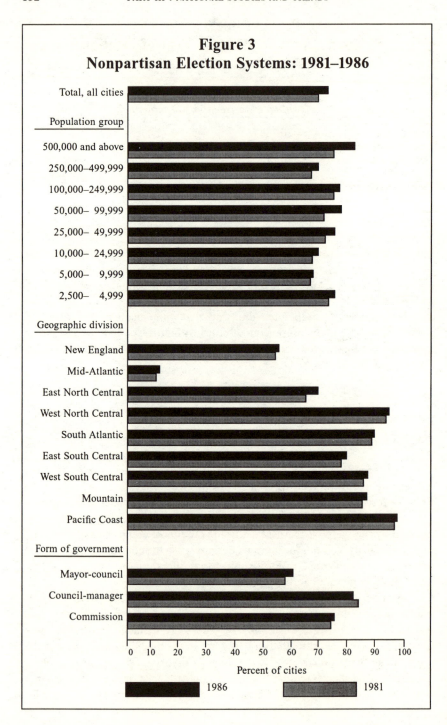

**Figure 3
Nonpartisan Election Systems: 1981–1986**

Total, all cities

Population group

500,000 and above
250,000–499,999
100,000–249,999
50,000– 99,999
25,000– 49,999
10,000– 24,999
5,000– 9,999
2,500– 4,999

Geographic division

New England
Mid-Atlantic
East North Central
West North Central
South Atlantic
East South Central
West South Central
Mountain
Pacific Coast

Form of government

Mayor-council
Council-manager
Commission

0   10   20   30   40   50   60   70   80   90   100

Percent of cities

■ 1986   ▨ 1981

for which there should be controls in order to determine the independent effect of municipal election procedures. Other researchers[9] have used an elaborate array of statistical controls in their analysis. In this project, however, the single control variable used is the percentage of each city's black population. This is collapsed in the same manner as the percentage of blacks on the councils. Cities with less than 20% black population are included in the low category. Those with at least 20% but less than 40% are in the medium group, and those with 40% or more are considered high.

Tables 6, 7, and 8 compare black representation on the councils by at-large, district, and mixed election systems for cities with low, medium, and high black populations. It is clear that method of election does not affect black representation on councils for cities with a low (less than 20%) black population. Of the 1,584 cities in this group, 94% have low black representation on their councils regardless of the type of election method they use. For cities with a medium-size black population (between 20% and 40%), the proportion of blacks on city councils appears to be related to the type of election system. Only 32.5% of the cities with district systems in this group had low black representation compared with 36.9% of those with mixed systems and 41.4% of those with at-large systems. For cities with a large black population, this tendency is especially dramatic. Among this group, 29.4% of the cities with at-large elections have low black representation on their councils compared with 17.3% for mixed systems, and only 9.7% for district elections. The systems with high black representation are at-large (35.3%), mixed (38.5%), and district methods (74.2%). Therefore, cities with high black populations that use district elections are more than twice as likely to have a high proportion of blacks on their city council as those that use at-large elections.

The data in Table 9 present the significance test and correlation figures for the relationship between election system and black representation for each of the three levels of black populations. The Cramer's V measure of association value of 0.236 indicates that the relationship is not very strong.

Table 10 presents data for partisan and nonpartisan elections relative to the level of black representation on the council. While few critics of nonpartisan elections have maintained that nonpartisan elections directly discriminate against minority representation in legislative bodies, it is possible that one could be associated with the other. If partisan elections actually stimulate voter interest and turnout as some scholars such as Frank Sorauf[10] have suggested, then it could be that partisan elections have an effect on the proportion of blacks elected to public office. This could also be the case if political party as a voting cue mitigates the impact of race as a voting cue.

The data in Table 10 are less conclusive than the data for at-large, mixed, and district elections. It is clear that the differences in minority representation are almost nonexistent for cities with low black populations. Over 90% of these cities using either procedure have councils that are less than 20% black.

Table 6
Black Representation on Councils in Cities
with a Low Black Population*

| | | Election form | | | | | |
| | | At-large | | District | | Mixed | |
Levels	No. of cities reporting	No. (A)	% of total (A)	No. (B)	% of total (B)	No. (C)	% of total (C)
Total, all cities	1,584	955	100.0	204	100.0	425	100.0
Black representation on council							
Low	1,491	901	94.3	192	94.1	398	93.6
Medium	89	51	5.3	12	5.9	26	6.1
High	4	3	0.3	0	0.0	1	0.2

*Less than 20%.

Table 7
Black Representation on Councils in Cities
with a Medium Black Population*

| | | Election form | | | | | |
| | | At-large | | District | | Mixed | |
Levels	No. of cities reporting	No. (A)	% of total (A)	No. (B)	% of total (B)	No. (C)	% of total (C)
Total, all cities	259	116	100.0	40	100.0	103	100.0
Black representation on council							
Low	99	48	41.4	13	32.5	38	36.9
Medium	132	55	47.4	19	47.5	58	56.3
High	28	13	11.2	8	20.0	7	6.8

*Between 20% and 39%.

For cities with medium-size minority population (Table 11), nonpartisan elections seem to be associated (albeit rather weakly) with more black representation. Only 35.9% of those using the nonpartisan system in this group have low black representation on the council. This compares with 48.4% of cities with partisan elections. However, in the group with the highest proportion of blacks (Table 12), partisan elections are associated with higher black council

Table 8
Black Representation on Councils in Cities
with a High Black Population*

| | | Election form | | | | | |
| | | At-large | | District | | Mixed | |
Levels	No. of cities reporting	No. (A)	% of total (A)	No. (B)	% of total (B)	No. (C)	% of total (C)
Total, all cities	151	68	100.0	31	100.0	52	100.0
Black representation on council							
Low	32	20	29.4	3	9.7	9	17.3
Medium	52	24	35.3	5	16.1	23	44.2
High	67	24	35.3	23	74.2	20	38.5

*Forty percent and over.

Table 9
Relationship Between Election Method*
and Black Representation†

| | Chi square | | | Cramer's V |
Variable	Value	Degree of freedom	Significance	Value
Low black population	1.024	4	0.906	0.018
Medium black population	6.328	4	0.176	0.111
High black population	16.843	4	0.002	0.236

*Election method refers to at-large, district, or mixed.
†Controlling for black population.

percentages. Almost 70% of cities with this procedure have high black representation compared to under 40% for nonpartisan election cities. Table 13 presents the significance test and correlation data for the relationship between type of election system (partisan, nonpartisan) and black representation for each of the three levels of black population. As with the data discussed above for at-large, district, and mixed election systems, partisanship in election procedures is significantly related to proportion of blacks on city councils for cities with 40% or greater black population but not below that level. The results in that category would have only occurred two times in a thousand (0.002) by chance if the variables were actually unrelated. The strength of this relationship

Table 10
Type* of Election in Cities
with a Low† Black Population

		Party affiliation on ballot			
		Yes		No	
	No. of		% of		% of
	cities	No.	total	No.	total
Levels	reporting	(A)	(A)	(B)	(B)
Total, all cities	1,581	424	100.0	1,157	100.0
Black representation on council					
Low	1,489	405	95.5	1,084	93.7
Medium	88	18	4.2	70	6.1
High	4	1	0.2	3	0.3

*Partisan or nonpartisan.
†Less than 20%.

Table 11
Type* of Election in Cities
with a Medium† Black Population

		Party affiliation on ballot			
		Yes		No	
	No. of		% of		% of
	cities	No.	total	No.	total
Levels	reporting	(A)	(A)	(B)	(B)
Total, all cities	262	64	100.0	198	100.0
Black representation on council					
Low	102	31	48.4	71	35.9
Medium	133	28	43.8	105	53.0
High	27	5	7.8	22	11.1

*Partisan or nonpartisan.
†Between 20% and 39%.

is comparatively weak (0.284 by Cramer's V). One of the major limitations to analyzing the effect of partisan or nonpartisan elections on minority representation using cross-tabulations is that researchers are limited in the number of statistical controls used. Before any firm conclusions are drawn about the independent impact of election systems on black representation on the council,

Table 12
Type* of Election in Cities
with a High† Black Population

| | | Party affiliation on ballot | | | |
| | | Yes | | No | |
Levels	No. of cities reporting	No. (A)	% of total (A)	No. (B)	% of total (B)
Total, all cities	151	37	100.0	114	100.0
Black representation on council					
Low	30	2	5.4	28	24.6
Medium	54	10	27.0	44	38.6
High	67	25	67.6	42	36.8

*Partisan or nonpartisan.
†Forty percent and over.

Table 13
Relationship Between Type* of Election and
Black Representation on City Councils†

| | Chi square | | | Cramer's V |
Variable	Value	Degree of freedom	Significance	Value
Low black population	1.932	2	0.381	0.035
Medium black population	3.297	2	0.192	0.112
High black population	12.148	2	0.002	0.284

*Type refers to partisan or nonpartisan.
†Controlling for black population.

a much more thorough attempt should be made to weed out the independent effect of the election systems variable.

Conclusion

This research has examined the cross-sectional patterns and longitudinal changes in municipal election systems. At-large elections were found to be most common among cities with smaller populations, western cities (particularly the Pacific Coast), suburban cities, and those with commission or council-manager forms of government. The overall national proportion of at-large systems decreased from the 1981 to the 1986 surveys from 66.5% to 60.4%. This decrease was the most substantial for cities in the South Atlantic and West South Central divisions.

The proportion of cities with nonpartisan elections was not found to vary much by population, but regional and form of government differences were readily apparent. Nonpartisan systems are least likely in the Northeast and most likely in the West. They are also more heavily concentrated in commission and council-manager cities than in mayor-council cities. However, there were few changes between 1981 and 1986 in these patterns or in the national percentage of cities using nonpartisan elections.

The latter section of this research analyzed the impact of election systems on minority representation in city councils, controlling for level of black population. Type of election procedure made little difference in the proportion of black city council members for cities with low (below 20%) black populations. However, for those with medium-size (20% to 40%) and especially high (40% and above) black populations, district elections were associated with the largest proportions of black council members followed by mixed and at-large systems, respectively.

The examination of partisan and nonpartisan elections found no substantial difference in black representation for cities with low black populations. Nonpartisan elections were associated with more equitable numbers of black council members for the medium black population cities. However, in the group with the largest black populations, cities with partisan elections were found to have the highest proportion of black council members.

The goal of this research was to analyze the most recent and comprehensive data available on municipal election systems. It was not designed to provide a definitive empirical test of any hypotheses regarding election systems and minority representation. The lack of statistical controls used clearly limits the extent to which we can make conclusive inferences from the data. Many other socioeconomic variables could be producing this relationship. However, despite these limitations, the findings of this research are basically consistent with those of other less comprehensive but more empirically rigorous projects.

Appendix: Methodology

The data used in this research were collected through the International City Management Association's 1986 Form of Government survey. The survey was mailed to city clerks in 7,062 municipalities in the United States. This represents all cities with a population of 2,500 and above plus 417 cities with less than 2,500 people that are recognized by ICMA as having the council-manager form of government or providing for a position of professional management. After a second request to those jurisdictions that did not return the first mailing, a total of 4,631 responses (65.6% of the total universe) was obtained. (Interested researchers can obtain the data set from ICMA.)

In this analysis, however, cities with under 2,500 people and those with town meeting or representative town meeting forms of government were not included. The purpose of this decision was to insure that the data were comparable to that reported from the 1981 Form of Government survey.

Table 14 presents ICMA's standard survey response table. It is clear from this data that the response rate was by no means uniform across the population, regional and metro status categories. Medium sized cities, for example, were more likely to return the questionnaire than small and large cities. The Mid-Atlantic and East South Central regions appear to be under-represented in the sample and the West North Central, Mountain and Pacific Coast areas are over-represented. In addition, central cities had the highest response rate, followed by suburban and independent cities. The patterns to this survey response bias, however, are very similar to those in the 1981 Form of Government survey. The comparable response table for that survey is presented in Table 15.

The chi-square statistics used in this research are significance tests for cross-tabulation data. Significance tests indicate the probability that the results of a researcher's sample would have occurred by chance if there was really no relationship between the variables. Researchers typically establish a significance level prior to conducting their research. If the results of one's test are less likely than the significance level used, then one rejects the notion that they occurred randomly. The conventional significance levels used are .05, .01, and .001.

Cramer's V, however, is a measure of association. It indicates the strength of a relationship. When Cramer's V is zero, there is no association whatsoever between the two variables under examination. If it equals one (1.0), then there is a perfect association between the two. In most real world social and policy research the value falls somewhere between the two extremes.

Notes

1. Robert L. Lineberry and Edmund P. Fowler, "Reformism and Public Policies in American Cities," *American Political Science Review* 61 (September 1967): 715.

2. *Cities* is used throughout this article to refer to cities, villages, towns, townships, and boroughs.

3. William Lyons, "Reform and Response in American Cities: Structure and Policy Reconsidered." *Social Science Quarterly* 59 (June 1987): 118.

Table 14
Survey Response: 1986

Classification	No. of cities surveyed (A)	No. of cities responding	
		No.	% of (A)
Total, all cities	7,062	4,631	65.6
Population group			
500,000 and over	23	14	60.9
250,000– 499,999	34	23	67.6
100,000– 249,999	113	96	85.0
50,000– 99,999	279	235	84.2
25,000– 49,999	619	505	81.6
10,000– 24,999	1,545	1,124	72.8
5,000– 9,999	1,747	1,080	61.8
2,500– 4,999	2,285	1,286	56.3
Under 2,500	417	268	64.3
Geographic division			
New England	797	491	61.6
Mid-Atlantic	1,168	637	54.5
East North Central	1,332	871	65.4
West North Central	712	547	76.8
South Atlantic	854	587	68.7
East South Central	472	260	55.1
West South Central	743	459	61.8
Mountain	359	264	73.5
Pacific Coast	625	515	82.4
Metro status			
Central	509	388	76.2
Suburban	3,775	2,476	65.6
Independent	2,778	1,767	63.6

4. Interview with the author on June 8, 1987.

5. *Regions: Northeast*—the New England and Mid-Atlantic divisions; *North Central*—the East and West North Central divisions; *South*—the South Atlantic and the East and West South Central divisions; *West*—the Mountain and Pacific Coast divisions. See footnote 6 for states included in the divisions.

6. *Divisions:* New England—the states of Connecticut, Maine, Massachusetts, New Hampshire, Rhode Island, and Vermont; *Mid-Atlantic*—the states of New Jersey, New York, and Pennsylvania; *East North Central*—the states of Illinois, Indiana, Michigan, Ohio, and Wisconsin; *West North Central*—the states of Iowa, Kansas, Minnesota, Missouri, Nebraska, North Dakota, and South Dakota; *South Atlantic*—the states of Delaware, Florida, Georgia, Maryland, North Carolina, South Carolina, Virginia and West Virginia, plus the District of Columbia; *East South Central*—the

Table 15
Survey Response: 1981

Classification	No. of cities surveyed (A)	No. of cities responding	
		No.	% of (A)
Total, all cities	6,761	4,659	68.9
Population group			
500,000 and over	24	15	62.5
250,000– 499,999	34	27	79.4
100,000– 249,999	105	85	81.0
50,000– 99,999	258	222	86.0
25,000– 49,999	590	458	77.6
10,000– 24,999	1,486	1,093	73.6
5,000– 9,999	1,664	1,098	66.0
2,500– 4,999	2,215	1,408	63.6
Under 2,500	385	253	65.7
Geographic division			
New England	771	536	69.5
Mid-Atlantic	1,169	684	58.5
East North Central	1,289	891	69.1
West North Central	680	502	73.8
South Atlantic	817	594	72.7
East South Central	445	260	58.4
West South Central	685	456	66.6
Mountain	325	236	72.6
Pacific Coast	580	500	86.2
Metro status			
Central	391	314	80.3
Suburban	3,465	2,409	69.5
Independent	2,905	1,936	66.6

states of Alabama, Kentucky, Mississippi, and Tennessee; *West South Central*—the states of Arkansas, Louisiana, Oklahoma, and Texas; *Mountain*—the states of Arizona, Colorado, Idaho, Montana, Nevada, New Mexico, Utah, and Wyoming; *Pacific Coast*—the states of Alaska, California, Hawaii, Oregon and Washington.

7. *Metro status: Central*—core city of an MSA; *Suburban*—incorporated city located within an MSA; *Independent*—city located outside of an MSA.

8. *Forms of government* include the following; *Mayor-council*—an elected council serves as the legislative body with a separately elected head of government; *Council-manager*—the mayor and council make policy and an appointed administrator is responsible for the administration of the city; *Commission*—a board of elected commissioners serves as the legislative body and each commissioner is responsible for administration of one or more departments; *Town meeting*—qualified

voters meet to make basic policy and choose a board of selectmen to carry out the policy; *Representative town meeting*—representatives selected by citizens vote at meetings, which may be attended by all town citizens.

9. See Susan A. MacManus, "City Council Election Procedures and Minority Representation: Are They Related?" *Social Science Quarterly*, 59 (June 1978): 153–61; Albert Karnig, "Black Representation on City Councils: The Impact of District Elections and Socioeconomic Factors," *Urban Affairs Quarterly* 12 (December 1976): 223–242; Theodore P. Robinson and Thomas R. Dye, "Reformism and Black Representation on City Councils," *Social Science Quarterly*, 59 (June 1978): 133–141; and Margaret K. Latimer, "Black Political Representation in Southern Cities: Election Systems and Their Causal Variables," *Urban Affairs Quarterly* 15 (September 1979): 65–86.

10. Frank J. Sorauf, *Party Politics in America* (Boston: Little, Brown Inc., 1984).

Constituency Size and Minority Representation

Susan A. MacManus

In amending Section 2 of the Voting Rights Act in 1982, Congress established a "totality of the circumstances" test to be used when assessing the fairness of an electoral system. It set forth seven major and two minor elements for the courts to consider in determining whether a jurisdiction's electoral system reduces the opportunity of minorities to participate equally in the political process and to elect candidates of their own choice. Among the major factors to be considered is the extent to which a state or political subdivision has used *unusually large election districts*.[1] The premise is that larger districts reduce the ability of minorities to participate in the political process and to elect representatives of their own choice.

Unfortunately, neither Congress nor the courts has clearly delineated what is meant by an "unusually large election district." It is not clear whether size is defined solely in terms of the number of constituents represented by an elected official or if it is merely a surrogate for the type of election system (at-large vs. single-member district system). The pattern of most lawsuits under Section 2 has been to equate at-large elections with larger constituency size, but there is no empirical evidence to legitimize this assumption. Nor is there empirical evidence documenting that larger constituency size has an independent negative effect on minority election to city councils. The purpose of this research is to determine whether these common assumptions are valid in 713 cities in the United States with populations 25,000 and above.

Reprinted with permission from State and Local Government Review, *Vol. 19, No. 1, Winter, 1987. Published by the Carl Vinson Institute of Government, University of Georgia, Athens, Georgia.*

Importance of Constituency Size

The relationship between constituency size and minority electoral success has been alleged to be a strong and negative one. Larger constituency size is presumed to require greater campaign expenditures, putting less affluent minority candidates at a disadvantage. A number of studies have indicated that a larger constituency necessitates expensive media-based campaigns (Patterson 1974; Karnig and Welch 1980; Jewell 1982; Davidson and Fraga 1984).

The literature has also equated larger constituency size with at-large elections. Councilmembers in at-large election systems are perceived to represent larger constituencies than councilmembers in single-member district election systems. Campaign cost is still the primary reason why some researchers hypothesize a negative relationship between at-large elections and minority electoral defeats. For example, Davidson and Fraga (1984, 122–23) in their description of Abilene, Texas, argue: "The costs of running for office at-large are greater than from single-member districts. Had Abilene had six single-member districts of equal size, 'shoe leather'—door-to-door canvassing by candidates—could have substituted for the costs of TV, radio, and newspaper ads." Thus, minority candidates are perceived by some to be disadvantaged by at-large elections because of the alleged larger constituency size involved.

Other studies have not found a strong linkage between constituency size, at-large elections, and campaign costs. Welch (1976) tested the hypothesis that "money per capita is more effective the larger the district" and found it invalid. He concluded that "there are no economies or diseconomies of scale in district size" (348).

Analysis by the Lyndon B. Johnson School of Public Affairs of the actual change in campaign costs in three Texas cities—Dallas, Ft. Worth, and Houston—concludes that "a change from an at-large system to some form of district system does not guarantee lower average campaign costs." The study reports that the costs per vote actually increased in several jurisdictions because when there is no incumbent in the race but a larger number of candidates, a candidate has to spend heavily to familiarize voters with his/her name. In other cases, "after only one or two district elections, incumbency reasserts itself, and council campaign costs edge up to their previous levels as challengers have to compete more vigorously to unseat an incumbent" (LBJ School 1984, 68).

Heilig and Mundt (1984, 76) in their study of cities which have changed election systems also found that "contrary to our hypothesis, there is no evidence that a district system serves to hold down the influence of money on election results." Winners merely spend more than losers, they find.

Arrington and Ingalls (1984a, 117) actually found that "campaign spending plays a stronger role in single-member district elections than in multiple seat [at-large] elections." And in another study, they observed that "black candidates are as well financed as whites because black contributors concentrate their funds exclusively on the small[er] number of black candidates" (Arrington and Ingalls 1984b, 583).

These newer studies suggest that the link between constituency size and minority electoral success may not be as strong as originally perceived, since campaign costs may not be significantly different in at-large and single-member district systems. These studies also suggest that the use of at-large systems as a surrogate for larger constituency size may be fallacious. The LBJ School study (1984) cites examples, usually large cities, where district councilmembers actually represent larger constituencies than at-large councilmembers, even when the size of the council is larger in the district system. Thus, it appears that sorting out the relationship between constituency size, type of election system, and size of the city council (number of seats) is an integral step in determining the independent effect of constituency size on minority electoral success.

The Study

The purpose of this study is to examine the linkage between constituency size and the election of blacks to city councils in the United States. The units of analysis are the 713 cities, in 1980, of 25,000 population and over, with at-large or single-member district electoral systems. (Cities with mixed systems are excluded from the analysis, because their inclusion would have necessitated averaging the constituency size of at-large and district-based councilmembers—a theoretically invalid approach.) The dependent variable (percentage of blacks on city council, 1985) was obtained through a telephone survey of city clerks in January and February 1985, as were the data identifying the type of electoral system utilized by each city (pure at-large; at-large from posts; at-large, residency requirements; or single-member district).

Constituency size for at-large councilmembers is the total city population as of 1980. For district-based councilmembers, constituency size is calculated by dividing the 1980 population by the number of council seats.

Controlling for Minority Population
Size and Size of Council

In sorting out the independent effects of constituency size on the election of blacks to city councils, it is important to control for other factors found to be associated with minority election rates, namely, the size (percentage) of the minority (black) population and the number of seats on the council.

In virtually every study using the proportion of minorities on a legislative body as the dependent variable, the independent variable with the most explanatory power, if it is included, is minority makeup in the population (Engstrom and McDonald 1981). Thus, we include the black population percentage in 1980 as a major control variable. If it turns out to be a more powerful predictor of minority representation than constituency size, it may show constituency size to be rather insignificant in affecting minority representation levels in most jurisdictions, given a minority's proportional makeup in the population. Likewise, several studies have speculated that the number of council seats is a powerful predictor of minority representation (Taebel 1978). It, too, is often assumed to be a surrogate for constituency size, an assumption that we will test.

Controlling for Type of Electoral System and Size of Black Population

Engstrom and McDonald (1981) found that the relationship between the black population percentage and the percentage of city council seats held by blacks differed across election system types. They concluded that the relationship between the size of the black population and its relative representation on city councils was *conditional*. To determine whether the impact of constituency size is conditioned by the type of electoral system, we regress black council representation on constituency size and the two other variables hypothesized to be important predictors of minority electoral success (size of black population, size of council).

Within each type of electoral system, we also control for the size of the black population. Structure is alleged to have a greater impact than socioeconomic characteristics when the black population is over 15 percent (Engstrom and McDonald 1981). We control for the size of the black population by dividing the observations into two groups: cities with black populations of less than 15 percent and those with black populations 15 percent or larger. By comparing the slopes for the two groups, we will be able to determine whether the relationship between constituency size and black representation is truly absent or is conditional upon structural and population characteristics.

Results

Constituency size has little effect on black city council representation levels across these cities. The more significant factor appears to be the size of the black population. For every increase of one percent in black population, blacks attain .83 percent of city council seats when constituency size is held constant. In other words, blacks hold about 83 percent of the city council seats that one would expect given their proportional makeup in the population. In contrast, for every 10,000–person increase in constituency size, blacks lose .01 percent of the council seats when the black population percentage is held constant. Constituency size is not at all an effective predictor of black makeup on city councils when the percentage of black population is held constant. In this two-variable additive model, constituency size accounts for only .2 percent of the explained variance, whereas the black population percentage accounts for 72 percent.

In an additive model including size of the black population and size of the city council along with constituency size (Table 1), constituency size still fails to reach significance as a predictor of black city council representation level. In this model black population size still explains virtually all of the variance (72 percent), although size of the council is significant at the .05 level. For every additional council seat, blacks gain .16 percent of the council seat. These relationships may vary, however, depending upon the type of election system employed by a city.

The Intervening Role of Electoral Systems

The impact of constituency size on minority representation is not strongly conditioned by the type of city council election system. As the results in Table 2 indicate, constituency size is not significantly related to minority representation in cities with pure-at-large, at-large residency requirement, or single-member-district systems. It is significant only in at-large-by-post systems, a relatively small number of the cites over 25,000 population. However, the relationship between constituency size and minority electoral success in these cities is positive, not negative as is commonly alleged. Thus, even where it does make a difference, it is a positive one. Regardless of the type of election system, the size of the black population is the most powerful predictor of minority electoral success. It is the only one of the three factors examined here that is significant across all four election types. By itself, it explains most of the variance in each model.

The impact of constituency size is also not strongly conditioned by the interaction between the size of the black population and the type of electoral system (Table 3). There is some evidence that constituency size plays a more important role in predicting minority electoral success where the black population is smaller. In pure-at-large and single-member district cities, with black populations smaller than 15 percent, there is a significant relationship between constituency size and the percentage of blacks elected to city council. But again, the relationship is *positive*, not negative as commonly perceived. Generally, the models are much less explanatory for the jurisdictions with smaller black populations, regardless of election system. However, in models which

Table 1
The Effect of Constituency Size
on Black City Council Representation Levels:
U.S. Cities 25,000 and Above, 1985

Variable	b	Standard Error
Constituency size	-.00000007	.000004
Percentage black population	.83†	.02
Council size	.16*	.07
Intercept -1.80		
R² = .72		
Adjusted R² = .72		

* = significant at .05 level.
† = significant at .001 level.

Table 2
Relationships Between Structure, Population,
and Minority Representation Under Different
Types of Council Election Systems

Variable	Pure At-Large	At-Large Post	At-Large Residency	Single-Member District
Intercept	-5.10	-9.97	2.49	-.48
Structure				
Size of council	.72*	1.34	-.50	-.02
		(.90)	(.43)	(.09)
Constituency size	-.000005	.00006*	-.000004	.00004
	(.000005)	(.00002)	(.000008)	(.00002)
Population				
Percent black population	.85†	.36†	.79†	.87†
	(.03)	(.10)		(.03)
R²	.69	.57	.75	.81
Adjusted R²	.69	.33	.73	.80
N	410	46	51	206

Notes: All models are significant at the .001 level. The slope and intercept estimates are for the impact of the independent variables within each type of council election system on the percentage of blacks elected to city council.
* = significant at .05 level.
† = significant at .001 level.

merely look at the influence of constituency size, council size, and black population size on black city council representation in cities with black populations under 15 percent and then those over 15 percent, constituency size does not achieve statistical significance in either group.

Conclusion

Constituency size is not found to be significantly related to minority electoral success in U.S. cities of 25,000 and larger. By far the most powerful predictor is the size of the black population.

The notion that larger constituencies are a disadvantage to minority candidates is heavily based on premises equating larger constituencies with at-large election systems and smaller city councils. This research has shown that such premises are generally erroneous. The linkages between electoral system type, size of council, and constituency size are weak and often insignificant.

Finally, this study has revealed that even in the election systems where constituency size is found to be statistically significantly related to minority electoral success, the relationship is *positive*, not negative, and it is still a far less powerful explanatory variable than the size of the black population.

Thus, it appears that, along with staggered terms and majority vote requirements, constituency size was included by Congress and the courts in the laundry list of minority vote dilution devices with no aggregate-level empirical justification (Bullock and Johnson 1985; Bullock and MacManus 1987; Butler 1985; LBJ School 1984; McDonald 1985; Stanley 1985).

For a city placed in the position of formulating a defense on the constituency size factor, there is very little aggregate-level evidence to give any guidance as to what is an "optimal" or acceptable constituency size. One can assume that for plaintiffs attacking any election system (at-large or district), it is simply less than the current constituency size. Unfortunately for defendants, no magic threshold number is available by which they can defend themselves, although as has been shown here, there is little empirical evidence to link constituency size with black city council representational levels, in cities with populations of 25,000 or more.

Note

1. Constituency size is actually one factor in Major Element #3 which instructs the courts to consider the extent to which the state or political subdivision has used unusually large election districts, majority vote requirements, anti-single shot provisions, or other voting practices or procedures that may enhance the opportunity for discrimination against the minority group.

Table 3

Relationships between Structure and Black Population Size and Black Representation on City Councils for Different Black Population Thresholds and Electoral Systems

	Type of Election System							
	Pure At-Large		At-Large Post		At-Large Residency		Single-Member District	
			Black Population					
Variable	Under 15%	15% or Above	Under 15%	15% or Above	Under 15%	15% or Above	Under 15%	15% or Above
Intercept	-.209	-25.5	-5.50	-17.91	-.86	-2.64	-1.69	-2.34
Structure								
Size of city council	.18	2.98†	.53	4.43	.24	-1.06	.12	-.04
	(.18)	(.97)	(.69)	(2.86)	(.47)	(.80)	(.13)	(.16)
Constituency size	.00001†	-.00002	.00005	.00005	-.000003	-.00001	.00009*	.00004
	(.000005)	(.00001)	(.00003)	(.00004)	(.000006)	(.00004)	(.00004)	(.00004)
Population								
Percentage black population	.66§	1.09§	.39	.17	.58	1.04§	.81§	.92§
	(.08)	(.11)	(.32)	(.33)	(.31)	(.16)	(.12)	(.08)
R^2	.23	.61	.17	.27	.12	.81	.33	.70
Adjusted R^2	.22	.59	.07	.09	.04	.76	.32	.68
N	335	75	30	16	36	15	137	69
			n.s.	n.s.	n.s.			

Notes: Models are significant at the .001 level unless otherwise noted. The slope and intercept estimates are for the impact of the independent variables within each type of council election system and black population category on the percentage of blacks elected to city council.
* = significant at the .05 level. † = significant at the .01 level. § = significant at the .001 level. n.s. = not significant.

References

Arrington, Theodore S., and Gerald L. Ingalls. 1984a. Effects of campaign spending on local elections: The Charlotte case. *American Politics Quarterly* 12 (January): 117–27.
_____. 1984b. Race and campaign finance in Charlotte, N.C. *Western Political Quarterly* 37 (December): 578–83.
Bullock, Charles S., and Loch K. Johnson. 1985. Runoff elections in Georgia. *Journal of Politics* 47 (August): 937–46.
Bullock, Charles S. III, and Susan A. MacManus. 1987. The impact of staggered terms on minority representation. *Journal of Politics.* Forthcoming.
Butler, Katharine Inglis. 1985. The majority vote requirement: The case against its wholesale elimination. *The Urban Lawyer* 17 (Summer): 441–55.
Davidson, Chandler, and Luis Ricardo Fraga. 1984. Nonpartisan slating groups in an at-large setting. In *Minority vote dilution,* 119–43. Chandler Davidson, ed. Washington, D.C.: Howard University Press.
Engstrom, Richard L., and Michael D. McDonald. 1981. The election of blacks to city councils: Clarifying the impact of electoral arrangements on the seats/population relationship. *American Political Science Review* 75: 344–54.
Heilig, Peggy, and Robert J. Mundt. 1984. *Your voice at city hall.* Albany: State University of New York Press.
Jewell, Malcolm E. 1982. The consequences of single- and multimember districting. In *Representation and redistricting,* 129–42. Bernard Grofman et al., eds. Lexington Mass.: Lexington Books.
Karnig, Albert K., and Susan Welch. 1980. *Black representation and urban policy.* Chicago, Ill.: University of Chicago Press.
Lyndon B. Johnson (LBJ) School of Public Affairs. 1984. *Local government election systems.* Policy Research Project Report #62. Austin: The University of Texas.
McDonald, Laughlin. 1985. The majority vote requirement: Its use and abuse in the south. Paper prepared for the Voting Rights and Democratic Process Conference, Tulane Law School.
Patterson, Ernest. 1974. *Black city politics.* New York: Dodd, Mead, & Co.
Stanley, Harold. 1985. Race and the runoff. Paper presented at the Southwestern Political Science Association meeting. March 20–23, Houston, Texas.
Taebel, Delbert. 1978. Minority representation on city councils. *Social Science Quarterly* 59 (June): 142–52.
Welch, W.P. 1976. The effectiveness of expenditures in state legislative races. *American Politics Quarterly* 4 (July): 333–56.

Diversity of Representation and Election Systems

Susan A. MacManus and Charles S. Bullock III

Record numbers of women and minorities are running for mayor and city council—and winning. Today, we have more women and minority mayors and council members than at any time in the nation's history. This trend bodes well for more diverse representation at higher levels—governor's offices, state legislatures, Congress, and even the presidency. There is ample evidence that local elective posts are excellent training grounds for women and minorities who yearn to hold higher officer.[1]

While most mayors and council members are still white males, women and minorities have won local elective office in many jurisdictions. This chapter highlights these successes and identifies the conditions that appear to promote diversification of municipal representation.

Methodology

This chapter draws on extensive research, as reflected in the notes that follow it. In addition, data are drawn from a 1991 "Form of Government" survey conducted by the International City/County Management Association (ICMA). In October 1991, ICMA mailed the survey to all U.S. municipalities 2,500 and over in population and to municipalities under 2,500 in population that are recognized by ICMA as having the council-manager form of government or as providing for a professional manager. Municipalities that did not

Reprinted with permission from Municipal Year Book 1993. *Published by the International City/County Management Association, Washington, D.C.*

respond to the first survey received a second mailing in December 1991. Of the 7,141 municipalities surveyed, 4,967 (69.6%) responded (Table 1).

Gender of Mayors

Women are capturing mayoral posts in increasing numbers. One national study found that as of August 1991 in U.S. cities with populations 10,000 and over, women occupied 374 (14.3%) of the 2,610 mayoral posts or their equivalents.[2] By January 1992, 19 of the 100 largest cities in the United States had elected women mayors.[3] When women do run, there is little evidence that they have a tougher time than men, even in raising money or gaining newspaper endorsements.[4] Women mayoral candidates often receive stronger support from their political party than male mayoral candidates.[5]

A study of female mayors in Florida uncovered some additional dimensions to their candidacies.[6] First, very few had held another elective post prior to being elected mayor; many were path breakers for other women running for municipal office.[7] However, if a female mayor had held previous office, she had most often filled a council seat. Second, women running for mayor are no less successful than those running for council posts.[8] Thus, it is not surprising that women mayoral candidates increasingly face female opponents when they seek office. The biggest challenge is getting women to run.[9]

There is growing evidence that "women and men [mayors] see their political environments—the constituency and the problems their constituencies face—in the same way."[10] A study contrasting the views of male and female mayors who have served the same city concludes: "It is not surprising that men and women who have been active for, campaigned in and led the same city, would be in close agreement.... [T]hese are people who knew their cities well enough to win the confidence of the electorate."[11] Nonetheless, in comparing themselves with their gender opposite, male mayors tend to attribute differences to personality whereas female mayors link differences to their gender.

Population Size

In spite of the growing number of women mayors, men continue to dominate the ranks of those in this position. Of the 4,860 cities that reported gender in the ICMA survey, approximately seven of every eight are led by a man. Men hold all of the mayoral positions in the ten largest cities reporting (populations of 500,000 and above). Women are most likely to head up the cities in the next two categories, cities with populations from 250,000 to 499,999 (31.3%) and from 100,000 to 249,999 (20%) (Table 2). However, among women mayors themselves, the overwhelming majority hold positions in jurisdictions

Table 1
Survey Response

Classification	No. of cities surveyed (A)	No. reporting	% of (A)
Total, all cities*	7,141	4,967	69.6
Population group			
Over 1,000,000	8	2	25.0
500,000–1,000,000	16	8	50.0
250,000–499,999	40	32	80.0
100,000–249,999	133	100	75.2
50,000–99,999	334	255	76.4
25,000–49,999	674	517	76.7
10,000–24,999	1,590	1,128	70.9
5,000–9,999	1,794	1,228	68.5
2,500–4,999	1,990	1,311	65.9
Under 2,500†	562	386	68.7
Geographic division§			
New England	794	530	66.8
Mid-Atlantic	1,180	713	60.4
East North Central	1,350	952	70.5
West North Central	720	558	77.4
South Atlantic	869	640	73.7
East South Central	470	282	60.0
West South Central	746	502	67.3
Mountain	368	263	71.5
Pacific Coast	643	527	82.0
Metro status**			
Central	511	382	74.8
Suburban	3,828	2,663	69.6
Independent	2,802	1,922	68.6

*The term *cities* refers also to towns, villages, boroughs, and townships.
†Limited to cities recognized by ICMA as providing for the council-manager plan or for a general management position.
§*Divisions: New England*—the states of Connecticut, Maine, Massachusetts, New Hampshire, Rhode Island, and Vermont; *Mid-Atlantic*—the states of New Jersey, New York, and Pennsylvania; *East North Central*—the states of Illinois, Indiana, Michigan, Ohio, and Wisconsin; *West North Central*—the states of Iowa, Kansas, Minnesota, Missouri, Nebraska, North Dakota, and South Dakota; *South Atlantic*—the states of Delaware, Florida, Georgia, Maryland, North Carolina, South Carolina, Virginia, and West Virginia, plus the District of Columbia; *East South Central*—the states of Alabama, Kentucky, Mississippi, and Tennessee; *West South Central*—the states of Arkansas, Louisiana, Oklahoma, and Texas; *Mountain*—the states of Arizona, Colorado, Idaho, Montana, Nevada, New Mexico, Utah, and Wyoming; *Pacific Coast*—the states of Alaska, California, Hawaii, Oregon, and Washington.
***Metro status: Central*—core city of an MSA; *Suburban*—incorporated city located within an MSA; *Independent*—city located outside of an MSA.

Table 2
Gender of Mayor

Classification	No. reporting (A)	Male No.	Male % of (A)	Female No.	Female % of (A)
Total, all cities	4,860	4,226	87.0	634	13.0
Population group					
Over 1,000,000	2	2	100.0	0	0.0
500,000–1,000,000	8	8	100.0	0	0.0
250,000–499,999	32	22	68.8	10	31.3
100,000–249,999	100	80	80.0	20	20.0
50,000–99,999	252	210	83.3	42	16.7
25,000–49,999	512	426	83.2	86	16.8
10,000–24,999	1,099	949	86.4	150	13.6
5,000–9,999	1,192	1,044	87.6	148	12.4
2,500–4,999	1,283	1,144	89.2	139	10.8
Under 2,500	380	341	89.7	39	10.3
Geographic division					
New England	451	363	80.5	88	19.5
Mid-Atlantic	701	619	88.3	82	11.7
East North Central	946	826	87.3	120	12.7
West North Central	557	495	88.9	62	11.1
South Atlantic	636	558	87.7	78	12.3
East South Central	280	263	93.9	17	6.1
West South Central	502	450	89.6	52	10.4
Mountain	262	229	87.4	33	12.6
Pacific Coast	525	423	80.6	102	19.4
Metro status					
Central	379	321	84.7	58	15.3
Suburban	2,597	2,203	84.8	394	15.2
Independent	1,884	1,702	90.3	182	9.7
Form of government					
Mayor-council	2,193	1,974	90.0	219	10.0
Council-manager	2,338	1,980	84.7	358	15.3
Commission	92	82	89.1	10	10.9
Town meeting	205	163	79.5	42	20.5
Rep. town meeting	32	27	84.4	5	15.6

with populations below 25,000 simply because there are more jurisdictions of this size.

Although data from the survey suggest that women have not captured mayoral offices in the nation's very largest cities, caution is in order about making conclusive inferences from "snapshot" data. (Only 2 of the 8 cities with populations over 1 million responded to the survey, and only 8 of the 16 cities with populations from 500,000 to 1 million responded.) Indeed, women *have* held mayoral posts in some of the nation's biggest cities, such as Chicago, Houston, Dallas, San Francisco, and San Antonio.

Geographic Patterns

Women mayors are most frequently found in New England and along the Pacific Coast. In these two geographic divisions women fill just under one of every five mayors' offices. At the opposite extreme, only 6% of the chief executives in the East South Central division are women. The political culture in this geographic area tends to be more traditional than in the other parts of the country.[12] Nonetheless, women are gaining political ground here, too.

Form of Government

There is relatively little variation in the proportions of male and female mayors in jurisdictions when form of government is considered. Men least often serve as mayors in town meeting jurisdictions but still constitute almost 80% of those mayors. Men dominate mayor-council and commission jurisdictions, holding approximately 90% of those mayoral posts. The post of mayor is most powerful in mayor-council jurisdictions where mayors are directly elected and have major budgetary, appointment, and policy initiation responsibilities.

Ethnic Distribution

Few female mayors in the ICMA survey are from racial or ethnic minorities (not shown). Of the 634 jurisdictions reporting a female mayor, 630 provided information on race and ethnicity. Of these, 96% were white. Of the remaining 25, 14 were black, 9 Hispanic, and 1 each was a Native American and an Asian. The distribution of males across the ethnic categories was almost identical to that of females, with whites making up 95.5% of the male mayors. Blacks were the second largest category with 2.1%.

One of the few studies to examine the careers of minority women mayors found that black women are often mayors of smaller, poorer towns. These women "see themselves as using different leadership styles and having different ways of solving problems" from men and as more committed to addressing problems of the economically disadvantaged.[13] They are often "firsts"—the first woman mayor and the first black mayor of their towns. When interviewed, "black women mayors—like their white counterparts—said that the people of the community felt very comfortable talking to them, they were accessible to the public, and the constituents could talk more freely to them than to previous mayors."[14] Many were school teachers, community activists, and church leaders.

Education Level

In American politics, it has always been the case that regardless of gender, "candidates and public officials are much better educated than most of the general population and they tend to be drawn disproportionately from managerial and professional occupations."[15] For quite some time now, women office-holders, particularly in larger jurisdictions, have been better educated on average than their male counterparts. Part of the reason for this is that women politicians, more than men, tend to be drawn from the ranks of those who have worked in the field of education.[16]

Figure 1 shows that while the general distribution of mayors across education levels is similar for males and females, women are slightly better educated overall. Although the bachelors degree is the modal category for both sexes, a higher percentage of women than men (5 percentage points) have some college education; the same pattern holds true for masters degrees. Conversely, more men (21.7%) than women (18.8%) have no more than a high school diploma.

Within each gender, there is often substantial variation in the proportion of the respondents who have a particular level of education (not shown). For example, among women, the municipalities having the smallest proportion of mayors with college degrees are those communities having populations from 2,500 to 4,999. Only about 40% of the female mayors in these communities have a bachelors degree or more. In each of the three groups of cities with fewer than 10,000 people less than 50% of the women mayors have college degrees. In larger cities with at least 100,000 residents, 87% of the female mayors are college graduates. The same pattern, although not as marked, characterizes male mayors.

Although women are increasingly attending law school, the law continues to be a male-dominated occupation. It is, therefore, not surprising that a higher proportion of male mayors (7.8%) than female mayors (4.1%) have law degrees. However, the relatively low percentage of lawyers in mayoral posts indicates that a law degree is not nearly as important for local office holders as it appears to be for state legislative positions.

Structure of the Mayoral Position

Data from the 1991 ICMA survey were examined to determine whether there are any gender patterns relative to mayor's service on the council, the full-time or part-time nature of the position, method of mayoral selection, or mayoral voting or veto power.

Service on the Council. It is not unusual for a mayor to serve as a member of the council, particularly in jurisdictions with the council-manager or commission form of government. For example, the 1986 ICMA "Form of

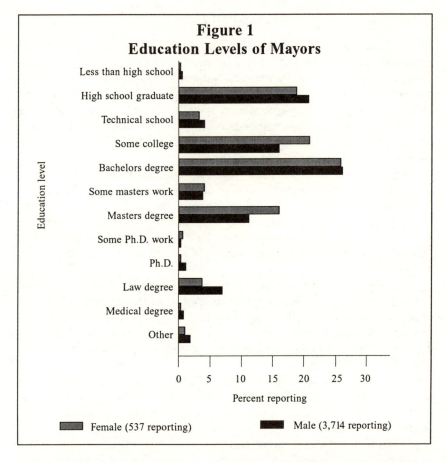

Figure 1
Education Levels of Mayors

Female (537 reporting)   Male (3,714 reporting)

Government" survey found that mayors were members of council in 96.6% of the commission jurisdictions and 85.6% of the council-manager jurisdictions but in only 33.2% of those with mayor-council charters.[17] A similar pattern is observable in the 1991 survey, with 97.8% of the mayors in commission jurisdictions and 82% of the mayors in council-manager jurisdictions serving on the council. In mayor-council jurisdictions, only 34.6% of the mayors sit on the council.

In 61.1% of the cities that reported in 1991, the mayor is a member of the council (not shown). Women mayors serve on city councils in a somewhat larger percentage (67.3%) than do male mayors (60.2%). The greater percentage of female mayors serving on the council generally holds for all but the smallest of municipalities. The patterns for male and female mayors are similar across forms of government.

Full-Time or Part-Time Position. Only 15.5% of the mayors serve full-time, regardless of gender (not shown). For men and women, the likelihood that the mayor is full-time increases with population. Full-time mayoral positions are most common in mayor-council and town meeting jurisdictions and least frequent in council-manager governments.

Method of Mayoral Selection. More than three-quarters of all mayors (77.1%) are elected directly by the voters, and 21.1% are chosen by the council (not shown). More female than male mayors are chosen by the council (26.3% compared with 20.3%) (Table 3). Mayors selected by the council tend to have as their primary role serving as a presiding officer rather than acting as a strong independent chief executive with major policy initiation responsibilities.[18]

Mayoral Voting Power. Women are substantially more likely to lead cities in which the mayor is allowed to vote on *all* issues (Table 4). Almost 60% of the female mayors but less than half of the male mayors have this power. This is evidence that women are not precluded from achieving powerful positions. More male (40%) than female (28.7%) mayors are restricted to voting only in the case of a tie. Approximately the same proportion of men and women mayors are not permitted to vote under any circumstance (9%). Except for very large cities (populations of 500,000 and over), where the number responding was very small, mayors more often enjoy voting rights in larger than smaller municipalities.

The biggest gender difference with regard to mayoral voting powers among forms of government occurs in commission municipalities. Women who are mayors in such municipalities are more likely to have full voting privileges than are men in comparable communities.

While women mayors are more likely to have full voting rights in most geographic divisions, the disparity is particularly large in the Mountain, West South Central, Mid-Atlantic, and East North Central states. In the Mountain states 69.7% of the female mayors but only 44.5% of the male mayors are able to vote on all issues. Women are also more likely to have full mayoral voting rights in municipalities with populations from 2,500 to 9,999 and in those with from 25,000 to 49,999 people. Greater concentrations of municipalities of these sizes are in the geographic divisions cited above. Just the opposite pattern characterizes the smallest communities, those with fewer than 2,500 people.

Mayoral Veto Power. Less than one-third of all mayors have veto power over council-passed measures. Those with such power are usually strong executives in larger cites with mayor-council governments (Table 5). Male mayors are somewhat more likely to have a veto (31.9%) than are women (26.3%) because more of them head larger mayor-council cities. The heavier concentrations of mayor-council governments in the midwestern cities help explain the higher incidence of veto power among male and female mayors in the East North Central and West North Central divisions.

Table 3
Mayoral Selection Method, by Gender and Ethnicity

	Male			Female		
		D*	C†		D	C
	No. reporting	% of	% of	No. reporting	% of	% of
Classification	(A)	(A)	(A)	(B)	(B)	(B)
Total, all cities	4,207	78.2	20.3	632	70.3	26.3
Population group						
Over 1,000,000	2	100.0	0.0	0	0.0	0.0
500,000–1,000,000	8	100.0	0.0	0	0.0	0.0
250,000–499,999	22	90.9	0.0	10	100.0	0.0
100,000–249,999	80	90.0	10.0	20	75.0	25.0
50,000–99,999	208	75.0	23.6	42	66.7	26.2
25,000–49,999	424	72.6	25.5	86	57.0	39.5
10,000–24,999	943	74.2	24.5	150	72.0	26.0
5,000–9,999	1,041	78.6	19.8	147	71.4	25.2
2,500–4,999	1,139	84.1	14.7	138	76.8	21.7
Under 2,500	340	72.6	25.3	39	59.0	25.6
Geographic division						
New England	348	54.9	37.9	87	51.7	31.0
Mid-Atlantic	618	75.2	23.1	82	75.6	24.4
East North Central	825	84.2	14.8	120	83.3	15.3
West North Central	495	89.3	10.1	62	83.9	16.1
South Atlantic	558	83.9	15.1	78	83.3	15.4
East South Central	262	87.4	12.2	17	100.0	0.0
West South Central	450	86.4	13.6	52	80.8	19.2
Mountain	229	84.3	15.7	33	66.7	33.3
Pacific Coast	422	51.4	46.4	101	38.6	56.4
Metro status						
Central	320	85.9	12.5	58	81.0	17.2
Suburban	2,191	75.4	23.1	394	70.8	26.4
Independent	1,696	80.3	18.3	180	65.6	28.9
Form of government						
Mayor-council	1,972	96.7	3.1	218	96.8	3.2
Council-manager	1,972	62.3	35.9	358	54.7	40.8
Commission	81	72.8	23.5	10	70.0	30.0
Town meeting	157	52.9	36.3	41	65.9	19.5
Rep. town meeting	25	52.0	44.0	5	60.0	40.0

Note: Row percentages may not total 100 because some respondents use a selection method not reported in this table.
*Direct election of the mayor by voters.
†Council selection of the mayor from among its members.

Table 3 (cont.)
Mayoral Selection Method, by Gender and Ethnicity

| | *Black* | | | *White* | | | *Hispanic* | |
| | *D* | *C* | | *D* | *C* | | *D* | *C* |
No. reporting (E)	*% of (E)*	*% of (E)*	*No. reporting (F)*	*% of (F)*	*% of (F)*	*No. reporting (G)*	*% of (G)*	*% of (G)*
101	71.3	26.7	4,590	77.6	20.7	86	61.6	34.9
Population group								
2	100.0	0.0	0	0.0	0.0	0	0.0	0.0
0	0.0	0.0	8	100.0	0.0	0	0.0	0.0
6	83.3	0.0	24	95.8	0.0	2	100.0	0.0
8	87.5	12.5	89	86.5	13.5	1	100.0	0.0
11	63.6	27.3	231	74.9	23.8	6	50.0	16.7
10	80.0	20.0	483	70.2	27.5	10	50.0	50.0
26	65.4	34.6	1,035	74.3	24.3	21	66.7	33.3
16	62.5	37.5	1,133	78.3	19.8	26	61.5	38.5
18	72.2	27.3	1,226	84.1	14.9	14	57.1	35.7
4	75.0	25.0	361	70.6	25.8	6	66.7	33.3
Geographic division								
4	75.0	25.0	424	54.5	36.6	5	60.0	40.0
13	76.9	23.1	675	75.3	23.3	5	60.0	0.0
19	68.4	21.1	912	84.5	14.8	1	0.0	100.0
6	100.0	0.0	548	88.9	10.6	5	80.0	0.0
32	68.8	31.3	590	84.6	14.4	1	100.0	0.0
7	71.4	28.6	270	88.1	11.5	25	84.0	16.0
7	71.4	28.6	462	86.1	13.9	18	77.8	22.2
2	100.0	0.0	239	82.0	18.0	26	26.9	69.2
11	54.5	45.5	470	49.8	47.4			
Metro status								
21	76.2	14.3	345	85.8	13.3	8	75.0	12.5
51	68.6	31.4	2,452	75.2	23.1	50	58.0	38.0
29	72.4	27.6	1,793	79.3	18.9	28	64.3	35.7
Form of government								
38	100.0	0.0	2,091	96.7	3.1	29	96.6	3.4
60	53.3	43.3	2,192	61.9	36.0	56	42.9	51.8
3	66.7	33.3	86	70.9	25.6	1	100.0	0.0
0	0.0	0.0	191	56.5	32.5	0	0.0	0.0
0	0.0	0.0	30	53.3	43.3	0	0.0	0.0

Composition of the Council

Although there is some research showing that women typically head jurisdictions in which there are few or no female council members, these studies were conducted before the recent surge in the election of women to city councils. The results of the 1991 ICMA survey show that where there are women mayors, there is a higher proportion of women on council. In jurisdictions with women mayors an average of 1.79 of the council members are female versus an average of 1.07 councilwomen in jurisdictions led by men (not shown). This pattern holds true across every population category. The average size of councils in jurisdictions with female mayors is 6.08; for those headed by males, it is 6.15. Broader female representation may be greater in areas with higher concentrations of older female populations (Sunbelt communities with more widowed retirees).[19]

Years in Office

The relatively recent entry of women into mayoral positions explains to a large degree the comparatively longer average years in office for male mayors. The average male mayor in the 1991 ICMA survey has been in office since mid–1986, compared with the average female mayor, who has been in office since 1988—a difference of approximately 1.5 years. Although a handful of the men have served as mayor since the late 1940s, the longest serving female chief executives have been in office only since the late 1950s (not shown).

With one exception, male mayors have greater seniority in municipalities of all sizes. Only in 29 cities reporting with populations from 250,000 to 499,999 has tenure for women been longer than for men, and the difference is less than three months.

Term Limits

Only 5% of all mayors face term limits, and this barrier is equally likely to be faced by men and women chief executives. For both sexes, term limits are most frequent in municipalities having 50,000 or more people; at least 10% of these larger communities restrict a mayor's right of succession. When term limits are imposed, the median and mean values are in the two- to three-year range. Only 5.8% of women and 5.2% of men served as mayors in municipalities with term limits.

Race/Ethnicity of the Mayor

Research has suggested that minority mayoral election success is generally higher when the minority population is larger and more cohesive and

Table 4
Mayoral Voting in Council, by Gender

	Male				Female			
	No. reporting (A)	*All* % of (A)*	*Tie† % of (A)*	*No§ % of (A)*	*No. reporting (B)*	*All % of (B)*	*Tie % of (B)*	*No % of (B)*
Classification								
Total, all cities	4,185	48.9	40.2	8.9	630	59.8	28.7	9.0
Population group								
Over 1,000,000	2	0.0	0.0	100.0	0	0.0	0.0	0.0
500,000–1,000,000	8	25.0	12.5	62.5	0	0.0	0.0	0.0
250,000–499,999	22	59.1	0.0	40.9	10	70.0	0.0	20.0
100,000–249,999	80	63.8	12.5	20.0	20	65.0	10.0	20.0
50,000–99,999	209	63.2	12.0	22.0	41	70.7	9.8	17.1
25,000–49,999	419	58.5	22.9	14.6	86	72.1	16.3	10.5
10,000–24,999	940	54.6	31.5	10.9	149	61.1	26.2	10.7
5,000–9,999	1,034	48.0	44.2	6.4	146	61.6	32.9	4.1
2,500–4,999	1,131	37.8	56.9	4.2	139	50.4	41.7	4.3
Under 2,500	340	48.8	45.0	5.0	39	38.5	41.0	17.9
Geographic division								
New England	335	69.3	11.9	17.9	86	68.6	4.7	24.4
Mid-Atlantic	616	45.5	45.8	6.2	81	58.0	25.9	13.6
East North Central	821	38.2	43.1	14.1	120	50.8	35.8	9.2
West North Central	495	40.2	42.6	15.8	61	41.0	49.2	9.8
South Atlantic	556	49.8	44.6	4.0	78	53.8	37.2	6.4
East South Central	263	46.4	42.6	8.7	17	47.1	47.1	5.9
West South Central	449	41.4	53.5	3.8	52	53.8	42.3	1.9
Mountain	229	44.5	51.1	4.4	33	69.7	24.2	3.0
Pacific Coast	421	79.3	18.3	1.9	102	82.4	15.7	.0
Metro status								
Central	319	48.3	18.8	29.5	58	60.3	13.8	20.7
Suburban	2,176	54.6	36.1	7.1	391	63.7	26.9	7.9
Independent	1,690	41.6	49.5	7.3	181	51.4	37.6	7.7
Form of government								
Mayor-council	1,962	20.9	59.9	16.3	217	20.3	57.6	18.9
Council-manager	1,976	71.9	24.5	2.1	358	79.9	15.6	2.5
Commission	82	89.0	11.0	0.0	10	100.0	0.0	0.0
Town meeting	142	86.6	6.3	6.3	40	82.5	0.0	15.0
Rep. town meeting	23	82.6	13.0	4.3	5	80.0	0.0	20.0

Note: Row percentages may not total 100 because the "other" category is not reported in this table.
*Mayor can vote on all issues.
†Mayor votes only to break a tie.
§Mayor is never allowed to vote.

minority voter turnout is equal to or higher than white turnout.[20] Minority mayoral election successes in cities in which a racial or ethnic group is less than a majority of the population are often a consequence of coalitions with liberal white voters.[21] Occasionally, although increasingly less common, coalitions between racial/ethnic groups launch minority candidates into the

Table 5
Mayoral Veto Powers, by Gender

| | Mayors with veto power | | | |
| | Male | | Female | |
Classification	No.	%	No.	%
Total, all cities	1,307	31.9	160	26.3
Population group				
Over 1,000,000	2	100.0	0	0.0
500,000–1,000,000	6	75.0	0	0.0
250,000–499,999	10	45.5	4	40.0
100,000–249,999	29	36.3	6	30.0
50,000–99,999	74	35.9	11	26.2
25,000–49,999	141	33.5	19	22.4
10,000–24,999	286	30.9	41	28.5
5,000–9,999	360	35.6	37	27.0
2,500–4,999	327	30.0	34	25.6
Under 2,500	72	22.1	8	21.1
Geographic division				
New England	51	15.5	7	9.2
Mid-Atlantic	236	39.5	23	30.3
East North Central	371	46.4	47	39.8
West North Central	222	46.2	31	50.8
South Atlantic	82	15.0	16	20.5
East South Central	105	41.3	7	43.8
West South Central	131	29.7	12	23.5
Mountain	58	25.6	2	6.1
Pacific Coast	51	12.2	15	15.0
Form of government				
Mayor-council	1,059	55.7	125	59.2
Council-manager	244	12.5	34	9.6
Commission	3	3.8	0	0.0
Town meeting	0	0.0	1	3.2
Rep. town meeting	1	4.5	0	0.0

*Note: 4,092 jurisdiction with male mayors provided information on their veto authority, and 609 jurisdictions with female mayors provided such data.

mayorship. Coalitions of blacks and Hispanics are becoming particularly difficult to build and sustain.[22]

According to the 1991 ICMA survey, non–Hispanic whites continue to dominate the office of mayor. Of the 4,825 jurisdictions reporting, 95.6% have a white mayor (Table 6). Of four other ethnic/racial groups considered, the minority most likely to serve as mayor are blacks, who held 101 (2.1%) of the mayorships. Blacks are closely followed by Hispanics who account for 87

(1.8%) of the mayors. The Asians or Pacific Islanders (9) and Native Americans (16) serving as mayor account for 0.5% combined.

Geographic Patterns

The geographic distribution of minority chief executives is as would be expected. That is, Hispanic mayors are clustered in the West South Central, Mountain, and Pacific Coast divisions, which have larger concentrations of Hispanic populations. In each of these areas, Hispanics hold at least 5% of the mayoral posts, more than two and one-half times their share of mayorships nationwide. These three geographic divisions account for 69 of the 87 Hispanic mayors (79.3%).

The only category of jurisdictions in which Hispanic chief executives are disproportionately found are those with populations from 250,000 to 499,999, in which Hispanics hold 6.3% of the mayoral offices. (Two of the 32 cities reporting have Hispanic mayors.)

The 16 Native American mayors serve in municipalities of less than 25,000, mostly in the West South Central and Pacific Coast divisions, where there are larger concentrations of Native Americans.

Black mayors are most concentrated in the South Atlantic division, where 5.1% of the municipalities report a black mayor. In no other division does the proportion of black mayors substantially exceed the nationwide figure. The New England and Mountain divisions have the smallest proportion of black mayors—less than 1%. These divisions have more municipalities with small black populations than the other divisions.

Population Size

Size of jurisdiction is associated with the likelihood of a black serving as mayor. Both of the cities reporting with more than 1 million residents are led by a black. Blacks also hold 18.8% of the mayorships in cities with populations from 250,000 to 499,999 and 8.1% of the posts in cities from 100,000 to 249,999. Less than 2% of the jurisdictions with populations under 10,000 have a black chief executive. These small jurisdictions tend to have relatively small black populations. Other studies have found that "the size of the African-American population ... contributes exponentially toward growth in proportions of black elected officials."[23]

Form of Government

Form of government is only weakly associated with the race or ethnicity of the mayor. Whites lead all but one of the jurisdictions with town meeting or representative town meeting governments. The highest percentage of black mayors is found in jurisdictions with the commission form of government,

Table 6
Ethnicity of Mayor

| | | Ethnic background of mayor | | | |
| | | Native American | | Hispanic | |
Classification	No. reporting (A)	No.	% of (A)	No.	% of (A)
Total, all cities	4,825	16	0.3	87	1.8
Population group					
Over 1,000,000	2	0	0.0	0	0.0
500,000–1,000,000	8	0	0.0	0	0.0
250,000–499,999	32	0	0.0	2	6.3
100,000–249,999	99	0	0.0	1	1.0
50,000–99,999	252	0	0.0	6	2.4
25,000–49,999	506	0	0.0	10	2.0
10,000–24,999	1,090	1	0.1	21	1.9
5,000–9,999	1,187	5	0.4	26	2.2
2,500–4,999	1,272	6	0.5	15	1.2
Under 2,500	377	4	1.1	6	1.6
Geographic division					
New England	446	1	0.2	0	0.0
Mid-Atlantic	694	0	0.0	5	0.7
East North Central	939	1	0.1	6	0.6
West North Central	556	0	0.0	1	0.2
South Atlantic	629	2	0.3	5	0.8
East South Central	279	0	0.0	1	0.4
West South Central	500	5	1.0	25	5.0
Mountain	262	1	0.4	18	6.9
Pacific Coast	520	6	1.2	26	5.0
Metro status					
Central	377	0	0.0	8	2.1
Suburban	2,577	6	0.2	51	2.0
Independent	1,871	10	0.5	28	1.5
Form of government					
Mayor-council	2,175	9	0.4	29	1.3
Council-manager	2,326	5	0.2	57	2.5
Commission	92	1	1.1	1	1.1
Town meeting	200	1	0.5	0	0.0
Rep. town meeting	32	0	0.0	0	0.0

Table 6 (cont.)
Ethnicity of Mayor

Ethnic background of mayor

	Asian		White		Black
No.	% of (A)	No.	% of (A)	No.	% of (A)
9	0.2	4,612	95.6	101	2.1
Population group					
0	0.0		0.0	2	100.0
0	0.0	8	100.0	0	0.0
0	0.0	24	75.0	6	18.8
1	1.0	89	89.9	8	8.1
2	0.8	233	92.5	11	4.4
1	0.2	485	95.8	10	2.0
1	0.1	1,041	95.5	26	2.4
2	0.2	1,138	95.9	16	1.3
1	0.1	1,232	96.9	18	1.4
1	0.3	362	96.0	4	1.1
Geographic division					
0	0.0	441	98.9	4	0.9
0	0.0	676	97.4	13	1.9
0	0.0	913	97.2	19	2.0
1	0.2	548	98.6	6	1.1
0	0.0	590	93.8	32	5.1
0	0.0	271	97.1	7	2.5
1	0.2	462	92.4	7	1.4
2	0.8	239	91.2	2	0.8
5	1.0	472	90.8	11	2.1
Metro status					
2	0.5	346	91.8	21	5.6
5	0.2	2,464	95.6	51	2.0
2	0.1	1,802	96.3	29	1.5
Form of government					
4	0.2	2,095	96.3	38	1.7
5	0.2	2,199	94.5	60	2.6
0	0.0	87	94.6	3	3.3
0	0.0	199	99.5	0	0.0
0	0.0	32	100.0	0	0.0

while Hispanic mayors most frequently serve in council-manager jurisdictions.

Table 6 shows that while there is some variation in the share of minority mayors across types of jurisdictions, the range is narrow. Notwithstanding a larger proportion of black mayors in commission governments, blacks lead only 3.3% of those jurisdictions. The range is even narrower for other minority groups, with Hispanics holding no more than 2.5% of the mayor positions under any electoral format.

Education Level

Generally, mayors are somewhat more educated than the constituencies they represent regardless of race or ethnicity. Mayors in municipalities where the position is demanding and full-time are more likely to be college educated and to have a professional degree. It is more difficult for persons in salaried jobs (as opposed to those who are self-employed or work on commission) to run for such positions because they cannot as easily take time off to run for and hold office.[24] Historically, this has tended to pose a greater problem for minorities, more of whom were salaried. But studies of minority elected officials in such jurisdictions have found that "except for race, they are virtually indistinguishable from the white majority with respect to economic and social status backgrounds."[25] However, there are still many mayoral positions that are not full-time in nature and thus more easily permit salaried individuals to run for them.

A majority of the white mayors have at least a college education and almost one-fourth of them have one or more advanced degrees. Approximately 1 in 14 white mayors have a law degree while one-fifth (20.7%) of the white mayors have only a high school diploma. As a group, Asian American mayors are the best educated, although only nine reported; all have at least a bachelors degree. Four of the Asian American mayors have a graduate degree.

Table 7 shows that the general level of education of black mayors exceeds that of whites. Two-thirds of the black mayors have college degrees; about 40% have done graduate work; and about one-third have a masters degree or more. A greater proportion of black than white mayors hold positions in larger cities, where being better educated may make a candidate more appealing and in a stronger position to deal with urban complexities.

Hispanic mayors report less education than whites and blacks. But they are more likely to govern in a council-manager jurisdiction where the position tends to be part-time in nature and they primarily preside over the council. About two-thirds of the Hispanic mayors have gone to college although only one-third have at least a bachelors degree. More than one-fourth have done some graduate work, with 21.6% having earned a masters or more.

Table 7
Education Level of Mayor, by Race/Ethnicity

	Race/ethnicity				
Highest education level achieved	*White (%)*	*Asian (%)*	*Black (%)*	*Hispanic (%)*	*Native American (%)*
No high school diploma	0.8	0.0	0.0	1.3	0.0
High school graduate	20.7	0.0	10.0	29.1	25.0
Some college	21.6*	0.0	20.0	35.4*	50.0
Bachelor's degree	26.9	44.4	25.0	7.6	12.5
Some master's work	4.1	11.1	6.3	3.8	0.0
Master's degree	12.6	22.2	17.5	13.9	6.3
Law degree	7.4	11.1	8.8	5.1	0.0
Ph.D.	1.4	0.0	6.3	1.3	0.0
Medical degree	1.5	11.1	2.5	1.3	0.0
Other	2.2	0.0	2.5	0.0	6.3

Note: Numbers responding were: white, 4,042; Asian, 9; black, 80; Hispanic, 79; Native American, 16.
*Includes post-high school technical.

Native American mayors are least likely to have a college degree or to have done graduate work. However, 75% of the 16 reporting have some college education—well in excess of the Native American population at-large.[26] They hold office in smaller cities of the Southwest with large concentrations of Native Americans.

Years in Office

In terms of length of service, a few mayors have been in office more than 40 years, with the longest serving respondent having been in office since 1947 (not shown). At the other extreme, there were, not surprisingly, a number of mayors elected in 1991. The average length of service is between five and six years. Of the three largest ethnic groups, whites have the longest average seniority (5.3 years). The averages for blacks and Hispanics (4.2 years) are almost identical.

There is virtually no variation in the length of service of incumbent mayors across city size, geographic division, or form of government. For all categories with at least ten cities, the average length of service is between four and six years.

Structure of the Mayoral Position

Data from the 1991 ICMA survey were examined to determine whether there are any racial/ethnic patterns relative to mayoral service on the council, the full-time or part-time nature of the position, method of mayoral selection, or other characteristics of the mayoral position.

Service on the Council. Most mayors serve as a member of the council. Almost three-fourths of the 85 Hispanic mayors, two-thirds of the 9 Asian mayors, 63% of the 100 black mayors, and 60% of the 4,491 white mayors serve on the council (not shown). The ethnic group whose mayors are least likely to serve on council are the Native Americans but even here a majority of the 15 reporting are council members.

In mayor-council jurisdictions, only about a third of the mayors serve as council members. In council-manager jurisdictions, by contrast, more than 80% of the chief executives also sit with the council. The variations across city size and geographic division in the frequency with which mayors serve on the council are probably linked to the incidence of mayor-council or council-manager arrangements within the area.

Full-Time or Part-Time Position. For the vast majority of jurisdictions the office of mayor is a part-time position. Just over 90% of the Hispanic mayors, 84.7% of the white mayors, and almost three-fourths of the black mayors serve part-time. Generally the smaller the jurisdiction, the more likely that the position of mayor will be part-time. Regardless of the ethnicity of the mayor, just over 10% of the jurisdictions with fewer than 10,000 people have full-time chief executives. Only in the cities with populations 250,000 and above is being mayor a full-time responsibility in half or more of the cases (not shown).

Method of Mayoral Selection. Overall, about 77% of mayors are elected directly by the voters (not shown). Among ethnic groups, this is true for 77.6% of white mayors and 71.3% of black mayors but for only 61.6% of Hispanic mayors (Table 3).

While a variety of other methods exist for choosing mayors, the only other method used with any frequency is selection from among the council membership. Minorities have been somewhat more likely to achieve their positions via this approach than have whites. A third of the Hispanics and Asians, one quarter of the Native Americans, and 25.7% of the black mayors were chosen from the council. In contrast, just over 20% of the white mayors were selected by other members of the council. There is, then, some indication that ethnic minorities, like women, are more likely to become the chief executive through the indirect approach of support from among council members, while whites are more likely to be elected directly by the public at-large.

The choice of the mayor by the council is most frequently found in council-manager jurisdictions and is rare in mayor-council jurisdictions.

Length of Term. Among jurisdictions responding to the survey, the term of mayor ranges from one to eight years, with four years being the most common (the mode). Almost 45% of the jurisdictions responding elect mayors for four years while in 37.3% of the jurisdictions the mayor's term is two years.

The minority group most likely to have mayors serving four-year terms are blacks, 52.5% of whom have these relatively long terms. For the other minority groups, the mode is two years. In part this is because many of the Hispanic, Native American, and Asian mayors come from the West South Central or Pacific Coast geographic divisions in which the most frequent tenure is two years. Black mayors come from a wider geographical range and a number of them are from areas in which mayors' terms are longer. Black mayors are also advantaged in term length vis-à-vis whites, only 44.7% of whom have four year terms.

As noted earlier, white mayors average longer tenure than do their black or Hispanic peers. One might infer that white mayors have been more successful in winning reelection than have black chief executives or that whites have a longer mean tenure because minorities have only relatively recently succeeded in winning mayorships.

Term Limits. There is no variation among ethnic groups in whether they serve in municipalities that limit the number of consecutive terms for a mayor. For every ethnic group, from 86% to 95% of the mayors can succeed themselves for as long as they win the favor of the public. For most categories of municipalities that do impose a limit, the median is two terms.

Mayoral Voting Power. The majority of mayors have the authority to vote on all issues, although almost 40% are limited to casting votes only when the council is tied (not shown). Hispanic mayors are most likely to have full voting privileges (see Table 8), while Native Americans are the only group in which substantially less than half of the mayors can vote on all issues.[27] (Native Americans are not reported in Table 8; 15 responded.)

Restricting the vote of the mayor most often occurs in mayor-council jurisdictions, in which most Native American mayors (9 of 15) and a substantial proportion of the white mayors (45.4%) serve. In contrast, only one-third of the Hispanic mayors and 37.6% of the black mayors serve in mayor-council jurisdictions. Thus it appears to be form of government rather than ethnicity of the chief executive that is likely to circumscribe the mayor's voting authority.

Mayoral Veto Power. For all ethnic groups and in most types of municipalities, the mayor lacks authority to veto council-passed legislation (not shown). Possession of the veto is most common for black (34.3%) and white (31.6%) mayors. Among other ethnic groups, no more than 27% of the mayors can exercise a veto; among Hispanic mayors, that figure is 15.1%. Again, the key to the ethnic differences that do exist is probably form of government, since a majority of the mayors in mayor-council municipalities have a veto while almost 90% of the mayors in other types of government lack this power. As previously noted, most Hispanic mayors serve in council-manager municipalities while a higher proportion of white mayors and of other groups serve in mayor-council municipalities.

Table 8
Mayoral Voting in Council, by Ethnicity

	Black				White				Hispanic			
	No. reporting (A)	All* % of (A)	Tie† % of (A)	No§ % of (A)	No. reporting (B)	All % of (B)	Tie % of (B)	No % of (B)	No. reporting (C)	All % of (C)	Tie % of (C)	No % of (C)
Classification												
Total, all cities	101	53.5	28.7	14.9	4,568	50.0	39.1	8.8	87	62.1	29.9	5.7
Population group												
Over 1,000,000	2	0.0	0.0	100.0	0	0.0	0.0	0.0	0	0.0	0.0	0.0
500,000–1,000,000	8	0.0	0.0	0.0	8	25.0	12.5	62.5	0	0.0	0.0	0.0
250,000–499,999	6	50.0	0.0	50.0	24	66.7	0.0	29.2	2	50.0	0.0	50.0
100,000–249,999	8	50.0	0.0	37.5	89	65.2	13.5	19.1	1	0.0	0.0	0.0
50,000–99,999	11	63.6	0.0	27.3	231	63.6	12.6	21.2	6	100.0	0.0	0.0
25,000–49,999	10	60.0	30.0	10.0	478	60.0	22.2	14.0	10	80.0	10.0	10.0
10,000–24,999	26	65.4	26.9	7.7	1,032	54.8	31.1	10.9	21	61.9	28.6	9.5
5,000–9,999	16	56.3	37.5	6.3	1,125	49.2	43.2	6.1	26	65.4	30.8	3.8
2,500–4,999	18	38.9	55.6	0.0	1,220	39.2	55.3	4.3	15	40.0	53.3	0.0
Under 2,500	4	25.0	75.0	0.0	361	48.8	43.5	6.4	6	50.0	50.0	0.0
Geographic division												
New England	4	25.0	25.0	50.0	412	69.7	10.4	18.7	0	0.0	0.0	0.0
Mid-Atlantic	13	46.2	15.4	30.8	672	46.6	44.5	6.4	5	80.0	0.0	20.0
East North Central	19	52.6	26.3	15.8	907	39.5	42.8	13.2	6	50.0	33.3	16.7

West North Central	6	33.3	66.7	0.0	547	40.2	43.3	15.2	1	100.0	0.0	0.0
South Atlantic	32	56.3	34.4	6.3	588	49.7	44.7	3.9	5	60.0	0.0	40.0
East South Central	7	42.9	42.9	14.3	271	46.5	42.8	8.5	1	100.0	0.0	0.0
West South Central	7	42.9	42.9	14.3	461	42.7	52.3	3.7	25	48.0	48.0	0.0
Mountain	2	50.0	0.0	50.0	239	49.4	46.4	3.8	18	33.3	61.1	5.6
Pacific Coast	11	90.9	0.0	9.1	471	79.0	18.9	1.5	26	92.3	3.8	0.0
Metro status												
Central	21	42.9	4.8	47.6	344	50.3	19.5	26.7	8	62.5	0.0	25.0
Suburban	51	60.8	25.5	9.8	2,436	55.4	35.3	7.2	51	70.6	23.5	5.9
Independent	29	48.3	51.7	0.0	1,788	42.5	48.2	7.6	28	46.4	50.0	0.0
Form of government												
Mayor-council	38	13.2	50.0	31.6	433	20.8	59.9	16.3	29	20.7	62.1	17.2
Council-manager	60	78.3	15.0	5.0	1,594	72.6	23.8	2.2	57	84.2	12.3	0.0
Commission	3	66.7	33.3	0.0	80	92.0	8.0	0.0	1	0.0	100.0	0.0
Town meeting	0	0.0	0.0	0.0	153	86.4	5.1	7.3	0	0.0	0.0	0.0
Rep. town meeting	0	0.0	0.0	0.0	23	82.1	10.7	7.1	0	0.0	0.0	0.0

Note: Row percentages may not total 100 because the "other" category is not reported in this table.
*Mayor can vote on all issues.
†Mayor votes only to break a tie.
§Mayor is never allowed to vote.

Gender of Council Members

Many jurisdictions now have at least one female council member (70% of those responding to the 1991 ICMA Survey). By 1991, approximately one-fifth of all council members were women.[28] In spite of tremendous gains in a relatively short period of time,[29] women are still underrepresented compared to their proportional representation in the electorate at-large. Thus, much attention has been placed on determining whether certain electoral system characteristics impede women from being elected to city councils across the United States.[30] Among the more commonly examined aspects are the method of electing council members (at-large, single-member district, mixed or combination);[31] the size of the council itself;[32] the term length;[33] and whether elections are partisan or nonpartisan,[34] staggered, or held simultaneously.[35] The question of whether women council candidates fare better in larger cities has also been raised.[36]

Population Size

Are women more successful in winning council posts in smaller or larger jurisdictions? Those who believe they win more often in smaller jurisdictions base their opinions on research suggesting that "women's representation is negatively related to the prestige of office" thereby making it easier for women to win office in smaller jurisdictions where such posts are less prestigious and competition less keen.[37] Others assert just the opposite—that women win more council seats in larger jurisdiction: "Larger communities tend to be more cosmopolitan and less traditional, thus perhaps more open to women officeholders. In larger towns, there are more likely to be groups such as the League of Women Voters, the National Women's Political Caucus, and the American Association of University Women that would give support to women candidates."[38] Yet another view is that size of jurisdiction makes little difference in the competitiveness (prestigiousness) of council seats.[39]

Among municipalities responding to the 1991 ICMA survey, women fill 18.7% of all council slots (Table 9). Women are more likely to serve in cities with populations of 25,000 or more. In all population categories of this magnitude, women hold at least 22% of the council seats, while the mean for the smaller jurisdictions is 19% or less. This pattern in Table 9 conforms with the hypothesis that small communities may have more traditional views of gender roles, which could make the election of female councilors more difficult.[40]

Geographic Patterns

In which regions of the country do we find the highest and lowest levels of representation of women on city councils? Several decades ago we would

Table 9
Proportion of Female Council Members

Classification	No. reporting	Average % female
Total, all cities	4,896	18.7
Population group		
Over 1,000,000	2	24.4
500,000–1,000,000	7	24.1
250,000–499,999	32	25.9
100,000–249,999	99	27.4
50,000–99,999	248	22.2
25,000–49,999	510	22.4
10,000–24,999	1,118	19.0
5,000–9,999	1,207	17.7
2,500–4,999	1,292	17.0
Under 2,500	381	16.3
Geographic division		
New England	501	19.4
Mid-Atlantic	706	17.3
East North Central	943	19.8
West North Central	555	16.7
South Atlantic	633	18.0
East South Central	280	12.7
West South Central	495	15.1
Mountain	261	21.2
Pacific Coast	522	26.2
Metro status		
Central	371	21.6
Suburban	2,627	20.5
Independent	1,898	15.6
Form of Government		
Mayor-council	2,174	17.4
Council-manager	2,346	20.2
Commission	94	10.3
Town meeting	245	18.4
Rep. town meeting	37	24.2

have expected the Deep South to have far lower levels than the rest of the nation because people in this region have more traditional views of the "proper role of women."[41] However, more recent studies have shown that, while female representation levels are lower in the South than the national average, the proportion of women represents a marked change from the past. According to one survey, females are the most evident on city councils in the West and appear the least in the Northeast.[42] (It is important to note that these studies focused on larger cities—those with populations over 25,000—and did not break the four regions down into their subparts.)

In the 1991 ICMA survey (more inclusive in terms of population size and more precise in terms of subregional analysis), the South and Midwest rank below the Northeast. Geographic divisions ranking below the national average (18.7% females on council) are: East South Central (12.7%); West South Central (15.1%); West North Central (16.7%); Mid-Atlantic (17.3%); and South Atlantic (18%). Women's council representation is highest in cities in the Mountain and Pacific Coast states—the very states that first extended to women the right to vote, with a number of them adopting that reform before the ratification of the Nineteenth Amendment. Several students of state political cultures have found that although the women's suffrage movement originated in the Northeast, its initial successes occurred in the West.[43] But it is evident that the regional gaps in female council representation are closing.

Form of Government

Are women better represented on councils in municipalities with mayor-council, council-manager, commission, or various kinds of town meeting governments? Little research exists to guide us on this point, other than indirect evidence linking population size and geographic division to various forms of government. Mayor-council governments are the dominant form for cities 500,000 and above. The highest proportions of mayor-council governments are located in the East South Central, East and West North Central, and Mid-Atlantic geographic divisions. Commission governments are more common in smaller jurisdictions (under 25,000) in the Mid-Atlantic, East South Central, and West North Central divisions. Town meeting and representative town meeting municipalities are most common in the New England states. Council-manager government is most prevalent among mid-sized cities (25,000 to 249,999) of the South and West. Typically, councils are largest on average in bigger cities with the mayor-council form of government (not shown). Councils are smallest in commission and town meeting governments.

Taking into account the relationships among form of government, jurisdiction size, council size, and geographic division, and the previous finding that women fare better in bigger jurisdictions with larger councils and in smaller jurisdictions in New England and the West, we would expect female council representation levels to be highest in large mayor-council governments and town meeting-type jurisdictions, followed (in order) by council-manager and commission jurisdictions.

The 1991 survey results confirm some of our expectations. Women council members are least frequently found in commission jurisdictions, where they make up just over 10% of all councilors. The combination of legislative and administrative responsibilities in the hands of commissioners may make council seats especially attractive in commission jurisdiction, and greater competition for commission seats could account for the lower proportion of females. The historically lower participation rates of women in the regions where commission forms are more common may also contribute to this phenomenon.

Women councilors are best represented in jurisdictions governed by representative town meeting, holding almost one quarter of the council seats. They fare second best in council-manager jurisdictions, where they constitute one in five councilors, followed by town meeting (18.4%), and mayor-council jurisdictions (17.4%). But if female representation on councils in mayor-council cities over 500,000 (23.7%) is separated from that in mayor-council cities under 500,000 (17.3%), the picture is quite distinct. Mayor-council governments in very large cities yield higher female representation levels.

Partisan and Nonpartisan Elections

Nearly three-fourths of all U.S. cities have nonpartisan elections.[44] Critics of nonpartisan elections argue that they decrease female council representation. They base their opinions on research that has identified a Republican, higher socioeconomic, white, male bias among candidates elected in nonpartisan races.[45] But proponents of nonpartisan elections argue that women are often advantaged in such settings for several reasons.[46] First, in nonpartisan settings, candidates must rely more on networks of friends, fellow workers, and associates than on a political party.[47] Women traditionally have been active in civic activities, especially in smaller communities. Second, even in nonpartisan settings, political partisanship is often evident in local elections.[48] Women tend to be active in local party organizations and are equally likely to be recruited to office by party leaders. These phenomena, then, would suggest that nonpartisan elections may actually help women council candidates or, at the very least, have no impact.

The 1991 ICMA survey shows that there is essentially no difference in the proportion of female councilors between jurisdictions that elect by party and those that are nonpartisan (Table 10). In nonpartisan jurisdictions, women hold 18.9% of the council seats compared with 18.1% in jurisdictions that elect by party. In New England, however, women are more likely to serve in partisan (23.6%) than in nonpartisan (17.7%) jurisdictions, especially those with town meetings.

Method of Council Election

A perennial question is whether women fare better when running for council in single-member districts, in pure at-large (multimember) formats, or in cities with other methods of electing council members (e.g., mixed systems where some are elected at-large and others from single-member districts; or at-large systems with residency requirements whereby a person must live

Table 10
Gender Composition of Council in
Partisan and Nonpartisan Cities

Election method	No. reporting	Composition of council (%)	
		Male	Female
Partisan	1,232	81.9	18.1
Nonpartisan	3,590	81.1	18.9

in a specific district but is voted upon citywide). This line of inquiry has also been followed by scholars studying the election of racial and ethnic minorities to city council. However, the findings have been quite different. For women, at-large electoral formats have generally been found to *promote* their election, albeit only weakly. In contrast, for racial/ethnic minorities the effect may be the opposite depending upon the size of the group, their geographic concentration, their political cohesiveness, and their ability to coalesce with other groups. (This will be discussed later.)

The first study to examine that impact of at-large elections on female city council representation argued that "voters would be more prone to support women, in multimember [at-large] than in single-member districts."[49] The authors' rationale was that in multimember districts, voters would be less likely to see the election in zero-sum terms and, consequently, would be more likely to vote for a woman, perhaps out of a sense of fairness. But neither they, nor those who replicated their study using a variety of data bases and time points, found a very strong linkage between electoral format and female council representation levels, even for black and Hispanic females.[50]

The 1991 ICMA survey results show a weak linkage between electoral format and the election of women to city council. Although female representation is slightly higher in municipalities with at-large formats, the percentage of women on council does not vary greatly depending upon the method of districting. Table 11 shows that in municipalities where all council members are nominated and elected at-large (a pure at-large system), women hold 19.7% of the seats; this is slightly higher than for other formats. Where council members are nominated and elected by district (a single-member district format), women are least prevalent, holding 16.3% of the seats. In municipalities that nominate by ward but elect at-large, women hold 17.4% of the seats—the same proportion as in municipalities that use other formats.

Table 11
Gender Composition of Council,
by Method of Election

Election method	No. reporting	Composition of council (%)	
		Male	Female
Nominated and elected at-large	2,527	80.3	19.7
Nominated by district, elected at-large	179	82.6	17.4
Nominated and elected by district	504	83.7	16.3
Other	156	82.7	17.4

Council Size

Are women council candidates more successful if they run for larger or smaller councils? Some argue that it is easier to win where there are more council seats because competition is less, leading to the conclusion that the office is less prestigious.[51] But there is little empirical evidence to support this "less desirable" premise, perhaps because larger councils are found in larger cities, where virtually no office is considered to be lacking in prestige if for no other reason than heavier media exposure. A more plausible explanation for greater female representation on larger councils relates to the fact that larger councils are found in bigger cities where women candidates benefit considerably from the more cosmopolitan nature of the electorate and the presence of more female political support groups.

The 1991 ICMA survey reveals a positive, although weak, relationship between the size of council and the proportion of females serving (Table 12). In the smallest councils, i.e. those with less than four members, women hold only 14.9% of the seats. In the modal category, councils with from four to six members, women hold 18.3% of the seats. Women occupy 19.6% of the seats in councils that have between seven and nine members. Females are most prevalent on councils that have more than nine members, holding 20.8% of these seats.

Length of Term

Are women more successful in winning seats on councils with shorter or longer terms of office? In general, the longer the term, the more desirable, prestigious, and competitive an elective office is presumed to be. Therefore, we would expect to see more women serving in council positions with shorter terms. However, few studies examining this relationship have found any significant linkage between the length of term and the proportion of women serving on a council.[52]

The 1991 ICMA survey data indicate that for women serving on councils

Table 12
Gender Composition of Council,
by Size of Council

Size of council	No. reporting	Composition of council (%)	
		Male	Female
Fewer than 4	243	85.1	14.9
4–6	2,781	81.7	18.3
7–9	1,685	80.4	19.6
More than 9	187	79.2	20.8

in jurisdictions in which the term is from one to four years (the overwhelming majority), the proportion of women on the council falls within a narrow range—from 16.7% to 20% (not shown). Only in 58 jurisdictions with *exceptionally* long council terms (five years or longer) are there considerably lower proportions of women on the council (11.1%).

Staggered and Simultaneous Terms

Is running for council in a community that staggers the election of its councilors better for women candidates than seeking election in a community that elects all its council members at the same time? Those who favor staggered terms argue that they make it easier for challengers (many of whom are women) to gain name recognition and to beat incumbents, especially in smaller jurisdictions. Conversely, advocates of simultaneous elections maintain that such an arrangement makes slating and group coalition building easier and also reduces campaign costs if group advertising is utilized. Research empirically examining the question has found that the term structure has little impact on female council representation levels.[53]

The results of the 1991 ICMA survey show that women are slightly better represented in municipalities with staggered council terms. As reported in Table 13, women hold 19.1% of the seats on councils whose terms are staggered (smaller municipalities) as compared with 16.9% of the seats on councils where terms for all members are simultaneous (larger municipalities).[54]

Policy Agendas and Governing Styles

Just as is the case with mayors, the policy agendas of men and women councilors are seen by many as remarkably similar. One study has observed that "the convergence between ... councilwomen and councilmen in defining priority issues in their communities is striking. Almost without exception, they identify the same concerns—taxes, development and the quality of life."[55] The

Table 13
Gender Composition of Council with
Staggered and Simultaneous Terms

Type of term	No. reporting	Composition of council (%)	
		Male	Female
Staggered	3,933	80.9	19.1
Simultaneous	920	83.1	16.9

same study found that male and female council members are very similar in their positions, tenure, and partisanship. But they differ on how "they perceive and respond to citizen concerns and complaints, how they gather and use information and how they feel about political maneuvering,"[56] although both men and women councilors view women as more responsive to constituents.[57]

Research suggests that women as a group appear to have less policy impact than racial/ethnic council members, perhaps because gender is not as powerful a priority or voting cue for councilors as race/ethnicity. However, there is evidence that for certain issues such as day care, domestic violence, and sexual assault, councilwomen have successfully initiated policy proposals and, in the process, raised the sensitivity level of their male colleagues.[58]

Race/Ethnicity of Council Members

The relative scarcity of blacks, Hispanics, Asians, and Native Americans in elective city council posts has captured the attention of many scholars, civil rights advocacy groups, and the courts, particularly following passage of the federal Voting Rights Act in 1965 with its subsequent amendments (1975, 1982).[59] The major thrust of the inquiry has been to determine the extent to which various electoral structures inhibit the election of minorities.

The greatest attention has been focused on various types of at-large election formats,[60] but there have also been examinations of the effect of nonpartisan elections,[61] small councils,[62] staggered council terms,[63] and majority vote requirements[64] on minority council representation. Conclusions as to the effects of each have varied, depending on the group of jurisdictions analyzed, the time frame of the data analysis, the methodology employed, and the specific racial/ethnic minority group (and gender within each group[65]) being studied. Within a community, the size of a minority group and its geographical concentration, political cohesiveness, coalitional capacities, and resources also have been found to affect the relationship between various structures and minority council representation.

As is the case for mayors, the 1991 ICMA survey shows that the vast majority of council members are white. Blacks are the second largest group but they fail to account for even 5% of all council members. The third largest group, Hispanics, constitute about 2% of the council members with barely a trace of Native Americans and Asians on the councils (Table 14).

Geographic Patterns

As should be expected, and as Table 14 shows, there are geographic patterns to the presence of minority groups, with blacks being most numerous on councils in the South Atlantic, East South Central, and West South Central states (the traditional South). Hispanics are found on councils almost exclusively in the West South Central, Mountain, and Pacific Coast states. While far less numerous than Hispanics, Native American council members tend to be concentrated in the same three divisions. Asians are most frequently found along the Pacific Coast, but even here hold a tiny share of the seats. In each instance, electoral success tracks closely with a group's regional population concentration patterns.

Population Size

The larger the city, the more diversity we would expect on the council, paralleling greater racial/ethnic diversity in the population at large. The 1991 survey results support this hypothesis, While whites hold a majority of the council seats in all categories of municipalities, they are least dominant in the very largest cities (which also have the largest councils, as noted earlier). Whites hold just 52.2% of the seats in the two cities over 1 million population in this sample and have just under two-thirds of the seats in the seven cities with populations from 500,000 to 1 million. In contrast, whites hold more than 90% of the seats in municipalities with populations below 50,000.

Form of Government

The strong relationships among geographic division, population size, council size, and form of government noted earlier, in combination with regional concentrations of different racial/ethnic groups, explain the representational patterns observable in jurisdictions with different forms of government. Black council representation is highest in central cities with mayor-council governments (and larger councils) and in cities in the Deep South with large black populations. Hispanic representation is greatest in larger central cities with council-manager governments located in the Southwest and Far West. Asian representation is highest among larger council-manager central cities of the Pacific Coast division. Native Americans are best represented

Table 14
Racial Composition of Councils

	No. reporting	White (%)	Black (%)	Hispanic (%)	Asian (%)	Native American (%)
Total, all cities	4,719	92.5	4.8	2.3	0.2	0.3
Population group						
Over 1,000,000	2	52.2	37.8	6.7	3.3	0.0
500,000–1,000,000	7	63.4	11.6	14.2	10.8	0.0
250,000–499,999	31	72.7	16.7	9.8	0.8	0.0
100,000–249,999	97	80.6	13.3	5.0	0.6	0.5
50,000–99,999	243	89.3	7.4	3.0	0.4	0.0
25,000–49,999	488	90.9	5.9	2.8	0.3	0.2
10,000–24,999	1,071	92.1	5.3	2.3	0.2	0.1
5,000–9,999	1,174	92.8	4.2	2.5	0.2	0.3
2,500–4,999	1,234	94.6	3.5	1.3	0.1	0.5
Under 2,500	372	95.0	2.9	1.6	0.1	0.4
Geographic division						
New England	473	98.8	0.9	0.2	0.1	0.0
Mid-Atlantic	676	95.8	3.4	0.6	0.1	0.2
East North Central	903	96.5	2.8	0.4	0.1	0.2
West North Central	543	98.1	1.4	0.3	0.1	0.1
South Atlantic	614	85.7	13.4	0.8	0.1	0.2
East South Central	268	87.8	11.8	0.4	0.0	0.0
West South Central	481	82.6	8.2	8.2	0.1	1.0
Mountain	257	90.2	1.2	8.1	0.5	0.1
Pacific Coast	504	90.1	1.9	6.1	1.1	0.9
Metro status						
Central	361	82.9	12.6	3.8	0.6	0.1
Suburban	2,530	94.1	3.3	2.3	0.2	0.2
Independent	1,828	92.1	5.4	1.9	0.1	0.5
Form of government						
Mayor-council	2,099	92.8	5.2	1.5	0.2	0.3
Council-manager	2,267	91.4	4.9	3.2	0.3	0.3
Commission	88	91.9	4.6	2.4	0.0	1.1
Town meeting	229	99.7	0.2	0.1	0.0	0.0
Rep. town meeting	36	98.9	0.6	0.6	0.0	0.0

in very small communities (villages) with commission governments located in the West South Central and Pacific Coast regions.

Partisan and Nonpartisan Elections

The expected impacts of partisan and nonpartisan elections, as well as other election procedures, on racial/ethnic city council representation are very similar to those noted in the discussion of female council representation. (In the literature, studies of racial/ethnic minority representation actually served as a guide to those examining female council representation rather than vice versa.)

Proponents of partisan council elections cite research showing a socioeconomic bias in the types of individuals elected from nonpartisan formats as justification for their position. In contrast, proponents of nonpartisan elections note that local party organizations may not necessarily provide minority candidates access to party nominations and support, in which case minority candidates "might find it easier to run for office and be elected in nonpartisan systems, despite their socioeconomic disadvantage."[66] Few studies have found strong evidence that nonpartisan elections disadvantage minority council candidates.[67] Nor does the 1991 ICMA survey.

As Table 15 shows, there is little variation in the racial composition on partisan and nonpartisan councils. The percentages of whites, Asians, and Native Americans on councils are nearly identical in partisan and nonpartisan settings. The largest difference is for Hispanics, who appear to benefit somewhat from nonpartisan electoral formats. This is not unexpected in light of the fact that Hispanics fare better under council-manager governments in the West, where nonpartisan formats are used extensively.

Method of Council Election. Much of the literature on minority city council representation has examined whether at-large elections, more than single-member-district or mixed (some at-large seats, some district-based seats) elections, disadvantage minority candidates. There has also been considerable inquiry into whether similar formats affect all racial/ethnic minority groups in the same manner.

Critics of at-large elections maintain that since minority candidates run most strongly among minority voters they are disadvantaged in citywide contests where the electorate is predominantly white. Also, the greater expense of campaigning throughout a jurisdiction is alleged to handicap minority candidates if their supporters are less affluent.[68] For these reasons, the critics believe that minority candidates have a better chance of election from single-member districts or combination systems (in jurisdictions where a minority group is more residentially dispersed).[69]

Supporters of at-large elections point to a wide range of studies showing that at-large elections have significant negative impacts on minority council candidates only when the minority population is large, geographically concentrated, and politically cohesive and the majority (white) population consistently votes as a bloc to defeat minority candidates. This view has been endorsed by the federal courts.

There is also considerable evidence that the size of the minority electorate within a community is the *best* predictor of the group's proportional representation on city council, far more powerful than the electoral format. Furthermore, research has shown that at-large elections differentially affect blacks,

Table 15
Racial/Ethnic Composition of
Council in Partisan and Nonpartisan Cities

Election method	No. reporting	Composition of council (%)				
		White	Black	Hispanic	Asian	Native American
Partisan	1,179	94.0	4.8	0.9	0.1	0.1
Nonpartisan	3,471	92.0	4.7	2.7	0.2	0.4

Hispanics, and Asians seeking council office primarily as a consequence of group differences in residential patterns, resources (political and economic), citizenship rates, and ability to coalesce with white or other racial/ethnic group voters. Historically, blacks have been more negatively affected by at-large elections than Hispanics[70] or Asians.[71] However, as black populations have grown, especially in large central cities, as black political participation rates (registration and turnout) have equaled or exceeded those of whites, and as successful black candidates have paved the way for others, the independent effect of electoral structure on black council representation levels has waned in certain parts of the country.[72] (There have been few studies of Native American council representation.)

The results of the 1991 ICMA survey confirm this trend. As reflected in Table 16, the proportional representation of each racial/ethnic group varies little across different electoral formats, although the historical patterns are still somewhat observable. Whites are most prevalent on councils that are nominated and elected at-large, where they hold 94.1% of the seats. Whites hold the smallest share of the seats (90.6%) in municipalities that do not nominate and elect all seats at-large or from single-member districts or nominate by district and elect at-large.

Table 16 further shows that blacks are somewhat more heavily represented on councils in which at least part of the selection process occurs at the district level. They make up 6.9% of the council members in cities elected from single-member district formats and 6.3% in cities where candidates run from a district but are elected citywide (an at-large with residency requirements system). Blacks are least frequent on councils nominated and elected at-large, where they hold only 3% of the seats.

Hispanics, as anticipated, fare best in jurisdictions with "other" (usually combination) electoral formats or at-large elections, where they hold 3.0% and 2.4% of the positions respectively. Hispanics occupy the smallest shares of seats in jurisdictions using single-member districts (1.4%) or at-large residency formats (1%).

The method of electing council members does not appear to have an

Table 16
Racial/Ethnic Composition of Council,
by Method of Election

Election method	No. reporting	Composition of council (%)				
		White	Black	Hispanic	Asian	Native American
Nominated and elected at-large	2,465	94.1	3.0	2.4	0.2	0.3
Nominated by district, elected at-large	174	92.3	6.3	1.0	0.0	0.4
Nominated and elected by district	490	91.3	6.9	1.4	0.2	0.2
Other	152	90.6	4.5	3.0	0.0	1.9

impact on Asian council candidates, consistent with the findings of other researchers. Native Americans are more prevalent on councils in jurisdictions without either pure at-large or pure single-member district systems.

Roles and Impacts

There is some evidence that minority council members perceive their roles a bit differently than their white counterparts. One study has found that "black city council members spend more time ... servicing their districts, hold more meetings with their constituents, ... and target different parts of their constituents as important."[73] The presence of racial/ethnic minorities on council also has been shown to have an impact on public policy decisions, most notably municipal hiring decisions.[74] However, the ability of minority council members to "deliver tangible, material rewards to their constituents" may be limited if "they are not part of the dominant political coalition" governing a jurisdiction.[75] A study has found that coalition building is "much more difficult in segregated than in nonsegregated communities.... In segregated cities blacks will have little opportunity to join the dominant coalition in either ward or at-large communities."[76]

Council Size

The argument is often made that the larger the council, the greater the number of minority members who will be elected. Large councils in jurisdictions with district-based electoral formats are thought to promote minority council representation. In such settings, it is presumed that it will be easier to create more minority districts (where minority populations are geographically concentrated), fewer districts where minority candidates have to face nonminority candidates, and smaller districts (to reduce the costs of campaigns, the need for civic group and media endorsements, and community-wide name recognition). In at-large settings, larger councils are also presumed to promote more minority candidate successes for two reasons. First, it is assumed that the more seats up for election, the more white voters will be likely to support a minority candidate out of a sense of fairness. Second, "single-shot" voting by minority groups may be more effective when more seats are up for consideration.[77]

Previous research has found a weak, although slightly positive, independent relationship between council size and black representation. There is little evidence that council size affects Hispanic or Asian council representation, although larger councils may "provide a greater chance for Asian recruitment."[78]

The results of the 1991 survey generally confirm these patterns. Table 17 shows that the proportion of white council members decreases slightly with council size. Among minorities, the pattern of greater representation on larger councils is sharpest for blacks.

Staggered and Simultaneous Terms

The earlier discussion of female city council representation identified the pros and cons of staggered terms from the perspective of minorities. Generally, staggered terms are thought to make it easier for nonincumbents to gain name recognition and beat incumbents, especially in smaller jurisdictions. On the other hand, they have the potential to make slating and group coalition building more difficult and to increase campaign costs if group advertising cannot be utilized as efficiently. Previous research on this issue has produced some support, although weak, for simultaneous (rather than staggered) terms for Hispanics running for office but only in cities with very large Hispanic populations.[79] Simultaneous terms have been found not to help blacks, except in the South.[80] (There have been no studies of the impact of this structure on Asians and Native Americans.)

Somewhat different linkages between term structure and black and Hispanic council representation are evident in the results of the 1991 ICMA survey. As shown in Table 18, black representation is higher (9.5%) in cities with simultaneous council elections, mostly in the South,[81] than where elections are staggered (3.7%). Hispanic representation is slightly higher in cities with staggered council elections because staggered terms are more commonly associated with council-manager governments[82] and cities in the West[83] (where more Hispanics serve on council).

Table 17
Racial/Ethnic Composition of Council,
by Size of Council

Size of council	No. reporting	White	Black	Hispanic	Asian	Native American
Less than 4	232	97.8	1.2	0.9	0.1	0.0
4–6	2,699	91.8	4.8	2.8	0.3	0.4
7–9	1,638	92.3	5.5	1.8	0.2	0.3
More than 9	180	90.5	7.9	1.2	0.3	0.1

(Composition of council (%))

Table 18
Racial/Ethnic Composition of Council
with Staggered and Simultaneous Terms

Election method	No. reporting	White	Black	Hispanic	Asian	Native American
Staggered	3,806	93.3	3.7	2.5	0.2	0.3
Simultaneous	876	88.9	9.5	1.2	0.1	0.2

(Composition of council (%))

Length of Term

Shorter council terms are thought by some to promote higher levels of minority representation for two reasons. First, it is alleged that shorter terms promote turnover, thereby increasing the number of open seats and weakening the white incumbency factor. Second, election costs are presumed to be lower the shorter the term. Others argue that longer terms are better at promoting minority council representation because they attract stronger minority candidates with more resources to run, i.e., better educated, more affluent individuals who are willing to risk campaigning for office if they do not have to run for reelection every other year. To date, no study has found that the length of term is significantly related to minority council representation levels. The results of the 1991 ICMA survey also do not reveal any such relationship.

Inspection of the proportion of different ethnic groups on city council after controlling for length of term does not reveal a consistent relationship between term length and racial makeup. Only in those few jurisdictions in which the term is five years or longer is there any indication that minorities may be less represented.

Conclusion

This chapter has examined the jurisdictional settings in which women and minority candidates for mayor and city council have been most successful. Patterns of representation have been discussed in the context of a very large body of literature covering several decades, much of which has focused on the impact of various governmental and electoral structural arrangements on female and minority representation.[84] We have presented information showing that as women and minorities have ventured into municipal electoral politics as candidates, they have, for the most part, been as successful as white males. Governmental and electoral structures seldom have an independent *unconditional* negative impact on representational levels. Minority electoral successes appear to be less a consequence of election system structure than of the size of a minority group and its demographic, socioeconomic, and political attributes relative to other groups within the same community. However, the major barrier to increasing female and minority representation in U.S. municipalities still seems to be that of getting women and minorities to run for office.

Notes

1. See Timothy Bledsoe and Mary Herring, "Victims of Circumstances: Women in Pursuit of Political Office." *American Political Science Review* 84 (1990): 213–23; William E. Nelson, Jr. and Phillip J. Meranto, *Electing Black Mayors* (Columbus, Oh.; Ohio State University Press, 1977); Rodney E. Hero, *Latinos and the U.S. Political System* (Philadelphia; Temple University Press, 1992); Sucheng Chan, *Asian Americans: An Interpretive History* (Boston; Twayne, 1991); and Sharon O'Brien, *American Indian Tribal Governments* (Norman; University of Oklahoma Press, 1989).

2. Center for the American Woman and Politics, "Women in Elective Office 1992: Fact Sheet." National Information Bank on Women in Public Office, Eagleton Institute of Politics, Rutgers University, 1992; 2. Data obtained from the National League of Cities.

3. In order of population, the cities were: San Diego, CA; San Jose, CA; Washington, DC; Fort Worth, TX; Virginia Beach, VA; Pittsburgh, PA; Sacramento, CA; Fresno, CA; Mesa, AZ; Tampa, FL; Las Vegas, NV; Corpus Christi, TX; Riverside, CA; Stockton, CA; Shreveport, LA; Glendale, CA; Spokane, WA; Tacoma, WA; and Little Rock, AR. Ibid.

4. See, for example, Charles S. Bullock III and Susan A. MacManus, "Voting Patterns in a Tri-Ethnic Community: Conflict or Cohesion? The Case of Austin, Texas 1975–1985," *National Civic Review* 79 (January–February 1990): 23–36.

5. Susan Carroll and Wendy Strimling, *Women's Routes to Elective Office* (New Brunswick, NJ.: Rutgers University, Center for the American Woman and Politics, 1983).

6. See Susan A. MacManus, "How to Get More Women in Office: The Perspectives of Local Elected Officials (Mayors and City Councilors)," *Urban Affairs Quarterly* 28 (September 1992): 159–70.

7. Ibid.: also see Susan A. MacManus, "A City's First Female Office Holder: 'Coattails' for Future Office Seekers?" *Western Political Quarterly* 34 (1981): 88–99.

8. MacManus, "How to Get More Women in Office."

9. Ibid.

10. Sue Tolleson Rinehart, "Do Women Leaders Make a Difference? Substance, Style, and Perceptions," in Debra L. Dodson, ed., *Gender and Policy Making: Studies of Women in Office* (Center for the American Woman and Politics, Eagleton Institute of Politics, Rutgers University, 1991), 93–102.

11. Ibid., 96.

12. Cf. David B. Hill, "Political Culture and Female Representation," *Journal of Politics* 43 (1981): 151–68; Joan S. Carver, "Women in Florida," *Journal of Politics* 41 (1979): 911–55; Eleanor C. Main, Gerald S. Gryski, and Beth Schapiro, "Different Perspectives: Southern State Legislators' Attitudes Among Women in Politics," *Social Science Journal* 21 (1984): 21–8; and Susan A. MacManus and Charles S. Bullock III, "Women on Southern City Councils: A Decade of Change," *Journal of Political Science* 17 (Spring 1989): 32–49.

13. Jeannette Jennings, "Black Women Mayors: Reflections on Race and Gender," in Dodson, ed., *Gender and Policy Making.* 73–9.

14. Ibid., 77.

15 Susan J. Carroll, *Women as Candidates in American Politics* (Bloomington: Indiana University Press, 1985), 66.

16. Ibid.

17. Charles R. Adrian, "Forms of City Government in American History," in International City Management Association, *The Municipal Yearbook 1988* (Washington, D.C.: ICMA. 1988), 10.

18. Ibid.

19. See Susan A. MacManus, "It's Never Too Late To Run—and Win! The Graying of Women in Local Politics," *National Civic Review* 80 (Summer 1991): 294–311.

20. See Robert B. Albritton, George Amadee, Keenana Grenell, and Don-Terry Veal, "A New Look at the New Black Politics," paper presented at the 1992 annual meeting of the American Political Science Association; David L. Lublin, and Katherine Tate, "Black Office Seeking and Voter Turnout in Mayoral Elections," paper presenting at the 1992 annual meeting of the American Political Science Association; Nelson and Meranto, *Electing Black Mayors*; Paul Kleppner, *Chicago Divided: The Making of a Black Mayor* (DeKalb, IL.: Northern Illinois University Press, 1985); Lawrence Bobo and Franklin D. Gilliam, Jr., "Race, Sociopolitical Participation, and Black Empowerment," *American Political Science Review* 84 (June 1990): 377–93; Albert K. Karnig and Susan Welch, *Black Representation and Urban Policy* (Chicago: University Chicago Press, 1980); Harvey Marshall and Debra Meyer, "Assimilation and the Election of Minority Candidates: The Case of Black Mayors," *Sociology and Social Science Research* 60 (October 1975): 1–21; Georgia A. Persons, "Racial Politics and Black Power in the Cities," in George C. Galster and Edward W. Hill, eds., *The Metropolis in Black & White* (New Brunswick, NJ: Center for Urban Research, Rutgers, 1992): 166–89; Michael B. Preston, ed., "Symposium: Big City Black Mayors: Have They Made a Difference?" in Lucius L. Barker, ed., *Black Electoral Politics, The National Political Science Review* 2 (New Brunswick, NJ; Transaction, 1990).

21. See Albritton et al., "A New Look at the New Black Politics"; Lublin and Tate, "Black Office Seeking"; Rufus P. Browning, Dale Rodgers Marshall, and David H. Tabb, *Protest is Not Enough* (Berkeley; University of California Press, 1984);

Rufus P. Browning, Dale Rodgers Marshall, and David H. Tabb, eds., *Racial Politics in American Cities* (New York: Longman, 1990); Huey L. Perry, "The Evolution and Impact of Bi-racial Coalitions and Black Mayors in Birmingham and New Orleans," in Browning, Marshall, and Tabb, eds., *Racial Politics,* 140–52: Richard A. Keiser, "The Rise of a Bi-racial Coalition in Philadelphia," in Browning, Marshall, and Tabb, eds., *Racial Politics,* 49–72; Robert L. Starks and Michael B. Preston, "Harold Washington and the Politics of Reform in Chicago: 1983–1987," in Browning, Marshall, and Tabb, eds., *Racial Politics,* 88–107; Clarence N. Stone, "Race and Regime in Atlanta," in Browning, Marshall, and Tabb, eds., *Racial Politics*, 125–39; Raphael J. Sonenshein, "Bi-racial Coalition Politics in Los Angeles," in Browning, Marshall, and Tabb, eds., *Racial Politics,* 33–48; Carlos Munoz, Jr. and Charles P. Henry, "Coalition Politics in San Antonio and Denver: The Cisneros and Pena Mayoral Campaigns," in Browning, Marshall, and Tabb, eds., *Racial Politics,* 179–90; Rodney E. Hero, "The Election of Hispanics in City Government: An Examination of Election of Federico Pena as Mayor of Denver," *Western Political Quarterly* 40 (March 1987): 93–105; Rodney B. Hero, "The Election of Federico Pena as Mayor of Denver: Analysis and Implications," *Social Science Quarterly* 70 (June 1989): 93–106; and Charles S. Bullock III and Susan MacManus, "Voting Patterns in a Tri-Ethnic Community," 5–22.

22. See Browning, Marshall, and Tabb, *Protest is Not Enough.* Also see Raphael J. Sonenshein, "Bi-racial Coalitions in Big Cities: Why They Succeed, Why They Fail," in Browning, Marshall, and Tabb, eds., *Racial Politics,* 193–211; Christopher L. Warren, John G. Corbett, and John F. Stack, Jr., "Hispanic Ascendancy and Tripartite Politics in Miami," in Browning, Marshall, and Tabb, eds., *Racial Politics,* 155–78; John Mollenkopf, "New York: The Great Anomaly," in Browning, Marshall, and Tabb, eds., *Racial Politics,* 75–87; Charles P. Henry, "Black-Chicano Coalitions: Possibilities and Problems," *Western Journal of Black Studies* 4 (Winter 1980): 222–32; Charles Henry and Carlos Munoz, Jr., "Ideological and Interests Linkages in California Rainbow Politics," in Bryan O. Jackson and Michael B. Preston, eds., *Racial and Ethnic Politics in California* (Berkeley: Institute of Governmental Studies Press, University of California at Berkeley, 1991), 323–38; and Carole J. Uhlaner, "Perceived Discrimination and Prejudice and the Coalition Prospects of Blacks, Latinos, and Asian Americans," in Jackson and Preston, eds., *Racial and Ethnic Politics*, 339–71.

23. Albritton et al., "A New Look at the New Black Politics," 6.

24. See Karnig and Welch, *Black Representation and Urban Policy,* 54.

25. Albritton et al., "A New Look at the New Black Politics," 12.

26. John W. Tippeconnie III, "American Indians: Education, Demographics, and the 1990s," in Gale E. Thomas, *U.S. Race Relations in the 1980s and 1990s: Challenges and Alternatives* (New York: Hemisphere, 1990), 249–57.

27. Of 4,758 white mayors, 2,286 can vote on all issues. This is under half (49.978%) so that to be absolutely precise, fewer than half of the Anglo mayors have an unrestricted vote.

28. "Women in Elective Office 1992: Fact Sheet," 1992. This figure is consistent with that observed among respondents to the 1991 ICMA survey.

29. The percentage of women holding municipal and township offices (including mayoral positions) more than tripled from 1975 to 1985 alone, increasing from 4% to 14.3%. Ibid.

30. For excellent summaries of these studies, see: Charles S. Bullock III and Susan MacManus, "Municipal Electoral Structure and the Election of Council-

women," *Journal of Politics* 53 (February 1991): 75–89; Robert Darcy, Susan Welch, and Janet Clark, *Women, Elections, and Representation* (New York: Longman, 1987); Wilma Rule and Joseph F. Zimmerman, eds., *United States Electoral Systems: Their Impact Woman and Minorities* (New York: Greenwood Press, 1992); and Lois L. Duke, ed., *Women and Politics: Have the Outsiders Become Insiders?* (Englewood Cliffs, NJ: Prentice-Hall, 1993).

31. Bullock and MacManus, "Municipals Electoral Structure and the Election of Councilwomen"; Susan A. MacManus, and Charles S. Bullock III, "Women of Southern City Councils: A Decade of Change," *Journal of Political Science* 17 (1989): 32–49; Susan A. MacManus and Charles S. Bullock III, "Minorities and Women *Do* Win At-Large!" *National Civic Review* 77 (May–June 1988): 231–44; Susan Welch and Rebekah Herrick, "The Impact of At-Large Elections on the Representation of Minority Women," in Rule and Zimmerman, eds., *United States Electoral Systems,* 153–66; Susan A. MacManus and Charles S. Bullock III, "Electing Women to City Council: A Focus on Small Cities in Florida," in Rule and Zimmerman, eds., *United States Electoral Systems,* 167–81; Susan Welch and Albert Karnig, "Correlates of Female Office-Holding in City Politics," *Journal of Politics* 41 (May 1979): 478–91; Albert K. Karnig and Susan Welch, "Sex and Ethnic Differences in Municipal Representation," *Social Science Quarterly* 60 (December 1979): 465–81; and Albert Karnig and B. Oliver Walter, "Election of Women to City Councils," *Social Science Quarterly* 56 (March 1976): 605–13.

32. Bullock and MacManus, "Municipal Electoral Structure and the Election of Councilwomen"; Welch and Karnig, "Correlates of Female Office-Holding"; and MacManus and Bullock, "Women on Southern City Councils."

33. Welch and Karnig, "Correlates of Female Office-Holding"; MacManus and Bullock, "Women on Southern City Councils"; Bullock and MacManus, "Municipal Electoral Structure and the Election of Councilwomen"; MacManus and Bullock, "Electing Women to City Council"; and MacManus, "How to Get More Women in Office."

34. Karnig and Walter, "Election of Women to City Councils"; Welch and Karnig, "Correlates of Female Office-Holding"; Darcy, Welch, and Clark, *Women, Elections, and Representation*; MacManus and Bullock, "Electing Women to City Council"; and MacManus, "How to Get More Women in Office."

35. MacManus and Bullock, "Women on Southern City Councils"; Bullock and MacManus, "Municipal Electoral Structure and the Election of Councilwomen"; MacManus and Bullock, "Electing Women to City Council"; and MacManus, "How to Get More Women in Office."

36. Karnig and Walter, "Election of Women to City Councils"; MacManus and Bullock, "Minorities and Women *Do* Win At-Large" ; Darcy, Welch and Clark, *Women, Elections, and Representation*; Welch and Karnig, "Correlates of Female Office-Holding"; Bullock and MacManus, "Municipal Electoral Structure"; and MacManus and Bullock, "Electing Women to City Council."

37. Karnig and Walter, 609.

38. Darcy, Welch, and Clark, 40.

39. MacManus and Bullock, "Electing Women to City Council." But it is important to note that this study was limited to a single state (Florida).

40. This finding confirms earlier findings reported by Karnig and Walter, "Election of Women," Welch and Karnig, "Correlates of Female Office-Holding," and Bullock and MacManus, "Municipal Electoral Structure" using national data sets.

41. Carver, "Women in Florida."

42. Bullock and MacManus, "Municipal Electoral Structure." However, this study was limited to cities over 25,000 population.

43. Hill, "Political Culture and Female Representation"; and Alan Grimes, *The Puritan Ethnic and Women Suffrage* (New York: Oxford University Press, 1967).

44. Charles R. Adrian, "Forms of City Government in American History."

45. Carol A. Cassel, "Social Background Characteristics of Nonpartisan City Council Members: A Research Note," *Western Political Quarterly* (September 1985): 495–501; and Susan Welch and Timothy Bledsoe, *Urban Reform and its Consequences* (Chicago: University of Chicago Press, 1988).

46. Welch and Karnig, "Correlates of Female Office-Holding."

47. Darcy, Welch, and Clark, *Women, Representation and Elections,* 32.

48. Cassel, "Social Background Characteristics"; Welch and Bledsoe, *Urban Reform*; and Bledsoe and Herring, "Victims of Circumstances."

49. Karnig and Walter, 610.

50. See for example, Welch and Karnig, "Correlates of Female Office-Holding"; Bullock and MacManus, "Municipal Electoral Structure"; Susan Welch and Donley Studlar, "Multimember Districts and the Representation of Women: Evidence from Britain and the United States," *Journal of Politics* 52 (May 1990): 391–412; Karnig and Welch, "Sex and Ethnic Differences in Municipal Representation"; and Welch and Herrick, "The Impact of At-Large Elections on the Representation of Minority Women."

51. This argument is articulated in Welch and Karnig, "Correlates of Female Office-Holding."

52. Welch and Karnig, "Correlates of Female Office-Holding"; MacManus and Bullock, "Women on Southern City Councils"; and Bullock and MacManus, "Municipal Electoral Structure."

53. Bullock and MacManus, "Municipal Electoral Structure"; and MacManus and Bullock, "Women on Southern City Councils."

54. More than half of the cities with populations over 500,000 have simultaneous council terms. The overwhelming majority of cities with populations below 250,000 have staggered terms.

55. Susan Abrams Beck, "Rethinking Municipal Governance: Gender Distinctions on Local Councils," in Dodson, ed., *Gender and Policy Making,* 105.

56. Ibid., 103. The study found that "women dislike the back stabbing and dirty politics; men complain about irate constituents. Men often express frustration that women ask too many questions, while women see themselves as well-prepared and think their male colleagues are often 'winging it.' Most of the women claim to have experienced discrimination of some kind, and most seem to have altered their behavior in some ways in response to perceived differences with their male colleagues."

57. This phenomenon was also found in Sue Thomas, "The Effects of Race and Gender on Constituency Service," *Western Political Quarterly* 45 (March 1992): 169–80.

58. See Janet K. Boles, "Advancing the Women's Agenda Within Local Legislatures: The Role of Female Elected Officials," in Dodson, ed., *Gender and Policy Making,* 39–48.

59. Various interpretations of the impact of the Voting Rights Act on minority political participation and representation can be found in: Lorn Foster, ed., *The Voting Rights Act: Consequences and Implications* (New York: Praeger, 1985); Abigail M. Thernstrom, *Whose Votes Count? Affirmative Action and Minority Voting Rights* (Cambridge, MA: Harvard University Press, 1987); Chandler Davidson, ed.,

Minority Vote Dilution (Washington, D.C.: Joint Center for Political Studies, Howard University Press, 1984); and Bernard Grofman and Chandler Davidson, eds., *Controversies in Minority Voting: The Voting Rights Act in Perspective* (Washington, D.C.: The Brooking Institution, 1992).

60. Among the most widely cited are: Charles S. Bullock III and Susan A. MacManus, "Testing Assumptions of the Totality-of-the-Circumstances Test: An Analysis of the Impact of Structures on Black Descriptive Representation," *American Political Quarterly* (1993); Charles S. Bullock III and Susan A. MacManus, "Structural Features of Municipalities and the Incidence of Hispanic Councilmembers," *Social Science Quarterly* 71 (December 1990): 665–81; Susan Welch, "The Impact of At-Large Elections on the Representation of Blacks and Hispanics," *Journal of Politics* 52 (November 1990): 1050–76; Tari Renner, "Municipal Election Processes: The Impact on Minority Representation," in *The Municipal Yearbook 1988* (Washington, D.C.: International City Management Association), 13–22; Nicholas O. Alozie, "The Election of Asians to City Councils," *Social Science Quarterly* 73 (March 1992): 90–100; Kenneth R. Mladenka, "Blacks and Hispanics in Urban Politics," *American Political Science Review* 83 (March 1989): 165–91; Jerry L. Polinard, Robert D. Wrinkle, and Thomas Longoria, Jr., "The Impact of District Elections on the Mexican American Community: The Electoral Perspective," *Social Science Quarterly* 72 (September 1991): 608–14; Albert Karnig and Susan Welch, "Electoral Structure and Black Representation on City Councils," *Social Science Quarterly* 63 (March 1982): 99–114; Susan A. MacManus, "City Council Election Procedures and Minority Representation: Are They Related?" *Social Science Quarterly* 59 (June 1978): 133–41; Theodore Robinson and Thomas R. Dye, "Reformism and Black Representation on City Councils," *Social Science Quarterly* 59 (June 1978): 133–41; Delbert Taebel, "Minority Representation on City Councils," *Social Science Quarterly* 59 (June 1978): 142–52;Chandler Davidson and George Korbel, "At-Large Election and Minority Group Representation: A Reexamination of Historical and Contemporary Evidence," *Journal of Politics* 43 (1981): 982–1005; Richard L. Engstrom and Michael D. McDonald, "The Election of Blacks to City Councils: Clarifying the Impact of Electoral Arrangements on the Seats/Population Relationship," *American Political Science Review* 75 (June 1981): 344–54; Peggy Heilig and Robert J. Mundt, *Your Voice at City Hall* (Albany: State University of New York Press, 1984); Albert K. Karnig and Susan Welch, *Black Representation and Urban Policy;* Jeffrey S. Zax, "Election Methods and Black and Hispanic City Council Membership," *Social Science Quarterly* 71 (June 1990): 339–55; Arnold Vedlitz and Charles A. Johnson, "Community Racial Segregation, Electoral Structure, and Minority Representation," *Social Science Quarterly* 63 (December): 729–36; Browning, Marshall, and Tabb, *Protest is Not Enough*; Karnig and Welch, "Sex and Ethnic Differences"; Lyndon B. Johnson (LBJ) School of Public Affairs, *Local Government Election Systems* (Austin: University of Texas, 1984); Leonard Cole, "Electing Blacks to Municipal Office: Structural and Social Determinants," *Urban Affairs Quarterly* 8 (1974): 17–39; Albert Karnig, "Black Representation on City Councils," *Urban Affairs Quarterly* 11 (1976): 223–42; and Albert Karnig, "Black Resources and City Council Representation," *Journal of Politics* 41 (1979): 134–49.

61. Renner, "Municipals Election Processes"; Robinson and Dye, "Reformism and Black Representation of City Councils"; Karnig and Welch, *Black Representation and Urban Policy*; and Carol A. Cassel, "The Nonpartisan Ballot in the United States," in Bernard Grofman and Arend Lijphart, eds., *Electoral Laws and Their Political Consequences* (New York: Agathon Press, 1986), 226–41.

62. Clinton B. Jones, "The Impact of Local Election Systems on Black Political Representation," *Urban Affairs Quarterly* 11 (March 1976): 345–56; Taebel, "Minority Representation on City Councils"; Karnig, "Black Resources"; Margaret K. Latimer, "Black Political Representation in Southern Cities: Elections Systems and Other Casual Variables," *Urban Affairs Quarterly* 15 (September 1979): 65–86; Karnig and Welch, *Black Representation and Urban Policy*; Vedlitz and Johnson, "Community Racial Segregation"; Susan A. MacManus, "Constituency Size and Minority Representation," *State and Local Government Review* 19 (Winter 1987): 3–7; Bullock and MacManus, "Testing Assumptions"; Charles S. Bullock III and Susan A. MacManus, "The Impact of Staggered Terms on Minority Representation," *Journal of Politics* 49 (May 1987): 543–52; Bullock and MacManus, "Structural Features of Municipalities"; Browning, Marshall, and Tabb, *Protest Is Not Enough*; LBJ School, *Local Government Election Systems*; Alozie, "The Election of Asians"; Welch, "The Impact of At-Large Elections"; and Zax, "Election Methods."

63. Bullock and MacManus, "Municipal Electoral Structure"; MacManus and Bullock, "Women on Southern City Councils"; and Bullock and MacManus, "Testing Assumptions."

64. Arnold Fleischmann and Lana Stein, "Minority and Female Success in Municipal Runoff Elections," *Social Science Quarterly* 68 (June 1987): 378–85; Bullock and MacManus, "Structural Features of Municipalities"; and Bullock and MacManus, "Testing Assumptions."

65. Karnig and Welch, "Sex and Ethnic Differences"; Welch and Herrick, "The Impact of At-Large Elections"; Rebekah Herrick and Susan Welch, "The Impact of At-Large Elections on the Representation of Black and White Women," in Lucius J. Barker, ed., *Ethnic Politics and Civil Liberties: National Political Review* 3 (New Brunswick, NJ: Transaction, 1992): 62–77; Robert Darcy and Charles D. Hadley, "Black Women in Politics: The Puzzle of Success," *Social Science Quarterly* (September 1988): 629–45; and Bullock and MacManus, "Municipal Electoral Structure."

66. Cassel, "The Nonpartisan Ballot," 237.

67. See Cassel, ibid., and Welch and Bledsoe, *Urban Reform and Its Consequences*, for excellent reviews of this research.

68. However, a growing body of literature shows that campaign costs do not necessarily decline significantly after a jurisdiction moves from an at-large to a single-member district electoral format. Changing an electoral format often creates open seats and large candidate fields. Thus, a candidate has to spend considerably more than the previous office-holder to gain name recognition. And in large cities it is increasingly coming essential to rely on expensive electronic media (TV and radio) even in running for single-member district seats. See LBJ School, *Local Government Election Systems*; Heilig and Mundt, *Your Voice at City Hall*; and Michael V. Haselswerdt, "Voter and Candidate Reaction to District and At-Large Elections, Buffalo, New York," *Urban Affairs Quarterly* 20 (September 1984): 31–45.

69. For an in-depth discussion of the pros and cons of combination systems, see Susan A. MacManus, "Mixed Electoral Systems Offer Opportunities for Representation Diversity," in Susan A. MacManus, ed., *Reapportionment and Representation in Florida: A Historical Collection* (Tampa, FL: Intrabay Innovation Institute, University of South Florida, 1991), 635–43.

70. See Bullock and MacManus, "Structural Features of Municipalities"; and Welch and Herrick, "The Impact of At-Large Elections on the Representation of Minority Women."

71. See Alozie, "The Election of Asians to City Councils."

72. See Welch, "The Impact of At-Large Elections on the Representation of Blacks and Hispanics"; Bullock and MacManus, "Testing Assumptions"; and Alozie, "The Election of Asians."

73. Thomas, "The Effects of Race and Gender on Constituency Service," 176–77.

74. For an excellent review of this research and additional empirical support, see Mladenka, "Blacks and Hispanics in Urban Politics."

75. Ibid., 179; also Browning, Marshall, and Tabb, *Protest Is Not Enough* and *Racial Politics in American Cities*

76. Mladenka, "Blacks and Hispanics in Urban Politics," 180.

77. Single-shot, or bullet voting, permits minority voters, if they so choose, to vote for only one candidate (usually a minority candidate) out of a list of candidates, thereby denying votes to the nonminority candidates.

78. Alozie, "The Election of Asians," 90.

79. Bullock and MacManus, "Structural Features of Municipalities."

80. Bullock and MacManus, "The Impact of Staggered Terms on Minority Representation"; and "Testing Assumptions."

81. The highest incidence of simultaneous council terms occurs in the East South Central region were 71.6% of the cities use them.

82. Over 90% of the council-manager jurisdictions have staggered terms. Comparative figures for jurisdictions with other forms of government are: town meeting (79.3%); representative town meeting (78.4%); mayor-council (72.2%); and commission (58.7%).

83. From a regional perspective, the highest incidence of staggered council terms appears among cities in the Pacific Coast (98.7%) and Mountain (97.7%) regions.

84. We did not, however, examine the impact of the interaction of percent minority population in a city with a particular electoral structure. The inclusion of interactive terms in research of this type is characteristic of the more current empirically based research, including ours. We expect that once controls are made for the racial composition of the city, the differences in female and racial/ethnic minority representation across various electoral formats, which we have often found in this chapter to be minor, will be even narrower.

Minority Vote Dilution and Election Systems

C.E. Teasley III

Perhaps no civil rights legislation has enjoyed an impact equivalent to that of the Voting Rights Act of 1965. In 1960, just prior to its passage, black voting registration rates in the South were estimated to be 28 percent (U.S. Civil Rights Commission 1961). Over the course of 20 years, corresponding estimates had more than doubled by 1980 to 59.3 percent (U.S. Bureau of the Census 1982). Even so, considerable debate remains over both the purpose and the scope of the law. Conflicting opinions are manifested in federal court decisions, the congressional debates during the passage of the 1982 amendments to the act, and in professional periodicals (Blumstein 1983; Derfner 1984; Howard and Howard 1983). It is, indeed, an irony that a public policy characterized by such high levels of conflict and ambiguity could have been so successful.

A substantial part of the controversy involves the use of at-large elections in local governments. The history of political reform in this country is familiar by now to most students of urban politics. Gaining impetus as a means of thwarting political machines in the Northeast, nonpartisan and at-large election systems were utilized to promote a "business" approach to government. While perhaps neutral on its face, some evidence indicates that, under at-large election systems, minority groups experience lower levels of representation in terms of their proportion of representatives to their percentage of the population than under single-member systems (Berry and Dye 1983; Davidson and Korbel 1981; Engstrom and McDonald 1981, 1982; Robinson and Dye, 1978; Taebel 1978; Vedlitz and Johnson 1982). Some researchers have suggested that

Reprinted with permission from State and Local Government Review, *Vol. 19, No. 3, Fall, 1987. Published by the Carl Vinson Institute of Government, University of Georgia, Athens, Georgia.*

election system *per se* is not the causative factor (MacManus 1978; Taebel 1978; Karnig and Welch 1982). A methodological issue has augmented the debate because different measures of representation have been employed to assess the impact of election system on minority representation.

The central question confronting jurists and community leaders alike is: Does this underrepresentation constitute the illegal dilution, i.e., "watering down," of minority votes? Mere underrepresentation is insufficient to sustain a claim of minority vote dilution. Additional evidence of discrimination is necessary to find a system guilty of vote dilution based on the "totality of circumstances." Much of the additional evidence involves a theoretical, but as yet untested, relationship among the existence of past discriminatory practices, resulting socioeconomic discrepancies along racial lines, and political participation. The major effort here is directed toward testing of this legislative-judicial theory of participation by determining what effect some of the various "circumstances" contribute to minority representation.

Minority Vote Dilution and the Voting Rights Act

The Voting Rights Act of 1965 (Public Law 89–110) was passed on August 6 of that year "[t]o enforce the fifteenth amendment to the Constitution of the United States...." Section 2 of the act is a virtual paraphrase of the amendment. It sates that

> No voting qualification or prerequisite to voting, or standard, practice or procedure shall be imposed or applied by any State or political subdivision to deny or abridge the right of any citizen of the United States to vote on account of race or color.

The 1965 version of Section 2 is relatively clear, and indeed, the U.S. Supreme Court has held that "it is apparent that the language of §2 no more than elaborates upon that of the Fifteenth Amendment...." (*Mobile v. Bolden*, 446 U.S. at 60). While court decisions paid little attention to Section 2 prior to its 1982 amendments, subsequent decisions have been based directly on court interpretations of legislative intent when the amendments were adopted. Thus, a review of court decisions and legislative history is critical to understanding the test which is currently applied to determine minority vote dilution.

Initial court decisions evolved to a general acceptance of the so-called "Zimmer factors" as sufficient to infer discriminatory intent. In the case of *Zimmer v. McKeithen* (485 F.2d 1297), several types of circumstantial evidence were deemed acceptable to prove "purposeful" vote dilution. As the Supreme Court became increasingly conservative during the 1970s and early

1980s, however, it began to require direct evidence of intent to substantiate a claim of purposeful discrimination. While initiated in other civil rights areas, the strong requirement for evidence of intent was formally stated with regard to vote dilution of April 22, 1980, in *The City of Mobile v. Bolden* (446 U.S. 55).

In his dissenting opinion, Justice Thurgood Marshall observed that the Court's decision meant that "the right to vote provides the politically power-less with nothing more than the right to cast meaningless ballots" (104). Justice Stewart, writing for the plurality, countered that

> The theory of this dissenting opinion ... appears to be that every "political group," or at least every such group that is in the minority, has a federal constitutional right to elect candidates in proportion to its numbers.... Whatever appeal the dissenting opinion's view may have as a matter of political theory, it is not the law (75).

The congressional debates during the passage of the 1982 amendments to the act reflect this same theme because they were largely generated by the Court's controversial decision in *Mobile*. Civil rights activists successfully lobbied for a "results" rather than the "intent" criterion required by the *Mobile* decision. The results criterion was strongly opposed by many congressmen, especially from the South, who were concerned that the voting rights amendments would require racially proportional representation. Their concerns were assuaged when Senator Robert Dole, R-Kansas, assured them that the Section 2 amendments meant only that minorities were guaranteed equal access to the political process and nothing more. According to Dole,

> It was generally agreed that the concept of certain identifiable groups having a right to be elected in proportion to their voting potential was repugnant to the democratic principles upon which our society is based (*Report of the Committee on the Judiciary, U.S. Senate on §1992 [Senate Report]* 1982, 193).

The resulting amendment to Section 2, therefore reflects the same constraint on proportional representation. That constraint is reflected in the following paragraph added to the section.

> (b) A violation ... is established, if based on the totality of the circumstances, it is shown that the political processes leading to nomination or election in the state or political subdivision are not equally open to participation by a class of citizens protected by subsection (a) in that its members have less opportunity than other members of the electorate to participate in the political process and to elect representatives of their choice. The extent to which members of the protected class have been elected to office in the State or political subdivision is one "circumstance" which may be considered, *provided that nothing in this subsection establishes a right to have members of a*

protected class elected in numbers equal to their proportion of the population (Public Law 97–205) (emphasis added).

As a result, Section 2 now states both that underrepresentation is an indication of illegal discrimination and that there is no legal entitlement to a given level of election success. Hence, proportional representation is merely one factor that may be considered in cases charging vote dilution. Given the absence of proportional representation, plaintiffs would then be required to demonstrate the contribution of other discriminatory factors to substantiate a dilutionary claim against an at-large system .

Methods of Legal Proof:
The Totality-of-Circumstances Test

While the limit on proportional representation is clear in the statute, equal access to the political process can only be determined by reviewing the appropriate methods of proof. The Zimmer factors are embodied as the "Totality-of-Circumstances Test" in the congressional debates concerning the revised Section 2. The "typical factors" include

1. [t]he extent of any history of official discrimination in the state or political subdivision that touched on the right of the members of the minority group to register, to vote or otherwise to participate in the democratic process;
2. the extent to which voting in elections of the state or political subdivision is racially polarized;
3. the extent to which the state or political subdivision has used unusually large election districts, majority vote requirements, ... or other voting practices or procedures that may enhance the opportunity for discrimination...;
4. if there is a candidate slating process, whether the members of the minority group have been denied access to the process;
5. the extent to which members of the minority group in the state or political subdivision bear the effects of discrimination in such areas as education, employment and health, which hinder their ability to participate effectively in the political process;
6. whether political campaigns have been characterized by overt or subtle racial appeals; (and)
7. the extent to which members of the minority group have been elected to public office in the jurisdiction (*Senate Report* 1982, 28–29).

A behavioral theory of minority vote dilution may be derived from the "results" test sanctioned in legislative reports and applied by federal courts.

In jurisdictions practicing discrimination, there should be, among other findings, a formal history of voting discrimination, and a discrepancy between the socioeconomic conditions of blacks and whites. When the lingering effects of socioeconomic discrimination are combined with racially polarized voting and an at-large election system, it should diminish the ability of minorities to compete equally in the political process to the point that their votes are, in effect, less valuable or diluted. Thus, the legislatively endorsed judicial standard for determining the existence of minority vote dilution would hold that at-large election systems are discriminatory only when other factors, such as an official history of discrimination or the resulting socioeconomic disadvantages, contribute to the denial to protected groups of the right to participate equally in the political process. Although implicitly logical, these hypotheses have not yet been empirically tested. The adoption of this untested theory of political participation is well exemplified by the following passage.

> The courts have recognized that disproportionate educational, employment, income level and living conditions arising from past discrimination tend to depress minority political participation, e.g., *White* 412 U.S. at 768; ... Where these conditions are shown, and where the level of black participation in politics is depressed, plaintiffs need not prove any further causal nexus between their disparate socioeconomic status and the depressed level of political participation (*Senate Report* 1982, 29).

While courts may require no further proof of the causal relationship between discrimination, socioeconomic factors, and political participation, that relationship has been studied often by political scientists and should be of concern in the setting of public policy.

Research Design

The central cities of standard metropolitan statistical areas constitute the units of analysis for this study. A 1976 survey of the 243 cities, conducted by Dye, provides the basis for assessing the electoral system and representation level for blacks in the cities being studied. While the act provides protection for other minorities, the dilution of black votes has been a central theme of litigation and will be the major focus of this study.

Since the chief theoretical concern with the at-large systems is their discriminatory impact when minorities constitute a sizable minority, but not a majority, of the community, only cities with black populations of 10 percent or more are analyzed here. Early studies concluded that discriminatory behavior increased with the size of the black population (Key 1949; Matthews and Prothro 1967). Furthermore, it is only when there is a sizable percentage of minority population that any group might expect to win seats on the jurisdiction's

elected council. Additionally, Engstrom and McDonald (1981, 348–49) conclude from their analysis that "one could consider 10 percent to be a threshold or critical point at which at-large elections can be expected to have an
adverse impact on black representation." Engstrom and McDonald (1981; 1982)
adopt a standard of dropping those cities with black populations of greater
than 50 percent from their analysis. Since a black population of 50 percent
does not mean a black electorate of 50 percent, the courts have normally viewed
districts with substantially more than 50 percent black to be "safe." In other
words, the effects of discrimination may well affect majority black cities with
regard to equal access to the political process. Thus, it would seem unwarranted
to eliminate them from this analysis. The criterion adopted brought the size
of the study group to slightly more than half (*N=141*) of the original group.

Representation

The dependent variable in this study is representation. It is employed here
to indicate equal access to the political process. The appropriate method for
measuring representation has received much attention in previous studies. Earlier studies have used ratio (e.g., Robinson and Dye 1978) or subtractive (e.g.,
MacManus 1978) measures of representation. Criticisms of these measures
have led subsequent researchers to concentrate on the slope coefficients resulting from regressing the representation percent on the population percent
(Engstrom and McDonald 1981, 1982; Vedlitz and Johnson 1982). Thus, representation is measured by the slope coefficient in this study, although when
relatively high thresholds are employed, the type of measure is of little consequence (Engstrom and McDonald 1981).

Electoral System

A jurisdiction's electoral system was divided into two levels. At-large
systems are those where the entire council was elected by the electorate as a
whole. Single-member systems include those where each council member was
elected by a geographically defined subset of the population, and mixed systems had a majority of council members elected by population subsets and a
few members elected at-large. The major concern from a legal perspective is
with the dilutionary impact of pure at-large systems. Thus, electoral system
is treated here as a dummy variable, with a city coded as 1 when it possessed
an at-large system and 0 when it did not.

History of Official Discrimination

Normally, the South has served as a proxy for discrimination (e.g.,
Engstrom and McDonald 1982), but all southern jurisdictions were not equal

in their denial of minority participation. Of course, discrimination occurred in various forms, but the primary interest here is with regard to voting participation. Consequently, registration discrimination was indicated by the city's being included as one pointed out by the original Voting Rights Act of 1965 for utilizing a test for registration and also having low voter participation rates. Jurisdictions in seven southern states, along with 40 counties in North Carolina, constitute the bulk of cities included in this category of discrimination. Coverage of the act was extended in subsequent years, but the extension dealt largely with minority language provisions which are not directly considered here. Thus, the cities included in this study exercised a specific form of voting discrimination with an empirical impact on participation.

Socioeconomically Depressed Participation

The lingering effects of past discrimination, or socioeconomically depressed participation, are normally measured by the differences between white and black levels of education, income, and housing conditions compared in the same communities. That approach was employed here because of its consistency with data as they are typically admitted into court proceedings. Data provided by the 1980 census were employed in this study. That census was closer to the year of the original Dye study than were the corresponding data from the 1970 census used in most previous studies. The effects of past discrimination are indicated by black and white differences in mean family income. Income was selected over other measures of the impact of discrimination because of its direct impact on the ability of blacks to support candidates for political office and because it had received the most consideration from previous studies (Engstrom and McDonald 1982; Karnig 1979).

Findings

The findings from Table 1 offer a good overview of the characteristics of cities under the three different election structures. First, the average black population percent varies little from one election system to another, but the black council percent increases steadily with the percent of council elected from single-member districts. Second, while no election system offers exactly equal representation to blacks, the "pure" at-large system offers minorities much less representation than either the mixed or single-member system. Analysis of the unstandardized slope coefficients indicates the rate at which black population percent translates into black percent on the elected council. In this study, there is no significant difference in the level of representation offered by pure and mixed single-member system cities. This finding differs from Engstrom and McDonald (1981) who dropped cities with over 50 percent black populations,

Table 1
Minority Representation, Past Discrimination, and Socioeconomic Differences by Election System in SMSA Central Cities with Greater Than 10 Percent Black Populations (N = 141)

	Election System		
	At-Large	Mixed	Single-Member
Black council percent, 1976	11.66	18.49	18.96
Black population percent, 1980	28.77	28.55	27.51
Representation: Unstandardized slope coefficient	.53	.78§	.71§
Registration discrimination (in percent of cities)	57.6	20.0§	30.0§
Mean family income difference by race (in $100s)	$94.04	$87.17	$91.58
N	66	45	30

Sources: Compiled from 1976 Dye survey of SMSA cities and the 1980 U.S. Census.
*P ≤ .05
†P ≤ .01
§P ≤ .001

but is consistent with the findings of Vedlitz and Johnson (1982) who did not. It may well be that majority black single-member cities do not transfer black votes into election victory comparatively as well as those with lower black population percentages. Overall, however, one finding is clear. Pure at-large election systems offer significantly lower levels of representation to blacks, and there is little difference between the level of representation offered minorities by mixed and pure single-member systems for the subset of large cities studied here.

Table 1 also addresses the history of official discrimination and socioeconomic discrepancies between blacks and whites in the SMSA cities. As expected, at-large cities were more likely to have a history of discrimination, due in large measure to the greater use of that structure in the South.

A different finding is true with regard to socioeconomic discrepancies. While there are some marginal differences between the mean family incomes of blacks and whites with regard to election structure, they are not significant. In this regard, the greatest difference is in cities that employ at-large systems, with the smallest difference occurring in cities with mixed systems.

Results shown in Table 2 reinforce many of those in Table 1. Table 2 reports the results of an ordinary least squares regression procedure. Election structure is treated as a specifying variable. Since mixed systems and single-member systems appeared to differ from at-large systems in similar ways in

Table 2
The Effects of Election Structure, Registration Discrimination, and Black/White Income Differential on Minority Representation in SMSA Cities with Black Populations Greater Than 10 Percent (N = 141)

Independent Variable	Black Council Percent: Representation
Black Population Percent	
Unstandardized slope coefficient	.70
Standardized slope coefficient	.70
Standard error	.06
Significance (t-test)	.000
At-Large Election Structure	
Unstandardized slope coefficient	-6.64
Standardized slope coefficient	-.23
Standard error	1.78
Significance (t-test)	.000
Registration Discrimination	
Unstandardized slope coefficient	-2.35
Standardized slope coefficient	-.08
Standard error	2.25
Significance (t-test)	.297
Black/White Income Differential	
Unstandardized slope coefficient	-.005
Standardized slope coefficient	-.01
Standard error	.03
Significance (t-test)	.855
Intercept	.0003
Multiple R	.71
R-Square	.51

Sources: Compiled from the 1976 Dye survey of SMSA cities and the 1980 U.S. Census.

Table 1 and since court decisions have often accepted them as nondilutionary, at-large election system was included as a single dummy variable. The existence of registration discrimination was included as a second dummy variable, and the black/white family income differential was entered in the respective $100 amounts. This analysis allows for the assessment of each variable's contributions to the model as it is included.

As with Table 1, socioeconomic differences contribute no significant increase in the level of minority representation. This finding differs from that of prior research (Engstrom and McDonald 1981, 1982). Prior research, however, did not include both registration discrimination and election system as specifying variables along with black/white income differential. It may well be that these other variables account for the decline in importance of resource discrepancies.

Another test involves accounting for the increase in total variance explained in black representation by the addition of past discrimination and black/white income disparities to the model. The R-Square for the full model with election structure, registration discrimination, and black/white income differential is virtually the same as for the restricted model which includes only election structure. The R-Square change when the model including registration discrimination and resource discrepancy is compared to a model excluding these two independent variables is a paltry .01. Thus, past discrimination and resource discrepancy add no significant explanatory power to the model. While the particular election system employed in a city has a significant impact on representation, the history of official past discrimination and its lingering socioeconomic disadvantages have little significant additive impact.

The model may be analyzed in a more practical manner. Given that the intercept is negligible, *Black Council Percent = 70 percent* (of the city's black population percent) *-6.64 percent* (if the city has an at-large system) *-2.35 percent* (if the city had an official history of past discrimination) *-.005 percent* (for every $100 difference between black and white mean family incomes). Hence, election system accounts for nearly three times the percentage loss in representation that is accounted for by official past discrimination and its lingering effects added together, provided that the average income discrepancy is reasonably close to the mean for all cities.

Conclusions

The major purpose of this research was to test a legislatively and judicially sanctioned theory of political participation. As such, its focus centers on the legal test employed in court challenges of discriminatory vote dilution, not on the philosophy of democratic representation.

The legislative history surrounding the passage of the 1982 extension to the Voting Rights Act made one point abundantly clear. "The mere combination of an at-large election and the lack of proportional representation is not enough to invalidate that election method" (*Senate Report* 1982, 16). A system would be judged discriminatory if in the totality of circumstances it denied equal access to the political process to groups protected by the act. A substantial part of the "result" prescribed by Congress and the courts involves an assumed causal relationship between past discrimination and political participation.

The testing of all the "typical factors" is not possible in this study. Those parts of the test that make up a theory of political participation are analyzed since they often assume an air of objectivity, based as they usually are on the presentation of empirical data. Supporters of the revised Section 2 reinforced the lofty status of the "results" test when they observed that "the court would assess the impact of the challenged structure or practice on the basis of objective factors, rather than making a determination about the motivations which lay behind its adoption or maintenance" (*Senate Report* 1982, 205).

In order to test the theory of political participation employed to determine equal access to the political process, an analysis was made of central SMSA cities in the United States. Those cities with 10 percent or greater black populations were analyzed to determine the relative effects on minority representation of the city's election system, its history of official discrimination, and the lingering effects of that discrimination in terms of socioeconomic discrepancies between blacks and whites.

The results of this study offer little support to the totality-of-circumstances test employed in suits alleging minority vote dilution. While there is a clear relationship between the type of election system and black representation in the cities studied, neither a history of past discrimination nor the lingering effects of it contribute any significant additional explanatory power to the model. Thus, serious concern deserves to be raised over whether or not the current standard for determining minority vote dilution is indeed appropriate.

References

Berry, Barbara L., and Thomas R. Dye. 1979. The discriminatory effects of at-large elections. *Florida State Law Review* 7:85–122.

Blumstein, James F. 1983. Defining and proving race discrimination: Perspectives on the purpose vs. results approach from the Voting Rights Act. *Virginia Law Review* 69: 633–714.

Davidson, Chandler, and George Korbel. 1981. At-large elections and minority group representation: A re-examination of historical and contemporary evidence. *Journal of Politics* 43: 983–1005.

Derfner, Armand. 1984. Vote dilution and the Voting Rights Act amendments of 1982. In *Minority Vote Dilution*. 145–66. Chandler Davidson ed. Washington, D.C.: Howard University Press.

Engstrom, Richard L., and Michael D. McDonald. 1981. The election of blacks to city councils: Clarifying the impact of electoral arrangements on the seats/population relationship. *American Political Science Review* 75 (June): 344–54.

_____. 1982. The underrepresentation of blacks on city councils: Comparing the structural and socioeconomic explanations for south/nonsouth differences. *Journal of Politics* 44: 1088–99.

Howard, Alan, and Bruce Howard. 1983. The dilemma of the Voting Rights Act— Recognizing the emerging political equality norm. *Columbia Law Review* 83 (November): 1615–63.

Karnig, Albert K. 1979. Black resources and city council representation. *Journal of Politics* 41 (February): 34–49.

_____, and Susan Welch. 1980. *Black Representation and Urban Policy.* Chicago: University of Chicago Press.

Key, V. O. Jr. 1949. *Southern Politics in State and Nation,* New York: Alfred A. Knopf.

Matthews, Donald R., and James W. Prothro. 1967. Social and economic factors and negro voter registration in the South. In *Negro Politics in America,* 178–210. Harry A. Bailey, ed. Columbus, Ohio: Charles E. Merrill.

MacManus, Susan. 1978. City council election procedures and minority representation: Are they related? *Social Science Quarterly* 59 (June): 153–61.

Report of the Committee on the Judiciary United States Senate on § 1992. 1982. Washington, D.C.: U.S. Government Printing Office.

Robinson, Theodore P., and Thomas R. Dye. 1978. Reformism and black representation on city councils. *Social Science Quarterly* 59 (June): 133–41.

Senate Report. 1982. See *Report of the Committee on the Judiciary.*

Taebel, Delbert. 1978. Minority representation on city councils. *Social Science Quarterly* 59 (June): 143–52.

U.S. Bureau of Census. 1981. *Voting and Registration in the Election of 1980.* Washington, D.C.: U.S. Government Printing Office.

U.S. Commission on Civil Rights. 1961. *Voting.* Washington, D.C.: U.S. Government Printing Office.

Vedlitz, Arnold, and Charles A. Johnson. 1982. Community racial segregation, electoral structure, and minority representation. *Social Science Quarterly* 63 (December): 729–36.

Social Backgrounds of Nonpartisan City Council Members

Carol A. Cassel

In roughly two-thirds of U.S. municipal elections, candidates run for office without party labels.[1] Such nonpartisan elections are a product of the municipal reform movement of the early twentieth century, which attempted to limit the power of corrupt party machines, insulate local elections from the influence of state and national party politics, facilitate more efficient and businesslike administration of local government, and encourage recruitment of superior candidates, who might be reluctant to associate themselves with party organizations (Lee 1960). Nonpartisan elections provide an interesting contrast with elections where party labels are present.

Behaviorally oriented political scientists of the mid-twentieth century questioned the validity of the reformers' good government theory of nonpartisan elections. A revisionist theory developed based on observations of nonpartisan elections in practice and a theoretical recognition of the functions of political parties in political systems. The classic reassessment was made by Adrian (1952), who hypothesized that nonpartisan elections weakened political parties, tended to be issueless in nature, advantaged incumbents and made them less accountable to the public, and restricted recruitment to higher political office. Subsequent studies of California cities (Lee 1960; Hawley 1973) also asserted that nonpartisan systems tended to over-recruit members of the business community and Republicans, thus reducing the representativeness of local government. This is plausible on any of several grounds: high–SES socioeconomic status candidates (and Republicans) may be more willing to run for

Reprinted with permission from Western Political Quarterly, *Vol. 83, No. 3, September, 1985. Published by the University of Utah, Salt Lake City, Utah.*

office in nonpartisan systems; high–SES candidates may be more likely to have the resources to win without the aid of a party label; or lower turnout in nonpartisan elections may bias the voting electorate in favor of high–SES candidates.

To date, none of this has been tested with a nationwide survey. This chapter makes a beginning toward remedying that omission. Drawing on a survey of all U.S. cities with a population of 2,500 or more, I test the revisionist assertion that high–SES candidates are elected more frequently in nonpartisan elections. In addition, I examine the relationship between ballot form and several other characteristics previously found to be related to it.

The survey from which I take my data, *Form of Government-1981*, was conducted by the International City Management Association, Washington, D.C. Using a mail questionnaire, the ICMA surveyed all U.S. cities size 2,500 and above, with a response rate of 69 percent.[2] The survey items include measures of municipal government structures and of social background characteristics of incumbent council members, including occupation, education, and age.[3]

Background

As a Progressive reform of the early twentieth century, the nonpartisan ballot is strongly related to region for historical reasons. Cities in the Northeast, formed early in U.S. history, are only 32 percent nonpartisan. Younger cities in the West were more likely to be influenced by the Progressive movement. Thus the proportion of nonpartisan cities in the West is over twice that in the Northeast.[4] Given this geographic and historical basis it is not surprising that ballot form, when considered nationally, has little relationship to other demographic factors. Despite assertions that nonpartisan elections occur more frequently in smaller and more middle-class cities, we find no evidence of significant relationships between ballot form and city size or income. The proportion of nonpartisan ballots is the same among large, medium, and small size cities.[5] Nor does income seem to make any difference. In 1980, the median annual income in nonpartisan cities was $10,355, while that in partisan cities was $10,260.[6]

A majority of all forms of government (mayor-council, council-manager, etc.) have nonpartisan elections, although the nonpartisan ballot is more frequently associated with the reform model form of government (council-manager). Likewise, the nonpartisan ballot is used in a majority of all council constituency types, but occurs most frequently with the most common reform model constituency type (at-large). When the three reform structures are considered together, the nature of city government is characterized more by diversity than by the "reformed" or "unreformed" model. Only 28 percent of U.S. cities have adopted all three reform structures (nonpartisan ballot, council-manager form of government, and at-large elections), and only 5 percent use all three unreformed structures (partisan ballot, mayor-council form of government, and ward elections).[7]

Since ballot form is not associated with city size or income, comparative studies such as the analysis presented below need not control for these factors. The relationship between ballot form and other municipal reform structures, however, suggest a need to control for other municipal reform structures to assess the relationship between ballot form and other variables.

Previous Studies of Social Background

Despite the revisionist claim that nonpartisan systems are biased toward high–SES officeholders, only a few studies have examined social backgrounds of elected officials in nonpartisan systems. Lee (1960: 171) found the nonpartisan system "pretty bad" in terms of the representativeness of local elective officials. Affluent white Protestant males were clearly advantaged in California municipal elections (all nonpartisan). As Lee noted, however, there was no evidence to determine whether successful candidates in cities with partisan elections would be any different. Rogers and Arman (1971) found that officials elected in nonpartisan systems in Ohio have higher status occupations and higher income than officials elected in partisan systems there. Their study was based on a 1967 questionnaire sent to all mayors and council members in Ohio cities with populations of 25,000 or more. Since nonpartisan systems tend to co-occur with at-large elections, which also may produce more affluent council members, at-largism is a potential confounding factor here. In another study, Feld and Lutz (1977) compared background characteristics of individuals recruited to run for the nonpartisan Houston City Council and the partisan Texas legislature from approximately the same electoral area. They found the nonpartisan city council to contain more members of the business community than the partisan state legislative seats from the same geographic areas. This difference cannot be attributed to varying district size, although the nature of the office being sought may be a confounding factor.

Related to the thesis that nonpartisan elections benefit high–SES candidates is the thesis that nonpartisan elections benefit Republican candidates, on the assumption that high–SES candidates tend to be Republican. Alternatively, the lower turnout that seems to characterize nonpartisan elections may help explain the apparent Republican (and high–SES) advantage. Hawley (1973), who tested the thesis most systematically, found that nonpartisanship does benefit Republicans, although the bias is substantial only in cities with a population of 50,000 or more.

Previous studies also have found that officials elected in nonpartisan elections are generally older and are more often attorneys than those elected in partisan systems (Rogers and Arman 1971; Feld and Lutz 1977). In explanation, Rogers and Arman suggest that it may simply take longer to develop the notability necessary for electoral success without a party label. Another possibility is that nonpartisan offices have lower career utility for ambitious politicians. If so, one might expect to find fewer young members and attorneys on nonpartisan councils. Feld and Lutz conclude that nonpartisan councils may attract "an older, more established man seeking a prestigious diversion," whereas partisan councils may attract "a young breed of politician" (1977: 927).[8]

Analysis

The present data enable us to test some of these hypotheses more definitively than previously has been possible. To address the proposition that nonpartisan city councils contain a higher proportion of persons of high socioeconomic status, Table 1 compares the occupational status and education of council members in nonpartisan city councils.[9] The data show occupational but not educational differences. The occupational differences are consistent and significant, although not dramatic: 51 percent of nonpartisan council members but only 44 percent of partisan council members have "high" occupational status.[10]

Since the association of the nonpartisan ballot with at-large constituencies leaves a suspicion of spuriousness (more affluent candidates may be better able to afford a citywide campaign), Table 2 adds controls for council constituency. Without these controls, high occupational status is 7 or 8 percent greater in nonpartisan than in partisan cities (Table 1). With council constituency controlled, it remains 6 or 7 percent greater, on average, within each category of constituency (at-large, combination, or district). At the extremes, reformed cities with both nonpartisan and at-large elections have a majority of elites on their councils (54 percent); and unreformed cities with both partisan and district elections have a clear minority of elites on their councils (37 percent). This difference does not vary with city size.[11]

Previous findings that officials elected in nonpartisan systems are older and less likely to be attorneys find no support here. Table 3 shows that the average age of city council members is virtually identical in nonpartisan and partisan cities, even for cities with a population of 25,000 or more, where such differences may be more important.[12] Similarly, there is virtually no difference in the proportion of attorneys elected in partisan and nonpartisan systems.

Table 1
Percent High Occupational Status and Average Education in Nonpartisan and Partisan City Councils by City Size

City size		Percent high occupational status*	Average education†
2,500 and above	nonpartisan	51.1 (2636)	14.5 (2139)
	partisan	44.4 (1131)	14.3 (962)
25,000 and above	nonpartisan	53.9 (529)	15.4 (430)
	partisan	45.7 (214)	15.0 (162)

Note: The figures in parentheses are the number of cases on which percentages are based.
*High occupational status = professionals, business executives and managers. The remainder are business or industry employees, homemakers, teachers and other educational personnel and clergy. Farmers or ranchers, retired persons and other are excluded.
†The survey item measuring education is categorical. The actual years of schooling are estimated by coding under high school graduate = 10, high school graduate = 12, post high school technical = 15, 1 to 3 years of college = 14, bachelor's degree = 16, master's degree = 17, doctor's degree and medical degree = 20, law degree = 19. Other is excluded.

Table 2
Percent High Occupational Status by Council Constituency in Nonpartisan and Partisan Cities by City Size

City size	Council constituency	High occupational status	
		Nonpartisan	Partisan
2,500 and above	at large	53.8 (1189)	47.5 (684)
	combination	45.8 (413)	40.9 (230)
	district	43.8 (413)	37.7 (203)
25,000 and above	at large	56.7 (361)	50.0 (98)
	combination	48.1 (120)	44.0 (74)
	district	47.6 (45)	36.9 (40)

Note: The figures in parentheses are number of cases on which percentages are based.

Conclusions

This chapter provides more conclusive evidence that nonpartisan elections produce higher status council members than partisan elections. The combination of nonpartisanship with at-largism, as opposed to the combination of partisanship with ward elections, exaggerates this difference. On the other

Table 3
Average Age and Percent Attorney in
Nonpartisan and Partisan City Councils by City Size

City size		Average age*	Percent attorney
2,500 and above	nonpartisan	47.9 (2650)	3.8 (2672)
	partisan	47.3 (1106)	4.1 (1145)
25,000 and above	nonpartisan	47.8 (528)	7.9 (532)
	partisan	46.3 (205)	7.7 (214)

Note: The figures in parentheses are the number of cases on which percentages are based.
*The survey item which measures age is categorical. Average age is estimated by coding under 22 = 21, 22–29 = 25.5, 30–99 = 34.5, 40–49 = 44.5, 50–59 = 54.5 and 60 and over = 65.

hand, anticipated differences in education level, age, and proportion of attorneys on partisan and nonpartisan councils do not appear.

These findings may help clarify the role of local partisan elections as providers of access to political office for nonelite candidates. They also afford a firmer empirical basis for the revisionist critique of nonpartisan elections as tending to produce less representative municipal legislatures.

Notes

1. Sixty-three percent, by a weighted estimate from the *Form of Government–1981* survey described below.
2. The ICMA surveyed 6,761 cities, 4,659 of which responded. Regional response rate varied considerably, ranging from 63 percent in the Northeast to 81 percent in the West. See Sanders (1982: 178–79). Because of the strong association between ballot form and region (see footnote 4), the survey is weighted by regional response rate to estimate the proportion of nonpartisan cities in the U.S. reported above. The same figure (63 percent) is obtained when weighting by the form of government item (response rate is highest among council-manager cities). Because these varying response rates bias this survey and previous surveys, the incidence of municipal reform structures (nonpartisan elections, council-manager form of government, and at-large elections) may be exaggerated slightly in reported studies. For example, when the 1981 survey is not weighted for response bias, it appears that 70 percent of U.S. cities have nonpartisan elections. Previous ICMA surveys of U.S. cities were conducted in 1962, 1971, 1974 and 1977.
3. Examples of several relevant items the survey asks: "Does political party affiliation of candidates appear on the ballot in a general election? Yes_____ No_____" and "Please specify the number of present city council members that have achieved the following levels of education.
_____ a. under high school graduate
_____ b. high school graduate

_____ c. post high school technical
_____ d. 1 to 3 years of college
_____ e. Bachelor's degree
_____ f. Master's degree
_____ g. Doctor's degree
_____ h. medical degree
_____ i. law degree
_____ j. other (specify)

4. Based on the Census definition of region, the figures 32 percent nonpartisan in the Northeast (N = 1084), 74 percent nonpartisan in the North Central region (N = 1297), 85 percent nonpartisan in the South (N = 1221) and 93 percent nonpartisan in the West (N = 694). The regional variation in nonpartisan response rate (see footnote 2) may exaggerate these differences somewhat.

5. Cities of 250,000 and above are 69.3 percent nonpartisan (N = 39), cities size 25,000 to 249,999 are 70.5 percent nonpartisan (N = 794), and cities 2,500 to 24,999 are 69.5 percent nonpartisan. These figures are based on the *Form of Government–1981* survey merged with 1980 Census data, also provided by the ICMA.

6. Source: Sanders (1982), Table 4/2. The estimate is obtained by coding under $8,000 = $7,000; $8,000–$10,000 = $9,000; $10,000–$12,000 = $11,000; $12,000–$14,000 = $13,000; and over $14,000 = $15,000.

7. Source: *Form of Government–1981*.

8. Engstrom and Perant (1975) also find a link between progressive ambitions and attorney occupation in a study of candidates for city council in New Orleans. For a more thorough review of the literature which examines the effect of the nonpartisan ballot on municipal elections in the U.S., see Cassel (1985).

9. The opposite of "high status" is not necessarily "low." Non-high status officials tend to be occupationally average or even above. Although some teachers, clergy, etc. might reasonably be considered high occupational status, and some professionals and business executives or managers middle-status, the data to differentiate within occupational categories are not available. Farmers, retired persons, and others whose occupational status is ambiguous are excluded.

10. The percentage differences are significant at the .001 and .05 levels in cities with populations of 2,500 or more and with populations of 25,000 or more respectively.

11. Though not statistically significant by conventional criteria, these differences are consistent and in the expected direction. Although the differences in Table 2 are similar in magnitude to those in Table 1, they fail to attain significance because they are based on smaller n's.

12. The hypotheses examined in Tables 2 and 3 also were tested in cities with population 50,000 or more. Differences between partisan and nonpartisan city councils do not increase with city size.

References

Adrian, C., 1951. "Some General Characteristics of Nonpartisan Elections." *American Political Science Review* 46 (September): 766–76.

Cassel, C., 1985. "The Nonpartisan Ballot in the United States," in B. Grofman and A. Lijphart, eds., *Electoral Laws and Their Political Consequences*. New York: Agathon.

Engstrom, R., and J. Perant, 1975. "Candidate Attraction to the Politicized Councilmanic Office: A Note on New Orleans." *Social Science Quarterly* (March): 975–82.

Feld, R., and D. Lutz, 1972. "Recruitment to the Houston City Council." *Journal of Politics* 34 (August): 924–33.

Hawley, W., 1973. *Nonpartisan Elections and the Case for Party Politics.* New York: Wiley.

Karnig, A., and B. O. Walter, 1977. "Municipal Elections: Registration, Incumbent Success, and Voter Participation." *The Municipal Yearbook 1977,* pp. 66–72. Washington, D.C.: International City Management Association.

Lee, E., 1960. *The Politics of Nonpartisanship: A Study of California City Elections.* Berkeley: University of California Press.

_____. 1963. "City Elections: A Statistical Profile." *The Municipal Yearbook 1963,* Washington, D.C.: International City Management Association, pp. 74–84.

Rogers, C., and H. Arman, 1971. "Nonpartisanship and Election to City Office." *Social Science Quarterly* 51 (March): 941–45.

Sanders, H.T., 1979. "Governmental Structure in American Cities." *The Municipal Yearbook 1979,* pp. 97–112. Washington, D.C.: International City Management Association.

_____. 1982. "The Government of American Cities: Continuity and Change in Structure." *The Municipal Yearbook 1982,* pp. 178–86. Washington D.C.: International City Management Association.

Blacks and Hispanics in Urban Politics

Kenneth R. Mladenka

After decades of demand and protest, are racial minorities any closer to achieving an equitable share of public sector resources? After numerous legal victories, legislative successes, and affirmative action initiatives, are blacks and Hispanics reaping tangible material rewards as just recompense for their labors? Does the political process work? If racial minorities elect mayors and council members, can they expect an increased flow of benefits from local public office? Does a heavy and consistent investment in the political system pay substantial dividends?

Given the crucial importance of the questions, surprisingly little research addresses the issue. One group of researchers does find that the election of blacks to office produces increased benefits for the black community (Campbell and Feagin 1977; Cole 1976; Keech 1968; Levine 1974). However, Karnig and Welch (1980) examine municipal expenditure patterns and discover that while black mayors had a relatively small effect upon policy, black council members did not. In addition, the literature on the distribution of urban public services reveals that resources are distributed in accordance with bureaucratic decision rules and technical-rational criteria rather than in response to political factors (Lineberry 1977; Mladenka 1980),

However, several recent examinations of the minority share of city jobs make a strong claim for the efficacy of black political power. It is reasonable to assume that blacks would focus their political energies on public sector jobs since according to Browning, Marshall, and Tabb (1984, 169), "governmental employment has long been an important goal and point of early access

Reprinted with permission from American Political Science Review, *Vol. 83, No. 1, March, 1989. Published by the American Political Science Association, Washington, D.C.*

for excluded groups in American society." These authors further observe that "discrimination in employment was one of the prime targets of black protests in the early Sixties. Several federal programs included in their stated goals the elimination of discrimination in public employment or the employment of the poor in general or of minorities in particular. Among these were the poverty program (1964), Model Cities (1967), and Equal Employment Opportunity (1972). At the local level significant minority political activity focused on changing city policy regarding government employment (p. 169).

A variety of studies provide varying degrees of support for the argument that vigorous efforts to increase the number of black elected officials in municipal government have had a demonstrable effect upon the minority share of city jobs. Dye and Renick (1981) find that although black representation on city council exerts no influence upon the black proportion of total city employment, it is the *most* significant determinant of administrative, professional, and protective service (policemen and firemen) positions. They conclude that "employment in top city jobs appears to be a function of political power, as it is reflected in city council representation. Representation on city council is more important in gaining city employment in administrative, professional and protective positions than any other single factor.... We believe that black representation on city councils is a crucial link in improving black employment opportunities in city government" (pp. 484–85).

Eisinger (1982) has also discovered that the number of black elected officials is unimportant in accounting for the variation in the minority share of *total* city jobs. The important variable here is the size of the black population. For decisionmaking and professional positions, however, Eisinger finds that the presence of a black mayor has a significant impact upon increasing the level of black employment. Although the black population was again the single, most important determinant of minority job success, a black chief executive did make a difference. Eisinger concludes that "the presence of a black mayor has a modest incremental effect on levels of black employment ... enabling us ultimately to conclude that a small but discernible portion of black employment is a product of black political authority" (p. 391).

In yet another study, Stein (1986, 702) analyzes the variation in the minority share of the workforce for the total jobs variable. Although percentage minority population was the most significant factor, Stein also finds that "political factors ... play significant roles." Specifically, the presence of a minority mayor and a mayor-council form of government were important variables in accounting for the variation in the employment of racial minorities.

Browning, Marshall, and Tabb (1984) study 10 California cities and find that the level of black representation on council was much more important than either demographic or bureaucratic factors in accounting for increases in black employment. They observe that they "find little support for the hypothesis that socioeconomic or demographic variables are more important than political variables in explaining policy; variations in city government responsiveness are not well explained by the proportion of minorities in the population. Cities with relatively small proportions of minorities were sometimes more responsive than cities with larger minority populations. Other factors more directly political in nature ... yield a much stronger explanation" (pp. 199–200).

In a related vein, Saltzstein (1986) analyzed female employment patterns in a number of cities. Her results also provide support for the argument that minority political power makes a substantial difference. Specifically, she found that the presence of a female mayor had a significant impact on increasing the level of female employment in nonclerical and professional-administrative jobs.

The conclusion that the political process works for blacks is an important finding. It is reassuring to learn that if racial minorities travel the electoral route, they can translate ballot success into tangible, material rewards. Black mayors mean more jobs for the black community. These jobs, in turn, will increase minority influence upon public policy. Eisinger (1982, 391) goes so far as to say that job progress will "contribute to the formation of black bureaucratic middle class." I conclude from this line of research that the election of minority officials, particularly mayors, will improve the chances of their constituents in the competitive struggle for scarce public resources. However, some lingering doubts remain.

First, the sample sizes in the studies described are generally small. Dye and Renick analyze only 42 cities, Eisinger includes 43 in his study, and Browning, Marshall, and Tabb study 10 cities. Stein examines employment patterns in 134 cities. Second, only Eisinger (1982) analyzes the impact of both black mayors and council members upon employment patterns. Dye and Renick limit their study to an examination of minority council while Stein analyzes only minority executives. In addition, the various studies examine different dependent variables. Only Dye and Renick analyze the full range of employment categories: total jobs, official-administrator positions, professional positions, and protective service workers. Eisinger does not include protective service positions in his analysis, while Stein limits her study to the total jobs variable. Further, the small sample sizes preclude the possibility of more detailed analysis. For example, the significance of region in accounting for variation in minority employment patterns cannot be ascertained. In addition, the various studies differ with respect to the relative importance of black political power. Browning, Marshall, and Tabb (1984) conclude that minority representation provides the dominant explanation of black employment levels, while Eisinger (1982, 391) finds that the "presence of a black mayor has a modest incremental effect." Further, very little research has examined the relationship between Hispanic political representation and employment outcomes. Welch, Karnig, and Eribes (1983) find, however, that neither Hispanic mayors nor council members were able to influence employment patterns. Finally, with only one exception (Stein 1986), past research has not considered the interaction among such important variables as local political institutions and the effectiveness of minority political power.

Methodology

The Equal Employment Opportunity Act of 1972 requires all cities with 99 or more employees to submit a report each year to the U.S. Equal Employment Opportunity Commission. The report, known as EEO-4, provides information on the race and sex of employees in eight different job categories. Since the law prohibits the release of employment data for individual cities, it is necessary to obtain the information directly from the city. A request was sent to all cities over 10 thousand in population for copies of their EEO-4 report for 1984. Two follow-up mailings generated a response from 1,350 of the 1,913 cities. Eventually, 1,224 cities were coded for analysis for a response rate of 64%. The cities in the study are highly representative of national employment patterns. Aggregate figures released by EEOC for 1984 reveal that 20.9% of all municipal jobs were held by blacks, while 10.7% of administrative, 14.6% of professional, and 12.6% of protective service positions were filled by blacks. In the sample of cities, 20.1% of all jobs were held by blacks while the comparable figures for administrative, professional, and protective service positions are 9.6%, 12.6% and 12.21% respectively. In addition, 75% of all black mayor cities (over 15 thousand in population) are included in the study.[1]

The eight job categories are officials-administrators, professionals, protective service workers, office and clerical, para-professionals, skilled craftsmen, service-maintenance workers, and technicians.[2] In the analysis that follows we will concentrate upon the black and Hispanic share of total jobs, officials-administrators, professionals, and protective service workers. These three job categories are particularly significant for several reasons. First, these positions pay considerably more than clerical and service-maintenance jobs. Second, blacks and Hispanics in official-administrator (department heads, directors) and professional positions have great potential to influence the recruitment and advancement of minority employees. In addition, the presence of minorities in key decisionmaking positions significantly increases minority influence in vital areas of city government such as spending, taxing, zoning, regulation, housing, and public services. Finally, blacks and Hispanics in protective service positions (police officers) can have major substantive as well as symbolic value with respect to the treatment of minorities in police-citizen encounters.

Independent Variables

Several different sets of independent variables were employed in the analysis. They include the following:

Demographic
total population
percentage black population
percentage Hispanic population
education level
median income
median housing value

Political Power
presence of a black or Hispanic mayor
percentage of city council that is black or Hispanic
black or Hispanic council representative ratio

Political Structure
reform index
percentage of council elected from wards and at-large

Region
Northeast, Midwest, South, West

Composition of Municipal Workforce
percentage of all city jobs accounted for by service-maintenance and clerical positions

Percentage of Workforce That Is Black

Residency Requirements
type of residency requirements in effect as a condition of employment

Previous research reveals that the size of the minority population is a major determinant of the variation in employment levels. Specifically, the percentage black and Hispanic variables were most significant in accounting for the minority share of total jobs and less important for official-administrator, professional, and protective service positions. The explanation advanced is that market factors will determine the level of black employment for less important jobs while political influence will assume increasing significance for key positions. According to this assumption, whites are not interested in many city jobs. Consequently, the size of the black and Hispanic population will determine the level of minority employment for these positions. Decision making, professional, and police positions, however, will be targets of minority political activity, at least for blacks. Therefore, we should expect that the percentage black population variable will be significant for total employment but that political factors will become important for key city jobs. The research evidence suggests that the level of political representation will be less significant for Hispanics (Welch, Karnig, Eribes 1983).

The environment in large cities with wealthier, better educated populations should also provide more employment opportunities for blacks and Hispanics. More cosmopolitan cities are apt to be somewhat more tolerant of racial minorities (Dye and Renick 1981; Stein 1986). It is hypothesized, therefore, that large cities with higher family incomes, housing values, and educational levels will hire more minorities in all employment categories. Because of the multicollinearity among these variables and for reasons of parsimony, z-scores were calculated to create a housing-income-education index. This index will be employed in each of the regression models.

Past research suggests that black elected officials will exert an impact upon employment levels, particularly with respect to key decisionmaking and professional positions. In particular, black mayors will reward their constituents with more jobs (Eisinger 1980, 1982; Stein 1986). Nelson and Meranto (1977) find that Carl Stokes in Cleveland and Richard Hatcher in Gary were able to improve black employment in city government during their terms in office. Saltzstein (1983) has discovered that the mayor's choice of personnel administrators was crucial to effective affirmative action programs.

Black representation on city council should also influence employment levels. Dye and Renick (1981) have discovered, in fact, that black council representation was the most significant determinant of the minority share of decisionmaking and professional positions. However, Eisinger (1982, 388) reports no such effect. Instead, he finds "that seats on the city council offer black representatives little opportunity for influence over personnel policies" and that this "suggests the degree to which employment policy is an executive rather than a legislative function." In a related vein, Karnig and Welch (1980) find that black council members have no effect upon policy expenditures. On the basis of the available evidence it is reasonable to expect that minority mayors, who are apparently well positioned to influence the hiring process, will exert a larger impact upon black employment levels than minority council members. There is less reason to expect that the level of Hispanic political representation will influence employment policy. Welch, Karnig, and Eribes (1983) find that Hispanic mayors and council members have no effect upon employment patterns.

In measuring the level of minority political representation I had to decide which year to employ. Once elected to office, how long will it take before minority public officials are in a position to influence employment policy significantly? The problem is complicated by the fact that in some cities minority representation in office is not continuous. Periods of a minority presence in government are interrupted by years in which no blacks or Hispanics hold public office. Since I could find no compelling reason to prefer one year or method over another I decided to measure the level of minority political representation during three separate periods: 1979, 1982, and 1984. The analysis revealed similar results for each year. Therefore, I will report findings for 1984 only.

A final political power variable is the council representation ratio. This measure was calculated by dividing the percentage black or Hispanic on council by the percentage black or Hispanic in the city population. The intent is to assess the extent to which councils where the minority share of the seats approaches the minority share of the population are able to influence employment patterns.

The political structure variables include election type, form of government, and percentage of council members elected from wards. I then combined these to create a reformism index. Municipal elections were coded as either partisan or nonpartisan. Partisan elections typically imply that the electoral process is contested by opposing political parties. Nominations are controlled by the parties, issues achieve greater significance, and candidates are identified on the ballot according to party designation. Nonpartisan elections tend to be dominated by personalities rather than issues. No political organization exists to provide support for public officials attempting to adopt innovative, redistributive, or controversial policies. In addition, voter turnout is lower in nonpartisan systems than in partisan ones, particularly among lower-income voters (Alford and Lee 1968; Hamilton 1971). The absence of political parties depresses turnout because the activity engaged in by parties stimulates interest, dramatizes issues, and mobilizes the voters. In addition, the lack of candidate designation on the ballot according to party affiliation contributes to voter frustration on the part of low-income citizens. It is probable, therefore, that the active electorate in nonpartisan cities will be dominated by conservative voters. Consequently, redistributive policies are unlikely to discover a sympathetic reception in such an environment.

The literature also suggests that form of government will influence public policy. Generally, mayor-council cities are thought to be more responsive to racial minorities (Lineberry and Fowler 1967) than council-manager cities. The latter type of government, with its professional city manager, is thought to emphasize middle-class values of efficiency and effectiveness and is seen as less sensitive to the demands of minority groups. Further, Stein (1986) finds that minority employment levels were somewhat higher in mayor-council cities. It should be noted, however, that other researchers have discovered that form of government exerts little impact upon municipal policy (Morgan and Pelissero 1980).

The representational system may also make a difference. Cities select council members by wards, at-large, or by a combination of the two. Generally, it is thought that ward systems are representative of neighborhood interests while at-large arrangements work to the advantage of business and upper-class interests. The empirical evidence tends to support the conclusion that minority representation on city council increases in a ward system (Engstrom and McDonald 1981; Hamilton 1978; Robins and Dye 1978; Vedlitz and Johnson 1982). However, others have found no such relationship (Karnig 1979; MacManus 1978).

Given the nature of the evidence, we can expect that cities with mayor-council government, partisan elections, and ward systems will be somewhat more likely to hire minorities than cities with council-manager forms, non-partisan elections, and at-large arrangements. In addition, the interactive effects among the variables may well be significant. Stein (1986) finds that minority employment levels are higher in mayor-council cities with a minority mayor than in council-manager cities with a white manager-mayor.

It should be noted, however, that form of government, partisanship, and election type all measure a more general dimension of reformism. Following the example of Lyons (1978, 123) I summed the number of reformed structures in each city (city manager, nonpartisan elections, percentage of council at-large) and assigned a reform score on that basis. These scores ranged from 0 to 3. I classified a city as reformed if its score exceeded 1.5 and unreformed if it had a score of 1.5 or less. For example, I considered a city reformed if it had a manager or nonpartisan elections and if at least 50% of the city council was elected from at-large positions.

Each of the 1,224 cities was also coded according to its regional location: Northeast, Midwest, South, and West. Although the sample sizes in most previous studies have not been large enough to control for the influence of region upon employment patterns, Saltzstein (1986) reports a negative effect for the Northeast for female jobs, while Stein (1986) has discovered higher minority employment rates in Sunbelt cities. In addition, Welch, Karnig, and Eribes (1983) analyze south-western cities and find that individual state locations are significant in accounting for variations in Hispanic employment levels.

Another variable included in the analysis is percentage of the total workforce accounted for by service-maintenance and clerical positions. This factor was thought to be important because some municipal workforces are composed of a higher percentage of menial jobs than others. It is also the case that blacks tend to disproportionately occupy these positions. Therefore, some cities may employ more blacks than others because a larger share of the public sector workforce is accounted for by service-maintenance and clerical jobs. In fact, Saltzstein (1986) finds that the proportion of total employment that is clerical is a significant predictor of the variation in female employment levels.

For Hispanics, I also consider percentage of the workforce that is black. Hall and Saltzstein (1976) find a negative relationship between proportion of Hispanics and blacks in the municipal workforce. Welch, Karnig, and Eribes

(1983) have discovered that Hispanic employment declined in cities with a large percentage of blacks on the workforce.

The effects of residency requirements upon the minority share of city jobs were also analyzed. Little is known about the impact of such ordinances on employment outcomes. However, on the basis of knowledge of the exclusionary effects of zoning regulations, I speculate that such ordinances are significant. In fact, Stein (1986, 702) finds that "the presence of a residency requirement ... has a favorable effect on minority hiring." Data on residency requirements were obtained from the personnel directors or city clerks in all 1,224 cities. Initially, it was anticipated that they would be relatively simple in nature. Instead, U.S. cities employ a bewildering variety of residency requirements as conditions of obtaining and holding jobs with city government. They include the following:

1. All or some employees have to move into the city within a specified period of time *after* they are hired.

2. Some employees, such as policemen and firemen, have to live within a certain number of miles or minutes of travel time to the city.

3. All employees have to be residents of the city a certain number of months or years before they are eligible to apply for a job.

4. Residents are given extra points on civil service exams.

5. Residents are hired before nonresidents.

6. The city has no residency requirement.

7. Certain employees, such as policemen and firemen, have to be residents of the city a number of months or years before they are eligible to apply for a job.

8. Certain employees, such as policemen and firemen, have to be residents of the *county* a number of months or years before they are eligible to apply for a job.

9. The city has multiple residency requirements consisting of various combinations of the conditions specified above.

The interpretation of these requirements poses some difficulties. For example, an ordinance that requires a new employee to move into the city within a few months may be just as exclusionary as one that requires applicants to be residents of the jurisdiction. A black resident of the inner city would lack the resources to move to a suburban location even if he or she happened to be qualified for the job on other grounds. Therefore, various combinations of residency requirements were coded for analysis and employed as dummy variables. A brief description of each follows.

Residency 1   0 = no residency requirement,
             1 = preemployment requirement

Residency 2   0 = no residency requirement,
              1 = pre- and postemployment requirement
Residency 3   0 = no residency requirement and postemployment
                  requirement,
              1 = preemployment requirement
Residency 4   0 = no requirement,
              1 = preemployment requirement and unspecified resident
                  preference
Residency 5   0 = no residency requirement and post employment
                  requirement,
              1 = preemployment requirement and unspecified resi-
                  dent preference.

Black Employment

An examination of Table 1 provides only limited support for the argument that black success at the ballot box translates into tangible rewards in the form of city jobs. The black mayor and black representation ratio variables exhibit a consistently weak relationship with employment outcomes in all four job categories. The black mayor coefficients are only .00 for total employment, .11 for officials-administrators, .05 for professionals, and .06 for protective service positions. However, the black council variable makes a greater difference. The council coefficients are .21 for officials-administrators and .14 for professional positions.

The political structure of city government is unrelated to how well blacks fare in the struggle for municipal jobs. An examination of the table reveals that none of the coefficients for the reform index rises above .02. It was also expected that percentage of the municipal workforce composed of clerical and service-maintenance jobs would prove to be a significant determinant of the variation in black employment. However, the evidence demonstrates that not to be the case. The same is true for the various categories of residency requirements imposed as a condition of city employment. The regression models reveal them to be consistently without effect.

Similarly, the total population variable and the income-housing-education index make little difference. The largest coefficient for the former variable is .11 while the strongest for the latter is .10. Instead, it is the size of the black population that is of overwhelming importance in each of the regression models. The coefficients for percentage black are .80 for total employment, .54 for officials-administrators, .62 for professionals, and .83 for protective service positions. What we can conclude is that it doesn't appear to make much difference whether a city is large or small, rich or poor. Further, the primary determinant of the variation in black employment levels

Table 1
Multiple Regression of Black
Employment Categories, All Cities

Variable	Total Employment	Officials- Administrators	Professionals	Protective Service Workers
Total population	.02	.04	.11†	-.01
Percentage black population	.80†	.54†	.62†	.83†
Black mayor	.00	.11†	.05†	.06
Percentage black council	.05*	.21†	.14†	.01
Percentage workforce clerical and service	.04†	.01	.03	.02
Reform index	-.02	.01	.00	-.02
Income-housing-education index	.10†	.01	.04	.06*
Black representation ratio	.00	-.06†	-.03	-.01
R²	.85	.56	.58	.72

*Significant at .05 level.
†Significant at .01 level.

apparently has little to do with whether the city has a black or white mayor, whether the governmental structure is reformed or unreformed, or whether the black share of seats on council approaches the black proportion of the population. Instead, black employment is a function of the size of the black population. Cities with a large black community hire more blacks than cities with a smaller black population. This powerful relationship holds for all four employment categories.

However, the level of black representation does make a difference. Although black control of the mayor's office was not an important factor, the black share of council seats did achieve modest significance. Even here, however, the influence of black representation upon employment levels is not uniform across all employment categories. Only for official-administrator and professional positions do minority council members exert an impact.

Another perspective on the relationship between the demographic, political, and employment variables is provided by eliminating from the analysis those cities with less than 10% black population. Generally, past research has excluded cities with a small black community based upon the assumption that a minimum threshold is necessary before black expectations with respect to electoral success and political power can be realized. When this is accomplished and the data are re-examined, the size of the black population again provides the dominant explanation of the variation in black job success in all four employment categories. In addition, the conclusion that the presence of a black mayor has no impact upon minority employment levels is reaffirmed. Further, the importance of the black council variable for professional positions declines to the point where it is no longer statistically significant. On the other hand, the regression coefficient for black council for officials-administrators increases from .21 for all cities to .26 for cities with large minority populations.

In general, when the analysis is limited to cites with larger black populations, the results support the findings reported for the full sample. The size of the black population continues to provide the dominant explanation of minority employment success in the public sector. This variable alone tends to dwarf in importance the political representation factors. In addition, no evidence was uncovered to challenge the conclusion that the presence of a black mayor makes little difference. However, there are two exceptions to the observation that the results for the two samples are essentially identical. First, the black council variable is no longer a significant factor in accounting for variation in professional positions. Second, the level of black representation on council increases in importance for official-administrator positions.

The finding that black political power is not particularly significant in terms of its impact upon minority employment levels is surprising. Could it be that the full sample of cities conceals considerable variation on a regional basis with respect to the effectiveness of minority political activity? Since the sample is so large, separate analyses make it possible to examine hundreds of cities in each region. When this is accomplished, some significant findings emerge. An examination of Table 2 reveals that the level of black political representation is of major importance in accounting for black job success in the West and is consistently significant in the Northeast. However, the black power variable only occasionally achieves significance in the Midwest and South.

Minority representation clearly makes a difference in northeastern cities. Although the size of the black population remains the dominant variable for all job categories, the percentage of the council that is black becomes the next-most-significant variable in the model. The regression coefficients for black council are .18 for total jobs, .36 for officials-administrators, and .29 for professional positions. Further, the presence of a black mayor becomes a significant factor in the regression model for protective service positions. The coefficient for the black mayor variable is .20. For northeastern cities, the variation in the level of minority employment is clearly a function of two factors: black population and the level of black political representation.

But while political power makes a substantial difference in determining who gets what in the Northeast, it doesn't count for much in the Midwest. The strongest relationship is noted for the black council variable and professional positions (.26). Neither black mayors nor black council members are capable of producing favorable and consistent employment outcomes in midwestern cities. Black political power also fails to make much of a dent in employment patterns in southern cities. The strongest relationships are observed for official-administrator positions where the regression coefficients are .27 for black mayor and .15 for the black council variable. Although demography rather than politics determines employment outcomes in southern cities, when politics does count, it is black mayors rather than black council members who are able to achieve favorable results for their constituents.

In the West the effectiveness of black political power is most dramatically realized. In fact, politics rivals the size of the black population as the key factor in accounting for the variation in minority job success. In western cities, the black share of council seats is a crucial variable in determining why blacks fare well in some municipalities and abysmally in others. For example, the regression coefficients for percentage black council are .35 for total employment, .44 for officials-administrators, .45 for professionals, and .44 for protective service positions. Again, however, the black mayor variable is not significant. The largest mayoral coefficient is only .07.

The separate regional analyses provide some striking evidence with respect to the effectiveness of the political process. What we can conclude is that minority investment in the political process returns substantial dividends in some parts of the country but not in others. In the West, black representation on council provides more than a simple boost to black employment chances. It is a decisive factor. In northeastern cities black political clout is an important but not dominant factor in the scramble for city jobs. In the South and Midwest political representation has some slight effect, but that impact is limited at best. In addition, the earlier finding that black mayors fail to contribute substantially to their constituents' employment success is reaffirmed. However, there are two notable exceptions to this pattern. In the North, the presence of a black mayor exerts a significant influence upon the level of minority employment for protective service positions. Similarly, black mayors make a difference for official-administrator positions in southern cities.

The examination of cities according to regional divisions strongly suggests that interpretations based solely upon an evaluation of findings derived from a national sample may well be misleading. The discovery in the full sample of 1,224 cities of a modest relationship between the level of black representation on council and job success does not hold when regional biases are included in the model. Instead, politics exerts a powerful and consistent effect in the West, substantial impact in the Northeast, and only limited influence in the South and Midwest.

Table 2
Multiple Regression of Black Employment Categories, Northeast and West

Variable	Total Employment		Officials-Administrators		Professionals		Protective Service Workers	
	Northeast	West	Northeast	West	Northeast	West	Northeast	West
Total Population	.06	.06	.00	.09*	.12	-.06	-.02	.02
Percentage black population	.77†	.64†	.63†	.46†	.58†	.55†	.76†	.48†
Black mayor	.01	.02	-.07	.07	-.02	-.06	.20†	.06
Percentage black council	.18*	.35†	.36†	.44†	.29*	.45†	-.03	.44†
Percentage workforce clerical and service	.04	.09†	.02	.03	-.07	.11†	-.07	.08†
Reform index	.00	.01	.04	-.01	-.10	-.02	-.04	-.01
Income-housing-education index	.14†	.09†	.06	-.04	.09	.05	.05	.05
Black representation ratio	-.02	-.09†	-.10	-.14†	-.11	-.10*	.04	-.11†
R²	.87	.88	.69	.78	.67	.73	.79	.77

*Significant at .05 level.
†Significant at .01 level.

Region and Political Structure

To conclude that the effectiveness of black political power varies considerably on the basis of region is not a particularly satisfying explanation. Do regional distinctions simply mask certain attributes that clusters of cities share in common? For example, do western cities exhibit a similar pattern of behavior because cities in that region have tended to adopt reformed rather than unreformed governmental structures? The regional distinctions we have uncovered might decline in significance if controls were instituted for additional variables.

The nature of local political institutions is a likely candidate for exploration in this area. The literature is replete with findings strongly suggesting that unreformed governments are more open and responsive to the diverse racial and socioeconomic groups in the city. It will be recalled that an examination of the various regression models revealed that the reform index variable was consistently without effect. Unreformed cities do not provide the black community with a larger share of public jobs. However, an interactive effect may be present. Although unreformed institutions and structures may not directly influence the level of minority employment, it may be the case that black elected officials are more effective in responding to constituent demands in unreformed cities.

In order to explore this possibility, I divided the entire sample into reformed and unreformed cities and conducted separate analyses of each group. An examination of the results reveals that the black council variable does, in fact, exert greater impact upon the level of minority employment in unreformed than in reformed governments. The coefficients for black council in unreformed communities are .31 for professionals and .23 for protective service positions (both of which are significant at the .01 level). The corresponding coefficients in reformed cities are only .09 and -.07.

The impact of unreformed structures upon enhancing the effectiveness of black public officials becomes dramatically apparent when we concentrate on cities with large black populations. An examination of Table 3 reveals that for unreformed cities with 10% or more black population the black council variable becomes the *most* significant determinant of minority employment for official-administrator and professional positions. With coefficients of .55 and .58, it is level of black representation on council rather than the black population variable that provides the dominant explanation in unreformed cities of why some governments hire more black decision makers and professionals than others. In reformed communities, however, black officials exert little effect upon minority employment success. In fact, for protective service positions the coefficient for the black council variable is actually negative (-.29).

Do these significant variations in black political effectiveness on the basis of differences in governmental structures also hold within individual regions?

Table 3
Multiple Regression of Black
Employment Categories, Unreformed
Cities with 10% or More Black

Variable	Total Jobs	Officials-Administrators	Professionals	Protective Service
Total population	.12	-.11	.35*	.04
Percentage black population	.45†	.19	.32*	.60†
Black mayor	-.04	.07	-.01	-.07
Percentage black council	.39*	.55*	.58†	.38
Percentage workforce clerical and service	.09	-.08	-.01	-.08
Income-housing-education index	.02	.23	-.16	.01
Black representation ratio	-.17	-.32	-.25	-.11
R²	.78	.45	.66	.71

*Significant at .05 level.
†Significant at .01 level.

I divided southern, midwestern, and northeastern cities into reformed and unreformed categories and conducted separate analyses of each group. (The West was excluded from this process since only a few cities in that region have adopted unreformed structures.) An examination of the results reveals that unreformed political institutions significantly enhance the effectiveness of black political power. In the South, the regression coefficients in unreformed cities for the black council variable are .48 for officials-administrators, .40 for professional positions, and .29 for protective service jobs. In reformed cities the same coefficients are .13, -.06, and -.20 respectively. A similar though less consistent pattern emerges in the Midwest. In that region the coefficients in unreformed cities for black council are .60 for professional positions and .36 for protective service jogs. The corresponding relationships in reformed cities are only .18 and .03. In northeastern cities, however, governmental structure appears to exert little impact upon the effectiveness of minority political representation. The variability of effects across the various employment categories in the region does not support an unambiguous interpretation with respect to the role of local political institutions.

The conclusion to be drawn from these various analyses is that it is not sufficient for blacks to elect one or more of their number to city council. The governmental structure under which minority officials operate also makes a very considerable difference. Apparently, the greater sensitivity of unreformed governments to the diverse racial and class groups that populate the city translates into enhanced political effectiveness for the black community. In fact, the interaction between structures and representation exerts a major impact on minority job success in southern and midwestern cities. It will be recalled that no political effects were noted in the South and Midwest in the initial regional analysis. That finding was misleading. Politics makes a very real difference in *unreformed* southern and midwestern communities. But is there another explanation lurking beneath the surface of unreformed structures? To maintain that unreformed governments are simply more open and responsive to minorities is too imprecise a solution to be compelling. Perhaps a more satisfactory answer is to be found in the nature of local electoral systems.

Wards, At-large, and Black Political Effectiveness

A major component of the reformism index is the type of electoral arrangement. Reformed cities elect members of the council at-large while unreformed governments select these public officials from wards or districts. One major line of inquiry in the study of urban politics has examined the extent to which ward electoral systems enhance and at-large arrangements depress the level of black representation. Generally, the evidence supports the conclusion that minorities fare better in ward cities (Engstrom and McDonald 1981; Robinson and Dye 1978; Vedlitz and Johnson 1982). The extent to which wards actually contribute to favorable policy outcomes for blacks is an issue that has received much less scholarly attention. In general, the findings suggest that policy differences between ward and at-large cities are unlikely to be particularly dramatic (Heilig and Mundt 1984). It should be pointed out, however, that no previous study has examined the effects of electoral arrangements upon employment outcomes.

In order to explore the possibility that there is an interactive effect between the nature of the electoral system and the effectiveness of black public officials, each of the 1,224 cities was classified into one of three groups: ward, at-large, or mixed. Again, separate analyses were conducted for each category. The results provide considerable support for the argument that minority elected officials are able to exert substantially more influence on employment outcomes in ward as opposed to at-large cities. In cities with ward systems the coefficients for the black council variable are .18 for total employment, .34 for professional positions, and .23 for protective service jobs (all significant at the .01 level). However, the corresponding coefficients in at-large cities are .00, .05, and -.10 respectively. As might be expected, cities with both ward and at-large council seats occupy the middle ground. The coefficients in those cities for total jobs, professionals, and protective service positions are .06, .27, and .11 respectively. The only exception to the pattern of greater minority influence in ward cities occurs for official-administrator positions. In that instance the largest coefficient is noted for cities with mixed arrangements (.28). An examination of the data, however, reveals that black council members in mixed systems tend to be elected from the ward rather than the at-large seats. Consequently, the finding of enhanced black power in ward systems is reinforced.

The fitting of the next piece of the puzzle revolves around the issue of regional differences. Does the interaction between black public officials and electoral type hold within regions? Again, the sample of cities was classified according to regional variations and further categorized on the basis of ward, at-large, and mixed systems. Then separate analyses were performed for each of the three groups within each of the four regions. An examination of the results continues to provide strong support for the argument that wards enhance minority political effectiveness while at-large arrangements stymie black efforts to influence employment outcomes. This pattern is particularly evident in southern cities. Tables 4–5 demonstrate that election in a ward system in the South significantly increases black political power for professional and protective service positions. The coefficients for the black council variable and professionals are .48 for wards, .27 for mixed, and -.16 for at-large systems, while the corresponding coefficients for protective service jobs are .34 for wards, .06 for mixed and -.24 for at-large. A similar pattern is also noted for officials-administrators. The coefficient in southern cities for the black council variable and decision-making positions is .42.

Clearly, then it makes a very considerable difference in southern cities whether black public officials are elected from wards or at-large. Ward arrangements dramatically enhance minority political effectiveness while at-large systems seriously damage the ability of black members of the council to deliver tangible, material rewards to their constituents. The importance of the ward system to black effectiveness is demonstrated by the fact that for decision-making and professional positions the black council variable in ward cities becomes one of the dominant factors in the regression models. With coefficients of .42 and .48, it actually rivals the significance of the black population variable in terms of accounting for variation in employment outcomes.

However, the finding that ward systems are crucial to black employment success in the South does not hold at all in western cities. Further examination of Tables 4–5 reveals, in fact, that the reverse is true. The relationships for the black council variable and the employment categories in the West are consistently negative in ward cities with coefficients of -.27 for professional, -.07 for protective service positions, and -.11 for officials-administrators. Instead, it is at-large electoral arrangements that dramatically boost black employment fortunes. The coefficients for the black council variable in at-large western cities are .53 for professionals, .45 for protective service positions, and .59 for officials-administrators. In fact, the black power variable becomes the key factor in all three regression equations and exceeds the

Table 4
Multiple Regression of Black
Professionals by Region

Variable	South			West*	
	Ward	At-Large	Mixed	Ward	At-Large
Total population	-.01	.11	.31	.12	-.05
Percentage black population	.45§	.72§	.48§	.81§	.42§
Black mayor	.01	.13†	.10	.00	.03
Percentage black council	.48†	-.16	.27	-.27†	.53§
Percentage workforce clerical and service	.02	.02	.10†	.04	.10
Income-housing-education index	.05	.17†	-.13	.05	.02
Black representation ratio	-.13	.11	-.06	.26†	-.12†
R^2	.56	.47	.75	.86	.77

*There were too few mixed cities in the West to make the regression analysis meaningful.
†Significant at .05 level.
§Significant at .01 level.

Table 5
Multiple Regression of Black
Protective Service Positions by Region

Variable	South			West*	
	Ward	At-Large	Mixed	Ward	At-Large
Total population	-.10	-.03	.19	.12	.00
Percentage black population	.77§	.85§	.83§	.82§	.42§
Black mayor	.00	.15§	.00	.00	.15†
Percentage black council	.34†	-.24§	.06	-.07	.45§
Percentage workforce clerical and service	.00	.01	-.08	-.06	.08†
Income-housing-education index	.09	.14§	-.17	-.05	.05
Black representation ratio	-.13	.10	-.05	.08	-.12†
R^2	.82	.72	.78	.84	.80

*There were too few mixed cities in the West to make the regression analysis meaningful.
†Significant at .05 level.
§Significant at .01 level.

significance of black population in each instance. For example, the coefficient for the black council variable for officials-administrators is .59, while the coefficient for black population is only .31.

Thus, governmental structure makes a very substantial difference. The nature of local political institutions and the type of electoral arrangement do matter and in fact matter a great deal. However, neither form of government or electoral system exerts an independent impact upon black employment patterns. Instead, structural arrangements and political institutions operate to either enhance or limit the effectiveness of black political leaders. Significantly, the substantial impact of these institutional conditions also holds across regions.

But why do electoral systems exert a differential impact on black political effectiveness in southern and western cities? Why do ward systems enhance black power in the South but detract from it in the West? Our efforts at developing a theory to account for these differences should begin with a consideration of the work of Browning, Marshall, and Tabb (1984). In their study of 10 California cities they concluded that black political effectiveness was a direct function of membership in the dominant political coalition. Black members of the council who were part of the dominant coalition in city government exerted a significant impact upon minority employment policy. Exclusion from the political coalition that controlled public policy severely retarded the ability of blacks on council to influence outcomes.

The concept of dominant political coalitions is an important contribution to the study of minority employment policy. However, two important questions remain unanswered. First, is black membership in the dominant coalition a realistic possibility in southern cites? Second, what is the relationship between electoral system and the likelihood of building coalitions that include minorities? The 10 cities in the Browning, Marshall, and Tabb study are not representative of all cities in the country. One important dimension on which cities differ is the extent of residential segregation and the likelihood of racial polarization. The interactive effect between racial segregation, electoral system, and coalition building may be crucial.

Vedlitz and Johnson (1982, 734) find ward systems have a major impact upon the election of blacks to council in segregated cities. In fact, they find that "in the segregated cities black representation in single-member district communities was nearly three times more favorable than in at-large communities." However, the type of electoral system makes no difference in nonsegregated cities with respect to black representation on council. Vedlitz and Johnson offer two explanations for this finding. First, racial segregation may also imply racial polarization in some cities. Such conflict may limit the likelihood of black electoral success in at-large systems. Second, at-large arrangements may require blacks to form coalitions with whites and building such coalitions will be difficult in segregated cities.

The conclusions reached in these two studies are relevant to the issue at hand. However, both a considerable refinement and an extension of the findings are in order. Clearly, coalition building should prove to be a more difficult task in segregated than in nonsegregated communities. In addition, the political effectiveness of blacks is likely to vary on the basis of two dimensions: segregation and the nature of the electoral system. In segregated cities blacks will have little opportunity to join the dominant coalition in either ward or at-large communities. Since the white majority will be unwilling to share substantial power with them, blacks will be forced to rely upon other means to influence policy outcomes. These alternative methods may include attempts to develop alliances with other minorities and disaffected white liberals as well as efforts to increase the minority share of council seats. In segregated and racially polarized communities black political power will prove to be the most effective in ward systems.

Minorities elected under at-large arrangements in segregated cities will exert little influence upon policy because they will be excluded from the dominant political coalition. In addition, they will have little opportunity to explore alternative means of enhancing their power because at-large systems in segregated communities severely depress the election of minorities.

Differences are also likely to exist between ward and at-large cities with respect to the types of coalitions formed and the style of black leaders elected. The coalitions built in segregated communities under at-large arrangements are not apt to survive the electoral stage. Also, blacks recruited to run as coalition candidates in at-large contests must be acceptable to the white majority. Consequently, it is unlikely that such candidates will vigorously champion a redistributive agenda on behalf of their constituents. On the other hand, blacks elected from wards in racially polarized cities will almost certainly take office with a clearly defined set of policy objectives. As a result, one can expect that in segregated communities blacks elected from wards will exert a greater influence on employment outcomes than leaders selected at-large.

In nonsegregated cities, however, the ward system may actually work to the disadvantage of blacks. In communities where little racial polarization exists, blacks elected from wards may have no incentive to engage in coalition building. As a result, they may be ignored by the dominant coalition. Black members of the city council in nonsegregated communities will experience their greatest success in terms of influencing employment outcomes in at-large systems where exclusion is not a goal of the dominant majority but where coalition building is nonetheless essential to electoral victory.

This interpretation of the interaction between black political effectiveness, segregation, and electoral system is highly consistent with the data. Although segregation indexes were not available for each city, I was able to obtain such data for the major cities in the sample (Vedlitz and Johnson 1982). I relied on these indexes of residential segregation to calculate a mean segregation score for each region. An examination of the results reveals that the South is the most segregated region in the country, followed by the Midwest, with the West and the Northeast ranking as the least segregated. As we have seen, black political power in segregated southern communities is much more effective in ward systems than under at-large arrangements, while in the West the reverse is the case. Black influence upon employment policy is dramatically enhanced in at-large western cities but severely limited in ward systems. The logical explanation is that blacks in segregated southern cities have little opportunity to effectively participate in the dominant coalition that controls public policy in either ward or at-large systems. Consequently, ward structures enhance black political effectiveness because they significantly improve the prospects of minority electoral success. Once elected in ward cities black officials can then use other means to influence policy choices (forming coalitions with other minorities and disaffected whites). In at-large segregated cities, however, blacks on council exert no influence on employment patterns. Not only do at-large systems in segregated communities severely depress the level of black representation on council, they also attract black candidates who, while acceptable to the white majority, are unlikely to press for a redistributive agenda once elected to office.

In less segregated cities, however, at-large systems appear to operate to the advantage of blacks. In the West, black political power is much more effective in at-large than in ward cities. According to our interpretation, less segregated communities are also less racially polarized. Therefore, the dominant majority has relatively little incentive to engage in a politics of minority exclusion. Blacks elected under at-large systems will be more likely to gain access to the dominant coalition because of the need to attract community-wide support during the electoral contest. On the other hand, a ward structure may tend to isolate black officials in nonsegregated cities and reduce their political influence and policy effectiveness. Since there are few incentives to build electoral coalitions in ward systems, the likelihood of joining the dominant policy coalition once elected to office may be greatly reduced.

Hispanic Employment

What role does politics play in determining employment outcomes for Hispanics? An examination of Table 6 reveals that for the entire sample of 1,224 cities political factors are more significant for Hispanics than for blacks. Although Hispanic mayors are not particularly important (the largest mayoral coefficients are only .12 and .13), the Hispanic council variable exerts a consistent if moderate effect across all employment categories. The coefficients for Hispanic council for all cities are .21 for total employment, .29 for officials-administrators, .20 for professionals, and .19 for protective service positions.

As was the case for blacks, however, the minority population variable provides the dominant explanation of the variation in employment patterns. The coefficients for the percent Hispanic population variable and the four employment categories are .79, .55, .57, and .72 respectively.

Hispanic councils exert an even greater impact on employment outcomes in cities with a substantial Hispanic population. A further examination of Table 6 reveals that in cities with 10% or more Hispanics the coefficients are .21 for total employment, .40 for officials-administrators, .36 for professionals, and .31 for protective service workers. Again, the relationships between political power and employment patterns are considerably stronger for Hispanics than for blacks.

In general, the analysis supports the conclusion that the determinants of the variation in public employment are similar for both minority groups. The size of the minority community is the best predictor of how well blacks and Hispanics will fare in the distributional struggle over finite resources. None of the other demographic variables makes a difference. However, an exception to the observation that minority employment outcomes can be traced to the same set of causal factors is the finding that Hispanic councils are considerably and consistently more influential than black councils. This differential impact is particularly pronounced in cities with a substantial minority population. It should also be noted that minority employment does not appear to be a zero-sum game for blacks and Hispanics. It is not the case that Hispanics fare poorly in those cities where blacks hold a sizable share of the municipal jobs.

What impact do regional distinctions have upon Hispanic employment patterns? Since northeastern and midwestern cities have small Hispanic populations, these two regions were eliminated from the analysis. I will focus on the South and West. Further, the states of California, Texas, New Mexico, and Arizona were combined to form a southwest region. An examination of the results reveals that the Hispanic council variable is crucial to the employment success of Hispanics in southwestern and western cities. This finding is particularly pronounced in cities with substantial Hispanic populations. For southwestern cities with 10% or more Hispanics the regression coefficients for the council variable are .31 for total employment, .52 for officials-administrators, .49 for professionals ,and .42 for protective service positions. In fact, for decision-making and professional positions (Tables 7–8) the proportion of council seats controlled by Hispanics exceeds the significance of the size of the Hispanic population in determining employment outcomes. Again, however, Hispanic mayors are not particularly influential. The coefficients for the mayoral variable are .08, .15, .16, and .12 respectively.

An examination of western cities reveals that the Hispanic share of council seats is similarly crucial to minority employment success. In cities with 10% or more Hispanics, the coefficients for the council variable are .40 for

Table 6
Multiple Regression of Hispanic Employment Categories, All Cities and Cities 10% or More Hispanic

Variable	Total Jobs		Officials-Administrators		Professionals		Protective Service Workers	
	All Cities	10% or More	All Cities	10% or More	All Cities	10% or More	All Cities	10% or More
Total Population	-.03	-.05	.05*	-.08	-.04	-.05	-.05†	-.11
Percentage Hispanic population	.79†	.65†	.55†	.50†	.57†	.47†	.72†	.65†
Hispanic mayor	.04†	.06	.12†	.12*	.13†	.13*	.09†	.09
Percentage Hispanic council	.15†	.21†	.29†	.40†	.20†	.36†	.19†	.31†
Percentage workforce clerical and service	.03†	.08*	.00	.02	-.03	-.09	.00	-.01
Reform index	.01	.01	.00	-.05	.00	.03	.00	.00
Income-housing-education index	.07†	.04	.04	.06	.05	.00	.07†	.12*
Percentage black workers	-.05†	-.06	-.03	.00	-.02	.00	.00	.04
Hispanic representation ratio	-.02*	-.06	-.06†	-.19†	-.05*	-.23†	-.04†	-.16†
R²	.87	.84	.69	.72	.61	.63	.81	.78

*Significant at .05 level.
†Significant at .01 level.

Table 7
Multiple Regression of Hispanic
Officials-Administrators by Region

Variable	Southwest		South		West	
	All Cities	10% or More	All Cities	10% or More	All Cities	10% or More
Total population	-.11*	-.08	-.04	-.11	-.15*	-.13
Percentage Hispanic population	.45†	.46†	.77†	.85†	.39†	.27†
Hispanic mayor	.15†	.15†	.13†	.12	.09	.12
Percentage Hispanic council	.44†	.52†	.10	.11	.42†	.69†
Percentage workforce clerical and service	.04	.03	-.02	-.03	.05	.07
Reform index	-.04	-.05	-.03	-.03	.00	-.04
Income-housing-education index	.07	.05	-.03	.04	.13*	.06
Percentage black workers	-.02	.00	.00	.11	.03	.02
Hispanic representation ratio	-.17*	-.25†	-.09†	-.16	.05	-.30•
R^2	.72	.76	.82	.85	.56	.60

*Significant at .05 level.
†Significant at .01 level.

total employment, .69 for officials-administrators, .68 for professionals, and .40 for protective service positions. Again, politics is more important than demography with respect to accounting for the variation in decision-making and professional positions. The coefficients for Hispanic council for these employment categories are .69 and .68, while the coefficients for the size of the Hispanic population are only .27 and .18. Clearly, Hispanic political power as measured by the minority share of council seats is the dominant influence in determining how well the Hispanic community fares in the struggle for key decision-making and professional positions in city government. Politics counts in southwestern and western cities and it counts heavily.

A different story can be told for southern cities. Neither the Hispanic mayor nor Hispanic council variables make much difference in either the full sample or in those cities with at least 10% Hispanic population. The largest coefficient to achieve statistical significance is noted for the relationship between Hispanic council and protective service positions (.20). It should be pointed out, however, that with the exception of Texas and Florida, southern cities have relatively small Hispanic populations. The fact remains that in those cities with substantial numbers of Hispanics (cities which are

Table 8
Multiple Regression of Hispanic
Professionals by Region

Variable	Southwest		South		West	
	All Cities	10% or More	All Cities	10% or More	All Cities	10% or More
Total population	-.10	-.03	-.06	-.11	-.09	.02
Percentage Hispanic population	.48†	.42†	.78†	.90†	.41†	.18
Hispanic mayor	.15†	.16†	.04	-.10	.15†	.22†
Percentage Hispanic council	.36†	.49†	.14	.30	.24†	.68†
Percentage workforce clerical and service	-.05	-.06	-.07†	-.25†	-.01	.03
Reform index	.03	.04	-.01	.14	.05	.08
Income-housing-education index	.08	-.01	.00	.08	.09	-.10
Percentage black workers	.00	.00	.03	.21*	.03	.00
Hispanic representation ratio	-.16*	-.29†	-.08*	-.25	-.04	-.45†
R^2	.62	.66	.77	.79	.40	.49

*Significant at .05 level.
†Significant at .01 level.

disproportionately concentrated in the West and Southwest) political power provides a powerful explanation of the variation in distributional outcomes.

For blacks the structural and institutional characteristics of local governments significantly enhance—or limit—the effectiveness of minority political power. Further, the interaction between structure and political power varies dramatically on a regional basis. This differential impact could be attributed to the level of residential segregation in a community. It is reasonable to expect that a similar causal relationship is present with respect to Hispanic employment patterns. Unfortunately, the small sample sizes preclude the possibility of examining the interaction between governmental structure, segregation, and political effectiveness at the regional level. Although analyses were conducted for individual regions, the volatility of the regression coefficients does not allow for any confidence in the results. Therefore, I will limit the discussion of the findings to an analysis of all cities.

It will be recalled that for blacks the ward system enhanced political effectiveness in segregated cities but seriously weakened it in at-large cities. The reverse was the case in nonsegregated communities where at-large arrangements dramatically strengthened the influence of black political leaders but where wards isolated minority officials and retarded their effectiveness. Can we expect an identical set of findings for Hispanics? Probably not. Although data are not available on the extent of Hispanic residential segregation for cities in the sample, there is considerable evidence to support the conclusion that Hispanics are less segregated than blacks. In fact, Anglo-Hispanic groupings exhibit the lowest levels of residential segregation while Anglo-black groupings show the highest (Hwang and Murdock 1982; Lopez 1981; Moore and Mittelbach 1966). Lopez (1981, 55) analyzed changes in segregation levels in 56 southwestern cities between 1960 and 1970 and found that "the difference in Mexican-American-Anglo segregation has narrowed while Mexican-American-black segregation has become more pronounced. It would appear that the segregation of Mexican-Americans from Anglos is becoming more like that of European ethnics ... and less like that of blacks."

Not only are Hispanics less segregated than blacks, but the perceived social distance between Hispanics and Anglos is less than it is between blacks and whites. Anglos have a greater tolerance toward Hispanics than toward blacks (Davidson and Gaitz 1973; Pickney 1970), and Hispanics are more frequently thought of as white by Anglos (Lopez 1981). Given the reduced levels of segregation for Hispanics and the greater acceptance of Hispanics by Anglos, we should expect that the interaction between electoral system and residential segregation will differ for each minority group. Specifically, Hispanic political power should be most effective under at-large arrangements and least influential in ward systems. This assumption is based upon the finding from the black analysis that at-large electoral structures in nonsegregated cities visibly strengthen minority political effectiveness while ward arrangements in nonsegregated cities severely limit that effectiveness.

When all 1,224 cities are classified according to ward and at-large systems and separate analyses are conducted of each, in fact, at-large electoral structures do significantly enhance Hispanic political effectiveness. An examination of Table 9 reveals that in every employment category the Hispanic council variable exerts a much greater influence in at-large than in ward cities. The coefficients for Hispanic council in at-large communities are .27 for total employment, .34 for officials-administrators, .30 for professionals, and .27 for protective service positions. The corresponding coefficients in ward systems are only .04, -.11, -.29 and .11 respectively.

Implications

The research reported here significantly advances the debate concerning the impact of local political institutions upon policy outcomes. Political structure does make a difference. Sometimes, in fact, it becomes the decisive factor in determining winners and losers in the distributional struggle. It should be emphasized, however, that the nature and characteristics of local political

Table 9
Multiple Regression of Hispanic Employment Categories by Electoral System

Variable	Total Jobs			Officials-Administrators			Professionals			Protective Service Workers		
	Ward	At-Large	Mixed	Ward	At-Large	Mixed	Ward	At-Large	Mixed	Ward	At-Large	Mixed
Total population	-.01	-.02	-.10*	-.04	-.04	.00	-.01	-.01	-.07	-.02	-.02	-.10
Percentage Hispanic population	.91†	.69†	.87†	.77†	.38†	.51†	.80†	.39†	.62†	.86†	.63†	.84†
Hispanic mayor	—	.04	.09†	—	.28†	-.13†	—	.24†	-.07*	—	.14†	.02
Percentage Hispanic council	.04	.27†	-.04	-.11†	.34†	.53†	-.29	.30†	.40†	.11†	.27†	.12*
Percentage workforce clerical and service	.01	.03	.06	-.01	.02	.04	-.04	.03	.02	-.02	.00	.05
Income-housing-education index	-.06†	.09†	.10†	-.01	.06	.00	-.05	.07	.07	-.01	.09†	.10*
Percentage black workers	-.03	-.04*	-.07*	-.03	.00	-.08	-.03	.00	-.03	.00	.00	-.03
Hispanic representation ratio	-.02	-.05†	-.02	.05	-.09†	-.16†	.09†	-.09†	-.14†	-.03	-.08†	-.04
R²	.92	.87	.93	.80	.71	.85	.75	.61	.82	.88	.81	.87

*Significant at .05 level.
†Significant at .01 level.

institutions do not directly influence employment patterns. Instead, they operate to create an environment which serves to either enhance or retard the effectiveness of minority political power. These findings challenge the assumption that electoral coalitions and election outcomes do not really matter, that political institutions (form of government, electoral system) are only historical curiosities with little policy relevance, and that city councils as decision-making bodies are inactive at worst or reactive at best. Minority political efforts can pay substantial dividends. Blacks and Hispanics are not helpless. The election of black and Hispanic representatives to the city council can produce more and better jobs for the minority community. However, that effectiveness is mediated by a powerful set of factors that includes the form of government, the level of racial segregation, and the nature of the electoral system.

The finding that minority mayors are unable to influence employment policy but that both black and Hispanic representatives on city council exert a major impact upon employment patterns also deserves comment. Traditionally, minority mayors have been perceived to be in the best position to reward their constituents. In some cities, at least, they appoint personnel directors, affirmative action officers, and department heads. They have the potential to set the tone of government and influence the administration and implementation of personnel policy. But there is reason to doubt the conventional wisdom. Karnig and Welch (1980) observe that black, as well as white, mayors are limited by the fiscal condition of the city and by the federal and state roles. In addition, black mayors tend to represent cities in the worst financial condition. Finally, whites will oppose attempts on the part of minority mayors to substantially redistribute resources. To this I might add that black mayors will likely find it necessary to court a citywide constituency and may find it exceedingly difficult to respond to the particularistic demands of the minority community.

On the other hand, the literature has not been kind to city councils. The research on municipal budgeting paints a picture of a council eager to defer to the expertise of the executive and the bureaucrat, while the recruitment literature (Prewitt 1970) reinforces the images of council members as motivated by a sense of civic obligation and "voluntarism." Successful candidates assume office without the benefit of a clearly defined policy agenda. Consequently, they are easy prey for the expert and experienced mayor, city manager, and administrator. Typically, city councils are described as reactive institutions characterized by high turnover and inadequate staff support. Individual council members are poorly paid and inexperienced, devote only a few hours a week to the job, take office without clear policy goals, are little interested in staying in office, and are no match for professional politicians, managers, and administrators.

However, this bleak picture of the policy role of city councils is likely overdrawn. First, these conclusions are generally based on findings from case studies of only one or a few cities and may not be representative of all communities. Second, the available research has largely ignored minority council members who are apt to be much more diligent in their pursuit of redistributive policy objectives than white businessmen who seek office out of a sense of civic obligation. Third, the literature has generally failed to distinguish between ward and at-large councils. We have seen that ward systems significantly enhance the effectiveness of black political power in segregated communities while at-large arrangements boost minority influence in non-segregated cities. It is probable that the behavior, activities, and influence of council members with respect to other policy agendas also varies significantly on the basis of electoral system difference. Studies that have ignored the substantial impact of these differences on council behavior and effectiveness may have produced a distorted picture of the policy role of local legislatures.

In fact, several recent studies suggest that city councils may exert a greater influence upon policy outcomes than was previously thought to be the case. Abney and Lauth (1986, 188) in a survey of department heads in cities over 50 thousand in population find that 32% of department heads "perceived contacts by council members on behalf of constituents to result in a distortion of their priorities." Thirty-seven percent reported that "requests from council members are important in their decisions about the pattern of service delivery," and 42% of the department heads in reformed cities ranked the council as having the *most* impact on their departments when compared to the chief executive and interest groups. Thomas Baylis (1983) studied the San Antonio council and finds that in addition to the selection of the city manager and the approval of the budget, the council exerted significant influence on the allocation of federal funds and on appointments to major municipal boards and commissions. Dye and Renick (1981) analyze employment patterns in 42 cities and conclude that the level of minority representation on council was the most significant determinant of the variation in minority employment. Finally Browning, Marshall, and Tabb (1984) in their study of 10 California cities find that the primary explanation of differences in minority share of public jobs is the extent to which minority council members have gained entry to the dominant political coalition.

Although the research literature does not allow us to resurrect the city council as the dominant policy-making institution, the evidence is sufficiently extensive to cast doubt on conventional wisdom. Councils are something more than reactive bodies manipulated at will by executives and bureaucrats and disinclined to press their own policy agendas. At a minimum, the research reported here, as well as the work of others (Browning, Marshall, and Tabb 1984; Dye and Renick 1981) reveals that minority council members play a crucial role with respect to employment policy.

Another point deserves consideration. Why does the level of Hispanic political representation exert a greater impact upon employment than black representation? Although we do not have data on the variety of factors that might account for this differential effectiveness, I can suggest one possibility. Browning, Marshall, and Tabb (1984) argue that one factor that will cause minority officials to take action with respect to employment policy is the severity of the problem; that is, minority council members are more likely to press for a redistribution of resources in cities where the minority share of the workforce lags far behind the minority proportion of the population. If this interpretation is correct, we should expect that the gap between share of the municipal workforce and proportion of the population will be greater for Hispanics than for blacks. Parity ratios were calculated by dividing the percentage black or Hispanic in each of the four employment categories by the minority share of the total population. Higher scores indicate a move toward parity while declining scores suggest an underrepresentation of minorities. An examination of the results reveals that while both blacks and Hispanics are underrepresented in terms of their share of municipal jobs, the parity gap is considerably greater for Hispanics than for blacks. The ratios for blacks are .52 for officials-administrators, .76 for professionals, and .73 for protective service positions. However, the corresponding scores for Hispanics are only .36, .45 and .58 respectively. If minority elected officials are moved to act on the basis of their perception of the severity of the problem, we can conclude that Hispanic council members will more vigorously press for a redistribution of public jobs. Although alternative explanations need to be explored, this interpretation is certainly consistent with the data. Hispanic representatives exert a greater impact upon employment policy because the gap between the Hispanic share of the workforce and their proportion of the total population is greater than it is for blacks.

Conclusion

I return to the original question: Does the political process work for blacks and Hispanics? The answer is *yes*—under certain conditions. Racial minorities are not helpless in their quest for more of the public benefits city government has within its power to withhold or bestow. Their fate does not depend completely upon the largess of the federal government or the sympathy and support of white allies. They are not captives of powerful forces beyond their ability to shape and control. If blacks and Hispanics organize, compete in the electoral arena, and elect one or more of their number to city council, they can lay claim to a larger slice of the public pie. In the process, however, minority influence is powerfully constrained by local political institutions.

When all cities were analyzed, the results reveal that the size of the minority population rather than minority political power provides the dominant explanation of why some municipal governments hire many more blacks and Hispanics than others. It is when we turned to an analysis of employment patterns on a regional basis that we discovered very substantial differences in the effectiveness of minority political representation. Region, in turn, was found to mask significant variations both within and across regions with respect to the influence of form of government and electoral system.

For example, when all southern cities were analyzed, we saw that black elected officials exert little impact upon employment outcomes. If we had left the matter at that, the inescapable conclusion would have been that politics doesn't make a difference in the South. However, further examination of the data revealed a powerful interactive effect between form of government, electoral system, and black political effectiveness. When southern communities were divided into reformed and unreformed governments we saw that black council members were much more effective in terms of influencing employment outcomes in unreformed cities. The evidence supports the argument that unreformed political institutions are more open and responsive to the diverse groups within the city. In addition, hiring decisions are more apt to be sensitive to the demands of elected officials in unreformed communities, while personnel matters in reformed governments will likely be controlled by the city manager and professional staff.

The nature of the electoral system was also found to be of major significance. In southern cities black political effectiveness was greatly enhanced by ward arrangements and severely retarded by at-large systems. The reverse was the case in the West where at-large elections provided a powerful boost to black influence and ward arrangements imposed significant limits on the effectiveness of minority council members. In both regions the political structure variable exerted a major and sometimes even dominant influence upon minority employment levels.

The failure in past research to examine the interaction between residential segregation, electoral system, and minority political effectiveness concealed the powerful role played by black and Hispanic council members. It is not that politics is of little significance in arraying winners and losers in the distributional contest. Rather, minority political representation makes absolutely no difference under some institutional arrangements but is of decisive importance under others.

I also suggest that a critical reevaluation of the respective policy roles of the mayor and city council is in order. Traditionally, councils have been perceived as reactive bodies easily manipulated by the executive and quick to defer to the expertise of the professional administrator. This perspective holds that only a strong, aggressive mayor has both the vision and requisite political skills and resources to confer significant public benefits upon the minority community. However, the findings reported in this chapter reveal that minority council members rather than mayors are the key actors in the policy process.

It is important to point out once again, however, that the nature of the local governmental and electoral system is crucial to both enhancing and limiting that effectiveness. The influence of minority council members is conditioned and medicated by a complex of factors that includes the extent of racial polarization and the type of structural arrangement.

Notes

Appreciation is expressed to Arnold Vedlitz, Charles Johnson, Norm Luttbeg, Harvey Tucker, Bryan Jones, Keith Hamm, and David Whaley for valuable advice and assistance on this chapter.

1. Most of the large cities with black mayors are found in the sample. These include Philadelphia, Atlanta, New Orleans, Detroit, Chicago, Los Angeles, Newark, and Richmond. The mean percentage black in all the black mayor cities was 43.0%.

2. *Officials and Administrators.* Occupations in which employees set broad policies and exercise overall responsibility for execution of these policies or direct individual departments or special phases of the agency's operations. Includes department heads, bureau chiefs, division chiefs, directors, deputy directors. *Professionals.* Occupations requiring specialized and theoretical knowledge usually acquired through college training or work experience. Includes personnel and labor relations workers, social workers, doctors, economists, lawyers, engineers, teachers, accountants, police and fire captains, and lieutenants. *Protective Service Workers.* Occupations in which workers are entrusted with public safety and security. Includes police officers, fire fighters, guards, correctional officers, detectives. *Service-Maintenance Workers.* Includes refuse collectors, construction laborers, bus drivers, custodial personnel, grounds keepers.

3. The regions were composed of the following states: Northeast (Connecticut, Maine, Massachusetts, New Hampshire, New Jersey, New York, Pennsylvania, Rhode Island, Vermont); Midwest (Illinois, Indiana, Iowa, Kansas, Michigan, Minnesota, Missouri, Nebraska, North Dakota, Ohio, South Dakota, Wisconsin); South (Alabama, Arkansas, Delaware, District of Columbia, Florida, Georgia, Kentucky, Louisiana, Maryland, Mississippi, North Carolina, Oklahoma, South Carolina, Tennessee, Texas, Virginia, West Virginia); West (Alaska, Arizona, California, Colorado, Hawaii, Idaho, Montana, Nevada, New Mexico, Oregon, Utah, Washington, Wyoming).

References

Abney, Glenn, and Thomas P. Lauth. 1986. *The Politics of State and City Administration.* Albany: State University of New York Press.

Alford, Robert P., and Eugene C. Lee. 1968. "Voting Turnout in American Cities." *American Political Science Review* 62: 796–813.

Baylis, Thomas A. 1983. "Leadership Change in Contemporary San Antonio." In *The Politics of San Antonio,* eds. David R. Johnson, John A. Booth, and Richard J. Harris. Lincoln: University of Nebraska Press.

Browning, Rufus P., Dale Rogers Marshall, and David H. Tabb. 1984. *Protest Is Not Enough.* Berkeley: University of California Press.

Campbell, David, and Joe R. Feagin. 1975. "Black Politics in the South: A Descriptive Analysis." *Journal of Politics* 37: 129–59.

Cole, Leonard. 1976. *Blacks in Power: A Comparative Study of Black and White Elected Officials*. Princeton, NJ: Princeton University Press.

Davidson, Chandler, and Charles M. Gaitz. 1973. "Ethnic Attitudes As a Basis for Minority Cooperation in a Southwestern Metropolis." *Social Science Quarterly* 53: 738–48.

Dye, Thomas R., and James Renick. 1981. "Political Power and City Jobs: Determinants of Minority Employment." *Social Science Quarterly* 62: 475–86.

Eisinger, Peter K. 1980. *Politics of Displacement: Racial and Ethnic Transition in Three American Cities*. New York: Academic.

Eisinger, Peter K. 1982. "Black Employment in Municipal Jobs: The Impact of Black Political Power." *American Political Science Review* 76: 380–92.

Engstrom, Richard L., and Michael E. McDonald. 1981. "The Election of Blacks to City Council: Clarifying the Impact of Electoral Arrangements on the Seats/ Population Relationship." *American Political Science Review* 75: 344–54.

Hall, Grace, and Al Saltzstein. 1976. "Equal Employment Opportunity for Minorities in Municipal Government." *Social Science Quarterly* 57: 865–71.

Hamilton, Howard D. 1971. "The Municipal Voter: Voting and Nonvoting in City Elections." *American Political Science Review* 65: 1135–40.

Hamilton, Howard D. 1978. "Electing the Cincinnati City Council: An Examination of Alternative Electoral Representation Systems." Cincinnati: Stephen H. Wilder Foundation.

Heilig, Peggy, and Robert J. Mundt. 1984. *Your Voice at City Hall*. Albany: State University of New York Press.

Hwang Sean-shong, and Steve H. Murdock. 1982. "Residential Segregation in Texas in 1980." *Social Science Quarterly* 63; 737–48.

Karnig, Albert. 1979. "Black Resources and City Council Representation." *Journal of Politics* 41: 134–49.

Karnig, Albert, and Susan Welch. 1980. *Black Representation and Urban Policy*. Chicago: University of Chicago Press.

Keech, William R. 1968. *The Impact of Negro Voting: The Role of the Vote in the Quest for Equality*. Chicago: Rand McNally.

Levine, Charles H. 1974. *Racial Conflict and the American Mayor*. Lexington, MA: Lexington Books.

Lineberry, Robert L. 1977. *Equality and Urban Policy: The Distribution of Municipal Public Services*. Beverly Hills, CA: Sage.

Lineberry, Robert L., and Edmund P. Fowler. 1967. "Reformism and Public Policy in American Cities." *American Political Science Review* 67: 701–16.

Lopez, Manuel. 1981. "Patterns of Interethnic Residential Segregation in the Urban Southwest, 1960 and 1970." *Social Science Quarterly* 62: 50–63.

Lyons, William. 1978. "Reform and Response in American Cities: Structure and Policy Reconsidered." *Social Science Quarterly* 59: 118–32.

MacManus, Susan S. 1978. "City Council Election Procedures and Minority Representation: Are They Related?" *Social Science Quarterly* 59: 153–61.

Mladenka, Kenneth R. 1980. "The Urban Bureaucracy and the Chicago Political Machine: Who Gets What and the Limits to Political Control." *American Political Science Review* 74: 991–98.

Moore, Joan W., and Fred G. Mittelbach. 1966. *Residential Segregation in the Urban Southwest*. Los Angeles: University of California Press.

Morgan, David R., and John P. Pelissero. 1980. "Urban Policy: Does Political Structure Matter?" *American Political Science Review* 74: 999–1006.

Nelson, William E., Jr., and Philip J. Meranto. 1977. *Electing Black Mayors: Political Action in the Black Community.* Columbus: Ohio State University Press.

Prewitt, Kenneth. 1970. *The Recruitment of Political Leaders: A Study of Citizen-Politicians.* Indianapolis: Bobbs-Merrill.

Pickney, Alphonso. 1970. "Prejudice toward Mexican and Negro Americans." In *Mexican-Americans in the United States,* ed. John H. Burma. Cambridge, MA: Schenkman.

Robinson, Theodore P., and Thomas R. Dye. 1978. "Reformism and Black Representation on City Councils." *Social Science Quarterly* 59: 133–41.

Saltzstein, Grace H. 1983. "Personnel Directors and Female Employment Representation: A New Addition to Models of Equal Employment Opportunity Policy." *Social Science Quarterly* 64: 734–46.

Saltzstein, Grace H. 1986. "Female Mayors and Women in Municipal Jobs." *American Journal of Political Science* 30: 140–64.

Stein, Lana. 1986. "Representative Local Government: Minorities in the Municipal Workforce." *Journal of Politics* 48: 694–713.

Vedlitz, Arnold, and Charles A. Johnson. 1982. "Community Racial Segregation, Electoral Structure, and Minority Representation." *Social Science Quarterly* 63: 729–36.

Welch, Susan, Albert K. Karnig, and Richard Eribes. 1983. "Changes in Hispanic Local Public Employment in the Southwest." *Western Political Quarterly* 36: 660–73.

District Elections and Municipal Employee Unions

Stephen L. Mehay and Rodolfo A. Gonzalez

I. Introduction

Social scientists have begun to pay closer attention to the role played by the institutional structure of municipal government in influencing the behavior of elected local officials. One important element of the political structure that has drawn scant attention is the method used to elect city council members. City council members may be selected from districts or wards; city-wide in at-large elections; or via a mixture of district and at-large elections. Prior to the early 1900s, the majority of cities used district elections, but at that time the political reform movement convinced most communities to adopt at-large seats. In recent years, efforts to improve minority representation on municipal governing bodies has sparked a return to district elections.[1]

The choice of election method could significantly affect the power of special interest groups to influence municipal decisions. This chapter focuses on the interaction between the electoral system and the power of municipal employees to affect compensation and employment levels. A key factor in the analysis is that, in general, public employees in district-election environments can influence city council candidates or members at lower costs than in at-large election cities. District elections could enhance the power of other interest groups as well. Municipal employees are considered here because they are an easily identifiable group with well-defined and measurable goals who frequently pursue their objectives through unions. Furthermore, public employees are directly affected by local fiscal decisions and have relatively high voting participation rates in typically low-turnout local elections.[2]

Reprinted with permission from Journal of Labor Research, *Vol. XV, No. 4, Fall, 1994. Published by George Mason University, Fairfax, Virginia.*

In the empirical section, U.S. cities are classified by election method. Municipal wage and employment models are specified as a function of the election system and other features of the institutional structure, as well as labor market conditions for public employees. Both structural and reduced form wage and employment equations are estimated. The empirical results, in contrast to prior research, are consistent with the hypothesis that municipal employees tend to have greater influence over employment conditions in cities with district elections, and this power tends to be enhanced when employees are unionized.

II. Background

Although a number of previous studies have examined "reform" city government, most have concentrated on the effects on tax and expenditure decisions. A reform government can be defined along various dimensions but often includes one or more of the following attributes: at-large elections, a city manager executive, and nonpartisan ballots. The findings of these studies have been mixed. Some report that reform governments tend to reduce tax and spending levels (Lineberry and Fowler, 1967; Lyons, 1978), whereas others have observed few such effects (Morgan and Pelissero, 1980). One aspect of reform government structure—the city manager type of government—has been examined independently of other reform elements and consistently has been found to have little effect on public sector outcomes (Deno and Mehay, 1987; Hayes and Chang, 1990).

Farnham (1987) analyzed the effect of the three major reform elements— city manager, at-large and nonpartisan elections—on city spending. The value of the reform index for each city ranged from zero to three depending on the number of reform elements present. Based on estimates of four separate equations for the subset of cities with different values of the reform index, Farnham concluded that reform-type government structures tend to dilute the role of the median voter in determining city expenditures.[3] However, when all cities were pooled and dummy variables were included for each separate reform element, their individual effects on expenditures were not significant. Moreover, the F–tests for pooling indicated no differences in the coefficients of the independent variables across cities with different values of the reform index. Farnham (1987, p. 580) concluded that "government structural characteristics play only a moderate role in affecting local public expenditures." These results were echoed by Reid (1991) who used micro-level data from Massachusetts to examine deviations between actual city expenditures and the median voter's expenditure demand. Reid found little evidence that elements of government structure influenced expenditure deviations.

While much of the prior literature has concentrated on the spending effects of the institutional structure of municipal government,[4] the wage and employment conditions of public workers also may be affected by the electoral system. The magnitude of these effects will be dictated by the extent to which the election system enhances or impairs the ability of public employee groups to engage in political activities. O'Brien (1992) provides evidence that certain types of advocacy by public workers tend to enhance employee compensation and employment.[5] Thus, if district elections increase the ease with which such activities are conducted, or increase the overall effectiveness of a given level of activity, the electoral system could play a significant role in determining the power of public workers to influence employment conditions.

Only one previous study has examined the relationship between reform government and wage and employment conditions of municipal workers. Zax (1990) argued that reform governments—defined as those with both at-large elections and nonpartisan ballots—weaken the political influence of conventional constituencies, such as neighborhoods and traditional political parties, thus enhancing the relative influence of other special interest groups, such as municipal employees. As a result, reform cities will be characterized by higher compensation and larger work forces (which provided job security), a prediction that was supported by his empirical results.

One flaw in Zax's approach is the failure to consider the possibility that at-large elections could weaken the power of *all* special interest groups, including public employees. When council members are chosen in ward, rather than at-large elections, the costs to public employees of engaging in political activities aimed at candidates for office and at voters are substantially lower. Compare, for example, two cities with equal populations (1,000) that have an equal number of city council seats to be filled (4), but that differ in the election method—city A uses at-large elections, and city B uses district elections. Suppose further that the district-election city (B) is divided into four equal-size districts of 250 voters each. Under these conditions, a group seeking to elect (or defeat) a majority of candidates to the city council in the at-large city (A) would need to attract a majority (501 votes) of the entire city electorate for *each* of three candidates; that is, they must garner a total of 1,503 potential votes. In the district case (city B), the interest group needs to attract a majority of the electorate for their candidate in only three of the city's districts. Thus, in district elections the group will need to attract only 126 votes in three districts, or a total of 378 votes.[6] Therefore, the total cost of political activities in time and outlays are lower, and the effectiveness of any given level of effort are higher, in district election cities.[7] Furthermore, it is more credible for organized public employees to target a single candidate for defeat in district-election cities because carrying out that threat requires influencing a smaller proportion of the electorate. Using the previous illustration, defeating any single candidate requires persuading only 126 voters in a district election city, but requires persuading 501 in an at-large city.[8]

The ability of public employees to influence electoral outcomes and their own pay and working conditions is constrained by a number of factors. Courant, et al. (1979) have demonstrated analytically that even where conditions are most favorable to public employees—public sector workers can influence the demand for municipal output and output demand is price inelastic—the threat of outmigration by local residents via the Tiebout process constrains public spending. Nevertheless, there is some empirical evidence that, within the range of existing budget and tax levels, public employee groups, especially unionized groups, have been able to influence municipal spending levels and the demand for their own services.[9] Because unorganized employees face free-rider problems that discourage collective action, one would expect the ability of public employees to influence employment conditions to be greater when represented by unions. However, as O'Brien (1991) points out, free-rider problems may constrain nonunionized employee groups from engaging in political activities, but do not prevent them from doing so.

Prior research in this specific area has analyzed the relationship between unionization and outcomes in the public sector labor market (Trejo, 1991) and the direct effect of union political activities (O'Brien, 1992). Only Zax (1990) tested the relationship between the electoral system structure and public sector labor outcomes. Zax, however, is silent on the potentially significant differences in the costs of influencing municipal elections in the two types of voting structures, differences which act to strengthen employee power in district election environments.[10] This chapter tests whether the cost differences enhance the ability of municipal employees to effectively carry out political activities and to extract significant economic rents. Zax also did not examine the role of unions in that process. This chapter attempts to provide more reliable estimates of the relationship between public employee power and election method and to integrate the role of unionized employees.

III. Empirical Analysis

To test the hypothesized differences between electoral systems, we specify a two-equation simultaneous model of the municipal labor market in which wage and employment levels are endogenous. The demand for city employees is derived, in turn, from the demand for municipal services, which is a function of the income and perceived tax-price of city residents and of factors that affect residents' preferences for local services. In the aggregate, the supply of employees is a function of the offered wage rate, the private opportunity wage, and the conditions of municipal employment.

To specify the structural model, average monthly compensation (*COMP*) and total employment (*EMPLOY*) are treated as endogenous variables. The demand equation is specified as:[11]

$$EMPLOY = \alpha_0 + \alpha_1 COMP + \alpha_2 ATLARGE + \alpha_3 POP + \alpha_4 INC + \alpha_5 DEN \text{ (1)}$$
$$+ \alpha_6 OWN + \alpha_7 CITYMGR + \alpha_8 AID + \alpha_9 CITYDEN + \alpha_{10} UNION + \varepsilon_d$$

where ε is a random error term. Per capita income (*INC*) and the percentage of housing owner-occupied (*OWN*) represent income and "tax-price" effects, respectively, on the demand for public services. The conventional assumption is that because local property taxes are more visible to homeowners than to renters, homeowners are more sensitive to changes in property tax rates; *OWN* serves as a proxy for this difference. The amount of per capita intergovernmental aid (AID) tends to alter the proportion of revenue that must be raised locally. Thus, *AID* enters equation (1) because it affects residents' tax prices and service demand. City characteristics that reflect community preferences for municipal services include city size (*POP*) and population density (*DEN*). A dummy variable for the city manager (*CITYMGR*) form of government tests for possible effects of management structure on the relative utilization of labor and capital in producing public services and thus on labor demand. *CITYDEN* is the number of municipalities per square mile of county area; its purpose is to capture potential Tiebout-style competition among communities within a given geographic area. The rationale is that the larger the number of communities in a geographic area, the greater the competitive constraints on local decisionmakers. Finally, a dummy variable for unionization (*UNION*) is included because, regardless of the municipal election method, unions may shift the entire demand curve for labor services.

The (inverse) supply equation is specified as:

$$COMP = \beta_0 + \beta_1 EMPLOY + \beta_2 ATLARGE + \beta_3 MFGWAGE + \beta_4 DEN$$
$$+ \beta_5 COPOP + \beta_6 UNEMP + \beta_7 UNION + \beta_8 NCENT$$
$$+ \beta_9 NEAST + \beta_{10} SOUTH + \varepsilon_s. \qquad (2)$$

In equation (2) several variables represent conditions in the local labor market, which is the county in which each city is located. The manufacturing wage (*MFGWAGE*) in the county proxies the opportunity wage for municipal workers. Second, the relative attractiveness of public employment also may be affected by the availability of alternative private sector employment. Tightness or slack in the local job market is captured by the county unemployment rate (*UNEMP*). If public employment is less cyclical than private employment, we would expect $\beta_6 < 0$. Third, county population (*COPOP*) accounts for the size of the local labor market and, because larger markets tend to be more competitive, we expect $\beta_5 > 0$. Regional dummy variables are entered as proxies for regional differences in pay practices and the cost of living. Population density (*DEN*) also proxies for the attractiveness of public employment, although the direction of the effect cannot be predicted ex ante.[12] Finally, we control for the effect of unionization by including a dummy variable (*UNION*) that equals unity for cities in which the percent of full-time employees, in all functions, belonging to a labor organization exceeds 50 percent.[13] All of the continuous variables in both equations are measured in logarithmic form.

Demographic and spending data are taken from the U.S. Bureau of the Census' *County and City Data Book 1982* computer tape. Information on government structure was obtained from the International City Management Association's *Municipal Yearbook 1982*. Because the ICMA information was based on a survey, the usable sample varied depending on the number of cities that responded to the questions used to construct specific variables. Thus, although 957 U.S. cities have populations greater than 25,000, the sample used here was smaller due to lack of data for some variables and the imposition of various restrictions.

Many cities have a mixed election system, with some city council seats filled by at-large elections and some via district elections. Our sample is restricted to cities in which *all* city council seats are filled via one of these methods; "mixed-election" cities which fill council seats by both types of elections are deleted. The reason for this restriction is that it is not clear that the hypothesized election effect occurs along an election "continuum," nor how the continuum should be defined.[14] Restricting the sample in this manner is an improvement over previous studies (Zax, 1990; Farnham, 1987) that included cities with mixed election (and nomination) structures, which clouded the interpretation of the direct effect of the election system. Our sample is also restricted to district-election cities with single-member districts. These restrictions reduced the usable sample to 561 cities.

To test the hypothesized effect of the election system, a dummy variable is created (*ATLARGE*), which equals unity for cities with at-large elections. If the power of municipal employees to extract economic rents is weakened by at-large elections, *ATLARGE* will have a negative coefficient in the demand equation. On the supply side, there is no compelling *a priori* reason to expect that the election system is an important determinant of labor supply. It is possible, however, that changes in the election system could benefit employees by improving working conditions, which would increase labor supply. In addition to the structural estimates, reduced form compensation and employment equations are estimated. Also, a separate reduced form equation for total city payroll is estimated to identify the net impact of the separate wage and employment effects. Based on our analysis of the structural effects noted above, we expect a negative effect of *ATLARGE* in both the reduced form employment and payroll equations. If labor supply is positively sloped, we also expect the impact of at-large elections on wages to be negative in a reduced form model.

Table 1 provides variable definitions and means for the full sample, a subsample of union cities only, and a subsample of nonunion cities. Table 1 indicates that at-large elections are slightly more common among union cities. Unionized cities tend to be larger and denser than their nonunion counterparts

Table 1
Variable Names, Descriptions, and Means

Variable Name	Description	Full sample (N = 438)	Union cities (N = 230)	Nonunion cities (N = 208)
ATLARGE	= 1 if all council members elected at large	.77	.80	.73
UNION	= 1 if percent city employees organized ≥.50	.53	—	—
CITYDEN	Cities per square mile (of county area)	.01	.01	.01
POP	City population	94,427	96,635	91,986
INC	Per capita income ($)	7,862	7,926	7,792
OWN	Owner-occupied housing (%)	.59	.57	.60
DEN	Population density	399.7	453.3	340.3
COMP	Average monthly compensation ($)	1,582	1,700	1,449
EMPLOY	Total municipal employment	1,324	1,262	1,394
CITYMGR	= 1 if use city manager executive	.72	.67	.77
COPOP	County population (mil.)	1,325	1,461	1,175
AID	Intergovernmental aid per capita ($)	148.03	155.12	140.19
MFGWAGE	Average annual compensation of manufacturing workers ($)	12,979	13,671	12,212
UNEMP	County unemployment rate	.09	.10	.09
NEAST	= 1 for cities in Northeast	.13	.21	.05
NCENT	= 1 for cities in Midwest	.22	.24	.20
SOUTH	= 1 for cities in South	.27	.08	.48
WEST	= 1 for cities in West	.35	.45	.24

Sources: U.S. Bureau of the Census, "County and City Data Book, 1982" computer tape; "Census of Government 1982" computer tape; International City Management Association, *Municipal Yearbook 1982.*

and are more likely to be located in the Northeast and West; also, compensation is about 18 percent higher in unionized cities. Nonunion cities are somewhat more likely to have a city manager.

Due to the wide range of city sizes in the data, heteroscedasticity appeared to be a likely problem. This was confirmed by two standard tests for heteroscedasticity—the Park test and White's test[15]—which indicated that the error variances of the estimated models varied directly with population size. Accordingly, the structural models were estimated using Kmenta's (1986, pp. 704–706) weighted two-stage least squares (W2SLS). The W2SLS results are presented in Table 2; the weighted OLS estimates of the three reduced form equations are presented in Table 3.

All coefficients in the estimated structural labor demand equation have the expected signs and most are statistically significant (Table 2, column 1); only the coefficient of the variable for interjurisdictional competition (*CITY-DEN*) is insignificant. The income elasticity is 1.08, and the price (compensation) elasticity is -2.5, both of which are somewhat higher than those estimated in prior municipal labor demand studies. The coefficient of the *ATLARGE* dummy variable indicates that employment demand is approximately 10 percent lower in cities with at-large elections versus those with district elections. This contrasts with Zax's finding that reform (at-large) city councils are associated with higher employment levels. The two results, however, are not strictly comparable as Zax's "reform" government measure incorporated both at-large elections and nonpartisan ballots; also, his sample included cities with mixed at-large and ward election (and nomination) procedures. These differences noted, our results indicate that municipal employees are more successful in increasing labor demand in cities with district (nonreform) elections than in cities with at-large (reform) elections.

Significant differences in the effect of the electoral system are noted when the full sample is disaggregated into union and nonunion cities and the model reestimated.[16] For union cities, the negative effect of at-large elections is statistically significant and large in magnitude; for nonunion cities the coefficient is insignificantly different from zero. It appears that, as hypothesized, the election system has a greater effect on employment conditions when employees are represented by unions. Some other differences between the two subsamples are illuminating. Among union cities, a city manager has no effect on labor demand, whereas in nonunion cities a city manager tends to increase demand. This suggests that the power of unions may neutralize whatever initial effects the city manager may have on labor demand.

In the supply equation in Table 3, the coefficient of *EMPLOY* in column 1 is positive and significant, as is the variable representing the opportunity wage in the area, *MFGWAGE*. The regional dummy variables indicate that, compared to the omitted West region, municipal employment is relatively more attractive in the other three major Census regions. As expected, all else equal, the compensation of unionized employees is about 7 percent higher than nonunion employees. County population (*COPOP*) also is associated with higher compensation levels, which represent *decreases* in the supply of labor. The coefficient on county unemployment indicates that labor supply is greater in areas of higher unemployment. The coefficient of *ATLARGE* in the supply equation is not significantly different from zero, confirming our hypothesis that the election method does not affect municipal labor supply.

When the supply model is estimated separately for union and nonunion cities in columns 2 and 3, the results are not altered. The coefficient of

Table 2
Weighted 2SLS Estimates of Demand Equation
Dependent Variable = log (EMPLOY)

Variable	Full Sample	Union Cities	Nonunion Cities
COMP	-2.530***	-1.943***	-2.931***
	(12.47)	(7.07)	(9.06)
ATLARGE	-.108***	-.166***	-.061
	(2.33)	(3.08)	(0.82)
POP	1.151***	1.099***	1.194***
	(41.176)	(34.34)	(24.79)
INC	1.089***	.963***	1.197***
	(9.16)	(7.36)	(6.01)
DEN	-.067*	-.101**	.036
	(1.86)	(2.55)	(0.51)
OWN	-.404***	-.538***	-.225
	(4.40)	(5.50)	(1.37)
CITYMGR	.135***	.046	.203***
	(2.67)	(0.73)	(2.25)
AID	.414***	.474***	.364***
	(13.94)	(12.96)	(7.64)
CITYDEN	.0001	-.015	-.006
	(0.01)	(0.74)	(0.24)
UNION	.177***	—	—
	(3.58)		
Intercept	21.034	14.764	24.609
R^2 adj.	.86	.90	.82
F-stat	273.34	251.02	105.33
N	432	230	202

Notes: absolute value of t-statistics in parentheses; *** (**, *) indicates significance at .01(.05, .10) levels.

ATLARGE never reaches conventional significance levels in either subsample. Moreover, even though there are some interesting differences between the subsamples, the F–test for pooling did not reject the hypothesis of identical coefficients, $F(10,412) = 1.25$. In nonunion cities population density is associated with lower labor supply, whereas in unionized cities density has no effect. Working conditions may be less attractive in denser cities, and unions may be able to offset these undesirable conditions via collective bargaining. Also, the negative coefficient of unemployment is significant only in the nonunion sample.

Table 3
Weighted 2SLS Estimates of Supply Equation
Dependent Variable = log (COMP)

Variable	Full Sample	Union Cities	Nonunion Cities
EMPLOY	.014**	.012	.013
	(2.08)	(1.43)	(1.27)
ATLARGE	.006	-.002	.017
	(0.40)	(0.12)	(0.77)
MFGWAGE	.124***	.089**	.157***
	(3.64)	(2.01)	(2.95)
DEN	.008	-.011	.32*
	(0.79)	(0.82)	(1.79)
COPOP	.043***	.043***	.041***
	(7.89)	(5.60)	(5.09)
UNEMP	-.050**	-.039	-.060*
	(2.37)	(1.31)	(1.91)
UNION	.079***	—	—
	(5.38)		
NCENT	-.047***	-.063***	-.028
	(2.62)	(2.63)	(0.99)
NEAST	-.235***	-.241***	-.235***
	(10.96)	(10.34)	(4.41)
SOUTH	-.224***	-.204***	-.215***
	(11.30)	(6.35)	(7.61)
Intercept	12.305	12.873	11.848
R^2 adj.	.61	.52	.57
F-stat	71.19	29.20	30.77
N	432	230	202

Notes: See Table 2.

The results of the reduced form compensation, employment, and payroll equations are displayed in Tables 4–6. With only a few exceptions, the results in Table 4 for the full sample tend to be consistent with the structural estimates for the full sample (see Table 2, column 1). One noteworthy exception is that the unemployment variable in the reduced form compensation equation in both the full and nonunion samples is insignificant despite the fact that the structural estimates indicate that higher unemployment increases labor supply. One possible explanation for this result is that when unemployment rises, voters demand an increase in public services, which increases

Table 4
Reduced Form Models: Full Sample (N = 432)

Variable	Employment Equation		Payroll Equation		Compensation Equation	
	Coeff.	t-stat	Coeff.	t-stat	Coeff.	t-stat
ATLARGE	-.089	1.93	-.097	2.03	-.011	0.80
MFGWAGE	-.222	2.03	-.169	1.50	.046	1.43
POP	1.086	37.22	1.119	37.19	.029	5.45
INC	.539	5.35	.784	7.56	.245	8.16
DEN	-.128	3.34	-.118	2.98	.010	0.85
OWN	-.311	3.13	-.367	3.58	-.053	1.81
CITYMGR	-.340	0.70	.047	0.92	.082	5.54
AID	.417	12.58	.408	12.06	-.006	0.61
NCENT	.106	1.85	.072	1.22	-.030	1.76
NEAST	.521	7.18	.378	5.05	-.146	6.77
SOUTH	.529	8.72	.331	5.37	-.194	10.91
COPOP	-.054	2.94	-.024	1.30	.029	5.45
UNEMP	.105	1.51	.132	1.84	.021	1.04
UNION	-.040	0.79	.029	0.64	.080	6.03
CITYDEN	.001	0.10	.001	0.03	-.001	0.16
Intercept	-5.949	4.95	4.802	3.88	10.818	30.20
R^2 adj.	.86		.85		.69	
F-stat.	184.62		167.03		66.45	

government employment (see Dudley and Montmarquette, 1984). The unexpected positive effect of the city manager variable in the reduced form compensation equation may result from city managers hiring a more skilled work force (see footnote 11). As expected from the structural estimates, at-large elections have a negative effect in both the reduced form employment and payroll equations.[17] Differences between the reduced form and structural equations for the union and nonunion samples tend to mirror the differences noted for the full sample.

IV. Summary and Conclusions

At-large election methods raise the cost to public employees of affecting the outcome of city council elections. This cost difference reduces (increases) the ability of employee groups to affect wages, job security, and employment in at-large (district) cities. The impact of the difference in the governmental structure will be more pronounced when employees are organized, which offsets the free-rider problem and promotes political action. The empirical results confirm these simple hypotheses. Unlike other attributes of municipal

Table 5
Reduced Form Models: Union Sample (N = 230)

Variable	Employment Equation		Payroll Equation		Compensation Equation	
	Coeff.	*t-stat*	*Coeff.*	*t-stat*	*Coeff.*	*t-stat*
ATLARGE	-.154	2.90	-.161	2.88	-.006	0.33
MFGWAGE	-.168	1.40	-.136	1.08	.032	0.71
POP	1.043	32.59	1.068	31.75	.025	2.07
INC	.616	5.08	.798	6.26	.182	3.98
DEN	-.120	2.92	-.126	2.92	-.006	0.38
OWN	-.446	4.11	-.445	3.91	.001	0.20
CITYMGR	-.055	1.00	.008	0.15	.064	3.06
AID	.478	12.23	.487	11.87	-.009	0.64
NCENT	.107	1.62	.049	0.70	-.058	2.33
NEAST	.458	6.51	.286	3.86	-.172	6.47
SOUTH	.365	4.46	.182	2.11	-.183	5.94
COPOP	-.002	0.09	.033	1.32	.031	3.45
UNEMP	-.070	0.82	-.049	0.55	.020	0.64
CITYDEN	-.057	2.34	-.052	2.03	-.004	0.54
Intercept	-8.093	5.46	3.770	2.42	11.863	21.22
R^2 adj.	.91		.90		.60	
F-stat.	168.93		150.55		23.39	

reform government, such as the city manager type of executive, which have been found to have little effect on public sector behavior, our results suggest that the electoral system *does* make a difference. In reform governments in which city council members are chosen in city-wide elections, public employee groups may wield less influence over municipal decisionmakers than in cities using district elections. However, public employees in district-election cities appear to have greater power when they are unionized.[18]

Notes

*The authors acknowledge the helpful comments of Tim Sass, Tom Means, and participants in a session at the 1991 Public Choice Society meetings.
   1. Lyons and Jewell (1988) discuss some of the constitutional and legal issues involving minority representation and the election methods for local governing bodies.
   2. Municipal employees, especially unionized employees, have been the focus of several previous studies; O'Brien (1992) provides a recent survey.
   3. We do not know how Farnham's reform index classified the numerous cities that use a mixture of at-large and district elections.
   4. Dalenberg and Duffy-Deno (1991) focused on the impact of election method on municipal capital outlays. They argued that district elections present greater

Table 6
Reduced Form Models:
Non-Union Sample (N = 202)

Variable	Employment Equation		Payroll Equation		Compensation Equation	
	Coeff.	t-stat	Coeff.	t-stat	Coeff.	t-stat
ATLARGE	-.032	0.43	-.048	0.64	-.016	0.88
MFGWAGE	-.105	0.56	-.039	0.20	.065	1.36
POP	1.139	23.03	1.181	23.22	.041	3.25
INC	.440	2.73	.716	4.32	.276	6.65
DEN	-.086	1.24	-.052	0.74	.033	1.87
OWN	.013	0.08	-.097	0.54	-.111	2.48
CITYMGR	-.060	0.71	.060	0.69	.120	5.55
AID	.346	6.46	.326	6.09	-.020	1.49
NCENT	.218	2.20	.202	1.99	-.015	0.59
NEAST	.821	4.45	.660	3.48	-.161	3.39
SOUTH	.680	7.40	.483	5.12	-.196	8.31
COPOP	-.088	3.03	-.063	2.13	.024	3.26
UNEMP	.337	2.96	.360	3.08	.023	0.80
CITYDEN	-.002	0.75	.004	0.18	-.003	0.43
Intercept	-6.120	3.23	3.975	2.04	10.095	20.73
R^2 adj.	.84		.82		.72	
F-stat.	73.39		64.45		34.68	

opportunities for logrolling among council members, which will be more intensive for capital spending projects that benefit individual districts but spread the costs city-wide. While their empirical analysis found that public capital stocks are higher in district-election cities, their cumulative capital stock measure did not distinguish between those capital projects that benefited the entire city versus those that benefited individual districts. Therefore, they were not able to distinguish between the logrolling effect and other forces that may have caused differences in capital stocks across cities.

5. Examples of political activities include endorsement of candidates, financial contributions to candidates, in-kind campaign contributions, and publicity campaigns, among others.

6. This has been the conventional argument against the at-large system advanced by candidates from districts with sizable minority populations. Using the example above, when minority candidates are forced to run in city-wide elections they must attract 501 votes from voters—most of whom are not minorities—across the city to be successful. If they are instead able to run in their own district (suppose, for example, that one of the four districts is composed mostly of minorities), they need to attract only 126 votes, and only from a largely minority electorate.

7. This result holds even if there are economies of scale in vote-getting.

8. This cost difference arises strictly due to the election method—district versus at-large—and is not related to the type of ballot (partisan versus nonpartisan). In contrast, Zax assumed that employee power depends on the interaction of the election method and the type of ballot. However, it is unlikely that the type of ballot

affects public employee power since candidates for office can easily convey their true party affiliation via other means. Thus, there is no compelling reason to include the type of ballot in the model, and even less reason to interact it with the election method. To test this hypothesis, we experimented with a nonpartisan election variable in our empirical estimates and, as expected, the variable was never significant.

9. Trejo (1991) summarizes this literature.

10. Flaws in the empirical tests also raise questions concerning the reliability of Zax's results. Zax estimated compensation, employment, and hourly wage equations using time series, cross-sectional data consisting of observations for four separate local services by year and by city. The implicit assumption of homogeneity across functional areas may be unwarranted since the effect of increases in municipal employee power is likely to vary across municipal labor markets (police versus sanitation, for example). Perhaps more important, the independent variables are not available for all three of the time periods used in the analysis. Although the explanatory variables exhibit cross sectional variation, the temporal variation is limited and inconsistent. Also, the point in time at which the independent variables are measured often differs; for example, government structure is measured as of 1981, but most of the demographic control variables are based on 1970 data. While local public sector studies are often plagued by a similar lack of contemporaneous data, differences in time periods of the magnitude in the Zax study are especially troublesome. As a result, the models cannot be expected to reflect the true contemporaneous relationships among the variables.

11. The model is similar to those in prior research of municipal labor markets (Hirsch and Rufolo, 1985; Gonzalez et al., 1991).

12. The form of city executive could affect the supply curve by altering employer-employee relationships and the attributes of public employment. To account for this possibility, we estimated the supply equation with a dummy variable. *CITYMGR*, equal to one for cities with professional managers. The results of this estimation indicated that compensation was higher in city manager-type governments. However, the other coefficients in the supply equation were not appreciably affected by inclusion of the city manager variable.

13. Although this definition is somewhat arbitrary, we experimented with alternative threshold values of percent unionized for all employees, and the percent unionized for police and fire personnel, the two main service functions. The use of these alternative definitions had little effect on the basic empirical results. The unionization data were kindly provided by Prof. Stephen Trejo. The data are based on the *Annual Survey of Governments* for October 1980 and are discussed in Trejo (1991) and U.S. Department of Commerce (1981).

14. This restriction reduced the sample by about one-half because often cities that use district representation also elect some council members at-large (Sanders, 1982).

15. These tests are described in Kmenta (1986) and Maddala (1992).

16. An F–test rejected the null hypothesis of identical coefficients between the union and nonunion samples of the demand (*EMPLOY*) equation, $F(10,412)=2.60$.

17. The insignificant effect of at-large elections in the reduced form compensation equation can be attributed to the high estimated labor supply elasticity.

18. It should be noted that cross-sectional data are not ideal for evaluating the impact of electoral systems as cities will be observed in various stages of adjusting to prior shifts in electoral processes and responding to the incentive structure presented by those shifts. Longitudinal data, or at least retrospective information on the

length of time elapsed since the introduction of a change in the electoral system, would be preferable.

References

Bennet, James, and William Orzechowski. "The Voting Behavior of Bureaucrats: Some Empirical Evidence." *Public Choice* 41 (1983): 271–83.

Courant, Paul, Edward Gramlich, and Daniel Rubinfeld. "Public Employee Market Power and the Level of Government Spending." *American Economic Review* 69 (December 1979): 806–17.

Dalenberg, Douglas R., and Kevin Duffy-Deno. "At-Large Versus Ward Elections: Implications for Public Infrastructure." *Public Choice* 70 (June 1991): 335–42.

Deno, Kevin T., and Stephen L. Mehay. "Municipal Management Structure and Fiscal Performance: Do City Managers Make a Difference?" *Southern Economic Journal* 54 (January 1987): 627–42.

Dudley, Leonard, and Claude Montmarquette. "The Effects of Non-Clearing Labor Markets on the Demand for Public Spending." *Economic Inquiry* 22 (April 1984): 151–70.

Farnham, Paul G. "Form of Government and the Median Voter." *Social Science Quarterly* 68 (September 1987): 569–82.

Gonzalez, Rodolfo, Stephen Mehay, and Kevin Duffy-Deno. "Municipal Residency Laws: Effects on Police Employment, Compensation, and Productivity" *Journal of Labor Research* 12 (Fall 1991): 439–52.

Hayes, Kathy, and Semoon Chang. "The Relative Efficiency of City Managers and Mayor-Council Forms of Government." *Southern Economic Journal* 57 (July 1990): 167–77.

Hirsch, Werner, and Anthony Rufolo. "Economic Effect of Residence Laws on Municipal Police." *Journal of Urban Economics* 17 (July 1985): 335–48.

Lineberry, Robert L., and Edmund P. Fowler. "Reformism and Public Policies in American Cities." *American Political Science Review* 61 (September 1967): 701–16.

Kmenta, Jan. *Elements of Econometrics* 2d. ed. New York: MacMillan, 1986.

Lyons, William. "Reform and Response in American Cities: Structure and Policy Reconsidered." *Social Science Quarterly* 59 (June 1978): 118–32.

_____. and Malcolm Jewell. "Minority Representation and the Drawing of City Council Districts." *Urban Affairs Quarterly* 23 (March 1988): 432–47.

Maddala, G. S. *Introduction to Econometrics* 2d. ed. New York: MacMillan, 1992.

Morgan, David R., and John P. Pelissero. "Urban Policy: Does Political Structure Matter?" *American Political Science Review* 74 (December 1980): 199–1006.

O'Brien, Kevin M. "Compensation, Employment, and the Political Activity of Public Employee Unions." *Journal of Labor Research* 13 (Spring 1992): 189–204.

Reid, Gary J. "Tests of Institutional Versus Non-Institutional Models of Local Expenditure Determination." *Public Choice* 70 (June 1991): 315–33.

Sanders, Heywood T. "The Government of American Cities," in the *Municipal Yearbook, 1982.* Washington, D.C.: International City Management Association, 1982.

Trejo, Stephen J. "Public Sector Unions and Municipal Employment." *Industrial and Labor Relations Review* 45 (October 1991): 166–80.

U.S. Department of Commerce. *Labor-Management Relations in State and Local Governments: 1980.* Washington, D.C.: U.S. Government Printing Office, 1980.
Zax, Jeffrey S. "Reform City Councils and Municipal Employees." *Public Choice* 64 (February 1990): 167–78.

Term Limits and Turnover Among Elected Officials

Victor S. DeSantis and Tari Renner

The American public's concern about the accountability of government officials appears to have grown in recent years. Large numbers of voters continue to indicate in public opinion surveys that they are frustrated with government actions and suspicious of elected officeholders.

In 1992, voters defeated an incumbent president and registered a near-record protest vote for an antiestablishment third party candidate. Ross Perot's 19% of the vote was the highest received by any non-major-party candidate since Theodore Roosevelt ran as the Progressive Bull Moose nominee in 1912. The number of incumbent members of the U.S. House of Representatives who were defeated for reelection increased substantially in 1992. This reversed a generation-long trend toward decreasing competitiveness in House elections where incumbents sought another term. As a result, there were more new members in the House after the 1992 elections than in any election year since 1948.

The state and local elections of 1993 showed few signs that voter anger with incumbents and the status quo had subsided. The two states holding off-year gubernatorial elections (New Jersey and Virginia) shifted political party control of the chief executive office from Democratic to Republican hands. The nation's two largest cities (New York and Los Angeles) also shifted party control of their mayoral positions by defeating either the incumbent or the incumbent party.

Perhaps the most important long-run consequence of the 1993 elections, however, was the adoption of term limitations on public officials through referendums in several states. This marks the fourth year in a row that additional states have instituted term limits. Only one referendum attempt has failed

Reprinted with permission from Municipal Year Book 1994. *Published by the International City/County Management Association, Washington, D.C.*

during this period (Washington State in 1991), and that decision was reversed by the voters in a subsequent election.

These reforms appear to be the most effective strategy to ensure that the tenure of public officials is limited and, therefore, that turnover is maximized. Voters seeking mandatory turnover among their elected officials have supported these restrictions apparently to save themselves from their own decisions at the ballot box. The assumption seems to be that policy-making institutions need constant membership change to remain responsive because incumbents over time become increasingly insulated from their constituents' interests.

This research project explores the patterns of turnover and term limitations among local government elected officials and turnover among appointed managers/chief administrative officers (CAOs). Although there is a substantial body of research in the field examining turnover and incumbency reelection prospects among executive and legislative officials at other levels of government, there is very little systematic evidence regarding local public officeholders.

The situation at the local level is unique and particularly warrants separate attention because many municipalities have nonelected, appointed chief executives with generally unspecified terms of service. In addition, the patterns and trends apparent for elected incumbents at other levels may not exist among local government officials. The advantages of incumbency, for example, may not be as strong given that incumbents' name recognition is likely to be lower, their constituencies smaller, and campaign costs lower than at other levels. It may be comparatively easy (from both an organizational and financial perspective) to successfully challenge an incumbent under these circumstances. It is also possible that the tendency for local public service positions to be part-time and volunteer, rather than full-time and career, results in more voluntary turnover of incumbents and less longevity than at other levels of government.

Methodology

The data for this exploratory research were collected through ICMA's 1991 *Municipal Form of Government* survey. The survey instrument was sent to city clerks in all 6,579 jurisdictions with populations of 2,500 and over and to 562 jurisdictions with fewer than 2,500 people that ICMA recognizes as providing for a position of professional management. Officials who did not respond to the first survey instrument received a second survey instrument. This chapter is based on the responses from jurisdictions with a population of 25,000 and above; 914 responded out of 1,205 for a 75% response rate (Table 1).

Table 1
Survey Response

Classification	No. of cities surveyed (A)	No. reporting	% of (A)
Total, all cities	1,205	914	75.9
Population group			
Over 1,000,000	8	2	25.0
500,000–1,000,000	16	8	50.0
250,000–499,999	40	32	80.0
100,000–249,999	133	100	75.2
50,000–99,999	334	255	76.4
25,000–49,999	674	517	76.7

Length of Mayoral Terms

Overall, a plurality (48.4%) of mayors have terms of four or more years (Table 2). Approximately one-third of the responding municipalities indicate that their mayors have two-year terms (33.1%). One– and three-year terms are the least likely to be reported with 14.8% and 3.7% respectively.

Although we cannot be certain from the data presented, the single-year mayoral term is probably found in jurisdictions in which the position rotates annually among members of the elected legislative body or in which the legislature elects the mayor from among its members. When the data are arrayed by form of government, the results are consistent with this possibility. While almost no mayor-council municipalities (1.7%) have one-year terms, more than one-fifth of the municipalities with other forms of government report one-year terms. Previous research using ICMA data has shown that choosing a mayor from among the council members and/or rotating the mayoral position among council members are common selection methods in all forms of government except mayor-council. In fact, the percentages of jurisdictions using these techniques of mayoral selection within each form of government are very similar to the percentages with single-year terms.[1] The patterns of mayoral terms vary by population group. Odd-year terms (one and three years) are least likely to be found in the largest cities. The percentages of respondents reporting four-year terms, on the other hand, consistently decline with population size, from 100% in jurisdictions with populations greater than 1,000,000 to 46% in jurisdictions with populations from 25,000 to 49,999. There appears to be no consistent pattern among population groups for jurisdictions using two-year terms.

The geographic patterns are not as clear-cut. Single-year terms are most likely to be found among Pacific Coast municipalities where a plurality (37.6%) of the 197 responding jurisdictions report one-year mayoral terms. They are least likely among cities in the East South Central division where none of the respondents indicates using one-year terms. Three-year terms are unlikely in all areas of the country. It is only in West South Central jurisdictions that the proportion exceeds 10%. Two-year terms are reported in the overwhelming majority of New England jurisdictions (73.8%) and by a smaller majority (56.6%) of West South Central jurisdictions. They are least likely in the East South Central division. Four-year terms are comparatively common in all geographic divisions except New England (7.5%). They are most likely, however, to be found in jurisdictions in the East South Central division (90.3%).

The distribution of responses by form of government shows that more than three-fourths (76.2%) of the mayor-council cities have four-year terms. Virtually all jurisdictions that do not report four-year terms have two-year terms (21.6%). A small plurality of council-manager cities (39.9%) report having two-year terms rather than four-year terms (34.1%). As noted earlier, a disproportionate number of jurisdictions with other forms of government report single-year mayoral terms.

Length of City Council Terms

Tables 3 and 4 show the term length data for city councils elected at-large and by district, respectively. The data are separated by election system type because the patterns differ for each. None of the responding jurisdictions indicates that any at-large council members have single-year terms; only one jurisdiction with election by district reports a one-year term. A solid majority (70.5%) of jurisdictions with at-large council members elect members to four-year terms and 22.4% elect them to two-year terms. Only 7.4% use three-year intervals. This contrasts with the aggregate pattern for council members elected by ward or district. Although the majority of respondents (59.3%) with district elections report four-year terms, the percent is lower than the percent reporting four-year terms and at-large elections for council members (70.5%). Alternatively, the proportion of respondents reporting council members serving two-year terms is higher for those elected by district (36.6%) than at-large (22.4%). Only 3.9% of responding jurisdictions holding district elections report three-year terms for council members. It is also apparent that, regardless of election system, council members are much less likely than mayors to serve in odd-year intervals.

Use of four-year terms appears to decline slightly with population size for council members elected at large; the decline is less consistent for council members elected by district. The geographic division patterns are similar for both election systems. New England communities are the most likely to

Table 2
Length of Term for Mayor

Length of term for mayor

Classification	No. reporting (A)	One year		Two years		Three years		Four years or more	
		No.	% of (A)	No.	% of (A)	No.	% of (A)	No.	% of (A)
Total, all cities*	891	132	14.8	295	33.1	33	3.7	431	48.4
Population group									
Over 1,000,000	2	0	0.0	0	0.0	0	0.0	2	100.0
500,000–1,000,000	8	0	0.0	2	25.0	0	0.0	6	75.0
250,000–499,999	32	0	0.0	9	28.1	1	3.1	22	68.8
100,000–249,999	99	7	7.1	36	36.4	4	4.0	52	52.5
50,000–99,999	248	35	14.1	85	34.3	10	4.0	118	47.6
25,000–49,999	502	90	17.9	163	32.5	18	3.6	231	46.0
Geographic division†									
New England	80	9	11.3	59	73.8	6	7.5	6	7.5
Mid-Atlantic	104	19	18.3	17	16.3	0	0.0	68	65.4
East North Central	158	9	5.7	34	21.5	1	0.6	114	72.2
West North Central	71	5	7.0	18	25.4	2	2.8	46	64.8
South Atlantic	110	11	10.0	39	35.5	8	7.3	52	47.3
East South Central	31	0	0.0	3	9.7	0	0.0	28	90.3
West South Central	83	2	2.4	47	56.6	15	18.1	19	22.9

Mountain	57	3	5.3	20	35.1	0	0.0	34	59.6
Pacific Coast	197	74	37.6	58	29.4	1	0.5	64	32.5

Form of government§

Mayor-council	303	5	1.7	65	21.5	2	0.7	231	76.2
Council-manager	566	119	21.0	226	39.9	28	4.9	193	34.1
Commission	13	4	30.8	2	15.4	0	0.0	7	53.8
Town meeting	1	1	100.0	0	0.0	0	0.0	0	0.0
Rep. town meeting	8	3	37.5	2	25.0	3	37.5	0	0.0

*The term cities refers also to towns, villages, boroughs, and townships.

†Divisions: New England—the states of Connecticut, Maine, Massachusetts, New Hampshire, Rhode Island, and Vermont; Mid-Atlantic—the states of New Jersey, New York, and Pennsylvania; East North Central—the states of Illinois, Indiana, Michigan, Ohio, and Wisconsin; West North Central—the states of Iowa, Kansas, Minnesota, Missouri, Nebraska, North Dakota, and South Dakota; South Atlantic—the states of Delaware, Florida, Georgia, Maryland, North Carolina, South Carolina, Virginia, and West Virginia, plus the District of Columbia; East South Central—the states of Alabama, Kentucky, Mississippi, and Tennessee; West South Central—the states of Arkansas, Louisiana, Oklahoma, and Texas; Mountain—the states of Arizona, Colorado, Idaho, Montana, Nevada, New Mexico, Utah, and Wyoming; Pacific Coast—the states of Alaska, California, Hawaii, Oregon, and Washington.

§Form of government: Mayor-council—an elected council serves as the legislative body with a separately elected head of government; Council-manager—the mayor and council make policy and an appointed administrator is responsible for the administration of the city; Commission—a board of elected commissioners serves as the legislative body and each commissioner is responsible for administration of one or more departments; Town meeting—qualified voters meet to make basic policy and choose a board of selectmen to carry out the policy; Representative town meeting—representatives selected by citizens vote at meetings, which may be attended by all town citizens.

Table 3
Length of Term for Council Members Elected At Large

	No. reporting (A)	Length of term* for council members elected at large					
		Two years		Three years		Four years or more	
Classification		No.	% of (A)	No.	% of (A)	No.	% of (A)
Total, all cities	706	158	22.4	50	7.1	498	70.5
Population group							
Over 1,000,000	2	0	0.0	0	0.0	2	100.0
500,000–1,000,000	3	0	0.0	0	0.0	3	100.0
250,000–499,999	23	5	21.7	1	4.3	17	73.9
100,000–249,999	71	16	22.5	3	4.2	52	73.2
50,000–99,999	211	51	24.2	12	5.7	148	70.1
25,000–49,999	396	86	21.7	34	8.6	276	69.7
Geographic division							
New England	77	56	72.7	18	23.4	3	3.9
Mid-Atlantic	81	3	3.7	5	6.2	73	90.1
East North Central	116	27	23.3	1	0.9	88	75.9
West North Central	46	6	13.0	1	2.2	39	84.8
South Atlantic	87	23	26.4	10	11.5	54	62.1
East South Central	15	5	33.3	0	0.0	10	66.7
West South Central	64	36	56.3	15	23.4	13	20.3
Mountain	37	1	2.7	0	0.0	36	97.3
Pacific Coast	183	1	0.5	0	0.0	182	99.5
Form of government							
Mayor-council	204	64	31.4	4	2.0	136	66.7
Council-manager	479	92	19.2	33	6.9	354	73.9
Commission	11	1	9.1	2	18.2	8	72.7
Town meeting	3	0	0.0	3	100.0	0	0.0
Rep. town meeting	9	1	11.1	8	88.9	0	0.0

*Not one respondent reported a one-year term.

use two-year terms, although the proportion of district legislators serving two-year terms (89.6%) is noticeably higher than the proportion of at-large legislators (72.7%) serving two-year terms. Pacific Coast and Mountain jurisdictions report the highest use of four-year terms for at-large council members (99.5% and 97.3%, respectively). Mountain and East South Central cities report the highest proportions of council members elected by district for four-year terms (94.4% and 89.5%, respectively). The form-of-government differences show that council-manager jurisdictions are slightly more likely than mayor-council jurisdictions to use four-year terms for their council members, regardless of election method.

Term Limitations for Mayors

It is clear that the overwhelming majority of cities with populations 25,000 and over (89%) do not have term limits on the mayor (Table 5). The 11% that report term limits are not uniformly distributed among different types of cities. The reporting of these restrictions appears to be positively associated with population size (with the exception of the two respondents with populations more than one million). One-half of the cities reporting with populations from 500,000 to 1,000,000 indicate mayoral term limits. This figure declines consistently with population size down to 7.9% for the jurisdictions with populations from 25,000 to 49,999.

The variation from the 11% average is even less dramatic among geographic divisions for jurisdictions with term limits. The proportion with mayoral term limits ranges from a high of 22.0% in the West South Central area to 3.6% in New England. Overall, the northern tier respondents are less likely to report having term limitations than the Sun Belt and western respondents.

Council-manager jurisdictions are the most likely to have mayoral term limits (12.7%) followed by mayor-council jurisdictions (8.9%). No jurisdiction with the commission, town meeting, or representative town meeting form of government reports mayoral term limits.

City Council

Table 6 displays the data for legal limitations on consecutive council terms. Overall, a slightly smaller proportion of municipalities have term limits on council members than on mayors. Only 8.4% of respondents report having term limits for the council.

City council term limits, like mayoral term limits, are positively related to the population size of the responding jurisdictions (with the exception of the two cities responding with populations greater than one million). One-half of the cities with populations from 500,000 to 1,000,000 report term limits for council members. This proportion consistently declines until it reaches 6.5% in the population group from 25,000 to 49,999.

The differences in council limits by geographic division are similar, but not identical, to those of mayoral limits. The range is from 16.9% in the West South Central division to 0.0% in the East South Central division. The overall geographic pattern appears to reflect an East/West distinction for council limits with the latter the most likely to report having term restrictions. The mayoral differences reflect a Frost Belt/Sun Belt distinction.

Table 4
Term Length for Council Elected by Ward or District

Length of term for council elected by ward or district

Classification	No. reporting (A)	One year No.	One year % of (A)	Two years No.	Two years % of (A)	Three years No.	Three years % of (A)	Four years or more No.	Four years or more % of (A)
Total, all cities	413	1	0.2	151	36.6	16	3.9	245	59.3
Population group									
500,000–1,000,000	6	0	0.0	2	33.3	0	0.0	4	66.7
250,000–499,999	22	0	0.0	7	31.8	0	0.0	15	68.2
100,000–249,999	51	0	0.0	12	23.5	2	3.9	37	72.5
50,000–99,999	120	0	0.0	48	40.0	7	5.8	65	54.2
25,000–49,999	214	1	0.5	82	38.3	7	3.3	124	57.9
Geographic division†									
New England	48	0	0.0	43	89.6	2	4.2	3	6.3
Mid-Atlantic	45	0	0.0	11	24.4	0	0.0	34	75.6
East North Central	88	0	0.0	32	36.4	2	2.3	54	61.4
West North Central	49	0	0.0	17	34.7	3	6.1	29	59.2
South Atlantic	55	0	0.0	16	29.1	3	5.5	36	65.5
East South Central	19	0	0.0	2	10.5	0	0.0	17	89.5
West South Central	48	0	0.0	26	54.2	5	10.4	17	35.4
Mountain	36	1	2.8	1	2.8	0	0.0	34	94.4
Pacific Coast	25	0	0.0	3	12.0	1	4.0	21	84.0
Form of government*									
Mayor-council	206	0	0.0	83	40.3	5	2.4	118	57.3
Council-manager	206	1	0.5	67	32.5	11	5.3	127	61.7
Commission	1	0	0.0	1	100.0	0	0.0	0	0.0

*Town meeting and rep. town meeting jurisdictions report only at-large elections.

Table 5
Legal Limit on Consecutive Terms for Mayor

Classification	No. reporting (A)	Legal limit on consecutive terms for mayor			
		Yes		No	
		No.	% of (A)	No.	% of (A)
Total, all cities	896	99	11.0	797	89.0
Population group					
Over 1,000,000	2	0	0.0	2	100.0
500,000–1,000,000	8	4	50.0	4	50.0
250,000–499,999	32	10	31.3	22	68.8
100,000–249,999	98	17	17.3	81	82.7
50,000–99,999	251	28	11.2	223	88.8
25,000–49,999	505	40	7.9	465	92.1
Geographic division					
New England	84	3	3.6	81	96.4
Mid-Atlantic	104	7	6.7	97	93.3
East North Central	156	10	6.4	146	93.6
West North Central	72	5	6.9	67	93.1
South Atlantic	109	18	16.5	91	83.5
East South Central	31	5	16.1	26	83.9
West South Central	82	18	22.0	64	78.0
Mountain	57	9	15.8	48	84.2
Pacific Coast	201	24	11.9	177	88.1
Form of government					
Mayor-council	303	27	8.9	276	91.1
Council-manager	569	72	12.7	497	87.3
Commission	13	0	0.0	13	100.0
Town meeting	2	0	0.0	2	100.0
Rep. town meeting	9	0	0.0	9	100.0

The form-of-government differences that relate to city council term limitations are virtually identical to those of mayors. Council-manager cities are the most likely to report having these restrictions (11.4%). Only 3.3% of mayor-council communities have term limits for city council members. Not one respondent with commission, town meeting, or representative town meeting form of government reports a limit on consecutive terms for council members.

Table 6
Limit on Consecutive Terms of Council Members

Classification	No. reporting (A)	Legal on consecutive terms of council members			
		Yes		No	
		No.	% of (A)	No.	% of (A)
Total, all cities	898	75	8.4	823	91.6
Population group					
Over 1,000,000	2	0	0.0	2	100.0
500,000–1,000,000	8	4	50.0	4	50.0
250,000–499,999	32	6	18.8	26	81.3
100,000–249,999	99	13	13.1	86	86.9
50,000–99,999	250	19	7.6	231	92.4
25,000–49,999	507	33	6.5	474	93.5
Geographic division					
New England	87	3	3.4	84	96.6
Mid-Atlantic	104	1	1.0	103	99.0
East North Central	156	8	5.1	148	94.9
West North Central	71	4	5.6	67	94.4
South Atlantic	108	8	7.4	100	92.6
East South Central	31	0	0.0	31	100.0
West South Central	83	14	16.9	69	83.1
Mountain	57	7	12.3	50	87.7
Pacific Coast	201	30	14.9	171	85.1
Form of government					
Mayor-council	300	10	3.3	290	96.7
Council-manager	572	65	11.4	507	88.6
Commission	13	0	0.0	13	100.0
Town meeting	3	0	0.0	3	100.0
Rep. town meeting	10	0	0.0	10	100.0

Turnover and Tenure

Turnover can, of course, be either voluntary or involuntary regardless of whether the official is a mayor, city council member, or city manager. Even without term limits, involuntary turnover may occur when voters defeat an incumbent elected official or when the city council votes to fire a city manager or place pressure upon the manager to resign. On the other hand, elected officials may decide not to seek reelection in order to retire or to pursue other ventures, including higher office. The same can be said of city managers, who may leave voluntarily because of retirement, other personal reasons, or to advance their careers by serving another, usually larger, community.

Mayors

The longevity of mayors is examined in Table 7, which shows the number of years that the incumbent has served. The overall average is 5.43 years. The maximum is 36 years and the minimum is zero (apparently for newly elected mayors).

The two cities with populations greater than 1,000,000 report incumbents with 18 and 19 years of service, for an average of 18.5 years. However, the consistency of average years of mayoral service by each of the other population, geographic, and form-of-government categories is surprising. There is remarkably little variation regardless of these characteristics.

City Managers

Survey respondents were asked in which year their current city manager/CAO was appointed. Table 8 shows the data on appointments in 1991. Jurisdictions with newly created city manager or CAO positions were excluded from this analysis. Only those reporting new appointments that related to turnover are included.

Overall, turnover was reported in 29.1% of the jurisdictions. This closely corresponds to the findings of a recent study of Florida cities conducted by Ruth DeHoog and Gordon Whitaker in which they found that approximately one-fourth of the jurisdictions had manager turnover in a one-year period.[2]

The limited number of cases in the top two population categories does not permit us to draw meaningful conclusions from the ICMA survey data. Below that level, however, it appears that incidence of manager turnover tends to decline with population size. Respondents from cities with populations from 25,000 to 49,999, for example, show the lowest rate of turnover among the four lower population categories, with jurisdictions with populations from 250,000 to 499,999 showing the highest.

Among the geographic divisions, the East South Central cities report no manager turnovers in 1991. The respondents from New England have the highest among the categories (37.9%).

The form-of-government figures indicate that greater turnover occurred among appointed executives in mayor-council communities (36.5%) than in council-manager jurisdictions (28.0%). This is consistent with anecdotal evidence and case studies that suggest turnover among mayors influences the likelihood of city manager turnover. The remaining categories have too few cases to draw substantive conclusions.

Table 7
Years in Office of Current Mayor

Classification	No. reporting	Years in office of current mayor		
		Average no.	Maximum no.	Minimum no.
Total, all cities	839	5.43	36.00	0.00
Population group				
Over 1,000,000	2	18.50	19.00	18.00
500,000–1,000,000	8	2.25	8.00	1.00
250,000–499,999	29	3.72	11.00	1.00
100,000–249,999	94	5.45	28.00	1.00
50,000–99,999	234	5.52	32.00	0.00
25,000–49,999	472	5.49	36.00	0.00
Geographic division				
New England	78	4.94	21.00	1.00
Mid-Atlantic	98	5.77	34.00	0.00
East North Central	148	5.54	31.00	0.00
West North Central	71	5.68	30.00	1.00
South Atlantic	102	5.42	22.00	1.00
East South Central	31	6.10	23.00	1.00
West South Central	77	4.42	18.00	1.00
Mountain	52	4.19	24.00	0.00
Pacific Coast	182	5.96	36.00	1.00
Form of government				
Mayor-council	283	5.95	29.00	0.00
Council-manager	533	5.15	36.00	0.00
Commission	13	4.92	23.00	1.00
Town meeting	2	6.50	7.00	6.00
Rep. town meeting	8	6.75	19.00	2.00

City Councils

An examination of city councils must include the individual council members. The analysis, therefore, requires slightly different data to examine longevity and turnover. Table 9 presents the average percent of council members that are serving all or part of one, two, three, four, or more than four terms. Overall, an average of 47.0% are in their first term, 24.2% in their second term, 13.8% in their third term, and 6.0% in their fourth term. An average of only 9% are serving more than four terms. The jurisdictions with populations greater than 1,000,000 report the highest percentage (53.3%) of council members serving more than four terms, but the most consistent population differences are apparent for the one- and two-term categories. Perhaps consistent with political norms of volunteerism (as opposed to careerism) in smaller jurisdictions, cities

Table 8
City Manager/CAO Turnover in 1991

Classification	No. reporting (A)	City manager/CAO turnover in 1991			
		No turnover occurred		*Turnover occurred*	
		No.	*% of (A)*	*No.*	*% of (A)*
Total, all cities	375	266	70.9	109	29.1
Population group					
Over 1,000,000	1	1	100.0	0	0.0
500,000–1,000,000	2	0	0.0	2	100.0
250,000–499,999	11	6	54.5	5	45.5
100,000–249,999	50	35	70.0	15	30.0
50,000–99,999	112	74	66.1	38	33.9
25,000–49,999	199	150	75.4	49	24.6
Geographic division					
New England	29	18	62.1	11	37.9
Mid-Atlantic	34	24	70.6	10	29.4
East North Central	49	36	73.5	13	26.5
West North Central	35	29	82.9	6	17.1
South Atlantic	51	34	66.7	17	33.3
East South Central	7	7	100.0	0	0.0
West South Central	42	29	69.0	13	31.0
Mountain	27	18	66.7	9	33.3
Pacific Coast	101	71	70.3	30	29.7
Form of government					
Mayor-council	52	33	63.5	19	36.5
Council-manager	318	229	72.0	89	28.0
Commission	1	1	100.0	0	0.0
Town meeting	3	3	100.0	0	0.0
Rep. town meeting	1	0	0.0	1	100.0

with populations less than 500,000 appear to have more members in their first or second terms than do the larger jurisdictions. However, these differences may exist because incumbents are more likely to be reelected in larger cities than in smaller ones, not because of more voluntary decisions not to seek reelection. Although they are less consistent, the same could be said of the slight regional and form-of-government differences. Since few communities have term limitations on their city councils, are the seniority differences between jurisdictions a function of voluntary retirements or of varying reelection patterns of incumbents?

Table 9
Number of Terms Served by Council Members

| Classification | Council members serving all or part of | | | | |
| | One term | Two terms | Three terms | Four terms | More than four terms |
	Mean %	Mean %	Mean %	Mean %	Mean %
Total, all cities	47.0	24.2	13.8	6.0	9.0
Population group					
Over 1,000,000	26.7	13.3	3.3	3.3	53.3
500,000–1,000,000	42.0	20.4	17.0	8.8	11.9
250,000–499,999	45.1	26.6	14.5	7.3	6.6
100,000–249,999	46.9	24.0	15.2	5.7	8.3
50,000–99,999	43.3	24.8	14.8	7.1	10.1
25,000–49,999	49.3	23.9	13.0	5.4	8.4
Geographic division					
New England	40.0	20.5	18.4	7.6	13.5
Mid-Atlantic	52.6	21.3	12.0	4.6	9.5
East North Central	43.4	25.1	14.6	6.1	10.8
West North Central	46.7	24.6	12.2	5.4	11.1
South Atlantic	39.9	26.4	13.6	8.1	12.0
East South Central	43.7	28.7	8.6	5.5	13.5
West South Central	48.4	25.2	13.7	5.8	6.9
Mountain	54.9	24.7	11.4	5.0	4.0
Pacific Coast	51.6	23.7	14.4	5.4	4.8
Form of government					
Mayor-council	44.7	23.5	14.2	6.7	11.1
Council-manager	48.3	24.7	13.5	5.7	7.8
Commission	45.5	21.8	9.1	5.5	18.2
Town meeting	46.7	26.7	6.7	6.7	13.3
Rep. town meeting	51.7	16.7	27.5	4.2	0.0

This and other questions regarding city council incumbency and turnover are important and cannot be definitively addressed in this project. However, the data in Table 10 provide some clues. Overall, nearly 84% of city council incumbents were successful in their reelection bids, and only 16% were defeated. This is actually lower than the reelection rates for the U.S. House of Representatives and appears more comparable to the lower rate among U.S. Senators. Perhaps more important is the minimal variation in council incumbency reelection patterns by either population group, geographic division, or form of government.

Table 10
Incumbents Successful in Reelection Bids

Classification	No. reporting	Successful incumbents Average (%)	Maximum (%)	Minimum (%)
Total, all cities	782	83.89	100.00	14.29
Population group				
Over 1,000,000	1	87.50	87.50	87.50
500,000–1,000,000	8	82.97	100.00	50.00
250,000–499,999	28	81.76	100.00	33.33
100,000–249,999	93	82.36	100.00	20.00
50,000–99,999	218	83.49	100.00	20.00
25,000–49,999	434	84.56	100.00	14.29
Geographic division				
New England	80	86.20	100.00	28.57
Mid-Atlantic	75	80.72	100.00	20.00
East North Central	144	84.98	100.00	16.67
West North Central	67	83.40	100.00	20.00
South Atlantic	95	84.89	100.00	25.00
East South Central	28	79.86	100.00	20.00
West South Central	74	87.41	100.00	33.33
Mountain	49	81.31	100.00	14.29
Pacific Coast	170	82.76	100.00	33.33
Form of government				
Mayor-council	268	82.00	100.00	14.29
Council-manager	495	84.57	100.00	16.67
Commission	10	86.00	100.00	50.00
Town meeting	2	100.00	100.00	100.00
Rep. town meeting	7	100.00	100.00	100.00

Causes of Turnover

There is little systematic research examining the causes, characteristics, and consequences of turnover among local government officials. What factors appear to produce high or low turnover? Does turnover depend upon whether the officials are elected or appointed?

City Councils

Although there is little controversy about what constitutes voluntary or involuntary retirement of city council members (those who do not seek reelection voluntarily retire, those defeated involuntarily retire), virtually all the systematic evidence that exists on the subject focuses exclusively on a single jurisdiction or region. James Vanderleeuw, for example, has recently examined city council incumbency reelection patterns in New Orleans from 1965 to 1985.[3]

In this project, we seek to explore whether the likelihood of council incumbency defeat in a jurisdiction's most recent election is associated with any of the following:

1. Form of government
2. Mayoral veto power
3. Existence of standing committees on the council
4. Whether the elections for council seats are staggered or simultaneous
5. Partisan elections
6. Election system type (at-large, mixed, district)
7. Geographic region, metropolitan status, and population size of the jurisdiction

The form-of-government and mayoral veto power variables are included in order to examine the impact of basic structural differences on the reelection success of council incumbents. We expect lower reelection rates in council-manager and commission jurisdictions than in mayor-council governments because without a separation of powers we assume that responsibility is more clearly concentrated in the council as a unit and that incumbents are less likely to be able to fashion a style that is individual and independent of city government.

The structural characteristics of the councils are included to distinguish them on the basis of activity and institutionalization. We suggest that incumbency will be more valuable as institutionalization increases. It is possible that as city councils come to resemble state legislatures or Congress in activity, the council member positions become more secure. A member's name recognition, ability to raise campaign contributions, and obtain interest group endorsements will presumably increase as a result.

The election system characteristics of the jurisdiction are presumed to have several effects. Simultaneous election of all council members should result in lower incumbency reelection than staggered elections. Because the council is perceived as a unit when all members are elected at the same time, it is difficult to present individual style. Partisan elections and at-large elections are also expected to be associated with lower incumbency reelection success. Political party organizations and labels on the ballot are presumed to increase competition and reduce the probability that an incumbent will get a free ride. At the very least, something other than simple name recognition exists as a possible voting cue in partisan systems. At-large elections are hypothesized to have a harmful effect upon an incumbent's reelection prospects because the constituencies are likely to be broader and more diverse.

Alternatively, at-large could be more costly than district elections and incumbents could have an easier time because of their greater ability to raise money.

Each of the three demographic variables included in the model is also hypothesized to have an impact. Southern cities are presumed to be more likely to reelect incumbents than non–southern communities. The traditionalist political background of the region is expected to produce greater deference to the status quo. Population size is hypothesized to have a negative effect upon incumbency reelection due to the larger, more diverse constituency. Larger and more diverse constituencies may, however, increase campaign costs and thereby increase the incumbent advantage. Metropolitan central jurisdictions are assumed to have more competition and more vulnerable incumbents than suburban jurisdictions. And the latter are expected to have lower incumbency reelection rates than nonmetropolitan independent jurisdictions.

Table 11 shows the data on reelection of city council incumbents. The patterns are generally in the directions hypothesized, but most of the differences are not substantial. The gap between categories exceeds 10% for population size, form of government, election systems, election timetable (staggered-simultaneous) and whether or not the city has partisan or nonpartisan elections. On the other hand, region and the presence of permanent standing committees on a council appear to have a negligible effect upon whether any incumbents are defeated in a jurisdiction.

One pattern that stands out is the consistent decrease in incumbency reelection rates from at-large to mixed and district election systems. This suggests that incumbents may benefit from at-large elections because challengers may be less able to raise funds. It is also possible, of course, that these differences are attributable to something else, such as partisanship. Since we know that at-large systems are disproportionately nonpartisan, it may be the latter and not the former variable that is having the real effect. This underscores the need for a preliminary multivariate analysis including all of the possible factors.

Table 12 presents the data in a logistic regression (logit) model. It examines the reelection of city council incumbents as a function of all of the other variables combined and of each individually. A logistic regression enables an analysis of the effect of combined variables or of individual variables by controlling for each of the other variables. The impact of the combined variables in the model is statistically significant at the .0001 level, which means that the probability is one in ten thousand that patterns in the data could have occurred by chance. However, the goodness of the fit measure is weak (.3664). Goodness of fit indicates strength of the correlation between the *combined* variables and ranges from a low of .0000 to a high of 1.000. Because the goodness of the fit is weak, we can conclude that although the patterns in the data probably did not occur by chance, the effect of the combined variables upon the reelection of council incumbents is weak.

Table 11
City Council Incumbency Reelection Patterns

Variables	At least one council incumbent defeated in last election (%)
Total, all variables	53.1
Demographic variables	
Population	
500,000 and over	90.0
250,000–499,999	62.5
100,000–249,999	54.5
50,000–99,999	54.7
25,000–49,999	50.8
Region	
South	50.4
Non-south	54.0
Metropolitan status	
Central	57.7
Suburban	50.6
Independent	47.9
Structural variables	
Form of government	
Mayor-council	62.0
Council-manager	48.6
Election systems	
At-large	49.3
Mixed	54.1
District	61.6
Election timetable	
Staggered	47.6
Simultaneous	67.5
Party labels	
Partisan	63.4
Non-partisan	49.9
Mayoral veto	
No	50.3
Yes	58.9
Council standing committees	
No	52.6
Yes	53.6

Table 12
Logit Analysis of City Council Incumbency

Model significance = .0000
Goodness of fit = .3664

Structural variables	Significance
Form of government	0.0741
Partisan elections	0.0995
Staggered/simultaneous elections	0.0007
At-large elections (%)	0.9306
Council meetings	0.7440
Mayoral veto	0.2836
Council size	0.3331
Standing committees	0.1795
Demographic variables	
Population size	0.0934
Region	0.1300
Central/noncentral city	0.6749
Independent/nonindependent city	0.6626

The only independent variable that is significant at the .05 level is whether the elections are staggered or simultaneous. There is a significant decrease in reelection of incumbents in jurisdictions with simultaneous elections. Three other independent variables—form of government, party on ballot, and population size—result in relationships that are likely to occur by chance only between 5% and 10% of the time. The remaining variables are not significant, using any of the conventional significance levels. Significance tests indicate the probability of obtaining a particular sample result of pattern by chance if there is really no relationship in the population from which the sample was drawn.

It is clear that there are other factors than those included in this model that account for the diversity of reelection patterns for council incumbents. We are unable to make good predictions about city council incumbent reelection using the factors in our model. Subsequent research might seek to examine additional socioeconomic characteristics such as education, income and unemployment levels or population diversity, personal and occupational characteristics of the incumbents themselves, or policy outputs of the city such as per capita taxation and municipal debt.

City Managers

It is clear from the existing research on city manager turnover that it is difficult to distinguish between voluntary and involuntary turnover. Few managers are overtly fired by their councils. But this does not mean that they are not pushed into resignation to avoid formal dismissal from their position. Others may choose to resign before potential disagreements escalate. Of course, a manager's resignation may also be voluntary. Recent research by DeHoog and Whitaker suggests, however, that a clear majority of manager turnovers are involuntary.[4]

Although determinations about reasons for turnover are difficult to make, the existing research suggests possible causes. DeHoog and Whitaker have found clear linkages between manager turnover and elections that change the composition of the city council.[5] In addition, the existence of a separately elected mayor appears to conditionally affect the relationship between city council and manager turnover. Apparently, "elections were likely to change the balance on the council only in cities with elected mayors who opposed the manager."[6] While the results of DeHoog and Whitaker's projects are limited by their small number of cases and the fact that they all come from Florida, a more recent national study supports most of their conclusions and finds that (1) the greater the length of time an elected mayor has served, the less likely the jurisdiction has experienced city manager turnover; (2) managers with greater budgetary authority are less likely to experience turnover than those with weaker authority; but (3) the appointment power of managers is not significantly associated with manager turnover.[7]

Conclusion

This exploratory research project seeks to shed some light on term limitations and turnover among local government officials.

It is our hope that future scholars will give this subject the attention it deserves. Local governments are clearly at the front line of virtually every major policy area in America. They are responsible for implementing many, if not most, federal and state programs. It is, therefore, vital for scholars, practitioners and activists to obtain an understanding of the selection and accountability processes within these often ignored governments.

Notes

1. See Tari Renner, *Elected Executives: Authority and Responsibility*, Baseline Data Report vol. 20, no. 3 (Washington, D.C.: International City/County Management Association, May/June 1988):7.

2. Ruth Hoogland DeHoog and Gordon Whitaker, "Political Conflict or Advancement: Alternative Explanations of City Manager Turnover," *Journal of Urban Affairs* vol. 12, no. 4 (1990): 361–77.

3. James Vanderleeuw, "The Influence of Racial Transition on Incumbency Advantage in Local Elections," *Urban Affairs Quarterly* vol. 27 (1991): 36–50.

4. See DeHoog and Whitaker, 1990.

5. See DeHoog and Whitaker, 1990, and DeHoog and Whitaker, "City Managers Under Fire: How Conflict Leads to Turnover," *Public Administration Review* vol. 51, no. 2 (1991): 156–65.

6. DeHoog and Whitaker, 1991: 162.

7. Tari Renner and Victor DeSantis, "City Manager Authority and Turnover: Is There a Linkage?" Paper presented at the 1993 annual meeting of the American Political Science Association, Washington, D.C.

The Coming of Municipal Term Limits

John Clayton Thomas

Term limits have captured the fancy of American voters like no electoral reform in recent history. The November 1992 elections saw 14 states pass measures limiting the number of terms state legislators and/or U.S. Senators and congressional representatives may serve.[1]

With all the concern over state and federal term limits, a parallel movement at the local level has largely escaped notice. Yet, term limits are proving to be a popular municipal reform, too.

Although local government administrators are not the targets of term limits, they do need to understand what term limits can mean for them and their local governments. This chapter explores what is known about municipal term limits, and what those limits might mean for managers and administrators. The conclusions are based on a survey of term limit adoptions and related issues in 60 U.S. cities with populations of more than 250,000 people.[2]

The Spread of Local Term Limits

Municipal term limits have spread rapidly. Even before the November 1992 elections, 11 of the 60 largest U.S. cities had adopted term limits in just the 1989–91 period with seven adoptions occurring in 1991 alone. At least 32 percent of these cities now have term limits, almost quadrupling the 8.3 percent reported in a mid–1980s ICMA survey, and the numbers still are growing.

Municipal term limits reflect more than simply a spillover of the

Reprinted with permission from Public Management, *Vol. 75, No. 7, July, 1993. Published by the International City/County Management Association, Washington, D.C.*

enthusiasm for limits at higher levels of government. By imposing limits, voters appear to be reacting against elected municipal officials who have served extended periods of time in office. Of the nine cities that recently have adopted term limit initiatives (in every case over the opposition of the council), 60 percent of the elected officials had served more than the eight years which a typical local term allowed.

But long tenures in office are only part of the story. Municipal term limits also appear, at least initially, to be following the path of early twentieth century "public-interest" reforms (e.g., council-manager government, at-large and nonpartisan elections, initiative, and referendum). Like those earlier reforms, municipal term limits have taken root in the West or adjacent to the Mississippi River where the vast majority of cities only recently adopted or considered term limits. In a related manner, term limits also are proving increasingly popular in council-manager rather than mayor-council cities. These patterns suggest that voters in reformed cities may view extended elective tenures as undermining concern for citywide and countrywide interests.

Municipal term limits principally have been a big city phenomenon. Although only inconclusive data is available on smaller cities, most municipal term limit adoptions have occurred in cities over 250,000 in population. On the other hand, the appeal of term limits could broaden since the initiative mechanism under which limits have traditionally been adopted is available in most U.S. cities, or specifically 81 percent of the largest cities. Term limits already appear to be migrating eastward where Cincinnati, Ohio, and Jacksonville, Florida, imposed limits in 1991. Limits also have been adopted in the mayor-council cities of Houston and New Orleans, and in the smaller cities, Englewood, Colorado, and Rockville, Maryland.

For the moment, however, these findings imply for administrators that the likelihood of successful local term limit movements will be greatest if a local government (1) has a majority of local elected officials who have served for more than eight years, (2) permits adoption of ordinances by voter initiative, (3) is governed by the council-manager form of government, and/or (4) has a population of over 250,000 people.

When Limits Become an Issue

When term limits become an issue, the community should be encouraged to debate the issue before taking action. Leaders of the first communities that adopted term limits have lamented that the limits "passed without sufficient debate or public consideration" of their merits.[3]

The debate might begin by asking whether the community has a problem that limits might address. Are multiple local elective officials serving extended tenures? Term limits may represent overkill if adopted where, as in some recent cases, only one or two officials have served longer than limits permit.

If extended tenures are common, are citizens dissatisfied with how the long-term officeholders are governing? Term limits appear to be a questionable reform unless there is broad dissatisfaction. The community also must be made aware that term limits judge only on the basis of tenure in office, making no discrimination between good and bad officials, and they may bring inexperienced individuals to government, reducing the experience that officials can bring to bear on the community's problems.

The community also should be told that term limits do not guarantee more competitive elections. Proponents contend that term limits will create more open seats where incumbents are prohibited from running for reelection; and more open seats will attract more candidates, making elections more competitive. That competitiveness also may depend in part on the other incentives to run for office. One can wonder, for example, whether term limits will attract more candidates in a city like Colorado Springs, Colorado, where councilmembers do not receive a salary.

Forms of Term Limits

If support for term limits develops, the community should be encouraged to ask about the various possible forms. Although often perceived as a single reform, term limits actually come in a variety of forms, each potentially producing different results. The questions to ask include:

1. How long is too long? Cities, for example, typically limit officials to eight consecutive years in the same office, but San Antonio and Houston limit officials to four years (two two-year terms). Is four years long enough to attract good candidates? Is it long enough for individuals to become effective officeholders?

2. Lifetime or not? Most term limits allow an individual who has served the maximum tenure to run again after sitting out one or two terms (usually four years), but some limits prohibit the individual from ever running again for that office. These lifetime limits can be expected to reduce the availability of experienced individuals who might return to local government at a later point.

3. Any exceptions? In some cities, an individual who has reached the maximum tenure may run as a write-in candidate; the term limit measure only bars the candidate's name from appearing on the ballot. Houston, for example, permits an elected official who has served the maximum tenure to regain a place on the ballot by obtaining a requisite number of voter signatures on a petition.

4. Run for other local government offices? Almost all local governments permit a councilmember who has served the maximum tenure to run for mayor (or vice versa), the only exceptions being council-manager communities where the mayor is not separately elected. Several cities (New Orleans, for example) with mixed district and at-large city councils also permit a councilmember to run for a different kind of council seat. These opportunities may increase the candidate pool for various offices, thereby increasing electoral competition. In Kansas City, Missouri, for example, three councilmembers who were prohibited by term limits from running for reelection chose, in 1991, to run for mayor.

Impact on Municipal Administration

What do term limits, where adopted, mean for municipal administration? With little experience to draw upon, a definitive answer is impossible, but some educated guesses can be made.

1. More turnover in elective offices? Since most term-limited cities have many officials who have served extended tenures, term limits should increase turnover in elected offices. That effect may not be seen immediately, however, because time served prior to the passage of limits usually does not count toward the maximum time allowed. As a consequence, long-term officeholders usually may run for additional terms even after the adoption of limits.

2. Increased or threatened administrative power? There has been widespread speculation that term limits will increase administrative power. Some argue that knowledgeable administrators will supposedly gain the upper hand when term limits replace experienced officeholders with the inexperienced.

There are a number of holes in that argument. First, the replacements may include such individuals as neighborhood activists and other civic leaders, who are, in fact, knowledgeable about the workings of local government. Second, these newcomers may have different agendas than their predecessors, agendas that may challenge precedents.

As a consequence, term limits may be as likely to threaten as to enhance administrative power. Managers and chief administrative officers may face the greatest threat since electoral turnover traditionally has been the principal catalyst for managerial turnover.[4]

A Brief Agenda for Managers

Term limits lie so clearly in the realm of politics that managers should mostly steer clear of debates about their merits. Still, there are at least two ways in which managers can prepare for debates and possible adoptions of limits.

First, although it is not the place of managers and administrators to make recommendations on term limits, it may be appropriate to suggest to community leaders the need for debate as well as the range of available options. These suggestions probably should be made only informally by managers working behind the scenes, with the goal of encouraging an open debate, not any particular course of action.

Where term limits are passed, municipal administrators may want to plan greater orientation of new councilmembers and mayors. New elected officials may become more sympathetic if they understand at the outset why the local government operates as it does. They may quickly become antagonistic, however, should they perceive these sessions as designed to manipulate rather than to inform.

What is clear, in any event, is that term limits are becoming a fact of life for an increasing number of U.S. local governments. Managers must begin to think about what that fact will mean for them.

Notes

1. As reported by U.S. Term Limits: Jeffery Langan, "Memorandum: Citizen Lobby Campaigns," Washington, D.C., January 26, 1993.

2. Also see John Clayton Thomas, "The Term Limitations Movement in U.S. Cities," *National Civic Review,* 81 (Spring–Summer 1992), pp. 155–73.

3. See Laurie Hirschfeld Zeller and John Calhoon, "Term Limitations for Local Officials: A Citizens' Guide to Constructive Dialogue." Denver: National Civic League, 1992, p. 11.

4. See Gordon P. Whitaker and Ruth Hoogland DeHoog, "City Managers Under Fire: How Conflict Leads to Turnover," *Public Administration Review,* 51 (March/April 1991), 156–65, pp. 161–62.

PART IV
State Studies and Trends

Writing Home-Rule Charters

Susan B. Hannah

Increased charter revision activity in Michigan presents a timely opportunity to study the process of local constitution-making or "writing your own government" as one commissioner put it. Michigan was the seventh state in the Union to adopt the principle of home rule. Under provisions of the 1908 Constitution and the Home Rule Cities and Villages Acts of 1909, the citizens of every Michigan city and village enjoy broad "power and authority to frame, adopt, and amend its charter."[1] The 1963 Constitution further declared the meaning of home rule "shall be liberally construed" in the citizens' favor.[2]

As a result of these generous provisions, all but one of Michigan's 266 municipalities and 48 villages have adopted the home-rule charters. Every year some 20 to 30 communities are engaged in studying, developing, rewriting, revising, or amending their charters to fit changes in state law and judicial opinions and to respond to shifts in social, economic and political circumstances.[3]

To learn more about the process of "writing your own government," the Michigan Municipal League (MML) and the Michigan Association of Municipal Attorneys (MAMA) sponsored a survey of all elected charter-study committees active in 1992. Resulting information about who serves on commissions, how commissions operate, and what issues they address were summarized in *Charter Revision Activity in Michigan,* published by the Michigan Municipal League Foundation in 1993.[4]

The present study expands on the 1992 survey by focusing on the issue of success: Which of the charter commissions went on to see their proposals adopted by the voters and which did not? What are the differences in successful and unsuccessful charter-revision efforts? Does the nature of the community matter? The characteristics of the commissioners? The way the commissioners

Reprinted with permission from National Civic Review, *Vol. 84, No. 2, Spring, 1995. Published by the National Civic League Press, Denver, Colorado.*

go about their work? The issues they consider? Answers to these questions will contribute to an improved understanding of the dynamics of local constitution writing and its relationship to the political life of the community.

A growing collection of case studies on municipal charter reform suggests that the unique political history of the city, the goals of revision, timing, and the community's "mood about change" affect the process and content of charter revision.[5] These studies confirm conventional wisdom that a city's size, political history, culture, and socio-economic characteristics are closely related to its governmental structure.[6]

Mediated by culture and leadership, changes in environment have often meant changes in governmental structure. In a study of charter amendments in Michigan cities which had experienced significant population growth and decline, this author previously found that the greater the shift in population, the greater the change in government structure.[7] More precisely, Maser's national study of charter revision tied structural reforms intended to enhance representation to increases in the proportion of the nonwhite population.[8] Benjamin and Mauro conclude that in contrast to classical reform, these contemporary initiatives aim for greater democracy rather than greater efficiency.[9]

Research on the consequences of charter reform shows that changes in the structure of local government has altered who gets elected to city councils and how government operates, but has not necessarily influenced municipal policy outcomes.[10] There is also evidence that the new wave of charter writing is blurring the clear distinctions between the mayor-council and the council-manager forms under concurrent demands for political leadership, professional management and representative governance. City managers make room for directly elected mayors in reformed cities under pressure for political leadership; strong mayors appoint CAO's to provide professional managers to assure accountability; and citizens adopt single-member districts and partisan elections or institute residency requirements to enhance representation.[11]

The Charter-Writing Process in Michigan

Michigan's Home Rule Cities Act specifies the process for developing and amending a charter and establishing mandatory, permissive and prohibited municipal powers and functions. The Act requires that each home-rule city be a body corporate, have a legislative body, a mayor, a clerk, a treasurer, and an assessor. Citizens may decide how to elect the legislative body, whether by wards, at-large, or a combination. They may choose to select the mayor or any other officer by election or by appointment. Elections may be partisan or nonpartisan and nominations may be by primary election, petition, affidavit, or convention. The charter establishes the administrative structure of the city and the qualifications, duties and compensation of its officers. Other required provisions address tax rates, taxing procedures, ordinance adoption, accounting systems, and public records.

The Act also includes an extensive list of permissive provisions concerning city powers, administrative structure and council rules, and establishes the rules for incorporation, consolidation and annexation. Final provisions of the Act spell out the procedure for charter commission selection and operation and for the adoption and amendment of charters.[12]

To initiate the process, the electors of a city or village must first vote upon whether or not to revise or, following state law regarding incorporation, write an initial charter. If the vote is positive, citizens then elect nine (five for a village) charter commissioners (often the resolution vote and the election occur simultaneously), who have three years to propose a charter. The proposed charter must be reviewed by the Attorney General, acting for the Governor, and submitted to the voters for approval. Cities sometimes begin with a charter study committee, appointed by the mayor or city council, to explore the need for charter adoption or revision. The committee's recommendation then becomes the basis for the initial ballot resolution on revision.

1992 Charter Commission Survey Results

The large majority of the charter commission members who responded to the 1992 MML-MAMA survey were white, middle-aged, well educated males. They earned middle- to upper-middle class incomes as professionals or managers and were long-time community activists and home owners. Retirees made up a significant portion of commission membership in many cities. Commissioners were less diverse, better educated and more highly paid than the citizens they represented.

In general, commission members were satisfied that legal requirements regarding commission size and time allotment were adequate for the task. Most commissions adopted their own rules, met twice a month, worked as a committee of the whole, received no compensation, and had little or no funding to support their work. As a result, commissioners depended on themselves or city staff for research, drafting and clerical support. The primary research resources were surveys of other cities, the National Civic League's *Model City Charter* and state-specific materials provided by the Michigan Municipal League.

Commissioners expressed concern about the lack of public interest and involvement in charter development, although commissions varied in the degree of effort they made to solicit community participation. Few commissions actually campaigned during the charter referendum and the support of city officials and employees appeared to be important for adoption.

Commissions varied significantly in the degree of conflict or controversy they experienced.

The most frequently discussed charter issues concerned the structure of local government, its officers and their powers. Selection issues—term length, residency requirements, council selection, advisory board appointment—were rated next. The third set of issues were related to city finances and administrative operations. "Newer" ideas, such as sunset provisions and ethics codes, were least discussed.

The great majority of charter-review commissioners felt positively about their charter-writing experiences and believed that it was educational and rewarding.

Comparison of Successful and Unsuccessful Commissions

Thirteen of the 20 study commissions (65 percent) were successful in seeing the charter they had written approved by voters in a special election as required by the Home Rule Cities Act.[13] Seven (35 percent) were unsuccessful—either their proposed charters were voted down or never reached the referendum stage. To compare their work, survey responses were sorted by city and supplemented with demographic information from the 1990 census. Table 1 reports comparisons of the demographic characteristics of the cities involved, the characteristics of the commissioners, the nature of commission operations, and the charter issues under discussion. Chi-square analysis was used to identify which differences were statistically significant.

Community Characteristics. Interestingly, the demographic characteristics of the community do not appear to be related to charter-revision success. Neither the size of the city, its unemployment rate, percentage of minority residents, degree of population change, nor median education level appear to affect the failure or success of charter revision.

Commission Characteristics. Of the variables describing the characteristics of the charter commissioners themselves, only the self-reported evaluation of the experience appears to distinguish between successful and unsuccessful commissions. The median levels of commission members' education, income or political and community involvement were not related to a successful outcome. Commissioners whose work was eventually adopted by the voters, however, did offer much more positive evaluations of the entire charter-writing experience. These results are all the more striking since the survey was distributed before most charter referenda were completed.

Commission Operations. Commission success is also related to commission operations. Commissioners on successful commissions rated their

Table 1
Comparison of Successful and Unsuccessful Charter Commissions (Selected Variables)

Variable	X^2
Nature of the Community	
Population	1.17
Unemployment Rate	1.17
Percentage Minority Population	1.56
Percentage with BA or Higher	.04
Population Change	1.98
Characteristics of the Commissioners	
Median Level of Education	.01
Median Level of Income	.04
Degree of Political Involvement	.29
Degree of Community Involvement	1.97
Rating of Experience	5.50*
Commission Operations	
Staff Support	10.20*
Leadership	9.29*
Time to Organize	.46
Internal Operations	8.81*
Internal Conflict	6.28*
Public Input	.18
Effort to Involve Public	.29
Conflict with the Community	1.17
Charter Issues	
Type of Government	6.28*
Council Powers	3.97*
Mayor's Powers	8.81*
Manager's Powers	1.90
Council Terms	.02
Ward Elections	1.99
Tax Rates	.04
Staff Issues	1.56
New Issues	2.03

*Significant at .05

staff support, leadership and internal operations much more positively than did commissioners whose proposals eventually failed. Successful commissions also experienced much less conflict. Members of both types of commissions rated the level of public input as unsatisfactory, although there was no difference in their efforts to solicit community participation.

Issues. Structural issues such as form of government or mayoral and council powers clearly distinguished successful from unsuccessful commissions. Commissions that took on these core structural and leadership issues were much more likely to be unsuccessful than those focusing on mere operational provisions. Table 2 compares the list of major topics discussed by successful commissions with those discussed by commissions that were not.

Content of Charter Reform. Of the 13 successful commissions, four had proposed significant reforms: two to a council-manager form from a strong mayor, one the reverse, and one from village to city status (which was only narrowly approved). Two others adopted term limits for their mayor and council positions and one changed from elected to appointed clerk and treasurer positions (also only narrowly approved). The remaining revisions consisted largely of updates to bring the charter into conformance with state law or improvements in administrative operations (increasing purchasing limits, spelling out administrative officers).

By comparison, all but one of the seven unsuccessful commissions had proposed major structural or financial change. One proposed changing to a council-manager form (only 200 out of 5,300 registered voters even voted); another proposed moving in the opposite direction to a strong mayor. One wanted to strengthen the manager's role over department head appointments, while another proposed to check the manager by changing to a directly elected mayor. Another proposed raising the tax limit. One commission did not finish its work within the three-year limit, and for another this was the second defeat in a row. Only one unsuccessful commission reported that its revisions consisted largely of updates.

Conclusion

Charter writing in Michigan is carried out by a familiar political elite and successful revisions are more incremental than radical. Successful commissions take on relatively minor revision issues, have smooth internal operations, and rate their experience very positively. Unsuccessful commissions address core issues of structure and power, endure greater conflict, rate staff support, leadership and internal operations less highly, and are less positive about their overall charter-writing experience.

Other studies have shown the relationship between significant structural revision and the socio-political environment: the greater the shift in these environmental and leadership factors, the greater the likelihood of structural reform. The results here help explain why. Working in relative isolation and with little financial or staff support, the political elites who write new charters face significant obstacles if they propose radical change in the status quo. To be successful, charter commissioners must make sure there is a compelling

Table 2
Major Charter Issues as Reported by Successful and Unsuccessful Charter Commissions

Issue	Percent Listing Issue as "Major"	
	Successful Commissions (N = 13)	Unsuccessful Commissions (N = 7)
Structure of government (council manager v. mayor-council)	30.8%	85.7%
Powers of mayor	15.4	100.0
Selection of mayor	7.7	71.4
Length of mayor's term	15.4	14.2
Mayor's compensation	15.4	14.2
Council powers	84.6	85.7
Council selection by ward	15.4	57.1
Council selection at-large	23.1	57.1
Council selection mixed	30.8	57.1
Length of council terms	38.5	28.5
Staggered terms	15.4	14.2
Manager powers	69.2	100.0
Employee residency	38.5	28.5
Selection of clerk	30.8	57.1
Selection of treasurer	30.8	28.5
Selection of assessor	15.4	14.2
Selection of Board of Review	15.4	14.2
Residency for elected officials	30.8	28.5
Selection of advisory boards	0.0	14.2
Powers of advisory boards	7.7	0.0
Property tax rates	38.5	28.5
Mission statement	7.7	28.5
Ombudsman	0.0	0.0
Ethics code	15.4	42.8
Planning process	7.7	14.2
Environmental issues	7.7	0.0
Sunset provisions	0.0	0.0
Intergovernmental cooperation	0.0	28.5
Purchasing/bidding	38.5	57.1

and widely accepted reason for whatever changes they propose. Success is more likely if the changes are incremental, staff support strong, internal operations smooth, and conflict limited. The more radical the proposal, the weaker the internal operations, the less the staff support and the greater the conflict, the more likely the charter-revision effort will fail.

Notes

1. CL 1948 #117.4j, MSA 5.2083 (3).
2. *Michigan Constitution,* Article VII, Section 21 (1963).
3. W.L. Steude, General Counsel, Michigan Municipal League, "Home Rule in Michigan: Why Charters Are Important," a paper presented at the meeting of the Michigan Public Management Institute, Lansing, May 1993; updated in a report to the League's Charter Focus Group, Ann Arbor, January 1995.
4. S.B. Hannah, *Charter Revision Activity in Michigan* (Ann Arbor: Michigan Municipal League Foundation, 1993).
5. For example, for New York City, see E. Lane, "The Practical Lessons of Charter Reform," *Proceedings of the Academy of Political Science* 37 (1989), pp. 31–44; for Illinois, see J.M. Banovetz and T.W. Kelty, *Home Rule in Illinois* (Springfield: Illinois Issues, 1987); for Lafayette Parish, see M.W. Mallory, "Home Rule in Lafayette Parish: A New Beginning," *National Civic Review* 73 (1984), pp. 556–570, 574; for Maine, see R. Josephson and G. Herman, "Municipal Charters: A Comparative Analysis of 75 Maine Charters," *Maine Townsman,* August 1992, pp. 5–15; and for Syracuse, see J.M. Harkin, "Structural Change and Municipal Government: The Syracuse Case," *State and Local Government Review* 15 (1983), pp. 3–9.
6. C.R. Adrian, "Forms of City Government in American History," *Municipal Year Book 1988* (Washington, D.C.: International City Management Association, 1988).
7. S.B. Hannah "Checks and Balances in Local Government: City Charter Amendments and Revisions in Michigan, 1960–1985," *Journal of Urban Affairs* 9 (1987), pp. 337–353.
8. S.M. Maser, "Demographic Factors Affecting Constitutional Decisions: The Case of Municipal Charters," *Public Choice* 47 (1985), pp. 121–162. See also Maser's more recent paper, "Analyzing Constitutions as Relational Contracts or Why People Negotiate Procedural Safeguards in Municipal Charters," presented at the Midwest Political Science Association Meetings, Chicago, April 1994.
9. G. Benjamin and F.J. Mauro, "The Reemergence of Municipal Reform," *Proceedings of the Academy of Political Science* 37 (1989), pp. 1–15.
10. For the impact of structure on representation, see W. Welch and T. Bledsoe, *Urban Reform and Its Consequences* (Chicago: University of Chicago Press, 1988); for impact on operations see J.H. Svara, *Official Leadership in the City* (New York: Oxford University Press, 1990); for impact on outcomes see T.N. Clark, *City Money: Political Processes, Fiscal Strain, and Retrenchment* (New York: Columbia University Press, 1983), K. Hayes and S. Chang, "The Relative Efficiency of City Manager and Mayor Council Forms of Government," *Southern Economic Journal* 57 (1990), pp. 167–177, and T.R. Sass, "The Choice of Municipal Government Structure and Public Expenditures," *Public Choice* 71 (1991), pp. 71–87.
11. J.M. Banovetz, "City Managers: Will They Reject Policy Leadership?" *Public Productivity and Management Review* XVII (1994), pp. 313–324.
12. D. Morris, *The Nature and Purpose of a Home Rule City Charter* (Detroit: Citizens Research Council in Michigan, 1971). Updated by W.L. Steude and D.C. Matsen in *The Nature and Purpose of a Home Rule City Charter,* Report No. 311 (Ann Arbor: Michigan Municipal League and Detroit: Citizens Research Council of Michigan, 1993).
13. Note that two of the 13 won by narrow margins (.6 percent and 5.8 percent, respectively).

The Impact of Cumulative Voting

Robert Brischetto

> The Voting Rights Act and its grant of authority to the Federal courts to uncover official efforts to abridge minorities' right to vote have been of vital importance in eradicating invidious discrimination from the electoral process and enhancing the legitimacy of our political institutions... As a Nation, we share both the obligation and the aspiration of working toward this end. This end is neither assured nor well served, however, by carving electorates into racial blocs. (*Justice Kennedy, majority opinion,* Miller v. Johnson, *6/29/95*).

With those words a divided, predominantly conservative Supreme Court declared a black-majority congressional district in Georgia illegally drawn to segregate voters on the basis of race and ruled that drawing electoral district lines chiefly on the basis of race can be presumed unconstitutional, absent some compelling state interest.

Two years ago the high court had called into question a "bizarrely" shaped North Carolina congressional district in *Shaw v. Reno* and warned that "Racial classifications with respect to voting carry particular dangers. Racial gerrymandering, even for remedial purposes, may balkanize us into competing racial factions; it threatens to carry us further from the goal of a political system in which race no longer matters..."(*Shaw v. Reno,* 1993).

For voting rights advocates, *Shaw* and *Miller* were bitter pills to take. For almost three decades they had been drawing districts chiefly on the basis of race in order to level the playing field and allow minorities an opportunity to elect candidates of their own choice. Indeed, the creation of majority-minority districts largely explains why there are 38 African Americans and 17 Latinos in the House of Representatives today.

Reprinted with permission from Voting & Democracy Report 1995. *Published by the Center for Voting and Democracy, Washington, D.C.*

Growing Interest in PR Alternative

After *Shaw* and *Miller*, the "radical" alternatives to districting presented by legal scholar Lani Guinier, whose nomination as Assistant Attorney General for Civil Rights was withdrawn by President Clinton, are looking increasingly relevant. In the wake of these decisions, voting rights advocates are seeking solutions that would provide better representation for minorities without resorting to racial gerrymandering. Some have turned to voting systems that approximate proportional representation in multiseat elections: cumulative voting, limited voting and preference voting.

The search for alternatives to districting has engendered a long-overdue national debate on more basic questions about how well our democracy works and how we choose our elected officials. The United States is one of only a few modern democracies that have not adopted some form of proportional representation. As Birmingham civil rights attorney Edward Still puts it: "Surely any majoritarian system that can leave 49 percent of the people ... with nothing to show for having gone to the polls except a patriotic feeling is not the answer."

More than a hundred local governments throughout the country—cities, counties and school districts—now employ these alternatives to districting, most in response to vote dilution law suits filed in the past decade. This chapter focuses on *cumulative voting,* particularly as it has been applied in cities and school boards in Texas.

The Cumulative Voting Alternative

Cumulative voting allows each voter as many votes as seats to be filled in a given election. In that way, it is the same as simple at-large systems. However, under cumulative voting, a voter may distribute votes among candidates in any combination, even distributing all votes to one candidate.

Although relatively rare, this system is not new to the American political scene. From 1870 to 1980, Illinois elected members of their general assembly by cumulative voting. Each legislative district had three representatives and a voter could cast one vote for each of three candidates, one and one-half votes for each of the two candidates or three votes for one candidate. Cumulative voting has also been used for decades to elect members of many corporate boards of directors.

Within this tradition, during the past decade some three dozen local jurisdictions have adopted cumulative voting as a remedy for minority vote dilution. For blacks in Peoria (IL), Hispanics in Alamogordo (NM), Native Americans in Sisseton (SD), blacks in Chilton Co., Centre, Guin and Myrtlewood

(AL) and for Latinos in more than two dozen local jurisdictions in Texas, it is a means of obtaining at least some representation. A federal judge last year was the first to *order* cumulative voting as a remedy in a case against Worcester County, MD (*Cane v. Worcester County*).

Cumulative Voting in Texas

Except for the use of limited voting in the small town of Grapeland, cumulative voting is the only modified at-large system in Texas that currently addresses the problem of minority vote dilution. In 1991, the Lockhart Independent School District settled a case of minority vote dilution by adopting four single-member districts and electing the remaining three board members by cumulative voting. In 1992 cumulative voting was adopted to settle lawsuits against the city of Yorktown and Yorktown Independent School District. Since then at least twenty-four small cities and school districts in the Texas panhandle and the Permian Basin have settled lawsuits with cumulative voting, most of them brought by San Antonio attorney Rolando Rios on behalf of the League of United Latin American Citizens (LULAC).

In Atlanta, an East Texas town of 6,000 near Texarkana, no black candidate had ever won a school board election—until May. In election after election, whenever blacks ran for office, the number of votes they received approximated the number of black voters. And that was always fewer than was needed to win.

Determined to address their lack of representation in school district matters, Atlanta's black community leaders sought help from local attorney Clyde Lee and the national office of the NAACP. A suit was filed in March of 1992.

In its initial response to the lawsuit, the school board offered five single-member districts with one majority black district and two at-large seats; but the plan did not pass muster with the Justice Department. The plaintiffs produced a seven-district plan with two majority-black districts and the school board promptly rejected it. No agreement was reached and it looked as if the case would go to trial on May 1, 1995.

In mid–March, NAACP national legal director Dennis Hays traveled to Atlanta with an expert on voting systems, hoping to negotiate a settlement. On March 23, six weeks before the next election, Federal District Judge John Hannah signed an agreement between the two parties for a cumulative voting system.

May 1995 Cumulative Voting Elections Study

The May 6, 1995 election provided a rare opportunity to test the effectiveness of cumulative voting in Texas. Twenty-six small cities and school districts

328 PART IV : STATE STUDIES AND TRENDS

in Texas held elections under cumulative voting that day, most for the first time, all in response to litigation. In sixteen of these jurisdictions, minority candidates were competing against Anglos; in ten jurisdictions, minority candidates did not file.

Fifteen of the sixteen jurisdictions studied had Latino candidates on the ballot. The Hispanic Research Center at the University of Texas at San Antonio conducted polling in these cities and school districts. Bilingual teams of pollsters went to these jurisdictions with bilingual questionnaires to gather data from 3,615 voters on how they cast their ballots, how well they understood and how they evaluated the new system of voting.

Atlanta Independent School District (ISD) held the only election in which a black candidate was running. The Atlanta survey of 569 voters was a cooperative effort by experts for the plaintiffs and defendants. The political science department at Texarkana College conducted the field work.

The study analyzes the exit polls of 4,184 voters in the sixteen jurisdictions in which minorities ran for office under cumulative voting (see Table 1). The study addresses several questions:

1. Was there racially polarized voting? Were there clear differences between minority and Anglo voters in their preferred candidates? Did minority voters vote as a bloc?
2. Did cumulative voting work to elect minority-preferred candidates? If not, why not?
3. Did voters understand cumulative voting?
4. Did voters accept cumulative voting?

Racially Polarized Voting

Knowing whether voters polarize along racial lines is pivotal in voting rights cases since in the absence of polarization there can be no claim of minority vote dilution.

In Atlanta ISD white and black voters could not have been much more polarized in their choices of candidates. Veloria Nanze came in last among white voters, but first among African American voters. Fewer than 3% of white voters cast even one of their four votes for Nanze; 94% of all votes cast by blacks went to Nanze.

The same general pattern of polarization between Anglos and Latinos was found in the jurisdictions with Latino candidates, but it was less severe. Except in two cases, Latino candidates were the top choices of Latino voters and ranked last or next to last among Anglo voters.

Threshold of Exclusion

In the worse case scenario of totally polarized voting, one can predict the outcome for a racial or ethnic group under cumulative voting by a simple calculation of the "threshold of exclusion." The *threshold of exclusion* is the percentage of votes that any group of voters must exceed in order to elect a candidate of its choice, regardless of how the rest of the voters cast their ballots. It is calculated as simply one divided by one more than the number of seats to be filled.

With four seats up in the 1995 election to Atlanta school board, the threshold of exclusion was 1/(4+1) or 20%. That meant that, even if Veloria Nanze did not get a single white vote—and if white voters were spread evenly among just four candidates—she could win as long as black voters comprised at least 20% of the total voters and concentrated their votes on her.

Blacks in Atlanta comprised 21% of the voting age population in 1990 and 31% of the voters in 1995, which means that voter turnout among blacks in this election apparently was much higher than among whites. In next year's election, when three seats are open on the school board, the threshold of exclusion will be 25% and it is likely that blacks will elect another representative (as long as two or more black candidates do not split the vote).

The Results Under Cumulative Voting

In the case of Atlanta ISD, cumulative voting worked as it should have for black voters seeking to elect one candidate. The African American community not only elected their candidate with almost no white support, but they voted together, placing almost all their votes on Nanze, who came in a close second among five candidates in a race that elected the top four choices.

In the 15 contests involving Latino candidates, on first glance the results seem mixed: 8 wins and 7 loses. A closer examination of the contests involving Latinos reveals that cumulative voting worked almost precisely as expected in polarized communities. In each of the jurisdictions where Latino candidates lost, there were not enough Latino voters to rise above the threshold of exclusion.

• In Andrews school district, Latinos were 32% of the total population but only 16% of the registered voters and 8% of all voters in the election. Since three seats were up, the threshold of exclusion was set at 25% not low enough for Latino voters to elect their preferred candidate.

• In Denver City ISD, Latinos were 36% of the total population and 15% of the registered voters, but only 4% of those who came out to vote. Two seats were up in the election, setting the threshold of exclusion at 33%, far above what was possible for Latino voters to elect someone.

Table 1

Cumulative Voting Election Outcomes in Jurisdictions with Minority Candidates: May 6, 1995

	Total Candidates	Rank of Minority Candidate(s) by: Minority Voters	Rank of Minority Candidate(s) by: Anglo Voters	Positions Elected	Exclusion Threshold	% Minority of Voters	% Over (+) or Under (-) Threshold	Minority Elected?
Minorities Won:								
Atlanta ISD	5	1	5	4	20%	31%	+11%	Yes
Anton	8	1	5	3	25%	30%	+5%	Yes
Morton	4	1,2	3,4	3	25%	26%	+1%	Yes (1)
Morton ISD	7	1,2	6,7	3	25%	23%	-2%	Yes (1)
Roscoe	8	1	6	5	17%	17%	0%	Yes
Rotan	8	1,2	7,8	5	17%	32%	+15%	Yes (2)
Rotan ISD	5	1	5	3	25%	25%	0%	Yes
Yorktown	2	1	2	2	33%	43%	+10%	Yes
Olton	6	1	6	2	33%	22%	-11%	Yes
Minorities Lost:								
Andrews ISD	7	1	6	3	25%	8%	-17%	No
Denver City ISD	5	2	4	2	33%	4%	-29%	No
Dumas ISD	7	2	6	2	33%	2%	-31%	No
Earth	6	1,4	5,6	3	25%	16%	-9%	No
Friona	6	1	5	3	25%	12%	-13%	No
Friona ISD	6	1	6	2	33%	7%	-26%	No
Stamford ISD	5	1	4	3	25%	7%	-18%	No

"Minority" refers to African Americans in the case of Atlanta ISD, where Latinos are fewer than 0.5% of voters. In the other 15 jurisdictions, "minority" refers to Latinos; blacks are only 1.2% of voters in these jurisdictions.

• In Dumas ISD, Latinos comprise 33% of the total population, but only 2% of the voters in the May 6 election. There were two seats up for election and the threshold of exclusion was set at 32%.
• In the city of Earth, Latinos are 51% of the total population, 31% of registered voters and 16% of actual voters. With three seats up for election May 6, the threshold of exclusion was 25%.
• In the city of Friona, Latinos are 51% of the total population, 37% of the registered voters and 12% of the voters in the May 6 election. With three seats up, the threshold of exclusion was 25%.
• In Friona ISD, Latinos are 45% of the total population, 21% of the registered voters and 7% of those who came out to vote.
• In Stamford ISD, Latinos are 22% of the total population, 14% of the registered voters and 7% of those who voted.

All seven losses could have been avoided either by lowering the threshold of exclusion or raising the level of minority participation in the election. The thresholds could have been reduced by agreement between the parties designing the cumulative voting system, realizing that the more seats up in an election, the lower the threshold. (In school districts with seven seats, if all seats were up at once, the threshold would be 1/(7+1) or 12.5%.)

The Key Role of Community Organizing

The other strategy for winning is somewhat more difficult: raising the level of voter participation through voter registration and education, minority candidate recruitment and get-out-the vote efforts. Where minority candidates were elected under cumulative voting, voter education and mobilization were apparent. In Atlanta, blacks launched door-to-door voter education and get-out-the-vote drives in black neighborhoods. In Morton, Roscoe and Rotan, where as many as five jurisdictions had Latino winners, the Southwest Voter Registration Education Project provided training on voter mobilization under cumulative voting. In Yorktown, where Concerned Citizens for Voting had begun mobilizing under their first cumulative voting election in 1992, a Latino was running as an incumbent.

In stark contrast, where Latino candidates lost, minority voter participation was low. The average turnout rate among Latinos registered to vote in the seven jurisdictions in which Latino candidates lost was one-half the turnout rate for non–Latino voters.

Finally, for a group or party to win under cumulative voting in a highly polarized political contest, they must vote together as a group. This may require planning to limit the number of minority candidates so as not to split their votes and placing all their votes on their preferred candidate (this problem is avoided by preference voting).

Placing all one's votes on a single candidate, or "plumping," is a practice that may enable minority voters to concentrate the strength of their group's vote and improve their chances of electing at least one candidate of their choice. African American voters in Atlanta, Texas, planned their effort very carefully in only a few weeks by agreeing to field only one candidate and conducting door-to-door voter-education drives in the black community and get-out-the-vote drives and early voting on election day. The poll found that 90% of blacks in Atlanta ISD "plumped" their votes for Veloria Nanze.

Is Cumulative Voting Understood and Accepted?

Ten of the sixteen jurisdictions were holding elections under cumulative voting for the first time; five for only the second time. Beyond the success of minority candidates, we wanted to know how all voters responded to the cumulative voting system. Did they understand the new voting system? How do both minority and white voters perceive cumulative voting?

Since all sixteen jurisdictions polled had been sued for minority vote dilution, it is likely that white voters harbored much resentment at being forced to adopt a settlement over which they had no control. Yet our polls found greater understanding and acceptance of cumulative voting than might be expected. More than nine in ten voters of each ethnic group knew they could concentrate all their votes on a single candidate. Asked to compare cumulative voting with previous election systems, more said that cumulative voting was easier than said it was more difficult.

There were large ethnic differences in evaluations of cumulative voting with regard to difficulty. More than twice as many minority as Anglo voters felt cumulative voting was easier compared to other elections in which they had voted; even so, fewer than two in ten white voters found this election system more difficult than previous voting methods they had used.

Contrary to our expectations, cumulative voting was not rejected by the majority of white voters. We found slightly more agreement than disagreement among whites with the statement that "the voting system used today gives everyone a fair chance to elect officials of their choice." Almost nine in ten blacks and eight in ten Latinos agreed that it was a fair system. However, there were a number of whites—between one in five and one in four—who strongly disagreed with that statement.

Conclusions and Recommendations

Lawsuits were settled with cumulative voting schemes in at least 26 jurisdictions in Texas during the past three years, many without regard for local community input or organizing. We studied 16 of these cities and school districts with exit polls on election day, May 6, 1995, all jurisdictions with cumulative voting where minority candidates were on ballot. In ten places with cumulative, minority candidates were not even fielded in the 1995 elections. Where there was a minority community initiative and the threshold of exclusion was exceeded, the minority candidate won. In those cases where minority candidates lost, there was no organized effort to get out the minority vote and the threshold of exclusion was too high.

The results of our study show that cumulative voting results in a more diverse city council or school board. In those cases where cumulative voting did not result in minority victories, it was not that the method did not work as predicted, but rather because it was not applied correctly.

The study sheds some light on this little-known alternative to districting and offers advice to those considering its adoption.

• Racial bloc voting was found to be extensive in all cities and school districts studied. In such a racially polarized context, the traditional winner-take-all at-large election system effectively precludes minority groups from electing candidates of their choice.

• Before fashioning an alternative to districting, such as cumulative voting, one must calculate the relative size of the eligible minority voting group. This proportion determines what "threshold of exclusion" is needed in the settlement. For Latino communities, population figures generally will not be an accurate measure of the size of the Latino vote; a better measure is the count of Spanish surnames on the list of registered voters for the jurisdiction.

• The number of seats up at any one time is crucial to determining a minority group's ability to elect since it is used to calculate the "threshold of exclusion." If terms of office are staggered, the chance that a minority group can elect a candidate of its choice will be diminished.

• The ability to elect candidates of their choice issues from the education of minority voters on how the system can work for them and lots of shoe leather. If there is not sufficient local mobilization to get out the minority vote in excess of the calculated threshold of exclusion, the minority's candidate is not likely to win.

• All of the jurisdictions which have adopted cumulative voting in Texas are small. A modified at-large election system was viewed by election administrators as a far more desirable alternative than carving their small communities into even smaller single-member districts. From this limited field experiment, it is not clear whether single-member districts in larger communities would work as well or better.

• Finally, if any numeric minority—racial, gender, country club crowd, bubbas, the militia—meets the magic threshold and votes as a block, they can elect a candidate of their choice.

Perhaps this last point is why the system is so controversial.

Women on Southern City Councils

Susan A. MacManus and
Charles S. Bullock III

Over a decade ago in the first empirical study of the level of female representation on U.S. city councils, Karnig and Walter reported that women were elected to less than 10 percent of the over 4,000 municipal posts. The authors concluded that "in local politics, sex is even more critical than race in impeding equitable representation."[1]

In probing into the question of why so few females are represented on local bodies (state and national, as well), scholars have focused on three major categories of explanations. The first, and most common, has been on factors restricting the candidacy of female officeseekers. These factors include attitudinal barriers, generally sex-role stereotyping on the part of voters, party leaders, and the potential candidates themselves, the effect being to restrict female candidacies and successes.[2]

Another common approach to the study of the success rate of female candidates has been to focus on environmental determinants, namely community demographic, socioeconomic, and political-cultural characteristics.[3] For example, Karnig and Walter looked at the relationship between women's candidacy and election rates and city size, southern location, and various income and education measures. But unlike the literature on the determinants of racial and ethnic minority candidate success, they found that these independent measures "have only feeble impact on female candidacy and election levels."[4] No single variable accounted for as much as 5 percent of the variance in any of the women's votes. Subsequent studies by other scholars produced similar

Reprinted with permission from Journal of Political Science, *Vol. 17, 1989. Published by the South Carolina Political Science Association, Clemson University, Clemson, South Carolina.*

results.[5] Demographic and socioeconomic models have *consistently* been poor predictors of female success in getting elected to city councils throughout the U.S. As noted, this is a different result than that produced by the literature examining the socioeconomic factors associated with racial and ethnic minority electoral success.[6]

A third approach to the study of the determinants of female city council representation has been to look at the relationship between various governmental structural arrangements, such as at-large elections, council size, term of office, and pay for office.[7] In general, governmental structural variables, like demographic and socioeconomic variables, have not been very powerful predictors of female electoral success.[8] For example, Karnig and Walter reported only a weak correlation (.12) between the percent candidates elected at large and the overall women's election rate; MacManus reported similarly weak coefficients.[9] Welch and Karnig found that even when socioeconomic and office prestige factors were controlled for, "election type explained less than one percent of the variance in female representation."[10]

Interestingly, however, in light of their findings, Welch and Karnig predicted that "in the long run women might do better in district than in at-large races because of the greater name recognition and financial support necessary even to get the nomination in at-large contests."[11] The purpose of our research is to determine whether their prediction has, in fact, come true.

The Study

Using data from nearly a decade later (1986), we test whether Welch and Karnig's prediction has yet been realized with regard to greater female representation under single member district election systems. We also examine the impact of other governmental structural variables on female city council representation: council size, incumbency return rate, length of term, staggered terms, and majority vote requirements. Each of these structures has been suggested in earlier research to have a detrimental effect on levels of female city council representation.[12] We are curious as to whether these structures have become more important determinants as larger numbers of women have gained political office,[13] gender-based stereotypes have eroded,[14] and the socioeconomic gap has narrowed somewhat.[15]

We also examine whether these structures have significantly different impacts on black females. Research on black women has often posited that they are doubly disadvantaged in the political arena by race and gender.[16] Other research suggests this interaction between race and sex is not as powerful as previously suggested.[17] There has not been much evidence to suggest that electoral structures serve as a significant deterrent to the election of black females.

Our data were gathered in the spring of 1986 from the 211 cities with 1980 populations over 25,000 in 11 southern states (Alabama, Arkansas, Florida, Georgia, Louisiana, Mississippi, North Carolina, South Carolina, Tennessee, Texas, and Virginia). Some studies have suggested that the South is "the region most likely to manifest differences between males and females toward the role of women and politics."[18] As noted by Carver, "opportunities for women have been particularly limited in the South, where the myth of the southern lady has served as a golden cord binding women to traditional roles."[19] Each of the earlier studies that used regional location as a predictor variable found that female representation levels were slightly lower in the South, but that the bivariate relationship between southern location and the percent of females elected was very weak (statistically insignificant). Consequently, if we find no support for relationships between structural variables and female representation in the South, we would not expect these relationships to be significant in other regions.

Governmental Structures and Women

The previous review of the literature examining the relationship between various governmental structural arrangements and female representation in the 1970's reported only weak correlations. A decade later, we reexamine these relationships. We begin with a review of the hypothesized directions of impact.

Electoral Format: At-Large v. District Elections

Traditionally, scholars have found that at-large elections are more "women-friendly" than district-based election systems.[20] Weaver states that:

> Any type of multimember district is more hospitable to women than the single-member district system. This includes at-large systems, semi-proportional systems, such as the single transferable vote (rank order), or party list/proportional representation. The single-member district system, by contrast, favors males from the largest ethnic group in each district.[21]

Weaver and others hypothesize that voters "are more apt to give one of several votes to a woman when they are limited to only one vote."[22] Likewise, nominations are easier to come by in multiple seat settings because party and organizational slating groups are more prone to see the advantages of "balanced tickets." Thus, we hypothesize that:

H1: At-large election systems will be characterized by higher percentages of female council members than district-based systems.
H1a: Purer at-large systems (non-district based) such as pure at-large and at-large, from posts will be characterized by higher percentages of female

council members than at-large systems with geographical residency requirements or mixed systems (some at-large; some single-member district seats).

H2: At-large election systems will have the same positive effect on black
female representation as on white female representation. At-large election systems will be characterized by higher percentages of black female council members than district-based systems.

Majority Vote Requirement (Runoffs)

This structural feature was alleged to have a discriminatory impact on
female representation by Smeal (1984), although she offered no reasons
why.[23] We do, however, have some notion of why racial minorities view runoffs as deterrents to electoral success. In his 1984 presidential campaign,
Jesse Jackson alleged that runoffs offer whites the ability to coalesce and defeat
a black that wins a primary with a plurality when the white vote was splintered.

Contrary to the speculations made by Smeal and Jackson, recent empirically based research has not found their claims to be warranted. In their analyses of primary runoffs in Georgia between 1965 and 1982, Bullock and Johnson
found that black and female party leaders fared as well in runoffs as white
male and front runners.[24] In the only study of the impact of runoffs at the
municipal level, Fleischmann and Stein also found "no systematic bias against
minority and female front-runners forced into runoffs."[25] Thus, we hypothesize that:

H3: Female representation levels on city council in cities that have majority vote requirements will not differ significantly from levels in cities that have
plurality systems.

H4: Black female city council representation levels in cities that have
majority-vote requirements will not differ significantly from levels in cities
that have plurality systems.

Staggered Terms

Staggered terms have not been the focus of study with regard to their
impact on females, but rather on minorities. Davidson described a scenario in
which staggered terms could have a discriminatory impact, namely in anti-
single shot systems (at-large, by post; at-large with residency districts). He
suggested that staggered terms could effectively limit a minority group's ability to single-shot vote by reducing the number of positions.[26] But a large scale
empirical test of his hypothesis revealed no statistically significant difference
between black representation levels in cities with staggered terms and those
without.[27] Therefore we hypothesize that:

H5: Female representation levels in cities with staggered terms will not differ significantly from levels in cities with simultaneous terms.

H6: Black female representation levels in cities with staggered terms will not differ significantly from levels in cities with simultaneous terms.

Size of Council

Welch and Karnig hypothesized that larger councils would yield greater levels of female representation.[28] Their hypothesis was based on Diamond's study of state legislatures. Diamond's theory was that larger councils were indicative of an office being "less desirable and less important" which would enhance females' chances of winning it.[29] The results of Welch and Karnig's study did not confirm this hypothesis. The correlation coefficient between number of council seats and the female council proportion was a statistically insignificant .06.

While there is not much evidence of council size having an impact on female representation, there is some data suggesting larger councils enhance minority representation.[30] However, recent research suggests that the size of the council appears to be a structural feature whose impact on minority representation is rather weak and conditional, first on the size of the minority population,[31] and second on geographical residential patterns.[32] We hypothesize that:

H7: Council size is not a significant predictor of female representation on city councils.

H8: Black female representation on city councils will not be enhanced by larger council size.

Length of Term

Longer terms of office are viewed as more attractive than shorter terms. It is another of what Welch and Karnig view as an indicator of the desirability and importance of a political office.[33] Thus, they hypothesized that there would be a negative relationship between length of term and female representation levels. However, their results showed an even weaker and insignificant relationship between length of term and female representation (–.00) than council size. Therefore, we do not expect to find a relationship either.

H9: Length of term is not a significant predictor of female representation on city councils.

There is also very little evidence of longer terms being disadvantageous to blacks.[34] The argument in favor of longer terms is often related to election costs. Karnig and Welch actually found higher levels of black representation in cities with longer council terms, although not a significantly greater number. They attributed this to the attractiveness and prestige of the longer term. In a later study based on 1986 data, Bullock and MacManus found that length of term was not a significant predictor of black representation.[35] Therefore, we hypothesize that:

H10: Length of term is not a significant predictor of black female representation.

Incumbency

Most studies recognize incumbency as powerful in explaining municipal electoral outcomes, particularly in nonpartisan settings.[36] High incumbency return rates are still a deterrent to the entry of women and minorities into political office, especially where there are none at present.[37] But where women and blacks are represented, incumbency has no significant racial-or-gender-based differentials in its impact. For example, Bullock found that incumbency advantages both minorities and whites.[38] Black incumbents tend to get more white crossover votes each time they run, perhaps because white fears are eased by a successful performance.[39]

Incumbency works the same across gender groups according to Darcy, Welch, and Clark.[40] Women incumbents have just about the same advantage as male incumbents. Therefore, based on studies showing no gender or racial-biased differentials in incumbency return rates (the measure we use in our study), we hypothesize that:

H11: Incumbency return rate is not a significant predictor of female city council representational level.

H12: Incumbency return rate is not a significant predictor of black female city council representational level.

In summary, we expect to find higher levels of female city council representation in the 1980's but little support for governmental structures as determinants of electoral success.

Findings

Across the 211 cities in the 11 southern states, there were 252 women on city councils in the spring of 1986. The average percent of females on city councils was 17, up considerably from the figures reported in studies based on data from the 1970's (Karnig and Walter, mid–1975—9.7%; MacManus,

1976—10%; Welch and Karnig, 1978—13%) although those were national averages, not just from the South.[41] In the aggregate, only one-third of our cities had no female representation. In contrast, Welch and Karnig's study showed a much larger percent of councils without any women (44 percent).[42] However, as the figures in Table 1 show, the percentage of cities with no women on their councils varies sharply across the 11 southern states. Women have achieved representation on a larger number of councils in Virginia, North Carolina, and Florida. They have fared badly in Alabama and Arkansas.

In 11 of our cities, women constituted at least half the council. The highest percentage of women councilmembers occurred in Orlando and North Miami where women made up two-thirds of the councils. Table 1 shows that the share of council seats held by women varies across states. At the low end were Alabama, Arkansas, Tennessee, and Louisiana where the average proportion of councilwomen was less than 12%. At the upper end were North Carolina, Florida, and Virginia. In each of these states women averaged more than one in five council seats and in North Carolina, the figure was closer to one in three.

The states where larger percentages of women serve on city councils are those characterized by higher population growth rates. Some scholars have found that the in-migration of persons from other regions has helped break down racial and gender stereotypes in the South.[43]

Electoral Districting Format

There is less range in the proportion of females across the five types of electoral formats. Women were somewhat more likely to serve in cities in which elections were pure at-large, from single-member districts, or in which some members were elected at-large while others ran in single-member districts. Fewer women were chosen when elections were citywide but individuals ran for a specific post or were required to live in a residency district. However, as Table 2 demonstrates, the range is narrow, with the mean running from 13 to 19%. Each type of system included some cities in which no female served in 1986. It appears, then, that the type of election system is still not a significant predictor of female city council representation. Welch and Karnig's predictions about single member districts yielding greater representation has not yet come true, although the gap between pure at-large and districts has narrowed. (Welch and Karnig's 1978 data showed an average of 10% elected under single-member district systems and 15% under pure at-large[44]; our 1986 data shows 17% for single-member districts and 19% for at-large.)

Majority Vote Requirement (Runoffs)

More than 80% of the cities had a runoff provision. Despite former NOW President Eleanor Smeal's contention that runoffs are "no help to women,"[45]

Table 1
Incidence of Women on City Councils by State

	Number of Cities	Incidence of Women			% with No Female on Council
		Minimum	Maximum	Mean	
Alabama	15	0%	44%	7%	73%
Arkansas	10	0	29	8	70
Florida	48	0	67	25	19
Georgia	12	0	33	17	25
Louisiana	12	0	43	11	50
Mississippi	9	0	33	13	44
North Carolina	17	0	63	31	18
South Carolina	8	0	33	14	25
Tennessee	13	0	23	10	31
Texas	52	0	50	13	38
Virginia	15	0	44	21	13

Table 2
Incidence of Women on City Councils
by Type of Electoral Districting

	Number of Cities	Incidence of Women		
		Minimum	Maximum	Mean
Pure At-Large	54	0%	67%	19%
At-Large by Post	32	0	40	13
At-Large by Residency	23	0	43	13
Mixed	54	0	55	18
Single-Member Districts	48	0	67	17

there is no evidence that having to poll a majority reduces the presence of women on the council. The mean for runoff and plurality cities is identical, confirming what Fleischmann and Stein found in Texas cities.[46] While the means in Table 3 are identical, all of the cities with the largest percentages of women employ a runoff. No plurality city has a female majority; seven runoff cities had a female majority.

Staggered Terms

The use of staggered terms, like a majority vote requirement, bears no consistent relationship to the size of the female component on a city council.

Table 3
Incidence of Women on City Councils
by Share of Vote Needed for Election

	Number of Cities	Incidence of Women		
		Minimum	*Maximum*	*Mean*
Plurality Vote	33	0%	50%	17%
Majority Vote	178	0	67	17

Table 4 reports that the range in percent female in cities that stagger terms and those that elect all members simultaneously is almost identical, confirming our hypothesis. The difference in means for the two groups is less than four percentage points.

Size of Council

The size of council bears no relationship to the incidence of women. The slope when percent female is regressed on size of council is (.0015) which is half as large as its standard error (.0032).

Length of Term

The presence of female councilors is unaffected by the length of a city's council terms. While there is a slight indication that women councilors are less frequent in cities in which terms are longer (b= −.005), the relationship is not statistically significant from zero (standard error .012).

The insignificant relationships between the size of the council and length of council term suggest that the office-prestige theory as an explanation for female representation is not well supported, at least at the municipal level.

Incumbency

The rate at which incumbents were returned in the previous elections is not related to the percent women on the council. When percent female is regressed on the proportion of incumbents reelected, the slope (.033) is somewhat smaller than its standard error (.042). This result confirms our hypothesis and the findings of other scholars.

Multivariate Analysis

The results of the bivariate analysis offers little reason to expect that the set of independent variables used here will be successful in predicting in the

Table 4
Incidence of Women on City Councils
by Whether Terms Are Staggered

	Number of Cities	Incidence of Women		
		Minimum	*Maximum*	*Mean*
Simultaneous Terms	83	0%	63%	15%
Staggered Terms	128	0	67	18

incidence of female councilors. Our expectations are borne out. A number of combinations of predictors were tried and the most successful one included three predictors: the dichotomous variables indicating the presence of staggered terms, election at-large to posts and election at-large but with a residency requirement. This model explains only 3% of the variance and none of the predictors has a coefficient twice as large as its standard error. The signs for the predictors indicate a weak tendency for women to serve in cities that have staggered terms and do not elect at-large for specific posts or from residency districts.

Black Female Councilmembers

Of the 252 women serving on southern city councils, 51 (20 percent) were black. Despite the small number of black women on councils, an exploration was launched to determine if their presence was systematically related to the three election-related variables considered in this chapter. We hypothesized that they would not be. It is assumed that the primary factor in the election of black women is the percentage black in the city. This assumption is based on the large body of literature cited earlier that examines the determinants of black city council representation. Therefore the percent black in a city's population is interacted with dichotomous variables for each of several features relating to electoral formats. Since each interaction term includes percent black, it is not possible to estimate a single equation as was done in the preceding section. (A model that includes percent black with terms for electoral districting, majority vote and use of staggered terms has serious collinearity problems.)

The model that incorporates measures of electoral format explains 9% of the variance. The coefficients for interaction terms created by multiplying percent black and three of the electoral systems (pure at-large, at-large with residency requirements and mixed) were twice as large as their standard errors. No other terms in Table 5 were statistically significant. The impact of the interaction terms for pure at-large elections (BLPURE) and at-large with residency

Table 5
Model for Percentage of Black
Councilwomen and Types of Elections

% Black Women = .034 + .123 BLPURE + .219 BLRESIDE + .096 BLMIXED
               (.055)   (.103)   (.041)

+ .022 BLSMD + .117 BLPOST - .013 PURE
  (.039)   (.076)   (.019)

-.011 POST - .032 RESIDE + .002 SIZE
(.020)   (.024)   (.001)

-.006 LENGTH - .023 PCTINC
(.005)   (.016)

$R^2 = .14$ Adjusted $R^2 = .09$

BLPURE	= percent black in population * pure at-large elections
BLRESIDE	= percent black in population * at-large with residency requirement
BLMIXED	= percent black in population * mixed systems
BLSMD	= percent black in population * single-member districts
BLPOST	= percent black in population * at-large, run for posts
PURE	= dummy variable for pure at-large elections
POST	= dummy variable for at-large elections in which candidates run for specific posts
RESIDE	= dummy variable for at-large election systems that have residency requirements
SIZE	= number of council seats
LENGTH	= length of council terms
PCTINC	= proportion of incumbents returned in most recent election

requirements (BLRESIDE) is reduced when we adjust for the negative values of the dummy variables associated with those terms (that is, PURE and RESIDE).[47] It is interesting that single-member districts (BLSMD) are not strongly associated with the election of black women, again confirming our hypothesis. An extensive literature has reported that single-member districts in the South are generally more conducive than other formats to the election of blacks.[48] Indeed in an earlier analysis of this data set in which black presence on city councils without regard for sex was considered, single-member districts were associated with a higher incidence of blacks in the South but not in other regions.[49] The dynamics associated with the election of black women are, therefore, still different than those linked to the election of black men. Darcy and Hadley attribute most of this to black females' greater political ambition and activism in civic, educational, religious, and civil rights groups.[50]

Table 6 reports a model that interacts percent black with majority and plurality vote systems. Both interaction terms were statistically significant and size of the council just missed being significant at the .05 level. While the slope for plurality systems is slightly larger than the slope for majority vote cities, the difference in predictions produced by the model is reduced if the positive value for the dummy variable indicating that a city has a runoff provision (MAJVOTE) is included. Predictions for runoff and plurality cities comparable on the other components included on the model diverge as the percent black in the city increases. The low R-square signals that predictions based on this model will often be wide of the mark. Therefore it would be dangerous to conclude that either a majority vote requirement or a particular type of districting is related in a consistent fashion to higher or lower levels of black female council presence.

Other variables considered had only weak relationships with the percentage of black councilwomen. Interaction terms for staggered and non-staggered terms were not statistically different from zero. As shown in Tables 5 and 6, the proportion of incumbents returned in the last election was weakly related to the presence of black women on councils while black women were slightly more likely on larger councils and when terms were shorter. None of these variables yielded values statistically different from zero.

Because of the small number of black councilwomen, even when the regression model produces statistically significant coefficients, there is no substantive difference for most of the range in percent black across cities. Thus the percentage of black women predicted for southern councils for each of the types of electoral formats are all within a few percentage points of each other.

Conclusions

In this chapter the impact of several structural variables on the incidence of women on the city councils of the South has been explored to determine if structure has become more important over time. While we occasionally observed variations across the categories considered, the overwhelming thrust of our findings is that structural features are not associated with whether women serve as council members. The same conclusion is appropriate for the incidence of black female councilors.

In the South, women are not disadvantaged by majority vote requirements or the use of staggered terms. Nor are they especially likely to serve on the councils of cities that elect some or all members from single-member districts. In some contexts, women and racial or ethnic minorities are lumped

Table 6
Model for Percentage of Black
Councilwomen and Majority Vote Requirement

% Black Women = .010 + .117 BLMAJVOT + .204 BLPLUVOT
                      (.029)   (.078)

+ .011 MAJVOTE + .002 SIZE - .006 LENGTH
    (.022)   (.001)   (.005)

-.021 PCTINC
 (.016)

$R^2 = .14$ Adjusted $R^2 = .11$

BLMAJVOT	= percent black * majority vote required
BLPLUVOT	= percent black * plurality vote system
MAJVOTE	= majority vote required for election
SIZE	= number of council seats
LENGTH	= length of council terms
PCTINC	= proportion of incumbents returned in most recent election

together as groups that are disadvantaged vis-à-vis white males. The structural features listed above are often pointed to as ones that dilute the ability of blacks and Hispanics to elect the candidates they prefer. We have previously found that at least in the South, there is some indication that blacks are more likely to serve on city councils elected from single-member districts. [51] Thus at least for that electoral feature, the impact on women and blacks is different. But this finding merely confirms what other researchers had already reported in an earlier decade. On the other features, the findings for this set of cities is essentially the same for women and blacks.

Just as the 1970's, our research shows that structural features are not significant determinants of female representation on city councils (nor black female representation). This holds true in spite of growing numbers of women on councils. Gender may still be somewhat of an impediment to representation—but electoral structures are not.

Notes

1. Albert K. Karnig and Oliver Walter, "Election of Women to City Councils," *Social Science Quarterly,* Vol. 56, 1976, p. 107.

2. See for example: Jeane Kirkpatrick, *Political Women,* New York: Basic Books, 1974; Marcia Manning Lee, "Why Few Women Hold Public Office: Democracy

and Sexual Roles," *Political Science Quarterly*, Vol. 91, Summer 1976, pp. 297–314; Sharyne Merritt, "Winners and Losers: Sex Differences in Municipal Elections," *American Journal of Political Science*, Vol. 21, November 1977, pp. 731–44; Irene Diamond, *Sex Roles in the Statehouse*, New Haven: Yale University Press, 1977; Susan Welch, "Recruitment of Women to Political Office: A Discriminant Analysis," *Western Political Quarterly*, Vol. 31, September 1978, pp. 372–380; Susan G. Mezey, "The Effects of Sex on Recruitment: Connecticut Local Offices," in Debra W. Stewart, ed., *Women in Local Politics*, Metuchen, NJ: Scarecrow Press, 1980; Diane L. Fowlkes, Jerry Perkins, and Sue Tolleson Rinehart, "Gender Roles and Party Roles," *American Political Science Review*, Vol. 73, September 1979, pp. 772–780; Ronald D. Hedlund, Patricia K. Freeman, Keith E. Hamm, and Robert M. Stein, "The Electability of Women Candidates: The Effect of Sex Role Stereotypes," *Journal of Politics*, Vol. 41, May 1979, pp. 513–524; Wilma Rule, "Why Women Don't Run: The Critical Contextual Factors in Women's Legislative Recruitment," *Western Political Quarterly*, Vol. 34, March 1981, pp. 60–77; Laurie E. Ekstrand and William A. Eckert, "The Impact of Candidate's Sex on Voter Choice," *Western Political Quarterly*, Vol. 34, March 1981, pp. 78–87; Susan Carroll and Wendy Strimling, *Women's Routes to Elective Office*, New Brunswick, NJ: Rutgers University, CAWP, 1983; Jerry Perkins, "Political Ambition Among Black and White Women: An Intragender Test of the Socialization Model," *Women and Politics*, Vol. 6, Spring 1986, pp. 27–40; Audrey Seiss Wells and Eleanor Catri Smeal, "Women's Attitudes Towards Women in Politics: A Survey of Urban Registered Voters and Party Committee-women," in Jane S. Jaquette, ed., *Women in Politics*, New York: John Wiley, 1974, pp. 54–72; Trudy Haffron and Susan Gluck Mezey, "Support for Feminist Goals Among Leaders of Women's Community Groups," *Signs*, Vol. 6, 1981, pp. 737–748; Keith T. Poole and L. Harmon Zeigler, *Women, Public Opinion, and Politics: The Changing Political Attitudes of American Women*, New York: Longman, 1985.

3. See Karnig and Walter, op. cit.; Susan A. MacManus, "Determinants of the Equitability of Female Representation on 243 City Councils," paper presented at the annual meeting of the American Political Science Association, 1976; Welch, op. cit.; Susan Welch and Albert Karnig, "Correlates of Female Office Holding in City Politics," *Journal of Politics*, Vol. 41, 1979, pp. 478–491. Albert K. Karnig and Susan Welch, "Sex and Ethnic Differences in Municipal Representation," *Social Science Quarterly*, Vol. 60, 1979, pp. 465–481; David B. Hill, "Political Culture and Female Representation," *Journal of Politics*, Vol. 43, February 1981, pp. 151–168.

4. Karnig and Walter, op. cit., p. 610.

5. MacManus, 1976, op. cit.; Karnig and Welch, 1979, op. cit.

6. See for example, Leonard Cole, "Electing Blacks to Municipal Office: Structural and Social Determinants," *Urban Affairs Quarterly*, Vol. 10, September 1974, pp. 17–39; Albert K. Karnig, "Black Representation on City Councils: The Impact of District Elections and Socioeconomic Factors," *Urban Affairs Quarterly*, Vol. 12, December 1976, pp. 223–242; Susan A. MacManus, "City Council Election Procedures and Minority Representation: Are They Related?" *Social Science Quarterly*, Vol. 59, June 1978, pp. 153–161; Theodore Robinson and Thomas R. Dye, "Reformism and Black Representation on City Councils," *Social Science Quarterly*, Vol. 59, June 1978, pp. 133–141; Delbert Taebel, "Minority Representation on City Councils," *Social Science Quarterly*, Vol. 59, June 1978, pp. 142–152; Albert K. Karnig and Susan Welch, *Black Representation and Urban Policy*, Chicago: University of Chicago Press, 1980; Richard L. Engstrom and Michael D. McDonald, "The Election of Blacks to City Councils: Clarifying the Impact of Electoral Arrangements

on the Seats/Population Relationship," *American Political Science Review,* Vol. 75, June 1981, pp. 344–354; Albert K. Karnig and Susan Welch, "Electoral Structure and Black Representation on City Councils," *Social Science Quarterly,* Vol. 63, March 1982, pp. 99–114.

7. See Karnig and Walter, op. cit.; MacManus, 1976, op. cit.; Welch, op. cit.; Welch and Karnig, 1979, op. cit.

8. Karnig and Walter, op. cit.

9. MacManus, 1976, op. cit.

10. Welch and Karnig, op. cit., p. 490

11. Welch and Karnig, op. cit., p. 491

12. See Karnig and Welch, op. cit.; Welch and Karnig, op. cit.; Eleanor Smeal, "Eleanor Smeal Report," *Eleanor Smeal Newsletter,* Vol. 2, June 28, 1984, p. 1.

13. Center for the American Woman and Politics, *Women in Elective Office 1975–1980,* New Brunswick, NJ: Rutgers University, CAWP, 1981; Denise Antolini, "Women in Local Government: An Overview," in Janet Flammang, ed., *Political Women,* Beverly Hills, CA: Sage, 1984.

14. Susan Welch and Lee Sigelman, "Changes in Attitudes Toward Women in Politics," *Social Science Quarterly,* Vol. 63, June 1982, pp. 312–322; Lee Sigelman and Susan Welch, "Race, Gender, and Opinion Toward Black and Female Candidates," *Public Opinion Quarterly,* Vol. 48, Summer 1984, pp. 467–475.

15. Sara E. Rix, ed., *The American Women 1987–88: A Report in Depth,* New York: W. W. Norton & Co., 1987.

16. See for example: Shirley Chisholm, *Unbought and Unbossed,* Boston: Houghton-Mifflin, 1970; Elizabeth M. Almquist, "Untangling the Effects of Race and Sex: The Disadvantaged Status of Black Women," *Social Science Quarterly,* Vol. 56, June 1975, pp. 129–142; Mae C. King, "Oppression and Power: The Unique Status of the Black Woman in the American Political System," *Social Science Quarterly,* Vol. 56, June 1975, pp. 116–128; Karnig and Welch, 1979, op. cit.; Susan Welch and Philip Secret, "Sex, Race, and Political Participation," *Western Political Quarterly,* Vol. 34, March 1981, pp. 5–16; Richard D. Shingles, "The Black Gender Gap: Double Jeopardy and Politicization," paper presented at the annual meeting of the Midwest Political Science Association, 1986.

17. Sandra Baxter and Marjorie Lansing, *Women and Politics: The Invisible Majority,* Ann Arbor: University of Michigan Press, 1981; Sigelman and Welch, op. cit.; Allen Wilhite and John Theilmann, "Gender Differences in Voting for Female Candidates: Evidence from the 1982 Election," *Public Opinion Quarterly,* Vol. 49, Summer 1985, pp. 179–197.

18. See for example: Joan S. Carver, "Women in Florida," *Journal of Politics,* Vol. 41, August 1979, pp. 941–955; Eleanor C. Main, Gerald S. Gryski, and Beth Schapiro, "Different Perspectives: Southern State Legislators' Attitudes About Women in Politics," *Social Science Journal,* January 1984, pp. 21–28.

19. Carver, op. cit. p. 941.

20. See Enid Lakeman, "Electoral Systems and Women in Parliament," *Parliamentarian,* Vol. 67, July 1976, pp. 159–162; R. Darcy, Susan Welch, and Janet Clark, *Women, Elections and Representation,* New York: Longman, 1987.

21. Cited in Wilma Rule, "Does the Electoral System Discriminate Against Women?" *PS,* Fall, 1986, p. 30.

22. Ibid.

23. Smeal, op. cit.

24. Bullock and Johnson, op. cit.; Charles S. Bullock, III and Loch Johnson,

"Runoff Elections in Georgia," *Journal of Politics*, Vol. 47, August 1985, pp. 937–946.

25. Arnold Fleischmann and Lana Stein, "Minority and Female Success in Municipal Runoff Elections," *Social Science Quarterly*, Vol. 68, June 1987, pp. 378–385.

26. Chandler Davidson, "Minority Vote Dilution: An Overview" in Chandler Davidson, ed., *Minority Vote Dilution*, Washington, DC: Howard University Press, 1984 , pp. 1–23.

27. Charles S. Bullock, III and Susan A. MacManus, "The Impact of Staggered Terms on Minority Representation," *Journal of Politics*, Vol. 49, May 1987, pp. 543–552.

28. Welch and Karnig, 1979, op. cit.

29. Diamond, op. cit.

30. See for example: Taebel, op. cit.; Karnig and Welch, 1980, op. cit.; Robert J. Mundt and Peggy Heilig, "District Representation Demands and Effects in the Urban South," *Journal of Politics*, Vol. 44, November 1982, pp. 1035–1048.

31. See Michael D. McDonald and Richard L. Engstrom, "Council Size and the Election of Blacks from Single-Member Districts: Classifying an Apparent Inconsistency Between Theory and Data," paper presented at the 13th World Congress of the International Political Science Association, 1985; Bullock and MacManus, op. cit.

32. See Taebel, op. cit.; Arnold Vedlitz and Charles A. Johnson, "Community Racial Segregation, Electoral Structure, and Minority Representation," *Social Science Quarterly*, Vol. 63, December 1982, pp. 729–736.

33. Welch and Karnig, 1979, op. cit.

34. John Kramer, "The Election of Blacks to City Councils: A 1970 Status Report and a Prolegomenon," *Journal of Black Studies*, Vol. 1, June 1971, pp. 443–476; Karnig and Welch, 1980, op. cit.

35. Charles S. Bullock, III and Susan A. MacManus, "Structural Features of Municipal Elections and Black Representation," paper presented at the annual meeting of the Southern Political Science Association, 1987.

36. Welch, op. cit.

37. Darcy, Welch and Clark, op. cit., p. 150.

38. Charles S. Bullock, III, "Racial Crossover Voting and the Election of Black Officials," *Journal of Politics*, Vol. 46, February 1984, pp. 238–251.

39. William E. Nelson, Jr., and Philip J. Meranto, *Electing Black Mayors*, Columbus, OH: Ohio State University Press, 1977.

40. Darcy, Welch, and Clark, op. cit.

41. Karnig and Walter, op. cit.; MacManus, 1976, op. cit.; Welch and Karnig, 1978, op. cit.

42. Welch and Karnig, 1978, op. cit.

43. See for example: Carver, op. cit.; Albert K. Karnig and Paula D. McClain, "The New South and Black Economic and Political Development: Changes from 1970 to 1980," *Western Political Quarterly*, Vol. 38, December 1985, pp. 539–550.

44. Welch and Karnig, 1978, op. cit.

45. Smeal, op. cit.

46. Fleischmann and Stein, op. cit.

47. A dummy variable for mixed electoral systems is not reported since inclusion of that variable produces unacceptable levels of collinearity.

48. See Engstrom and McDonald, 1981, op. cit.; Chandler Davidson and George

Korbel, "At-Large Elections and Minority Group Representation: A Reexamination of Historical Contemporary Evidence," *Journal of Politics*, Vol. 43, 1981, pp. 932–1005.

49. Bullock and MacManus, 1987, op. cit.

50. R. Darcy and Charles D. Hadley, "Black Women in Politics: The Puzzle of Success," *Social Science Quarterly*, forthcoming, 1988.

51. Bullock and MacManus, 1987, op. cit.

Term Limits and Local Elected Officials

James Fay and Roy Christman

With a righteous fury, the term limits movement has arrived in California. Like earlier reform spasms of the Progressive era, this movement is likely to have a lasting impact on certain institutions of government.[1] Its most recent manifestation was Proposition 164, adopted in November of 1992, limiting California's U.S. Representatives to three terms and U.S. Senators to two terms. In 1990 California state legislators and statewide officials had their terms in office capped by Proposition 140, whose essential provisions have been upheld by the California Supreme Court.[2] Proposition 164 has not yet been tested.

The idea of term limits for public office holders is not new. As Mark Petracca has noted, it goes back to the Ancient Greek city-states. During the first years of American government, Thomas Jefferson, among many others, was a devoted supporter of the principle of "rotation in office," as term limits then were called. Then as now, term limits were seen as a check on the advantages of incumbency and aloofness.[3]

Term Limits and Higher Office

We have ample evidence of the incumbency advantages that enable members of Congress and state legislators to hold office for a long time. Prior to the 1992 election, 16 percent of California's congressional delegation had held office for 20 years or more, and 71 percent had been in Congress for at least a decade. State Senator Ralph Dills began his legislative tenure in 1938, Senator Nick Petris in 1958, and Assemblyman Willie Brown in 1964. Although

Reprinted with permission from National Civic Review, *Vol. 83, No. 1, Winter/Spring, 1994. Published by the National Civic League Press, Denver, Colorado.*

turnover among state legislators is higher than in the state's congressional delegation, 39 percent of the California Assembly members and 48 percent of state senators holding office in 1981 were still there a decade later.

Term Limits for City Councils

The underlying assumptions of the local term-limit movement are that unconscionable numbers of city and county officials also cling to their jobs with the tenacity of barnacles, and only mandated restrictions on office holding will dislodge them. Based on these assumptions, local activists and reformers have been crafting—and voters have been approving—initiatives to limit the terms of their city council members. Last November, voters in Long Beach, Torrance and Anaheim imposed term limits on their council members. At least 28 of California's home rule cities and nine general law cities now have term limits.

Unfortunately for the reformers, local government in the state may lack the legal authority to set such limits. Several California Appellate Court decisions[4] have held that California local governments have no constitutional or statutory authority to limit the terms of their elected officials, although one appeals court recently ruled that charter cities may impose such limits.[5] To eliminate this legal uncertainty, bills have been introduced in both the state senate and assembly to explicitly enable all local governments and special districts to impose their own term limits by popular vote. Neither measure has yet become law.

Turnover in City Government

Are these efforts to limit political loitering in local office really needed? Is the turnover rate of locally elected officials so dismally low that term limits are needed? No one has provided convincing evidence to justify them.[6]

To determine whether the drive for term limits at the city level is justified by compelling evidence rather than faddishness, we examined turnover patterns for elected office holders in California's cities during the past two decades. We looked at all the mayors and council members in 1971, 1981, 1985, and 1989 to determine how many were still in office in 1991.[7] To our surprise, of the 2,177 mayors and council members holding office in 1971 only 50 (2.3 percent) were still on the job 20 years later. Of those in office in 1981, only 14.6 percent were still serving ten years later. Of the 1985 contingent, fewer than one-third were in office six years later. Finally, of those holding office in 1989, 66 percent remained in 1991 (Table 1).

These numbers suggest a rather substantial rate of turnover in local office:

Table 1
Mayor/Council Member Turnover,
1971–1991

	Holding office as of 1971 and remaining in office in 1991	Holding office as of 1981 and remaining in office in 1991	Holding office as of 1985 and remaining in office in 1991	Holding office as of 1989 and remaining in office in 1991
N	50 of 2,177	331 of 2,267	733 of 2,302	1,556 of 2,357
%	2.3	14.6	31.8	66.0

almost 98 percent in 20 years, 85 percent in ten years, 68 percent in six years, and 34 percent in just two years. But there were substantial differences *among* the cities for each time period. One city in particular of the 469 cities in the state stands out for the tenure of its elected officials: Los Angeles. There, six council members (38 percent) serving in 1971 were still in office two decades later. Only two other cities in the state—Vernon (the smallest city in California) and Lorma Linda (located in San Bernardino County)—approach Los Angeles's pattern of long-time incumbency.

The visibility of Los Angeles city officials may account for the inaccurate public perception that California as a whole has a problem with council member turnover.

Term Limits and Female Office Holders

Will term limits have a greater impact on female city council members?[8] The answer is yes, but the difference is marginal. Of the women holding office in 1971 only two percent were still in office 20 years later, versus 2.3 percent of the men. By contrast, 18 percent of the women in office in 1981 were serving in 1991, as opposed to 14 percent of the men. Of the 1985 contingent, 36 percent of the women but only 31 percent of the men still held their seats in 1991. Finally, of the women in office in 1989, 71 percent were in office two years later versus 64 percent of the male office holders (Table 2).

Term limits, therefore, could have a slightly greater negative effect on female office holders. Of course, if a large number of California cities enact term limits, more male than female incumbents would be forced out of office, simply because more men now hold office. This would result in a larger number of available seats, increasing opportunities for men and women alike. The same logic applies to minority candidates.[9]

Table 2
Mayor/Council Member Turnover,
by Gender, 1971–1991

	Holding office as of 1971 and remaining in office in 1991	Holding office as of 1981 and remaining in office in 1991	Holding office as of 1985 and remaining in office in 1991	Holding office as of 1989 and remaining in office in 1991
WOMEN:				
N	2 of 100	73 of 398	172 of 482	395 of 554
%	2.0	18.3	35.7	71.3
MEN:				
N	48 of 2,077	258 of 1,869	561 of 1,820	1,161 of 1,803
%	2.3	13.8	30.8	64.4

Turnover in County Office

This research also analyzed all of the 296 county supervisors holding office in 1971, 1979, 1983, and 1987 to determine longevity in office at the county level in 1991.[10] Of 296 county supervisors in office in 1971, only five (two percent) retained their seats as of the fall of 1991 (Table 3). One of these long-time incumbents was Supervisor Kenneth Hahn of Los Angeles County. Placer County had two 20-year veterans on the county board, and Riverside and Tehama Counties had one each.

While a large proportion (17 percent) of supervisors elected in 1979 still were holding their seats in 1991, 83 percent had retired to the private sector, died, or moved on to higher office. Of the supervisors elected to office in 1983, only 107 (36 percent) held their seats eight years later. Finally, 189 (64 percent) of the 296 county supervisors holding office in 1987 were in office four years later.

Turnover in Large Counties

Supervisors in the most populous counties have a measurable tendency to stay in office longer than supervisors in the less populous ones. Comparisons of turnover rates in the 15 largest counties (populations over 500,000) to those of the 43 other counties reveals significant differences. Twenty-five percent of the supervisors in large counties who were elected in 1979 were still in office in 1991 (Table 4). The average for the smaller counties is 14 percent. Of large-county supervisors elected in 1983, 51 percent still held office eight years later. The average for the smaller counties was 31 percent. Finally,

Table 3
Turnover of County Supervisors,
1971–1991

	Holding office as of 1971 and remaining in office in 1991	*Holding office as of 1979 and remaining in office in 1991*	*Holding office as of 1981 and remaining in office in 1991*	*Holding office as of 1983 and remaining in office in 1991*	*Holding office as of 1987 and remaining in office in 1991*
N	5 of 296	50 of 296	79 of 296	107 of 296	189 of 296
%	2	17	27	36	64

Table 4
Turnover of County Supervisors,
by Size of County, 1971–1991

	Holding office as of 1971 and remaining in office in 1991	*Holding office as of 1979 and remaining in office in 1991*	*Holding office as of 1981 and remaining in office in 1991*	*Holding office as of 1983 and remaining in office in 1991*	*Holding office as of 1987 and remaining in office in 1991*
COUNTY POPULATION OVER 500,000:					
N	2 of 81	20 of 81	32 of 81	41 of 81	64 of 81
%	2	25	40	51	79
COUNTY POPULATION UNDER 500,000:					
N	3 of 215	30 of 215	47 of 215	66 of 215	125 of 215
%	1	14	22	31	58
STATEWIDE:					
N	5 of 296	50 of 296	79 of 296	107 of 296	189 of 296
%	2	17	27	36	64

79 percent of large-county supervisors elected in 1987 still held office after four years. The average for the smaller counties was 58 percent.

The reason supervisors in the 15 largest counties remain in office longer than those in the 43 other counties may reside in different political recruitment mechanisms, the wider variety of decision-making challenges, more staff assistance, and higher public visibility and prestige. Alternatively, it may be a simple question of money. Supervisors in the 15 largest counties are, on average, better paid than their counterparts in the other 43. Those in the 15 largest counties pay themselves an average of $56,000 annually, plus assorted benefits. In the 43 smaller counties, the annual compensation of supervisors is only $27,000.

The Impact of Term Limits on Female Supervisors

Female supervisors, who have been elected in large numbers only since the late 1970s, are staying in office considerably longer than their male colleagues (Table 5). For example, only 16 percent of male supervisors elected in 1979 were still in office 12 years later, while 24 percent of the women had not left their posts. Thirty-two percent of the male but 58 percent of the female supervisors elected in 1983 were still on the job in 1991, and 59 percent of male but 81 percent of female supervisors elected in 1987 continued in office four years later.

Term limits on supervisors, then, will have a greater impact on women than on men. The overall impact will be greatest on women who hold office in the counties with populations over 500,000, since these women (with the exception of the 1987 contingent) exhibit a more pronounced tendency toward multiple terms than their counterparts in smaller counties (Table 6). (The number of minority supervisors has not been large enough until recent years to invite generalizations about the impact of term limits on their political careers.)

Conclusion

The policy question for state legislators and citizens is whether mandatory term limits should be imposed to prevent a small number of incumbents, particularly in the larger cities and heavily populated counties, from holding their positions for extended periods.

If the legislature permits, more city and county governments will inevitably adopt term limits. But such limits, unlike tenure limits on members of Congress and state legislators, will have little effect; *the turnover rates already are high.*

Because term limits will have little practical effect, they will probably do no harm. There may even be assorted benefits to a variety of political actors and analysts. For example, there may be therapeutic benefits to the public psyche. Ambitious politicians will be better able to plan their careers as local offices open up regularly. Academics, journalists and the public at large will have more interesting and competitive elections to observe, and the economy will be greatly stimulated by the campaign activity engendered by a higher proportion of contested open seats.

Ultimately, each citizen must weigh the desirability of legislative experience, contacts and institutional memory against the need for vitality, new ideas and fresh talent, as well as the palpable reality of abundant turnover in the existing system.

Table 5
Turnover of County Supervisors, by Gender, 1971–1991

	Holding office as of *1971* and remaining in office in 1991	Holding office as of *1981* and remaining in office in 1991	Holding office as of *1985* and remaining in office in 1991	Holding office as of *1989* and remaining in office in 1991
WOMEN:				
N	0 of 7	11 of 46	29 of 50	48 of 59
%	0	24	58	813
MEN:				
N	5 of 289	39 of 250	78 of 246	141 of 237
%	2	16	32	59

Table 6
Turnover of Female County Supervisors by Size of County, 1971–1991

	Holding office as of *1971* and remaining in office in 1991	Holding office as of *1979* and remaining in office in 1991	Holding office as of *1981* and remaining in office in 1991	Holding office as of *1983* and remaining in office in 1991	Holding office as of *1987* and remaining in office in 1991
COUNTY POPULATION OVER 500,000:					
N	0 of 3	7 of 13	13 of 20	17 of 25	23 of 29
%	0	54	65	68	79
COUNTY POPULATION UNDER 500,000:					
N	0 of 4	4 of 33	9 of 28	12 of 25	25 of 30
%	0	11	25	48	83
STATEWIDE:					
N	0 of 7	11 of 46	22 of 48	29 of 50	48 of 59
%	0	22	45	58	81

Notes

1. Olin C. Spencer, Jr., *California's Prodigal Sons: Hiram Johnson and the Progressives, 1911–1917* (Berkeley: University of California Press, 1968); George E. Mowry, *The California Progressives* (Berkeley: University of California Press, 1951).

2. *Legislature v. Eu* 54 Cal. 3d 492 (1991); certiorari denied, 112 S.Ct. 1292 (1992).

3. Mark P. Petracca, "Rotation in Office: The History of an Idea" in Gerald Benjamin and Michael J. Malbin, *Limiting Legislative Terms* (Washington, D.C.: Congressional Quarterly Press, 1992).

4. *Younger v. Board of Supervisors* 93 Cal. App. 3rd 864 (1979); *Steinkamp v.*

Teglia 210 Cal. App. 3d 402 (1989); *Polis v. City of La Palma* 10 Cal. App. 4th 25 (1992).

5. *Cawdrey v. Redondo Beach* 15 Cal. App. 1212 (1991).

6. See John Clayton Thomas, "The Term Limitations Movement in U.S. Cities," *National Civic Review*, 81:2, Spring–Summer 1992, pp. 160–173. Thomas's data suggest that passage of local term limits is associated with the long tenure (over eight years) of elected city council members.

7. California Secretary of State, *California Roster* (various editions).

8. Joel A. Thompson and Gary Moncrief, "The Implications of Terms Limits for Women and Minorities: Some Evidence from the States," *Social Science Quarterly*, 74:2, June 1993. The authors' data suggest that term limits will have little impact on African-American or Hispanic state legislators and little impact on women serving in lower houses. However, term limits may have a negative impact on women serving in upper houses, where female legislators tend to serve longer than their male counterparts.

9. The authors could find no comparable longitudinal data on minority mayors and council members in California.

10. California Secretary of State, *California Roster* (various editions); California Supervisors Association, *Roster* (various editions). Only San Mateo, San Francisco and Santa Clara of California's 58 counties currently have term limits on their supervisors.

PART V
County and City Studies and Trends

Minorities and Women
Do Win At-Large

*Susan A. MacManus and
Charles S. Bullock III*

Nonpartisan, at-large election systems have come under heavy attack in recent decades. Today, these once-honored centerpieces of early civic reform, once actively espoused by groups like the National Civic League are often maligned for inherently discriminating against minority and female candidates. Allegedly, such "good government" formulae all but guarantee conservative, business-led, white male-dominated elections while discouraging women, blacks, Hispanics and other minorities from running for local office, and deprive them of effective support when they do.

This chapter directly challenges such widespread—and, we would argue, destructive—assumptions with results from a study of elections in a "reformed" city—Austin, Texas—conducted between 1975 and 1985. Our research aims to determine rigorously: 1) how often minority group members and females ran for office in Austin; 2) whether such candidates gained essential backing in their campaigns; and 3) the minority success rate compared to that of Anglo males. Our findings clearly show that reformed structures per se do not shut minorities and women out of the election process.

Austin selects its council and mayor in nonpartisan, at-large elections. In 1980, its population was 71% Anglo, 18% Hispanic, and 11% black. Over the previous decade, Hispanics had gained 65%, whites 44%, and blacks 41%. During the period studied, three elections were held for the seven-member council (which includes the mayor). In the 21 contests, black candidates won 2 seats, Hispanics 1, and women 6. A white woman became mayor in 1977 and

*Reprinted with permission from National Civic Review, *Vol. 77, No. 3, May/June, 1988. Published by the National Civic League Press, Denver, Colorado.*

was re-elected in 1981. The question we address here is how, under purportedly unfavorable reform conditions, this community avoided a white, male representative monopoly.

Our study identified five specific factors which are widely used to explain candidate success. These "predictors" are: campaign spending; newspaper endorsements; citizen-group endorsements; party endorsements; and incumbency.

Before presenting our findings, it is important to understand what other researchers and commentators have said about the availability of such resources to minority and female candidates and the impact of each upon election results.

Campaign Spending

It is widely believed that the candidate "who spends the most wins the most." Some claim that spending is particularly important in at-large systems where candidates rely more on the electronic and print media to reach larger constituencies.[1] Heilig and Mundt state what is obvious to most politicians: "Winners generally spend more than losers,"[2] regardless of the type of election system.

The difficulties of disentangling the effects of incumbency, campaign spending, and other factors are well documented. As Heilig and Mundt note, "It is nearly impossible to single out the effect of funding when in the real world it is confounded by incumbency, turnout levels, closeness of competition, and other factors."[3] It is also difficult to determine the chain of events. "Good candidacies get lots of contributors. Which produces the victory—the money or the characteristics that drew the money?"[4]

Most multivariate analysis shows no strong connection between campaign spending and incumbency, gender, and race. Arrington and Ingalls, for example, concluded that "the variations of spending within each of the groups is much greater than the differences between them."[5] While race may help to align contributor and candidate, it appears that "black candidates are as well financed as whites because black contributors concentrate their funds exclusively on the small number of black candidates."[6] There is also evidence that female candidates are no longer disadvantaged in fund raising.

Endorsements

Newspapers may provide voting cues for independent, politically attentive, better-educated voters. Citizen and political groups may influence voters who share priorities and ideologies with the endorsing organization. The endorsement process may also distinguish serious candidates. One expects that broader endorsements (in terms of ideology and the appeal of the source) facilitate election. Our study is the first to test this assumption.

Newspapers. In a comparative study of six cities between 1950 and 1980, Stein and Fleischmann report that a daily paper endorsement is worth 10 to 20 percent of the vote to city council candidates. They found that while publishers showed no "systematic bias against either minorities or females,"[7] they did have excellent track records in supporting winners. Banfield and Wilson in their classic work, *City Politics* (1963), underlined the power of the press in large, nonpartisan cities when numerous candidates lack wide voter recognition. Yet, they observed, this power breaks down when "voters group the newspapers, the professional politicians, and the business elite together as a 'power structure' which they then repudiate—perhaps because of economic stagnation, accumulated grievance, or a general disaffection from local politics."[8]

Editorial endorsements are on the wane nationally. Some publishers believe "if you endorse too early in the campaign, you place a burden on your reporters because the politicians and the readers perceive them as no longer being totally objective, as reflecting your editorial position."[9] Despite the trend, the Austin *American Statesman* (a major daily) endorses candidates, but usually not until the weekend before the election.

The effect of newspaper endorsements is often questioned. Fewer than one-third of all readers seriously consider editorial pages. Nonetheless, this third is weighted toward the more educated and politically attentive. In a city like Austin (home of the University of Texas and the state capitol), with a high proportion of college graduates, we expected the press to carry weight. Political activists we interviewed cited the paper as a major factor in defeating a conservative-backed mayoral candidate in 1985.

Citizen Groups. The political clout of citizen groups in local politics, especially in nonpartisan settings, was also recognized by Banfield and Wilson. "In many cities elections are won by organizations, or alliances of organizations, or other well defined, well disciplined, city-wide parties."[10]

Austin has two ideologically based citizen groups: the liberals, or progressives, and the conservatives. An umbrella organization, the River City Coordinating Council (RC3) represents the liberal component. While RC3 does not formally endorse candidates, its founder and other activists confirm that "informal advisements" are given to member groups upon request. There is no equivalent formal umbrella organization for conservative groups, although local experts attribute such a role to the Austin Area Research Organization (AARO). Austin's liberal and conservative leaders generally agreed which candidates the two groups supported.

Some scholars claim that conservative groups dominate the political scene in nonpartisan, at-large settings. Nonetheless, a comparative study asserts only that reformed cities (nonpartisan, at-large, city manager), especially those in the Sunbelt with higher socioeconomic status (like Austin), are most likely to be characterized by group politics in which "influence is dispersed among a range of community groups and organizations."[11]

Few multivariate studies of municipal electoral outcomes have examined citizen group endorsements. To probe this factor, we focused on the RC3 and AARO which are ideologically distinct, have extensive voter bases, and are reputed to be influential. While they often disagreed, on 13 occasions progressives and conservatives backed the same candidates.

Mason's (1973) study of endorsement patterns in state legislative races found that both citizen group and special interest group (labor, agricultural) endorsements were important determinants of electoral outcomes, leading us to expect similar results in Austin.

The only study to contrast group support by race relied on assessments by candidates and "found no evidence in these self-reports that black candidates receive less support from several major interest groups (labor, business, neighborhood, racial or ethnic, and party)."[12] Indeed, Bledsoe and Welch (1985) conclude that blacks elected to urban councils have broader bases of support than whites. They also note that there is no evidence that neighborhood groups, relatively new arrivals on the urban political scene, discriminate against black candidates. The focus of such groups, regardless of socioeconomic or racial composition, is on neighborhood preservation and improvement of its quality of life (streets, parks, public safety, etc.).

Austin's liberal and conservative leaders saw no particular partisan or ideological bias in the city's 400 neighborhood groups which focus instead on growth and environmental issues. Correspondingly, all serious candidates generally projected themselves as "friends of neighborhoods."

Thus in Austin, the distinguishing endorsements are those of citizen groups—or are ideological rather than neighborhood-based.

Party. While formally discouraged, party influence in nonpartisan systems is widely acknowledged. Thus, we expected party backing to play a significant role in outcomes.

In Austin, Democratic party endorsements are actually made under the banner of the Austin Progressive Coalition (APC). To gain APC backing, a candidate must be supported by both the Travis County Democrats and the University Democrats. APC endorsements are similar, but not identical, to those of the liberal citizen group. Candidates with Democratic backing invariably received RC3 endorsement, but not vice versa; there is no Republican equivalent to the Democrats' APC.

Candidate Race/Ethnicity

Despite impressionistic evidence that nonpartisan, at-large election systems work against minority candidacies (especially those of blacks), the size of minority populations proves a better predictor of outcomes. Most research on this question has postulated that minorities vote for minority candidates and Anglos for Anglo candidates. In other words, it is widely held that race/ethnicity are the predominant voting cues. If true, this situation would make it very difficult for minorities to win at-large contests in most communities.

Several studies challenge that assertion. When other factors are considered (e.g., council size, the minority population, residential dispersion patterns, and coalition patterns) a candidate's race often becomes less significant.

A growing literature based on recent socioeconomic and political data shows increasing class and political fragmentation among blacks and casts serious doubt on their ability to act as a cohesive voting bloc. For their part, Mexican Americans are generally known to split along generational, class, and partisan lines.

Studies that use candidate race/ethnicity as an explanatory variable show that minority status is negatively related to total vote share. However, when multivariate models are used to test alternative explanations, race per se proves less significant. In such cases, partisanship, newspaper endorsements, incumbency, and other factors emerge as important determinants of success and white crossover voting.

In Austin, black and Hispanic candidates have succeeded in coalition building, although the choice of partners shifts from election to election. Since Austin's minority populations are more residentially dispersed than in many other cities, this ability proves critical.

Gender

Partisan issues seem to have little effect on women's election chances. Recent studies show that influential groups (partisan and citizen) strive to recruit women to balance their slates, an affirmative action strategy designed to pull in the votes of Independent women for whom gender may be an important voting cue.

While women still do not run in proportion to their numbers, at-large or multimember electoral structures may favor them. The larger the number of seats at stake, the more likely are slating groups to recruit and endorse women. On the fund-raising side, women now appear on a par with men. Welch, Clark, Darcy and Ambrosius (1985) conclude that "in primary elections women are more fully equal with men; they are just as likely to run unopposed and when opposed they do equally well in gaining voter support."[13]

Bullock and Johnson (1985) found that women who won pluralities in primaries were more likely to win runoffs than were male primary leaders in all-male runoffs.[14] In nonschool board elections, women receive an average of four to seven percent more votes than men, according to Arrington and Ingalls

(1984).[15] We predicted, therefore, that in Austin, gender would have little effect on electoral success.

Incumbency

Most studies recognize that office holders have a distinct advantage in regaining their seats. In the nonpartisan environment, "the voter often resorts to selecting a familiar name on the ballot in the absence of party labels."[16]

Controlling for incumbency, many racial and gender differences evaporate. For example, Arrington and Ingalls observed that in at-large elections, incumbency plays a stronger role than campaign spending, party, gender, or race.[17] Regardless of the type of election, the authors reported that incumbents received between 3 and 20 percent more votes than challengers.

In addition, it appears that incumbency helps both blacks and whites. Black office-holders tended to get more white crossover votes each time they ran, perhaps because white fears were eased by successful performance.[18] The same holds true for women. An analysis of Austin city elections from 1973 to 1983 by the LBJ School reports a strong preference for incumbents.[19]

Findings

We analyzed 209 candidacies in primary and run-off elections, eliminating people who did not file expenditure reports. Campaign expenditures were determined from candidate filing, with amounts for primaries separated from the total spending of candidates who participated in both a primary and runoff. Newspaper endorsements were culled from newspaper files. Democratic endorsements were determined through interviews.

We used two indicators of candidate success to chart results: 1) the share of the vote received by a candidate; and 2) a measure of whether the candidate won either the election or a plurality of the primary vote. With multivariate regression analysis, we evaluated the relative impact of endorsements, spending, and incumbency for each candidate category.

In sum, the minorities and women who have entered the fray have done quite well in Austin electoral politics. One inference is that female or minority candidates have been more credible as a group than the average Anglo male candidates. Female candidates have averaged 31 percent of the voters, about the same as the percentage of blacks and substantially less than the 37 percent average for Hispanic candidates. A third of the women were elected or led fields of primary candidates, compared to only a quarter of the men. Hispanics were most successful, winning 42 percent of the time, ahead of blacks who won 37 percent of their contests and Anglos who won only 23 percent of theirs (see Table 1).

Table 1
Electoral Success of Candidates
in Austin, Texas, 1975–85

	Gender of Candidates		Race/Ethnicity of Candidates		
	Women	*Men*	*Blacks*	*Hispanics*	*Anglos*
Number of candidates	33	168	19	19	163
Average percentage of votes per candidate	31.2	23.9	30.5	36.7	22.9
Percentage of candidates who won	33.3	24.6	36.8	42.1	22.8
Average campaign spending	$18,386	$13,314	$10,269	$14,667	$14,555
Percentage of group endorsed by:					
Liberals	30.3	24.1	42.1	47.4	20.2
Conservatives	27.3	27.1	36.8	47.4	23.3
Democrats	14.2	28.0	21.4	36.4	26.6
Press	39.4	23.4	36.8	57.9	20.5

The women and minorities candidates were also successful at raising money and obtaining endorsements. The mean spending for females was almost $18,400, or $5,000 more than for males. Table 1 also indicates that average campaign spending by Hispanic candidates slightly exceeded that of Anglos. However, black spending lagged, making the good performance of black candidates all the more impressive.

Generally, women, blacks, and Hispanics received more endorsements than Anglo males, supporting Bledsoe and Welch's observation that minority candidates tend to have broader bases of support than Anglos.[20]

As one might expect, liberal groups endorsed blacks and Hispanics at higher rates than Anglos. Surprisingly, the same pattern maintains for conservatives. At times they may simply have acknowledged the inevitable, for example by supporting an incumbent Hispanic who received between 61 and 82 percent of the vote. In other contests where conservatives backed Hispanic candidates, there is reason to believe that the Hispanic was more conservative than at least some of the Anglo competitors. Political activists told us that while liberals generally labeled minority and female candidates as progressive, this expectation is not always correct in Austin.

Indications that the press frequently fails to support minority and female candidates proved inaccurate for Austin. Blacks and Hispanics were far more likely to get newspaper backing than were Anglos, and women were more often endorsed than men.

Of the endorsing groups, only the Democratic party showed a tendency to support Anglos and males more frequently. In light of contrary RC3 positions, this response underscores the independence of citizen and partisan group endorsement patterns. It may also indicate that women were less active in the Party. However, a similar explanation seems less likely for blacks. Perhaps local Democrats, with concerns at other levels of government, faced pressures to balance endorsements.

Minority and Female Candidates

Further analysis confirms that women, blacks, and Hispanics polled slightly larger shares of the vote than did males and whites. This result is not surprising since throughout the period studied, at least one woman, black, and Hispanic sat on the council.

Incumbency and endorsement rates were significant predictors of female vote share. Neither spending nor the type of election proved significant.

Models for blacks and Hispanics provide less stable estimates because of smaller numbers of cases. With that caveat in mind, black success was also linked to endorsement and spending levels. Endorsements provide the strongest indicator of Hispanic vote percentage.

Incumbency was worth 17.7 percentage points for minority candidates, and each endorsement provided an additional 11 points. When separate group endorsements were substituted for the overall total, all except support from conservatives were statistically significant, with press endorsements being the most valuable. The only significant predictor of whether women and minorities would win was the number of endorsements received. With this single variable one can correctly predict 85 percent of the minority candidate outcomes.

Successful Candidates

In our model for successful candidates, the variable factors of press endorsements, incumbency, and the number of candidates competing for each position tended to relate strongly to the vote shares of winners:

• Successful incumbents received nine percent more of the vote than successful novices;
• Newspaper endorsements were worth more than eight percentage points;
• Within individual races for office, each additional candidate reduced the winner's vote share by 2.5 percent.

The model for successful candidates resembles that for women and minorities. Both models include incumbency, which has a stronger effect in the model for women and minorities. In our model for women and minorities, the number of endorsements is a better predictor than any single endorsing group alone, while among successful candidates, the press had a significant effect that was not present when the sum of endorsements was used.

Finally, spending was not a factor among successful candidates. Some of the differences, particularly the spending variable, may be due to the greater variation in the data on women and minorities. Some of these candidates won while most lost, so that the range in the share of votes received went from almost 0 to 90 percent. Spending was not a factor among winners, since all of them were relatively well funded, while among women and minorities, some raised hundreds of thousands of dollars and others ran on shoestring budgets.

Among successful candidates, the racial, ethnic and gender/ethnic identity were not useful predictors when added to the model.

Conclusions

Despite widespread assumptions that minorities and women are electorally disadvantaged in nonpartisan at-large settings, these groups have been consistently elected in Austin. Women, blacks, and Hispanics have received average shares of the vote that exceed the figures for Anglo males. Larger percentages of minority and female candidacies have succeeded.

Austin's minorities and women enjoy access equaling that of Anglo males to key ingredients for political success. They raise large sums of money, are frequently endorsed, and often enjoy the advantages of incumbency. Three different blacks have been elected to the council and five women were elected during the period under study, including one who served as mayor. Holding office is not, however, a prerequisite for minority success.

It seems clear that in Austin none of the structural elements—nonpartisan, at-large, majority vote elections—frequently alleged to dilute minority influence is a serious impediment. Since Austin's black and Hispanic populations are relatively small and have had trouble building coalitions, Anglo support is a key ingredient to their electoral success.

The reform movement and community power literature which dominated political science 20 years ago produced some very influential theories about governmental structure and representative democracy, most of which have been tested only periodically on a cross-sectional, piecemeal basis for a single racial, ethnic, or gender group.

Our findings, based on longitudinal, comparative analysis of the relative impact of various factors on different minority groups within the same reform community, show the negativism attributed to reform structures may be waning. One reason for this change may be the growing tendency of whites to cross over and support minority candidates as the population becomes more educated and color/gender blind in their voting patterns. Another reason may be that political interest groups are now more open in their candidate recruitment and endorsement policies, recognizing that inclusion of minorities may offset similar actions by opposing groups. Third, and perhaps most important, minorities and women appear to be gaining skills which enable them to tap traditional power resources more effectively.

So women and minorities *do* win at-large elections, out of all proportion to the number of candidates. The only open question is whether more women and minorities might *win* in greater numbers in a district-based structure. With one-third of the voting population (and growing) and only 19 percent (38/201) of the candidates, minorities are not offering themselves for election in proportion to their numbers. Similarly, with half the population and only 16 percent (33/201) of the candidacies, women are even more shy about running for office.

Notes

1. Davidson, Chandler and Luis Recardo Fraga. "Nonpartisan Slating Groups in an At-Large Setting," in *Minority Vote Dilution*, Chandler Davidson, ed. (Washington, D.C.: Howard University Press, 1984), pp. 119–43.

2. Heilig, Peggy and Robert J. Mundt. *Your Voice at City Hall* (Albany: State University of New York Press, 1984), p. 73.

3. *Ibid.*, p. 73.

4. Arrington, Theodore S. "Race and Campaign Finance in Charlotte, N.C.," *Western Political Quarterly*, December, 1984, pp. 578–83.

5. Arrington, Theodore S. and Gerald L. Ingalls. "Effects of Campaign Spending on Local Elections: The Charlotte Case," *American Politics Quarterly*, January, 1984, pp. 115–27.

6. *Op. cit.,* Arrington, pp. 578–83.

7. Stein, Lana and Arnold Fleischmann. "Newspaper and Business Endorsements in Municipal Elections: A Test of the Conventional Wisdom," *Journal of Urban Affairs,* September, 1987, pp. 325–36.

8. Banfield, Edward C. and James Q. Wilson. *City Politics* (New York: Vintage, 1963), p. 325.

9. Shaw, Danald L. and Maxwell E. McCombs. *The Emergence of American Political Issues: The Agenda-Setting Function of the Press* (St. Paul: West Publishing Co., 1977), p. 55.

10. *Op. cit.*, Banfield and Wilson, p. 128.

11. Dutton, William H. and Alana Northrop. "Municipal Reform and the Changing Pattern of Urban Party Politics," *American Politics Quarterly,* October, 1978, pp. 429–52.

12. Bledsoe, Timothy and Susan Welch. "The Effect of Political Structures on the Socioeconomic Characteristics of Urban City Council Members," *American Politics Quarterly*, November, 1985, pp. 467–483.

13. Welch, Susan and Timothy Bledsoe. "Perceived Sources of Electoral Support for Black and White City Council Members," *Journal of Urban Affairs,* Fall, 1985, pp. 1–12.

14. Bullock, Charles S., III and Loch Johnson. "Sex and the Second Primary," *Social Science Quarterly*, December, 1986, pp. 933–44.

15. Arrington and Ingalls, *American Politics Quarterly,* pp. 117–27.

16. Cassel, Carol A. "The Nonpartisan Ballot in the United States," in *Electoral Law and Their Political Consequences*, Bernard Grofman and Arend Lijphard, eds. (New York: Agathon Press, 1986), pp. 226–41.

17. Arrington and Ingalls, *American Politics Quarterly*, pp. 117–27.

18. Bullock Charles S., III. "Racial Crossover Voting and the Election of Black Officials," *Journal of Politics*, February, 1984, pp. 239–51.

19. Lyndon Baines Johnson School of Public Affairs. *Local Government Election Systems*, Policy Project Report No. 62 (Austin: University of Texas, 1984).

20. *Op. cit.,* Bledsoe and Welch, pp. 467–83.

Cumulative Voting as a Remedy for Minority Vote Dilution

Richard L. Engstrom, Delbert A. Taebel, and Richard L. Cole

Many local legislative bodies in the United States are elected through the use of at-large election systems. Each voter in a particular political jurisdiction (e.g., city, county, school district) is allowed to cast a vote for as many candidates as there are legislative seats to be filled.[1] The seats are then awarded to the candidates who have received votes from a plurality (or sometimes majority) of all of the voters in the jurisdiction.[2] These at-large systems, not surprisingly, have been the subject of complaints by racial and language minority groups within many of these local units. Blacks, Hispanics, and Native Americans, for example, have alleged that at-large election systems "dilute" their voting strength by submerging it into that of the white or Anglo majority.[3] When voting is divided along group lines, they correctly note, the at-large format seriously impairs their ability to elect candidates favored by them.[4]

If the voting power of a racial or language minority is diluted as a result of an at-large structure, that local election system is vulnerable to invalidation under the federal Voting Rights Act.[5] Section 2 of the Act, as amended in 1982, prohibits the use of electoral arrangements having this discriminatory effect.[6] Specifically, Section 2 forbids state and local governments from structuring electoral competition in a manner that results in minority voters having "less opportunity than other members of the electorate to participate in the political process and to elect representatives of their choice."[7] This provision

Reprinted with permission from The Journal of Law & Politics, *Vol. V, No. 3, Spring, 1989. Published by the University of Virginia School of Law, Charlottesville, Virginia.*

has been the basis for many successful challenges to at-large systems by black,[8] Hispanic,[9] and Native American voters.[10]

The remedy adopted to cure the dilution found to result from election at-large has almost invariably been election by district.[11] Single-member districts are chosen as the medium for selecting the entire local legislature, or at least a major portion of it. These districting arrangements have been, as a general matter, effective remedies. Given the levels of residential segregation common in this country, single-member districting schemes have usually resulted in minority voters constituting a majority in one or more of the new districts. These "majority minority" districts have in turn resulted in the election of minority representative in setting after setting.[12]

Single-member districts will not, however, provide an adequate remedy in all situations. In some circumstances, minority voters are too geographically dispersed for a districting plan to result in many if any, "majority minority" districts. This is reportedly the situation frequently faced by Hispanics in the southwestern portion of the United States,[13] and sometimes by blacks in rural areas of the South.[14] While somewhat dispersed residentially, these groups are often cohesive politically, and their voting strength can be diluted by an at-large system just as seriously as that of a residentially concentrated minority.

Despite being equally susceptible to dilution by submergence as more concentrated minorities, dispersed minorities may not share equally in Section 2's protection against that type of electoral discrimination. The inability to remedy the submergence through a single-member district arrangement may now, as a consequence of a recent ruling by the Supreme Court in *Thornburg v. Gingles*,[15] place Section 2's protection beyond their reach. This judicially granted exemption from the statutory prohibition against dilutive systems is both unfortunate and unnecessary.

The ability to create at least one "majority minority" single-member district was held by the Court in *Thornburg v. Gingles*, its first decision involving the amended Section 2, to be a "*necessary precondition*" to a valid claim of dilution by submergence.[16] The Court stated, in effect, that if dilution cannot be cured by single-member districting, then minority voters may not complain that a system that submerges their votes is impermissible.[17] This holding is extremely unfortunate. The absence of a single-member district remedy of course in no way negates the presence of dilution. Minority votes are still submerged within the at-large electorate. The holding is also unnecessary, because single-member districting is not the only electoral arrangement through which dilution by submergence can be measured and remedied. Other electoral systems which are at least as democratic as single-member districts may be employed to provide minority voters with a reasonable opportunity to elect representatives of their choice.[18] The following, after reviewing the Court's holding in *Thornburg,* identifies one such alternative system, *cumulative voting,* and reports on the first adoption and application of that system as a remedy for minority vote dilution in this country.

I. Thornburg v. Gingles

The single-member district precondition was enunciated by the Supreme Court in *Thornburg v. Gingles*, a case involving an allegation that several multimember state legislative districts in North Carolina unfairly submerged the voting power of the black minorities within them (the same dilution issue, in effect, as in cases involving at-large election systems).[19] Plaintiffs were able to show to the Court's satisfaction that voting in each of these multimember districts (from which three to eight legislators were elected) was racially polarized, and that each could be subdivided into smaller single-member districts in a way that would result in at least one district with a black majority.[20] This combination of circumstances led the Court to conclude that the multimember format impaired the ability of blacks to elect candidates of their choice, and the state was therefore enjoined from continuing to use these districts.[21]

In elaborating on the evidentiary requirements for demonstrating unlawful submergence, the Court focused most of its attention on the issue of whether voting had been "racially polarized."[22] The definition and measurement of this phenomenon had become a central and controversial factor in Section 2 litigation,[23] and the Court clarified the matter considerably.[24] Yet satisfactory proof that voting within a multimember district or at-large system is polarized and that the candidates preferred by minority voters therefore usually (or will usually) lose—i.e., proof of dilution—was held to be insufficient to invalidate that arrangement.[25] In order to sustain a claim that the system itself was the proximate cause of the relative inability to elect candidates, the Court held that "the minority group must be able to demonstrate that it is sufficiently large and geographically compact to constitute a majority in a single-member district."[26]

The rationale for this requirement, described as a "threshold matter,"[27] was expressed in a footnote as follows:

> Unless minority voters possess the *potential* to elect representatives in the absence of the challenged structure or practice, they cannot claim to have been injured by that structure or practice. The single-member district is generally the appropriate standard against which to measure minority group potential to elect because it is the smallest political unit from which representatives are elected.[28]

Given the single-member district as the "standard,"[29] the Court further noted:

> Thus, if the minority group is spread evenly throughout a multimember district, or if, although geographically compact, the minority group is so small in relation to the surrounding white population that it could not constitute a majority in a single-member district, these minority voters cannot maintain that they would have been able to elect representatives of their choice in the absence of the multimember electoral structure.[30]

While single-member districts have often been compared and contrasted, along a variety of dimensions, with at-large elections and multimember districts,[31] they are by no means the *only* alternative electoral system through which to assess a minority group's "potential to elect representatives." Other democratic systems can be employed, within the multiple seat context, to provide politically cohesive but residentially dispersed minorities with an opportunity to elect candidates.[32] These are not systems which guarantee minorities "proportional representation," but only the opportunity, despite polarized voting, to elect a candidate or some candidates favored by them.[33] In the case of one such system—cumulative voting—this theoretical potential was recently confirmed empirically.[34]

When single-member districting will not alleviate dilution by submergence, these alternative systems should be examined before a court concludes that a minority group does not have "the *potential* to elect representative[s] in the absence of the challenged structure."[35] To do otherwise will result in meritorious, remediable claims of dilution being left outside Section 2's coverage.[36] Dilution, in short, has never been a problem confined to "geographically insular" minority groups;[37] neither, therefore, should Section 2's protection against it be limited by that geographical constraint.

II. Cumulative Voting

Cumulative voting is a system that may be employed any time more than one person is to be elected from a specified geographical area.[38] Just as in the more traditional at-large or multimember district context, each voter is allowed to cast as many votes as there are positions to be filled. In other words, if three people are to be elected, every voter has three votes. The distinguishing feature of cumulative voting, however, is that voters are not restricted to casting only a single vote for any particular candidate, but may instead cumulate or aggregate their votes behind one or more candidates if they wish. For example, in the three-vote context, a voter may vote in the traditional fashion, casting one vote each for three different candidates, or may cast two votes for one candidate and one for another, or even cast all three of his votes for a single candidate (a phenomenon called "plumping").[39] Cumulative voting, in short, allows voters to express their preferences more flexibly than does the more traditional one-vote-per-candidate format. If voters intensely prefer to be represented by one or more of the candidates to the others, they may reflect that intensity in their vote. The winning candidates are determined, as in most multiseat contexts, by a simple plurality rule: the top X vote recipients are elected to the X available seats.

Cumulative voting complies fully with the "one person, one vote" rule.[40] As in the more traditional one-vote-per-candidate system, every individual enters the voting booth with the same voting power. Indeed, cumulative voting is arguably more democratic than the one-vote-per-candidate format because it allows voters to cast ballots that more fully reflect their preferences among the candidates. It is also less likely to dilute the voting strength of a minority group. Minority voters who would be submerged in the more traditional context may, through cumulative voting, have an opportunity to elect a candidate or candidates of their choice within the multimember context despite polarized voting. This opportunity is contingent upon minority voters being politically cohesive, but *not* upon them being residentially concentrated.

The *"potential* to elect representatives" favored by minority voters under cumulative voting is readily illustrated by a coefficient called the *threshold of exclusion*.[41] This coefficient identifies the percentage or proportion of the electorate that a group must exceed in order to elect a candidate of its choice, *regardless of how the rest of the electorate votes*. The coefficient is based on a set of "worst case" (from the minority's perspective) assumptions about the behavior of majority group voters. In the context of cumulative voting, these assumptions are: (1) majority group voters cast all of the votes available to them, (2) none of these votes are cast for the minority's preferred candidate, but rather (3) they are concentrated entirely on a number of candidates equal to the number of seats or positions to be filled, and (4) they are divided evenly across those candidates.

In a three votes, three seat election with cumulative voting, for example, the threshold of exclusion is 25%. This means that any group that constitutes more than 25% of the voters, regardless of where those voters live, can elect a candidate if they "plump" for that candidate. This can be demonstrated by the following hypothetical. Assume that 1,000 people have voted, and that 25% plus one of them, or 251, have plumped for candidate A. Assume further that the remaining 749 voters have voted according to the worst case assumptions, i.e., all 749 cast three votes, none of which are cast for candidate A but instead are divided evenly across only three other candidates, B, C, and D. Under these assumptions, A receives 753 votes while B, C, and D each receive 749, and therefore A is elected. If any of these assumptions about majority voters' behavior is relaxed, candidate A's vote is still sufficient to win one of the three seats. For example, if majority voters do not support the three candidates evenly, but instead give B and C 754 votes each, then D can receive at most 739 and A still wins a seat. In the three seat context, therefore, any group that exceeds 25% of those voting can, by concentrating their support behind a particular candidate, elect that candidate regardless of how the rest of the voters cast their ballots.

In a cumulative voting system the threshold of exclusion varies inversely with the number of seats or positions being filled; in other words, the greater the number of seats at issue, the smaller will be the threshold. If five seats are being filled, for example, the value of the threshold is only 16.7%; for seven seats, it is 12.5% (see Table 1). The value of the threshold, expressed as a percentage, can be calculated through the following formula:

$$\text{Threshold of Exclusion} = \frac{1}{1 + (\text{Number of Seats})} \times 100$$

The threshold of exclusion illustrates that with cumulative voting a relatively small and residentially dispersed minority group does have the potential, provided they are politically cohesive, to elect representatives of their choice in a multiseat electoral context. Single-member districts, in short, are not the only democratic electoral alternative to dilution by submergence, and not the only system through which "to measure minority group potential to elect."[42] *Thornburg's* "precondition"[43] therefore need not be, nor should it be, operationalized so narrowly. It must also be remembered that the threshold of exclusion is the point beyond which a cohesive minority can elect a candidate *regardless of how majority voters behave.* If the behavior of the majority voters in any way deviates from the worst case assumptions, the minority group may be smaller, less cohesive, or both, and still have a realistic opportunity to elect a candidate of its choice through cumulative voting.

This opportunity to convert, through cumulative voting, minority votes into minority preferred representatives was demonstrated empirically in Alamogordo, New Mexico recently. Cumulative voting was adopted in that city in 1987 as the medium for settling a vote dilution lawsuit challenging, under Section 2 of the Voting Rights Act, the use of at-large elections.[44] On July 21, 1987, that system was used for the first time to elect three members at-large to the Alamogordo city council. Reported below are both ecological and survey data demonstrating that Hispanic voters, by voting cohesively and intensively for a particular candidate that day, successfully converted their voting strength into the election of an Hispanic to that council.

III. Cumulative Voting in Alamogordo

In 1983, the City of Alamogordo (population: 24,030) adopted through referendum a new mixed electoral system for selecting its city council. Four council members were to be elected from single-member districts and three at-large. The district members were elected initially in 1984 to four-year terms,[45] and the at-large members were to have been elected in 1986, also to four-year terms. This at-large election was to have been conducted under a one-vote-per-candidate rule, with the top three vote recipients awarded the seats.[46] This arrangement replaced the previous all at-large system in which five council members were elected on a staggered basis, each to a particular place or seat on the council.[47]

Table 1
Threshold of Exclusion Values
for Cumulative Voting Systems

Number of Seats or Positions	Value (%) of Threshold of Exclusion
2	33.3
3	25.0
4	20.0
5	16.7
6	14.3
7	12.5
8	11.1
9	10.0

Hispanic and black voters objected to the continued use of the at-large format in Alamogordo. Although minorities constituted, according to the 1980 census, 29.3% of the city's population (24.0% Hispanic and 5.3% black) and 25.9% of its voting age population (21.0% Hispanic, 4.9% black), no minority person had been elected to the council under the old at-large system since 1970.[48] Minority voters maintained that the continued use of that format, even without the place provision, would be discriminatory. Hispanic and black plaintiffs therefore filed suit prior to the 1986 at-large elections, seeking to have the new system declared invalid under Section 2, and a preliminary injunction postponing the election was granted.[49]

A cumulative voting system for the three at-large seats was agreed to by the parties and, after a hearing, approved by the District Court.[50] The only change in the city's election system was the manner in which ballots could be cast in the at-large election.[51] This agreement allowed the city to continue its mixed system of representation, with some council members accountable electorally to district constituencies and others to the entire city electorate. It also offered the city's minority residents a chance to elect a candidate at-large, provided they voted cohesively. Due to the relative dispersion of Hispanics across the city, the opportunity for minorities to elect representatives of their choice in this modified mixed arrangement was perceived to be equal to, if not better than, that offered by a seven single-member district system.

One of the four single-member districts used in the 1984 election was a majority minority district. The total population in this district was 53.9% Hispanic and black, but when the personnel and their dependents from a nearby Air Force base (few of whom participated in city elections) were excluded, the figure was estimated to be much higher, 67.3%[52] In the 1984 election, the voters in this district elected a black to represent them on the council.[53] Although a seven district plan with two majority minority districts was developed by plaintiffs, that majority was viewed as tenuous in one of them. One district would have a combined minority population of 54.7%, but the nonmilitary population in that district would be approximately 66% minority, close to that in the majority minority district in the four district scheme.[54] The other would have a minority population of 55.1%, but the nonmilitary population would only be about 60%.[55] The minority percentage of the nonmilitary voting age population, of course, would be lower. Given that minorities constituted about 30% of the total citywide population and 25% of the voting age population (*without* excluding the military personnel and their dependents), the chances of electing another minority council member through cumulative voting at-large appeared to be as good as, if not better than, that offered by a seven district arrangement. Plaintiffs therefore also opted for the modified mixed system.

IV. The 1987 Election

The first election for the three at-large seats using cumulative voting was held on July 21, 1987. Eight candidates sought the seats. Seven of the candidates were Anglos while the eighth was an Hispanic woman, Inez M. Moncada. The voting machine ballot was very straightforward. There were three voting levers over every candidate's name, and voters were informed (in both English and Spanish) that they could pull any three of the levers. Participation in the election was described as "heavier than normal" in Alamogordo, with 49.2% of the city's registered voters signing-in, and 2.98 votes being cast per voter.[56] The results were tallied within two hours of the closing of the polls.[57]

The total number of votes received by each candidate, along with their votes within each of the city's five polling places and from absentee ballots, are reported in Table 2. Anglo candidates finished first and second in total votes, while Ms. Moncada finished third. She was therefore awarded, under the plurality rule, one of the three at-large seats.

Ms. Moncada was the first Hispanic to be elected to the city council since 1968, and her election was quite clearly the result of Hispanic voters seizing the opportunity to cumulate their votes on her behalf. This is initially suggested by a comparison of the votes cast in the five different polling places. Sacramento School was the polling location for voters residing in the southwestern portion of the city, the most Hispanic area of Alamogordo. Ms. Moncada received 822 votes from the 492 voters signing in at that location. This was the only instance of a candidate receiving more votes than there were voters at a polling place. Her vote there exceeded that of the second place candidate by 631 votes. Most important, the voters at Sacramento School gave Ms. Moncada a 673-vote margin over Donald E. Carroll, who finished fourth in the city-wide vote, only 479 votes behind her.

Table 2
Results of the July 21, 1987 Election Using Cumulative Voting

	Total No. of People Signing-in	Total Number of Votes for Candidate							
		Downs	Moncada	Seamans	Welling	Watts	Riordan	Furrow	Carroll
Citywide	3,949	2,469	2,398	921	449	806	2,418	378	1,919
Polling Places									
Sacramento School	592	160	822	152	80	141	191	39	149
Mid High School	373	238	238	82	62	71	225	36	164
Sierra School	702	464	395	199	92	130	419	59	341
Buena Vista School	1,097	815	379	175	101	222	816	115	653
Heights School	1,057	738	516	301	103	198	652	122	520
Absentee Ballots	128	54	8	13	11	44	115	7	92

More detailed evidence from an exit poll conducted on election day confirms that Ms. Moncada's election was attributable primarily to "plumping" by Hispanic voters. An effort was made to have all voters respond to a confidential self-administered questionnaire on which they were asked to report, among other things, how they had voted.[58] The questionnaire was returned by 1,310 voters (33.2% of those who had signed-in), with 1,101 providing the requested information about their voting behavior. Reported in Table 3 are both the number of votes and the percentage of votes received by each candidate in the exit poll, along with their percentage of the actual vote (excluding absentee votes). The results of the survey are extremely close to those of the election itself. Not only are the same candidates "elected," but no candidate's percentage of the vote in the exit poll is more than 1.4 percentage points different from the percentage received on election day.

The voting choices revealed in the exit poll, reported in Table 4, show that the cumulative voting format was critical to Ms. Moncada's success. *Fewer voters* reported voting for her than for Mr. Carroll, the fourth place finisher in the election. Ms. Moncada did receive *more votes* than Mr. Carroll, however, as a result of a much higher percentage of her supporters (52.9%) cumulating votes for her than did his (27.4%) for him. Indeed, more voters reported "plumping" for Ms. Moncada than for any other candidate, and it was this phenomenon which allowed Ms. Moncada to surpass Mr. Carroll in total votes. It seems safe to conclude, therefore, that if Ms. Moncada's supporters had not had the ability to express, through plumping, the intensity with which they preferred her to the others, she would not have been elected to the city council. This would have been the case even if, in the more traditional one vote per candidate format, those voters casting two or three votes for her, or for another candidate, had chosen to "single-shot" vote for their most preferred candidate (i.e., cast one vote for that candidate but none for any of the competitors).[59]

Ms. Moncada's electoral support was by no means exclusively Hispanic, and some "crossover" vote from Anglos was necessary for her election. Reported in Table 5 are the total number of votes cast for each candidate by those respondents to the exit poll identifying themselves as Anglo, black, Hispanic, or "other." Hispanic participation was far short of the "threshold of exclusion" for a three-vote, three seat contest (Hispanic voters constituted only 13.7% of the respondents whose votes are tallied in this table), and although Hispanics overwhelmingly supported Ms. Moncada, not every Hispanic voter cast three votes for her. Yet Ms. Moncada was able to finish third and win a seat because Anglos dispersed their votes across the various candidates, with some of those votes cast for Ms. Moncada herself.[60] She is estimated to have received, based on the exit poll, votes from 21.8% of the Anglos participating in the election (13.8% reported giving her one vote, 3.0% two votes, and 5.0% three votes). While this crossover vote was in fact necessary for her election, it must still be noted that Ms. Moncada would *not* have won

Table 3
Votes Cast in Exit Poll,
Compared to Actual Vote on Election Day

| Candidate | Exit Poll | | % of Actual Votes[a] | % Point Difference (Poll-Actual) |
	No. of Votes	% of Votes		
Downs	737	22.4	21.2	1.2
Moncada	636	19.3	20.7	-1.4
Seamans	289	8.8	8.0	0.8
Welling	87	2.6	3.9	-1.3
Watts	233	7.1	6.7	0.4
Riordan	641	19.5	20.2	-0.7
Furrow	116	3.5	3.3	0.2
Carroll	552	16.8	16.1	0.7

[a]Absentee votes have been excluded from these calculations.

Table 4
Distribution of Votes Cast in Exit Poll

| Candidate's Name | Number of Voters Voting For | Number of Voters Giving Candidate | | | |
		1 Vote	2 Votes	3 Votes	Total Votes
Downs	433	243	76	114	737
Riordan	423	277	74	72	641
Carroll	391	284	53	54	552
Moncada	331	156	45	130	636
Seamans	184	119	25	40	289
Watts	127	66	16	45	233
Furrow	89	72	7	10	116
Welling	64	51	3	10	87

a seat on the council had the election been held only among Anglo voters. She was the fourth most preferred candidate among the Anglo voters. In contrast, she was the first choice, by a small margin, of black voters, and the first choice, by an enormous margin, among Hispanic voters. It was this large absolute margin among Hispanic voters, made possible by cumulative voting, that was critical to her third-place finish overall.

Without the cumulative voting option, Ms. Moncada's Hispanic supporters would not have been able to provide her with the margin of votes necessary for her victory. In the exit poll, 73.0% of the respondents identifying themselves as Hispanic voted for her; more important, 50.0% cast all three of

Table 5
Total Votes for Candidates
in Exit Poll, by Type of Voters

	Votes Received from[a]			
Candidate	Anglos (n = 861)	Blacks (n = 47)	Hispanics (n = 148)	Others (n = 25)
Downs	653	20	31	20
Riordan	583	8	29	12
Carroll	470	28	39	12
Moncada	300	36	268	6
Seamans	242	19	21	5
Watts	176	18	24	11
Furrow	96	7	8	5
Welling	58	4	19	3

[a]Twenty respondents who reported how they had cast their votes but did not report which of these group identifications applied to them are excluded from this table.

their votes for her, with another 8.1% casting two of their votes for her. In short, about three out of every four Hispanics voted for Ms. Moncada, and those voting for her gave her, on average, 2.6 votes apiece! It was this expression, through the ballot, of the intensity with which they preferred her to be their representative that allowed Hispanic voters to have a decisive impact on the election outcome. By taking advantage of the opportunity offered by cumulative voting, the Hispanic minority in Alamogordo was able to elect, at-large, a second representative of its choice to the city council, something that minority voters may not have been able to accomplish under a seven single-member district plan.

V. Conclusion

Section 2 of the Voting Rights Act prohibits electoral systems that dilute the voting strength of protected racial and language minorities.[61] This protection is most frequently invoked against at-large election systems that submerge minority voters into an electorate with a white or Anglo majority, thereby reducing the ability of minority voters to elect representatives of their choice. The Supreme Court, however, has recently restricted this protection against submergence, limiting its application to minority groups that are "geographically insular."[62] This geographical requirement is to be satisfied empirically by demonstrating that the minority in question could constitute a majority within a single-member district.[63] The explicit rationale for this requirement is that unless a district can be created that would give minority voters the ability, or at least potential ability, to elect a candidate of their choice, the challenged at-large arrangement should not be considered a cause of their electoral impotence.

The establishment of this geographic requirement is unfortunate, unnecessary, and unjustified. It has the effect, of course, of withdrawing Section 2's protection against dilution by submergence from minority voters who happen to be relatively dispersed residentially. This will leave, in particular, many Hispanic voters in the Southwest and some black voters in the rural South vulnerable to discriminatory at-large systems.[64] In establishing this requirement, the Court never suggested that dispersed minorities do not suffer from dilution. The Court argued, to the contrary, that when minorities are dispersed, the dilution appears to be beyond correction.[65] This, of course, is erroneous. Electoral competition can be structured in other ways that are equally (if not more) democratic as single-member districts and that will provide minority voters, regardless of how they happen to be distributed residentially, with the potential to translate their votes into representatives of their choice. Cumulative voting, as demonstrated recently in the Alamogordo election, is one such alternative. These alternatives should be examined before the judiciary grants exemptions from Section 2's coverage.[66]

The Court in *Thornburg* failed to cite anything in the legislative history of the amended Section 2 to suggest that Congress intended that Section's application to be limited in this manner. Nor did the Court refer to anything in the extensive case law concerning the dilutive consequences of at-large systems and large multimember districts that Congress expressly relied upon in fashioning the new Section 2.[67] The ability to create a majority-minority single-member district should be considered sufficient to demonstrate that an at-large system, if dilutive, is remediable. It should not, however, be treated as a necessary condition for either a showing of dilution or as a remedy for dilution. The fact that one of several possible remedies may not be applicable in a particular situation is not a justification for tolerating an electoral system that discriminates against minority voters.

Notes

1. Several states currently mandate at-large elections. See Cal. Const. art. XI, § 7; Conn. Gen. Stat. Ann. § 9–169c (West 1988); Ill. Rev. Stat. ch. ¶ 703 (1987); Ind. Code Ann. § 36–3–4–3 (Burns 1987); Ky. Rev. Stat. Ann. § 83A.040 (Michie/Bobbs–Merrill 1985); Md. State Gov't Code Ann. § 2–201 (1984); Mass. Gen. Laws Ann. ch. 43, § 50 (West 1987); Ohio Rev. Code Ann. § 705.72 (Page's 1988); Tenn. Code Ann. § 6–53–110 (1987).
2. The at-large format may be used to select an entire local legislative body, or only part thereof, and may be combined with a variety of other election rules and

requirements, such as full-slate laws, places or numbered posts with majority vote rules for nomination and/or election, geographical residency requirements for candidates, and staggered legislative terms. For the variation in at-large systems, see Engstrom & McDonald, "The Election of Blacks to Southern City Councils: The Dominant Impact of Electoral Arrangements," in *Blacks in Southern Politics* 245, 249–55 (L. Moreland, R. Steed & T. Baker 1987); MacManus, "City Council Election Procedures and Minority Representation: Are They Related?" 59 Soc. Sci. Q. 153, 154–57 (1978).

3. See generally Davidson, "Minority Vote Dilution: An Overview," in *Minority Vote Dilution* 1 (C. Davidson ed. 1984) [hereinafter *Minority Vote Dilution*] (defines "dilution" as a "process whereby election laws or practices, either singly or in concert, combine with systematic bloc voting among an identifiable group to diminish the voting strength of at least one other group." Id. at 4. "Ethnic or racial minority vote dilution is a special case, in which the voting strength of an ethnic or racial minority group is diminished or canceled out by the bloc vote of the majority." Id.) See also Engstrom & McDonald, "The Effect of At-Large Versus District Elections on Racial Representation in U.S. Municipalities," in *Electoral Laws and Their Political Consequences* 203 (B. Grofman & A. Lijphart eds. 1986) (analyzes the "new black reform movement" in electoral districting, which seeks to substitute single-member districts for the at-large arrangements, primarily in municipalities within the southern portion of the United States. District-based electoral systems, it is maintained, would provide blacks with a much more equitable opportunity to elect fellow blacks to city councils, a situation which in turn is expected to result in municipal government being more responsive to minority needs and interests. Id. at 223.); McDonald & Engstrom, "Minority Representation and Councilmanic Election Systems: A Black and Hispanic Comparison," in *Ethnic and Racial Minorities in Advance Industrial Societies* (A. Messina, L. Rhodebeck, F. Wright & L. Fraga eds. forthcoming).

4. See Minority Vote Dilution, supra not 3.

5. 42 U.S.C. §§ 1971, 1973 et seq. (1981), as amended by Pub. L. No. 97–205, § 3, 96 Stat. 131, 134 (1982) (codified as amended at 42 U.S.C. § 1973 (1982)).

6. Id. at § 2.

7. Id. Identified as "language minorities" by the Act are American Indians (Native Americans), Asian Americans, Alaskan Natives, and people of Spanish heritage. For the context and reasons for the 1982 amendment, see Derfner, "Vote Dilution and the Voting Rights Act Amendments," in *Minority Vote Dilution,* supra note 3, at 145; Engstrom, "Black Politics and the Voting Rights Act, 1965–1982," in *Contemporary Southern Politics* 83 (J. Lea ed. 1988).

Employing an electoral arrangement for the *purpose* of diluting minority voting strength is a violation of the fourteenth amendment to the United States Constitution. See Rogers v. Lodge, 458 U.S. 613 (1982); City of Mobile v. Bolden, 446 U.S. 55 (1980). For a review of fourteenth amendment litigation involving at-large elections, see Engstrom, "Racial Vote Dilution: The Concept and the Court," in *The Voting Rights Act: Consequences and Implications* 13 (L. Foster ed. 1985); Parker, "The 'Results' Test of Section 2 of the Voting Rights Act: Abandoning the Intent Standard," 69 Va. L. Rev. 715, 718–46 (1983).

8. See, e.g., Citizens for a Better Gretna v. Gretna, 834 F.2d 502 (5th Cir. 1987), reh'g denied, 849 F.2d 1471 (5th Cir. 1988), petition for cert. filed (Oct. 7, 1988).

9. See, e.g., Campos v. City of Baytown, 840 F.2d 1240 (5th Cir. 1988), reh'g denied, 849 F.2d 943 (5th Cir. 1988), petition for cert. filed (Oct. 5, 1988); Gomez v. City of Watsonville, 863 F.2d 1407 (9th Cir. July 27, 1988).

10. See, e.g., Windy Boy v. County of Big Horn, 647 F.Supp. 1002 (D. Mont. 1986).

11. See *Minority Vote Dilution,* supra note 3, at 5 ("When courts have found illegal vote dilution to exist, they have typically ordered a remedy consisting of the creation of single-member districts, on the assumption that if they are fairly drawn, they will increase the chances of minority groups to elect candidates of their choice." Id.).

12. See especially the before and after comparisons reported in Davidson & Korbel, "At-Large Elections and Minority Group Representation: A Re-Examination of Historical and Contemporary Evidence," 43 J. Pol. 982 (1981); Heilig and Mundt, "Changes in Representational Equity: The Effect of Adopting Districts," 64 Soc. Sci. Q. 393 (1983). See generally Lyons & Jewell, "Minority Representation and the Drawing of City Council Districts," 23 Urb. Aff. Q. 432 (1988).

13. See Taebel, "Minority Representation on City Councils: The Impact of Structure on Blacks and Hispanics," 59 Soc. Sci. Q. 142, 151 (1978); Karnig & Welch, "Sex and Ethnic Differences in Political Representation," 60 Soc. Sci. Q. 465, 474 (1979); Lyons and Jewell, supra note 12, at 441–42.

14. See Still, "Cumulative and Limited Voting in Alabama: The Aftermath of *Dillard v. Crenshaw County,*" paper presented at the 1988 annual meeting of the American Political Science Association 5–6 (Aug. 31–Sept. 4, 1988).

15. Thornburg v. Gingles, 478 U.S. 30 (1986) (affirmed in part and reversed in part the decision by the U.S. District Court of North Carolina that a legislative redistricting plan for the state's Senate and House of Representatives violated § 2(a) of the Voting Rights Act because it resulted in the dilution of black citizens' votes in six disputed districts).

16. Id. at 50.

17 "First, the minority group must be able to demonstrate that it is sufficiently large and geographically compact to constitute a majority in a single-member district. If it is not, as would be the case in a substantially integrated district, the *multimember* form of the district cannot be responsible for minority voters' inability to elect its candidates." Id. at 50.

18. See infra note 34 and accompanying text.

19. See, e.g., White v. Regester, 412 U.S. 755 (1973); United States v. Dallas County Com'n, 580 F.2d 1433 (11th Cir. 1988); Metropolitan Pittsburgh Crusade for Voters v. Pittsburgh, 686 F.Supp. 97 (W.D. Pa. 1988).

20. *Thornburg,* 478 U.S. at 50–51 (The Court also imposed two other preconditions upon minority plaintiffs: "Second, the minority group must be able to show that it is politically cohesive. If the minority group is not politically cohesive, it cannot be said that the selection of a multimember electoral structure thwarts distinctive minority group interests" and "Third, the minority must be able to demonstrate that the white majority votes sufficiently as a bloc to enable it—in the absence of special circumstances ...—usually to defeat the minority's preferred candidate ... In establishing this last circumstance, the minority group demonstrates that submergence in a white multimember district impeded it ability to elect its chosen representatives.").

21. In District 23, one of the multimember districts under contention, the Court reversed the decision of the District Court and held that black voters experienced "sustained success" in electing representatives in that district and that they had attained "persistent proportional representation." In the opinion of the Court, "this ... is inconsistent with appellee's allegation that the ability of black voters in District 23 to elect representatives of their choice is not equal to that enjoyed by the white majority." Id. at 77.

22. Id. at 52–74.

23. See, e.g., Engstrom, "The Reincarnation of the Intent Standard: Federal Judges and At-Large Election Cases," 28 How. J.J. 495 (1985); Grofman, "Criteria for Districting: A Social Science Perspective," 33 UCLA L. Rev. 77, 136–44 (1985).

24. *Thornburg*, 478 U.S. at 53 n.21 (citing the trial record at 160) (The definition given to "racially polarized" voting by Dr. Grofman, the appellee's expert witness, was adopted by the Court: "'racial polarization' exists where there is consistent relationship between [the] race of the voter and the way in which the voter votes ... or to put it differently, where 'black voters and white voters vote differently.'"). Compare, however, Wildgen, "Adding Thornburg to the Thicket: The Ecological Fallacy and Parameter Control in Vote Dilution Cases," 20 Urb. Law. 155 (1988) with Engstrom & MacDonald, "Definitions, Measurements, and Statistics: Weeding Wildgen's Thicket," 20 Urb. Law. 175 (1988).

25. *Thornburg*, 478 U.S. at 50–51 (The Court lists this as one of the "necessary preconditions" which must exist for a multimember district to impair the ability of minority voters to elect representatives of their choice.).

26. Id. at 50. A panel of the Seventh Circuit Court of Appeals has recently held that this requires that the minority group constitute a majority of the *voting age* population within the district. McNeil v. Springfield Park Dist., No. 87–2478 (7th Cr. July 8, 1988). See also Romero v. City of Pomona, 665 F.Supp. 853, 858–59 (C.D. Cal 1987) (both age and citizenship must be considered in determining whether Hispanics constitute a majority within the district).

27. *Thornburg*, 478 U.S. at 50 n.17.

28. Id. (emphasis in original).

29. Id.

30. Id.

31. See, e.g., Klain, "A New Look at the Constituencies: The Need for a Recount and a Reappraisal," 49 Am. Pol. Sci. Rev. 1105 (1955) (This piece traces the history of the development of multimember districts and single-member districts and takes issue with the claim that single-member districts were "the rule" at least in 1955. The author compares the two systems and determines that the evidence is too scant to decide which system is better, and he presents points in favor of both.); Silva, "Compared Values of the Single- and Multi-Member Legislative District," 27 W. Pol. Q. 504 (1964); M. Jewell, *Metropolitan Representation: State Legislative Redistricting in Urban Counties* (1969); Jewell, "The Consequences of Single- and Multimember Districts," in *Representation and Redistricting Issues* (B. Grofman, A. Lijphart, R. McKay & H. Scarrow eds. 1982); Niemi, Hill & Grofman, "The Impact of Multimember Districts on Party Representation in U.S. Legislatures," 10 Legis. Stud. Q. 441 (1985) (The effects of multimember districts on minority parties are mixed, according to the authors. While there are drawbacks to the multimember districting system, such as racial minorities often being underrepresented, this system does not necessarily have an adverse impact on the minority party in the district, as many claim. "The best way to view them," according to the authors, "is as tools sometimes used to suppress minority party representation, but not as prima facie evidence of discrimination against the minority party."; Grofman, Migalski & Noviello, "Effects of Multimember Districts on Black Representation in State Legislature," 14 Rev. Black Pol. Econ. 65 (1986); Engstrom & McDonald, "The Effect of At-Large Versus District Elections on Racial Representation in the U.S. Municipalities," in *Electoral Laws and Their Political Consequences* 203 (B. Grofman & A. Lijphart eds. 1986) (While it is not empirically clear that electing more black city

councilmen will increase the responsiveness of the city council to minority concerns, it is clear that using "district-based" rather than "at-large" council elections will help blacks gain more proportional representation on city councils. This latter proposition is, according to the authors, "among the best verified empirical generalizations in political science.").

32. There are a variety of alternative electoral systems that can be employed for this purpose. The "limited vote," whereby voters cast fewer votes than there are seats to be filled, and the "cumulative vote," whereby voters can cast more than one of their votes for a single candidate, are examples of such alternatives which are considered to be semi-proportional in nature. Grofman, "Criteria for Districting: A Social Science Perspective," supra note 23, at 162–170. See also E. Lakeman, *How Democracies Vote: A Study of Electoral Systems* (1974); Grofman, "Alternatives to Single Member Plurality Districts: Legal and Empirical Issues," 9 Pol. Stud. J. 875 (1981); Weaver, "Semi-Proportional and Proportional Representation Systems in the United States," in *Choosing an Electoral System* 191 (A. Lijphart & B. Grofman eds. 1984); Still, "Alternatives to Single-Member Districts," in *Minority Vote Dilution*, supra note 3, at 249; Lijphart, "Trying to Have the Best of Both Worlds: Semi-Proportional and Mixed Systems," in *Choosing an Electoral System* 207 (A. Lijphart & B. Grofman eds. 1984); Lijphart, Lopez Pintor & Stone, "The Limited Vote and the Single Nontransferable Vote: Lessons from the Japanese and Spanish Examples," in *Electoral Laws and Their Political Consequences* 154 (B. Grofman & A. Lijphart eds. 1986); Note, "Affirmative Action and Electoral Reform," 90 Yale L. J. 1811 (1981); Note, "Alternative Voting Systems as Remedies for Unlawful At-Large System," 92 Yale L.J. 144 (1982).

33. Section 2 does state that "...nothing in this section establishes a right to have members of a protected class elected in numbers equal to their proportion in the population."

34. See infra section on cumulative voting in Alamogordo, New Mexico.

35. *Thornburg*, 478 U.S. at 50 n.17.

36. This was recognized by the panel of the Seventh Circuit in McNeil v. Springfield Park Dist., 851 F.2d 957 (7th Cir. 1985).

37. *Thornburg*, 478 U.S. at 49.

38. Cumulative voting was used to elect the lower chamber of the Illinois House of Representatives from 1872 until 1980. Everson, "The Bullet Bites the Dust: Will the Cutback Amendment Bring Competition and Accountability?" 7 Ill. Issues 12 (1988) (proposition approved Nov. 1980, which reduced the membership of the General Assembly and brought cumulative voting to an end). It was abandoned in 1980 when Illinois voters, upset over a substantial pay raise that legislators had granted themselves, voted to reduce the number of seats in that chamber. D. Everson, J. Parker, W. Day, R. Harmony & K. Redfield, *The Cutback Amendment* 28 (1982) (describing history of cumulative voting in Illinois). Ten years earlier, the voters had supported the use of cumulative voting over a move to establish single-member districts. J. Cornelius, *Constitution Making in Illinois, 1818–1970,* at 162–63 (1972).

The cumulative voting system in Illinois has been the topic of much academic study. Blair, *Cumulative Voting: An Effective Device in Illinois Politics* (1960); Blair, "Cumulative Voting: Patterns of Party Allegiance and Rational Choice in Illinois State Legislative Contests," 52 Am. Pol. Sci. Rev. 123 (1958); Blair, "Cumulative Voting: An Effective Electoral Device for Fair and Minority Representation," in *Democratic Representation and Apportionment: Quantitative Methods, Measures, and Criteria* 20 (L. Papayanopoulos ed. 1973); Broh, "Utility Theory and Partisan Decision-

Making: Cumulative Voting in Illinois," 55 Soc. Sci. Q. 65 (1974); Dunn, "Cumulative Voting Problems in Illinois Legislative Elections," 9 Harv. J. Legis. 625 (1972); Hyneman & Morgan, "Cumulative Voting in Illinois," 32 Ill. L. Rev. 12 (1937); Klulinski, "Cumulative and Plurality Voting: An Analysis of Illinois' Unique Electoral System," 26 W. Pol. Q. 726 (1973); Sawyer & MacRae, "Game Theory and Cumulative Voting in Illinois: 1902–1954," 56 Am. Pol. Sci. Rev. 936 (1962); Moore, *The History of Cumulative Voting and Minority Representation in Illinois, 1818–1919* (1919); Wiggins & Petty, "Cumulative Voting and Electoral Competition: The Illinois House," 7 Am. Pol. Q. 345 (1979).

39. Voters may cast fewer than three votes if they wish, of course, and may also be allowed to cast fractions of votes (e.g., 1 1/2 and 1 1/2). "A cumulative voting system allows the strength of minority groups members' identity of interest to weigh against the greater number of the majority who share less well-defined interests." Note, "Alternative Voting Systems," supra not 32, at 154. The effects of the cumulative voting system have been studied in other contexts, most notably in the area of corporations law. Sanji & Brinkley, "Cumulative Voting: The Value of Minority Shareholding Voting Rights," 27 J. Law & Econ. 339 (1984) (economic analysis of effect of cumulative voting on representation).

40. See Wesberry v. Sanders, 376 U.S. 1 (1964) (establishing one person, one vote requirement for congressional districts); Reynolds v. Sims, 377 U.S. 533 (1964) (establishing one person, one vote requirement for state legislative districts); Avery v. Midland County, 390 U.S. 474 (1968) (establishing one person, one vote requirement for local governing bodies); Karcher v. Daggett, 462 U.S. 725 (1983) (congressional redistricting plan held unconstitutional as violation of the one person, one vote requirement); Brown v. Thomson, 462 U.S. 835 (1983) (upholding Wyoming's state legislative districts against challenge on one person, one vote grounds). On the development of the "one person, one vote" rule, see Engstrom, "Post-Census Representational Districting: The Supreme Court, 'One Person, One Vote,' and the Gerrymandering Issue," 7 S.U.L. Rev. 173 (1981) (placing the issue in historical and empirical perspective).

41. See Rae, Hanby & Loosemore, "Thresholds of Representation and Thresholds of Exclusion: An Analytic Note on Electoral Systems," 3 Comp. Pol. Stud. 1479 (1971).

42. *Thornburg*, 478 U.S. at 50 n.17.

43. Id., at 50–51, see supra note 20.

44. According to the terms of the settlement, each qualified voter in a municipal election involving an at-large election may cast as many votes as there are at-large positions to be filled. Voters have the option of casting all or some of their votes for any one candidate or candidates in the election. Vega v. City of Alamogordo, Civ. No. 86–0061–C (D.C.N.M. Mar. 2, 1987).

45. "Alamogordo Municipal Election Results and Appointments: 1950–Present 73–76" (compiled by A. Rahn, City Clerk, City of Alamogordo) [hereinafter Election Results]. See Deposition of Angie Rahn, Vega v. City of Alamogordo, Civ. No 86–0061–C, at 4 (D.C.N.M. 1987).

46. Alamogordo City Charter, articles VI–VII (1983).

47. See Election Results, supra note 45, at 9–68. See also Deposition of Guy Gallaway, Alamogordo City Commissioner, Vega v. City of Alamogordo, Civ. No. 86–0061–C, at 5–6 (D.C.N. 1987); Deposition of Sandra A. Grisham, Chairperson, City Charter Commission, Vega v. City of Alamogordo, Civ. No. 86–0061–C, at 6–8 (D.C.N.M. 1987).

48. Election Results, supra note 45, at 45–46.

49. Vega v. City of Alamogordo, Civ. No 86–0051–C (D.C.N.M. Feb. 10, 1986).

50. Vega, Civ. No. 86–0061–C.

51. Id.

52. Stipulated Findings of Fact and Conclusions of Law, Vega v. City of Alamogordo, Civ. No. 86–0061–C, at 11 (D.C.N.M. Mar. 2, 1987) [hereinafter Findings].

53. The district was District 3, and the person elected was Sylvester Mattox. Election Returns, supra note 45, at 75.

54. Findings, supra note 52, at 12–13.

55. Id.

56. *Albuquerque Journal,* July 23, 1987, at 1D, col. 6; *El Paso Times* (N.M. ed.), July 22, 1987, at 1A, col. 5.

57. *Alamogordo Daily News*, July 22, 1987, at 8, col. 6.

58. An effort was made to invite all of the voters to participate in the exit survey. The questionnaire, in both English and Spanish, was available at each polling place the entire period during which the polls were open. Respondents were requested to fold their completed questionnaires and deposit them in a "ballot box." The authors would like to thank Mr. Isaiah Scott, guidance counselor at Alamogordo Senior High School, and the members of the Key Club at that institution for assisting with the exit poll. Data from exit polls have been accepted as evidence of voters' candidate choices in voting rights litigation. See, e.g., Romero v. City of Pomona, 665 F.Supp. 853, 858–60 (C.D. Cal. 1987). On exit polling generally, see Asher, *Polling and the Public: What Every Citizen Should Know,* 98–102 (1988); Levy, "The Methodology and Performance of Election Day Polls," 47 Pub. Opinion Q. 54 (1983).

59. If the reported votes are adjusted so that those casting two or three votes for a particular candidate are assumed to have "single-shot" voted for the candidate, Mr. Carroll places third and Ms. Moncada fourth in the total vote. On the single-shot voting strategy, see Engstrom & McDonald, "The Election of Blacks to Southern City Councils," supra note 2; Engstrom & McDonald, *At-Large Plus: The Impact of "Enhancing Factors" on Black Councilmanic Representation* (1989) (paper presented at the Annual Meeting of the International Society for Political Psychology, June 18–23, 1989, Tel Aviv, Israel).

60. If Ms. Moncada had received all of the votes cast by Hispanic voters, she could have been elected without any "crossover" votes from Anglos, given the dispersion in the Anglo vote across the candidates.

61. Voting Rights Act, supra note 5.

62. *Thornburg*, 478 U.S. at 50.

63. Id.

64. See supra notes 13–14.

65. *Thornburg*, 478 U.S. at 50.

66. Cumulative voting also has been the basis for the settlement of at-large election cases involving five local governments in Alabama, and "limited voting" (in which voters may cast only one vote for any candidate but have fewer total votes than there are positions to be filled) has been the basis for settlements involving 21 other local governments in that state. See supra note 14. In addition, cumulative voting has been adopted as part of the settlement of a lawsuit involving the system for electing the city council in Peoria, Illinois, see Banks v. City of Peoria, No. 87–2371 (C.D. Ill. 1987), and the Sisseton School District No. 54–5 in Sisseton, South Dakota, see Buckanaga v. Sisseton Sch. Dist. No. 54–5, Civ. No 84–1025 (C.D.S.D. 1988); and limited voting has been ordered as a remedy for dilution in McGhee v. Granville

County, No. 87–28–CIV–5 (E.D.N.C. Feb. 5, 1988), rev'd and remanded, 860 F.2d 110 (4th Cir. 1988).

67. This case law centers on White v. Regester, 412 U.S. 755 (1973); Zimmer v. McKeithen, 485 2d 1297 (5th Cir. 1973), aff'd on other grounds sub nom. East Carroll Parish School Board v. Marshall, 424 U.S. 636 (1976). These cases served as the basis for the evidentiary considerations that Congress identified as "typical factors" in a vote dilution case to be litigated under the amended Section 2. S. Rep. No. 417, 97th Cong., 2d Sess. 28–29 (1982).

Voting Patterns in a Tri-Ethnic Community

Charles S. Bullock III and
Susan A. MacManus

Many southwestern and western communities are tri-ethnic.[1] Of the 499 cities in the South and West with over 25,000 population, seven percent now have black and brown populations exceeding 10 percent; three percent have 15 percent or greater. The emergence of tri-ethnic communities has raised important questions about ethnic voting patterns: 1) how often do minority groups (black, brown) align more closely with each other than with whites; 2) how often does a minority group (black, brown) more closely align with whites than with the other significant minority group; 3) how often does a plurality/majority of each group (black, brown, white) support the same candidate; and 4) what are some plausible explanations for the ethnic voting patterns which have emerged.

This research report examines the level of intragroup and intergroup electoral conflict and cohesion in municipal elections in a tri-ethnic community, Austin, Texas, from 1975–1985. In 1980 the city was 71 percent white, 18 percent Hispanic, and 11 percent black. Between 1970 and 1980, Austin's Hispanic population grew 65 percent, its white population 44 percent, and its black population 41 percent.

A black has been on the Austin City Council since 1971 and there has been a Hispanic member since 1975. The six council members and the mayor run for designated slots. There is a majority vote requirement for municipal elections with runoffs held when no candidate for a position receives a majority.

Reprinted with permission from National Civic Review, *Vol. 79, No. 1, January/ February, 1990. Published by the National Civic League Press, Denver, Colorado.*

We do not contend that Austin is representative of ethnic political patterns for Texas, or the Southwest, although it may be. The Austin data may, however, stimulate additional research into this area which would reveal whether the Austin experience is typical of America's emerging tri-ethnic communities.

Theories of Ethnic Voting Patterns

Most studies of ethnic and racial voting patterns have been bi-ethnic[2] or bi-racial.[3] Relatively little empirical work has compared electoral patterns of multiple ethnic groups within the same community since the studies of Tom Bradley's 1969 and 1973 mayoral election campaigns in Los Angeles.[4] Those studies found that Mexican American voting patterns more closely resembled those of whites than of blacks. Mexican Americans were a less cohesive voting block than blacks, but more cohesive than whites.

The Los Angeles election studies reported that black turnout exceeded that of Hispanics and whites.[5] This finding parallels other studies contrasting the organizational participation rates of whites, blacks, and/or Hispanics.[6] In general, black participation rates equal or exceed those of whites and far exceed those of Hispanics. The participation differentials are "explained" by assimilation-, generational-, socioeconomic-, cultural-, legal-, and relative deprivation-based theories, among others.[7]

Unfortunately, most of these studies are based on socioeconomic and participatory data from the 1960s and early 1970s. They do not reflect the vast improvements in minority socioeconomic status (especially education) which occurred in the 1970s. Nor do they reflect the significant gains in minority registration, turnout, and electoral success which followed passage of and amendments to the Voting Rights Act.

Ironically, in the period following the 1975 amendments to the Voting Rights Act the tendency of the courts, the U.S. Justice Department, and scholars has been to treat the concerns of minorities (racial and language—blacks and browns) as one and the same. A partial explanation for this tendency may be that the strategies followed by Hispanic activists in the 1970s seemed to parallel those successfully used by black activists in the 1960s.[8] Similar treatment of the preferences of blacks and browns was also an integral part of Jesse Jackson's rainbow coalition.[9] Yet, the 1984 CBS-*New York Times* exit polls of voters in the Democratic presidential primaries found that 78 percent of the blacks supported Jackson, compared with 14 percent among Hispanics, which was similar to the white vote for Jackson, nine percent. Should we really expect electoral preferences of the two groups to be identical when other literature suggests that *policy* preferences are not?[10] Even when there is a tendency for blacks and Hispanics to share policy preferences, this agreement may be overridden by the social distance between the two minority groups.[11] A closer look

at the premises underlying the formation of various ethnic coalitions is important to our understanding of this apparent inconsistency.

Premises of Ethnic Coalition Theories

Black-brown coalitions. The assumption that minority groups will coalesce is derived from the premise that since both groups have been discriminated against by whites, they will favor the same candidates in their search
for political and economic influence. The minority-supported candidates tend
to be minority, Democrat, and/or liberal, white candidates.[12]

Leaders of both minority groups have urged their members to "work
together on issues of common interest, such as affirmative action, employment, job training, housing, and health care."[13] The inference is that these common policy preferences are strong enough to stimulate formation of minority
electoral coalitions, particularly when candidates run against whites. (Interestingly, there have been few examinations of what happens to the coalition
when black and brown candidates run against each other or in races where all
three ethnic groups have at least one candidate.)

Minority-white coalitions. The assumption that the common experience
of ethnic discrimination or of being disproportionately disadvantaged economically suffices to unite blacks and Hispanics is suspect. The history of
other ethnic groups suggests, instead, that those who share common disadvantages may view one another as *competitors.* In the Northeast, for example, the Irish and Italians often were political opponents. Moreover, ethnics
have often adopted the stereotypes of other groups that WASPs had of them.
Myrdal found that immigrants often became more hostile toward blacks than
the native born population was.[14] Thus, despite both groups' being disadvantaged vis-à-vis whites, "their marginal status has also led to competition
between them, accompanied by rancor and mistrust."[15]

Using data from a statewide Texas poll conducted in mid–1986, Dyer and
Vedlitz conclude that "perhaps the most significant findings bearing on the
coalition potential between blacks and Hispanics is the relatively low acceptance between blacks and Hispanics. Both groups are more accepting of Anglos than they are of each other.[16] Dyer and Vedlitz see social distance as
impeding joint black–Hispanic action that could emerge from a general agreement on a number of spending priorities. Dreyfuss sees greater difficulty in
unifying blacks and Hispanics: "The major obstacle to political alliance is the
mistrust that the two groups have of each other. Other problems include
differences on key political issues, competition for federal funds, and a sense
of unequal power. While blacks are accustomed to complaining about their
lack of influence, many Chicano leaders view with envy the gains that blacks
have made."[17] Conflict over power and the policy agenda also characterizes
the relationship between Cuban Americans and blacks in Miami.[18]

Each group's leaders periodically accuse the other of not being genuinely concerned with "minority issues," and of aligning with whites against them to get ahead faster.[19] Most of these conflicts occur over allocational decisions. As Herzog notes, "When the objective is to secure common material goals, there are very definite tensions that test a coalition. For example, when the goal is better job opportunity, the competition for scarce rewards produces severe conflict."[20] He also observes that black-brown coalitions become more tenuous as the possibility of electoral success for each group improves. Under those circumstances, each group is more inclined to build electoral coalitions with whites than each other.

Black-white coalitions. There are a number of alternatives regarding black-white coalitions reflecting the different community socioeconomic conditions. Holloway reports that in some bi-ethnic, rural, lower-income communities, a basic strategy has been to form a liberal coalition linking blacks with "underdog whites" (poorer, less-educated) and white liberals.[21] This perspective assumes that "the 'underdogs' in the community are potentially a majority and should be able to unite in pursuit of common economic interests."[22] Hahn, Klingman, and Pachon refer to this strategy as "redistributive politics" that "aim to improve the position of persons at the bottom of the socioeconomic hierarchy at the expense of those who have been the traditional beneficiaries of public as well as private programs."[23] In other communities, the more pragmatic coalition may be among blacks and white élite (business and financial leaders, wealthier conservative whites).[24]

There is some evidence that black-white coalitions are more common than Mexican American-white coalitions, especially on issues.[25] Greater political sophistication of blacks in understanding the policy-formation process is the major explanation for this finding.[26]

Mexican American-white coalitions. Other studies have asserted that Mexican American-white coalitions are more common.[27] Lopez argues that "the trend in Mexican American attitudes is away from an association with blacks and toward an alignment with Anglos" because whites are more accepting of Mexican Americans than they are of blacks.[28] According to Ambrecht and Pachon, Mexican Americans, to a greater extent than blacks, have been assimilated into white middle class communities and schools.[29]

There is some evidence of Mexican American-white coalitions. As noted earlier, in the Los Angeles mayoral elections of 1969 and 1973, white and Mexican American preferences more closely resembled each other than those of blacks.[30] But just as with black-white coalitions, Hispanics are concerned about whether to coalesce with poor and liberal whites or the white élite.[31]

Shifting alignments. Some studies have shown that racial groupings shift depending upon the nature of the policy area.[32] "On employment, government services, and educational issues (distributional issues), Hispanics and blacks are found to be competitive or conflictual, whereas on civil rights and law-enforcement issues (authoritative issues) they tend to be consensual.[33] Holloway notes two other conditions under which coalitions shift: 1) when local leaders experiment with alliances; and 2) when leaders do not reflect the opinions of their group members.[34] In other words, differences in intragroup cohesion may explain shifting intergroup coalitions. Whites and Hispanics are far less likely to be cohesive within their group than are blacks.[35]

Another stimulant to shifting coalitions may be performance of minority candidates once elected. Sonenshein has observed that Tom Bradley's performance won over the white Republican business community and reduced the gap between blacks and moderate whites.[36] Finally, changes in the relative size of ethnic groups within a community may alter the nature of their electoral coalitions. "Group size can affect the extent of voter mobilization, expectations of success, range of alternatives, extent of sources, and intensity of incentives."[37]

There is, then, reason to expect that voting alignments in tri-ethnic communities may be dynamic rather than stable. There are five possible voting patterns in communities having three ethnic groups: 1) blacks and Hispanics uniting in opposition to whites; 2) blacks and whites uniting against Mexican Americans; 3) Hispanics and whites uniting against blacks; 4) blacks, Hispanics and whites sharing a common preference; and 5) each group having a unique preference. We do not expect a minority versus white coalition to have been exclusive and persistent in Austin city elections over the past decade.

Research Design

Two measures of voting patterns will be examined here. One is the frequency with which possible pairs of groups agree on a candidate in opposition to the third group. This assessment determines the percentage point differences in support for the candidate who gets a majority or plurality of the vote. Table 1 presents the number of times that each of the three possible pairings displayed the least difference. To illustrate, if the winning candidate got 38 percent of the black vote, 45 percent of the Hispanic vote, and 65 percent of the white vote, this would be counted as a situation in which blacks and Hispanics united against whites. The difference in support among blacks and Hispanics is seven points, compared with a 20-point spread between whites and blacks.

A second measure considers the number of times that an individual was the most preferred candidate within each group. This second approach allows for the possibility that a candidate may be the winner with all three ethnic groups, or that each group has a different choice.

The analysis uses data from six Austin municipal elections held between 1975 and 1985. The unit of analysis is the contest for a position of mayor or

Table 1
Frequency with Which Pairs of Ethnic Groups
Were Most Alike in Supporting Winning or
Leading Candidates, 1975–1985

	Hispanics and blacks	Hispanics and whites	Blacks and whites
All Contests	24	12	14
Ethnicity of Winner or Leader			
Hispanic	7	1	0
black	1	5	1
white	16	6	13
Ethnicity of Minority Candidates*			
Hispanic	1	2	5
black	2	2	0

*When a minority candidate lost to another candidate of the same ethnicity, the losing minorities have been excluded.

council member. Estimates of the support for candidates among voters in the three ethnic groups were generated using ecological regression.[38]

Findings

Of the 50 contests for mayor and city council, the vote for the leading candidate was more similar among blacks and Hispanics in 24 instances. As Table 1 shows, each of the other two possible patterns occurred in almost 25 percent of the elections. Therefore, while the most common pattern was for blacks and Hispanics to be more similar to each other than to whites, this is not the only pattern.

Minority group similarity may not be typical of all elections, but it may have been more common when there was a minority candidate. Although minorities voted together and less like whites in just under half of the elections, minority unity may have dominated contests in which there was a black or Hispanic candidate.

Analyses of voting patterns for minority candidates in Table 1 present two kinds of data. The first reports patterns for contests won by minority candidates; the second deals with minority candidates who lost.[39] In seven of eight contests in which a Hispanic triumphed (i.e., was a majority or plurality leader), Hispanics and blacks tended to vote together. There is, however, a distinctly different pattern in the seven contests won by blacks. In only one of these did blacks and Hispanics coalesce. The more common pattern was for less difference between Hispanic and white voting than between Hispanic and black voting. Of 35 elections won by whites, Hispanics and blacks were more alike 16 times while blacks and whites were most alike 13 times.

Turning to unsuccessful Hispanic candidates, for only one of these did blacks and Hispanics unite, while for two, Hispanics and whites voted more alike. The most common pattern was for blacks and whites to vote alike and this occurred five times. There were four blacks who lost to white candidates. For the two earlier ones, Hispanics and whites voted alike. In 1985, however, the least difference was between black and Hispanic voting. Black-brown coalitions were much less frequent for unsuccessful than successful minority candidates, occurring for only a quarter of the losing minority candidates.

While minorities vote together more than either group does with whites, this pattern accounts for just under half the elections studied. Even when there is a minority candidate and black-brown unity might be most likely, the minority candidate is opposed by a coalition of whites and the group of which the minority candidate is not a member in 16 of 27 contests. Black-brown agreements are most likely when there is a successful Hispanic candidate. Blacks support successful Hispanic candidates but Hispanics do not reciprocate when there is a black candidate. Instead, Hispanics tend to vote more like Anglos and less like blacks when there is a black candidate. If this pattern exists in the California cities studied by Browning, Marshall, and Tabb, it could further explain the animosities discovered between the two minority groups in some cities.[40] Not only might blacks complain that it appears Hispanics are more often given things that blacks have had to work for—initial Hispanic council representation in California was more often via an appointment than was initial black representation—but Hispanic voters are less supportive of black candidates.

The second perspective on voting patterns looks at whether a candidate was the leading vote getter with more than one ethnic group (see Table 2). The pattern for most favored candidates is different from that for differences in vote shares. Most frequently (48 percent of the time), a single candidate was the leader among all three groups of voters! The second most common pattern (one-third of the time), was for minorities to back one candidate while whites preferred someone else. Only once did each group have a unique preference.

Focusing on the favored candidate reveals even less of a minority/white split in the case of minority candidates than existed when we looked at vote shares. Most black and Hispanic candidates who attracted at least plurality support from more than one ethnic group were the leading vote getters among all three ethnic groups. This was true in all but one election won by a black and in five of nine contests in which Hispanics showed strength.[41] No black

Table 2
Frequency with Which Ethnic Groups Cast a Majority or Plurality of Their Votes for the Same Candidate, 1975–1985

	Hispanic and black	Hispanic and white	Black and white	Hispanic, black and white	Each group supported a different candidate
All Contests	16.5*	3.5*	5	24	1†
Ethnicity of Candidates§					
Hispanic	4	0	0	5	0
black	1	0	0	6	0
white	11.5*	3.5*	5	13	0

*In one contest the Hispanic vote was divided evenly between the candidate most popular with blacks and the candidate most popular with whites.
†The bulk of the Hispanic vote was cast for a Hispanic; whites and blacks favored two different white candidates.
§Candidate attracted plurality/majority support from more than one ethnic group.

who was not elected was the leading vote getter among *any* ethnic group; there was one Hispanic who was the preferred candidate among both minority groups but was defeated by the white vote.

Summary

Electoral results from Austin, Texas demonstrate that while blacks and Hispanics often share candidate preferences, tri-ethnic politics are not universally "minorities versus whites." If the distribution of voting patterns were random, minorities would vote most alike in terms of share of the vote one-third of the time. The minority coalition is particularly likely when a Hispanic is elected, but is infrequent when a black wins or when minority candidates lose.

If we look at ethnic voting patterns from another perspective, minority cohesion appears less important. *The most frequent pattern is for all three groups to support the same candidate.* Successful minority candidates—even more often than successful whites—evoke a positive response from all three sets of voters most of the time, but especially when a black is elected. In no instance would a white candidate have been elected in place of a black even if we discount the minority vote. Minority votes are more important to the political success of Hispanic candidates. In two instances white votes kept Hispanic candidates from winning majorities in the first primary, and in one instance minorities elected a Hispanic in a runoff over white opposition. Minority votes are more significant for Hispanic than black candidates because blacks are more likely to support Hispanic candidates than Hispanic voters are to support black candidates.

While minorities tend to unite behind winning Hispanic candidates, this pattern did not carry over to black candidates or even to unsuccessful Hispanics. And while black and brown support of successful Hispanics was more alike than either group was with whites, five of the nine successful Hispanics polled at least a plurality from all three ethnic groups. There is, then, no consistent evidence that minorities vote against whites, even when a minority candidate opposes a white.[42]

Since blacks and browns together constitute less than one-third of Austin's population, the willingness of whites to support some minority candidates is critical to the ethnic diversity of the city council. Hispanic and black members on the council ensure that there is descriptive representation of these groups, but, taken alone, do not guarantee substantive representation of minority interests.[43] Enactment of policies desired by blacks and/or Hispanics requires the votes of some white members. The support given by one or both minority groups to most white municipal officials suggests that policy concerns of minorities are advanced by more than just the black or Hispanic council members. The variety of voting patterns that have elected Austin's mayor and council members alert candidates to the possibility of alternative groupings that could produce electoral success. The interaction of supporting groups and enthusiasm within each group means that serious candidates—both incumbents and challengers—dare not take any of the three ethnic groups lightly.

Conclusion: Significance for Other Communities

Many American cities (and suburban communities) are becoming more ethnically diverse. The termination of immigration quotas in 1965, and a surge in the number of immigrants and political refugees from Latin America, Asia, and Africa has drastically changed the face of many U.S. communities. For example, in the 1950s, Europeans constituted 59 percent of all immigrants; by the 1970s this figure had dropped to 18 percent. At the same time, Hispanics rose from 22 percent to 41 percent of all legal immigrants, and Asians from 6 percent to 36 percent.[44] As new immigrants are assimilated into the political system, the political dynamics of the host community change. The importance of building coalitions and consensus can not be overstated. Studies such as this one of Austin, of who aligns with whom, when, and why can prove invaluable to community leaders responsible for building *effective* rainbow coalitions.

Notes

1. Much has been made of the differences in the terms "race" and "ethnicity." While some scholars argue that the terms are quite different, (Lipset, 1987) others have regarded the two terms as interchangeable. As Meister notes (1981, p. 86), "Most sociologists use 'ethnic' to include nationality, ethno-religious, and racial groups." Moreover, Horowitz (1985, p. 41) concludes that "comparison is facilitated by an inclusive conception of ethnicity that embraces differences identified by color, language, religion, or some other attribute of common origin."

2. See B.C.S. Ambrecht and H.P. Pachon, "Ethnic Mobilization in a Mexican American County: An Exploratory Study of East Los Angeles, 1965–1972," *Western Political Quarterly,* September, 1974, pp. 500–519; R. de la Garza, "Voting Patterns in Bi-Cultural El Paso: A Contextual Analysis of Mexican American Voting Behavior," in F. Garcia, ed., *La Causa Politica* (Notre Dame: University of Notre Dame Press, 1974), pp. 250–265; J.A. Garica, "Chicano Voting Patterns in School Board Elections: Bloc Voting and Internal Lines of Support for Chicano Candidates," *Atisbos: Journal of Chicano Research,* Winter 1976–77, pp. 1–13; and J.A. Garcia, "An Analysis of Chicano and Anglo Electoral Patterns in School Board Elections," *Ethnicity,* June 1979, pp. 168–183.

3. See H. Holloway, "Negro Political Strategy: Coalition or Independent Power Politics?" *Social Science Quarterly,* December 1969, pp. 534–547; B. Patterson, "Political Action of Negros in Los Angeles: A Study in the Attainment of Councilmanic Representation," *Phylon,* Summer 1969, pp. 170–183; C. Davidson, *Biracial Politics: Conflict and Coalition in the Metropolitan South* (Baton Rouge: The University of Louisiana Press, 1972); V. Jefferies and H.A. Ransford, "Ideology, Social Structure, and the Yorty-Bradley Mayoralty Election," *Social Problems,* Winter 1972, pp. 358–372; T.F. Pettigrew, "When a Black Runs for Mayor," in Harlan Hahn, ed., *People and Politics in Urban Society* (Beverly Hills: Sage Productions, 1972), pp. 95–117; R. Murray and A. Vedlitz, "Race, Socioeconomic Status and Voter Participation in Large Southern Cities," *Journal of Politics,* Vol. 39, 1977, pp. 1,064–1,072; R. Murray and A. Vedlitz, "Racial Voting Patterns in the South: An Analysis of Major Elections from 1960 to 1975 in Five Cities," *Annals,* September 1978, pp. 29–39; P. Kleppner, *Chicago Divided: The Making of a Black Mayor* (DeKalb: Northern Illinois University Press, 1985); and R.J. Sonenshein, "Bradley's People: Biracial Coalition Politics in Los Angeles" (presented at the 1985 annual meeting of the American Political Science Association).

4. See H. Hahn and T. Almy, "Ethnic Politics and Racial Issues: Voting in Los Angeles," *Western Political Quarterly,* December 1971, pp. 719–730; Ambrecht and Pachon, 1974; H. Hahn, D. Klingman and H. Pachon, "Cleavages, Coalitions and the Black Candidate: The Los Angeles Mayoralty Elections of 1969 and 1973," *Western Political Quarterly,* December 1976, pp. 507–520: R.M. Halley, A.C. Acock and T. Green, "Ethnicity and Social Class: Voting in the 1973 Los Angeles Municipal Elections," *Western Political Quarterly,* December 1976, pp. 521–530; and Sonenshein, 1985.

5. Halley, Acock, and Greene, 1976.

6. See J.A. Williams, Jr., N. Babchuk and D.R. Johnson, "Voluntary Associations and Minority Status: A Comparative Analysis of Anglo, Black, and Mexican Americans," *American Sociological Review,* Vol. 38, 1973, pp. 637–646; G. Antunes and C.M. Gaitz, "Ethnicity and Participation: A Study of Mexican Americans, Blacks and Whites," *American Journal of Sociology,* Vol. 80, 1975, pp. 1,192–1,211: S. Welch, J. Comer and M. Steinman, "Ethnic Differences in Social and Political Participation:

A Comparison of Some Anglo and Mexican Americans," *Pacific Sociological Review,* July 1975, pp. 361–382; S.M. Cohen and R.E. Kapsis, "Participation of Blacks, Puerto Ricans, and Whites in Voluntary Associations: A Test of Current Theories," *Social Forces,* June 1978, pp. 1,053–1,069; R.D. Shingles, "Black Consciousness and Political Participation: The Missing Link," *American Political Science Review,* Vol. 75, 1981, pp. 76–91; S.A. MacManus and C.A. Cassel, "Mexican Americans in City Politics: Participation, Representation, and Policy Preferences," *The Urban Interest,* Spring 1982, pp. 57–69; and T.M. Guterbock and B. London, "Race, Political Orientations, and Participation: An Empirical Test of Four Competing Theories," *American Sociological Review,* Vol. 43, 1983, pp. 439–453.

7. For good reviews of these theories, see Hahn and Almy, 1971; D.E. Nelson, "Ethnicity and Socioeconomic Status as Sources of Participation: The Case of Ethnic Political Culture," *American Political Science Review,* December 1979, pp. 1,024–1,038; and Guterbock and London, 1983.

8. R.P. Browning, D.R. Marshall and D.H. Tabb, *Protest Is Not Enough: Struggle of Blacks and Hispanics for Equality in Urban Politics* (Berkeley: University of California Press, 1984).

9. See T.E. Cavanagh, *The Impact of the Black Electorate* (Washington, D.C.: Joint Center for Political Studies, 1984); T.E. Cavanagh and L. Foster, *Jesse Jackson's Campaign: The Primaries and the Caucuses* (Washington, D.C.: Joint Center for Political Studies, 1984); R. Smothers, "Alabama Black Leaders Are Urging Pragmatism in Supporting Mondale," *New York Times,* March 12, 1984, p. B-9; and C.A. Broh, *A Horse of a Different Color* (Washington, D.C.: Joint Center for Political Studies, 1985).

10. See J. Florez, "Chicanos and Coalitions as a Force for Social Change," in Margaret M. Mangold, ed., *La Causa Chicana: Change* (New York: Family Service Association, 1972), pp. 78–86; C. Davidson and C.M. Gaitz, "Ethnic Attitudes as a Basis for Minority Cooperation in a Southwestern Metropolis," *Social Science Quarterly,* March 1973, pp. 738–748; S.J. Herzog, "Political Coalitions Among Ethnic Groups in the Southwest," in Rudolph O. Garcia, ed., *Chicanos and Native Americans: The Territorial Minorities* (Englewood Cliffs, N.J.: Prentice Hall, 1973), pp. 131–138; N. Lovrich, "Differing Priorities in the Urban Electorate: Service Preferences among Anglo, Black and Mexican American Voters," *Social Science Quarterly,* December 1974, pp. 704–717; J. Dreyfuss, "Blacks and Hispanics: Coalition or Confrontation?" *Black Enterprise,* July 1979, pp. 21–23; C.P. Henry, "Black-Chicano Coalitions: Possibilities and Problems," *Western Journal of Black Studies,* Winter 1980, pp. 222–232; MacManus and Cassel, 1982; S.A. MacManus, "Shifting to State Block Grants: The Priorities of Urban Minorities," *Journal of Urban Affairs,* Spring 1985, pp. 75–92.

11. J.A. Dyer and A. Vedlitz, "The Potential of Minority Coalition Building" (presented at the 1986 annual meeting of the Southeastern Political Science Association).

12. Hahn and Almy, 1971; Hahn, Klingman and Pachon, 1976; Halley, Acock, and Greene, 1976; Sonenshein, 1985.

13. Dreyfuss, 1979, p. 21. See also Lovrich, 1973; Herzog, 1973; Henry, 1980; Dyer and Vedlitz, 1986.

14. G. Myrdal, R. Sterner and A. Rose, *An American Dilemma* (New York: Harper, 1944), p. 603.

15. Davidson and Gaitz, 1973, p. 738.

16. Dyer and Vedlitz, 1986, p. 19.

17. Dreyfuss, 1972, p. 21.

18. C.L. Warren, J.F. Stack and J.G. Corbett, "Minority Mobilization in an International City: Rivalry and Conflict in Miami," *PS*, Summer 1986, pp. 626–634.

19. Florez, 1972; Ambrecht and Pachon, 1974; Dreyfuss, 1979; MacManus and Cassel, 1982; MacManus, 1985; J. Mollenkopf, "New York: The Great Anomaly," *PS*, Summer 1986, pp. 591–597.

20. Herzog, 1973, p. 133.

21. Halley, Acock and Greene, 1976.

22. Holloway, 1969, p. 537.

23. Hahn, Klingman and Pachon, 1976, p. 511.

24. Holloway, 1969; Sonenshein, 1985.

25. MacManus, 1985.

26. Dreyfuss, 1979.

27. Davidson and Gaitz, 1973.

28. M.M. Lopez, "Patterns of Interethnic Residential Segregation in the Urban Southwest," *Social Science Quarterly*, March 1981, p. 59.

29. Ambrecht and Pachon, 1974, p. 503.

30. Hahn and Almy, 1971; Hahn, Klingman and Pachon, 1976; Sonenshein, 1985.

31. See Henry, 1980 and Florez, 1973.

32. Henry, 1980; MacManus and Cassel, 1982.

33. MacManus, 1985, p. 85.

34. Holloway, 1969, p. 535.

35. See Hahn and Almy, 1971; Ambrecht and Pachon, 1974; Hahn, Klingman and Pachon, 1976; Halley, Acock and Greene, 1976.

36. Sonenshein, 1985.

37. Garcia, 1979, p. 181.

38. For discussions of ecological regression, see L. Goodman, "Some Alternatives to Ecological Correlation," *American Journal of Sociology*, Vol. 64, 1959, pp. 610–625; E.T. Jones, "Ecological Inference and Electoral Analysis," *Journal of Interdisciplinary History*, Vol. 2, 1972, pp. 249–269; J.W. Loewen, *Social Science in the Courtroom* (Lexington, Mass.: Lexington Books, 1982); and C.S. Bullock III and S.A. MacManus, "Measuring Racial Bloc Voting is Difficult for Small Jurisdictions," *National Civic Review*, 73:4, July–August, 1984.

39. Losing minority candidacies are limited to contests in which a minority was defeated by a white. Instances in which a minority lost to another minority are excluded.

40. Browning, Marshall and Tabb, 1984.

41. In the one instance in which blacks and Hispanics preferred one candidate while another candidate got the bulk of the white votes, the candidate preferred by most whites was also black. Therefore, in no instance have most whites opted for a white over a black candidate.

42. The attitudes uncovered by Dyer and Vedlitz prompt the conclusion that there exists "a complicated picture of coalition potential among Texas's various ethnic groups. There are elements of commonality between all or parts of the various groups which could serve as the basis for joint political activities, but there are also elements of division between these groups or group segments which would mitigate cooperation" (See Dyer and Vedlitz, 1986, p. 19). These statewide findings may be appropriate for Austin and, if so, would help account for the variety of voting patterns observed in municipal elections.

43. Browning, Marshall and Tabb, 1984.

44. B.E. Cain and D.R. Kiewiet, "California's Coming Minority Majority," *Public Opinion*, February–March, 1986, pp. 50–52.

The Election of Hispanics in City Government

Rodney Hero

While the election of ethnic and racial minorities to positions in city government has received considerable attention, there have been few analyses of the election of Hispanics (Taebel 1978; Browning, Marshall, and Tabb 1984; Henry and Munoz 1985; de la Garza 1974, 1977). The purpose of this chapter is to examine the election of Federico Peña, a Mexican-American, as mayor of Denver. This is important for several reasons. Available evidence indicates that the political orientation and achievements of Hispanics have been different from those of other groups, including blacks (Browning, Marshall, and Tabb 1984; Lovrich and Marenin 1976). Secondly, the Denver mayor holds a visible and powerful position. Denver has a strong mayor system. The formal powers of the Denver mayor appear stronger than those in most other cities, such as San Antonio, where Hispanic mayors have been elected and are probably greater than in most cities where minority mayors have been elected. Thus, the Denver mayor is in a favorable position to influence city policy. Finally, Denver has a relatively small Hispanic population (18–20 percent) and its overall minority population (30–35 percent Hispanic and black) is somewhat smaller than those of most other large cities with minority mayors.

How a Hispanic was elected to such a powerful position in a city with such a small minority population warrants attention. The analysis seeks to address this question as follows. First, a discussion of relevant scholarly literature is presented to provide a theoretical grounding for the subsequent analysis. The Peña campaign strategy is then discussed, followed by a consideration of the major themes of the Peña campaign and a general description of the campaign. This portion of the discussion draws upon a personal

Reprinted with permission from Western Political Quarterly, *Vol. 40, No. 1, March, 1987. Published by the University of Utah, Salt Lake City, Utah.*

interview with one of the major Peña campaign strategists, Peña campaign materials, and a close reading of the Denver newspaper with the largest circulation, the Denver *Post*, between January and July, 1983. An analysis draws upon precinct-level voting data and demographic and related data purchased from a public agency and a private vendor. Finally, the analysis will provide a baseline from which to compare other elections involving Hispanics to consider such matters as whether such campaigns raise unique issues, whether certain types of issues receive greater or lesser attention, and to compare electoral coalitions.

Theoretical Discussion

Research suggests that the electoral response to minority candidates is significantly influenced by such factors as the nature of the constituency in which they are running, the strategies that they pursue, and the particular circumstances of an election (Hahn, Klingman, and Pachon 1976). Scholars have identified several strategies that minority mayoral candidates have employed given different constituency contexts. Holloway (1968) describes three types of coalitions between minority (black) and white voters: the "conservative coalition," the "independent power politics" approach, and the "liberal coalition." The conservative coalition is a linkage between the minority community and powerful white business and financial interests. The independent power approach occurs when white votes are either unnecessary to secure a majority or seemingly impossible to obtain. The liberal coalition seeks to unite ethnic-racial minorities with low-income whites, labor unions, and white or Anglo liberals from the business and professional world.

A recent study found that the major factor leading to the election of blacks and Hispanics (primarily Mexican-Americans) in a group of northern California cities with small minority populations was the emergence of liberal coalitions (Browning, Marshall, and Tabb 1984). Such liberal coalitions were generally made up of ethnic-racial minorities, the poor, white liberals, particularly Democrats, and labor unions. De la Garza (1974), however, found that despite the "bi-cultural" image projected in El Paso, Texas, Anglos were reluctant to vote for Mexican-American candidates in state and local elections, particularly when the Mexican-American candidate made "ethnic" appeals (cf. Hahn, Klingman, and Pachon 1976; Vigil 1978).

Bullock and Campbell (1984) found considerable evidence of racial, as distinct from racist, voting in Atlanta municipal elections. That is, their evidence indicates that whites as well as blacks are likely to vote for persons of their own race in the absence of compelling reasons to do otherwise. Candidates' issue positions may be an important factor leading citizens to vote for candidates of another racial or ethnic background.

Previous research suggests, then, that when minority candidates run for office in a city where the minority population does not comprise a majority or near-majority of the electorate, they most frequently seek to develop a "liberal coalition," i.e., they tend to make broad-based and issue-oriented appeals and do not overly emphasize "ethnic" concerns which might entail redistributive policies (Hahn, Klingman and Pachon 1976; de la Garza 1974). Evidence also indicates that in the absence of compelling reasons, such as strong issue agreement, candidate image or personality and the like, voters will generally support candidates of their own racial-ethnic background. The implications of the foregoing will be considered relative to the Peña campaign.

The Peña Campaign

Strategies

The Peña election strategy had several components, which were developed after a careful analysis of mayoral elections in the city dating back to the mid–1970s. The Peña camp perceived that recent mayoral races in Denver had had lackluster campaigns whose candidates and policies failed sufficiently to excite many voters either to turn out at all or to vote for an alternative to the incumbent mayor. Data from state and national elections suggested that many of the white voters who did not usually turn out for city elections were moderate to liberal (Rocky Mountain *News*, January 10, 1983: B6; personal interview). The Peña campaign therefore sought to generate an exciting, dynamic contest, one which would increase turnout from the common 50 to 55 percent rage to 70 percent or more. This higher turnout, it was believed, would benefit Peña and upset the slim margins by which the incumbent had won in the past.

Another part of the Peña election strategy was to undertake a drive to register Hispanics and the poor, who had had the city's lowest registration rates (cf. Henry and Munoz 1985: 19, 22). Peña had previously worked for the Mexican-American Legal Defense and Education Fund and the Chicano Education Project. And, as a member of the state House of Representatives, Peña had strongly and visibly supported efforts to provide more equitable funding for education, a particular concern for Mexican-Americans and blacks. Given this background of support for minority concerns, the belief was that these constituencies were naturally Peña's (personal interview). Also, it was perceived that as a result of his state legislative activities and voting record Peña had built strong ties with labor, neighborhood organizations, environmentalists, the handicapped, young professionals and the elderly. Peña's voting record as a state legislator had been given high marks by labor, environmental, women's, and elderly groups.

Campaign Themes

The Peña campaign did not emphasize his ethnic heritage (see e.g., Denver *Post*, April 26, 1963: B7; June 12, 1983). However, his obviously ethnic name and previous record as a proponent of minority concerns were important. The major campaign themes focused on issues and leadership. The emphasis on issues served several purposes. First, it helped put Peña's views on record and attract news coverage which, with relatively scarce financial resources, was deemed essential. It also helped to establish an image of Peña as a forward-looking, bold leader and diminish his image as a "one-issue," namely minority-oriented, candidate (Denver *Post,* April 26, 1983 and *passim*; cf. Hahn, Pachon, and Klingman 1976). Some campaign material may help give a sense of this issue appeal. One piece of campaign material indicated the following concerns and goals for Peña's "first 100 days" in office, should he be elected:

1. "Denver is unprepared for the future. We have not planned or prepared adequately for the city's physical, economic, or social development." Peña claimed that he would: consolidate city agencies responsible for planning and development; restore planning and staff resources; review current zoning citywide; put forth an agenda for developing the city's major undeveloped parcels of land; evaluate Denver's economic base and future revenue sources through a blue ribbon panel.

2. "Denver's government lacks accountability and sound management." Peña claimed that he would: recruit qualified replacements for all cabinet positions; review all existing city leases and contracts; begin management and efficiency studies of each department; institute an open, performance-based budget process; conduct town meetings throughout the city.

3. "Denver must pursue cooperative relationships with suburban jurisdictions and the state." Peña specified a number of intergovernmental efforts he would undertake to address several intergovernmental issues facing the city, including air pollution.

Along with these and other concerns, Peña issued a number of detailed position papers dealing with various issues including airport expansion, neighborhood preservation, economic development and job creation, bringing a major league baseball team to the city, and the city's financial future.

It appears, then, that the campaign's strategy and themes were geared toward building an aggregate of electoral support or a "chowder of constituencies" (Denver *Post,* March 6, 1983: B1) most similar to what has previously been described as a "liberal coalition." It is also clear that these themes had a nondivisive, "distributive," or "developmental" politics flavor to them.

Particular Circumstances and the Campaign

Denver mayoral elections are held in odd-numbered years and thus separately from national and state elections. The elections are nonpartisan, although all the major candidates in 1983 were Democrats. The 1983 elections required a runoff because no candidate received a majority in the first general election. The candidates in the 1983 first election were the incumbent three-term mayor, the district attorney, who had previously run for mayor, two members of Governor Richard Lamm's cabinet, one of whom was black, and two other candidates, along with Federico Peña, the former two-term member of the state House of Representatives. Peña had served as the Democratic party leader during his second term.

Along with some of the issues noted above and several others, the campaign often focused on the incumbent administration's (alleged) lack of energy and leadership and its mismanagement, cronyism and the like. These allegations made the incumbent quite vulnerable and, along with related factors, made Denver "ripe for a change" (Henry and Munoz 1985: 20). In the course of the campaign Peña received a number of endorsements, most prominently from labor groups, including the American Federation of State, County, and Municipal Employees, the Denver Area Labor Federation and the local chapter of the International Brotherhood of Electrical Workers.

Other notable endorsements were an early one from a "respected Republican developer" who had "strong ties to the downtown business community" (Denver *Post*, March 3, 1983: B1) and from the Sierra Club (Denver *Post*, April 21, 1983: B4). Of the city's two major newspapers, the Denver *Post* and the Rocky Mountain *News*, the former endorsed the incumbent district attorney and the latter endorsed Peña but neither endorsed the incumbent mayor. Peña was also aided by the Southwest Voter Education Project's substantial efforts to register Mexican-American voters.

Peña surprised most observers by not only making the runoff but by leading the field in the first election. Peña won 36.4 percent of the vote; the district attorney received 30.8 percent to join Peña in the runoff election. The incumbent was third, receiving only 19.1 percent of the vote and thus not making the runoff. The black candidate, who was the last to enter the race, received 7.1 percent of the vote and none of the other candidates received more than 5 percent of the vote. Peña's success was attributed to several factors: his early entrance into the race and his relentless campaigning; a very well-organized campaign, which had large numbers of volunteers; new registrants and high turnout (see Table 1); and the highly effective use of relatively limited money in his media campaign (Denver *Post*, May 18, 1983: A10–A12).

Few major issues were introduced in the runoff election. Peña's runoff opponent raised an argument that had been made earlier in the campaign that Peña had little if any administrative experience. Peña responded that state

Table 1
Registration and Turnout in
Denver Mayoral Elections, 1975–1983

	Registration	Turnout	% Turnout
1975 May	227,478	121,478	53.4
1975 June	227,447	116,381	51.2
1979 May	203,016	108,142	53.3
1983 May	211,235	134,189	63.5
1983 June	217,313	155,895	71.7

legislative leadership had provided some experience. More significantly, however, Peña argued that his opponent had an overly managerial or technocratic perspective of the mayor's role. Peña contended that a mayor must be more than a manager; that person also must be "a leader, a policy maker, an advocate, a catalyst, an innovator, a promoter and a mediator." Peña's opponent also argued that as a state legislator Peña's voting record indicated that he was "soft on crime," a charge which Peña characterized as a "gross misrepresentation" of his (Peña's) voting record (Denver *Post,* May 25, 1983: A1).

Several other issues raised in the runoff can be noted. Peña's runoff opponent once suggested that Peña's "backers were mostly on the (political) left" (Denver *Post,* May 18, 1983: A15), and at other times called Peña a "liberal." Peña responded that his support was broad-based. Peña also contended that there were not strong philosophical differences between him and his opponent and that classifying "by philosophy" in a nonpartisan election was "unfortunate" and "inappropriate." Peña added that whether or not streets get paved, how airport expansion is done and how air pollution is reduced are not liberal or conservative issues (Denver *Post,* May 18, 1983: A15). Another point of contention concerned collective bargaining for city employees; Peña supported it, his opponent did not (Denver *Post,* June 14, 1983: B1).

Finally, Peña criticized his opponent for running a negative campaign. Among the points Peña raised in this regard were his opponent's misrepresentation of his (Peña's) voting record as a state legislator and his opponent's suggestion that if Peña were elected it might have effects on Denver similar to those which the election of Dennis Kucinich had had in Cleveland (Denver *Post,* June 3, 1983: A1). Moreover, Peña aides expressed annoyance that pollsters for his opponent had questioned citizens about whether they were concerned that Peña is Hispanic, about the possibility of homosexuals being appointed to city administrative positions, and other questions which his opponent later said were "inappropriate" (Denver *Post,* May 28, 1983: B1). Peña argued that, in contrast, his own campaign had been "positive and upbeat."

In the runoff, Peña received the endorsement of most of the candidates who had been defeated in the first election, including the black candidate. The defeated black candidate cited Peña's sensitivity to "affordable housing, pub-lic safety and helping the elderly" as reasons for his endorsement (Denver *Post*, May 21, 1983: A1). The defeated incumbent, who Peña had visited on election night shortly after the results of the first election were known, did not endorse either candidate. However, the defeated incumbent's brother, himself a former governor of the state, endorsed Peña. Many observers took this to be an implicit endorsement by the defeated incumbent. Another important devel-opment during the runoff campaign was a registration drive, which was pro-moted by Peña supporters. During the three-day period between the first and runoff elections that registration was allowed, over 6,200 persons registered (Denver *Post*, May 20, 1983: A1 and May 25, 1983: A12). Finally, Peña received a $10 thousand contribution from a highly prominent oil billionaire (Denver *Post*, May 29, 1983: B4). This seemed significant for reasons other than the obvious financial ones. This contributor had supported the defeated incum-bent mayor in past elections and his visibility and prominence in the business community probably enhanced Peña's status among supporters of the defeated incumbent and with business groups.

Peña won the runoff election by a narrow 51.4 to 48.6 percent margin. The election was notable in two respects: the election of the city's first Mex-ican-American mayor and a record turnout.

Analysis of Election Results

The success of Peña's campaign strategy, outlined above, is assessed by using two sources of data. First, the precinct-level election results were obtained from the City and County of Denver Election Commission.[1] Second, data on precinct-level demographic characteristics, party registration, and other information were purchased from a private vendor, Voter Contact Services. Because of possible limitations in the data[2] and the well-known problem of making inferences about individual behavior from aggregate-level data, in this case precincts, certain of the data presented below should be interpreted cau-tiously.

Evidence concerning the Peña strategy to increase registration and turnout is presented in Tables 1 and 2.

Table 1 indicates that the 1983 elections had considerably higher levels of registration than did the 1979 election. While the number of registered vot-ers for the 1975 election exceeded that of the 1983 election, that may partly be because Denver had a larger population in 1975; Denver's population declined over 4 percent during the 1970s. The turnout rate among registered voters for the first election in 1983 was a full 10 percentage points above that for any of the 1975 and 1979 elections. The runoff election turnout in 1983 was a record for Denver city elections.

Table 2
Relationships (R) Between Registration
and Turnout and Vote for Peña

Registration and Turnout Variables	% for Peña First Election	% for Peña Runoff
Registration between March* and May (first election)	.252	.362
% Registration between First and Runoff Election	.706	.595
% Registration between March* and June (runoff election)	.368	.452
% Turnout—First election	-.054	-.119
% Turnout—Runoff	-.049	-.185
Average Turnout in 1981 and 1979 State Primary Elections†	-.297	-.311

*March 1983, two months prior to the first election, was taken as a "baseline" period with which to compare subsequent registration.
†These elections are examined to consider how turnout in previous elections compared with that in the 1983 city elections.
Note: The analyses presented in this and subsequent tables are all based upon precinct-level data for all the variables.

Table 2 more specifically attempts to assess the extent to which (precinct-level) registration and turnout are correlated with the (precinct-level) vote for Peña. The data concerning registration indicate that, whatever period is considered, Peña benefited from new registration. The strongest relationships are those of registration between the first and runoff election and the vote for Peña. And the increase in registration during the three-day period between the first and runoff elections were strongly positively related (.706) to the vote for Peña in the first election; i.e., registration between the elections was generally greatest where Peña had done best in the first election. Moreover, the simple correlations between percent Spanish and new registration for the several time periods noted in Table 2 are .214, .739, and .361. These data on registration would suggest, then, that increased registration was quite important to Peña's ultimate victory (cf. Henry and Munoz 1985: 26).

The data in Table 2 also show negative, albeit weak, relationships between turnout and the vote for Peña. These findings must be considered in the context of the considerable new registration and the overall higher levels of turnout. That is, while high levels of turnout at the precinct-level are not positively related to the vote for Peña, it should be remembered that the precincts that had historically turned out at the highest levels were relatively affluent and conservative areas, areas presumably not supportive of minority candidates. Thus, if these affluent areas increased their turnout, somewhat, and the minority areas increased their turnout considerably—remembering that registration in these minority and poorer areas had also increased considerably—a negative relationship between turnout and vote for Peña is less surprising, particularly when those negative relationships are weak. And data support this speculation. The simple correlations between percent new registration from the first to the runoff election with percent nonminority is -.540 (Henry and Munoz 1985: 22). It is also important to note that the (positive) relationships between registration and vote for Peña are somewhat stronger than those (negative relationships) between turnout and vote for Peña.

The simple correlations between various demographic characteristics and other variables and the vote for Peña, shown in Table 3, provide evidence of a "liberal coalition." The correlation between percent Spanish and vote for Peña is rather strong for both elections. The relationship between the vote for Peña and percent black is rather strong and positive for the runoff election, although it is weakly negative for the first election. This negative relationship is almost certainly the result of the black candidate's presence and good showing among black voters. While the relationships between Peña's vote in the runoff and percent Spanish and black are strong, they may not be as strong as one might expect. However, Henry and Munoz, using aggregate data, claim that 96 percent of Hispanics and 86 percent of blacks who actually voted in the runoff supported Peña. The reason that these aggregate numbers do not translate into stronger correlations seems to be related to differences between groups in levels of registration and turnout. Henry and Munoz's data (26, 22) indicate that only about 42 percent of Latinos, as compared to 65 percent of blacks and 68 percent of whites, were registered for the runoff election. Thus, while Hispanic registration had increased substantially over previous city elections, it still lagged considerably behind that of other groups (cf. Lovrich and Marenin 1976). Similarly, while turnout among Hispanics increased over past elections, data suggest that Hispanics (and blacks) still turned out at much lower levels than did whites. As a result of lower registration and turnout, then, the strength of the relationship between percent Spanish and black and the vote for Peña is lessened.

The simple correlation between vote for Peña and percent nonminority is negative for both elections and is particularly strong in the runoff election. However, Henry and Munoz's aggregate analysis found that Peña received about 42 percent of the white vote in the runoff. In this instance, the especially high registration and turnout among whites generally may exaggerate the strength of the negative relationships. These and subsequent data indicate considerable "racial" voting. Despite the general lack of explicit emphasis in his campaign on ethnic concerns, Peña's name and record, along with several endorsements, brought him strong minority group support. There is also considerable evidence of racial voting among nonminorities which, as will be noted momentarily, was modified by several factors.

Table 3
Simple Correlation (R) of Vote
for Peña with Independent Variables

Variables (Precinct Level)	% for Peña First Election	% for Peña Runoff
% Spanish (18+ yrs. old)	.654	.519
% Black (18+ yrs. old)	-.199	.537
% Nonminority (18+ yrs. old)	-.359	-.776
Median Income	-.178	-.133
Median Value of Housing	-.006	.004
% Unemployed	.456	.586
% w/Some College	-.327	-.468
% Democratic Registration	.363	.743

The negative relationship with "percent with some college" and the rather strong relationship with "percent unemployed" provides further evidence that Peña fared relatively well among the less educated and lower status economic groups. While Denver elections are nonpartisan and all the major candidates in both elections were Democrats, it is clear that Peña did much better in Democratic areas of the city than the Republican ones (cf. Browning, Marshall, and Tabb 1984). This pattern, particularly notable in the runoff election, is important because Democrats comprise about 15 percent more of Denver's registered voters than do Republicans.

Some further, although tentative, evidence of the liberal coalition is the weak relationships between two measures of income, median income and median value of housing, and the vote for Peña. In previous elections, analyses by Peña campaign strategists suggested, the affluent had voted for relatively conservative candidates, most often the defeated incumbent mayor. That the relationship of these measures of income were not strongly related to the Peña vote would seem to suggest some success in gaining the support of professionals and the like. The findings in Table 3 are generally consistent with those of Browning, Marshall and Tabb. (The possible influence of the labor element of the liberal coalition could not be examined for lack of appropriate measures.)

Further multivariate analysis, such as regression analysis, might be desirable. However, substantial intercorrelation among several of the independent variables makes the utility of such an analysis questionable. Instead, several partial correlation analyses were undertaken; these are shown in Table 4 (cf. Hahn, Klingman, and Pachon 1976).

Controlling for median income and value of housing has rather little impact on the already weak simple relationship between vote for Peña and ethnic background. However, when education (percent with some college), percent unemployed, and party affiliation are controlled, the simple relationships

Table 4
Partial Correlations Analyses of Vote for
Peña Runoff with Independent Variables

A. Percent for Peña—Runoff with Ethnic-Racial Background Controlling
for Socioeconomic Variables and Party Affiliation

Controlling for	Ethnic-Racial Background		
	% Spanish	% Black	% Nonminority
(None)	.519	.537	-.776
Median Income	.502	.551	-.775
Median Value of Housing	.534	.541	-.794
% w/Some College	.336	.498	-.714
% Unemployed	.237	.497	-.644
% Democratic Registration	.182	.213	-.432

B. Percent for Peña—Runoff with Socioeconomic Variables
and Party Affiliation Controlling for Ethnic-Racial Background

Socioeconomic and Party Variables	Controlling for			
	(None)	% Spanish	% Black	% Nonminority
Median Income	-.133	-.028	-.196	-.023
Median Value of Housing	.004	.150	.001	.225
% w/Some College	-.468	-.209	-.403	.090
% Unemployed	.586	.404	.557	.163
% Democratic Registration	.743	.645	.634	.283

are affected considerably. When education is controlled, the positive relationships of vote for Peña with percent Spanish and black, particularly the former, are diminished. This would suggest some lack of cohesion among
Hispanics related to education levels (cf. Hahn, Klingman, and Pachon 1976).
Similarly, as shown in Part B. of the Table, when percent Spanish is controlled,
a weak negative relationship between vote for Peña and the education measure remains. A similar although stronger relationship results when percent
black is controlled, while controlling for percent nonminority makes the initial negative relationship disappear and become very weakly positive. That
controlling for education has rather strong impacts is not surprising given that
the simple relationships between percent with some college and percent Spanish, black, and nonminority voters who did not support Peña were probably
those with higher levels of education while among whites, education has a negligible or slightly positive affect overall on the vote for Peña.

Unemployment is related to the vote for Peña in ways somewhat similar
to education. Controlling for unemployment lessens the positive relationship
between vote for Peña and percent Spanish and black while controlling for

this variable lessens the negative relationship with percent nonminority. Relatedly, Part B indicates that controlling for percent Spanish weakens the relationship between percent unemployed and vote for Peña slightly, while controlling for percent black affects that relationship almost not at all. Controlling for percent nonminority considerably weakens the relationship between vote for Peña and percent unemployed, from .586 to .163 (cf. Hahn, Klingman, and Pachon 1976). Again, it should be noted that the simple relationships between percent unemployed and percent Spanish, black, and nonminority are .623, .262, and -.623, respectively.

Finally, the impact of Democratic party affiliation is similar to, but stronger than, that for education and percent unemployed. When this variable is controlled, the relationship of minority status (Spanish or black) to vote for Peña declines rather dramatically and that for nonminority becomes somewhat less negative. Similarly, the relationship between vote for Peña and Democratic registration drops substantially, from .743 to .283 when percent nonminority is controlled (cf. Browning, Marshall, and Tabb 1984). However, controlling for percent Spanish and black has relatively little impact on the simple relationships. Once again, the high correlations among the independent variables probably account for substantial changes that occur. The simple relationships between percent Democratic registration and percent Spanish, black, and nonminority are .562, .567, and -.831.

Conclusion

The description of the Peña campaign suggested that it sought to increase participation, especially among certain groups, and to develop something similar to a liberal coalition. The statistical evidence indicates the success of the campaign in generating increased registration, turnout and support among both minorities, especially Hispanics, and white liberals. The appeals to gain white liberal support stressed better management generally and better managed growth in particular. Peña was also apparently able to present a positive, dynamic image. With respect to minority voters, Peña's name and record along with his stated concern for "affordable housing" and other social issues were apparently quite important. This aggregate of support also indicates considerable racial voting, apparently modified by various factors such as issues and party affiliation. The term "aggregate of support" is used because the Peña campaign seemed to offer a "little something" for the several major groups whose support is sought, without directly confronting the question of whether these various goals might conflict.

Despite the overall indications of much "racial voting" (Bullock and Campbell 1984), there is some rather weak evidence that more educated Hispanics and blacks supported Peña less strongly than did the less educated ethnic minorities. Among whites, the impact of higher levels of education had either negligible or slightly positive impacts on the vote for Peña (cf. Hahn, Klingman, and Pachon 1976; de la Garza 1974). The tendency of racial voting was also modified by party affiliation and employment status. Economic status, as indicated by two measures of income, was weakly related to the vote for Peña, either directly or indirectly. Also, the coalition among Hispanics and blacks found here also has been found in some (Browning, Marshall, and Tabb 1984) but not all (Hahn, Klingman, and Pachon 1976) the previous research.

While these findings should be interpreted cautiously, they do indicate that the campaign appeals and electoral coalitions of minority candidates are quite important and may differ according to different constituency contexts and other factors (cf. Hahn, Klingman, and Pachon 1976; de la Garza 1974). The data also suggest that the response of minority groups to different candidates may differ within groups, often due to socioeconomic variables, between groups, and between groups of the same ethnic background in different cities (cf. Hahn, Klingman and Pachon 1976; Browning, Marshall and Tabb 1984; Henry and Munoz 1985).

The implications of these findings are unclear, but brief speculation can be offered. Hispanics and blacks strongly supported Peña and were crucial to his election. However, due to their relatively small proportion of Denver's population, lower levels of registration (for Hispanics), and low levels of turnout (for both minority groups), whites provided the major portion of the vote for Peña. Thus, despite the election of a Hispanic mayor it would appear difficult to alter substantive policy in ways which previous research suggests would be preferable to Denver's minorities (Lovrich 1974). This is due to the apparent constraints placed upon Peña by this electoral coalition, constraints that are probably even greater when actual issues of governance must be confronted (Stone 1980). Notably, Peña's top administrative appointees to date have been white (cf. Henry and Munoz 1985: 23). Beyond the likely symbolic importance and perhaps a different tone in city administration, and despite the considerable formal powers of the Denver mayor, it is unclear what the real impacts of Peña's election for minority groups will be. Further judgment on this probably should be withheld until a full term of office has been completed.

Further research is needed before the election and governing issues confronted by Hispanic candidates are better understood. That research should be sensitive to differences within and between ethnic-racial groups as well as to regional and historical factors. Until such research is undertaken, it will remain uncertain whether the election of Federico Peña is similar to or different than the election of Hispanics in other cities and offices, how Hispanics differ from other minority groups in terms of the electoral coalitions that they are able to construct, and the implications of these matters for successful governance. Despite impressive previous research, numerous significant questions such as these remain to be answered.

Notes

1. The total number of precincts is 389; however, the number of precincts used in the analyses in Tables 3 and 4 varies from 371 to 385 due to missing data.

2. The major data limitation is related to "reprecincting." Denver precincts are redrawn from time to time to accommodate the larger registration and turnout for state and national elections. Thus the precincts for which the electoral results were drawn, which are the "correct" precincts, and those from which the demographic and related data are drawn do not coincide exactly. However, if caution is taken in interpreting the results, the data are useful. Other evidence suggests that the statistical results produced can be used with considerable confidence. An examination by the author of the precinct maps before and after the re-precincting indicates that the affects appear minor. Also, assuming that the re-precincting is done randomly, which conversations with staff officials of the Denver Election Commission indicate is the case, the effect on the statistical output is probably minor. In any case, the potential data limitations noted here are not uncommon for analyses of municipal elections (cf. Bullock and Campbell 1984; Hahn 1969).

References

Browning, Rufus P., Dale Rogers Marshall, and David H. Tabb. 1984. *Protest Is Not Enough—The Struggle of Blacks and Hispanics for Equality in Urban Politics*. Berkeley: University of California Press.

Bullock, Charles S. III, and Bruce A. Campbell. 1984. "Racist or Racial Voting in the 1981 Atlanta Municipal Elections." *Urban Affairs Quarterly* 20 (December): 149–64.

de la Garza, Rudolph. 1974. "Voting Patterns in 'Bi-Cultural El Paso'—A Contextual Analysis of Chicano Voting Behavior." *Aztlan* 5 (Spring–Fall): 235–60.

_____. 1977. "Mexican-American Voters: A Responsible Electorate." In Frank L. Baird, ed., *Mexican Americans: Political Power, Influence, or Resources*, pp. 63–76. Lubbock: Texas Tech Press.

Garcia, F. Chris, and Rudolph O. de la Garza. 1977. *The Chicano Political Experience: Three Perspectives*. North Scituate, MA: Duxbury.

Hahn, Harlan. 1969. "Ethos and Social Class Referenda in Canadian Cities." *Polity* 2 (December): 295–315.

Hahn, Harlan, David Klingman, and Harry Pachon. 1976. "Cleavages, Coalitions, and the Black Candidate: The Los Angeles Mayoralty Elections of 1969 and 1973." *Western Political Quarterly* 55 (December): 507–20.

Holloway, Harry. 1968. "Negro Political Strategy: Coalition or Independent Power Politics?" *Social Science Quarterly* 49 (December): 534–47.

Henry, Charles P., and Carlos Munoz. 1985. "Under the Rainbow: Black and Latino Support for Minority Mayors." Paper presented at the Annual Meeting of the American Political Association, August 29–September 1, New Orleans, Louisiana.

Lovrich, Nicholas. 1974. "Differing Priorities in an Urban Electorate: Service Preference Among Anglo, Black and Mexican American Voters." *Social Science Quarterly* 55 (December): 704–17.

_____ and Otwin, Marenin. 1976. "A Comparison of Black and Mexican American

Voters in Denver: Assertive versus Acquiescent Political Orientations and Voting Behavior in an Urban Electorate." *Western Political Quarterly* 29 (June): 284–94.

Stone, Clarence. 1980. "Systemic Power in Community Decision Making: A Restatement of Stratification Theory." *American Political Science Review* 74: 978–90.

Taebel, Delbert. 1978. "Minority Representation on City Councils: The Impact of Structure on Blacks and Hispanics." *Social Science Quarterly* 59 (June): 142–52.

Vigil, Maurilio. 1978. "Jerry Apodaca and the 1974 Gubernatorial Election in New Mexico." *Aztlan* 9 (Spring, Summer, Fall): 133–50.

Wolfinger, Raymond. 1974. *The Politics of Progress*. Englewood Cliffs, NJ: Prentice-Hall.

The Impact of Proportional Representation

Bruce I. Petrie and Alfred J. Tuchfarber

Proportional representation[1] as the method of electing the nine members of city council has been but a spiritual presence in Cincinnati since its defeat at the polls in 1957 and replacement by a 9X at-large system.[2] In the intervening 33 years, many of PR's true believers have likewise departed the Cincinnati political scene on their way to whatever reward awaits stalwarts of local government reform.[3] During those years in Cincinnati, as in the rest of the nation, vast political changes have evolved from the civil rights and women's movements.

Despite PR's long absence, its memory has engendered in recent years a surprising amount of new attention, particularly as a possible alternative to the idea advanced by some that at-large voting should be abandoned in favor of districted voting. Thus, even with an under-funded and under-publicized campaign, PR showed strength in an initiative-based attempt at restoration in 1988.[4] To some political observers, it was a propitious time to test the efficacy of PR in the current political atmosphere and to encourage further public discussion and debate on a subject of vital long-range importance to Cincinnati.

Sponsored by the Murray and Agnes Seasongood Good Government Foundation,[5] the Institute for policy research of the University of Cincinnati considered various methods of measuring the difference, if any, between 9X and PR in Cincinnati's contemporary political climate. The Institute determined that an exit poll using a PR ballot, taken of a representative sample of voters—immediately after they had marked their 9X ballots for council at the November 1989 election—would offer the most reliable expression of the differences in councilmanic results attributable to the two methods of voting.

Reprinted with permission from National Civic Review, *Vol. 79, No. 1, January/ February, 1990. Published by the National Civic League Press, Denver, Colorado.*

It was, of course, recognized that no practical method for such an experiment could reflect the influence of 1) a political campaign specifically designed for a PR election, or 2) a variation in the number of candidates running on each party's ticket.[6] Yet, as it turned out, the very absence of such a campaign provided some revealing insights about the most important factors for election under the respective systems (e.g., the need for a strong core of supporters under PR).

In particular, it was anticipated that the exit poll might shed light on these questions about PR:

- Would more minority candidates be elected?
- Would more women be elected?
- Would more special interest candidates be elected?
- Would any entrenched incumbents be defeated?
- Would the voters understand PR well enough to use it?

The exit poll was conducted with slightly less than 1,000 randomly selected voters from 52 precincts which also were selected at random from each of the city's 26 wards or from a ward grouping.[7] The number of precincts selected from each ward or ward group was proportional to voter turnout in the 1987 council election. At the selected precincts poll takers asked every third voter to complete the exit poll, but refrained from interviewing the respondents. Those voters were given a pencil and clipboard with a questionnaire/ballot and printed instructions.[8] Completed ballots were then placed by the respondents in a ballot box labeled "UC Exit Poll."

Exit polling was done from early morning until shortly before the polls closed. Precincts were randomly assigned to morning, early afternoon, and late afternoon/evening time slots for interviewing.[9]

Of the total of 958 completed PR ballots, 881 were valid and 77 were invalid because voters gave the same rank to more than one candidate or made other mistakes which masked their intentions.

As to sampling validity, the sample of voters polled is representative of the entire voting population, within certain limits, and the results should be within approximately plus or minus three percent of the results that would have been recorded had every voter leaving the polls completed an exit-poll ballot.

The Voting Results: PR Versus 9X

Overall, the results of the two electoral methods are significantly different, although this was not the case among the leading vote getters (see Table 1). Mayor Luken (D) and Guy Guckenberger (I)[10] finished first and second under both systems. David Mann (D) and Reggie Williams (C), a black, reversed their finish; Williams finished third under PR and Mann a strong fourth, whereas under 9X Mann finished third and Williams a very strong fourth.

Steve Chabot (R) finished a strong fifth under both systems. Bobbie Sterne (C), a woman with long experience on council, was eighth under 9X, but moved up to sixth under PR. This move up, however, was not a major shift when compared to the actual 9X results. Sterne finished only 2,167 votes out of sixth place in the actual election.

The most significant difference between the results of the two electoral methods was Roxanne Qualls's (D) move from tenth under 9X to seventh under PR. Qualls finished almost 6,000 votes out of seventh place and 2,000 votes out of ninth place under 9X.

John Mirlisena (R) finished eighth under PR and seventh under 9X. Mirlisena received only 1,037 more votes than the eighth-placed finish under 9X. Thus, his move down one place has no great analytic significance.

In a very close race under PR, William Mallory, Jr. (D), a black (son of a long-time Ohio legislator), edged out Peter Strauss (D) for ninth place. Under 9X Mallory finished a relatively poor 12th, 8,559 votes out of ninth place. Mallory's strong finish under PR was due principally to his strong support among black voters. Although Reggie Williams, a black (and well known professional football player), received most of the first-choice black votes, Mallory received a large percentage of the second-choice votes.

The shift of Strauss, a relatively well known, multiterm veteran of the city council, from a strong sixth place finish under 9X to tenth under PR is almost the reverse of the Roxanne Qualls story. It is very important to note, however, that after all transfers, only two votes out of 881 ballots separated Mallory and Strauss for the ninth seat under PR. Given the potential for sampling error, it is best to consider Strauss and Mallory as essentially tied for ninth place. Notwithstanding, Strauss dropped three positions under PR and Mallory advanced three positions.

Jim Cissell (R) dropped from a ninth place election to council under 9X to a 12th place defeat under PR.

Paul Booth (R) finished 13th under PR compared to 11th under 9X. Although Booth is black, most first- and second-choice black votes went to other blacks, Reggie Williams and William Mallory, Jr.

David Altman (C) did slightly better with PR than 9X, 14th place vs. 16th, as did Tim Riker (D), 15th place vs. 17th. However, neither had a large enough core of solid supporters to make a major run at a top-nine finish. The other five candidates had neither a solid core of support, nor widespread name recognition.

Demographic Differences

As would be expected, various political and demographic groups cast their PR votes in different ways (see Tables 2 and 3).

Table 1
Vote Totals at End of Each Round of Transfers

	Actual 9X System votes, Nov. 1989 Election	Actual 9X System order of finish	PR Experimental order of finish	PR Experimental first choice votes	1. Transfer of Luken surplus	2. Transfer of Guckenberger surplus	3. Transfer of Williams surplus	4. Transfer of Condit votes	5. Transfer of Sunderman votes
Alan (R)	18,511	13	11	32	33	33	33	33	33
Altman (C)	14,548	16	14	8	9	9	9	9	10
Booth (R)	29,151	11	13	17	24	26	26	26	27
Chabot (R)	40,356	5	5	64	89*	89	89	89	89
Cheng (I)	8,026	18	18	5	5	5	5	5	5
Cissell (R)	35,203	9	12	16	24	26	28	28	30
Condit (Cin)	6,717	19	20	2	4	4	4	—	—
Garrett (R)	15,590	15	17	5	5	5	5	6	6
Guckenberger (R)	48,691	2	2	101*	89	89	89	89	89
Luken (D)	53,172	1	1	230*	88	88	88	88	88
Mallory (D)	26,444	12	9	30	38	38	38	38	38
Mann (D)	43,151	3	4	54	89*	89	89	89	89
Mirlisena (R)	39,089	7	8	51	63	68	68	69	69
Qualls (D)	33,196	10	7	66	76	77	77	77	77
Riker (D)	12,416	17	15	7	9	9	9	9	9
Sterne (C)	38,062	8	6	68	83	86	88	88	88
Strauss (D)	40,229	6	10	21	35	36	36	37	37
Sundermann (R)	16,956	14	19	3	5	5	5	5	—
Sweeney (Lib)	5,076	20	16	6	6	6	6	6	6
Williams (C)	42,718	4	3	96*	96	95	89	89	89

	6. Transfer of Cheng votes	7. Transfer of Garrett votes	8. Transfer of Sweeney votes	9. Transfer of Riker votes	10. Transfer of Altman votes	11. Transfer of Booth votes	12. Transfer of Cissell votes	13. Transfer of Allen votes
Alan (R)	33	33	34	35	35	35	40	—
Altman (C)	10	10	10	10	—	—	—	—
Booth (R)	27	27	27	27	28	—	—	—
Chabot (R)	89	89	89	89	89	89	89	89
Cheng (I)	—	—	—	—	—	—	—	—
Cissell (R)	32	34	35	35	36	39	—	—
Condit (Cin)	—	—	—	—	—	—	—	—
Garrett (R)	6	—	—	—	—	—	—	—
Guckenberger (R)	89	89	89	89	89	89	89	89
Luken (D)	88	88	88	88	88	88	88	88
Mallory (D)	38	39	40	42	43	50	54	64*
Mann (D)	89	89	89	89	89	89	89	89
Mirlisena (R)	70	72	73	73	74	77	87	89*
Qualls (D)	78	78	79	81	84	84	89*	89
Riker (D)	9	9	9	—	—	—	—	—
Sterne (C)	88	88	88	89	89*	89	89	89
Strauss (D)	37	38	38	40	41	44	51	62
Sundermann (R)	—	—	—	—	—	—	—	—
Sweeney (Lib)	6	6	—	—	—	—	—	—
Williams (C)	89	89	89	89	89	89	89	89

*The point at which the candidate was declared elected to one of the 9 seats. At the end of the final round of transfers, Mallory had more votes than Strauss and was declared elected to the ninth and last seat.

Notes: In the PR experiment, a total of 881 valid ballots were cast, thus 89 votes were needed to win. Luken had only 88 votes after the transfer of his surplus; this was caused by a minor anomaly in the way that surplus had to be transferred using the standard PR transfer rules.

Blacks were most likely to give Reggie Williams, a black, their *first* place votes. Well over one-half of the black voters ranked Williams among their *top nine* choices. Mayor Luken, a white, received the next highest number of *first* place exit poll votes from blacks. Bill Mallory, a black, finished third with David Mann, a white, as close fourth. Paul Booth, a black, was fifth and Bobbie Sterne, a white female, was sixth.

Whites gave twice as many *first* place votes to Luken as anyone else. Guy Guckenberger was a strong second, with Steve Chabot and Roxanne Qualls third and fourth.

When all the top *nine* votes of the whites were tallied, Luken was first, Guckenberger second, Chabot third, Mann fourth, Mirlisena fifth, and Strauss sixth. Reggie Williams finished eighth among whites, while Paul Booth finished 13th and Bill Mallory 12th.

All age groups gave Mayor Luken the largest fraction of their *first* and *top nine* place votes. Guy Guckenberger finished strongly with all age groups. Reggie Williams was also strong with all age groups.

David Mann was popular with all age groups, while Roxanne Qualls's support came strongly from younger voters. Bobbie Sterne was moderately strong with all age groups.

Among both males and females, Mayor Luken received far more first-place votes than any other candidate. Reggie Williams and Guy Guckenberger were also strong with both sexes. Roxanne Qualls and Bobbie Sterne (both women) did somewhat better with women than men. However, for the most part there were no enormous differences in how men and women voted. Gender was substantially less important in predicting voter choices than were race, age or party affiliation.

Breakdowns by party were, for the most part, predictable. Democrats voted for Democrats, Republicans for Republicans, Charterites for Charterites.

Some notable exceptions to the general rule of party voting were Guy Guckenberger's fifth place finish among Democrats (top nine vote totals), and Bobbie Stern's third place finish among the same group. Also of interest was Peter Strauss's seventh-place finish among the four respective party groups: Democrats, Republicans, Independents and Charterites.

Reggie Williams also showed great breadth of support with a fourth-place showing among Democrats, sixth place among Republicans, and third place among Independents.

Invalid Ballots and Voter Confusion

One of the great concerns about PR has been that voters will be confused by numerical voting. The PR experiment suggests that while such concerns may be overestimated, more voter education is required (see Table 4). More than 90 percent of those participating in the exit poll cast valid ballots, while eight percent were invalid.[11] The most frequent problems on invalid ballots were the voters' assigning the same rank to more than one candidate and voters' indicating one or more choices with an "X" or check mark instead of numbers. It must be noted that most voters had never used PR and there was no educational campaign prior to the exit poll.

Black voters were much more likely to cast invalid ballots. Older voters, 65 and over, were also more likely to have difficulty than the younger voters.

Conclusions and Implications

The PR exit-poll experiment confirms much of the conventional wisdom about PR as an electoral method. The main beneficiaries of PR compared to the 9X system are candidates who have a strong core of committed supporters, but who also have at least moderate appeal to other voters. The candidates harmed most severely by PR when compared to 9X are those with name recognition but only a small core of committed followers.

The 1989 Cincinnati City Council election PR experiment did not demonstrate in a conclusive fashion that more blacks would be elected under PR. Although William Mallory, Jr., a black Democrat, did substantially better under PR than he did under 9X, his "election" to the ninth seat was too narrow to come to a conclusion that PR would result in the election of several blacks to the city council. Paul Booth, a black Republican, did worse under PR compared to 9X and Reggie Williams, a black Charterite, finished with strength under both electoral methods.

Although Roxanne Qualls gained the most from PR, it is not demonstrable that she gained because she is a woman; rather, it is arguable that her long standing advocacy of community and environmental issues caused her to have the strong core of support so important under PR. Bobbie Sterne did not do substantially better under PR, and Lynn Sundermann, another woman, slipped significantly.

A switch to PR is likely to lead to the defeat of some incumbents. The 9X system rewards widespread name recognition. PR rewards widespread name recognition only if it is coupled with a strong core of support (i.e., first-place votes).

The voters themselves can cope with PR. Over 90 percent of participants cast valid ballots in the experiment. Since even a few invalid ballots is too many, any switch to PR must be accompanied by an extensive, multifaceted public education campaign. Special care must be taken to ensure that blacks and older persons receive ample education about the use of a PR ballot.

Although more analysis is desirable, it appears that the exit poll experiment

Table 2
PR Vote Experiment—Demographic Breakdowns of First-Place Votes

CANDIDATE	RACE black first place votes	rank	white first place votes	rank	AGE 18–29 first place votes	rank	30–45 first place votes	rank	46–64 first place votes	rank	65–above first place votes	rank
Allen (R)	2	13	30	8	5	8	15	8	7	10	5	8
Altman (C)	2	13	7	12	0	17	3	14	4	12	2	12
Booth (R)	14	5	1	18	2	12	3	14	4	12	5	8
Chabot (R)	2	13	59	3	16	3	19	7	12	7	15	3
Cheng (I)	1	17	4	16	4	9	1	19	1	15	0	17
Cissell (R)	4	10	11	11	1	16	6	12	8	9	0	17
Condit (Cin)	1	17	1	18	0	17	2	17	0	19	0	17
Garrett (R)	1	17	5	14	2	12	2	17	0	19	2	12
Guckenberger (I)	9	7	86	2	3	10	41	2	36	2	18	2
Luken (D)	46	2	173	1	40	1	84	1	62	1	38	1
Mallory (D)	24	3	7	12	6	7	11	11	10	8	5	8
Mann (D)	16	4	34	7	2	12	21	6	16	5	11	4
Mirlisena (R)	3	11	46	6	8	6	13	10	19	4	10	6
Qualls (D)	6	9	54	4	13	4	38	3	7	10	4	11
Riker (D)	1	17	5	14	2	12	4	13	1	15	0	17
Stern (C)	13	6	49	5	11	5	27	5	16	5	11	4
Strauss (D)	7	8	13	10	3	10	14	9	1	15	2	12
Sunderman (R)	2	13	1	18	0	17	0	20	1	15	2	12
Sweeney (Lib)	3	11	3	17	0	17	3	14	2	14	1	16
Williams (C)	61	1	25	9	21	2	36	4	25	3	8	7

CANDIDATE	SEX male first place votes	male rank	female first place votes	female rank	PARTY Democrats first place votes	Democrats rank	Republicans first place votes	Republicans rank	Independents first place votes	Independents rank
Allen (R)	19	9	13	10	3	14	19	5	7	6
Altman (C)	5	14	5	13	12	8	0	19	1	16
Booth (R)	9	12	5	13	12	8	0	19	1	16
Chabot (R)	32	4	30	6	11	10	34	3	13	3
Cheng (I)	4	15	2	18	1	18	3	12	2	14
Cissell (R)	7	13	8	12	4	13	7	8	4	10
Condit (Cin)	1	18	1	20	0	20	1	16	1	16
Garrett (R)	4	15	2	18	2	15	2	13	2	14
Guckenberger (I)	57	2	40	4	24	6	40	2	19	2
Luken (D)	93	1	132	1	105	1	60	1	30	1
Mallory (D)	15	10	16	9	24	6	2	13	3	11
Mann (D)	26	6	24	7	34	4	4	11	9	5
Mirlisena (R)	32	4	18	8	12	8	28	4	7	6
Qualls (D)	23	8	39	5	44	3	7	8	6	8
Riker (D)	1	18	5	13	2	15	1	16	3	11
Sterne (C)	24	7	41	2	29	5	16	7	5	9
Strauss (D)	11	11	9	11	9	11	5	10	3	11
Sunderman (R)	0	20	3	17	1	18	1	16	0	20
Sweeney (Lib)	2	17	4	16	2	15	2	13	1	16
Williams (C)	49	3	41	2	52	2	17	2	12	4

Table 3

PR Vote Experiment—Demographic Breakdowns of First to Ninth Votes

CANDIDATE	RACE black first to ninth votes	rank	white first to ninth votes	rank	AGE 18–29 first to ninth votes	rank	30–45 first to ninth votes	rank	46–64 first to ninth votes	rank	65–above first to ninth votes	rank
Allen (R)	12	16	134	11	18	13	69	13	42	13	21	13
Altman (C)	11	18	116	12	15	14	67	14	35	14	13	16
Booth (R)	103	5	98	14	33	11	77	12	62	11	36	11
Chabot (R)	42	11	308	3	70	4	120	9	103	6	63	5
Cheng (I)	8	20	51	18	14	15	25	17	15	20	6	19
Cissell (R)	40	12	235	9	42	10	93	10	94	8	53	8
Condit (Cin)	9	19	39	19	8	19	18	20	16	18	7	18
Garrett (R)	34	13	55	17	9	17	38	16	31	16	15	14
Guckenberger (I)	70	7	395	2	73	2	194	2	139	2	70	3
Luken (D)	119	2	404	1	94	1	207	1	142	1	93	1
Mallory (D)	97	6	103	13	32	12	88	11	53	12	35	12
Mann (D)	111	4	296	4	66	5	169	3	112	4	70	3
Mirlisena (R)	47	10	290	5	55	7	130	8	100	7	59	7
Qualls (D)	58	9	235	9	49	9	136	5	67	10	47	10
Riker (D)	13	5	58	16	9	17	38	16	17	17	9	17
Stern (C)	116	3	265	7	63	6	166	4	108	5	53	8
Strauss (D)	62	8	271	6	53	8	134	7	94	8	61	6
Sunderman (R)	14	14	87	15	10	16	45	15	34	15	15	14
Sweeney (Lib)	12	16	29	20	8	20	19	19	16	18	2	20
Williams (C)	168	1	245	8	77	2	151	5	123	3	73	2

CANDIDATE	SEX male first to ninth		female first to ninth		PARTY Democrats first to ninth		Republicans first to ninth		Independents first to ninth	
	votes	rank	votes	rank	votes	rank	votes	rank	votes	rank
Allen (R)	69	13	80	13	31	15	79	9	27	13
Altman (C)	65	14	66	14	59	13	26	16	23	14
Booth (R)	115	11	102	12	98	11	56	11	39	11
Chabot (R)	181	5	174	7	101	10	155	1	61	4
Cheng (I)	36	17	25	18	20	18	19	18	10	18
Cissell (R)	142	9	139	10	80	12	124	5	45	10
Condit (Cin)	30	19	18	20	13	20	20	17	10	18
Garrett (R)	49	15	43	16	24	16	40	14	19	15
Guckenberger (I)	248	1	228	3	184	5	152	3	81	2
Luken (D)	244	2	294	1	232	1	155	1	85	1
Mallory (D)	102	12	106	11	119	9	38	15	32	12
Mann (D)	185	4	234	2	217	2	82	8	58	5
Mirlisena (R)	177	6	166	9	110	8	143	4	53	7
Qualls (D)	126	10	172	8	167	6	48	13	46	9
Riker (D)	35	18	37	17	34	14	12	20	17	16
Sterne (C)	171	7	222	4	212	3	71	10	57	6
Strauss (D)	161	8	180	6	157	7	89	7	53	7
Sunderman (R)	49	15	55	15	23	17	54	12	14	17
Sweeney (Lib)	24	20	20	19	18	19	17	19	6	20
Williams (C)	201	3	204	5	197	4	103	6	67	3

Table 4
Analysis of Invalid Ballots

	Valid Ballots	Invalid Ballots
Party		
Democrat	43.2%	36.4%
Republican	28.8	28.6
Charterite	3.9	2.6
Independent	15.0	13.0
Other	6.3	7.8
No Answer	2.9	11.7
Age		
18–29	16.1	14.3
30–45	39.4	31.2
46–64	26.6	15.6
65 and over	15.9	29.9
No Answer	1.9	9.1
Gender		
Male	47.5	48.1
Female	50.4	46.8
No Answer	2.1	5.2
Race		
black	25.0	42.9
white	70.6	48.1
other	1.1	1.3
No Answer	3.2	7.8
	N = 875*	N = 77

*Six additional ballots were found to be usable for the PR manual count of ballots. The 875 valid ballots used for this analysis were valid under rules used for the computerized statistical analysis.

supports the belief that adopting PR for Cincinnati City Council elections would cause some changes in how campaigns are conducted, the size of the party tickets, who gets elected, and, to some degree, how the city is governed.

In summary, the PR experiment suggests that had PR been used instead of 9X, one, and perhaps two, seats on city council would be occupied by different people than is now the case. The Republicans would have lost one seat, the Democrats would have gained a net of one, and the charter presence would have remained the same. Instead of three Republicans, one Independent, three Democrats and two Charterites, council would have been divided two-one-four-two.

Appendix
University of Cincinnati Exit Poll

Thank you for agreeing to help us. Mark or circle your answers as noted.
Please don't hesitate to ask any questions you might have.

After you have completed the survey, please fold it and place it in the box marked
UNIVERSITY OF CINCINNATI EXIT POLL.

PART 1

Cincinnati City Council Election

DIRECTIONS

- Put the number 1 in the box next to the name of the person you MOST want to be elected to City Council.

- Put the number 2 in the box next to the name of the person who is your second choice.

- Put the number 3 next to your third choice, and so on.

- You may take as many choices as you wish.

- You cannot hurt any of those you prefer by making many choices, but you should not feel obliged to select any more people than you want.

- Please do NOT put the same number next to more than one name.

- If you make a mistake that you cannot correct by erasing it, just ask for a new ballot.

CANDIDATES FOR COUNCIL

Please read the directions before marking your choices.

	The Numbers Below Are For Tabulations Only
☐ James J. Condit, Jr.	(7)
☐ Len Garrett	(8)
☐ Guy C. Guckenberger	(9)
☐ Charles Luken	(10)
☐ William L. Mallory, Jr.	(11)
☐ David Mann	(12)
☐ John Mirlisena	(13)
☐ Roxanne Qualls	(14)
☐ Tim Riker	(15)
☐ Bobbie Sterne	(16)
☐ Peter Strauss	(17)
☐ Lynn K. Sundermann	(18)
☐ Gary K. Sweeney	(19)
☐ Reggie Williams	(20)
☐ Michael Allen	(21)
☐ Dave Altman	(22)
☐ Paul M. Booth	(23)
☐ Steve Chabot	(24)
☐ John Cheng	(25)
☐ James Cissell	(26)

PART 2

1. IN TERMS OF YOUR IDENTIFICATION WITH LOCAL POLITICS ... DO YOU CONSIDER YOURSELF CLOSER TO THE DEMOCRATS, REPUBLICANS, CHARTERITES, OR WHAT?

1. Democrats   4. Independents
2. Republicans   5. Other
3. Charterites   (27)

— — —

2. WHICH OF THE FOLLOWING AGE GROUPS DO YOU FALL INTO?

1. 18–29   3. 46–54
2. 30–45   4. 65 or over
                    (28)

— — —

3. WHAT IS YOUR SEX?

1. Male   2. Female
                    (29)

— — —

4. WHAT IS YOUR RACE?

1. black   3. other
2. white
                    (30)

Thank you for your help. Please fold the questionnaire and place it in the box marked
UNIVERSITY OF CINCINNATI EXIT POLL

As stated above, the authors recognize that, like many experiments, perfect correlation with reality could not be achieved. Nonetheless, for those interested in election systems, the PR exit poll offers significant data on how PR would function if its resuscitation were real.

Notes

1. The references to PR in this chapter are to the Hare System with the single transferable vote, and not to other systems of proportional representation with which it is sometimes confused.

2. PR succumbed after four other attacks, in 1936, 1939, 1947 and 1954, by the Hamilton County Republican organization. The 9X system is nine-seat at-large electoral system.

3. The principal supporters of PR were members of the Charter Committee, a coalition of independents, Republicans and Democrats, celebrated as an unusually long-lived municipal reform movement.

4. A total of 45.4 percent of the voters favored PR.

5. From 1931 to 1934, the late Murray Seasongood was President of the National Municipal League, now the National Civic League.

6. For example, in 1989 the Charter Committee ran only three candidates on its ticket; formerly, under PR, it ran nine.

7. Ward groupings consisted of small wards, contiguous and similar to other wards (e.g., 16, 17 and 18; 6 and 8; 10 and 11; 19 and 20; 21 and 22 were all grouped).

8. The form of the Exit Poll Ballot used in the PR experiment is reproduced in the Appendix (p. 431). There were 20 different versions with each candidate topping the list on one of the versions.

9. The weather in Cincinnati on Election Day, November 7, 1989, was inclement during part of the day.

10. Guckenberger, elected many times as a Republican candidate, lost his party's endorsement shortly before the election because of party differences, which simply served to give him additional visibility.

11. "Invalidity" was determined in accordance with the definitions used in the 1949 PR election (e.g., an entire ballot was "invalid" even if duplicated numbers were of the voter's lower choices).

The Impact of Municipal Term Limits

Mark P. Petracca and Karen Moore O'Brien

Term limits have come to city hall in a growing number of municipalities. At least 35 percent of the 60 largest U.S. cities, including New York, Los Angeles, Houston, New Orleans, San Antonio, and San Francisco, have adopted term limits for local elected officials in the last few years. This is more than four times the 8.3 percent reported by the International City Management Association for the same big cities in the mid–1980s. Countless smaller municipalities also have adopted term limits for locally elected officials.[1]

In some parts of the country, the movement to bring term limits to city hall has become a veritable contagion. Seven out of 31 cities in Orange County, California have been operating with municipal term limits for some time, in one case going back to the mid 1960s (Santa Ana). In 1992, four additional cities in Orange County adopted term limits and voters in two other approved advisory term-limitation initiatives as well. Other cities in the county currently are contemplating similar measures.

The pace of a the term-limits movement has been startling, surprising even some of its most ardent supporters. But precisely because of the rapid spread of this reform, there has been little opportunity to assess the impact of term limits on governance and public policy at the local level. This has frustrated a great many scholars, especially political scientists, who fear that inadequate emphasis has been placed on the potentially undesirable and unanticipated consequences of term limits.[2]

At the federal and state levels there is no modern experience with limits on legislative terms.[3] This makes it virtually impossible to evaluate the impact

Reprinted with permission from National Civic Review, *Vol. 83, No. 2, Spring/Summer, 1994. Published by the National Civic League Press, Denver, Colorado.*

legislative term limits may have on a wide range of political and governmental dynamics. It also has meant that much of the popular and even scholarly debate over term limits has not progressed very far since the awakening of the movement in the late 1980s.[4] Reviews of the recent literature on term limits reveal a stunning lack of analytical or empirical development.[5]

Nonetheless, term limits have been operating for some time at the municipal level in Orange County, offering at least a limited opportunity to evaluate their impact on local politics. We recognize that conclusions drawn from the experiences of term-limited cities are not applicable to what may await state legislatures or the U.S. Congress, once applicable statewide measures begin to influence incumbency. At this point in the movement, we can either learn what we can from cities that have been operating with term limits or continue to rehash the same old charges and promises until newly adopted state initiatives kick-in, which won't be until 1998 at the earliest.

Surveys of Local Elected Officials

In order to begin the process of assessing the impact of term limits on local governance, we conducted two surveys of elected officials in Orange County municipalities. The first survey was administered to all elected officials in the seven cities operating under term limits prior to 1992. The seven cities were Santa Ana, Seal Beach, Cypress, Villa Park, Huntington Beach, La Palma, and Irvine (see Table 1). Santa Ana has been operating with term limits since 1966, making it, we believe, the first city in the United States to adopt term limits. The first survey was mailed prior to California's June primary in the spring of 1992 and yielded a 56 percent response rate.

The second survey, posing a similar battery of questions, was sent at the same time as the first to elected officials in seven other cities where the adoption of term limits was under consideration. Cities in the second survey included Garden Grove, Anaheim, Orange, Tustin, Newport Beach, Dana Point, and Yorba Linda. Four of these cities adopted term limits in 1992, Dana Point in June and Anaheim, Newport Beach and Yorba Linda in November. The City of Orange adopted an advisory term-limitation measure in November of 1992 as well. Neither Garden Grove nor Tustin ended up putting a term-limits measure on the June or November ballots. Westminster, which was not surveyed, also approved an advisory term-limitation measure in November. A 57 percent response rate was received for the second survey.

The two surveys permit us to compare the attitudes of elected officials in term-limited cities with officials in cities considering term limits on a range of issues constituting the conventional critique of term limits. The surveys also provide additional comparative information about the causes of the term-limitation movement at the municipal level.

Orange County's Embrace of Term Limits

The fate of recently adopted term-limit initiatives for state and federal legislators undoubtedly rests with the courts, where opponents of term limits are attempting to overturn such measures on the basis of state and federal constitutional law.[6] Only time will tell whether term limits for state and federal legislators will withstand judicial scrutiny and eventually take effect. In Orange County, however, term limits already have stood the test of time, if not always judicial scrutiny.[7]

As noted above, term limits have been operating in Orange County since 1966 when Santa Ana, the county seat, adopted a term-limit initiative. Table 1 presents the Orange County cities currently operating under ordinances or charter amendments limiting the terms of city council members. In two cases, Irvine and Anaheim, term limits also apply to the directly elected mayor. Santa Ana's directly elected mayor is not subject to term limits, although such a proposal currently is under consideration. In all other cities, mayors are selected from among the members of the city council by the council members themselves.[8] Four out of the five largest cities in Orange County (i.e., Anaheim, Huntington Beach, Irvine, and Santa Ana) now operate with term limits.[9]

Popular support for term limits in Orange County has been exceedingly strong. In 1990, the vote supporting Proposition 140 from Orange County (imposing term limits on state legislators) made the difference in the narrow passage of California's first term-limits initiative. In 1992, support for the passage of Prop. 164, California's initiative to limit terms for federal legislators, exceeded 70 percent in Orange County. The voting record indicates that no local term-limitation initiative has ever failed to pass in Orange County,[10] and in only one city, Huntington Beach, has there ever been a ballot measure requesting the repeal of municipal term limits—which failed overwhelmingly.

Of the 11 cities in the county with term limits only two cities have deviated from the basic plan adopted by Santa Ana in 1966. Limited terms may sound restrictive, but in fact most cities in the county adhere to the rotative principle, prohibiting individuals from *consecutive* service on city council (usually of more than two terms). All terms for city council members in Orange County are four years.[11] After waiting out either one full term, or in some cases an unspecified period of time, the former council member may run for council again. Only two cities, Cypress and Villa Park, prohibit anyone from ever running for council again after serving a total of eight years in office.[12] Yorba Linda's term-limit ordinance also varies from the normal pattern by limiting the number of permissible consecutive terms to three, rather than two.

Table 1
Term-Limited Cities in Orange County*

City	Charter/ General Law	Year Enacted	Size of Council	Terms Limited To:	Partial Term Provision	Rotation	Other Offices Limited
Santa Ana	Charter	1966	6	2 Consecutive Terms	None Stated	None Specified	Mayor Not Included
Seal Beach	Charter	1974	5, Including Mayor†	2 Consecutive Terms	None Stated	None Specified	Planning Commission
Cypress	Charter	1977	5, Including Mayor†	8 Years Total	None Stated	None Specified	None
Villa Park	General Law	1978	5, Including Mayor†	8 Years Total	None Stated	None Specified	None
Huntington Beach	Charter	1978	7, Including Mayor†	2 Consecutive Terms	More Than 2 Years	Must Wait 2 Years	None
La Palma§	General Law	1982	5, Including Mayor†	2 Consecutive Terms	More Than 2 Years	Must Wait 1 Term	None
Irvine	Charter	1986	4	2 Consecutive Terms	None Stated	None Specified	Mayor
Dana Point	General Law	1992	5, Including Mayor†	2 Consecutive Terms	More Than 2 Years	Must Wait 1 Term	None
Anaheim	Charter	1992	4	2 Consecutive Terms	None Stated	None Specified	Mayor
Yorba Linda	General Law	1992	5, Including Mayor†	3 Consecutive Terms	2 Years	None Specified	None
Newport Beach	Charter	1992	7, Including Mayor†	2 Consecutive Terms	None Stated	Must Wait 1 Term	Planning Commission

*Two other cities, Westminster and Orange, also approved advisory term-limit measures in 1992.
†Mayor selected by city council members and subject to term-limit provisions.
§La Palma's term-limit ordinance was overturned by a California Court of Appeals decision in *Polis v. La Palma* (1992), but has not been repealed.

The Development of Local Term Limits in Orange County

Who was responsible for bringing term limits to city hall throughout the county and what motivated that demand? The documentary record necessary to answer either question is weak, to put it mildly. Cities don't have very good record-keeping procedures, and local newspapers have not been very attentive to the issue until recently. However, results from the two surveys suggest a few general answers to these questions.

Regarding who was responsible for term-limitation advocacy, in term-limited cities, 47.4 percent of responding elected officials said the request for term limits came from the city council, 32 percent said it came from a local citizens group, 11 percent said it came from the efforts of a single individual, and 11 percent said it came from another source. In the survey of elected officials from cities considering term limits, 62 percent of the respondents said the city council requested term limits and 38 percent said they were requested by local citizens groups.

Some additional insight on this question comes from how the term-limitation measure was placed on the ballot. In term-limited cities, 43 percent of the respondents said the proposal came about as a result of a citizen petition drive, and 29 percent said the council placed the measure on the ballot (i.e., by means of "referendum"). In 1992, this latter means was employed to place term-limitation measures on the ballot in Dana Point, Anaheim, Yorba Linda, Orange, and Westminster. In Newport Beach in that same year, a citizens group led by a first-term council member collected a sufficient number of signatures to place a term-limitation measure on the ballot (i.e., by means of the "initiative").

It is likely that state and national support for term limits by 1992 forced many otherwise reluctant council members to place term-limitations measures on the ballot rather than face angry citizens out gathering signatures to qualify a ballot initiative. This new, favorable atmosphere for term limits contrasts sharply with the experience of cities adopting limits prior to the 1990s.

What, then, motivated the demand for term limits, previously as well as in 1992? The surveys asked elected officials to respond to this question in an open-ended fashion. The responses of the two sets of informants (presented in Table 2), at times amusing as well as instructive, are virtually indistinguishable.

Both sets of explanations highlight citizen dissatisfaction with current office holders as a motivation for the adoption of term limits, despite the opportunity citizens have to vote incumbents out of office on election day. The need to do something about the advantages of incumbency is also a theme that runs through both sets of comments, although those of the first set stem from local

Table 2
Motivations for Adopting Term Limits
in Orange County Municipalities

Officials in Term-Limited Cities
- "Too much control by a few people affecting zoning and other major issues."
- "Dissatisfaction with representatives."
- "Unhappy with top government officials, only place to control was the city."
- "An old council member who fell asleep at meetings but continued to get elected."
- "Council members lost touch and weren't listening."
- "Preventing entrenchment and encouraging role for professional staff."
- "Politics."
- "The good ole' boys who would never step down."
- "One person who wanted on the council and felt the only way was through term limits."

Officials in Cities Without Term Limits
- "People who want to run for office."
- "Perceived lack of responsiveness, objectivity and reasonableness [among the current council]."
- "Dissatisfaction with long-term incumbents."
- "Incumbency advantage intimidates others who want to run for office."
- "Long-term incumbents (e.g., five and six terms)."
- "Lack of responsiveness by council; general dissatisfaction with government performance of legislators at high levels of office."
- "Previous mayor served 25 years, mayor pro tem served 20 years, council member 12 years."
- "Just a general feeling that the 'well water should be replenished' with new office holders."
- "Politics."
- "Primary source of motivation came from a frustrated former planning commissioner who could not beat an incumbent."
- "I brought it forward because I feel this is healthy and fair for our city."
- "National attention to abuses of Congress and [the] poor economy."

---

term-limitation movements that preceded the current national movement by a decade or more. Personal ambition for elected office, if the comments are to be believed, also played some role in motivating individuals to lead term-limitation petition drives.

For a variety of reasons, some related to the conservative proclivities of Orange County voters and others unique to specific municipalities, term limits were popular in Orange County years before anyone else was even discussing them as a viable political reform.[13]

Evaluating the Experience with Local Term Limits

The most frequently raised objections to term limits, which may be used as bases for empirical evaluation of the effects of the reform, can be summarized as rough propositions:

1. Term limits are not needed—legislative turnover is high enough already.
2. Term limits will reduce the quality of government.
3. Term limits will reduce the number of persons seeking election.
4. Term limits will depress the quality of candidates.
5. Term limits will reduce the level of political participation.
6. Term limits will enhance the power of the executive branch.
7. Term limits will enhance the power of legislative staff.
8. Term limits will increase the influence of special interest groups.

Both surveys asked officials to evaluate most of these arguments regarding the impact of term limits as applied to local government. The research methodology first sought the opinions of elected officials in term-limited cities on the conventional case against term limits, as summarized by the eight propositions listed above. Next, the attitudes of public officials already serving under term limits were compared to those of elected officials facing or "threatened by" term-limitation measures in upcoming elections. This strategy assumed that elected officials in cities considering term limits would be especially hostile toward them, given the prevalent view that most politicians do not want limits placed on how long they may serve in elected office. A survey of California state legislators conducted after the passage of Prop. 140 validates this view.[14]

What do elected officials in Orange County think about the impact of term limits on local legislators? Responses to the conventional case against term limits for the two surveys are presented in Tables 3 and 4. Generally, both groups of respondents were far more favorably disposed toward local term limits than we would have predicted, especially those council members facing the prospect of limits for the first time.

Beginning with the most dire overall prediction about the impact of term limits, that they will decrease the quality of local government, the survey revealed that contrary to this cataclysmic prediction, 77.3 percent of term-limited officials disagreed or strongly disagreed with that assessment. Moreover, 70 percent of the elected officials in cities considering limits felt the same way.

While the quality of government, however defined by the respondent, may not be diminished by term limits, there remains the question of whether or not municipalities *need* term limits. Of course, exactly what constitutes "need" is relative. There is no single percentage of turnover in any legislative body necessary for healthy and responsive political representation. That is a judgment call left to debate by individual analysts. Yet, an overwhelming 72.8 percent of term-limited officials agreed that term limits are needed at the local level. By comparison, a substantially smaller majority of officials in cities considering term limits, 57.1 percent, also agreed that term limits were necessary.

Even if there is a need for greater turnover at city hall, the critics claim

Table 3
Attitudes of Elected Officials*
in Term-Limited Cities

Proposition	SA	A	DISA	SDISA
	Percentages†			
There is a need for term limits on city council members.	45.5	27.3	18.2	9.1
Term limits will lead to a reduction in the quality of individuals running for city council.	4.5	9.1	50.0	36.4
Term limits have increased the number of individuals running for city council.	9.5	42.9	42.9	4.8
Term limits will enhance the power of the city manager.	13.6	31.8	50.0	4.5
Term limits will enhance the power of city staff.	13.6	27.3	54.5	4.5
Term limits will increase the influence of special interest groups in your city.	13.6	18.2	36.4	31.8
Term limits will decrease the quality of local government.	0.0	22.7	45.5	31.8

SA = Strongly Agree, A = Agree, DISA = Disagree, SDISA = Strongly Disagree

*N = 22.
†Percentages may not add up to 100 due to rounding.

term limits will reduce the number of persons seeking election, thereby diminishing electoral competition. The survey results show that 52.4 percent of term-limited officials believe term limits have increased the number of individuals running for city council, while 40 percent of officials in cities considering term limits agree that term limits will have this result.

How reliable were the elected officials' opinions? A consultation of Orange County voting records revealed that in every city with term limits prior to the 1992 fall elections the number of candidates for each available seat on council had, in fact, decreased. The same was true however, for all but one of the cities without term limits as of 1992. Thus, this may be one area where more empirical research is needed to settle the dispute between term-limitation advocates and opponents. It is clear, however, that term limits have not *increased* the average number of individuals seeking to serve on city councils in Orange County.[15]

What about the quality of individuals running for local elected office? Opponents claim term limits will reduce candidate quality. Elected officials in both surveys disagreed (see Tables 3 and 4); 86.4 percent of the term-limited officials disagreed or strongly disagreed with this claim, and 76.2 percent

Table 4
Attitudes of Elected Officials*
in Cities Considering Term Limits

Proposition	SA	A	DISA	SDISA
	Percentages†			
There is a need for term limits on city council members.	33.3	23.8	4.8	38.1
Term limits will lead to a reduction in the quality of individuals running for city council.	4.8	19.0	42.9	33.3
Term limits have increased the number of individuals running for city council.	6.7	33.3	40.0	20.0
Term limits will enhance the power of the city manager.	23.8	19.0	33.3	23.8
Term limits will enhance the power of city staff.	23.8	19.0	33.3	23.8
Term limits will increase the influence of special interest groups in your city.	19.0	14.3	33.3	33.3
Term limits will decrease the quality of local government.	15.0	15.0	30.0	40.0

SA = Strongly Agree, A = Agree, DISA = Disagree, SDISA = Strongly Disagree

*N = 21.
†Percentages may not add up to 100 due to rounding.

of officials in cities considering term limits felt the same way. Moreover, in contrast with the state legislators surveyed by Price and Neves, not a single respondent to either of our surveys said term limits would have dissuaded them from running for office when they first ran for city council.

By reducing the importance of elections due to the "safety" of term limits, critics argue that term limits will reduce political participation. This argument has been substantiated on a limited scale by David Rausch's study of term limits in San Mateo County, California. However, the research presented here on Orange County elections shows a different result. Table 5 presents the average level of voter turnout in the seven cities with term limits prior to 1992, before and after the adoption of term limits. In every case the averages include information from at least five elections held prior to the adoption of term limits for purposes of establishing a credible baseline.

In every city except Villa Park, the average voter turnout has increased following the adoption to term limits. In Cypress and La Palma, two small cities, turnout increased on average by 25 percent or more following the adoption of term limits. Even in large cities, such as Irvine and Huntington Beach, the increase in turnout after the adoption of term limits has been substantial, at 15 percent and 19 percent respectively.

Table 5
Average Level of Voter Turnout in Municipal Elections
Before and After Adoption of Term Limits

City	Year Adopted	Average Before (%)	Average After (%)	Difference
Santa Ana	1966	34.00	36.21	2.21
Seal Beach	1974	30.67	39.44	8.77
Cypress	1977	31.67	60.25	28.58
Villa Park	1978	64.20	62.67	-1.53
Huntington Beach	1978	39.33	58.40	19.07
La Palma	1982	34.17	73.40	38.23
Irvine	1986	48.63	64.00	15.37

We cannot conclude that term limits caused higher levels of voter turnout in these cities. Turnout could have increased for a number of reasons completely unrelated to term limits, such as the salience of local, state or national races, the presence of controversial ballot measures, or changes in the date on which municipal elections are held. However, it appears safe to conclude that the adoption of term limits in six of the seven cities under review in Orange County did not *reduce* voter turnout as the critics continue to allege.

Finally, what impact will term limits have on the relative distribution of political power at city hall? Opponents say the power of the executive, legislative staff, and special interests will increase with the arrival of inexperienced, term-limited legislators. In general, the results from both surveys, presented in Tables 3 and 4, do little to confirm these predictions.

Every city in Orange County has a council-manager form of government, even where the mayor is directly elected. There are no mayor-council governments in Orange County. Hence, the comparable power shift might be to the city manager. Will term limits enhance the power of the city manager? In term-limited cities, 54.5 percent of the officials disagreed or strongly disagreed with this assessment. An even higher percentage of officials from cities considering term limits, 57.1 percent, disagreed or strongly disagreed with that claim. It should be noted that a sizable percentage of officials in both surveys strongly agreed that term limits will enhance the power of the city manager. When it comes to greater power for city staff, 59 percent of term-limited officials disagreed or strongly disagreed with that argument and 57.1 percent of officials in the second survey group had the same opinion.

No one wants to introduce any reform that would unwittingly increase the influence of special interests, especially after campaign finance reforms in the early 1970s did precisely that, enabling the explosion of PAC power. But neither elected officials serving under term limits nor those in communities contemplating them think term limits will increase the influence of special interests. In term-limited cities, 68.2 percent of the officials disagreed or strongly disagreed with that assessment and 66.6 percent of the officials in the second survey shared the same view of this prediction.

On all three counts, regarding greater power for the city manager, city staff, or special interests, officials who have experienced term limits and those facing adoption of them rebutted the traditional case against term limitations.

Conclusion

We have sought to add the experience of Orange County municipalities with term limitations to the emerging body of knowledge concerning the politics of the term-limitation movement and the impact of term limits on representative democracy. With only a few important exceptions, this study shows that the conventional case against term limits is not sustained by the experience of elected officials serving in Orange County's term-limited cities. Neither were the negative consequences of term limits widely expected by elected officials serving in the cities actively considering term limits in 1992. Of course, showing that term limits do not produce the negative effects alleged by the critics is entirely different from proving that term limits produce the salutary effects claimed by proponents.

When it comes to assessing the impact of term limits, whether at the municipal, state or federal level of government, the attitudes of political participants may be suspect. California's state legislators were decidedly opposed to the passage of Prop. 140 and fearful of its consequences. This is to be expected. If members of the U.S. Congress were given a similar survey of the potential impact of term limits on that body, we would expect a similar set of attitudes. Both groups of elected officials, those operating with term limits and those anticipating this reform, confirm the need for municipal term limits and discount the arguments made against their adoption.

This study is intended to stimulate others to take municipalities seriously as a place to assess the political and policy consequences of the term-limitation reform.

Notes

1. See, John Clayton Thomas, "The Term Limits Movement in U.S. Cities," *National Civic Review*, 81:2, Spring-Summer 1992, pp. 155–173; John Clayton Thomas, "The Coming of Municipal Term Limits—Prepare for the Debate," *Public Management*, 75:7, July 1993, pp. 12–14; and Erica Gould, "The Municipal Term Limits Groundswell," *Term Limits Outlook Series* (Washington, D.C.: U.S. Term Limits, August 1993).

2. Recent examples of this perspective include Morris P. Fiorina, *Divided*

Government (New York: MacMillan, 1992); Thomas E. Mann, "Congressional Term Limits: A Bad Idea Whose Time Should Never Come," paper presented at the Conference of the Politics and Law of Term Limits, Cato Institute, Washington, D.C., December 1, 1993; Nelson W. Polsby, "Some Arguments Against Congressional Term Limitations," *Harvard Journal of Law and Public Policy*, Winter 1993, pp. 101–107; and David E. Price, *The Congressional Experience* (Boulder, Colo.: Westview Press, 1992). For a response to this view, see, Mark P. Petracca, "Predisposed to Oppose: Political Scientists and Term Limitations," *Polity*, Summer 1992, pp. 657–672.

3. There was, however, extensive experience with mandatory and voluntary rotation in America from the 17th through the late 19th centuries at various levels of government. See, Mark P. Petracca, "Rotation in Office: The History of the Idea," in *Limiting Legislative Terms*, Gerald Benjamin and Michael J. Malbin, eds. (Washington, D.C.: Congressional Research Quarterly, 1992).

4. The exception is the developing legal debate on the constitutionality of state-imposed term limits for members of Congress. A full set of citations for this debate can be found in Mark P. Petracca, "A New Defense of State-Imposed Congressional Term Limits," *PS: Political Science and Politics*, December 1993, pp. 700–705; and Daniel Hays Lowenstein, "Are Congressional Term Limits Constitutional?" paper presented at the annual meeting of the American Political Science Association, Washington, D.C. September 3, 1993.

5. Exceptions are A. Dick and J. Lott, "Reconciling Voters' Behavior and Legislative Term Limits," *Journal of Public Economics*, January 1993, pp. 1–14; Gary F. Moncrief, Joel A. Thompson, Michael Haddon, and Robert Hoyer, "For Whom the Bell Tolls: Term Limits and State Legislatures," *Legislative Studies Quarterly,* February 1992, pp. 37–47; W. Robert Reed and D. Eric Schansberg, "An Analysis of the Impact of Congressional Term Limits," *Economic Inquiry* (forthcoming); and John David Rausch, "Testing Legislative Term Limitations: The San Mateo Board of County Supervisors as Laboratory," *National Civic Review*, 82:2, Spring 1993, pp. 149–156.

6. The constitutionality of California's Prop. 140, the initiative passed in 1990 to limit term limits for state legislators, has already been upheld by both the California Supreme Court and the U.S. Supreme Court, see, Mark P. Petracca, "Do Term Limits 'Rob Voters' of Democratic Rights? An Evaluation and Response," *Western State University Law Review*, Spring 1993, pp. 547–567.

7. In two major decisions, California Appeals Courts have invalidated term-limitation ordinances in general-law cities, see, Mark P. Petracca, "Reining in Local Politicians with Term Limits," *Orange County Metropolitan*, 15 May 1993, p. 10.

8. As a matter of local convention, under this means of selection the office of mayor normally rotates among the council members on an annual basis.

9. The fourth-largest city in the county, Garden Grove, contemplated the adoption of term limits in 1992.

10. Nonetheless, some groups have found it difficult to gather the signatures necessary within the specified time period to qualify a term-limitation initiative for the local ballot. This was the case in 1990 and 1991 in the City of Newport Beach. A citizen initiative was successfully qualified in 1992 and went on to an easy victory in November.

11. Mayoral terms, where the mayor is directly elected, are either two or four years.

12. Likewise, California's Prop. 140 is "non-rotative" in that it establishes an

absolute limit on the number of years any person may serve in either the state assembly or state senate.

13. A detailed case study of Santa Ana's early adoption to term limits confirms the presence of similar motivations back in 1966, see, Craig Capon, "Term Limits in Santa Ana," unpublished paper, University of California at Irvine, December, 1993.

14. See, Charles Price and Helen Neves, "Term Limits: California's Gift (?) to the Nation," *California Journal*, December 1991, pp. 547–555. A new survey by Price reveals a different attitude toward term limits among the first class of California Assembly members elected after the adoption of Prop. 140, see Charles Price, "Class of '92: The Proposition 140 Babies," *California Journal*, April 1993, pp. 34–38.

15. This finding is consistent with the study of term limits in San Mateo County, California. See, for discussion, John David Rausch, "Testing Legislative Term Limitations: The San Mateo County Board of Supervisors as Laboratory," *National Civic Review*, 82:2, pp. 149–156.

PART VI
The Future

A Different Kind of Politics

David Mathews

America has a secret political life. We don't see it because it doesn't fit the conventional definition of politics. It is a public form of politics that offers different ways of dealing with old problems.

The conventional wisdom was set in stone a generation ago when Walter Lippmann pronounced the American public a political fiction, a phantom of our imagination. He meant that people lacked the sense of responsibility and intelligence needed to govern themselves. The only public he saw was "a bewildering herd" that had to be "put in its place."

Based on ten years of research at the Kettering Foundation and work with all kinds of Americans on all kinds of issues, I have come to the conclusion that Lippmann was wrong—not in his criticisms of popular passions and all the things that go wrong in our democracy—but in his conclusion about the public's place.[1]

There is a public—and it is more than just an elite five percent who are well educated and altruistic. It is people from all walks of life who take responsibility for what is happening in the country and act. They aren't always sure of how to act; often they are frustrated. Still, they care and they keep on trying.

As much as citizens like to blame "the government" and "the politicians," when they stop to think for a while, they know that citizens are themselves a large part of "the problem." Kettering research shows that, deep down, Americans recognize that change cannot take place unless people act. As two good citizens from Tennessee put it, "Nobody's going to come along and make everything better. It's us. We're the problem, we're the solution." More succinctly, a man from Texas said, "Nothing will change unless people act."

A new breed of citizen activism—what I would call public politics—is

Reprinted with permission from National Civic Review, *Vol. 83, No. 3, Summer/Fall, 1994. Published by the National Civic League Press, Denver, Colorado.*

being born out of people's sense of responsibility and their frustration with politics as usual. This *public politics is different in objectives, organization and strategies.* Public politics is focused on the well-being of a community as a whole, rather than single issues. People are trying to solve problems, not just by working on projects, but by strengthening the civic infrastructure of their cities and states [for a definition of civic infrastructure, see, John Parr, "Civic Infrastructure: A New Approach to Improving Community Life," *National Civic Review*, 82:2, Spring 1993, pp. 93–100]. Finding more productive ways of working together is an important objective. As one civic leader reasoned, "If all the people in the city are banded together to make it a better place to live, then it will be a better place to live." Broad-based organizations now are emerging with members who think of themselves as citizens rather than representatives of some group or interest. These organizations are spanning economic, social and geographic boundaries that have separated Americans from one another and balkanized conventional politics.

For example, a few years ago, Dorothy Stuck and her friends in Arkansas, concerned with problems that governments alone could not solve, formed a citizens organization unlike the typical blue-ribbon commission or coalition of organizations. Participants do not represent anyone but themselves. This organization, called the Wilowe Institute, does not hire expert planners to develop long lists of recommendations. The Institute is built around ongoing, state-wide conversation. The objective is to connect people and stimulate a host of cooperative efforts. Wilowe is a catalyst and political incubator. Ask Stuck about the results and she will point to the initiatives and new organizations that have grown out of Wilowe's work, such as a development group that strengthens the economy by utilizing indigenous capabilities. They call what they are doing "Building Arkansas from the bottom up."

While determined to get results, these new public groups have broader objectives than traditional organizations. In Grand Rapids, Michigan, a retired business executive, Carl Eschels, and Yvonne Sims, a school administrator, helped establish a network of more than 49 civic and educational organizations that addresses three common issues every year. The objective is not to promote particular projects, but to build more effective working relationships throughout the community. The network itself, now over ten years old, is a concrete accomplishment. It is a civic superhighway and, though not as visible as physical infrastructure, it is just as essential. It links various sectors of the community, creating new ties and strengthening norms of cooperation. It generates what political economists call "social capital." Conventional politics uses a lot of financial capital, yet its programs often fail to achieve their objectives because there is not enough of this other kind of capital to sustain them [see, for background, Robert D. Putnam, "What Makes Democracy Work?," *National Civic Review*, 82:2, Spring 1993, pp. 101–107].

Public politics is as different in its strategies as it is in its organization and objectives. Rather than merely trying to get people to vote or win converts to a special cause, practitioners of public politics concentrate on the things people have to do *before* they will vote. They are more concerned about the public's ability to make sound decisions on a range of issues than they are about enlisting advocates for one position on one issue. Some practitioners of public politics create gateways into politics and develop the skills needed for public action through a particular kind of forum. These are called National Issues Forums, even though they are locally sponsored and financed. They provide a setting where people can get their hands on issues and turn first impressions and personal reactions into shared, reflective judgments about how to act.

These are deliberative forums, not debates or discussions. What sets them apart is that people are challenged to work on making tough choices inherent to each issue under consideration. The forums are held merely to provide information or an opportunity to criticize decisions others have made. Participants have to "work through" the conflicts and contradictions themselves. They have to weigh carefully the costs and consequences of all of the options as well as the views of others. That is what deliberation means—weighing carefully. We can't really expect legislative bodies to be deliberative unless the public also appreciates and has a capacity for deliberation.

Our research shows that not just any kind of talk will do when Americans are deciding whether or not to act on an issue. In order to make these decisions, people need a deliberative dialogue and issues framed in public terms (i.e., framed in terms of what is valuable to people in everyday life, rather than in expert or ideological terms). They need this kind of conversation with one another to answer four "gateway" questions:

- *Does the issue affect my life?* People have to find a connection between the issue they hear about and their own sense of what is valuable before they will get involved. However, their interests go well beyond what happens to their pocketbooks.
- *Can I do anything?* Even if people are convinced that a problem is serious and poses a danger, they won't take the next step unless they can find some way to get a handle on the problem. Unless we can get our hands on a problem, we tend to give up. When we do find a handle—something we can do personally—we think we *might* make a difference. That sense of possibility is charged with political energy.
- *Who will join me?* People are unwilling to act unless they see that others are going to act with them. They want to know who will join them. Instinctively, we seem to know that we're powerless when we are alone and that change is more likely when we are banded together. Moreover, people reason, "If we start working together on little things, we can get together on bigger things."

• *What should we do?* In order to act together, people have to make choices about what they are going to do. And unless those choices are sound, they are not likely to act wisely. That is not a conclusion from research; it's just common sense. What research shows is that people understand the importance of deliberation in making sound choices. While they may never use the term, they know that making choices requires looking at the "gray areas" of issues, examining all the options, getting different perspectives, exploring alternatives rather than trying to score points, and carefully weighing trade-offs.

Often, we don't see what is different about public politics because we mistake it for conventional politics. The public I am talking about is not reducible to the supporters of protest candidates or groups insisting that nothing affect their backyards. The public is more than the interest groups and citizen activists who champion a particular cause or solution. It is not the silent majority or the many volunteers who care for the less fortunate. The public is political, not exclusively social. It is concerned about problem solving and building political communities that transcend neighbors and friends. Yet, public politics is more than local politics. The issues forums, for example, don't just deal with purely parochial interests. They deal with all the major national issues: health care, the deficit, welfare, our country's role in the world.

Public politics is even creeping into professions like journalism. Some newspapers, along with some radio and television stations (sometimes working together), are experimenting with different ways of covering issues and campaigns. They are trying to connect their reporting to the four questions that people ask before getting involved. As with the other examples of public politics, there is something distinctive about what these journalists are doing. They are not just *informing* a public; they are helping to *form* one. There is even a different name for what is happening at the Wichita *Eagle,* the *Oregonian* in Portland, the Dayton *Daily News,* and National Public Radio— to mention a few. It is called "public journalism."

While public politics is not ideal politics or an alternative to conventional politics, it does have the potential to supply some of what is missing from "politics as usual." For example, without a good measure of public deliberation, our political conversations easily degenerate into personal pleadings, sound bites, and partisan rancor. Without holding council with one another, people can't fashion and own their opinions. Opinions tend to become "store bought," prepackaged and unreflective. Without deliberation, the public has difficulty learning its own business.

Unfortunately, conventional politics doesn't seem to understand how the public learns the public's business. Much of what is done to "educate" people is counter-productive. Americans are bombarded with facts that don't connect to their concerns. Choices for dealing with issues usually are narrowed down to two: conservative and liberal, Democratic and Republican. Little time is allowed for the public to work its way through an issue. Plans are publicized and ready-made opinions are marketed like soap. There appears to be little appreciation of the necessity for people to form their own opinions so they will own and take responsibility for them. However, many of our problems—crime is at the top of the list—require an engaged and committed public that will act rather than a persuaded citizenry that only defers to the action of others.

We depend on public politics working as it should, not only for effective citizen action but for conventional politics to work as it should. Yet, when Kettering reports that citizens have their own ways of organizing and solving problems, the response is usually, "That's nice," implying "That really doesn't have anything to do with politics." Wrong. Public politics is the politics the public uses to meet its "undelegable" responsibilities. There are certain things that a democratic public must do in order for a representative government to work effectively. Only a public can define the public's interest. Only a public can give legitimacy to government by giving it direction. Only a public can create the common ground necessary for solving public problems. Only a public can generate the political will required for hard work and sacrifice. All require deliberative, public politics.

Perhaps the greatest contribution public politics can make is to change our understanding of the political. We have made conventional politics the special province of a few, a realm apart from everyday life. No wonder people feel excluded—currently, there isn't much place for them in the political system, except as consumers of government's services or properly outraged critics. Public politics, on the other hand, treats citizens as public actors, as people who have work to do, who have to produce, not just consume. The implication of that definition is that citizens have to hold one another, not just office holders, accountable. That's not a bad idea. Otherwise, politics remains a contest of "Us" versus "Them."

Notes

1. For an extended discussion of many of the concepts presented in this chapter, consult David Mathews's *Politics for People: Finding a Responsible Public Voice* (Urbana and Chicago: University of Illinois Press, 1994).

Effective Citizen Involvement

Charles K. Bens

Governance in the 1990s is quickly being transformed from an exercise in backroom decision making to an up-front, open, "we-want-in-on-the-decision-making" experience for citizens. The public is both frustrated with and angered by the inability of governing institutions to adequately address and resolve the wide range of difficult social and economic issues facing them. Accordingly, an ever-growing number of people have been asking—if not demanding—to be brought into the decision-making process in a meaningful way.

Citizens will not tolerate being informed after the fact, or merely being politely informed or consulted along the route toward important decisions. They want to be seriously involved, from the beginning to the end, in any project or issue-resolution process. Better yet, many citizens would welcome a more active role in the delivery of public services. For example, in many communities, low-income housing tenants now participate in housing authority governance; local parent groups are making school policy; welfare recipients are changing the system of counseling and training people to get off the dole; citizens are blocking undesirable public projects; and voters are forcing spending limitations on legislative bodies.

The literature is replete with stories of constructive citizen intervention in the decisions of government. The techniques used to accomplish these feats are fairly well documented. However, there is still much work to be done in bringing more citizens into the decision-making process in a constructive way. This chapter seeks to fill that need, with an eye toward saving time and effort on the part of community groups and governmental bodies seeking to quickly identify some of the proven techniques for involving citizens meaningfully.

Reprinted with permission from National Civic Review, *Vol. 83, No. 1, Winter/Spring, 1994. Published by the National Civic League Press, Denver, Colorado.*

The Conditions for Involvement

The actual conditions that provide an opportunity for increased community involvement will differ from one situation to another, and usually are determined by the severity of the circumstances and the receptivity and openness of the government to include the public in decisions is illustrated in Figure 1.

Governments at all three levels seem reluctant and even unable to include the public in most serious issues, because they do not trust the judgment of citizens. The excuse given—if any—often is a presumed unfamiliarity of the public with the content of the issue at hand. Another view suggests that the underlying reason is purely and simply the reluctance to share power.

Regardless of the root cause, the result usually is the same: Government officials (elected and appointed) retain the power to make the decision and often either don't make one, or make the wrong one. In a governance landscape characterized by numerous pressure groups, vacillating public opinion and a nervous bureaucracy, decisions are delayed or watered-down in an effort to please everyone and offend no one. Failure to develop an adequate solution results in a gradual worsening of the original circumstance, problem or issue. Here are some examples of the types of problems that defy solution in this ineffective decision-making environment:

- Quality, cost and accountability in education;
- Quality, cost and accountability in health care;
- Reduction and/or disposal of solid waste;
- Crime and the related issues of drugs and guns;
- Restructuring of the economy (and resulting unemployment);
- Public sector debt;
- Deterioration of the infrastructure; and
- Welfare reform.

These and other issues will remain unresolved until the public is finally and seriously brought into the decision-making process. The relative openness of governing institutions to citizen involvement may be located along a three-stage continuum, with each stage defined by a set of conditions, characteristics and elements:

Stage One: Closed System

- One strong political party
- Weak or insecure leadership
- Secretive bureaucracy

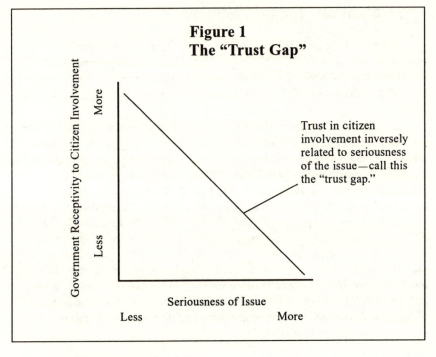

Figure 1
The "Trust Gap"

Government Receptivity to Citizen Involvement
More
Less

Trust in citizen involvement inversely related to seriousness of the issue—call this the "trust gap."

Seriousness of Issue
Less
More

- Special interest group-driven
- Media-controlled
- Unorganized citizens
- Poor information systems
- Strong, inflexible unions

Stage Two: Uncertain System

- Multiple influential political parties
- Leadership struggle
- Self-centered bureaucracy
- Alliances of interests
- Media not fully competent
- Some citizen groups, but little coherence
- Lax information systems
- Little or no labor organization

Stage Three: Open System

- Progressive, cooperative politicians
- Open and shared leadership

- Progressive, quality-oriented bureaucracy
- Community cooperation
- Competent, involved media
- Active, effective citizen groups
- Information collected and shared freely
- Strong, cooperative unions

Exemplary Profiles

There are literally thousands of examples of both good and poor community involvement experiences, but two brief community profiles help illustrate what can happen when the conditions are not right for citizen participation.

County B. This is a rural community whose economy is based primarily on tourism and farming. The elected officials are very conservative, with a history of regional differences and back room decision making. County B embarked on an expensive planning process which relied heavily on technical consulting services and very little front-end citizen involvement. Midway through the process, public meetings were called, but very poorly attended. Then, the county commissioners reluctantly invited citizens to attend a visioning session, but were dissatisfied with the vision adopted. County B now has spent $175,000 and several months on a planning process that has produced no agreement on where the community should go or how it should get there. The economy is dying fast and the welfare rolls are climbing. No strategy for tourism, farming or industry exists, and County B likely will continue to decline as the elected leaders argue and blame everyone but themselves.

County N. This is a rural community with some farming and tourism, as well as a small residential base of commuters to a nearby urban area. The elected officials are a mix of conservatives and progressives with a history of disagreement and reluctance to assume responsibility for regional issues. As part of their planning process, the county commissioners decided to invite active citizen participation from the beginning. The study process involved preparation of a very brief background document, which was quickly reviewed at an open public forum. Issues were jointly identified and numerous citizens volunteered to be active throughout the planning process. Citizens were trained in facilitation techniques so they could conduct local focus group discussions. A consultant supplied questionnaires and focus group questions, which could be amended as participants saw fit. The press was actively involved. The final public meeting put the stamp of approval on a vision statement, goals and objectives, as well as specific action plans on a wide range of planning topics. The only negative press was a letter to the editor from a disgruntled politician. The media and general public enthusiastically supported the plan, which now is being implemented. The total cost: $75,000.

Skills and Techniques for Community Involvement

The key distinctions between County B and County N were 1) the willingness of the county commission to involve citizens and 2) the skills to conduct a public participation process. There are many remedies for barriers to willingness, but they are complicated and involve changing the political climate and fundamental reform of how government interacts with citizens. Some of the literature recommended in the resource list at the end of the chapter deals with overcoming these substantial structural and social barriers. Below we discuss the more manageable problem of developing the skills to conduct effective public participation processes.

1. *Community assessment.* A good starting point in determining how much community involvement is desirable and feasible is some assessment of existing community strengths and weaknesses. An excellent tool for such an exercise is the National Civic League's Civic Index. The Index consists of ten components:

- Citizen Participation
- Community Leadership
- Government Performance
- Volunteerism and Philanthropy
- Intergroup Relations
- Civic Education
- Community Information Sharing
- Capacity for Cooperation and Consensus Building
- Community Vision and Pride
- Inter-Community Cooperation

2. *Civic infrastructure.* Infrastructure in this case refers to the structure of government as well as the mechanisms and practices of community involvement. How people are elected and how government is structured can exert significant influence on the extent and nature of community involvement. A structure based on an unrepresentative electoral system can be divisive, and a bureaucracy without a chief administrative officer can be fragmented and corrupt. Useful resources on this topic can be obtained from the International City/County Management Association and the National Civic League (see resource list).

3. *Leadership.* Nurturing and facilitative political leadership is vital to

effective community involvement. Some communities have serious leadership voids that only can be filled by new blood at the political level. Knowing what to look for in an elected leader is one of the keys to community success. A publication that can help in this exercise is *Cutting through Charisma: A Layman's Guide to Electing Better Politicians*, which provides a set of guidelines for assessing both incumbents and new candidates to help voters make more informed and objective decisions about their elected leadership (see resource list).

4. Research. In some instances involved citizens may need to distance themselves from government and rely on independent research mechanisms and agencies for information. Some government agencies have weak information-gathering skills, particularly in collecting comprehensive community input. *Enjoying Research*, available from the Ontario (Canada) Ministry of Tourism and Recreation, is an excellent "how to" manual covering such techniques as questionnaires, surveys and interviews. It also includes a step-by-step research guide (see resource list). The quality of community involvement often depends on the quality of information used to capture community attitudes and opinions. Consequently, understanding how to gather, analyze and present information is critical to the success of projects relying on citizen involvement.

5. Facilitation skills. Another skill needed to ensure successful community involvement is the ability to facilitate meetings. Getting active and comprehensive input from all participants at any gathering and reaching agreement on sensitive issues is not an easy task. Special skills are needed to lead problem-solving teams and few people possess such skills naturally. *Facilitation Skills for Team Leaders* is a handy resource for facilitators, but such skills cannot ordinarily be learned from a book (see resource list). Formal training in process facilitation is available in most metro areas.

6. Collaborative decision making. Many communities do not really understand how to design and conduct a collaborative problem-solving or decision-making process. Officials may know how to conduct public meetings or engage in debate, but these techniques result in decisions made by "decision makers," which may be unacceptable to a sizable segment of the community. A valuable beginning resource for groups and communities wishing to develop collaborative skills is the Spring 1991 issue of the *National Civic Review*, which presents both the theory of collaboration and some case studies and "how to" guidelines.

7. Problem solving. Within the collaborative problem solving and facilitation skills categories is a more specific skill set that merits special attention. The ability to actually follow a systematic problem-solving model is critical to the successful resolution of community issues. A good resource for problem-solving models is *Working with Volunteer Boards*, developed by the Ontario Ministry of Citizenship and Culture (see resource list). Effective problem-solving models use such tools as brainstorming, force-field analysis and decision grids to clearly define the problem and then systematically guide groups toward the most feasible and high-impact solutions. Such tools have the power to transform otherwise dysfunctional groups into high-performing teams.

8. *Conflict management.* Another special skill set within the collaborative problem-solving process involves the ability to successfully manage conflict. There are five common methods of managing conflict, ranging from avoidance to collaboration as diagrammed in Figure 2. There is an appropriate time and place for each conflict-management approach, and knowing when and how to use it is a key ingredient to successful community involvement. *Working with Volunteer Boards*, among other publications, offers useful beginning perspectives on conflict management (see resource list).

Conclusion: Customer-Oriented Government

The citizen-as-customer principle—which is transforming government into a more open and participatory institution—suggests we are all consumers of public services and policies and should be treated with appropriate respect and consideration. This is one of the central themes of Osborne and Gaebler's *Reinventing Government*, which supplies an excellent set of guidelines for any government agency committed to improving itself and meeting or exceeding the expectations of citizen-customers on a regular basis.

But high performance in public agencies is not the exclusive responsibility of government. Citizens have an important contribution to make, particularly in becoming better informed and more involved in the running of their governments. Community involvement is a key instrument in the process. Good citizenship is hard work, and implies much more than voting or attending an occasional public meeting. The price of not fulfilling the broader responsibilities of citizenship is dramatized in the failure of governing institutions to respond to the challenges facing society.

Healthy communities, with vibrant economies, safe streets and proactive policies to *prevent* problems rather than *fight* problems, are the product of effective leadership skills and well developed ethic of citizenship. The current clamor for better leadership conveniently ignores the source of at least half the fault.

Resource List

Publications

The Civic Index: A New Approach to Improving Community Life. Available from the National Civic League, 1445 Market Street, Suite 300, Denver, Colorado, 80202–1728.

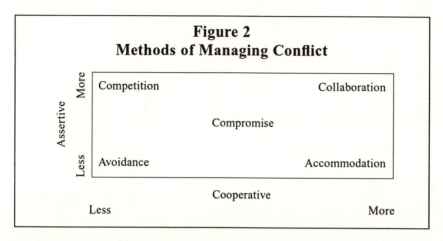

Figure 2
Methods of Managing Conflict

Cutting through Charisma: A Layman's Guide to Electing Better Politicians. Available from Advanced Performance Systems, 456 College Street, Toronto, Ontario, Canada M6G1A1.

Effective Project Planning, by W. Alan Randolph and Barry Z. Posner. Prentice Hall, Englewood Cliffs, New Jersey 07632.

Enjoying Research. Available from the Ministry of Tourism and Recreation, The Queens's Printer for Ontario, Queen's Park, Toronto, Ontario, Canada M7A2E.

Facilitation Skills for Team Leaders. Available from Advanced Performance Systems, 456 College Street, Toronto, Ontario, Canada M6G1A1.

Managing Change: A Guide to Producing Innovation from Within, by Sandra J. Hale and Mary M. Williams. The Urban Institute Press, 2100 M. Street, N.W., Washington, D.C. 20037.

National Civic Review (specific issues listed below). Available from the National Civic League, 1445 Market Street, Suite 300, Denver, Colorado 80202–1728.

The Achieving Organization (Vol. 79, No. 3, May-June 1990).

Civic Infrastructure (Vol. 82, No. 2, Spring 1993).

Collaborative Problem Solving (Vol. 80, No. 2, Spring 1991).

Making Citizen Democracy Work (Vol. 79, No. 5, September-October 1990).

Reinventing Government: How the Entrepreneurial Spirit is Transforming the Public Sector, by David Osborne and Ted Gaebler. Available from Penguin Books USA., Inc., 375 Hudson Street, New York, N.Y., 10014 (Penguin Books Canada, Ltd., 10 Alcorn Avenue, Toronto, Ontario, Canada M4V3B2).

Working with Volunteer Boards. Available from Ministry of Citizenship and Culture, Publications Service Section, Fifth Floor, Bay Street, Toronto, Ontario, Canada M7A1M8.

Organizations

Center for Living Democracy, RR#1 Black Fox Road, Brattleboro, Vermont 05301.

International City/County Management Association, 777 North Capitol Street, N.E., Suite 500, Washington, D.C. 20002–4201.

Study Circles Resource Center, Route 169, P.O. Box 203, Pomfret, Connecticut 06258. Supplies books, audio recordings, articles, and a newsletter on wide range of topics related to citizen involvement.

Reconnecting Citizens with Public Life

David D. Chrislip

A growing sense of anomie pervades the conventional wisdom regarding the role of citizens in politics. This way of thinking holds that citizens no longer care about public life. They have no sense of civic duty or public concerns. Efforts to counter this breakdown usually look no deeper than reforms designed to improve faith and participation in electoral politics. Few politicians take the time to listen to Americans or understand how they feel about politics and the role they want to play in public life.

A 1990 study conducted by Richard Harwood for the Kettering Foundation tells a very different story.[1] Rather than being apathetic or unconcerned, citizens are angry and frustrated by politics as usual. They feel cut out of the process and unheard; they do not see how they can have any real impact on public affairs. Thus, according to Harwood's focus group research, government lies beyond the reach of ordinary citizens. Governing institutions do not respond to the concerns and needs of individuals, neighborhoods or communities, but to interest groups and power players.

Nonetheless, citizens genuinely want to be heard, understood and considered. They want to have a sense that their involvement can make a difference, that the *public* defines the public interest, not government officials or narrow interest groups.

In 1989, the sprawling desert metropolis of Phoenix, Arizona launched a year-long, citizen-based strategic planning and community-assessment exercise called the Phoenix Futures Forum [see "The Phoenix Futures Forum: Creating Vision, Implanting Community," *National Civic Review*, 80:2, Spring 1991, pp. 135–157]. The purpose of the Forum, according to an organizer, was

Reprinted with permission from National Civic Review, *Vol. 83, No. 1, Winter/Spring, 1994. Published by the National Civic League Press, Denver, Colorado.*

to put government and citizens intimately in touch with each other, and so government is a reflection of the kind of community the people want.

Citizens call for forums that can provide constructive ways for them to work together with governments on common problems. They crave information and problem-solving opportunities that transcend the polarization of exclusive partisan positions. They want intimate and direct contact with the issues and problems that concern them. Most of all, they want a sense of community, a sense that all of us are in this together.

There is no lack of desire among citizens to participate in public affairs. "I want more say in my community," said a Phoenix citizen. "I want more say in what goes on." Fed up with gridlock and impotence, citizens are seeking new ways for public involvement. Faced with a paucity of formal options for engaging constructively with governing institutions around issues of shared concern, citizens are relying on themselves for leadership and initiative. They are tackling difficult problems not in anarchic or antagonistic ways, but in ways that reflect a new kind of democracy and sense of citizenship. It is a deeper, more intimate and inclusive kind of democracy—more direct than representative, more consensual than voting. This vision of public life constitutes a shift in the practice of democracy from hostility to civility, from advocacy to engagement, from confrontation to conversation, from debate to dialogue, and from separation to community.

This shift is occurring in many places on many issues. Citizens no longer defer to elected leaders or experts, trusting instead in their own capacity to work together and their deep sense of commitment to each other and where they live. These collaborative endeavors are engaging people in new ways that provide the role in public life citizens want, get results, empower people, build a new civic culture, and renew a sense of community.

Success and the "Civic Community"

Robert Putnam of Harvard University has written a somewhat obscure but profoundly important book, *Making Democracy Work: Civic Traditions in Modern Italy.*[2] In a seemingly innocuous, thoroughly researched, comparative study of the 20 governing regions of Italy established in 1970, Putnam discovered that the relative success or failure of each region was not determined by the usual measures of prosperity, such as access to natural resources, abundant capital wealth or levels of education. Instead, it was determined by the degree to which trust, reciprocity and, therefore, civic engagement were woven into the social fabric of the region. According to Putnam's research, success or failure depends on the extent to which "civic community" exists in the community.

The civic community, Putnam's name for these networks and norms of civic engagement, is marked by "active participation in public affairs," and a steady focus on the public good, rather than on narrower parochial ends. There is political equality—citizens are peers. There is a deep sense of individual rights, as well as obligations to the broader community. Citizens trust each other and remain helpful and respectful even when differences arise. There are deep, mutually reinforcing civic networks, associations and relationships that regularly bring citizens together in constructive ways. Putnam's findings were unambiguous: "Civic context matters for the way institutions work. By far the most important factor in explaining good government is the degree to which social and political life in a region approximates the ideal of the civic community."

Columnist Neal Peirce raised similar questions in his book *Citistates: How Urban America Can Prosper in a Competitive World*.[3] "Across America and across the globe," he writes, "Citistates are emerging as a critical focus of economic activity, of governance, of social organization for the 1990s and the century to come." He defines a "citistate" as a region consisting of a historic central city surrounded by cities and towns characterized by social, economic and environmental interdependence. He argues that America's future economic success depends on the ability of American citistates, such as Denver, Atlanta, Los Angeles, and Houston, to compete with international citistates like Hong Kong, Milan, Singapore, London, and Barcelona. He identifies three barriers facing American citistates as they struggle to compete: first, the deep socio-economic gulf between poor cities and affluent suburbs; second, physical sprawl and its damaging environmental and social consequences; and third, the inability to found effective systems of coordinated (i.e., regional) governance.

Peirce's conclusions about how to deal with these challenges sound very much like Putnam's. If America's citistates are to succeed, they must "undergird governance with a strong civic organization." The purpose of this region-wide organization would be to work "for the shared and common good over pressure from special interests and the parochial positions of fragmented local governments." These organizations would provide the forums for addressing the governance issues of regions, fostering the partnerships necessary for success and engaging *regional citizens* in the collective concerns of citistates.

The key question underlying the work of both Putnam and Peirce is whether civic community can be created. The deep historical roots of civic community found in Italy make Putnam less hopeful about creating it in places where it does not now exist. "Where norms and networks are lacking, the outlook for collective action appears bleak." Peirce is more optimistic. He believes citizens and civic leaders can plan for and develop civic networks and the new collaborative leadership skills necessary to address the problems and concerns of citistates.

Successful communities, we have learned, can develop a different kind of civic culture that can enhance their long-term problem-solving prospects. The development of civic community is an outgrowth of engaging successfully and collaboratively around public issues. When citizens succeed in working together to address common concerns, new networks and norms of civic engagement are established, and the primary focus of work shifts from parochial interests to the broader concerns of the community.

The Challenge of Leadership

Wherever one asks the question, "What makes leadership difficult on the issues your city faces?" the answers are similar whether the issue is education, health care, social injustice, economic development, or something else equally challenging. What are the typical answers? There are many people with the power to say no, but no single person or group with the power to act alone. People don't trust each other. There are hidden agendas. There is no larger vision that lends coherence to actions. No person or group has enough credibility to provide leadership. Nobody will assume a leadership role. People don't have the leadership capacities or group skills to work together constructively. There are not enough resources to address the problem. There are angry, frustrated citizens who can find no constructive way to engage in public life. Leaders and citizens avoid risk for fear of being attacked by others. The problems are complex and interdependent. They cross jurisdictional boundaries. No one is in charge. Many people don't know what the "real" problem is. Information about problems distorts understanding.

Most of these observations reflect the inability of people to work together constructively. They have to do with the process (or lack thereof) by which we engage each other on the issue at hand, not the substance or content of the problem. This is an important distinction: *it means that some citizens or civic leaders must focus on the "process" of how people work together to solve problems, not on the "content" of the problem itself.* In most communities, no one is paying attention to the process of how people engage on issues of public concern. They are too caught up in their own positions on the content or substance of the issue.

All of the answers to the question, "What makes leadership difficult?" are useful information for leaders. Each answer indicates an obstacle that must be addressed and suggests how a constructive process might be designed. For instance, if people don't know how to work together, teach them. If there is no agreement about the vision for the city or region, design an initiative whereby citizens can explore and agree on future needs and direction. If no one has the power to act unilaterally, or when no one is in charge, build a collaborative partnership. If no one person or group has the credibility to provide leadership, develop a structure for sharing leadership across the dividing lines of the community. When communities succeed in solving public issues these leadership challenges are consciously addressed.

Restoring Our Civic Will

In every city and town in America public opinion cries out for significant change in virtually every major area of community concern. Only in a few places does the political or institutional will exist to make any progress. Political leaders either fail to lead or cannot lead because they are hamstrung by competing interest groups. These leaders respond, citizens say, only to interest groups and power players who are more interested in the negative use of power—stopping others' actions that hurt them rather than moving forward on the public's concerns. The focus of leadership is on bringing together small groups of people or interest coalitions to overpower others and achieve narrow ends. As power becomes more fragmented this becomes more difficult. When it works it leaves people divided. When it does not work it leaves gridlock. The link between public opinion and political will is broken.

A new vision of civic action. Some places, however, are dealing with these challenges. In these places, citizens and civic leaders recognize a missing link between public opinion and political will—civic will. Rather than wasting time and energy on the futile hope of finding new and better candidates for office or reforming electoral politics, some citizens and a few elected leaders are using collaborative approaches to creating civic will. They understand that if the civic will exists then political and institutional will must follow. Public policy problem solving and decision making are shifting from politicians to citizens. They get results by creating a new way of doing business around public issues.

The initiative for generating civic will can come from both "ordinary" citizens and elected leaders. Many collaborative initiatives are begun by citizens who, frustrated by the failure of traditional politics, want to find constructive ways to address public concerns. The motivation for elected leaders is similar. Impeded by power players and interest groups in their attempts to lead, they look to citizens and civic will to overcome political gridlock and bureaucratic inertia. They understand that civic will is the force that can prompt and sustain needed change.

The advantages for leaders of coalescing with citizens was recognized in 1739, by the Marquis d'Argenson, a public servant in the government of Louis XV, King of France. D'Argenson outlined a "royal democracy" that could overcome the resistance to reform of the country's nobility.[4] He understood that "democracy is as much a friend of monarchy as the aristocracy is an enemy." This new kind of collective community—"a republic protected by a King"—would address the concerns of citizens while sustaining confidence in the monarchy. Unfortunately, his advice went unheeded and the citizens sent Louis XVI to the guillotine in 1793 when all faith in the monarchy disappeared during the French Revolution. In more recent time, American citizens have lost confidence in political leaders who attended primarily to the "aristocracy" of influence and interest. Many of the country's best known leaders have suffered similar, if less violent fates.

The collaborative premise. In every arena, organizations, communities and regions around the globe exhibit a powerful drive to overcome gridlock and allow broader interests to prevail over the parochial concerns that undermine efforts at renewal and change. The means used are fundamentally different from those traditionally practiced; rather than relying on hierarchy, exclusion and brute force to achieve narrow ends, they rely on trust, inclusion and constructive engagement to achieve a shared, common purpose.

There is a fundamental premise—the collaborative premise—that supports these efforts. This premise holds that *if you bring the appropriate people together in constructive ways with good information, they will generate authentic visions and strategies for addressing the shared concerns of the organization or community.* This constitutes a profound shift in our conception of how change is effected, and requires an equally profound shift in our conception of leadership. Rather than heroes who tell us what to do, we need servants to help us do the work ourselves.

New skills for citizens and civic leaders. Whether private citizens or elected officials, collaborative leaders operate under very different assumptions from those of traditional leaders. Instead of pitting groups or coalitions against each other, they look to the public for power and serve in a very different leadership role. They trust their fellow citizens in the collaborative process when it is inclusive, constructive and well informed. Their role is to convene, catalyze and facilitate the work of others. They inspire people to act, help them solve problems as peers, attract broad involvement, and sustain hope and participation. They also are willing to settle for no change. They know that the will to solve problems comes not from them or from elected leaders or "old boys," but from citizens engaged in addressing public issues.

Collaborative leaders possess new and different skills. They know how to analyze and understand the challenge of leadership and how to develop change strategies that will overcome resistance and inertia. They know how to bring citizens together and help them build trust and the skills for collaboration. They help design constructive processes to collaboratively solve problems and create shared visions.

Conclusion: Next Steps

American Renewal demands an overhaul of politics as it is traditionally practiced. This has implications both for leadership and citizenship. Individuals must acknowledge the leadership demands of active citizenship, and leaders, whether elected or informal, must recognize that collaboration in public life is necessary, and acquire the skills to unite and engage citizens in public problem solving when nothing else is working.

Notes

1. Richard Harwood, *Citizens and Politics: The View from Mainstreet America* (Dayton, Ohio: Kettering Foundation, 1991).

2. Robert D. Putnam et al., *Making Democracy Work: Civic Traditions in Modern Italy* (Princeton, N.J.: Princeton University Press, 1993).

3. Neal R. Peirce et al., *Citistates: How Urban America Can Prosper in a Competitive World* (Washington, D.C.: Seven Locks Press, 1993).

4. S. Schama, *Citizens: A Chronicle of the French Revolution* (New York: Vintage Books, 1989), p. 113.

Appendix A:
Model City Charter
Election Guidelines

Section 6.01. City Elections.

(a) **Regular Elections.** The regular city election shall be held at the time established by state law.

(b) **Registered Voter defined.** All citizens legally registered under the constitution and laws of the state of _____ to vote in the city shall be registered voters of the city within the meaning of this charter.

(c) **Conduct of Elections.** The provisions of the general election laws of the state of _____ shall apply to elections held under this charter. All elections provided for by the charter shall be conducted by the election authorities established by law. Candidates shall run for office without party designation. For the conduct of city elections, for the prevention of fraud in such elections and for the recount of ballots in cases of doubt or fraud, the city council shall adopt ordinances consistent with law and this charter, and the election authorities may adopt further regulations consistent with law and this charter and the ordinances of the council. Such ordinances and regulations pertaining to elections shall be publicized in the manner of city ordinances generally.

Section 6.02. Council Districts; Adjustment of Districts. (for use with Alternatives II, III and IV of §2.02)

(a) **Number of Districts.** There shall be _____ city council districts.

(b) **Districting Commission; Composition; Appointment; Terms; Vacancies; Compensation.**

Reprinted with permission from Model City Charter, 1996. *Published by the National Civic League Press, Denver, Colorado (telephone: 303-571-4343).*

(1) There shall be a districting commission consisting of five members. No more than two commission members may belong to the same political party. The city council shall appoint four members. These four members shall, with the affirmative vote of at least three, choose the fifth member who shall be chairman.

(2) No member of the commission shall be employed by the city or hold any other elected or appointed position in the city.

(3) The city council shall appoint the commission no later than one year and five months before the first general election of the city council after each federal decennial census. The commission's term shall end upon adoption of a districting plan, as set forth in §6.02(c).

(4) In the event of a vacancy on the commission by death, resignation or otherwise, the city council shall appoint a new member enrolled in the same political party from which his or her predecessor was selected, to serve the balance of the term remaining.

(5) No member of the districting commission shall be removed from office by the city council except for cause and upon notice and hearing.

(6) The members of the commission shall serve without compensation except that each member shall be allowed actual and necessary expenses to be audited in the same manner as other city charges.

(7) The commission may hire or contract for necessary staff assistance and may require agencies of city government to provide technical assistance. The commission shall have a budget as provided by the city council.

(c) Powers and Duties of the Commission; Hearings, Submissions and Approval of Plan.

(1) Following each decennial census, the commission shall consult the city council and shall prepare a plan for dividing the city into districts for the election of council members. In preparing the plan, the commission shall be guided by the criteria set forth in §6.02(d). The report on the plan shall include a map and description of districts recommended.

(2) The commission shall hold one or more public hearings not less than one month before it submits the plan to the city council. The commission shall make its plan available to the public for inspection and comment not less than one month before its public hearing.

(3) The commission shall submit its plan to the city council not less than one year before the first general election of the city council after each decennial census.

(4) The plan shall be deemed adopted by the city council unless disapproved within three weeks by the vote of the majority of all members of the city council. If the city council fails to adopt the plan, it shall return the plan to the commission with its objections, and with the objections of individual members of the council.

(5) Upon rejection of its plan, the commission shall prepare a revised plan and shall submit such revised plan to the city council no later than nine months before the first general election of the city council after the decennial census. Such revised plan shall be deemed adopted by the city council unless disapproved within two weeks by the vote of two-thirds of all of the members of the city council and unless, by a vote of two-thirds of all of its members, the city council votes to file a petition in the _____ Court, _____ County, for a determination that the plan fails to meet the requirements of this charter. The city council shall file its petition no later than ten days after its disapproval of the plan. Upon a final determination upon appeal, if any, that the plan meets the requirements of this charter, the plan shall be deemed adopted by the city council and the commission shall deliver the plan to the city clerk. The plan delivered to the city clerk shall include a map and description of the districts.

(6) If in any year population figures are not available at least one year and five months before the first general election following the decennial census, the city council may be local law shorten the time periods provided for districting commission action in subsections (2), (3), (4) and (5) of this section.

(d) Districting Plan; Criteria. In preparation of its plan for dividing the city into districts for the election of council members, the commission shall apply the following criteria which, to the extent practicable, shall be applied and given priority in the order in which they are herein set forth.

(1) Districts shall be equal in population except where deviations from equality result from the application of the provisions hereinafter set forth, but no such deviation may exceed five percent of the average population for all city council districts according to the figures available from the most recent census.

(2) Districts shall consist of contiguous territory; but land areas separated by waterways shall not be included in the same district unless said waterways are traversed by highway bridges,

tunnels or regularly scheduled ferry services both termini of
which are within the district, except that, population permitting, islands not connected to the mainland or to other islands
by bridge, tunnel or regular ferry services shall be included in
the same district as the nearest land area within the city and,
where such subdivisions exist, within the same ward or equivalent subdivision as described in subdivision (5), below.

(3) No city block shall be divided in the formation of districts.

(4) In cities whose territory encompasses more than one county or
portions of more than one county, the number of districts which
include territory in more than one county shall be as small as
possible.

(5) In the establishment of districts within cities whose territory is
divided into wards or equivalent subdivisions whose boundaries
have remained substantially unaltered for at least fifteen years,
the number of such wards or equivalent subdivisions whose territory is divided among more than one district shall be as small
as possible.

(6) Consistent with the foregoing provisions, the aggregate length
of all district boundaries shall be as short as possible.

   (e) Effect of Enactment. The new city council districts and boundaries
as of the date of enactment shall supersede previous council districts and
boundaries for all purposes of the next regular city election, including nominations. The new districts and boundaries shall supersede previous districts
and boundaries for all other purposes as of the date on which all council members elected at that regular city election take office.

[Section 6.03. Initiative and Referendum.
   The powers of initiative and referendum are hereby reserved to the electors of the city. The provisions of the election law of the state of _____, as
they currently exist or may hereafter be amended or superseded, shall govern
the exercise of the powers of initiative and referendum under this charter.]
   **Note: Section 6.03 is in brackets because not all states provide for the
initiative and referendum and it is possible that not all cities within the
states that do provide for it will choose to include the option in their charters.**

Commentary on Article VI

   In previous editions of the *Model* detailed provisions on the nomination
and election process were included. This edition recognizes that the election

laws of each state apply to municipalities whether or not they operate with a local charter. Areas of local discretion are few. Among those discretionary areas may be the provision of nonpartisan elections and the timing of elections. Operating within the limitations imposed by state law, the city may by ordinance adopt regulations deemed desirable.

§6.01. City Elections.

Although in most states local elections are regulated entirely or to a very substantial extent by state statutes, certain variations may be provided by local charter; for example, home rule charters may provide for nonpartisan local elections as provided in this section. When possible, it is particularly desirable to separate municipal from state and national elections. Therefore, municipal elections are frequently scheduled in the fall of odd-numbered years or in the spring of the year—both as a result of state election laws and of city charters. This separation is important whether elections are conducted on a partisan or nonpartisan basis. It is recommended that such timing be specified in the charter if it is permissible under the state election laws.

§6.02. Council Districts; Adjustment of Districts.

With three of the five alternatives provided for the election of the city council involving districts, the provision for drawing and redrawing district lines assumes particular importance.

This section is a substantial departure from that in the previous editions because of the necessity of complying with such legal mandates as *Baker v. Carr, Avery v. Midland County, Texas,* and the Voting Rights Act and its amendments. Rather than a two-part process with an advisory commission recommending a plan, followed by city council passage of a plan (which might or might not resemble that of the advisory commission), the *Model* provides for a more direct process—redistricting by an independent commission. The lead time for redistricting has been expanded to provide sufficient time to resolve some of the increasing number of local government redistricting suits as well as to provide for sufficient time to comply with the requirements of §5 of the Voting Rights Act where that is applicable. In addition, the *Model* provides for ordered, specific criteria for redistricting based on population rather than the "qualified voter" standard of the sixth edition.

The *Model* provides for a bi-partisan commission. Even cities with nonpartisan elections may have problems with political parties (either local or national) wanting to dominate the process to achieve advantage. The fact that the four council appointees (or at least three of the four) must be able to agree on the choice of chairman should facilitate the commission being able to work together.

To avoid the conflict of interest created when council members must consider new districts whose lines may materially affect their political futures, the council can neither approve nor veto the result. The council may, however, prevent implementation of the plan if it finds the plan in violation of the charter and files with the courts for such a determination.

The criteria mandated in this section are designed to preclude gerrymandering either to protect or punish incumbents or to prevent particular voting groups from gaining power. The criteria are unquestionably the most important part of the section. It has been suggested that with the proper ordered criteria, the redistricting process is less open to manipulation and flagrant gerrymandering will be almost impossible without a clear violation of the mandated criteria. The criteria concerning waterways and islands should be included in charters where appropriate. The exact terminology for election administration subdivisions (e.g., wards or equivalent subdivisions) should be adjusted to conform to state law.

There are cities which prefer to have redistricting done by the city council either because of a belief that the redistricting process essentially involves a series of political decisions and that attempts to separate the process from the politics is futile and foolish or because redistricting in the past has been satisfactorily accomplished by the city council and that there is no need for change. Where a city opts for redistricting by the city council, the following provisions should be substituted in §6.02, (b) and (c):

(b) Council to Redistrict. Following each decennial census, the city council shall, by ordinance, adjust the boundaries of the city council districts using the criteria set forth in §6.02(e).

(c) Procedures.
  (1) The city council shall hold one or more public hearings prior to bringing any proposed plan to a vote. Proposed plans must be available to the public for inspection and comment not less than one month before the first public hearing on said plan. The plan shall include a map and description of the districts recommended.
  (2) The city council shall approve a districting plan no later than 10 months (300 days) prior to the first regular city election following the decennial census.

(d) Failure to Enact Ordinance. If the city council fails to enact a redistricting plan within the required time, the city attorney shall, the following business day, inform the _____ Court, _____ County, and ask that a special master be appointed to do the redistricting. The special master shall, within 60 days, provide the court with a plan drawn in accordance with the criteria set forth in §6.02(e). That plan shall have the force of law unless the court finds it does not comply with said criteria. The court shall cause an approved plan to go into effect no later than 210 days prior to the first regular city election after the decennial census. The city shall be liable for all reasonable costs incurred by the special master in preparing the plan for the court.

Subsections 6.02(d) and (e) of the *Model* should be retained, relettered (e) and (f), and the words "city council" substituted for "commission."

§6.02(d) of the substitute language (*Failure to Enact Ordinance*), is particularly important because it is designed to be an incentive for the council to get redistricting completed on time. Failure to redistrict will not result in just another election with the same old district as was provided in the previous edition. Even the most divided of city councils would probably prefer to get down to the business of compromise than have a special master redistrict for them—and few would want to explain the additional cost of paying someone else to draw up a plan that probably would not be any more satisfactory than their own compromise.

Appendix B:
Model County Charter
Election Guidelines

Section 6.01. County Elections.

(a) **Regular Elections.** The regular county election shall be held at the time established by state law.

(b) **Registered Voter Defined.** All citizens legally registered under the constitution and laws of the state of _____ to vote in the county shall be registered voters of the county within the meaning of this charter.

(c) **Conduct of Elections.** The provisions of the general election laws of the state of _____ shall apply to elections held under this charter. All elections provided for by the charter shall be conducted by the election authorities established by law. For the conduct of county elections, for the prevention of fraud in such elections and for the recount of ballots in cases of doubt or fraud, the county council shall adopt ordinances consistent with law and this charter, and the election authorities may adopt further regulations consistent with law and this charter and the ordinances of the council. Such ordinances and regulations pertaining to elections shall be publicized in the manner of county ordinances generally.

Section 6.02. Council Districts; Adjustment of Districts. (for use with alternatives II, III and IV of §2.01)

(a) **Number of Districts.** There shall be _____ county council districts.

(b) **Districting Commission; Composition; Appointment; Terms; Vacancies; Compensation.**

Reprinted with permission from Model County Charter, 1990. *Published by the National Civic League Press, Denver, Colorado (telephone: 303-571-4343).*

(1) There shall be a districting commission consisting of five members. No more than two commission members may belong to the same political party. The county council shall appoint four members. These four members shall, with the affirmative vote of at least three, choose the fifth member who shall be chairman.

(2) No member of the commission shall be employed by the county or any political subdivision of the county, or hold any other elected or appointed position in the county or any political subdivision of the county.

(3) The county council shall appoint the commission no later than one year and five months before the first general election of the county council after each federal decennial census. The commission's term shall end upon adoption of a districting plan, as set forth in §6.02(c).

(4) In the event of a vacancy on the commission by death, resignation or otherwise, the county council shall appoint a new member enrolled in the same political party from which his or her predecessor was selected, to serve the balance of the term remaining.

(5) No member of the districting commission shall be removed from office by the county council except for cause and upon notice and hearing.

(6) The members of the commission shall serve without compensation except that each member shall be allowed actual and necessary expenses to be audited in the same manner as other county charges.

(7) The commission may hire or contract for necessary staff assistance and may require agencies of county government to provide technical assistance. The commission shall have a budget as provided by the county council.

(c) Powers and Duties of the Commission; Hearings, Submissions and Approval of Plan.

(1) Following each decennial census, the commission shall consult the county council and shall prepare a plan for dividing the county into districts for the election of council members. In preparing the plan, the commission shall be guided by the criteria set forth in §6.02(d). The report on the plan shall include a map and description of districts recommended.

(2) The commission shall hold one or more public hearings not less than one month before it submits the plan to the county council. The commission shall make its plan available to the public

for inspection and comment not less than one month before its public hearing.

(3) The commission shall submit its plan to the county council not less than one year before the first general election of the county council after each decennial census.

(4) The plan shall be deemed adopted by the county council unless disapproved within three weeks by the vote of the majority of all members of the county council. If the county council fails to adopt the plan, it shall return the plan to the commission with its objections, and with the objections of individual members of the council.

(5) Upon rejection of its plan, the commission shall prepare a revised plan and shall submit such revised plan to the county council no later than nine months before the first general election of the county council after the decennial census. Such revised plan shall be deemed adopted by the county council unless disapproved within two weeks by the vote of two-thirds of all of the members of the county council and unless, by a vote of two-thirds of all of its members, the county council votes to file a petition in the _____ Court, _____ County, for a determination that the plan fails to meet the requirements of this charter. The county council shall file its petition no later than ten days after its disapproval of the plan. Upon a final determination upon appeal, if any, that the plan meets the requirements of this charter, the plan shall be deemed adopted by the county council and the commission shall deliver the plan to the county clerk. The plan delivered to the county clerk shall include a map and description of the districts.

(6) If in any year population figures are not available at least one year and five months before the first general election following the decennial census, the county council may by ordinance shorten the time periods provided for districting commission action in subsections (2), (3), (4) and (5) of this section.

(d) Districting Plan; Criteria. In preparation of its plan for dividing the county into districts for the election of council members, the commission shall apply the following criteria which, to the extent practicable, shall be applied and given priority in the order in which they are herein set forth.

(1) Districts shall be equal in population except where deviations from equality result from the application of the provisions hereinafter set forth, but no such deviation may exceed five percent of the average population for all county council districts according to the figures available from the most recent census.

(2) Districts shall consist of contiguous territory; but land areas separated by waterways shall not be included in the same district unless said waterways are traversed by highway bridges, tunnels or regularly scheduled ferry services both termini of which are within the district, except that, population permitting, islands not connected to the mainland or to other islands by bridge, tunnel or regular ferry services shall be included in the same district as the nearest land area within the county and, where such subdivisions exist, within the same ward or equivalent subdivision as described in subsection (5), below.

(3) No city block shall be divided in the formation of districts.

(4) A municipality within a county shall be divided among as few districts as possible.

(5) In the establishment of districts within counties whose territory is divided into wards or equivalent subdivisions whose boundaries have remained substantially unaltered for at least fifteen years, the number of such wards or equivalent subdivisions whose territory is divided among more than one district shall be as small as possible.

(6) Consistent with the foregoing provisions, the aggregate length of all district boundaries shall be as short as possible.

(e) Effect of Enactment. The new county council districts and boundaries as of the date of enactment shall supersede previous council districts and boundaries for all purposes of the next regular county election, including nominations. The new districts and boundaries shall supersede previous districts and boundaries for all other purposes as of the date on which all council members elected at that regular county election take office.

[Section 6.03. Initiative and Referendum

The powers of initiative and referendum are hereby reserved to the electors of the county. The provisions of the election law of the state of _____, as they currently exist or may hereafter be amended or superseded, shall govern the exercise of the powers of initiative and referendum under this charter.]

Note: Section 6.03 is in brackets because not all states provide for the initiative and referendum and it is possible that not all counties within the states that do provide for it will choose to include the option in their charters.

Commentary on Article VI

In previous League models, detailed provisions on the nomination and election process were included. This edition recognizes that the election laws

of each state apply to counties whether or not they operate with a local charter. Areas of local discretion are few. Among those discretionary areas may be
the provision of nonpartisan elections and the timing of elections. Operating
within the limitations imposed by state law, the county may by ordinance adopt
regulations deemed desirable.

§6.01. County Elections.

Although in most states local elections are regulated entirely or to a very
substantial extent by state statutes, certain variations may be provided by local
charter; for example, home rule charters may provide for nonpartisan local
elections. When possible, it is particularly desirable to separate local from
state and national elections. Therefore, local elections are frequently scheduled in the fall of odd-numbered years or in the spring of the year—both as a
result of state election laws and of city and county charters. It is recommended
that such timing be specified in the charter if it is permissible under the state
election laws.

§6.02. Council Districts; Adjustment of Districts.

With three of the five alternatives provided for the election of the county
council involving districts, the provision for drawing and redrawing district
lines assumes particular importance.

This section is a substantial departure from that in the previous editions
because of the need to comply with such legal mandates as *Baker v. Carr, Avery
v. Midland County, Texas,* and the Voting Rights Act and its amendments.
Rather than a two-part process with an advisory commission recommending
a plan, followed by county council passage of a plan (which might or might
not resemble that of the advisory commission), the *Model* provides for a more
direct process—redistricting by an independent commission. The lead time for
redistricting has been expanded to provide sufficient time to resolve some of
the increasing number of local government redistricting suits as well as to
provide for sufficient time to comply with the requirements of §5 of the Voting
Rights Act where that is applicable. In addition, the *Model* provides for
ordered, specific criteria for redistricting based on population.

The *Model* provides for a bi-partisan commission. The fact that the four
council appointees (or at least three of the four) must be able to agree on the
choice of chairman should facilitate the commission being able to work
together.

To avoid the conflict of interest created when councilmembers must consider new districts whose lines may materially affect their political futures,
the council can neither approve nor veto the result. The council may, however,
prevent implementation of the plan if it finds the plan in violation of the charter and files with the courts for such a determination.

The criteria mandated in this section are designed to preclude gerrymandering either to protect or punish incumbents or to prevent particular voting groups from gaining power. The criteria are unquestionably the most important part of the section. It has been suggested that with the proper ordered criteria, the redistricting process is less open to manipulation and flagrant gerrymandering will be almost impossible without a clear violation of the mandated criteria. The criteria concerning waterways and islands should be included in charters where appropriate. The exact terminology for election administration subdivisions (e.g., wards or equivalent subdivisions) should be adjusted to conform to state law.

There are counties which prefer to have redistricting done by the county council either because of a belief that the redistricting process essentially involves a series of political decisions and that attempts to separate the process from the politics is futile and foolish or because redistricting in the past has been satisfactorily accomplished by the council and that there is no need for change. Where a county opts for redistricting by the council, the following provisions should be substituted in §6.02:

(b) Council to Redistrict. Following each decennial census, the county council shall, by ordinance, adjust the boundaries of the county council districts using the criteria set forth in §6.02(e).

(c) Procedures.
(1) The county council shall hold one or more public hearings prior to bringing any proposed plan to a vote. Proposed plans must be available to the public for inspection and comment not less than one month before the first public hearing on said plan. The plan shall include a map and description of the districts recommended.
(2) The county council shall approve a districting plan no later than 10 months (300 days) prior to the first regular county election following the decennial census.

(d) Failure to Enact Ordinance. If the county council fails to enact a redistricting plan within the required time, the county attorney shall, the following business day, inform the _____ Court, _____ County, and ask that a special master be appointed to do the redistricting. The special master shall, within 60 days, provide the court with a plan drawn in accordance with the criteria set forth in §6.02(e). That plan shall have the force of law unless the court finds it does not comply with said criteria. The court shall cause an approved plan to go into effect no later than 210 days prior to the first regular county election after the decennial census. The county shall be liable for all reasonable costs incurred by the special master in preparing the plan for the court.

Subsections 6.02(d) and (e) of the *Model* should be retained, relettered (e) and (f), and the words "county council" substituted for "commission."

§6.02(d) of the substitute language (*Failure to Enact Ordinance*), is particularly important because it is designed to be an incentive for the council to get redistricting completed on time. Failure to redistrict will not result in just another election with the same old districts as was provided in the previous edition. Even the most divided of councils would probably prefer to get down to the business of compromise than have a special master redistrict for them—and few would want to explain the additional cost of paying someone else to draw up a plan that probably would not be any more satisfactory than their own compromise.

About the Contributors

Affiliations are as of the time the articles were written.

Charles K. Bens, Consultant to Local Governments, Toronto, Canada, and a member of the Editorial Board of the *National Civic Review*.

Lee L. Blackman, Attorney and Partner, McDermott, Will & Emery, Los Angeles, California.

Robert Brischetto, Sociologist, Lakehills, Texas.

Charles S. Bullock III, Richard B. Russell Professor of Political Science, University of Georgia, Athens, Georgia.

Carol A. Cassel, Associate Professor of Political Science, University of Alabama, Huntsville, Alabama.

David D. Chrislip, Senior Associate, National Civic League, Denver, Colorado.

Roy Christman, Lecturer, Political Science Department, San Jose State University, San Jose, California.

Richard L. Cole, Professor of Urban Affairs and Political Science and Dean of the Institute of Urban Studies, University of Texas, Arlington, Texas.

Olethia Davis, Assistant Professor of Political Science, Southern University, Baton Rouge, Louisiana.

Victor S. DeSantis, Assistant Professor of Public Administration, University of North Texas, Denton, Texas.

Richard L. Engstrom, Research Professor of Political Science, University of New Orleans, New Orleans, Louisiana.

James Fay, Chairman, Political Science Department, California State University, Hayward, California.

Rodolfo A. Gonzalez, Professor of Economics, San Jose State University, San Jose, California.

Susan B. Hannah, Director, School of Public Affairs and Administration, Western Michigan University, Kalamazoo, Michigan.

Rodney Hero, Professor of Political Science, University of Colorado, Boulder, Colorado.

Pamela Karlan, Professor of Law, University of Virginia, Charlottesville, Virginia.

Erich R. Luschei, Attorney and Associate, McDermott, Will & Emery, Boston, Massachusetts.

Susan A. MacManus, Professor of Public Administration, University of South Florida, Tampa, Florida.

David Mathews, President, Kettering Foundation, Dayton, Ohio.

Stephen L. Mehay, Professor of Economics, U.S. Naval Postgraduate School, Monterey, California.

Kenneth R. Mladenka, Associate Professor of Political Science, Texas A & M University, College Station, Texas.

Karen Moore O'Brien, is a 1992 graduate of the University of California, Irvine, California, where she majored in political science.

Mark P. Petracca, Associate Professor of Political Science, University of California, Irvine, California.

Bruce I. Petrie, President, Murray and Agnes Seasongood Good Government Foundation, Cincinnati, Ohio.

Tari Renner, Chairman, Political Science Department, Illinois Wesleyan University, Bloomington, Illinois.

Robert Richie, Executive Director, Center for Voting and Democracy, Washington, D.C.

Edward Still, Attorney-at-Law, Birmingham, Alabama.

Delbert A. Taebel, Professor of Urban Affairs and Political Science, University of Texas, Arlington, Texas.

C. E. Teasley III, Associate Professor of Political Science, University of West Florida, Pensacola, Florida.

John Clayton Thomas, Professor and Director, School of Public Administration and Urban Studies, Georgia State University, Atlanta, Georgia.

Alfred J. Tuchfarber, Director, Institute for Policy Research, University of Cincinnati, Cincinnati, Ohio.

Richard A. Walawender, Contributing Editor, *Journal of Law Reform,* University of Michigan School of Law, Ann Arbor, Michigan.

Darrell Williams, Information Specialist, Municipal Reference Service, National League of Cities, Washington, D.C.

Joseph F. Zimmerman, Professor of Political Science, Graduate School of Public Affairs, State University of New York, Albany, New York.

Index